BE STILL and KNOW

BY MILDRED E. STAMM

Meditation Moments

Be Still and Know

BE STILL and KNOW

By MILLIE STAMM

ZONDERVAN PUBLISHING HOUSE
OF THE ZONDERVAN CORPORATION
GRAND RAPIDS, MICHIGAN 49506

Scripture quotations are from the *King James Version* unless otherwise designated. Modern translations used are:

The Amplified Old Testament, Part One—Genesis to Esther, © 1964 by the Zondervan Publishing House *(Amplified)*.

The Amplified Old Testament, Part Two—Job to Malachi, © 1962 by the Zondervan Publishing House *(Amplified)*

The Amplified New Testament, © 1958 by the Lochman Foundation, published by the Zondervan Publishing House *(Amplified)*

The Emphasized Bible, by Joseph Bryant Rotherham, © 1959 by Kregel Publications *(Rotherham)*

The Holy Bible, The Berkeley Version in Modern English, © 1959 by the Zondervan Publishing House *(Berkeley)*

The Living Bible, paraphrased, © 1971 by Tyndale House Publishers (LB)

The New English Bible, © 1961 by Oxford University Press (NEB)

The New Testament in Modern English, Revised Edition, by J. B. Phillips, © 1972 by the Macmillan Company *(Phillips)*

The New Testament in the Language of the People, by Charles B. Williams, © 1937 by Bruce Humphries, Inc., assigned to the Moody Bible Institute, 1949 *(Williams)*

Weymouth New Testament in Modern Speech, by Richard Francis Weymouth © by Harper & Brothers Publishers *(Weymouth)*

Zondervan Publishing House, 1415 Lake Drive, S.E., Grand Rapids, Michigan 49506

Library of Congress Cataloging in Publication Data

Stamm, Mildred.
Be still and know.

1. Devotional calendars. I. Title
BV4811.S78 242'.2 78-13125

Cloth: ISBN 0-310-32990-6
Paper: ISBN 0-310-32991-4

Printed in the United States of America

84 85 86 87 88 — 10 9 8

It is with heartfelt thanks that I lovingly
dedicate this book to
Helen Duff Baugh
and
Mary E. Clark
for the inspiration they have been to me and in appreciation for the spiritual strength and wise guidance they have offered me through the Stonecroft Ministries.

Preface

BE STILL! In the 20th Century? In the hustle and bustle of today's living, who has time to be still? Yet how needful it is.

The title comes from the familiar verse, "Be still, and know that I am God" (Ps. 46:10). My prayer for the book from the first has been that the devotionals would create a desire in the hearts of those who read them to know God in a more real and intimate way.

As I began writing, God didn't put me in quiet, peaceful surroundings that I might "Be still and know Him" as I wrote. He put me through one of the most difficult times of my life. I underwent two serious surgeries. My sister was critically ill and passed away just before the book was completed.

But through these experiences I came to know God in a deeper, more personal way than I had before. What I have written has come out of the experiences of "Being still and knowing God" during times of sorrow and pain.

As this book comes to you, my prayer is that the Lord will use it to encourage you to set apart time to be with Him. May they help you to "be still" before God and, as a result, your acquaintance with God will become more real.

Millie Stamm

Stonecroft
October, 1978

Acknowledgments

I wish to acknowledge here the untiring efforts of Genevieve Kesby as she has typed and re-typed the many pages of the manuscript. My thanks also go to Beth Ferris and Ruth Carpenter for their help in typing.

In this book I have interspersed with my own experiences and observations many helpful insights from others. I wish to thank those from whom I have quoted. In some cases I do not know to whom credit should be given. But in all cases, I extend my grateful appreciation.

BE STILL and KNOW

January
1

Be still, and know that I am God (Ps. 46:10).

We are living in a technological age geared to speed. Speed records are being set in travel enabling us to circle the globe in an unbelievably short time. This accelerated tempo is experienced in every area of living today. A twenty-four hour day is insufficient time to complete all we have scheduled on our calendars. We are always in a hurry, rushing from one thing to another. It is no wonder that tensions build up almost to the breaking point. We keep stereo, radio, and television on because we cannot stand the stillness. It is as if we are on a carousel revolving so rapidly we cannot get off.

As we are now crossing the threshold of a new year, it is an opportune time to reevaluate our lives in the light of the future. How are we going to use this year? For our own interests or for God's glory? Do we have our priorities in the right perspective? What has top priority? Are the things we are doing of most importance in the light of eternity?

Our Scripture verse for today says, "Be still, and KNOW that I am God." Ask yourself, "How well do I know God? How real is He to me? Is He only a casual acquaintance, or a dear, intimate friend?" Perhaps our greatest need this year is to deepen our friendship with Him. This will mean spending time with Him. The more time we spend with a person, the better we get to know him. We need a quiet time, a "Be Still" time, each day, alone with the Lord, to become better acquainted.

It is not easy to be perfectly still in God's presence. The harder we try, the more difficult it becomes. We remember something we have forgotten to do. The phone rings. The noise of the world about us becomes louder and louder. Yet times of quiet are necessary for our spiritual well-being. Dr. Gilbert Little, a Christian psychiatrist, was asked for a simple rule for mental health. He answered, "Be still, and know that I am God." Rest is not only important for our physical life, but for our spiritual life, too.

The world says, "Be active; be busy; be industrious." But God says, "BE STILL—be quiet; don't rush." This is not just a cessation of activities, but a quietness of heart and spirit in which we are aware of His presence. In the center of our soul is a place where God dwells, and where, if we enter and close out every other sound, He will speak to us. Someone has said, "It is not in the college or academy, but in the silence of the soul, that we learn the greater lessons of life—and quiet hearts are rare." Many times we do all the talking instead of being quiet enough to listen to Him.

As we continue to wait before Him, the sounds about us fade away; and we are aware of being in the quietness of His Holy Presence.

In 1 Kings 19:11 and 12, we read that it was not in the wind, nor the earthquake, nor the fire that God spoke to Elijah, but in a still small voice. It is in the stillness of the soul that God speaks to us.

An explorer went on a trek into the jungle with some nationals as guides. The first two days the group hurried so fast that they were able to cover many miles. On the third day the explorer planned to start at daybreak. When it was time to leave, he discovered the guides were not ready. He asked them what was wrong. They replied, "We must wait." "Wait?" he said "Wait for what?" They replied, "We have been going too fast. Now we must wait for our souls to catch up with our bodies." Have we been hurrying so fast that we, too, need to wait for our souls to catch up with our bodies?

May we take time this year to be still before Him that we may get to KNOW HIM in a more personal and real way. Be still and reduce self-activity; be still and quit rushing about.

"BE STILL. And know that I AM GOD."

January
2

Be still, and know that I am God (Ps. 46:10).

One day a little girl slipped into her father's study. Without saying a word, she quietly sat on the floor close beside him, watching him at work. After a while he said, "Honey, is there something you want?" "No," she replied, "I am just sitting here loving you." Soon she left as quietly as she had come in. Little did she know the lesson she had taught her father. She had not come to ask him for anything. She had just wanted to be near him and love him. The thought came to him, "How often do I spend time in God's presence, just loving Him and becoming acquainted with Him? Or do I only come to Him when I have a request to ask of Him?"

God not only wants us to bring our requests to Him, but He also wants us to spend time with Him. Yet we are so busy and have so many needs that we often rush into His presence, make our requests known, and rush out again without taking time to be quiet enough to hear Him. God says, "Be still, and KNOW THAT I AM GOD."

It has been said, "Quietness is not just the opposite of noise. It is not the absence of excitement, haste, and confusion. These dissipate strength while calmness conserves it. The world's mighty men have grown in solitude." As we study the lives of many Bible characters, we discover that they had a close friendship and walk with God. God spoke of Abraham as "My friend" (Isa. 41:8). David was known as "a man after Mine own heart" (Acts 13:22). In reading about the lives of Christians through the ages who were strong in their faith, we learn that they took time to BE STILL and become intimately acquainted with God.

Suppose each of us would pause and make a list of people that we know. What a long list of names we would have! Some we know only by name. Others we recognize by sight. Some are just casual speaking acquaintances. Then there are others who are very dear, intimate friends. We know their likes and dislikes. We enjoy their company. They know all about us and love us just as we are.

In which group of friends is Jesus classified in your life? Is He just a casual acquaintance, or a dear, close friend with whom you enjoy spending time?

Jesus Christ came that He might reveal God to us. "It is true that no one has ever seen God at any time. Yet the divine and only Son, who lives in the closest intimacy with the Father, has made him known" (John 1:18, *Phillips*).

To become better acquainted with God necessitates spending time with Him. It means more than hurriedly reading a verse or two of Scripture and quickly asking God to bless us. We need to enter our spiritual closet, close the door, and become quiet in His presence, meditating on who He is and what He has done for us.

As we become quiet before Him, He can begin to speak and reveal Himself to us. He may say, "Be still and know that I am the all-powerful God. Your need today is not too hard for Me or beyond My power." Or, "Be still and know that I love you. I know all about you, your weaknesses, failures, and mistakes; but I still love you. And My love is stedfast and unchanging." Or, "Be still and know that I am interested in every detail of your life. I want to enter into every need you have—even the need you have today." As we ponder on His greatness and His holiness, yet realize that His love and concern for each of us is very personal, our hearts are filled with worship and adoration.

Often we become so involved in the fast pace of life that we fail to take the necessary time for such fellowship with Him. How well do you know God?

As we begin the new year, may the prayer of our hearts be that we will take time to "Be still, and KNOW GOD."

January

3

"For I know the plans which I am planning for you," saith Jehovah, "plans of welfare and not of calamity, to give you a future and a hope" (Jer. 29:11, Rotherham).

The year we are now entering is one unknown to us, but known to God. He has a "custom-designed" plan for our lives. Included in His plan for us is the year ahead.

At the time Jeremiah wrote the above scripture, God's chosen people were in captivity. Jeremiah reminded them that God had not forgotten them, but in His own time would return them to their homeland. ". . . I know the plans I am planning for you . . ." Their captivity may have seemed like a calamity, but God assured them He had their welfare in mind.

We cannot see what lies ahead in the new year, but God can. ". . . I KNOW the plans I am planning for YOU . . ." His plans are for the PRESENT moment—NOW. "The plans I AM planning for you . . ." He knows "where" we are, the "why" of our circumstances, "how" His plans fit into our lives, and "what" His plans are to accomplish.

His plans are PURPOSEFUL. "Plans of welfare, not of calamity . . ." Often we see our circumstances as calamities, but not so with God. He loves us and desires only His best for us. We view our situations from where we are, but God sees them completed and fitted into His plans.

He has PROSPECTIVE plans for our FUTURE. We are to be WITH HIM in heaven. There we will experience no sorrow, nor pain. There all our tears will be wiped away. Knowing that one of these days He will return for us gives us HOPE today.

We can face the new year with peace of heart and mind, knowing that God is working out His plans not only for our life on earth but throughout eternity.

His plan for our lives finds completion and fulfillment in Jesus Christ. "Moreover we know that to those who love God, who are called according to HIS PLAN, everything that happens fits into a pattern for good. For God, in His foreknowledge, chose them to bear the family likeness of His Son" (Rom. 8:28-29, *Phillips*).

O Lord, thou hast searched me, and known me (Ps. 139:1).

How many times have you said, "There is no one who really knows and understands me"? How many people really do know you? Do they know the person you want them to know, or the REAL YOU?

David said, "O Lord, you have examined my heart and know everything about me" (Ps. 139:1, LB). When He searches us, we cannot hide our weaknesses, mistakes, and failures from Him. Our lives are completely open to Him. He knows that which we try to hide from even our best friends.

The all-knowing God knows where we are and what we are experiencing every moment. He knows our loneliness, discouragement, and disappointments. He knows when dear ones forsake us. He knows when our world seems to be falling apart about us and there is nothing we can do. Nothing takes Him by surprise.

He knows our ordinary, everyday movements, even our sitting and our standing. He knows our inward thoughts even before they mature in our minds. "You know when I sit or stand. When far away You know my every thought" (v. 2, LB).

He plans our paths ahead. "You chart the path ahead of me, and tell me where to stop and rest. Every moment You know where I am" (v. 3, LB). The King James translation reads, "Thou . . . art acquainted with all my ways."

Not only does He plan our walk, but He accompanies us on it. He surrounds us with His presence. "You both precede and follow me, and place Your hand of blessing on my head" (v. 5, LB).

Today God knows us better than any person knows us. He knows us better than we know ourselves. He knows our innermost longings and desires. He knows our motives and our purposes, which often those nearest us do not understand. He knows our weaknesses and failures, yet He loves us with a steadfast and unchanging love. Not only does He know us as we are, but He knows the potential of what we can be in Jesus Christ. Realizing this, we can say as the Psalmist did, "This is too glorious, too wonderful to believe" (v. 6, LB).

January
5

If I take the wings of the morning, and dwell in the uttermost parts of the sea; even there shall thy hand lead me, and thy right hand shall hold me (Ps. 139:9-10).

David not only recognized that God was all-knowing, but that He was all-seeing. David said, "I can never be lost to your Spirit! I can never get away from my God! If I go up to heaven, you are there; if I go down to the place of the dead, you are there. If I ride the morning winds to the farthest oceans, EVEN THERE Your hand will guide me, Your strength will support me" (Ps. 139:7-10, LB).

Since God is everywhere, it is impossible to escape from His presence. It has been said, "There are no God-deserted spots." "He knows about everyone, everywhere. Everything about us is bare and wide open to the all-seeing eyes of our living God; nothing can be hidden from Him to whom we must explain all that we have done" (Heb. 4:13, LB).

Sometimes we try to fly away and hide from our problems, our circumstances, even from people. Yet if we fly with the speed of the morning light from east to west and reach to the farthest corners of the world, we cannot get away from our pressures and frustrations. However, it is comforting to know that EVEN THERE in the midst of them He is with us. We may be in the depths of despair but EVEN THERE He will uphold us with His right hand of power.

Where are you today? Are you fretting about your circumstances? Are you trying to go your own way? Are you rebelling and resisting God's will? God is EVEN THERE waiting for you to let go of your own plans and let Him give you His. His are always best.

We must say as David did, "How precious it is, Lord, to realize that You are thinking about me constantly! I can't even count how many times a day Your thoughts turn toward me. And when I waken in the morning, You are still thinking of me" (Ps. 139:17-18, LB).

Search me, O God, and know my heart; test my thoughts. Point out anything you find in me that makes you sad, and lead me along the path of everlasting life" (Ps. 139:23-24, LB).

David realized that God knew all about him. "You . . . know everything about me" (Ps. 139:1, LB). Because he wanted his heart to be right before God, he asked for a divine examination. "Search me, O God, and know my heart; test my thoughts."

David asked God, "Search my life and show me anything that displeases You; even anything of which I might not be aware." David wanted an honest and open relationship between God and Himself. He wanted God to make a complete search—"me," "my heart," "my thoughts," "my ways." He wanted nothing to hinder his communication with God. David said, "He would not have listened if I had not confessed my sins" (Ps. 66:18, LB).

Are we willing for such divine examination and scrutiny of our lives? Do we say, "Search ME, O God, and know MY heart; test MY thoughts?" "Search me" means "God, YOU search me." True knowledge of self comes not from searching ourselves but from God's searching us, for He really knows our innermost being.

God may see a wrong attitude, a spirit of complaining or criticism that needs to be changed. A root of bitterness may have to be removed. We may be disobedient, self-willed, or self-seeking. We need to permit God to reveal anything in our lives that is hindering our spiritual growth. Not only is He the Great Revealer, but through Christ He gives us victory over our weaknesses.

David said: (1) "Search me." Am I willing for God to search me? (2) "Know me." Know my heart, my life, yes, even my thoughts. (3) "Try me." What are the results of this test on my life? (4) "See me." Does He see anything in my life that displeases Him? (5) "Lead me." In the path of everlasting life, the way that leads to heaven.

Life is centered around things that have either temporal or eternal value. May our prayer be that we not waste time on things that are transitory, but live each day with eternity's values in view.

January
7

Therefore if any man be in Christ, he is a new creature: old things are passed away; behold, all things are become new (2 Cor. 5:17).

As the old year draws to a close, we usually spend time in retrospection, recalling our failures and mistakes of the past year. Then we make a set of resolutions for the year ahead. We start out with a great determination to keep them, but before long we discover that they have been broken. It is not "turning over a new leaf" we need, but "living a new life"; not a "new year" but a "new you."

Paul wrote of this new life we have IN CHRIST—the life that makes us a new person. "When someone becomes a Christian he becomes a brand new person inside. He is not the same any more. A new life has begun." (2 Cor. 5:17, LB). This new life becomes ours the moment we personally invite Christ to become our Savior and Lord. We BECOME new creatures THEN!

This life of Christ within does more than make us ready for heaven. It gives a new power for daily living. With this new relationship comes a new nature, new standards, new desires, new attitudes, new motives, new goals, new actions and reactions. He doesn't try to improve our former life. He doesn't make us a better person but a different one. The Holy Spirit makes us a new person, producing the life of Jesus Christ within.

In Christ, every area of our lives is strengthened. Perhaps worry is a problem for us. Have you heard anyone say, "It is just my nature to worry," or "I'm a natural-born worrier"? Our own nature may be one to worry, but in Christ we can be free from worry. He said, "Peace I leave with you, My peace I give unto you" (John 14:27). His new nature can give victory in every area of our lives day by day as we yield to Him.

In Christ we have the resources for living an abundant life each day of this next year.

These things have I written unto you that believe on the name of the son of God; that ye may know that ye have eternal life, and that ye may believe on the name of the Son of God (1 John 5:13).

If you were asked today, "Are you a Christian?" what would you answer? Could you reply with certainty, "Yes, I know I am"? Many people do not have this assurance. They do not have the confidence of knowing that they have eternal life.

Assurance is defined as "sureness, confidence, certainty." In our spiritual lives assurance is the confidence of knowing that there is a right relationship between God and one's self. We can KNOW that we have eternal life. We can KNOW that we have the life of God within.

Eternal life is more than just a never ending duration of life. It is a quality of life, the life of Jesus Christ. "This is the record, that God hath given to us eternal life, and this life is in his Son" (1 John 5:11). It becomes ours NOW when we invite Jesus Christ into our lives. "He that hath the Son hath life; and he that hath not the Son of God hath not life" (v. 12).

After we receive Christ as our personal Savior, we have eternal life as a PRESENT possession. This assurance is not based on our feelings, but on God's word. "I write this to you who believe in (adhere to, trust in and rely on) the name of the Son of God . . . so that you may KNOW (with settled and absolute knowledge) that you [ALREADY] HAVE LIFE, yes, eternal life" (1 John 5:13, *Amplified*). The word used for "know" in this verse is a strong one, meaning "know with certainty."

Paul had this assurance. He said, "I KNOW WHOM I have believed" (2 Tim. 1:12). Not "I hope I believe," "I think I do," or "I am doing my best to," but "I KNOW."

Some are uncertain because they have never personally received Christ. "But as many as received him, to them gave he power to become the sons of God, even to them that believe on his name" (John 1:12).

On the authority of God's Word, can you say, as Paul, "I KNOW WHOM I have believed"?

January 9

To the praise of the glory of his grace, wherein he hath made us accepted in the beloved (Eph. 1:6).

Today many people have a great fear of not being accepted. They are constantly trying to gain favor with others. We are told that acceptance is a necessary element in our personality growth. We want to be noticed, appreciated, accepted. We want to belong. We want to be special to someone.

This is true in our religious life as well as in our social life. Not only do we want acceptance with people, but with God as well. We work diligently doing things to gain His favor. In some countries people even torture themselves trying to merit acceptance with God.

The real basis of our acceptance is through a personal relationship with Jesus Christ as Savior. ". . . wherein He hath made us ACCEPTED in the BELOVED." "Jesus saith unto him, 'I am the way, the truth, and the life: no man cometh unto the Father, but by me'" (John 14:6).

Some people base their acceptance on their feelings. But feelings change, actions change. Our acceptance doesn't depend on what we are or what we do. We are not accepted because of our character or conduct. God has promised that He will accept us in the Beloved. Of that we can be assured, for God never changes.

After my marriage I had free access to the home of my husband's parents, sharing the privileges my husband had. I wasn't accepted just because they liked me, although they did; nor because I did things for them, although I did. I was accepted as a member of their family because I had married their son. This illustrates our acceptance with God. We are accepted in His Son.

We must remember that when God accepts us into His family we have not "arrived" in our Christian life, we have only started. But in Christ we have found Someone who accepts us where we are and enables us to accept ourselves as we are. However, even though God loves us just as we are now, He isn't satisfied to leave us there. His purpose is to conform us to the image of His Son, a process that continues throughout our lifetime.

Wherefore God also hath highly exalted him, and given him a name which is above every name: that at the name of Jesus every knee should bow, of things in heaven, and things in earth, and things under the earth; and that every tongue should confess that Jesus Christ is Lord, to the glory of God the Father (Phil. 2:9-11).

In the early times of Christianity, the Romans were not only a strong military force, but a dominating power in religion. They worshiped their emperor as a god. The people were allowed to retain their own religion as long as they accepted "Emperor-worship," along with their own belief.

The Greek word "kurios" meaning "Lord" was used as a divine title for the emperor. This is the same word Paul used in speaking of Jesus as Lord.

After the death and resurrection of Jesus Christ, God highly exalted Him, giving Him "a name that is above every name." It is "THE name above every name," indicating that He is Lord. A day is coming when every knee will bow at His name and every tongue will confess Him as Lord.

One day Jesus said to His disciples, "Ye call me Master and Lord; and ye say well; for so I am" (John 13:13). But it is more than the bending of the knee and the confession of the lips that He desires. He wants the Lordship of our lives. He is more concerned that we confess Him as Lord with our hearts than with our lips.

When we acknowledge Him as Lord, we recognize His ownership of our lives.

In accepting His ownership, we must submit to His will. We must relinquish all rights to our lives, holding nothing back. There must be no reservations. "Then Jesus said to his disciples, 'If anyone wants to follow in my footsteps he must give up all right to himself, take up his cross and follow me'" (Matt. 16:24, *Phillips*).

Today, who is the Lord of your life: self or the Lord Jesus Christ? Just calling Him "Lord" doesn't mean you are allowing Him to be that. You must recognize His right to that place in your life. Is He Lord of your possessions? Your home? Your time? Your talents? Your career? Your business? Have you released your family to Him?

Christ Jesus, YOU ARE MY LORD!

January

11

Now the Lord said unto Abram, Get thee out of thy country, and from thy kindred, and from thy father's house, unto a land that I will shew thee (Gen. 12:1).

Abraham is a supreme example of a man with deep faith in God. God asked him to leave his country, home, and loved ones, and move to a land unknown to Abraham but known to God. God's call was sure. Abraham's trust in God was unwavering. Not knowing where he was bound, obediently "Abram departed, as the Lord had spoken unto him" (Gen. 12:4).

Not only did Abraham have faith IN God, but he was obedient TO God. "It was BY FAITH that Abraham OBEYED the summons to go out to a place which he would eventually possess, and he set out in complete ignorance of his destination" (Heb. 11:8, *Phillips*). He took God at His word.

Faith is trusting God when we cannot see where He is leading us, or what He is doing. It is committing our lives completely to Him with no strings attached. Someone has said, "Faith is marching under sealed orders willingly and joyfully." It is trusting Him, taking hands off our lives and obediently following His directions. No half-way obedience satisfies God.

Today is God moving you into a new land, situation, or activity? Are you in the midst of some new circumstance or problem? Is your path uncertain before you? Has He given you sealed marching orders and you do not know where He is leading you, nor do you understand why? Your faith will be demonstrated by your willingness to obey. It has been said, "We are not traveling by schedule but by faith."

F. B. Meyer said, "We may not have to leave home as Abraham did, but it will be necessary to withdraw our heart's deepest dependence from all earthly props if ever we are to learn what it is to trust simply and absolutely on the eternal God." God has to remove any support we may be leaning on to teach us complete reliance on Him.

1 Timothy 1:19 *(Amplified)* describes faith as "that leaning of the entire human personality on God in absolute trust and confidence."

He staggered not at the promise of God through unbelief; but was strong in faith, giving glory to God; and being fully persuaded that, what he had promised, he was able also to perform (Rom. 4:20-21).

One day God revealed to Abraham that he and Sarah were to have a son. Abraham knew it was a physical impossibility. Humanly speaking it could not be. But it was not in human hands. Someone has said, "Faith does not operate in the realm of the possible. There is no glory for God in that which is humanly possible. Faith begins where man's power ends."

Abraham was strong in his faith, for its basis was not God's promise to him, but the God who had given him His promise. Abraham, when hope was dead within him, went on hoping in faith, believing that he would become "the father of many nations." He relied on the word of God which definitely referred to "thy seed" (v. 18, *Phillips*). Without the God of Abraham, the faith of Abraham was nothing. From the human viewpoint, not one promise given Abraham was logical or possible, but he didn't limit God to what seemed reasonable. He believed God was able. It is as easy for God to do a difficult thing as an easy one. The strength of his faith was his confidence in God's ability.

We, too, are to "walk by faith, not by sight." Many times we face circumstances beyond human possibility. There is no way out for us. We may not be able to see where God is leading us, what He is doing, or why. But Abraham's God is our God. He who did the impossible for Abraham will do the same for us.

It is not the degree of our faith that is important but the object of our faith, God Himself. It is not great faith we need, but faith in a great God. By faith we put our dependence and reliance upon God.

One of the tribes in Africa spoke of faith as "leaning on God." Sometimes we lean so heavily on earthly props that God has to remove them until there is nothing on which we can lean but God. Then we learn we can put our entire weight on Him and find that He is enough. Someone has said, "Faith is our weakness leaning on God's strength."

January

13

And thine ears shall hear a word behind thee, saying, This is the way, walk ye in it, when ye turn to the right hand, and when ye turn to the left (Isa. 30:21).

Early one morning I was invited to go for a walk in the woods. It was a beautiful morning. The birds were singing, and the sun was shining through the trees along the trail, reflecting its rays on a lake close by.

The family dog went with us. However, he was not satisfied to stay on the path, but ran from one side to the other. As we returned, the dog was exhausted, panting as hard as he could. I said, "Do you know why your dog is worn out? It is from all the detours he took. He was off the trail more than he was on it."

We may become exhausted physically, mentally, and spiritually at times because of the detours we take from God's path. We run this way and that on paths of our own making.

The Lord has promised to be our personal Guide through life. His part is to open the way before us; our part is to walk in it. Whether the way be rough or smooth, dark or bright, easy or hard, we have Someone who knows each step of it. However, we must seek guidance from His Word and from prayer. He promised, "I will instruct thee and teach thee in the way which thou shalt go: I will guide thee with mine eye" (Ps. 32:8).

Many voices urge us to turn this way and that. Many things may distract from His way, but we must close our ears to them. We must stay close enough to hear His voice directing us. If the way is not clear before us, we must wait until it is.

Today are you uncertain which way to go? Perhaps the "traffic light" of your life is red, indicating you are to stop. Or it may be the yellow of caution. As you wait, in God's perfect timing, it will turn green; indicating that you can go ahead. You will hear the Lord say, "This is the way, walk ye in it, when you turn to the right hand, and when you turn to the left."

All scripture is given by inspiration of God, and is profitable for doctrine, for reproof, for correction, for instruction in righteousness: that the man of God may be perfect, thoroughly furnished unto all good works (2 Tim. 3:16-17).

As food is necessary for growth and development in our physical life, so God's Word is necessary for growth and maintenance of spiritual health. "Your words are what sustain me; they are food to my HUNGRY SOUL" (Jer. 15:16, LB).

Because the Bible is God-breathed, it is different from any other book. The secret of its power is that it is the direct revelation of the living God. It is His word of authority for our lives. Throughout its pages we read, "Thus saith the Lord."

The Bible is more than a book to impart knowledge. It reveals our need of a Savior, Jesus Christ. It is given for instruction, training, direction, and guidance in daily living. It gives us nourishment, maturing us into well-balanced Christians.

Paul reminded Timothy of the importance of knowing the Word of God and appropriating it as a guideline for life. He outlined for Timothy a four-fold way in which the Bible brings PROFIT to a life.

It is profitable, first, for doctrine—that is, for teaching. The Bible "is useful to teach us what is true" (2 Tim. 3:16, LB). Secondly, it is profitable for reproof—showing us where we are wrong, where we have deviated from God's plan. We need to be tested in the light of it to show us where we fall short, "to make us realize what is wrong in our lives" (v. 16, LB). Next, it is profitable for correction—setting and re-setting the direction of our lives in the right way. "It straightens us out" (v. 16, LB). It is also profitable for instruction in righteousness—how to keep us right. "And helps us do what is right" (v. 16, LB).

There is PURPOSE IN the Scripture. "It is God's way of making us well prepared at every point, fully equipped to do good to everyone" (v. 17, LB).

The principles for everyday living and the answers to life's needs are in the Bible.

What has the Bible done for your life? For mine? Is it your Guide Book?

January

15

Cast not away therefore your confidence, which hath great recompence of reward. For ye have need of patience, that, after ye have done the will of God, ye might receive the promise (Heb. 10:35-36).

I recall a young Christian couple who began their married life with a bright future. They purchased a beautiful home. They had a lovely family. They went into business. Everything was going well for them.

Then reverses came. They lost their business, home, car—everything. The young wife developed multiple sclerosis.

As trouble came, they turned to the Lord for help. They began seeking His will for their lives. As they committed their lives completely to Him, He became very real to them.

Through each new trial, their trust in the Lord deepened. Never once did they complain. If we voiced sympathy, they replied, "We wouldn't take anything for this experience. We know the Lord so much better than we did before."

Their difficulties left them unshaken, for their confidence was not in the things they had acquired. They had placed their trust and confidence—not in possessions—but in the PERSON JESUS CHRIST; and they discovered that HE was sufficient.

Instead of CASTING away their CONFIDENCE in the Lord, they "cast on HIM their CARES." "Casting all your care upon Him; for He careth for you" (1 Peter 5:7).

Confidence in the Lord means having trust, reliance, complete dependence on Him. Yet we so often become impatient when our needs are not met according to our time schedule. Sometimes our prayers are answered immediately. More often the answer is delayed. We may even have to wait for years.

Delay is a process God uses in our lives to teach us PATIENCE. He delays answering prayer to enlarge our capacity to receive the answer He wants to give us. He allows problems to come to strengthen our confidence in Him.

In Proverbs 3:26 we read, "THE LORD shall be THY confidence." Is He YOUR confidence today? Or are you casting it away? It is never a mistake to put your confidence in Him, for He NEVER fails.

Someone has said, "You keep your confidence, and He'll keep your cares."

There were the potters, and those that dwelt among plants and hedges: there they dwelt with the king for his work (1 Chron. 4:23).

On the television program "What's My Line?" many interesting and varied lines of work have been discovered. The program specialized in discovering and presenting people whose fields of activity were unusual.

God has varied fields of service for His children. He doesn't use all of them in the same place or give them the same work. Some serve in places of public activity; others in areas hidden from view.

In the midst of the long list of family names in 1 Chronicles 4, we find potters and gardeners mentioned as workers for the king. You might expect to find the king's workers in his palace, but not among the pottery, the plants and hedges. They may not have chosen this as a place of service for the king, but even THERE in a seemingly insignificant place, they dwelt WITH the king, FOR his work.

Today we may not be in the place of our choosing. Perhaps we are at home when our desire is for some public service for the Lord. Or we may be far from home in a place so hidden we wonder at times if God even remembers we are there. Wherever we are, we must remember God has a purpose in allowing us to be THERE—to DWELL there with the King to do His WORK.

However, we must be careful not to be so involved in working for Him that we overlook dwelling with Him. Before we can be effective workers for Him THERE, we must take time to commune with Him. When Jesus chose His disciples, we read, "And He ordained twelve, that they should be WITH HIM and that He might send them forth to preach" (Mark 3:14). We are not to dwell with the work, but with the king. We are not to dwell with our needs, our problems, our helplessness, our circumstances, but with the King.

We can be assured that wherever we are today, our King, the Lord Jesus Christ, is dwelling with us THERE. What a privilege is ours. First—DWELLERS with HIM; then—WORKERS for HIM.

January 17

Rejoicing in hope; patient in tribulation; continuing in prayer (Rom. 12:12).

We are not guaranteed a life of ease and happiness when we become Christians. Problems still come; adversity and affliction still strike. Paul has given a formula in today's Scripture verse to help maintain our spiritual radiance.

First, there is the "Radiance of Rejoicing." We are to rejoice in hope. Without hope, life can become unbearable. We hope things will be better tomorrow. We hope to be taken out of our present circumstances. The Christian can rejoice in this hope in his Christian life, for it becomes real through Jesus Christ. "Christ in you, the hope of glory" (Col. 1:27).

Our hope reaches beyond today, even beyond our present life. It reaches into eternity. This is the hope of His return. "Looking for that blessed hope" (Titus 2:13). We can rejoice in the midst of our trials today because our "Rejoicing Hope" is assured.

Next, there is the "Radiance of Patience." We are to be patient in tribulation. Tribulation literally means "pressing together," or "pressure." We need to learn patience. God uses tribulation to teach us patience—being patient under pressure.

To develop patience, we must be placed in situations where we are given opportunities to grow. The trial that requires patience in order to endure it, develops the patience to endure. In James 1:3 and 4 (LB) we read, "For when the way is rough, your patience has a chance to grow. So let it grow, and don't try to squirm out of your problems. For when your patience is finally in full bloom, then you will be ready for anything, strong in character, full and complete."

Then there is the "Radiance of Prayer." We are to continue steadfast in prayer. Prayer will keep our hope alive, and give endurance for our present needs. An effective prayer life lifts us above our circumstances. God has told us to pray; not "if you pray" but "when you pray."

In prayer we have communion and fellowship with God. But prayer is for more than fellowship. It is being in partnership with Him in accomplishing His great eternal purpose and plan.

Are we maintaining our spiritual radiance? Are we rejoicing in hope, patient in tribulation, and steadfast in prayer?

Therefore I say unto you, What things soever ye desire, when ye pray, believe that ye receive them, and ye shall have them (Mark 11:24).

Jesus said there is a faith in God that can move mountains (Mark 11:23). He did not necessarily refer to physical mountains, but mountains of fear, doubt, despair, and discouragement. He said that if we pray with "mountain-moving" faith, believing, we will receive answers.

You may have wondered what it means to pray, believing. There have been times when we have prayed for a great need in our lives. We committed this need to God; then we said, "Now I have faith to believe God is going to answer my prayer." We waited for the answer, yet nothing happened. We decided we lacked enough faith. The reason may have been that we were trying to generate our own faith. This we cannot do. Faith is not working up assurance by our will that prayer will be answered.

Faith to believe begins with God, the source of our faith. An increased knowledge of God strengthens our faith. Abraham's intimate relationship with God made him a man of strong faith. The stronger our faith in Him, the stronger will be our confidence as we come to Him in believing prayer, assured He will answer.

Martin Lloyd-Jones said, "Faith does not look at itself or the person exercising it. Faith looks at God, holding on to His faithfulness. The measure of the strength of a man's faith always is ultimately the measure of his knowledge of God."

A secret to believing and receiving prayer is the phrase, "what things soever ye desire." The psalmist said, "Delight thyself also IN THE LORD; and he shall give thee the DESIRES of THINE HEART" (Ps. 37:4). Can we say His desires are our desires? Can we say of each request, "I am praying this request with Him as His desire; I am praying it for His glory"?

Trust comes from confidence in the person trusted. We can pray in faith believing because we have complete trust in the One to whom we are praying.

January
19

But the God of all grace, who hath called us unto his eternal glory by Christ Jesus, after that ye have suffered a while, make you perfect, stablish, strengthen, settle you (1 Peter 5:10).

We are living in a trouble-filled world. Many people are facing problems almost insurmountable; many are undergoing great suffering. Trials are testing them almost to the limit of human endurance.

We need not be surprised when suffering comes—it is inevitable. Sometimes it extends through weeks, even years. To the suffering one it seems so long. But Peter said, "after we have suffered A LITTLE WHILE." It is a little while when compared with the glory of heaven. Our life on earth is brief compared with eternity. "For our light affliction, which is but for a moment, worketh for us a far more exceeding and eternal weight of glory" (2 Cor. 4:17).

In accomplishing His purpose, God will use suffering to perfect our lives. "Perfect," in today's verse, means to adjust, fit or join together, the same thought as a dislocated bone being put back into place. Our own wills need to be adjusted to God's. It is the God of all grace who does the adjusting.

The Lord uses strong winds of adversity and suffering to help establish us in our faith, making us steadfast, strengthening our character and settling us firmly on the foundation of Jesus Christ. The Lord "set my feet upon a rock, and established my goings" (Ps. 40:2).

It is said that the old Damascus blade, used for making swords, was so tempered by heating, cooling, and hammering that it would not break even though the point was bent back to the hilt. God uses suffering to temper our lives, perfecting, establishing, strengthening, and settling us so that we do not break under the pressures and tensions of life.

"After you have suffered a little while, our God, who is full of kindness through Christ, will give you His eternal glory. He personally will come and pick you up, and set you firmly in place, and make you stronger than ever" (1 Peter 5:10, LB).

The steps of a [*good*] *man are directed and established of the Lord, when He delights in his way* [*and He busies Himself with his every step*] *(Ps. 37:23,* Amplified).

Walking is made up of steps. In our walk of faith with God, He doesn't lead us a year, a month, or even a day at a time, but just step by step. "He busies Himself with his (our) every step."

When the children of Israel were on their way through the wilderness, God directed their steps with a cloud by day and a pillar of fire by night. When it moved, they moved. When it stopped, they did, too. It is important for us, also, to move at His pace, never running ahead of Him, nor lagging behind.

God may have unusual ways of directing our steps, and it is important to follow His guidance.

One evening I was returning to Denver by plane. I usually sat in the back of the plane. However, that night, to my surprise, my feet would not go in that direction. I found myself going to the front of the plane. Just before we took off, a woman hurried on board. She came to the front, taking a seat beside me. I could see she was distraught. She told me that she and her husband had received a long distance call from Denver, telling them their teen-age son was being rushed to the hospital for emergency surgery. Because he was having some emotional problems, she was unusually concerned.

Suddenly I found myself saying, "The Lord can take care of your need." As she looked at me, she said, "You're a Christian, aren't you?" "Yes, I am," I replied. Then she said, "I was so upset, that on the way to the airport I prayed, asking the Lord to put a Christian beside me." In flight, at the very time her son was undergoing surgery, we prayed for him. When we landed someone met her to tell her the operation had been successful.

God had directed my steps to His choice of seat that night, not mine. Where do our steps lead us? Do we let Him direct them? Where do our steps lead others?

"We should make no footprints of our own."

January
21

And she said unto her husband, Behold now, I perceive that this is an holy man of God, which passeth by us continually (2 Kings 4:9).

One day as Elisha was going through Shunem, a woman invited him to stop and eat with her and her husband. We aren't told her name, but she was a woman of influence. She was spoken of as "a great woman" (2 Kings 4:8). When Elisha left, she invited him to stop whenever he passed by.

This woman was discerning, for she recognized the spiritual depth of Elisha's life. She didn't speak of him as a great man, a successful man, or a brilliant man, but a holy man. It was not so much what he did or said that impressed her as what she saw in his life. She said to her husband, "I perceive that this is a holy man of God which passeth by us continually." A holy person is not pious, trying to impress people with his spirituality, but is genuine and real, one in whom people see the wonderful life of our Lord.

Elisha did not live as a recluse, but ministered to people wherever he went. His holy walk was continuous, not just when he felt like it, or when he thought he had time, but CONTINUALLY.

While Jesus lived on earth He passed along the roads through the villages where the people were. One day a blind beggar was sitting by the side of the road. Hearing the crowd of people on the road, he asked what the excitement was. "Jesus of Nazareth passeth by" (Luke 18:37), he was told.

Jesus is still "passing by" today in our lives. What do people say as we pass by? What do they see in our lives to remind them of the Lord Jesus? Does our conduct and conversation reflect His presence in us?

When asked what program of evangelism was carried on in an area of West Africa, a girl replied, "We send one or two Christian families to live in a village. When the villagers see what Christians are like, they want to become Christians."

All that some people know about God is what they see in our lives.

Be strong and courageous, be not afraid nor dismayed for the king of Assyria, nor for all the multitude that is with him: for there be more with us than with him: with him is an arm of flesh; but with us is the Lord our God to help us, and to fight our battles. And the people rested themselves upon the words of Hezekiah king of Judah (2 Chron. 32:7-8).

Sennacherib, King of Assyria, was waging war on Judah. The final attack was to be on Jerusalem. Hezekiah, King of Judah, didn't minimize the power of the enemy, yet he recognized that their great strength was only an arm of flesh. The army of Judah didn't have great human resources, but their trust was in GOD. "With him is an arm of flesh; BUT with US is the LORD OUR GOD to help us; and to fight our battles."

One time King Jehoshaphat faced a powerful enemy. Knowing he and his army lacked strength enough to overcome such a formidable foe, he went to his one certain source of help—God. He prayed, "For we have no might against this great company that cometh against us; neither know we what to do: BUT our eyes are upon thee." God answered, "Be not afraid nor dismayed by reason of this great multitude; for the battle is not yours, but God's" (2 Chron. 20:12, 15).

We, too, face a powerful foe. His attacks often come to us in very subtle ways. It may be a temptation or a feeling of defeat. Discouragement may overwhelm us. We may find ourselves in a place of danger. We may face insurmountable problems. We have no power of ourselves against such a strong enemy. We know not what to do. But the battle is not ours. With us is the LORD OUR GOD to fight it for us. As we keep our eyes upon Him we need not fear, for it is not too much for Him. Victory is not dependent on us, but on God.

More important than where we are or what we have is WHO is with us. It has been said, "Safety is not the absence of danger, but the presence of the Lord."

January

23

And therefore will the Lord wait, that he may be gracious unto you, and therefore will he be exalted, that he may have mercy upon you: for the Lord is a God of judgment: blessed are all they that wait for him (Isa. 30:18).

Today people are impatient. Before the traffic light is completely changed, the car behind has honked to hurry us up. When we enter a store or office we want immediate service.

This same impatience often carries over into our relationship with God. We bring a request to Him and expect an immediate answer. We become impatient when it is not forthcoming.

However, God knows the importance of our learning the lesson of waiting, not only our waiting on God, but His waiting on us. He may allow us to wait that we may be better prepared for the answer to our request. He may let us wait that our capacity to receive His answer may be enlarged. He may have things to accomplish in the lives of others before He can give us what we are asking. He may know that we are still too self-sufficient. But our waiting is never in vain.

There may be lessons of patience to learn which can come only through waiting. "But let patience have her perfect work, that ye may be perfect and entire, wanting nothing" (James 1:4). Sometimes we want our own way and are not willing to wait for His plan to be revealed to us. In our impatience we choose our way instead of God's. We miss God's best because of our unwillingness to wait.

To have a harvest of fruit, there must be a waiting period for the fruit to form and ripen on the trees. God often has to give us a waiting period for spiritual fruit to be produced in our lives. We may think He has forgotten us, but He knows when we are ready. He is never ahead of schedule, never late, but always on time. Remember, if He waits longer than you wish, it is only to make the blessing more abundant when it comes.

"God's delays are not always denials!"

Blessed is the man whose strength is in thee; in whose heart are the ways of them (Ps. 84:5).

In these days when we are pressured on every side, we often wonder how we will make it through the day. We need a strength beyond our own limited supply.

It is encouraging to know there is strength available for us, sufficient for today's need. The source of this strength is God Himself. "Blessed is the man whose strength is in THEE." The supply is inexhaustible, enough for everyone, and ready for us to draw upon at all times. We are not provided tomorrow's strength today, but we are given strength for today. The *Living Bible* (Ps. 84:5) reads, "Happy are those who are strong in the Lord, who want above all else to follow your steps."

Blessed also is the one "in whose heart are the ways of them." The words "of them" are in italics in the Bible. If we omit these two words we read "in whose heart are the ways." In the heart of the child of God are God's ways, His likenesses, His way of doing things. It is a heart guided and directed by God. It has been said, "God's ways must rule our hearts if our feet are to tread God's paths."

As trials come, we may find ourselves in the Valley of Baca, which means weeping. Our reaction to such experiences is important. We can become bitter, filled with self-pity, or we can let the valley be transformed into a blessing. "When they walk through the Valley of Weeping it will become a place of springs where pools of blessing and refreshment collect after rains!" (Ps. 84:6, LB).

Our tears can become wells of grace and springs of blessing. We might ask ourselves, "What am I leaving behind in the valley of weeping? Murmuring or complaining? Or praise and joy?"

In our physical life, we go from strength to weakness. But in the Lord, we go from strength to strength. Our strength may fail, but His is limitless. Paul wrote, "That is why we never give up. Though our bodies are dying, our inner strength in the Lord is growing every day" (2 Cor. 4:16, LB).

January
25

We are Christ's ambassadors. God is using us to speak to you; we beg you, as though Christ himself were here pleading with you, receive the love he offers you–be reconciled to God (2 Cor. 5:20, LB).

An ambassador is an authorized representative sent from one government to another to act on behalf of the country which sent him. His own interests, opinions, and ambitions must be put aside. The decisions he makes must be for the interest of his country, influenced in no way by personal ideas. His whole life is given completely to fulfilling this mission.

Paul was an ambassador for the Lord Jesus Christ. He had no desires, plans, or interests of his own. His whole-hearted loyalty and obedience was to Jesus Christ. The Greek word for ambassador has the meaning of "the one who spoke for the emperor." Paul had the authority to speak for Jesus Christ, the King of Kings. "We [as Christ's personal representatives] beg you for His sake to lay hold of the divine favor [now offered you] and be reconciled to God" (2 Cor. 5:20, *Amplified*).

We, too, as members of God's family, are personal representatives for Christ. It is a divine appointment. "As my Father hath sent me, even so send I you" (John 20:21). We are here in Christ's stead. "We beg you, as though CHRIST himself were here pleading with you" (2 Cor. 5:20, LB). We have a message to proclaim: ". . . be reconciled to God."

Living here today in Christ's place is a responsibility not to be taken lightly. It means putting aside our ambitions and aims. It means giving Him priority in our lives. We are His representatives in what we do, what we say, and where we go.

We aren't told to be His ambassadors when we feel like it, or when we want to, or if we feel qualified. It says "WE ARE." He doesn't use all of us in the same place. He may send some to faraway places, others He puts in a public ministry, or in a hidden place. Home may be the place of service for some.

Are you in your appointed place today, as His ambassador, in His stead? Or are you holding back from obeying His call?

For I have learned, in whatsoever state I am, therewith to be content (Phil. 4:11).

Contentment is defined as "satisfaction; the state of being happy with what one has or is." It has been described as "that which calms you down."

Have you ever said, "If I could have that dress (car, home, or business position), I could be content"? Yet after you obtained it, you were not satisfied. You wanted something else. You discovered that acquiring possessions does not bring contentment. Someone has said, "A person's life is a constant struggle to lift his earning power up to his yearning power."

People today are searching for that which will bring contentment. But because they seek in the wrong place for the wrong things, it eludes them.

Paul learned that there is contentment and it was not dependent on his outward condition, for he was in prison when he wrote Philippians. Translators inserted "therewith" in this verse, emphasizing that Paul was content with his circumstances. When we omit the word, "therewith," we discover that the emphasis is not on Paul being content WITH his circumstances, but being content IN them.

He learned that real contentment was in Jesus Christ, His sufficiency and satisfaction. "For he satisfieth the longing soul, and filleth the hungry soul with goodness" (Ps. 107:9).

Contentment is the inner satisfaction that enables us to live in quietness, peace, and acceptance. "Not that I am implying that I was in any personal want, for I have learned how to be content (satisfied to the point where I am not disturbed or disquieted) in whatever state I am" (Phil. 4:11, *Amplified*).

Have you learned to be content? Possession of material things, social position, fame, talent will not give you permanent contentment. But you can be contented today regardless of where you are, what you are, what you have or what you do not have. Real contentment for you can be had through the Lord Jesus Christ.

Paul wrote, "[And it is, indeed, a source of immense profit, for] godliness accompanied with contentment—that contentment which is a sense of inward sufficiency—is great and abundant gain" (1 Tim. 6:6, *Amplified*).

January

27

I will lift up my eyes to the hills [around Jerusalem, to sacred Mount Zion and Mount Moriah]. From whence shall my help come? My help comes from the Lord, Who made Heaven and earth (Ps. 121:1-2, Amplified).

For years I lived at the foot of the Rocky Mountains. They never ceased to thrill me to the depth of my soul as I viewed their grandeur and majesty, and felt their power and strength. But even though I sensed the awesomeness of their beauty, my thoughts would go beyond the hills to the One who made them. With an UPWARD LOOK to God, I would meditate on His greatness and power.

The psalmist must have experienced this same feeling as he looked up at the hills surrounding Jerusalem, for he said, "My help comes from the Lord who made heaven and earth."

Today many people are facing problems for which they are seeking help. Some have been left alone; others are in a mental depression; some have physical handicaps. There are single girls who want to be married. Many are turning for help to tranquilizers, sleeping pills, pep pills, alcohol, and dope. Increasing numbers are seeking the help of counselors, psychologists, and psychiatrists. Although God may use people to encourage us in our time of need, the one sure source of help is the Lord Himself. "MY HELP cometh from THE LORD."

Are you in the valley of despair, disappointment, discouragement, or disillusionment today? Are you looking for help? Human sources cannot be depended upon, but real help comes from the Lord. We need to "look up" beyond our needs to the Lord Jesus, the One who can meet them. If He is powerful enough to create the heavens and earth, cannot He help us with our problems? He may not remove us from our desperate situation, but will lead us through it, if we keep our eyes focused on Him. He comes to us bringing comfort, pouring His healing balm into our wounds. His arms of strength uphold us.

"God is our refuge and strength, a very PRESENT HELP in trouble" (Ps. 46:1).

This is the day which the Lord hath made; we will rejoice and be glad in it (Ps. 118:24).

How often, at the close of the day, have you said, "What a day this has been! I should never have gotten up this morning"? Probably most of us have had this experience.

Our attitude at the beginning of the day can set the pace for that day. If we begin with a spirit of complaining, dreading our day's schedule, wondering how we will have the strength and wisdom to meet its demands, soon we become filled with self-pity and discouragement.

What a difference it makes if we first look into the face of God as we waken. We can prepare ourselves for the day by committing it to Him; by asking Him to guard our conversation, actions, and thoughts, that they will be pleasing to Him; by taking time to tell Him we love Him. Remember that "THIS IS THE FIRST DAY OF THE REST OF OUR LIVES." We must ask God to fit it into His plan for us.

Each day offers new opportunities. There will be new choices to make, new decisions, new avenues of service for the Lord. It may even be a day filled with heartache and pain, a day filled with unsolved problems. How different our day will be if we begin with a rejoicing spirit, knowing it has been entrusted to us by the Lord!

God has given His promises to encourage us through the day. "And as thy DAYS, so shall thy strength be" (Deut. 33:25). "The Lord is good, a strong hold in the DAY of trouble" (Nah. 1:7).

Yesterday, with its successes and failures, is past. We are not to look back. We can rest in the knowledge that tomorrow is still in God's hand. Only today is ours to live for Him. So it is important how we use it, for "Today is part of my life work." Our joy is not in the day, but in "the Lord" who made the day.

The psalmist said, "Every day will I bless thee; and I will praise thy name for ever and ever" (Ps. 145:2). "Every day" includes today. "A DAY TO USE OR LOSE."

January
29

As newborn babes, desire the sincere milk of the word, that ye may grow thereby (1 Peter 2:2).

If we could measure our spiritual growth in the past year, would we be satisfied? Instead of looking back, may we look forward to new opportunities for spiritual growth this year.

Peter uses an interesting metaphor as an illustration of our Christian growth. He compares the Word of God to milk. Just as babies depend on milk for growth, the Christian must depend on the Word of God for spiritual nourishment. Jeremiah wrote, "Your words are what sustain me; they are food to my hungry soul. They bring joy to my sorrowing heart and delight me. How proud I am to bear your name, O Lord" (Jer. 15:16, LB).

A glass of milk sitting before us does us no good. To be nourished, we must drink it. So with our spiritual food. We must do more than desire it. We must eat it. "But he answered and said, It is written, Man shall not live by bread alone, but by every word that proceedeth out of the mouth of God" (Matt. 4:4). Many Christians are suffering from malnutrition because they do not regularly feed on the Word of God.

A healthy, normal person has an appetite for food. A healthy Christian will have a desire for God's Word. Loss of appetite is a warning in our physical life. So, also, if we have no desire for God's Word, there is a reason. The Holy Spirit will reveal and remove anything from our lives that is hindering our development if we let Him.

Sometimes a new Christian questions, "Why should I have to read the Bible and pray every day? Why should God make me do that?" God doesn't make us. But if we don't spend time with Him, we are the loser.

As we read and assimilate the Word of God, we grow in the knowledge of Jesus Christ. "But grow in grace, and in the knowledge of our Lord and Saviour Jesus Christ" (2 Peter 3:18).

Where the Bible is read not only with the eyes but with the mind and heart, the life is changed.

"Let the word of Christ dwell in you richly" (Col. 3:16).

Wherefore laying aside all malice, and all guile, and hypocrisies, and envies, and all evil speakings (1 Peter 2:1).

Yesterday we considered the necessity of the Word of God for spiritual growth. As a normal person has a hunger for food, so a normal Christian has a desire for God's Word. When there is no such appetite, something is wrong.

Peter enumerates a number of things which lessen the desire for the Word of God and hinder spiritual growth. They must be eliminated from our lives, if we are to mature spiritually.

First, malice must be put away. Malice is the harboring of unkind thoughts about others, an evil intent to harm others, a desire to get even. As we feed on malice, resentments and bitterness build up. This must be removed.

We must remove all guile, deceitfulness, and slyness. Of Jesus it is said, "Neither was guile found in his mouth" (1 Peter 2:22). Hypocrisy, pretense, insincerity, pretending to be what we are not, must be eliminated.

Sometimes we are envious of what others have, or of honors they receive. We become jealous of someone who receives a position we desired. This kind of spirit hinders our spiritual growth.

Evil speaking, gossip, and even slander can easily creep into our conversation. If you could play a tape of your conversation for the past week, would you want to change what you said? Our talk may hold back our spiritual development.

Have you recognized any of these hindrances in your life? Peter said they must all be removed, every one of them. Sometimes they are so deeply rooted, they have to be cut out.

If we do our part in confessing them, God does His part in forgiving and cleansing. "If we confess our sins, he is faithful and just to forgive us our sins, and to cleanse us from all unrighteousness" (1 John 1:9).

Not only are we to remove these hindrances from our lives, but we must nourish ourselves by feeding upon God's Word. Psalm 119:11 gives us the secret. "Thy word have I hid in mine heart, that I might not sin against thee." Job said, "I have esteemed the words of his mouth more than my necessary food" (Job. 23:12).

January
31

Preach the word; be instant in season, out of season; reprove, rebuke, exhort with all long suffering and doctrine (2 Tim. 4:2).

Recently a brand new year was placed in our hands. This year represents an investment of three hundred sixty five golden days, eighty seven hundred sixty silver hours, and five hundred twenty-five thousand six hundred diamond minutes. As we spend this time allotted to us, many opportunities and challenges will present themselves. Have you asked yourself, "How am I going to invest this year? For myself? For my family? For God?" It has been said that each day is a day to use or lose.

Paul challenged Timothy to communicate the gospel; to "preach the Word." The word used here for "preach" is a strong word, meaning "proclaim God's message with authority."

He encouraged Timothy to persevere. "Be instant in season, out of season;" "be urgent." Paul was an example of a life dedicated to sharing his faith. "So, much as in me is, I am ready to preach the gospel to you that are at Rome also." (Rom. 1:15).

The challenge is for us today. The Bible says, "GO YE into all the world, and preach the gospel to every creature" (Mark 16:15). We are to be in constant readiness to share the gospel, not occasionally, not just when we feel like it, nor when convenient. But day after day, at all times, we are to live for Him and make Him known to others: "to preach the Word of God urgently at all times, whenever you get the chance, in season and out, when it is convenient and when it is not" (2 Tim. 3:2, LB). It is a lifetime ministry; we are never on vacation.

The Duke of Wellington asked a British soldier slouching in his uniform, "Why do you stand in such an unbecoming position?" "I am off duty, sir," the man replied. "A British officer is never off duty," said the Duke. "Resume your military position."

So, too, in the service of the King of Kings, a Christian is never off duty, but is to be ready at all times to share with others the gospel of Jesus Christ.

"God doesn't want our spare time, but our precious time."

According to my earnest expectation and my hope, that in nothing I shall be ashamed, but that with all boldness, as always, so now also Christ shall be magnified in my body, whether it be by life, or by death (Phil. 1:20).

My husband's hobby was photography. Often we went into the high Rockies to take pictures of tiny flowers, many of them no larger than the head of a pin. By using high powered lens, the smallest flowers were magnified to fill the entire picture.

Paul desired Christ to be so magnified that He would fill his life; that at all times and in all places Christ might have the preeminence. "But that I will always be ready to speak out boldly for Christ while I am going through all these trials here, just as I have in the past; and that I will always be an honor to Christ, whether I live or whether I must die" (Phil. 1:20, LB).

Major Ian Thomas was asked what his purpose in life was. He replied, "To make the invisible Christ visible."

You may say, "This is my desire; that Christ be magnified in my life. I want Him to so fill my life that He may be seen by others. But it is difficult in my circumstances. If only I were in a different environment I could magnify Him. If I lived in another neighborhood, worked in another office, or had a different family situation, I could magnify Him."

At the time Paul wrote this, his circumstances were not conducive to such a life. He was in prison, yet he didn't complain or pray to be released. He rejoiced in the opportunities to magnify Christ there.

Because Paul had a single-hearted devotion to Jesus Christ, he had no desires or plans of his own. He could say, "If Christ will be magnified by my living, I want to live. If he will be magnified more by my death, I am ready to die." It has been said, "He had an aim worth living for and also worth dying for." Do we?

"O magnify the Lord with me, and let us exalt His name together" (Ps. 34:3).

February

2

And there was a famine in the land (Gen. 12:10).

At times have you followed what you thought was God's will, yet things didn't go as you expected? In fact, your circumstances became worse. You may have wondered if you had mistaken God's will.

God called Abraham to leave his home and move to Canaan. After his arrival, "there was a famine in the land"(Gen. 12:10). No rain fell, crops burned up, pasture land became brown and dry, food supplies diminished. Perhaps Abraham wondered if he had rightly understood God's call. Could he have been wrong in coming to Canaan?

Realizing the seriousness of the famine, he feared for the future of his family. Instead of trusting God to meet their needs, he decided to move to Egypt. "Abram went down into Egypt to sojourn there; for the famine was grievous in the land" (v. 10). Rather than wait for God to provide his needs, he made his own plans, thus missing an opportunity to learn new lessons of faith.

Perhaps you are facing difficulties you cannot understand. Your circumstances do not seem to agree with the guidance you thought God gave you. This is not proof that He is displeased with you, or that you are out of His will.

Our natural reaction is to look for a way out. We try to take things into our own hands as Abraham did. But God will assume the responsibility for working our situation out if we stay where He has placed us and wait on Him. He knows the reason for our difficulty. He knows the lessons we need to learn. He sees the end from the beginning in our lives. He knows the purpose He wants to accomplish even though we do not see or understand. He knows how the test of today can strengthen us for tomorrow. Instead of asking God to take us out of our trouble, we need to let Him teach us the lessons to be learned through it.

At such times we can say, "You brought me here. I will stay until You clearly show me what to do." How true is the statement, "It is better to walk in the dark with God than to walk alone by sight."

And call upon me in the day of trouble; I will deliver thee, and thou shalt glorify me (Ps. 50:15).

When doctors practice together, they usually take turns being "on call" evenings, weekends, and holidays. When patients call, they are referred to the particular doctor on duty.

God has a communication system between Himself and His children. He is always "on call," twenty-four hours a day. Regardless of the number of calls He receives, even many at the same time, He never misses one. He answers each one personally.

Trouble comes to all of us. "Yet man is born unto trouble, as the sparks fly upward" (Job. 5:7). It may strike very suddenly. But God is personally "on call." "Call upon Me in YOUR day of trouble." He hears even our weakest cry.

God has given His promise that when we call He will deliver. He doesn't say, "I may deliver," "I will try to deliver," "Perhaps I will deliver," "I will deliver if I feel like it," or "If I'm not too busy I will deliver," but "I WILL deliver."

He who promised to deliver, has the power to do it. "That power belongeth unto God" (Ps. 62:11). He will shake heaven and earth to deliver you if need be. God is the One who delivers, not people, although He often uses people.

What do we do when trouble comes? Do we try every human resource first? All we need do in the midst of trouble is call, and He is on the other end of the line. He assures us He will deliver, but He will do it in a way that will glorify Himself. He promises to deliver us, but He doesn't say when. It may be today, next week, or next year. He is not in a hurry, as we are. He knows the right moment.

After God listens to our need, He completes our call; He delivers us. Sometimes we are delivered from trouble. Sometimes we are delivered from defeat in the midst of trouble. Spurgeon said, "He has solemnly promised, and He will fully perform."

Today we are as close to God as a call. "Call unto ME—and I will deliver THEE."

February

4

Put on therefore, as the elect of God, holy and beloved, bowels of mercies, kindness, humbleness of mind, meekness, longsuffering (Col. 3:12).

Today's world is fashion conscious. Outfits are carefully selected and coordinated for each occasion. Even men's fashions have a new look.

More important than the proper selection of our outer wardrobe is our inner attire. The above Scripture mentions various articles of our spiritual wardrobe.

The first piece is "bowels of mercies," often translated "a heart of compassion." It is a heart of empathy, the ability to put ourselves in the place of others, touched by their suffering. An old Indian custom was to select judges to try an accused person of doing wrong. One judge said he would not judge an Indian until he had walked in his moccasins three weeks.

Our clothing must include kindness, gentleness, and a gracious disposition, both in word and deed. We are to be thoughtful of others, unselfish, encouraging those who need such help.

Our head covering is humbleness of mind. This is not just lowliness of attitude toward one's self; it is not thinking of self at all. Meekness is a part of our apparel. It is accepting without resistance God's dealings with us, recognizing they are for our good.

Longsuffering is part of our attire. It is suffering patiently without complaining, even when the suffering continues a long time.

A forgiving spirit adds beauty to our outfit; not only the willingness to forgive but also to forget (Col. 3:13).

When da Vinci was painting his great masterpiece, *The Last Supper,* he became angry with someone. When he returned to his fresco and began to paint the face of Jesus, he was unable to work on it. He had to find the man and ask forgiveness before he could continue.

The last piece of attire is love (v. 14); the love of Christ implanted in us and shed abroad by the Holy Spirit.

The Lord Jesus Himself set the example for the correct fashion for our spiritual wardrobe. This spiritual attire is available for us, but we must let the Holy Spirit adorn our lives with it.

Today are you wearing the spiritual outfit of the "well dressed" child of God?

God is our refuge and strength, a very present help in trouble (Ps. 46:1).

This is a Psalm of comfort and trust for a life filled with trouble. When problems arise and discouragements come, when there is no human source of help, we have the promise that God is "our refuge," "our strength," and "our help."

Refuge is defined as "shelter from danger or distress." The Lord Jesus Christ IS our refuge today (present tense). Hidden in the hollow of His all-mighty hand, we have a shelter that is safe and secure. This refuge is not a place where we escape from the situations and circumstances of life, but is a protection for us in the midst of them.

Not only is the Lord our refuge in time of trouble, but our strength to endure it. When we realize our limited strength is not sufficient, we discover He has a never-ending supply of strength on which we can draw. "And as thy days, so shall thy strength be" (Deut. 33:25).

He is also our help in trouble. Whatever our need may be, He wants us to know that, "I AM, right now, this very moment, not only your help in trouble, but a PRESENT help." It has been said, "It sometimes takes trouble for God to get our attention."

When we become Christians, we often assume our days of trouble are over. Soon we discover this is not true. God has a purpose to accomplish through difficulties in our lives. Some lessons can only be learned through trouble.

We are proved and tested in this way. "A very present and WELL PROVED HELP in trouble" (Ps. 46:1, *Amplified*). "A TESTED help in times of trouble" (LB). It has been said, "Trouble is His vote of confidence in us."

He is a "well-proved help," a "tested help." Are you testing and proving Him as your own personal refuge, strength, and help in your problems and trials of today?

There is a poem that begins, "He's helping me now, this moment; in ways that I know and I know not." He is our help today, whatever our day.

February
6

Wherefore seeing we also are compassed about with so great a cloud of witnesses, let us lay aside every weight, and the sin which doth so easily beset us, and let us run with patience the race that is set before us (Heb. 12:1).

Many illustrations are used in Scripture to describe the Christian life. One is the comparison of a Christian to a runner in a race. The writer of Hebrews very likely had in mind the great amphitheater where Greek games, including foot races, were held. Eager spectators crowded the sidelines to watch the participants as they expended every bit of energy in running it.

The Greeks realized the importance of a rigid physical fitness program to prepare for the race. It required proper diet, sufficient rest, and consistent exercise.

In the arena of life, each of us is running our race on the course God planned for us. ". . . let us run with patience the race that is set before us." A strong "spiritual fitness" program is necessary to run it successfully.

We need a properly balanced spiritual diet. Our basic food is God's Word. "But he answered and said, It is written, Man shall not live by bread alone, but by every word that proceedeth out of the mouth of God" (Matt. 4:4). A consistent prayer life gives the needed inner calm to face life quietly and courageously. The exercise of faith also strengthens us for the race. An inadequate training program will not properly condition us.

Every weight and sin impeding our spiritual progress must be relinquished. A career, ambitions, money, habits, friends, despondency, pride, anger, envy, or murmuring may be a hindrance in our lives. Although they may not be the same for each of us, any obstacle in our lives affecting our relationship with the Lord must be removed.

The word "lay aside" means to cast off deliberately, without hesitancy; to put off all non-essentials, when evaluated in the light of eternity.

Take time today to check your own personal race. Are you maintaining your spiritual fitness program? How do you rate as you check your spiritual diet, rest, and exercise? Are there any obstacles to be removed?

Today is part of your race of life.

Wherefore seeing we also are compassed about with so great a cloud of witnesses (Heb. 12:1).

In ancient times, eager spectators crowded the amphitheater, watching with great interest as the runners started their race. The above Scripture mentions witnesses watching us as we run our race of life. "Therefore then, since we are surrounded by so great a cloud of witnesses [who have borne testimony of the Truth]" (Heb. 12:1, *Amplified*).

In Hebrews 11 we find a list of some of God's family who have completed their race. They were ordinary people who faced problems and experienced difficult situations as we do. Yet they emerged victorious, strong in their faith. Their example can be a great inspiration and encouragement to us.

As I read the Bible, I search for lessons I can learn from the lives of such witnesses. From Abraham, I have learned lessons of faith. When God called him to leave his home, he obeyed, even though he didn't know where God was leading him. Noah walked with God in the midst of a people of whom God said, "The wickedness of man was great in the earth, and that every imagination of the thoughts of his heart was only evil continually" (Gen. 6:5). Elijah lived in close touch with God, an example of a great man of prayer.

From Mary I have learned the important secret of sitting at the feet of Jesus and listening to His Word. I have been encouraged by David's trust in the Lord, even when forsaken by family and friends. Job has given me comfort for the times of heartache and sorrow I have encountered on my course. The words of Paul have offered instruction, correction, and inspiration to assist in my race of patient endurance.

As I study their lives I realize they finished their race triumphantly because of their trust in the Lord God. This is an encouragement to me, knowing that as I, too, trust my life to Him, He will take me across the finish line victoriously. "But thanks be to God, which giveth us the victory through our Lord Jesus Christ" (1 Cor. 15:57).

February

8

And let us run with patience the race that is set before us (Heb. 12:1).

Our race of life is not always easy. At times we may long to drop out. Discouragements may turn us aside, but we must not give up. The *Amplified Bible* (Heb. 12:1) reads, "Let us run with patient endurance and steady and active persistence the appointed course of the race that is set before us."

Many of us run spasmodically. We start with a great burst of speed; but when the speed begins to wear off, we find it hard to keep going. Paul encouraged us with these words, "And let us not lose heart and grow weary and faint in acting nobly and doing right, for in due time and at the appointed season we shall reap, if we do not loosen and relax our courage and faint" (Gal. 6:9, *Amplified*).

In the legend of Princess Atalanta and the three golden apples, the princess announced she would not marry. However, she had so many suitors she finally promised to marry the young man who could win a foot race with her. Many tried and failed.

One day a young man challenged her to a race. Early in the race spectators could see he was no match for her. Suddenly he dropped a shining, golden apple. As she stopped to pick it up, he shot past her. A second and third time he tossed an apple in front of her which she paused to pick up. Straining every muscle, he crossed the finish line, winning Atalanta as his bride. The brief delays had cost her the race.

Have we become so involved in our own plans we have taken our eyes off the goal? Satan may throw "golden apples" of material prosperity, pleasure, or fame in our way to divert us from the race. Or we may have become so weary we are ready to give up.

It takes the utmost strength and endurance to continue our race to the end. But we must not quit when the going gets rough.

"When the way is rough, your patience has a chance to grow" (James 1:3, LB). We have One who runs the race with us and in Him we can persevere to the end.

Looking unto Jesus the author and finisher of our faith (Heb. 12:2).

It is interesting to watch a group of runners getting set for a race. The tension mounts as they wait for it to start. At the given signal, they are off like a shot, completely oblivious to everything about them, for they are in the race to win.

If they are to win the race, they must be sure of the direction of their goal and keep their eyes focused on it. A number of years ago a crowd of spectators watched a football player run for a touchdown. However, to their consternation, he ran in the opposite direction. As he crossed the goal line, he discovered that, although he had made a spectacular run, he had crossed the wrong goal.

Our goal is Jesus Christ, the Author and Finisher of our faith. Our eyes are to be centered on Him. "Simply fixing our gaze upon Jesus, the Leader and Perfector of our faith" (*Weymouth*). It is not enough to look up; we must look unto JESUS. It is not faith in our own faith we need, but faith in Jesus Christ.

The Lord knows our race course. He knows the obstacles along our way. He has the power to keep us on the course, avoiding the impediments that may hinder.

Sometimes detours cause us to take our eyes off the goal. We may be distracted by looking at obstacles, hindrances, circumstances, environment, or problems. We must keep our eyes focused on our goal, the Lord Jesus Christ. He who is with us at the beginning of the race and at the end of the race, accompanies us each mile of our way, strengthening and encouraging us.

When Blondin, the great tightrope walker, crossed Niagara Falls on a cable suspended over the falls, we are told he had a star fixed to the opposite side. Focusing his eyes on it, not looking down at the falls, he successfully crossed over.

Where are your eyes focused today? On yourself? Your obstacles? The race course? The secret of crossing the finish line victoriously is to keep "looking unto Jesus."

February
10

These things have I spoken unto you, that my joy might remain in you, and that your joy might be full (John 15:11).

As we look at the faces of people today, few reflect joy. This is understandable, for conditions in the world tend to produce fear instead of joy. People are seeking joy but in the wrong places. They are looking for it in outward circumstances, but to their great disappointment, they do not find it.

Not long before His crucifixion, the Lord Jesus shared with His beloved disciples words of encouragement. He knew life would not be easy for them; some would suffer great persecution. Yet He wanted them to know that even in trouble, they could have joy-filled lives.

The joy Jesus was talking about springs from a heart untouched by outer conditions. He had been talking with His disciples about the abiding life. "Abide in me, and I in you" (John 15:4). He used the vine and branch as an illustration. He had told them these things that they might know that such a relationship would give joy in the midst of trouble.

This same joy is possible for us today. From a vital union with Christ comes real joy for our lives—His joy—for He is its source. He said, ". . . that MY JOY might remain IN YOU." It is a supernatural joy produced in us by the Holy Spirit. We try to find joy in what we have or what we do, but real joy comes from constant abiding in the Lord.

Outward happiness is not permanent, but the joy of the Lord is. Jesus said, ". . . that my joy might REMAIN in you." When our joy is in Him, no one can take it from us.

The Lord does not do things in small measure. He promised, ". . . that your joy might be FULL." The *Living Bible* (John 15:11) reads, "Yes, your cup of joy will overflow." A container overflows with that which is within. When our lives are filled with His joy, it will overflow on others.

His joy, a joy you can experience in any circumstance, is for you personally today. "I have told you this so that YOU can share MY joy, and that YOUR joy may be complete" (John 15:11, *Phillips*).

And when Abram was ninety years old and nine, the Lord appeared to Abram, and said unto him, I am the Almighty God (Gen. 17:1).

What is your concept of God? When you think of Him, what comes to mind? Does He seem so far away He couldn't possibly know you exist? Does He seem impersonal to you? John B. Phillips has written a book entitled *Your God Is Too Small.* How big is your God? Is He too small?

God wanted to enlarge Abraham's concept of Himself, so from time to time He revealed some new aspect of Himself to Abraham. One day He said to him, "I am the almighty God." The Hebrew word for almighty God is El Shaddai, the all-sufficient One.

In effect He was saying, "Abraham, I am the almighty God. I am your El Shaddai; the God who is sufficient for all your needs; the God who is enough."

When we know God personally through Jesus Christ, God becomes our El Shaddai, our God who is sufficient for all our needs. Once when going through deep waters of trouble, I experienced a time of emotional disturbance. God seemed to be taking everything from me. I felt no one understood or cared. When it seemed I had reached the very end, when I had been stripped of everything, I discovered in a deeper way that my El Shaddai, the Lord Jesus Christ, was SUFFICIENT for MY need at that time. I learned that He, and He alone was enough—He was ALL I needed.

Are you wondering why some particular need has not been met? You have prayed a long time, yet the answer has not come? God has not forgotten you. Perhaps He is waiting to reveal some deeper aspect of His character to you. He wants you to know Him in a more intimate way. He wants you to experience that He is your El Shaddai. He says, "I am YOUR ALL-SUFFICIENCY, I am YOUR God who is enough, I am all YOU need today. I completely satisfy."

"When you have nothing left but God, then for the first time you become aware that God is enough."

February

12

And when Abram was ninety years old and nine, the Lord appeared to Abram, and said unto him, I am the Almighty God; walk before Me, and be thou perfect (Gen. 17:1).

When God appeared to Abraham one day saying, "I am the almighty God," He gave him some directives for his life.

He gave Abraham a STANDARD for his walk. "Walk and live habitually before Me, and be perfect—blameless, wholehearted, complete" (Gen. 17:1, *Amplified*). To walk before God is to be constantly aware of His presence. To be perfect is to have an undivided heart, a whole-hearted loyalty. "For the eyes of the Lord run to and fro throughout the whole earth, to shew himself strong in the behalf of them whose heart is perfect toward him" (2 Chron. 16:9).

Abraham could trust the SURENESS of God's promises. God reassured him that He would keep His promise to give them a son. "And I will bless her, and give thee a son also of her" (Gen. 17:16). Abraham had confidence in God's promise, for he had confidence in the One who gave the promise.

Abraham must learn to SURRENDER his desires to God. Instead of waiting for God to fulfill His promise, he and Sarah had devised their own way of obtaining a son. Then Abraham asked God to bless this son. "O that Ishmael might live before thee!" (v. 18). But God couldn't give His blessing on their plans.

We can learn from Abraham's experience. God has a standard for our walk today: "That ye might walk worthy of the Lord" (Col. 1:10). Our enabling for such a walk is not in ourselves but in the indwelling power of Jesus Christ. "As ye have therefore received Christ Jesus the Lord, so walk ye in Him" (Col. 2:6).

We, too, have the sureness of His promises. "There hath not failed one word of all his good promise" (1 Kings 8:56).

We must surrender our desires, our ambitions, our lives completely to Him. His will must be ours. Can we say as Jesus did, "Nevertheless not my will, but thine, be done"? (Luke 22:42).

It has been said, "What God claims, I yield; what I yield, He accepts; what He accepts, He fills; what He fills, He uses; what He uses, He blesses."

Lay not up for yourselves treasures upon earth, where moth and rust doth corrupt, and where thieves break through and steal: But lay up for yourselves treasures in heaven, where neither moth nor rust doth corrupt, and where thieves do not break through nor steal (Matt. 6:19-20).

Treasures are defined as "those things of great worth, things that are precious." How carefully we "store up" treasures that are valuable and precious to us.

Knowing that an instinct of human nature is accumulating possessions, Jesus warned against storing up earthly treasures, possessions, pleasures, persons, for they are transitory and can be quickly swept away. Only treasures stored in heaven cannot be taken from us.

A wealthy Christian lady, who spent her time and wealth on herself, dreamed one night she was in heaven. Seeing a large, lovely home, she was told it was her gardener's. To her surprise, her home was only a small cottage. When she questioned this, the angel replied, "We did our best with the materials you sent up."

What are your treasured possessions? Your family, home, car, position, time, talent? It is not wrong to have treasures, but it is important where you are storing them, on earth or in heaven.

In the early days of Standard Oil Company of New York, the company needed someone to represent them in China, someone who knew the people, spoke their language, and had their confidence. Dr. R. A. Jaffrey, a missionary to China, fulfilled these qualifications. They offered him the position with a salary of $5,000. At that time he was earning $300 a year. He refused. They offered him $10,000, then $20,000. Each time he refused. Finally they said, "Get him at any price." He replied, "You are offering me a big salary with a little job. I have a big job with a small salary, and I am content." His interest was in storing up heavenly treasures, not accumulating earthly wealth.

Are you laying up treasures in heaven which cannot be taken away? God can only store up for us that which we have deposited with him during our earthly life.

May we live each day with eternity's values in view.

February

14

Because the love of God is shed abroad in our hearts by the Holy Ghost which is given unto us" (Rom. 5:5).

February is valentine month, a special time for showing our love to dear ones. I remember some very special valentines I received and some very special ones I gave. Don't you?

God has selected us to be "Living Valentines," His living messengers. "YOU are a letter from Christ, written by us. It is not a letter written with pen and ink, but by the Spirit of the living God; not one carved on stone, but in human hearts" (2 Cor. 3:3, LB).

As His messengers, we are to carry His message of love wherever we go. This message is given in John 3:16, "For God so loved the world, that He gave His only begotten Son, that whosoever believeth in Him should not perish, but have everlasting life." This love is personal; it includes you and me.

God's love is real and genuine. "For God IS love" (1 John 4:8). It is a steadfast, unchanging love. "Having loved His own which were in the world, He loved them unto the end" (John 13:1). It is a powerful love, more powerful than all the powers and agencies of earth. "Who shall separate us from the love of Christ? Shall tribulation, or distress, or persecution, or famine, or nakedness, or peril, or sword? Nay, in all these things we are more than conquerors through Him that loved us" (Rom. 8:35, 37). His walk of love is an example for us daily. "And walk in love, as Christ also hath loved us, and hath given Himself for us" (Eph. 5:2).

This love of God is shed abroad, becoming real in our lives through the Holy Spirit.

As it fills our lives, it overflows from us into the lives of others. "BE FULL OF LOVE FOR OTHERS, following the example of Christ who loved you" (Eph. 5:2, LB). With His love we can love the unlovely.

May our hearts be so filled with His love that we will be Living Valentines, shedding His love abroad in our needy world, not just on Valentine Day, but each day of the year.

But God commendeth his love toward us, in that, while we were yet sinners, Christ died for us (Rom. 5:8).

One of our basic needs is to be loved; to have someone who cares for us. Recognizing the importance of love, doctors sometimes prescribe "tender, loving care" for emotionally upset patients.

It has been said that love cannot be defined; it has to be demonstrated; it has to be experienced. God has given us the greatest demonstration of love.

Before I knew God in a personal way through Jesus Christ, I thought that we had to attain a certain standard of goodness before God could love us. The more nearly perfect we lived, the greater His love for us. I wanted to be accepted by Him and know that He loved me. But I knew my life didn't reach His standard of acceptance, so I assumed He couldn't love me. Then I discovered that He did love me, and His love was not dependent on how I lived. He had proved His love in a most amazing way.

"And we can see that it was at the very time that we were powerless to help ourselves that Christ died for sinful men. . . . Yet the proof of God's amazing love is this: that it was while we were sinners that Christ died for us" (Rom. 5:6-8, *Phillips*).

Because He loved us, God sent His Son to become our Savior. The penalty for our sin had to be paid. This the Lord Jesus did, reconciling us to God by His death on the cross.

As we look back at the cross and behold Jesus dying there in our place for our sins, taking the punishment we deserved, our hearts are filled with worship and adoration.

The queen of England attended incognito the funeral of General William Booth, the founder of the Salvation Army. A poor woman came in and sat on the aisle, next to the queen. When the casket was brought down the aisle, the woman put two roses on it. Then she turned to the queen and said, "He cared for the likes of us." So the Lord Jesus "cared for the likes of us." "The Son of God, who loved me, and gave himself for me" (Gal. 2:20).

February

16

For if, when we were enemies, we were reconciled to God by the death of his Son, much more, being reconciled, we shall be saved by his life (Rom. 5:10).

When I became a Christian, my life was filled to overflowing with the joy and peace of his presence. My one desire was to try to live a life pleasing to Him. Some days I was satisfied with my efforts. Other days I failed miserably. My life seemed like an elevator, always going up and down. I wondered why I couldn't live a consistent Christian life. That was my problem. I was trying to live it in my own strength. I had to learn that the Lord Jesus wanted to live His life in me by the power of the Holy Spirit.

Many try to live the Christian life themselves, only to become defeated. Too often we accept defeat as the normal life. But there is MUCH MORE for us than failure and discouragement. In Christ we have a new dynamic, a new life, His resurrection life, which can deliver from the power of sin. "It is MUCH MORE [certain], now that we are reconciled, that we shall be saved [daily delivered from sin's dominion] through His [resurrection] life" (Rom. 5:10, *Amplified*).

John Hunter has said, "God did not save us to be failures: He did not save us to be defeated." The Holy Spirit will give us victory as we yield to Him.

It has been said, "He died on the cross to save us from our sins, and He rose again to dwell in our hearts to save us from ourselves. Through His saving life we are daily delivered from our self with its fears, worry, selfishness, and rebellion. Christ, our substitute on the cross, secures our forgiveness; Christ, our substitute within, secures constant victory day by day."

Ray Stedman has said, "Jesus has come to prepare us to live, to take life at its worst, its hardest, and to find in Him hidden streams of strength that make it possible to rejoice in all difficulties, hardships, trials, defeats, adverse circumstances, crushing disappointments, and heartaches because it is producing in us the very thing God is after and making us what He wants us to be."

And God remembered Noah, and every living thing, and all the cattle that was with him in the ark (Gen. 8:1).

Have you ever experienced a feeling of utter loneliness? You wondered if anyone really remembered you. Then one day the telephone rang. Someone on the other end of the line said, "I have been thinking about you. How are you?" Or one morning the mail brought a friendly note from someone for no other reason than the person was thinking of you. Suddenly a song came to your heart, a lilt to your voice, and a spring to your step. You were remembered!

The Bible tells of a time when God remembered Noah in a special way. God instructed him to build an ark as a place of safety for him and his family during the flood. There may have been times when Noah wondered if God still remembered him. But God did. "And GOD REMEMBERED Noah." He did not forget him for one moment. He knew where he was all the time.

At times we may feel forgotten. We wonder if anyone cares. As God remembered Noah, so He remembers us. "And God remembered . . . (your name)." How encouraging are these words when we are lonely, and apparently forgotten. God does care! He remembers!

One time I spent a weekend at a motel in an area where they were having heavy rainstorms. Rivers were nearly out of their banks in some places. Severe tornado warnings were out. Television newscasters were designating danger areas, giving the names of the counties involved. Being a stranger in the state, I didn't know whether I was in danger or not. The storm became increasingly worse. Finally I said, aloud, "Lord, just remember I am here." I experienced a quietness and peace that God gives at a time like that. Later I learned that a tornado had almost touched down close to my motel.

God's eye is always upon us. "He that keepeth thee will not slumber" (Ps. 121:3). Today do you seem to be forgotten? Remember, you aren't. God is saying to you, "I haven't forgotten you for one minute." Perhaps you are lonely. Listen to Him lovingly whisper, "I am with you—I remember YOU." Oh, the comfort of knowing GOD REMEMBERS!

February
18

May God who gives patience, steadiness, and encouragement help you to live in complete harmony with each other—each with the attitude of Christ toward each other. And then all of us can praise the Lord together with one voice, giving glory to God, the Father of our Lord Jesus Christ (Rom. 15:5-6, LB).

The Bible gives some guidelines for our relationships with others, in our family, neighborhood, place of business, church, and community.

Paul wrote that we are ". . . to live in COMPLETE HARMONY with each other." Because we have the mind of Christ we can have the right attitude toward others. But it is more than just having His mind. We must let it possess us, giving us His thoughts, His attitudes, His desires. "Let this mind be IN YOU, which was also in Christ Jesus" (Phil. 2:5).

God gives us the patience, steadfastness, and encouragement we need as we associate with others. Remembering how patient God is with us should help us be patient with others. God gives stability when we are discouraged and want to give up. God encourages us so we can encourage those with whom we minister.

Sometimes in listening to a group sing, we hear someone singing off key. How disturbing this is. One discordant note can spoil the melodious harmony of the group.

One person out of tune with God, having a critical attitude, can hinder the freedom of the Spirit at work. Oneness with God leads to oneness with others.

Romans 15:5 and 6 has been paraphrased, "Live in harmony with each other. Don't be snobbish but take a real interest in ordinary people. Don't get set in your own opinion."

When we live in harmony with each other whether in our home or in our community, our lives manifest to the world a clearer picture of God. Our lives are a song of praise to Him. "That ye may with one mind and one mouth glorify God" (Rom. 15:6). Is this what we manifest to the world? Do our lives make people think of God?

"So open your hearts to one another as Christ opens his heart to you, and God will be glorified" (v. 7, *Phillips*).

And God is able to make all grace abound toward you; that ye, always having all sufficiency in all things, may abound to every good work (2 Cor. 9:8).

We are living in days filled with tension and turmoil. Many are depressed and in despair. But God has made an abundant provision of His grace available for facing the complexities of life. Not only are we saved by His grace through faith in Jesus Christ, but an abundant supply is available for our daily living. "He giveth more grace" (James 4:6).

Jesus said, "I came that they may have and enjoy life, and have it in abundance—to the full, till it overflows" (John 10:10, *Amplified*). His grace is unlimited and inexhaustible—not a little grace, or some grace, but ALL grace.

The word for grace has been described as "graciousness of manner, the divine influence upon the heart, its reflections in the life." Someone has said, "Grace is all that God has made available for us in the life of Jesus Christ."

God's grace through the life of Christ abounds to us wherever we are. There is enough grace to meet every problem and need of our lives.

Not only is His grace always available for us, but it is all-sufficient for all life situations. There is no limit to what He can do for us—HE is all-sufficient. There is no limit on the time—it is always available. There is no limit to the amount—there is enough for our every need.

God not only provides the resources for an abounding life, but He has the power to make it real in our lives—"GOD IS ABLE." There is no difficulty beyond the reach of His grace and sufficiency, for He is all-powerful.

The Greek word for the grace of God has the two-fold meaning of not only graciousness of our manner but also of our actions. As we abound in the loveliness of the life of Jesus Christ within, the fragrance of His life will overflow from our lives in good works.

The abounding measure of His grace and sufficiency overflows in abundant supply. He provides all of the grace and sufficiency we need for abundant living.

February
20

And whatsoever ye shall ask in my name, that will I do, that the Father may be glorified in the Son (John 14:13).

Today many people believe in prayer who do not pray. Some people pray but do not expect an answer. They go through the ritual of "praying prayers," but do not pray from the heart in faith believing.

Prayer is defined in the Bible by such simple words as ask, cry, call. "Ask, and it shall be given you" (Matt. 7:7). This puts us in a position of dependence upon God. Jesus told His disciples to ask the Father in His name and they would receive. "IF YE ASK . . . I will do it" (John 14:14). God desires to answer prayer, and has given His promise that He will.

Two conditions are mentioned in today's Scripture verse for an effective prayer life. First, we are to pray "in His name." This is more than adding His name at the end of our prayer. Asking in His name gives authority to our prayers. As we come to Him, recognizing we have no merits of our own, He intercedes before the Father in our behalf. It is asking in accordance with His will. It is praying as He would pray.

The most important part of a check is the signature. Is the person reliable? Does he have an account in the bank? Are there sufficient funds? It is honored not because of the bearer, but because of the One who signed it.

All of God's resources are available to us. A supply of "heavenly checks" are issued from His "Bank of Heaven" to use in drawing upon Him for our needs. Jesus' signature gives them authority before the Father. Since His deposits are adequate, our checks are honored. God hears and answers our prayers not because we are deserving but because we have asked in the name of His Son.

Another condition for answered prayer is that the Father be glorified in the Son. Can we say of our prayer requests, "I am asking this in His name, that the Father be glorified?" Or are we asking it for our own desire?

What a great promise the Lord has given us: "Whatsoever ye shall ask in my name, that will I do." This glorifies the Father.

And God opened her eyes, and she saw a well of water; and she went, and filled the bottle with water, and gave the lad drink (Gen. 21:19).

As the result of a serious family situation, Abraham sent Hagar, a maid servant, and her son, Ishmael, away from their home. As they wandered across the desert, the burning rays of the sun beat down mercilessly upon them. At last their bottle of water was gone. In despair Hagar placed Ishmael in the shade of a bush, knowing he could not live long in the intense heat. Completely at the end of human resources, she began to weep.

Suddenly the angel of God called, "What aileth thee Hagar? fear not; for God hath heard the voice of the lad where he is. Arise, lift up the lad, and hold him in thine hand. . . . And God opened her eyes, and she saw a well of water; and she went, and filled the bottle with water, and gave the lad drink" (Gen. 21:17-19). Their thirst was quenched as they drank from the well.

We may find ourselves in a desert place, experiencing an intense thirst. Drinking from bottles of human sources will not quench our thirst. We may drink from the bottles of wealth, popularity, friends, talent, home, pleasures. They provide only a limited supply of water and after a time fail.

However, God has a well of the Water of Life from which we may drink. It has an unfailing supply, and always satisfies. Jesus said, "But whosoever drinketh of the water that I shall give him shall never thirst; but the water that I shall give him shall be in him a well of water springing up into everlasting life" (John 4:14). It is life-satisfying water that completely quenches our thirst. It is available for us, but there is a condition—we must drink.

Today are you drinking from bottles of human supply that do not quench your thirst? Or are you drinking from the Well of Water that never runs dry and always satisfies?

"And the Spirit and the bride say, Come. And let him that heareth say, Come. And let him that is athirst come. And whosoever will, let him take the water of life freely" (Rev. 22:17).

I am the least in my father's house (Judg. 6:15).

When God has a work to be done, He uses a person to accomplish it. When God wanted to deliver Israel from the Midianites, a strong, formidable foe, He chose Gideon. One day an angel of the Lord appeared to Gideon, saying, "The Lord is with thee, thou mighty man of valour." And Gideon said unto him, "Oh my Lord, IF the Lord be with us, WHY then is all this befallen us?" (Judg. 6:12-13). He was perplexed. If the Lord was with them, why were they being harrassed? Do we ever question "if" and "why"?

Knowing his human limitations, he couldn't believe God had made the right choice. He lacked the usual qualifications of a great military leader. He was timid, fearful, insecure, and considered himself the least of his family. However, Gideon failed to reckon with God.

The angel assured Gideon of the availability of GOD'S POWER. "Go in this thy MIGHT, and THOU shalt save Israel from the hand of the Midianites; have I not sent thee?" (v. 14). He was inadequate, but God saw the potential in Gideon; God saw what He could do in Gideon's life. Someone has said, "Gideon's might was in his weakness, for in his weakness he was strong in the power of God."

Not only was God's power available, but GOD'S PRESENCE would accompany him. "Surely I will be with thee, and thou shalt smite the Midianites AS ONE MAN" (v. 16).

We may be overwhelmed by the magnitude of the task God has chosen for us. We may be saying, "I am the least qualified." All God wants is our willingness to let Him do it. His power is available for us. "Be strong in the Lord, and in the power of HIS might" (Eph. 6:10). Not only is His power available to us, but His Presence will accompany us. "For He hath said, I will never leave thee, nor forsake thee" (Heb. 13:5).

God is looking for those to serve Him who recognize their insufficiency but are willing to be a vessel filled with His power and His Presence, a vessel He can use.

Someone has encouraged us by saying, "God never asks us to do anything He cannot do."

And the Lord said unto Gideon, The people that are with thee are too many for me to give the Midianites into their hands, lest Israel vaunt themselves against me, saying, Mine own hand hath saved me (Judg. 7:2).

When God recruited an army of volunteers to join Gideon, thirty-two thousand responded. Although Gideon's army was one-fourth the size of the enemy's army, Gideon heard God say, "The people that are with thee are too many for us to give the Midianites into their hands, lest Israel vaunt themselves against them, saying, Mine own hand hath saved me."

Through a series of unusual tests, God began His process of elimination, reducing Gideon's army to three hundred. What could Gideon do with such a small band? Humanly speaking he was helpless, but God wanted him to learn that the battle would not be won by human strength.

Their weapons were not the usual ones of earthly warfare, but trumpets, pitchers, and torches. Yet this band of men, few in number, equipped with strange weapons, put the enemy to rout.

God demonstrated through this victory what He can do with people who are weak, with no ability or wisdom of their own, but obedient to God. He displayed His power as the God of the impossible. Only God could have given the victory! Only God could receive the glory!

We, too, have a strong foe against whom we have no might. When we attempt to meet this enemy in our wisdom and strength, when we use our strategy as we face him, we are defeated before we begin. We must remember, the battle is not ours, but God's. When we are weak, He is strong. When we confess our weakness to God, it gives Him the opportunity to demonstrate His almighty power.

God never measures the victory by human strength or human resources, but by His power, that all the glory may be His.

"For ye see your calling, brethren, how that not many wise men after the flesh, not many mighty, not many noble, are called: But God hath chosen . . . the weak things of the world to confound the things which are mighty . . . that no flesh should glory in His presence" (1 Cor. 1:26-29).

February

24

In conclusion, be strong–not in yourselves but in the Lord, in the power of his boundless strength" (Eph. 6:10, Phillips).

Recognizing the importance of a strong national security, the national budget includes a large appropriation for a powerful defense for our country.

How important it is to have a strong defense for the spiritual conflict we are in. Our conflict is against the enemy of our souls. We must not underestimate his strength, but recognize him as a powerful foe, too strong to fight against. God has made full provision for our victory over him through Christ. "Greater is he that is in you, than he that is in the world" (1 John 4:4).

God has made available adequate resources for a life of victory. Though we are weak in ourselves, we can "BE STRONG IN THE LORD" (because of WHO HE IS); we can "BE STRONG IN HIS POWER AND MIGHT" (because of WHAT HE HAS DONE FOR US). This is not something we attain by our own efforts. It is ours through Jesus, in whom we have all the power of God available to defeat Satan in every situation we face. Through HIM, we are strengthened within, "strengthened with might by His Spirit in the inner man" (Eph. 3:16).

Not only is He our inner strength and power, He is our armor for protection when facing our foe. "Put on the whole armour of God" (Eph. 6:11). In Romans 13:14 we read, "But put ye on the Lord Jesus Christ."

Satan says, "Be weak; be fearful; be filled with self-pity; be discouraged; be nagging; be critical; be defending your own rights." God says, "Be strong; be restful; be at peace; be content; be rejoicing; be victorious."

We need not fear the foe, "for the battle is not ours, but God's." Jesus said, "All power is given unto Me in heaven and earth" (Matt. 28:18).

After being a Christian for many years, a person has no more power in himself to insure victory than when he first invited Christ into his life. Our strength must be Christ's strength from the beginning of our Christian walk to the end.

"Thanks be to God, which giveth us the victory through our Lord Jesus Christ" (1 Cor. 15:57).

Wherefore take unto you the whole armour of God, that ye may be able to withstand in the evil day, and having done all, to stand (Eph. 6:13).

We are in a conflict against an enemy over whom we have no power. Yet God has assured us of victory. God's armor is strong enough to protect us from any missile Satan hurls against us. "Put on the whole armour of God, that ye may be able to stand against the wiles of the devil" (Eph. 6:11).

God has provided a complete armor for the entire body. The first piece is the girdle of truth. Jesus said, "I am the truth." The truth of the Living Word revealed in the written Word must be applied to our lives.

The next piece of armor is the breastplate of righteousness, not our righteousness, but the righteousness of Christ. It is doing daily what is right before God.

Our feet must be properly equipped. "And having shod your feet in preparation [to face the enemy with the firm-footed stability, the promptness and readiness produced by the Good News] of the Gospel of peace" (Eph. 6:15, *Amplified*). We need a firm-footed stability as we face our enemy.

"Taking the shield of faith." Faith accepts and appropriates what God has provided and promised.

The helmet of salvation is necessary to protect the mind. "But we have the mind of Christ" (1 Cor. 2:16).

The Word of God is our Sword of the Spirit to use when tempted by Satan.

The armor of God is a complete and sufficient armor, for our use in battle. It can withstand any attack of Satan. Each piece of it is Christ Himself. God has provided it, but we put it on by faith. "Put on God's complete armour so that you can successfully resist all the devil's craftiness" (Eph. 6:11, *Phillips*). Omitting one part will make us vulnerable in battle. In His power, and protected by His armor, God fights our battles for us. In Him we have victory, not defeat.

"So use every piece of God's armor to resist the enemy whenever he attacks, and when it is all over, you will still be STANDING UP" (Eph. 6:13, LB).

February

26

Praying always with all prayer and supplication in the Spirit, and watching thereunto with all perseverance and supplication for all saints (Eph. 6:18).

We are in a spiritual warfare. Satan is a powerful foe and only God knows how to carry on a successful warfare against him. Someone has said that every spiritual battle is won or lost first in the prayer life. We are too weak to meet the onslaughts of Satan alone. In prayer we acknowledge our helplessness and our dependence upon God. Through earnest prayer we stand victorious in the conflict.

Prayer is God's communication system between Himself and His children. He knows how to carry on the warfare against our enemy. He knows his tactics and strategies. But we need to keep in close touch for His orders and assistance.

We are to PRAY ALWAYS—at all times, wherever we are, on our knees, when we are driving our car, while waiting for an appointment, or when we lie awake at night—pray always. First Thessalonians 5:17 reads, "Pray without ceasing."

We are to pray "with all prayer," all kinds of prayer. Sometimes we just worship the Lord in prayer; other times we have to make a confession. Sometimes our prayers are longer; other times the need is so urgent we have to send up a quick "SOS" prayer. Requests must be specific.

Prayer to be effectual must be in the power of the Holy Spirit. Often we are not sure how to pray; we do not know what is best. The Holy Spirit will guide us in what we are to pray for.

We must always be alert to the tactics of our enemy, watching with all perseverance. In many ways Satan tries to prevent our prayers—through weariness, neglect, forgetfulness, or business. He even tries to convince us that we can be self-sufficient.

Then we are to pray for other believers—"all saints." There is a great need to pray for each other, not only for those we know, but for ALL saints around the world.

Through prayer the armor is made effective and kept ready for instant use.

"The effectual fervent prayer of a righteous man availeth much" (James 5:16).

You have seen me tossing and turning through the night. You have collected all my tears and preserved them in your bottle! You have recorded every one in your book (Ps. 56:8, LB).

Are you an individual who has difficulty sleeping at night? The harder you try, the more you toss and turn. Sometimes our wakefulness is caused by sorrow, pain, or heartache. During the dark night hours the tears fall. Our hearts may be broken. Loneliness may overwhelm us.

David knew what it was to shed tears. "You have seen me tossing and turning during the night. You have collected all my tears and preserved them in your bottle." We read that in Persia and Egypt, tears were sometimes wiped from the eyes and cheeks of a mourner and preserved in a tear bottle. Often a person's tear bottle was buried with him. David asked God to preserve his tears in a bottle and record them in His book.

Sometimes a child will cry over a broken toy. As the parent mends it and returns it to the child, a smile breaks through the tears. Sometimes, however, it is broken beyond repair. Then the parent has to become a special comforter, for the toy will have to be replaced with something else.

Sometimes our tears come from a broken heart. God mends it, and we smile again through our tears. But sometimes God knows that for our own good He must remove something from our lives, something we may consider very dear. The tears may fall; we may not understand why, yet He does it for our good. However, He never removes anything from our lives without replacing it with something else. It has been said, "Our broken things lead us to His better things." God comforts as no one else does. He understands as no one else does.

A time is coming when all tears will be wiped from our eyes. One of these days, we will go to live with Him eternally. "And God shall wipe away ALL tears from their eyes; and there shall be no more death, neither sorrow, nor crying, neither shall there be any more pain: for the former things are passed away" (Rev. 21:4).

February

28

Whose adorning let it not be that outward adorning of plaiting the hair, and of wearing of gold, or of putting on of apparel; but let it be the hidden man of the heart, in that which is not corruptible, even the ornament of a meek and quiet spirit, which is in the sight of God of great price (1 Peter 3:3-4).

In verses 1 and 2 of this Scripture passage Peter has been reminding Christian wives of the influence of their lives upon their husbands. "OUR LIVES SPEAK LOUDER THAN OUR WORDS" is a true statement.

He continued on a subject of great interest to women—beauty. Most women have a natural desire to be attractive.

We are to be good representatives of Jesus Christ in the world today. This includes our entire person, outer as well as inner. However, the outer appearance is not the criterion for real beauty. Just outer attractiveness is not sufficient. There must be an inner loveliness. More important is the "hidden person of the heart." This is what God sees. "Man looketh on the outward appearance, but the Lord looketh on the heart" (1 Sam. 16:7).

It has been said that true beauty is Jesus Christ revealed in our lives. "They looked to Him and were radiant" (Ps. 34:5, *Amplified*).

We are to have a meek and quiet spirit. This does not mean a weak spirit, but a gentle one, taking no thought of self. We are not to complain, argue, nag, or domineer. We are to have a quietness of heart, a calmness when the pressures mount, a restfulness that comes from God.

As the years pass, our natural beauty begins to fade. Wrinkles come, the hair is streaked with gray, the amount of energy diminishes. Yet our inner loveliness remains through the years. In Song of Solomon 5:16 we read, "Yes, HE is altogether lovely." One definition of the word "altogether" is permanently. He is the One permanently lovely. His beauty, loveliness, and radiance in our lives can keep us permanently lovely.

His beauty within speaks more effectively through our lives than our words.

LET THE BEAUTY OF JESUS BE SEEN IN ME!

Acquaint now thyself with him, and be at peace: thereby good shall come unto thee (Job 22:21).

Once Mark Twain was invited to visit the Kaiser in Germany. His little daughter was greatly impressed and excitedly said to him, "Daddy, if it keeps on this way, soon there won't be anyone left for you to get acquainted with but God."

Today so few people really KNOW God. Many know about Him; some know Him in a casual way; but few have an intimate, close friendship with Him.

It was during a time of trouble that Job was encouraged to become acquainted with God. He had lost his possessions, family, everything. A friend advised Job, "Acquaint now thyself with Him."

In sorrow and disappointment as we wait before God, submissive to His will, we experience a deeper knowledge of Him and His love for us. "Acquaint now yourself with Him—agree with God and show yourself to be conformed to His will" (Job. 22:21, *Amplified*).

It was in the furnace of affliction and suffering that Job came to this deeper, more intimate acquaintance with God. He finally came to the place in his testing when he could say, "But he knoweth the way that I take: when he hath tried me, I shall come forth as gold" (Job 23:10).

A man once visited a factory where fine china was being made. The china, ready to have the color burned in, was not beautiful, for a drab looking blue and a dirty red paint had been applied. There were even touches of black paint. The design was smudged in spots. Then it was put in the furnace for the colors to be burned in. When it was removed from the furnace, the design was clear, and the colors were bright gold against the black, blue, and the wonderful red known as "Crown Derby."

God doesn't promise freedom from trials. But He gives us the privilege of experiencing a deeper knowledge and a closer fellowship with Him through each trial.

We discover that in the furnace of affliction He has allowed the beautiful design of His image to be burned into our lives.

March

1

But straightway Jesus spoke unto them, saying, Be of good cheer; it is I; be not afraid (Matt. 14:27).

One evening Jesus sent His disciples across the Sea of Galilee while He remained to pray. Suddenly a severe storm arose on the sea. The disciples realized they were in danger.

Was it not strange that Jesus sent them across the sea when He knew they would experience the storm? But He knew there were lessons of trust they would learn in no other way.

He had not forsaken them. He knew where they were and their need of help. "And HE SAW THEM toiling in rowing; for the wind was contrary unto them" (Mark 6:48). Trying as hard as they could to reach shore, they seemed to be getting nowhere. He delayed His coming to them that their faith might be strengthened. But in His perfect timing, He entered into the storm with them.

Between 3:00 and 4:00 in the morning, when the night is the darkest, Jesus came walking to them on the water. He appeared when they had reached the end of their resources and were in need of supernatural help. He timed it not too early for them to learn their lesson, but not too late for their deliverance.

Failing to recognize Him, they cried out in fear. Jesus calmed their fears, saying, "Be of good cheer; it is I; be not afraid." The very PRESENCE of Jesus Christ brings comfort and cheer.

Is a storm raging in your life today? Are contrary winds blowing? Are you "toiling in your rowing," getting nowhere? This does not necessarily prove we are out of God's will. In the center of God's will, storms may be raging about us. Even in our darkest hour, we are assured of the security of His Presence.

Regardless of the severity of the storm, He draws near with words of comfort and cheer. His presence goes with us, encouraging us as we go through them.

No matter how turbulent the storm, it becomes a pathway by which He draws near to us, saying, "Be of good cheer; it is I; be not afraid."

And Peter answered him and said, Lord, if it be thou, bid me come unto thee on the water. And he said, "Come" (Matt. 14:28-29).

Jesus appeared to the disciples at the darkest hour of the night, encouraging them with His PRESENCE. When Peter recognized the Lord, his fear left and his faith began to grow. He said, "Lord, if it be thou, bid me come unto thee on the water." In response, Jesus said, "Come."

Would we have replied as Peter, or would we have said, "I would like to come," or, "I'll think it over," or "I'll try it when I have enough courage"?

But Peter was confident that since the Lord had invited him to come, He would provide the POWER to make it possible. Peter didn't look at the waves, but fastened his eyes upon Jesus. Peter stepped out of the boat in complete trust and obedience to Jesus' command. He did the humanly impossible, that which was beyond the ability of any person except by the power of Christ.

Suddenly he looked from the Lord to the waves beating about him. He began to sink. He was in danger, not because he left the boat, not because he was in the storm, but because he had taken his eyes off the Lord. Doubt and fear filled Peter instead of faith and trust in Jesus.

He cried out, "Lord, save me." This short prayer of three words was sufficient to bring help from the Savior. Just one cry and immediately Jesus was there, reaching out his hand to Peter. He said, "O thou of little faith, wherefore didst thou doubt?" (Matt. 14:31).

When the storms are raging about us, when things seem darkest, we can either look at the waves of our circumstances and sink, or look to Him and rise above them.

He has the POWER to quiet the storms of our lives. But He can go beyond that and quiet the storms of our hearts, bringing calmness and quietness.

It has been said, "Christ is no security against storms, but a perfect security in storms. He does not promise us an easy voyage, but He does guarantee a safe landing."

March

3

I had fainted, unless I had believed to see the goodness of the Lord in the land of the living (Ps. 27:13).

God encourages us through His Word. In it He gives principles and guide lines for our lives—lives often filled with perplexities, uncertainties, and insecurities.

David experienced many of the same situations we face. Often he was faint of heart, falling into the depths of despair. Discouragement and disappointment were very real to him. He knew what it was to come to the end of himself. He said, "I had fainted."

But David had discovered a key word that changed his spirit of defeat to victory. "I had fainted UNLESS." Unless what? "I had BELIEVED to see the goodness of the Lord in the land of the living." It is often said, "Seeing is believing." But David believed God when he couldn't see the outcome. When he was almost fainting he looked to God, believing Him, trusting Him.

There was a time in my life when I went through deep waters. My husband was ill for many years and for some time he was depressed. Because of the strain of encouraging him and the lack of sleep, I became exhausted. Many times I felt I could not continue another day. Often it seemed I would faint beneath the load. I cried to the Lord day after day, telling Him I had reached the end.

I, too, learned the importance of the word "UNLESS." I would have fainted UNLESS I had learned to "believe to see the goodness of the Lord." I focused my eyes, not on my problem, but on the Lord. Instead of fainting, I experienced the rest that comes from trusting Him completely.

Are you fainting today beneath the load of your care? Do you feel you have reached the end? Instead of fainting, believe God. As you trust Him, your TROUBLES can become TRIUMPHS. It has been said, "God doesn't have problems, He has plans; and He will take our problems and convert them into His plans if we will let Him."

In Isaiah 40:29 we find God's remedy, "He giveth POWER to the FAINT; and to them that have no might he increaseth strength."

I am come that they might have life, and that they might have it more abundantly (John 10:10).

Eternal life is the gift God has provided mankind through personal faith in Jesus Christ. It is more than a quantity of life that endures throughout eternity; it is a quality of life, the very life of God, the life we receive the moment we believe on Christ.

But God's purpose is not only that He share His life with us, but that we receive it abundantly. The Amplified New Testament reads, "I came that they may have and enjoy life, and have it in abundance, to the full, till it overflows."

Every Christian has eternal life, but not every Christian has it abundantly in his daily experience. Abundant life is the life of Christ filling us to overflowing in every area of our lives. Any lack is not on His part in giving, but our part in possessing.

God intends that abundant life be the normal experience of every one of His children. Yet we often think of it as the unusual. As His life is made real in us, we will speak as He would speak; we will walk as He would walk; we will do what He would do; we will go where He would go; we will react to situations as He would; our motives will be His.

The life of Christ is available in abundance for every need. If we need peace, His abundant supply is available. When we need wisdom or patience, He gives abundantly. We may lack joy but His abundant supply can fill our hearts to overflowing. The abundant life provides power to overcome hatred, jealousy, selfishness. It gives strength to face disappointment and heartaches.

The abundant life is not just for a select few. It is God's desire that all His children live and enjoy an abundant life day by day. All of His resources are available for abundant living for everyone.

May we let Him live His life in our entire personality in such abundance that it overflows wherever we go. It is not our overwork but our overflow that blesses others.

March

5

And there went with him a band of men, whose hearts God had touched (1 Sam. 10:26).

When Saul returned home after being presented as the new king, ". . . a band of men went with him, WHOSE HEARTS GOD HAD TOUCHED."

While Jesus was on earth, He drew together a band of men, His disciples, whose hearts HE had touched to follow Him. "And he ordained twelve, that they should be with him, and that he might send them forth to preach" (Mark 3:14).

Down through the years God has used lives whom He has touched for the purpose of sharing the gospel: David Livingston, Mary Slessor, William Carey, Dwight L. Moody, and others.

God is looking for a band of God-touched lives today to reach a spiritually needy world for Jesus Christ. God's touch upon our lives begins with our own personal relationship with Jesus Christ. Then He touches us for the particular work He has planned for us to do.

It may not be what we would have chosen. I would not have selected writing as my particular work. It is difficult for me to write. Subjects pertaining to writing were my most difficult ones in school. Little did I realize when in school that I would be writing devotional material month after month for years. Yet God touched my life to write for Him. It has been said, "He never asks us to do anything HE cannot do." This is true in my life.

I am a timid and shy person in a crowd. I loved my home and was always content to spend much time there. Would I have chosen to live a life of travel, speaking to groups of people? Of course not. But God touched my life and I have followed where He has led me.

Have you let Him touch your life? Are you letting Him use you wherever you are today to accomplish His purpose in and through your life? It may not be in the place you would have chosen, but God-touched lives are willing to follow where He leads.

"My sheep hear My voice, and I know them, and they FOLLOW ME" (John 10:27).

Seek ye first the kingdom of God, and his righteousness; and all these things shall be added unto you (Matt. 6:33).

Priority is a word in common use today. Certain people are given priority ratings. Some reservations have top priority. Several times I have flown on the same plane with Big League ball teams. They were given priority when boarding.

Jesus reminded His disciples of the importance of keeping the priorities in their lives in proper order. If they gave God first place, they need not fret and worry over their daily needs. "But seek for (aim at and strive after) FIRST of all His kingdom, and His righteousness [His way of doing and being right], and then all these things taken together will be given you besides" (Matt. 6:33, *Amplified*).

A kingdom implies there is a king in control. Down through history there have been kings who were only figureheads. Another person or group of people had control of the power. The Kingdom of God is a spiritual kingdom. Jesus Christ desires to reign as King over our lives. He doesn't reign like an earthly ruler who rules with an iron hand, but His reign is one of love. His kingdom is one of righteousness, doing right and being right.

Seeking means more than looking for or even searching. It is seeking God and His kingdom as the prime objective with everything else in second place.

Have you checked your priority list recently? Do you have first things first? "Seek FIRST." Have you relinquished everything to the Lord Jesus? Is He reigning as King of your life? Have you allowed Him to take up residence in every area of your life?

A queen of England asked one of her subjects to leave his business to go on an important mission for her. He wondered what would happen to his business while he was gone. The queen assured him that if he would undertake her mission, she would see that his business was taken care of for him while he was gone.

". . . and He will give them to you if you give Him first place in your life" (Matt. 6:33, LB).

March
7

Though I walk in the midst of trouble, thou wilt revive me (Ps. 138:7).

When I became a Christian, I thought my troubles would be over. I assumed Christians were free from trouble. But I discovered that even they are not immune. Job said, "Yet man is born unto trouble, as the sparks fly upward" (Job 5:7). We have not been promised exemption from trouble, but we are assured help in the midst of it.

David had learned to turn to God in his times of difficulty. Although deliverance wasn't always immediate, God's presence was with him in the midst of his trouble. Though he was surrounded BY trouble, he was revived IN it.

We read in Daniel of the king's command that for thirty days everyone was to worship him or be thrown into a fiery furnace. Because three men defied his command, they were thrown into a furnace heated seven times hotter than usual. Suddenly four men were seen walking in the furnace. The king said, "The form of the fourth is like the Son of God" (Dan. 3:25). When they were brought out of the furnace, the fire had not touched them, their clothing was not scorched, their hair was not singed, they didn't even smell of smoke. Even as they walked in the midst of the fire, God walked with them, protecting them until He delivered them.

How often we find ourselves in the midst of trouble. God uses this in the process of accomplishing His purpose for our lives. David didn't say, "The Lord CAN perfect," but "The Lord WILL perfect that which concerneth me" (Ps. 138:8). In the very center of our trouble He revives us and gives us fresh courage and strength to continue.

Someone has said, "In time of trouble say: 'First, He brought me here; it is His will I am in this place; in that I will rest. Next, He will keep me here in His love and give me grace in this trial to act as His child. Then He will make the trial a blessing, teaching me the lessons He means for me to learn, and working in me the grace He intends for me. Last, in His good time, He can bring me out again. HOW and WHEN He already knows!'"

And he said to another, Follow me. But he said, Lord, suffer me first to go and bury my father (Luke 9:59).

One day a man came to Jesus, saying, "Lord, I will follow thee whithersoever thou goest" (Luke 9:57). Jesus reminded the man that a PRICE was attached to following Him. It would not be a life of comfort, ease, or earthly gain. He must consider the cost.

Jesus said to another, "Follow Me." The man replied, "Lord, suffer ME FIRST to go and bury my father" (v. 59). He wanted to follow Jesus, but his aged father was not dead yet. According to custom, he should return to him until his death. Instead of giving Jesus TOP PRIORITY, he said, "ME FIRST."

Another man said, "Lord, I will follow thee; BUT let me first go bid them farewell, which are at home at my house" (v. 61). He was willing, BUT wanted to POSTPONE the time. He wanted to do other THINGS first. But Jesus answered, "Anyone who lets himself be distracted from the work I plan for him is not fit for the Kingdom of God" (Luke 9:62, LB).

When the Lord calls us to follow Him, we must consider our willingness to pay the price before we answer. Is it CHRIST FIRST or ME FIRST? Are we willing to follow Him constantly wherever or whenever He leads us? Or do we say, "I would be willing to follow Him, BUT I can't give up my possessions or plans, or leave the place where I am right now"? If He is first, we will put Him first in every area of our lives.

Our commitment to follow Him is more than a promise to do His will when our circumstances are right, or when His plans do not interfere with our own. It must first be to the person of Jesus Christ, even before a particular task.

Total commitment doesn't necessarily mean we can't have a home, family, or earthly possessions. But it does mean Christ must be in His rightful place for everything else in our lives to be in their rightful places.

May this be our response: "Lord, I will follow You wherever You lead, wherever You ask me to go, whatever You ask me to do."

Be careful for nothing (Phil. 4:6).

If a poll were taken today, asking people what they desired more than anything else, many would reply, "Peace of heart and mind." Thousands of people are under the doctor's care whose physical problems are the result of emotional conflict. Although many doctors prescribe tranquilizers and sleeping pills, such medication does not give their patients peace.

Yet God's Word promises freedom from worry. There IS an inner peace for us today. It begins with a personal relationship with Jesus Christ by faith. "Therefore being justified by faith, we have peace WITH God through our Lord Jesus Christ" (Rom. 5:1).

When we are at peace WITH God we can experience the peace OF God in our daily living. However, the peace of God doesn't come automatically. Philippians 4:6 and 7 gives a formula by which we can experience it as a reality in our lives day by day.

First, "Don't worry about anything" (Phil. 4:6, LB). It has been said, "Worry is assuming responsibility God never intended us to have. It is carrying tomorrow's load with today's strength." When we worry, does it not indicate we think God is not big enough to handle our problem without our help?

He didn't say we are not to worry about most things, some things, or the easy things. We are not to worry about ANYTHING—NOT ONE THING. You may say, "It is just my nature to worry." Does worry accomplish anything for you? Since the Bible tells us we are not to worry, we are disobeying His Word when we do.

Today your life may be full of care. You may feel you have every reason to worry. Yet God's Word says, "Be CAREFUL for nothing. Don't worry about ANYTHING." Jesus said, "So don't be anxious about tomorrow. God will take care of your tomorrow too. Live one day at a time" (Matt. 6:34, LB).

In 1 Peter 5:7 *(Amplified)* we discover WHAT we are to do with our cares. "Casting the whole of your care—all your anxieties, all your worries, all your concerns, once and for all—on Him; for He cares for you affectionately, and cares about you watchfully."

Prayer is the channel by which we cast our cares upon Him.

TURN CARE TO PRAYER!

Don't worry about anything; instead, pray about everything; tell God your needs and don't forget to thank him for his answers (Phil. 4:6, LB*).*

How easy it is to say to someone, "Don't worry." But that does not give the person the comfort He needs, nor the solution to his problem.

God tells us not to worry about anything, but He doesn't stop there. He has a formula by which we can exchange worry for peace, a supernatural peace that passes understanding. The cure for worry is prayer—"PRAY about EVERYTHING."

The *Amplified Bible* reads "in EVERY circumstance and in EVERYTHING by prayer." If we are not to worry about anything, we must pray about everything. We must bring our requests to Him and leave them with Him. We are not to pray about just some things, or most things, but EVERYTHING.

Often when problems arise we go to a dear friend for help. Sometimes the friend can help; sometimes not. But through prayer we have access into the presence of the One who can answer every need. Nothing is impossible with Him. In our helplessness we not only come to Him with our burdens but leave them with Him. "In everything with PRAYER and SUPPLICATIONS let your requests be made known unto GOD."

If we are to pray about everything at all times, we must be sure to keep the line of communication open. Nothing must be allowed in our lives to cause a short circuit. Then when emergencies arise, requiring "SOS" prayers, we have instant contact with Him, finding HIM listening on the other end of the line.

We can develop the best plans to meet our needs, we can look to people for help, we can depend on our strongest resources, but they cannot be a substitute for prayer. God alone knows what we really need and how to supply it. He invites us to, "Call upon Me, and I will answer thee, and show thee great and mighty things, which thou knowest not" (Jer. 33:3).

What is the cure for worry? PRAYER. What are you worrying about today? "Tell God every detail of your needs in thankful prayer" (Phil. 4:6, *Phillips*).

March

11

Be careful for nothing; but in every thing by prayer and supplication with thanksgiving let your requests be made known unto God (Phil. 4:6).

Sometimes our lives are so filled with anxiety and care, we feel we have little to be thankful for. We forget the many everyday blessings that we take for granted. Yet as we begin to count our blessings, thanking Him for what He has given us and done for us, our list grows rapidly.

Paul reminds us that THANKSGIVING is one of the ingredients for inner peace. ". . . in everything by prayer and supplication with THANKSGIVING." Thanksgiving comes from a heart filled with an awareness of the goodness of the Lord. In Psalm 103:1 and 2 we read, "Bless the Lord, O my soul: and all that is within me, bless his holy name. Bless the Lord, O my soul, and forget not all his benefits."

How thankful we should be for the access we have into His presence; of the privilege of coming to Him with our needs. How often we bring Him our requests but forget to thank Him for what He has given us. In the story of the ten lepers whom Jesus cleansed, only one returned to thank Him.

When we pray, we must remember to thank God for past blessings. "It is a good thing to give thanks unto the Lord" (Ps. 92:1).

We are to thank Him in the midst of our difficulties and trials. "In EVERYTHING give thanks: for this is the will of God in Christ Jesus concerning you" (1 Thess. 5:18). This is not easy.

As we pause to thank Him for answers to prayer in the past, our faith is increased as we pray for present needs.

A. B. Simpson said, "Worry and anxiety flee as we come to Him with thanksgiving for past blessings and requests for present needs. As we commit them to Him, our hearts are filled with His peace."

Have you included thanksgiving in your prayer as you bring your requests to Him? "Don't forget to thank Him for His answers" (Phil. 4:6, LB).

If you do this you will experience God's peace, which is far more wonderful than the human mind can understand. His peace will keep your thoughts and your hearts quiet and at rest as you trust in Christ Jesus (Phil. 4:7, LB*).*

This verse begins with "If you would do THIS." Do what? Pray instead of worrying. Our problem may not always be removed, but we can have peace instead of anxiety.

It is easy to have peace when we have the security of a home, position, bank account, friends, and health. But God's peace sustains us when trouble comes and the heart is breaking.

Before Jesus left earth, He promised to leave His peace for us. He said, "Peace I leave with you, my peace I give unto you: not as the world giveth, give I unto you. Let not your heart be troubled, neither let it be afraid" (John 14:27). This is a supernatural peace, a peace that passeth our understanding, but not our experience.

Satan will do all in his power to keep us worried and upset. But Jesus keeps our hearts and minds at peace. In exchange for our problems He gives us His peace. "And the peace of God which transcends human understanding will keep constant guard over your hearts and minds as they rest in Christ Jesus" *(Phillips).* The word "keep" has the thought of acting as a guard. His peace mounts guard over our hearts and minds, preventing anything from upsetting our inner peace.

We can have an inner peace during the storms in our lives. This peace is Christ Himself, for "HE IS OUR PEACE. . . ." (Eph. 2:14).

Someone has said, "True peace is more than tranquility; it is perfect security in the midst of the storm. It is a quiet trust in God who only does His best for us."

His peace is personal—it will keep OUR hearts and minds.

A. B. Simpson has said, "The peace of God is His own calm, restful heart possessing ours and filling us with His divine stillness."

God's formula for "peace instead of worry" is: "Be careful for nothing; be prayerful in everything; be thankful for anything; be peaceful through all things."

March

13

Ye are our epistle written in our hearts, known and read of all men . . . written not with ink, but with the Spirit of the living God; not in tables of stone, but in fleshy tables of the heart (2 Cor. 3:2-3).

"What you do speaks so loudly, I cannot hear what you say." Many times my mother quoted that to me as I grew up. How closely people watch our lives!

Paul compares our lives to letters that are read. "[No, YOU] yourselves are our letters of recommendation (our credentials), written in your hearts, to be (perceived, recognized,) KNOWN and READ by EVERYBODY. You show and make obvious that YOU ARE A LETTER FROM CHRIST delivered by us, not written with ink but with [the] Spirit of [the] living God, not on tablets of stone but on tablets of human hearts" (2 Cor. 3:2-3, *Amplified*).

An author once said, "The reward of writing books is not the financial returns.—The real question is whether books pay the people who spend time reading them." As people read our lives, what do they read in them?

We are His letters of recommendation known and read by people. Someone said there are five gospels: Matthew, Mark, Luke, John, and the Gospel according to YOU. We may be the only Bible some people will ever read.

People detect inconsistencies in our lives and often judge the Gospel by what they see in us. We become God's message for the world as the Holy Spirit writes His message in our lives. "It is not a letter written with pen and ink, but by the Spirit of the living God; not one carved on stone, but in human hearts" (2 Cor. 3:3, LB).

Through the work of a missionary, a young man came to know Jesus Christ. When asked about his conversion, he said, "One day Jesus Christ became real to me and I invited HIM into my life as personal Savior." Then he said, "Do you know where I first met Him? In the life of the missionary."

What do people learn of Jesus Christ by reading our lives? "They can see that you are a letter from Christ" (v. 3, LB). Can they?

As it is written, How beautiful are the feet of them that preach the gospel of peace, and bring glad tidings of good things (Rom. 10:15).

When we have good news, how eager we are to share it with someone. This same eagerness should be ours as we carry the glad tidings of the gospel to others. God's Word says, "How beautiful are the feet of those who bring glad tidings! How welcome is the coming of those who preach the good news of His good things!" (Rom. 10:15, Amplified).

A century and a half ago one of God's greatest servants was a shoe repairman. As he studied the world map, more and more he was reminded of the thousands in such places as Africa and India who had never heard of Christ. As he prayed, God opened the way for William Carey to go to India. He became known as the father of modern missions. It could be said of him who had repaired shoes for other people's feet, "How beautiful were his feet as he went forth with the gospel."

God calls the feet of those who carry such Good News beautiful. We do not usually consider our feet as a beautiful part of our body. But God is not speaking of the shape and size of our feet, but of their use. God sees a special beauty in feet willing to serve Him wherever He may lead them, whether an obscure, hidden place of service or a prominent one. God sees the willing feet of those who walk His paths wherever He leads.

Once a Christian man was visiting some mission stations in Africa. One day he saw a man hobbling along ahead of him. The man's legs were swollen with the painful disease of elephantiasis. The visitor knew that the man was suffering intense pain, yet, undaunted by his suffering, he was carrying a bag of Bibles and tracts to be given out wherever he went. His feet, so misshapen and excruciatingly painful, were "beautiful" in the eyes of God as he went about giving the Good News.

Are our feet "beautiful" in God's eyes because of our dedication to giving out the gospel?

March

15

And ye shall seek me, and find me, when ye shall search for me with all your heart (Jer. 29:13).

While in captivity, God sent the children of Israel a message that they were to settle down in the land for seventy years. His purpose for them had not yet been accomplished. He said, "I know the plans which I am planning for you. . . . Plans of welfare and not of calamity, to give you a future and a hope" (Jer. 29:11, *Rotherham*).

From their viewpoint, this captivity looked like a calamity. But God was looking at it from His vantage point and knew it was for their welfare. They were looking at the immediate; God was looking at the ultimate.

Today we may be in a place of seeming captivity. From our viewpoint it may look like a calamity. But God sees and is planning for our ultimate welfare. God reassures us, "I know the plans I am planning for YOU." Then He gives us an answer for the immediate, for today. "IF ye seek ME, YE shall find ME." We may be seeking the answer to our problems in the wrong place. Instead of focusing on our situation, we are to seek HIM.

We are not to seek experiences, feelings, methods, plans, programs, financial security, or people. God may use these in our lives, but we are first to seek HIM. Feelings are not lasting; experiences fade; circumstances overwhelm us; environment may discourage us. But when we seek and find Him, He satisfies.

We may settle for something less than the Lord. We may settle for programs or plans instead of seeking the PERSON of the Lord Jesus Christ. He has promised that if we seek Him, we shall find Him, if we seek Him with all our heart.

Are you seeking for anything less than the Lord Himself? Don't stop short of Him. The Psalmist wrote, "The one thing I want from God, the thing I SEEK most of all, is the privilege of meditating in His Temple, living in His presence every day of my life, delighting in HIS incomparable perfections and glory" (Ps. 27:4, LB). It has been said, "Seeking hearts will not be disappointed by God; they will find HIM."

For it is God which worketh in you both to will and to do of his good pleasure (Phil. 2:13).

God has created us for His pleasure. "For thou hast created all things, and for thy pleasure they are and were created" (Rev. 4:11).

After we become God's child, He begins working out His plan for our lives. He knows we are incapable of accomplishing this in our own strength, so He provides His power. "[Not in your own strength] for it is God Who is all the while effectually at work in you—energizing and creating in you the power and desire—both to will and to work for His good pleasure and satisfaction and delight" (Phil. 2:13, *Amplified*).

Often we hear people talk about living for God and serving Him in their own weak way. If we are doing it in our own strength, it will be weak. But this is not what God wants. We need not depend on our own strength. We have God's power available and we can live triumphantly and victoriously through it.

This does not mean we will always have a spirit of exuberance. But it does mean that we will have peace and joy in the face of our life situations.

We can be assured that God will disclose His will to us. There may be times, however, when we are not willing to do His will. We may even be a little rebellious. God, in His great patience, is even willing to make us willing.

One day Mendelssohn went to see the great Freiburg organ. The custodian refused him permission to play upon it, not knowing who he was. Reluctantly he finally gave permission. Soon from the organ came the most beautiful music. The custodian was spellbound. He asked the great musician his name. Learning it, he said, "And I almost refused you permission to play on the organ."

Our Master Musician wants permission to play on the instrument of our lives. Only as we grant Him this permission will our lives be a pleasure to Him and a blessing to others.

March
17

Choose you this day whom ye will serve . . . but as for me and my house, we will serve the Lord (Josh. 24:15).

The early leaders of the state of Virginia were trained from their youth to involve themselves in the affairs of their state. Recognizing that their loyalty was to their state, they willingly accepted leadership without question, ready to serve wherever needed, regardless of the cost or inconvenience to their private business, or inconvenience to their own plans. It must come first in their lives, before their own desires, pleasures, or business. They made a total commitment to a cause they believed in.

If the affairs of state called for men willing to assume leadership regardless of cost, how much more does the work of sharing the gospel call for dedicated people.

In his farewell message to the children of Israel, Joshua said, "Now therefore fear the Lord, and serve him in sincerity and truth! . . . choose you this day whom ye will serve; . . . but as for ME and MY house, we will serve the Lord" (Josh. 24:14-15).

Today God is looking for people who will choose to serve HIM. We cannot go two directions at the same time. A choice has to be made. Jesus said, "No man can serve two masters: for either he will hate the one, and love the other; or else he will hold to the one, and despise the other. Ye cannot serve God and mammon" (Matt. 6:24).

As we choose to serve Him, we become His representative, seeing the world through His eyes, ministering to it with His compassion.

A newspaper columnist, visiting India, found a missionary working with the lepers. As he watched her, he said, "I wouldn't wash the wounds of those lepers for a million dollars." She replied, "Sir, neither would I." She had chosen to serve Jesus Christ wherever He would send her, doing whatever He gave her to do.

Have you chosen to serve HIM? This challenge is not for tomorrow, next week, or next year; it is a PRESENT challenge—choose you THIS DAY. This challenge is a PERSONAL one, "but as for ME." What has been your reply? The choice is yours.

Hear Me when I call, O God of my righteousness; thou hast enlarged me when I was in distress; have mercy upon me, and hear my prayer (Ps. 4:1).

David lived within calling distance of God. In time of need he lifted his SUPPLICATIONS to God. He recognized that out of his distress good could come. "You have freed me when I was hemmed in and enlarged me when I was in distress; have mercy upon me and hear my prayer" *(Amplified)*. Someone has said, "God allowed David to be in distress for He wanted to make him a bigger man for bigger tasks."

God had SET APART David for His own. "But know that the Lord hath set apart him that is godly for Himself" (Ps. 4:3). God has set us apart, too, for Himself, not because of who we are or what we are, but because of what we can become in Christ.

David could have become bitter, thinking of his foes. Instead, he said, "Stand in awe, and sin not; commune with your own heart upon your bed, and be STILL" (v. 4). As he became still within, he could hear God's gentle whisperings to him during the night watches.

David recognized the SECURITY of trusting the Lord. "Put your trust in the Lord" (v. 5). People may forsake you, circumstances may change. But God never forsakes. We can trust Him at all times.

In spite of his troubles, David experienced a SATISFIED HEART, one filled with God-given gladness. "Yes, the gladness you have given me is far greater than their joys at harvest time as they gaze at their bountiful crops" (Ps. 4:7, LB). Too often we look for joy and gladness in prosperity. But the gladness David wrote about had its source in God. It is a "more than" gladness in the midst of trials, a gladness dependent on God.

Trusting God, he could say, "I will lie down in peace and sleep, for though I am alone, O Lord, you will keep me safe" (v. 8, LB).

Regardless of our problems today, our hearts can be filled with a God-given gladness that completely satisfies.

March
19

And he led them forth by the right way, that they might go to a city of habitation (Ps. 107:7).

The first time my husband and I went to New York City, the hustle and bustle of the huge metropolis frightened me. How would we find our way about the city and see the many things that were of special interest to us? A simple solution was arranged. We were introduced to a man who lived in the city. He became our guide, taking us on a personally conducted tour.

The children of Israel are pictured in Psalm 107 as travelers, lost in a barren desert, hungry, thirsty, and lonely. When they cried to God in their helplessness, He delivered them; He became their Guide as "HE led them forth by the RIGHT way."

Today we may be wandering travelers, lost in a wilderness of loneliness, disappointment, discouragement, despair, fear. We may be wondering whether we are in the right way. Turning to Him in our desperation, He is ready to become our PERSONAL-GUIDE. We need not question His leading. His way is always the right way.

He knows where we are. What may be an unknown way to us is known to Him. It may not be easy; it may not be smooth. But His way is the best way. With Him we are safe.

Sometimes we become lost because we go our own way instead of God's. We must come back to the place where we left Him and be willing to again go His way.

How can we know the right way? We must have regular communion with the Lord, in His Word and in prayer. We must totally commit our lives to Him. We must hold nothing back. Then we must be obedient to the direction He reveals to us, even though we may not see more than the next step ahead.

With Him as our Guide, He will lead us in the way that will lead us to HIMSELF. In Him we will find complete satisfaction.

"For he satisfieth the longing soul, and filleth the hungry soul with goodness" (Ps. 107:9).

And he answered, Fear not: for they that be with us are more than they that be with them (2 Kings 6:16).

When Benhadad, the Syrian king, was waging war on Israel, his military secrets kept leaking out. Learning that Elisha was responsible, the king sent his soldiers to capture him. However, Benhadad failed to realize his schemes were nothing against a man who had an open line of communication with God.

One morning Elisha's servant discovered they were completely surrounded by Benhadad's army. Frightened, he hurried to Elisha, saying, "Alas my master! How shall we do?" "Elisha, WHAT shall we do."

To his surprise, Elisha did not panic, but was completely undisturbed. Elisha, having SPIRITUAL VISION, SAW the great INVISIBLE host of God around them. Elisha said, "FEAR NOT, but they that be with us are more than they that be with them." How ineffective were Benhadad's chances against a man who had the resources of heaven at his disposal.

Then Elisha prayed that his servant, also, might have SPIRITUAL VISION to see the invisible hosts. "Lord, I pray thee, open his eyes that he may see. And the Lord opened the eyes of the young man; and HE SAW: and, behold, the mountain was full of horses and chariots of fire around about Elisha" (2 Kings 6:17).

Today we may be facing problems and situations that have no visible solution. We may be looking at our problems with our physical eyes. We may be crying out, "Alas! WHAT shall WE do?" When our eyes are on our circumstances we panic. When they are on God we are at rest.

We need to let God open our eyes of faith, giving us SPIRITUAL VISION. By faith our inner eyes can see God's provision for us. "FEAR NOT; they that be with You are more than they that be with them." We may not see our way out of our problem, but we can trust God to encircle us with His invisible host in the midst of it.

With our physical eyes we see the enemy; with our spiritual eyes we see God's heavenly host standing ready to deliver us. "The angel of the Lord encampeth round about them that fear him, and delivereth them" (Ps. 34:7).

March

21

Let not your heart be troubled: ye believe in God, believe also in me (John 14:1).

Sometime ago I had a conversation with a young college student. He said, "We young people today might as well confess that we are afraid."

The world is filled with troubled hearts. People are worrying about everything—business, the stockmarket, world conditions, families, sickness, the uncertainty of the future. More people are seeking help from psychologists and psychiatrists than ever before.

At a time when Jesus was facing Calvary, He took time to comfort His disciples. He knew they would face trouble, persecution, or even death. He encouraged them with "LET NOT your heart be troubled" (John 14:1). Williams translates this verse "STOP LETTING your hearts be troubled."

Jesus gave the secret for an untroubled heart. Its source is not in outward circumstances, but in a personal faith in God revealed in Jesus Christ. He said, "Ye believe in God, believe also in me" (John 14:1). "Trust in God: trust in me also" *(Weymouth).* The answer for trouble is to trust in God and in Jesus Christ.

We can also have untroubled hearts because of His promise that one day He will return and take us to be with Him in heaven. What hope that gives us!

This message has been a source of comfort to believers through the ages. Jesus didn't say we would be free from trouble, but we must not let it disturb our hearts. It is easy to say, "Don't get upset," or "Don't worry," but not so easy to practice. However, Jesus said, "LET NOT," or "DO NOT LET." "Let" means to allow or permit. We are not to allow or permit our hearts to be troubled.

Is your heart troubled today? Are you LETTING your heart be troubled? Jesus said, "Peace I leave with you; My [own] peace I now give and bequeath to you. Not as the world gives do I give to you. DO NOT LET your heart be troubled, neither let it be afraid—stop allowing yourselves to be agitated and disturbed; and DO NOT PERMIT yourselves to be fearful and intimidated and cowardly and unsettled" (John 14:27, *Amplified*).

A troubled heart? A trustful heart? Which is yours?

Hitherto hath the Lord helped us (1 Sam. 7:12).

An old hymn of the church reads, "O God, our help in ages past; our hope for years to come; our shelter from the stormy blast; and our eternal home." It has been said that God is the God of every tense—past, present, and future. He is the help of our past, the hope of our future, and the great "I am" of today.

After the Israelites had defeated the Philistines, they planted a stone and called it Ebenezer, saying, "HITHERTO HATH THE LORD helped us." We, too, need to be reminded occasionally how the Lord has led in the past. If we placed a stone each time the Lord has helped us, what a wall we would have. God has been our help in the PAST.

As we look into the unknown future, with no clear path before us, we may become fearful. But God has provided for our future. One name for God is "Jehovah-jireh," "the Lord WILL provide" (Gen. 22:14). Paul wrote, "But my God SHALL supply all your need according to His riches in glory by Christ Jesus" (Phil. 4:19). It does not say "perhaps He will provide," or "He is able to," but He "shall provide." God is our hope for the FUTURE.

We can thank Him for the past and have confidence in Him for the future. Yet sometimes we find it difficult to trust Him for the needs of today. But we must remember He IS willing to do the same for us today as He did in the past and will do in the future. He is the great "I am" of today, the all-sufficient One for this very moment. "The Lord IS my helper" (Heb. 13:6).

Sometimes He takes us out of our situations, problems, or needs; other times He takes us THROUGH them. Regardless of the way He works in our lives, we can trust Him as our ever-present Guide for TODAY.

Hebrews 13:8 reads, "Jesus Christ the same yesterday, and today, and forever." George Mueller had a motto on his wall that read, "And Today." Each of us can claim "And Today" as our motto for each day.

March

23

Be clothed with humility: for God resisteth the proud, and giveth grace to the humble (1 Peter 5:5).

The story is told of a preacher who said he had a wonderful sermon on humility. He was waiting for a large enough crowd to which he could preach it.

Humility is a fruit of grace. God's Word says, "But he giveth more grace. Wherefore he saith, God resisteth the proud, but giveth grace unto the humble" (James 4:6).

Some people by their attitude seem to be proud of their humility. The Pharisees were an example of this. They wanted people to believe they were humble. Yet, they were boastful, desirous of self-glory, proud of their humility.

Some people are always depreciating themselves, talking of their unworthiness, weaknesses, and failures. They belittle themselves. Such attitudes do not come from genuine humility. It is a false humility.

A truly humble person is unconscious of his humility. He has no thought of self. He realizes he has nothing but that which he has received from God. He takes the lowest place; he is willing to work without recognition.

The proud trust in themselves. The humble recognize their dependence on the Lord and want Him to receive all the glory.

The more we are emptied of self, the more room there will be for the Lord. The closer we live to Him the more we will recognize our unworthiness.

Paul, who had every reason to be proud, said, "Yes, every advantage that I had gained I considered lost for Christ's sake. Yes, and I look upon everything as loss compared with the overwhelming gain of knowing Christ Jesus my Lord. For His sake I did in actual fact suffer the loss of everything but I considered it useless rubbish compared with being able to win Christ" (Phil. 3:7,8, *Phillips*).

In the presence of the living God we will humbly bow as David did, and say, "Thine, O Lord, is the greatness, and the power, and the glory, and the victory, and the majesty: for all that is in the heaven and in the earth is thine; thine is the kingdom, O Lord, and thou art exalted as head above all" (1 Chron. 29:11).

Therefore, my beloved brethren, be ye steadfast, unmoveable, always abounding in the work of the Lord, forasmuch as ye know that your labour is not in vain in the Lord (1 Cor. 15:58).

Most of us have experienced discouragements in our Christian activities. There is so much to do and so few to help that we can easily become frustrated. The above Scripture verse encourages us when we wonder if it is worth continuing.

Paul had written about the resurrection of Jesus Christ. The power of His resurrection life indwelling us has a transforming result in our lives. Through His resurrection power we can be steadfast in our daily walk. We can be unmoveable when pressures come and storms shake our lives. We can abound in the ministry of sharing the gospel.

We are assured that our labor will not be in vain. "Forasmuch as ye know that your labor is not in vain in the Lord." Whatever we do for Him is never lost, never wasted. "Knowing and being continually aware that your labor in the Lord is not futile—never wasted or to no purpose" (1 Cor. 15:58, *Amplified*). This is the result of working, not FOR the Lord, but IN the Lord. We will do more than is required, more than just enough to get by.

Once a missionary couple were returning on the same ship as a well-known celebrity. They were broken in health and discouraged. As the ship docked, a great crowd had gathered to give the celebrity an enthusiastic welcome. No one met the missionary couple. It was almost more than the husband could take. For several days he was in the depths of despair, thinking God had forgotten them, and their work had not been appreciated. One day after a time in prayer, he came out of the bedroom radiant. He said to his wife. "The Lord spoke to me and it is all right now. When I asked why, He said, 'You aren't home yet.'" This couple's welcome would come when they entered His presence in heaven.

It will be worth it all when we enter His presence and He welcomes us home with, "Well done, thou good and faithful servant" (Matt. 25:21).

March
25

Come unto me, all ye that labour and are heavy laden, and I will give you rest (Matt. 11:28).

There is a great spirit of restlessness in the world today. People are like the restless sea, seeking peace, but finding instead turmoil and tension, fear and frustration. The world is in a state of unrest because individuals are in a state of unrest. Inner strain and pressure build up as a result of a constant round of frenzied activity.

While Jesus was here on earth He was aware that many people were burdened with the cares of life. "And what pity he felt for the crowds that came, because their problems were so great and they didn't know what to do or where to go for help. They were like sheep without a shepherd" (Matt. 9:36, LB). He could also look down the corridor of time and see that, even today, people would be carrying heavy burdens; burdens of fear, loneliness, bitterness, inadequacy, sorrow, guilt, and sin.

From a heart filled with love and concern for people, He gave a simple invitation. "Come to Me, all you who labor and are heavy-laden, and over burdened, and I will cause you to rest—I will ease and relieve and refresh your souls" (Matt. 11:28, *Amplified*). Bible scholars tell us the word "come" appears in the Bible more than six hundred times. This invitation was not just for the people of that day. It was not just for a select few, but it included all people through all ages.

We do not find rest in the act of coming, but in the One to whom we come. He will release the tension and strain and GIVE us rest. Coming to Him indicates that we put our trust in Him. Rest comes as we give our burdens to our Rest-giver. Yet many have not appropriated His provision for heart rest.

One night a pastor was preaching a sermon on these verses. Toward the end of his message he said, "Come unto Me! What does that mean?" As he paused, a little girl sitting in the front lifted her hand. Asking her what she thought it meant, she said, "It means that He wants me." And He does—today.

Today the world is full of heavy-laden people. They may have a smile on their faces, but hidden behind the smile is a burden almost too heavy to bear. You may be one of these people. He is saying to you, "Come to me. I want YOU." Your part is to come; His to give you rest. He never turns anyone away.

Take my yoke upon you, and learn of me; for I am meek and lowly in heart: and ye shall find rest unto your souls (Matt. 11:29).

In this mechanized age, not many have seen a yoke in use. In Palestine, ox yokes were made of wood. After the ox was measured, the yoke was roughed out. Then it was adjusted to fit the ox perfectly. The Lord has a "custom-designed" yoke for each of us, one carefully adjusted to our own personal life. "Wear my yoke—for it fits perfectly" (Matt. 11:29, LB).

Jesus invited His disciples to yoke themselves with Him, "and let me TEACH YOU" (v. 29, LB). As we enroll in His school, we major in "Learning of Him;" we minor in "Discovering God's Will for Our Lives." Jesus, our Master Teacher, enrolls us in such classes as His love, power, protection, provision. In some classes we learn how faith is increased. Sometimes lessons on chastening are included. They are all designed to bring us to spiritual maturity, and reveal God's will for our lives.

Geometry was not one of my better subjects in school. When an examination included the writing of certain theorems from memory, I made a good grade for I had memorized them. However, when problems were included in the examination, I wasn't able to apply the theorems to solving the problems. I finally realized that I really did not know geometry.

In our spiritual lives we may know ABOUT God without experiencing the reality of His presence in our life situations. For example, I had a knowledge of the peace of God for I had memorized the Scriptures on peace, and had meditated on them. But when did I really KNOW the peace of God? One day the doctor told us that my husband had Hodgkin's disease. As we left his office, tears trickled down our cheeks. Suddenly we had a peace that only God can give, a peace that passeth understanding. Then we knew the peace of God in a way we had not known before. Not only did we know the peace of God but we had a deeper knowledge of the God of peace.

As we are yoked together with Him in quiet yielding, we learn of Him. In this way we can live a restful life.

March
27

For my yoke is easy, and my burden is light (Matt. 11:30).

One day a young woman, new in her Christian faith, was listening to a discussion on the subject of rest. She was concentrating intently on every word that was being said. Finally looking up through her tears, she said, "You mean there is rest for us in this hectic life of today?"

Yes, there is rest for us today, a rest that comes as we are yoked together with Him, in submission to His will. It has been said, "Jesus took the Father's yoke when He said, 'Lo, I come to do thy will, O God.' We take His yoke when we submit to His control of our lives." Instead of trying to do His will in our strength, we can rest in Him, allowing Him to fulfill God's plan for our lives.

A yoke is not a weight, but a means of distributing the weight. So it is not surprising that He could say, "MY yoke is easy, and MY burden is light." Our side of the yoke is easy and light, for He carries it for us.

His yoke is not one of a tyrant wanting to rule over us, but the yoke of One who loves us and has our best interests at heart. Yoked together with Him, we have inner peace, for He removes tension and turmoil, giving us rest. Although He wants us to take up His yoke, He puts no pressure on us. The decision is ours. There must be a willingness on our part.

A team is yoked together to do the same work. Sometimes, however, a team pulls against each other, hindering progress. In our daily walk, self-will may cause us to pull in the opposite direction, resulting in friction. However, if yielded to His control, we are released from frustration and anxiety, experiencing the ease of His yoke. Giving control of our lives to Him doesn't mean we will have nothing to do. There will be activity, but it will be a restful activity.

When the heart yields, Christ is Lord.
When He is Lord, there is rest.

He was a burning and shining light (John 5:35).

Jesus, in speaking of John the Baptist in this Scripture verse, called him a "burning and shining light." Wherever he went, John was a shining light, pointing others to Jesus Christ. Once he said, "He must increase, but I must decrease."

Throughout the centuries, many people have been burning and shining lights for Jesus Christ.

Today we are living in a world filled with spiritual darkness. People all about us are groping for something to bring light into their darkened lives. God has entrusted to us the ministry of being a shining light for Jesus Christ, the Light of the world. Paul wrote, "You are seen as bright lights—stars or beacons shining out clearly—in the [dark] world" (Phil. 2:15, *Amplified*). He doesn't place all of us in the same place to shine. Some may be called to shine in faraway places; others in their families, neighborhoods, and places of business.

Sometimes we are in such a dark place we think our small light cannot be seen. I remember the first time we visited Carlsbad Caverns. When we reached the deepest section, they turned off all the lights. We experienced a darkness that could almost be felt. Suddenly in the distance a light came on. It seemed so small, yet it shone brightly in that large area which had been dark just a moment before.

So Jesus, the Light of the world, shining through our lives, can bring light into the darkness wherever He has placed us, even though we think our light very small.

A little girl once visited the home where Abraham Lincoln had lived. She had heard many things about the great man who did so much for people. She was eager to see his house. As she approached it, she noticed lamps burning inside, just as they had been years before when he lived there. She said to her mother, "Mr. Lincoln left the lights on when he went away."

Many lights have been left on in the world by those whose lives shone briefly for God. Can He say to us, "They are lights, burning and shining for Me?"

March

29

But Noah found grace in the eyes of the Lord. . . . Noah was a just man and perfect in his generations, and Noah walked with God (Gen. 6:8-9).

Noah lived in the midst of a wicked people "The wickedness of man was great in the earth" (Gen. 6:5).

Yet he was an example of one who could live a godly life in an evil world; a life pleasing to God in his everyday environment. "But Noah found grace in the eyes of the Lord." His favor with the Lord was through no merit of his own, but through his personal faith in God.

God could see that Noah's life was upright. "He was the only truly righteous man living on the earth at that time" (Gen. 6:9, LB). God recognized Noah as a perfect man; not perfect in character, but in a life revealing a genuineness of faith in God.

We also read that "Noah walked [in habitual fellowship] with God (v. 9, *Amplified*). In the midst of wickedness, he was able to keep close fellowship with God. "He tried always to conduct his affairs according to God's will" (v. 9, LB). It is not the environment but the heart that determines one's walk with the Lord.

Noah was not as concerned with pleasing people as he was with pleasing God. "But Noah found grace in the eyes of the Lord."

We may question ourselves, "Do I find grace in the eyes of the Lord?" Remembering our weaknesses and failures we realize we have no merit by which God can accept us. But God knows all about us and has provided a way by which we can be accepted by Him. We find grace in God's sight through our relationship with Jesus Christ. God sees us perfect in Him.

We may find ourselves in a place not conducive to Christian living, just as Noah did. Even there, God gives us grace to live victoriously. "He giveth MORE GRACE" (James 4:6).

Ponder the words, "Noah found grace in the eyes of the Lord." In the eyes of the Lord, is MY life pleasing to Him today? Do I find grace in His sight?

Fear thou not; for I am with thee: be not dismayed; for I am thy God (Isa. 41:10).

As you begin a new day, do you wonder what it will hold? Because of the uncertainty and insecurity of life, fear of the unknown often fills our hearts. We may fear loss of employment, sickness, being left alone, or failure of being accepted in society. People are sometimes so gripped by fear they can't cope with life.

What place should fear have in the life of a Christian? If we are honest, we must admit that at some time each of us has experienced fear. Satan makes every effort to keep us fearful, robbing us of trust in the Lord. He will attempt to discredit the power of God to handle our situations and keep us from the assurance of His personal interest in us.

Fear is not of God. "For God hath not given us the spirit of fear" (2 Tim. 1:7). Throughout the Bible two simple, encouraging words, "Fear not," reassure us that we can TRUST GOD.

In today's Scripture verse we are reminded of two reasons why we need not fear. First, because "I AM WITH YOU." When fear comes He speaks these comforting words, "Fear not, for I am with YOU." It is easier, when going through trouble, if someone shares the burden with us. In our times of stress and strain God is our present Companion, easing our load and encouraging our hearts. He does not say, "I HAVE been with thee," or "I WILL be with thee," but "I AM with thee." Surely we need not fear when we have the companionship of the God of the universe.

Then we need have no fear because He is our personal God. "I am THY GOD." The all-powerful God, the Creator of heaven and earth, is interested in us and cares for us. Not one detail in our lives is unimportant to Him. He is saying, "Fear not; I am in control of your circumstances."

Paul reminds us of this same truth in 2 Corinthians 6:16. HIS PRESENCE in us: God said, "I WILL DWELL IN THEM, and walk in them." HIS PERSONAL INTEREST in us: "I will be THEIR GOD, and they shall be MY PEOPLE."

March
31

I will strengthen thee; yea, I will help thee; yea, I will uphold thee with the right hand of my righteousness (Isa. 41:10).

In our devotional yesterday we considered the fact that freedom from fear is possible because we have the PRESENCE of God indwelling us and He has a PERSONAL interest in us.

Freedom from fear is also possible because of WHAT He has promised to do for us. He promised the "I will" of strength—"I will strengthen thee." The secret of our strength is that in our weakness we are strong in Him. "For my strength is made perfect in weakness. . . . for when I am weak, then I am strong" (2 Cor. 12:9-10).

We are promised the "I will" of His help—"I will help THEE." Do you face an insurmountable obstacle today? Remember when you are at your extremity, you are in God's territory.

He promised the "I will" of upholding us. "I will hold you up . . . with My victorious right hand" (Isa. 41:10, *Amplified*). His unlimited power is available for our walk through life.

When a child is learning to walk, a parent holds his hand to prevent his falling. If the child stumbles, the parent lifts him up onto his feet again. Our heavenly Father holds our hand to steady us over the rough places of our road. If we stumble, He lifts us onto our feet again. With our hand in His, we are secure.

The "I AM" of WHO HE IS, and the "I WILL" of WHAT He can do for us, dispels fear. "For I, the Lord your God, hold your right hand; I, Who say to you, FEAR NOT, I will help you" (v. 13). He is our antidote for fear. It is not "something" we need, but "Someone," the ONE who is our peace, the Lord Jesus Christ. In Him we have freedom from fear.

As we let God remove fear from our lives, and give us HIS peace in the midst of our problems, people will recognize what God can do in a life. "That men may see, and know, and consider, and understand together, that the hand of the Lord has done this" (v. 20).

It is God which worketh in you both to will and to do of his good pleasure (Phil. 2:13).

In making a garment, a person selects a pattern suitable for the fabric. She places the pattern on the fabric, cuts, sews, and fits it to the person; finishing touches complete the garment.

God has a life pattern for us and begins to fit it to the fabric of our lives. Some rearranging may be necessary to make the pattern fit. Some attitudes, desires, or motives may have to be adjusted. As He begins to cut the fabric, some things will require cutting out completely. Other things will only need trimming. This process may hurt, but it is necessary in order to complete the garment for His good pleasure.

The pieces of our lives have to be fitted together to complete His purpose. "Moreover we know that to those who love God, who are called according to his plan, everything that happens fits into a pattern for good" (Rom. 8:28, *Phillips*).

God adds finishing touches to bring out His beauty in our lives. No two lives are designed alike; He has His own special pattern for each of us.

To make the garment, it took the pattern, fabric, scissors, thread, trimming. Yet not one of them had the power to cut, fit, or sew that garment. It took the power of a person to do it.

We cannot make our lives according to God's pattern. It takes His power. Ephesians 2:10 says, "For we are His workmanship, created in Christ Jesus unto good works, which God hath before ordained that we should walk in them."

Sometimes we are not willing to do His will. A little rebellion may enter in. But He can even make us willing to be made willing.

F. B. Meyer told of the time God asked him for the keys to the rooms of his life. One by one he gave them to Him—all but one key to a little closet room. This was the key to something he was not willing to turn over to God. No peace came until finally he prayed, "Lord, I am not willing to give you the key, but I am willing to be made willing."

"For it is God who is at work within you, giving you the will and the power to achieve his purpose" (Phil. 2:13, *Phillips*).

April

2

Fear not ye: for I know that ye seek Jesus, which was crucified. He is not here: for he is risen, as he said. Come, see the place where the Lord lay (Matt. 28:5-6).

Easter is a joyous season, commemorating the bodily resurrection of Jesus Christ from the dead.

The dark events surrounding His crucifixion had left His followers discouraged. They had expected an earthly kingdom to be set up. Instead, Jesus had been crucified. However, they didn't realize that what had seemed a tragedy to them would soon be turned into a triumph.

At daybreak some of the women went to the tomb to anoint the body of Jesus with sweet spices as their one last act of love and devotion. Not long before, they had been spectators at the crucifixion. Now with heavy hearts they were on their way to the tomb.

Imagine their surprise to find the stone already rolled away from the tomb and an angel saying, "Fear not ye: for I know that ye SEEK JESUS, which was crucified. He is not here: for He is risen, as he said; COME, SEE the place where the Lord lay." What joy we would experience if we received a message that a dear one whom we thought dead was alive. So these friends were overjoyed with the news that Jesus Christ had risen from the dead.

The message of the angel proclaimed the great victorious miracle—the victory of life over death. It dispels fear, bringing peace to our hearts. "FEAR NOT YE—He is not here." The message brings hope. "HE IS RISEN" means that He is alive. The message is reassuring. "AS HE SAID." This gives us confidence that His Word is true.

Victory, peace, and hope characterize our Christian faith because Jesus came forth triumphant over death. "I am he that liveth, and was dead; and, behold, I am alive for evermore" (Rev. 1:18). How we can praise God today for the personal knowledge that He is not only the living Savior and LORD of the world, but that He can be OURS personally.

The reality of this knowledge in our lives gives us the promise of life throughout eternity with Him. "Because I live, ye shall live also" (John 14:19).

And go quickly, and tell his disciples that he is risen from the dead; and, behold, he goeth before you into Galilee; there shall ye see him: lo, I have told you (Matt. 28:7).

When we find a new recipe we think is good or a book we enjoy, we want to share it with others.

This is true in our spiritual lives. When Christ becomes real to us, we want to share Him with others. In the above Scripture verse, the words "GO" and "TELL" give a directive for our lives—"something to do" and "something to say."

A famine had spread throughout the land of Samaria. Four lepers were at the city gate starving to death. They decided to go to the Syrian camp for food. Imagine their great suprise to find the camp evacuated but the supplies left behind. In excitement they went from tent to tent helping themselves to food, silver, gold, and clothing.

Finally they said, "We do not well: this day is a day of good tidings, and we hold our peace: if we tarry till the morning light, some mischief will come upon us: now therefore come that we may GO and TELL the king's household" (2 Kings 7:9).

They realized their responsibility to share with others from their provisions. "We do not well: this is a day of good tidings, and we hold our peace."

In a day when so many are searching for an answer to life, are we, too, holding our peace? This is the day of good tidings. Just before Jesus returned to His heavenly home, He said, "Go ye into all the world, and preach the gospel to every creature" (Mark 16:15).

Today many people are starving for spiritual food. We have the "Living Bread" to share with them. Jesus said, "I am the Bread of Life: he that cometh to me shall never hunger; and he that believeth on me shall never thirst" (John 6:35). Are we sharing this Good News, or are we holding our peace?

This is the day of good tidings! GO and TELL!

April
4

My presence shall go with thee, and I will give thee rest (Exod. 33:14).

What great comfort to our hearts is the assurance of God's presence with us. When deserted by friends and family, when lonely, when burdened with cares, what encouragement to hear God say, "MY presence shall go with THEE, and I will give thee rest."

While Moses was in the mount with God, the people turned from God to worship a golden calf.

Discouraged and disheartened, Moses cried to the Lord, saying, "Now therefore, I pray thee, if I have found grace in thy sight, show me now thy way, that I may know thee, that I may find grace in thy sight: and consider that this nation is thy people" (Exod. 33:13).

He knew God was his only source of help. His heart's cry was, "that I may know THEE."

Moses was reassured when God said, "My presence shall go with thee, and I will give thee rest." My presence—nothing less than the presence of God Himself! Moses could rest secure in this promise, "I SHALL go with thee." Sidlow Baxter has said, "God's blessings without Himself are not blessings at all to the God-hungry heart." "My presence" in the Septuagint is translated, "I myself will go with thee."

Are you disappointed and discouraged today? Did you start out on your Christian walk with excitement and expectancy? Then things fell apart? God promises you today, "My presence shall go with YOU, and I will give YOU rest." In the midst of your disappointment, discouragement, failure, and depression, He assures you that He knows about you and, wherever you go, whatever you are going through, He will not leave you.

Rest comes from releasing your plans to Him and receiving His plans. Rest comes from keeping your eyes fixed upon Him instead of your circumstances. Rest comes from ceasing to live for self and living in Him.

Rest will come, not from things or people, not from the removal of circumstances; rest will come from HIM.

It is a gift. "I will GIVE." It is a personal gift. "I will give YOU." But you must take it by faith.

April 5

That the trial of your faith, being much more precious than of gold that perisheth, though it be tried with fire, might be found unto praise and honour and glory at the appearing of Jesus Christ (1 Peter 1:7).

Many old popular songs are being revised, one of which is "Singing in the Rain." Paraphrasing this title, may we say that many Christians today are "Singing in the Fire." Even though they are going through fires of testing and trial, almost beyond measure, yet they have learned the secret of praising God at such times.

Peter compares with fire the METHOD used to purify our lives. The ancient goldsmith put crude gold ore in a vat. A heat seven times hotter than usual was turned on to refine gold, burning out the dross and purifying it. In the process, the refiner stood by the vat of gold, drawing off the dross, with his eyes constantly fixed on the molten metal. When he could see his image reflected in the gold, the fire was turned off.

The Master Refiner wants to bring out the beauty of the Lord in our lives. He turns on the fire of trial to burn out such unlovely characteristics as self-pity, selfishness, criticalness, pride, or jealousy in our lives. As the heat is turned on, God keeps His eye on us, watching for the image of Jesus Christ to be formed in our lives. It has been said, "Gold is refined in the fire, but God's fire never hurts His saints—it makes them."

We can SING IN THE FIRE if we remember that our trials are to perfect the loveliness of the Lord in us.

Faith enables us to face our trials with a spirit of calmness and joy. Instead of focusing our eyes on the trials, we must keep them looking to the Lord. Faith untried may be true faith, but great faith develops and grows under trials.

As a RESULT of the trials, God is making of our lives that which will bring praise, honor, and glory at His appearing. "So if your faith remains strong after being tried in the test tube of fiery trials, it will bring you much praise and glory and honor on the day of His return" (v. 7, LB).

Are you "Singing in the Fire" today? No faith is so precious as that which triumphs in adversity, a faith in God that gives a song of triumph when overwhelmed by trials.

TRIALS! Either OBSTACLES or OPPORTUNITIES!

April
6

Thy words were found, and I did eat them; and thy word was unto me the joy and rejoicing of mine heart: for I am called by thy name, O Lord God of hosts (Jer. 15:16).

Jeremiah was known as "The Weeping Prophet." His life was filled with trouble, loneliness, and discouragement. He endured great persecution.

Yet his life was filled with joy in spite of adverse circumstances, because of his spiritual diet on the Word of God. He said, "Your words are what sustain me; they are food to my hungry soul. They bring joy to my sorrowing heart and delight me. How proud I am to bear your name, O Lord" (Jer. 15:16, LB). Feeding upon it gave him the power he needed to overcome and rise above his obstacles.

As we need food for physical nourishment, so the Word of God is necessary for our spiritual well-being. It feeds the soul. Jesus said, "Man shall not live by bread alone, but by every word that proceedeth from the mouth of God" (Matt. 4:4).

However, to receive benefit, we must appropriate it for our daily living. It fortifies us to face problems. It gives wisdom and guidance for our life situations. It brings comfort when our hearts are breaking and tears are falling.

As I open His Word, I pray, "Open thou mine eyes, that I may behold wondrous things out of thy law" (Ps. 119:18). I read it with expectation, knowing He has something for me personally from it. I meditate over each word and phrase in a verse or portion. What does it mean? What is God saying to me? What guidance does it give for my present need?

The more I read it, the better acquainted I become with the Lord. My friendship with Him deepens as He reveals Himself to me from its pages each day. Although I read it regularly, I never let it become just a form or habit without personal meaning for my life that day.

Are you reading it regularly? Are you seeking HIM as you read it? It will then be the joy and rejoicing of your heart.

Because I live, ye shall live also (John 14:19).

In a world on the brink of collapse, gripped by hate and filled with despair, Easter has a powerful message. It brings a message of LOVE, PEACE, and HOPE, for it is a message of LIFE. "Jesus said unto her, I am the resurrection, and the life: he that believeth in me, though he were dead, yet shall he live" (John 11:25).

Men's biographies end with their death; not so with the story of Jesus. He rose from the dead, becoming the Living Savior. In Revelation 1:18 we read, "I am He that liveth, and was dead; and, behold, I am alive for evermore."

One day a man stood looking in a shop window at the picture of the crucifixion. Standing next to him was a ragged little street urchin, lost in contemplation of the picture. Wondering if the boy really understood its meaning, the man said, "Sonny, what does it mean?" "Don't you know?" the boy replied. "That man is Jesus. The woman crying is His mother. The others are the Roman soldiers." He paused, then continued, "They killed Him." The man turned away. In a moment he heard steps running after him. It was the little boy. Breathlessly the boy said, "Say, mister, I forgot to tell you. He rose from the dead."

Jesus' death and resurrection give us the promise of life everlasting. ". . . Because I LIVE, ye shall LIVE also."

The personal possession of the life of the Risen Savior gives peace, power, and purpose for our daily living. Jesus said, "I came that they may HAVE *(not will have)* and enjoy life, and have it in abundance—to the full, till it overflows" (John 10:10, *Amplified*). His life filling our lives gives us power to meet each situation and is sufficient for each day.

Has Easter lost any of the freshness and reality of its meaning for you? Is the presence of the Christ of Easter real to you? Knowing the nearness of His presence doesn't depend on our feelings; we accept it by faith. One of our lovely Easter songs asks the question "You ask me how I know He lives?" The answer, "HE LIVES WITHIN MY HEART."

April
8

But thou, O Lord, art a shield for me; my glory, and the lifter up of my head (Ps. 3:3).

King David was facing a time of great distress. His son, Absalom, had led a successful revolt against him. David, in deep despair, prayed, "Lord, how are they increased that trouble me! many are they that rise up against me. Many there be which say of my soul, 'There is no help for him in God.' Selah" (Ps. 3:1,2). His cause seemed hopeless.

But David knew where to go in time of trouble. He turned in confidence to God, his PRESENT source of help. "But THOU, O LORD, art (right now) a shield to me; my glory, and the lifter up of my head."

When the darts of his enemies were hurled at him, God was his shield. In the midst of his discouragement, he knew the glory of God's presence. God's presence was so real to him he could say of Him, "My glory." Even though he was downcast, God lifted his head, delivering him from despair.

David took his burden to the Lord and left it with Him. Because of his confident trust in God, he could say, "I laid me down and slept; I awaked; for the LORD sustained me" (v. 5).

Does your case seem hopeless? Do you feel everyone has turned against you? You have the same source of help at such times as David. "But THOU, O LORD."

We need not fear the attacks of the enemy for God surrounds us and protects us with Himself as our mighty shield. His presence within becomes our glory, bringing His beauty and splendor into our lives. When our heads and hearts are bowed down, our eyes overflowing with tears, He lovingly and tenderly lifts up our heads so we can see HIM. As we look into His face, we are comforted by Him. He wipes away our tears.

When we commit our problems to Him, we can say as David did, "I cried unto the Lord with my voice, and He heard me out of His holy hill. Selah" (v. 4). Then we can lie down and sleep, for we know, "The LORD sustained me" (v. 5).

"Mary!" Jesus said. She turned toward Him. "Master!" she exclaimed! (John 20:16, LB*).*

On the resurrection day as Mary waited at the tomb, Jesus appeared and spoke to her. One word: "Mary!" Immediately she knew Him.

Love and joy overflowed from her heart as she fell at His feet in adoring worship, calling Him "Master!" In calling Him Master she was expressing the whole attitude of her life toward Him as Lord and Master.

Today is He the Lord and Master of our lives? What should be some of the attitudes and motives in the life of a person to whom He is Master and Lord?

First, we should love Him from the depths of our innermost being. "Thou shalt love the Lord thy God with all thy heart, and with all thy soul, and with all thy mind" (Matt. 22:37). This kind of love is satisfied with nothing less than the Lord Himself. "Whom having not seen, ye love; in whom, though now ye see him not, yet believing, ye rejoice with joy unspeakable and full of glory" (1 Peter 1:8). It never counts the cost. Is this the kind of love we have for Him?

Another attitude should be adoration of Him. Our love for Him overflows in adoration and worship. Worship is being occupied with the Lord Himself, not just with His gifts and blessings. We are told to ". . . worship the Lord in the beauty of holiness" (1 Chron. 16:29). To worship Him we must spend time with Him.

Then we need to give Him our allegiance, living for Him with a singleness of heart and purpose, with undivided loyalty.

But real love, adoration, and allegiance respond in obedience to Him. "And what is the point of calling me, 'Lord, Lord,' without doing what I tell you to do?" (Luke 6:46, *Phillips*).

What is the attitude of our lives toward Him? Is He the object of our love, worship, allegiance, and obedience? By the measure of our obedience to Him, we reveal our love for Him. Not only are we to say, "Master"—"Lord," with our lips, but with our lives.

Can we truly call Him "MY Master"—"MY Lord"?

April

10

The Lord is my light and my salvation; whom shall I fear? the Lord is the strength of my life; of whom shall I be afraid? (Ps. 27:1).

Most of us must confess that we have been fearful at some time in our lives. Fear is a natural emotion, very real in our lives. If we are not careful, it can become a controlling power over us.

But God has promised freedom from fear, for the Lord is our LIGHT, and lightens our path before us step by step.

One dark night we were driving on a desolate road across the desert. No stars could be seen in the sky; the moon was hidden behind the clouds. Suddenly the car lights went out. For a moment fear gripped our hearts, for we could see nothing. Just as suddenly, the lights came on again and the fear was gone.

So in our lives, there are times when the lights go out. We are in complete darkness. We cannot see the way ahead. Fear grips our hearts. But God is with us in the darkness and His presence illuminates our lives. In His own time He shows us the next step ahead for us.

We can also be free from fear for He is our SALVATION. He is the all-powerful one in Whom we put our complete trust, confident that He can lead us safely along His path for us.

Then we can be free from fear for He is our STRENGTH. He is our constant source of power. Could anything be more powerful than our lives plus God? His all-powerfulness in our weakness.

He was our confidence in the past. "When the wicked, even mine enemies and my foes, came (past tense) upon me to eat up my flesh, they stumbled and fell" (Ps. 27:2). He is our confidence for the future. "Though an host should encamp against me, my heart shall (future tense) not fear" (v. 3). He is our confidence all through life. "I sought the Lord, and He heard me, and delivered me from ALL MY FEARS" (Ps. 34:4).

In the light of His presence I shall not fear; in the security of His presence I shall not be afraid.

And be ye kind one to another, tenderhearted, forgiving one another, even as God for Christ's sake hath forgiven you (Eph. 4:32).

Do you know someone to whom it is difficult to be kind? Someone you don't like? Someone toward whom you have a bitter and unforgiving spirit? Perhaps you have said, "I can forgive, but I can't forget." If so, do you really know the spirit of forgiveness? The life of a Christian should be an example of a forgiving spirit.

Peter once asked Jesus, "How oft shall my brother sin against me and I forgive him? Till seven times?" Peter thought he was being very generous. But Jesus answered, "I say not till seven times, but until seventy times seven." The spirit of forgiveness is beyond mathematical calculations. There is to be no limit in our readiness to forgive others. There is to be no limit in the greatness of the wrong we are to forgive.

What is our reaction when something is said about us, or our wishes are crossed? Not only are we to forgive, but forget.

God's forgiveness of us for Christ's sake is our pattern. When He has forgiven us so much, can we do less? Jesus said that if we bring our gift to the altar and the Holy Spirit reminds us of anyone who has anything against us, we must leave our gift and go to him, trying to make it right. Then we can return and offer our gift. The person who wronged us may not deserve our forgiveness, but neither do we deserve God's forgiveness.

The Holy Spirit provides the tenderness and kindness of Christ in our lives and then we can forgive others as God in Christ forgives us.

It has been said of Henry VI of England, "He never forgot anything but injuries." Emerson said of Lincoln, "His heart was as great as the world, but there was not room in it for the memory of a wrong." What are you giving room to in your heart? Bitterness? Resentment? Dislike? Or kindness? Love? Forgiveness?

"Be gentle and ready to forgive; never hold grudges. Remember, the Lord forgave you, so you must forgive others" (Col. 3:13, LB).

April
12

Verily, verily, I say unto you, Except a corn of wheat fall into the ground and die, it abideth alone: but if it die, it bringeth forth much fruit (John 12:24).

On a packet of flower seed are pictures of what can be expected from the seeds. If we put the packet away, all we can expect is a packet of individual seeds. Only when the seeds are planted will there be a harvest of flowers.

The above Scripture verse reveals the law of spiritual harvest. When a seed is planted in the ground, it dies. Yet from the seed eventually springs forth new life. Dying, it begins to live again. In time, from one little seed comes not one grain, but a harvest of grain.

The same principle of life out of death is true in the spiritual realm. "I must fall and die like a kernel of wheat that falls into the furrow of the earth. Unless I die I will be alone—a single seed. But my death will produce many new wheat kernels—a plentiful harvest of new lives" (John 12:24, LB).

Jesus used this as an illustration in referring to his own death and resurrection. As the corn of wheat must die to come forth in new life, He died that He might live again in resurrection life, imparting this life to His redeemed people. "For if, when we were enemies, we were reconciled to God by the death of His Son, much more, being reconciled, we shall be saved by His life" (Rom. 5:10).

The same principle is in effect in our lives. The way to fruitfulness is death to self. "When I die, I will be alone—a single seed." If we are willing to die to self, to our desires, thoughts, ambitions, successes, and failures, in order to reach souls for Christ, our lives will produce an abundant spiritual harvest for His glory.

Ask yourself this question today. "Am I producing a spiritual harvest, or am I abiding alone?" A kernel of wheat can only multiply itself by death. The only way to spiritual fruitfulness is death to self.

When you stand before Jesus Christ will you be empty-handed, or will you have an abundant spiritual harvest?

Order my steps in thy word: let not any iniquity have dominion over me (Ps. 119:133).

How many steps do you take in a day? By evening most of us feel we have taken too many. Regardless of the number, we only take them one at a time. A Chinese proverb says, "A journey of a thousand miles begins with one step."

The steps of our spiritual walk are important. If our steps are to go in the right direction, they must be ordered in God's Word. "Establish my steps and direct them by (means of) Your Word" (Ps. 119:133, *Amplified*).

When being trained for a new work we must first read and study the textbooks. We must absorb and familiarize ourselves with the subject matter. Then we begin doing what we have been instructed and trained to do. So in our Christian life. The Bible is our Book of Instructions. To walk in God's path, we must know His instructions from His Word. "The entrance of thy words giveth light; it giveth understanding unto the simple" (Ps. 119:130).

As we appropriate His Word into our lives, the Holy Spirit will guide our steps. "He will keep the feet of his saints" (1 Sam. 2:9).

A young pastor was impressed with his own knowledge of God's Word. He was invited to visit an older pastor who was not a great scholar, but was a real man of God. The young man thought it would be an opportunity to display his understanding of the Bible. However, as the older gentleman picked up his Bible, he put his hand tenderly and gently on the opened page. The young pastor recognized the deep love this man had for the Bible and its Author, God Himself. This was the turning point in the young man's life. He realized his intellectual knowledge of the Bible was not enough. He needed the deep intimate love not only for the Bible, but for its Author, that the older pastor had.

Do you have a deep love like this for the Bible? Do you have a real desire to know its Author in a deeper, more real way? Do you desire that your steps be directed by it? "The steps of a good man are ordered of the Lord" (Ps. 37:23).

April
14

Thou wilt keep him in perfect peace, whose mind is stayed on thee: because he trusteth in thee (Isa. 26:3).

One evening a young man being interviewed on television was asked for his definition of happiness. He paused a moment, then answered, "I would define happiness as having inner peace." Today many people are seeking a peace of heart and mind.

God's Word assures us that there is a STATE of perfect peace. "Thou wilt keep him in perfect peace." We can have perfect peace in the midst of life's turmoil. It gives no place to worry. It does not come from human effort or circumstances. It is a state of continual, unbroken peace. "You will guard him and keep him in perfect and constant peace" (Isa. 26:3, *Amplified*).

It is a supernatural peace with its source in God Himself—"THOU will keep." It is available to us in the person of Jesus Christ. The promise of it is certain, "thou WILT keep."

The SECRET of peace is ". . . a mind stayed on thee." In this verse, the word for "mind" includes the thoughts and imaginations of the mind. Fear and distress can fill our minds, causing anxiety and worry as a result of our imaginings. Satan often attacks the mind, for he knows a distressed mind can cause a distraught life.

The STEADFASTNESS of this peace comes from trusting Him. "Because he trusteth in THEE." The trusting is our part, the keeping His.

We may receive distressing news. Trouble may befall us. Our lives may be completely shaken. God's promise of perfect peace is for us in the midst of these difficulties. God enables us to remain calm during such experiences.

Two artists each painted a picture illustrating rest. The first artist painted a scene showing a still lake of water among the far-off mountains. The second artist drew a thundering waterfall with a slender branch of a tree bending over the foam. At the fork of the branch, almost wet with spray from the waterfall, sat a robin on its nest. This was the real picture of rest in the midst of storm and turbulence.

"Oh, for the peace of a perfect trust, my loving God in Thee; unwavering faith that never doubts. Thou choosest best for me."

"MENTAL REST BRINGS HEART PEACE."

And in the morning, rising up a great while before day, he went out, and departed into a solitary place, and there prayed (Mark 1:35).

It has been said, "Life is so fragile we must handle it with prayer."

What do the early morning hours find us doing? As we awaken, do our thoughts turn to our heavenly Father? Do we thank Him for a new day, committing it and ourselves to Him? Do we spend time reading His Word and praying before we face the day with others? Or are we so weary from the strenuous day before, we feel we deserve extra rest?

Jesus lived a busy life. His daily schedule was full. Yet as we follow His ministry, we discover He never seemed hurried and tense. Everywhere He went multitudes followed Him. People pressed upon Him constantly, seeking His help. He always had time for each individual. With the pressures of such busy days it must have been difficult for Him to find time for communion with His Heavenly Father. But He had learned the importance of "The Solitude of Prayer." Prayer to Him was not "incidental" but "fundamental." He rose early in the morning for time alone with His Heavenly Father in prayer.

In today's complex way of life it may not be possible to "rise up a great while before day." Dr. Edman gave a helpful comment on this. He said, "There should be the 'sunrise' of the soul each day, no matter what the hour of the day may be for the believer."

It was said of John Wesley, "He thought prayer to be more his business than anything else. I have seen him come out of his prayer closet with a serenity of face next to shining."

Regardless of what time of day is best for us, it is vital to our spiritual life to go "into the solitary place" with God. Our needs may be many, problems may seem insurmountable, strength may be limited. In the solitary place of prayer, help comes from God. In His presence, tensions are relieved, courage is renewed. Calmness of spirit comes as we rest in the Lord.

April
16

And he said unto them, Come ye yourselves apart into a desert place, and rest a while (Mark 6:31).

We are familiar with the well-known slogan of the Coca-Cola Company, "The Pause that Refreshes."

In these days of tension, we are looking for ways to relax and refresh ourselves. Tremendous amounts of sleeping pills and relaxers are consumed nightly to induce sleep. But nothing can be of greater refreshment to our tired bodies than a good night of natural sleep.

As sleep rests the body, so prayer rests the inner person. Jesus recognized the great refreshing power that comes from prayer. He took time for it in His own life, drawing apart for times of communion with His Heavenly Father.

He knew, also, that times of prayer were important for His disciples. "And he said unto them, Come ye yourselves apart into a desert place, and rest a while; for there were many coming and going, and they had no leisure so much as to eat."

We, too, need a time for refreshing our inner being. The tensions of life begin to bring pressure. Problems, heartaches, and sorrows mount. Physically we are exhausted. Yet we need more than physical rest. It isn't sufficient just to go to a quiet place and rest. We need the renewed strength that comes from spending time with Him in prayer. He invites us to COME (not GO). As we come to Him and rest in His presence, His blessing is upon us and we are revived within.

We read in Isaiah 40:31 *(Amplified)*, "But those who wait for the Lord—who expect, look for and hope in Him—shall change and renew strength and power; they shall lift their wings and mount up [close to God] as eagles [mount up to the sun]; they shall run and not be weary; they shall walk and not faint or become tired."

Someone has said, "There is no time lost in waiting if our waiting is on the Lord."

"There is a place of quiet rest, near to the heart of God; a place where sin cannot molest, near to the heart of God."

And as he prayed, the fashion of his countenance was altered, and his raiment was white and glistering (Luke 9:29).

One day Jesus took Peter, James, and John up to a mountain top to pray. There the disciples were witnesses to a great transformation. "And AS HE PRAYED, the fashion of his countenance was altered, and his raiment was white and glistering." It was His deity from within shining forth in resplendent glory. It revealed the glory of God in Him. "And as he was praying, his face began to shine" (Luke 9:29, LB).

The place of prayer on the mountain became a place of transformation for His disciples that day. "And when they had lifted up their eyes, they saw no man, SAVE JESUS ONLY" (Matt. 17:8). The direction of their eyes was drawn to Him. With their vision filled with Him, they were ready to go back into service.

We, too, need the transformation that comes from prayer. Fellowship with Christ through prayer transforms our character so that we reflect the glory of the Lord. When we see Him we lose sight of ourselves and others. All else fades and He completely fills our vision. Our place of prayer becomes our place of transformation.

In Psalm 34:5 *(Amplified)* we read, "They looked to Him, and were radiant." From our prayer time His radiance becomes ours. It has been said, "There will be more reflection of Christ when there is more reflection on Him."

But we are not to stay on the mountain top. It is a preparation for us to return to the fields below, ready for fruitful service for Him.

A company in England made a special type of firebrick. Their slogan was, "For every hour of saturation, there is a corresponding hour of illumination." The brick was soaked before used. The number of hours of illumination corresponded with the number of hours of saturation. This illustrates the effect of prayer on our lives. If we are to reflect the image of Christ, we must spend time with Him in prayer. We must remove anything that limits or diminishes our vision of Him.

"The negative of Christ is developed in the dark room of prayer."

April
18

In returning and rest shall ye be saved; in quietness and in confidence shall be your strength: and ye would not (Isa. 30:15).

Does quietness describe your life today? Or is it filled with tension and turmoil? Such tension can bring depression of spirit, draining of energy, and depleting of strength. Important, therefore, is an inner stability to carry us through the pressure times of life.

The children of Israel were in danger of an attack by the Assyrians. Instead of going to the Lord for help, they turned to Egypt. God warned them through the prophet, Isaiah, that only in returning to God and resting in Him, could they find safety and security.

When problems arise in our lives, we begin to seek ways of solving them ourselves. We turn to people whom we think can give us assistance. We try plans and methods we think may handle our situation. But none of our self-seeking plans are adequate. This is not God's way.

WE must CEASE from OUR feverish activity, our self-effort, and rest in Him. Quiet tension is not trust. It is simply compressed anxiety. Only in returning to God and resting in Him will we have quietness in place of fear and a confidence in God that will be our strength.

In a partnership, each partner shares in the work. In our partnership with God, God does the work, but He uses our lives to accomplish it. Our part is to be available.

God reminded the Israelites, ". . . and ye would not." Sometimes we learn our most valuable lessons when "we would not." We may have to learn the hard way. When we rebel against returning to the Lord for His help, He lets us experience the failure of going our own way.

Strength for meeting life each day becomes ours as we wait in His presence. It is there we learn of Him; we discover His direction for our lives and are empowered of Him to accomplish it. From this comes His quietness and confidence that strengthens us, knowing that all is well in God's hands.

"Ye would!" "Ye would not!" The choice is ours.

The Lord is thy keeper: the Lord is thy shade upon thy right hand (Ps. 121:5).

Recently I listened to a commercial on television advertising the effectiveness of a certain burglar alarm system to insure safety for the home. We use various methods for providing safety and protection of life. We rent safety deposit boxes for our valuables, we deposit our money in banks, we insure our lives and possessions to protect from loss.

The psalmist had learned that beyond all human devices for safety, our one sure security is the Lord Himself. "The LORD is thy keeper." He can keep us in all places at all times. He guards us carefully, never relaxing His watch over us.

If we have to sit up through the night with a loved one we find it difficult to stay awake, but our Keeper never slumbers nor sleeps. There is never a moment when His eye is not on us.

If He is to be our Keeper, we must commit ourselves to Him. It has been said, "Everything is safe which we commit to Him, and nothing is really safe that is not committed." Paul wrote, "I know whom I have believed, and am persuaded that he is able to keep that which I have COMMITTED unto Him against that day" (2 Tim. 1:12).

Committal has been illustrated in this way. When we write a letter, we have confidence that the postal department will deliver it. So we write it, put it in an envelope, address it, seal it, and stamp it. We take it to the mail box. But we have not really committed it to them for delivery until we let go of it completely, and let it drop into the mail box.

Have you committed your life completely to His keeping, holding nothing back? Have you let go of your loved ones, committing them completely to God? Only as we let go of our lives and of those near and dear to us can God take over and bring His will to pass.

His keeping power is personal—THY keeper. It is a constant keeping. "The Lord shall preserve thy going out and thy coming in from this time forth, and even for evermore" (Ps. 121:8).

April

20

Now thanks be unto God, which always causeth us to triumph in Christ, and maketh manifest the savour of his knowledge by us in every place (2 Cor. 2:14).

In the time of Paul, when a Roman emperor or general was successful in battle, he was privileged to return home with his victorious army and march down the Via Sacra, which was the road leading from the beginning of the Roman Forum to the great temple that stood on the Capitoline Hill in Rome. The streets were filled with enthusiastic throngs of people watching the leader and his army march by. Great torches of incense were carried by incense burners on the victorious march.

Behind the victorious army came the unfortunate captives chained to the chariots.

As the army marched triumphantly through the streets, the incense spread its fragrance all around. To the victors it spelled victory; to the captives, defeat.

With this in mind, Paul writes, "But thanks be to God, Who in Christ always leads us in triumph" (2 Cor. 2:14, *Amplified*).

Our victory is not in ourselves, not in friends, not in circumstances, not in our easy times, but IN HIM. Victory is not just for some days, not just for our good days, not just for our problem-free days. It is for us "ALWAYS," in all things, at all times.

Victory is more than winning the battle in times of crisis; it is being victorious in our everyday situations. Victory is being content with our home when we desire a larger one. Victory is answering sweetly the barbed remarks of someone in the office. Victory is having patience with the children when they track mud on your clean floor. Victory is a peaceful spirit when another receives the promotion you deserved.

Victory centers in the Lord Jesus Himself. "But thanks be to God, Who in Christ ALWAYS LEADS US in triumph—as trophies of Christ's victory—and through us spreads and makes evident the fragrance of the knowledge of God everywhere" *(Amplified).*

When we become a "captive" of Christ we are liberated from defeat and failure and become liberated to a life of victory in Christ.

Know therefore that the Lord thy God, he is God, the faithful God, which keepeth covenant and mercy with them that love him and keep his commandments to a thousand generations (Deut. 7:9).

Friends are an important part of our lives. Some are casual acquaintances; others close friends; still others more intimate, dear ones. How we appreciate those whom we characterize as "faithful friends," friends who are steadfastly loyal, friends on whom we can depend at all times and for every need.

Yet most of us have experienced the hurt that comes from friends who are unfaithful. Even members of our family may prove unfaithful.

How reassuring to know there IS One who is FAITHFUL—FAITHFUL ALWAYS and faithful in EVERYTHING. "Know therefore that the Lord thy God, He is God, the FAITHFUL GOD." Because of His very nature, He could not be God and ever be unfaithful. We read in 2 Timothy 2:13, "If we believe not, yet He abideth faithful; he cannot deny Himself." Phillips paraphrases, "Yet if we are faithless He always remains faithful. He cannot deny His own nature." He never changes. He never fails. He never goes back on one of His promises. God, being who He is, cannot cease to be what He is. He cannot act out of character with Himself. Because He is faithful, He will be faithful in His actions.

At times we may forget His faithfulness to us. When trials and testings come, it may seem as if God has surely forgotten us. When friends fail us and our lives are falling apart, we may feel He has forsaken us. There seem to be so few people we can trust. Many people do not keep their word. Our faith in human nature becomes shaken, and we wonder if anyone is honest.

Yet there is One, the faithful God, on whom we can depend. He will never let us down. He has promised, "I will NEVER leave thee, nor forsake thee" (Heb. 13:5).

He can always be trusted. He will never disappoint us. To His unchanging faithfulness, we can respond, "His compassions fail not. They are new every morning: great is THY faithfulness" (Lam. 3:22,23).

April
22

Now when he had left speaking, He said unto Simon, Launch out into the deep, and let down your nets for a draught (Luke 5:4).

Some of Jesus' disciples had been fishing all night with no success. They were ready to quit when Jesus said to Peter, "Launch out into the deep, and let down your nets for a draught." Peter must have been surprised at His command. "What does Jesus know of fishing?" he may have thought. "Doesn't He know the best time for fishing is at night?"

But Peter had to admit, "Master, we have toiled all night and have taken NOTHING." When we do the toiling, it always adds up to nothing.

Peter's response revealed his faith in Christ. He said, "Nevertheless at THY WORD I will let down the net."

The results were different when he fished at Jesus' command. The Lord's "Launch out" and Peter's "I will" linked human effort with sovereign power and a miracle took place. Then Jesus said, "From henceforth thou shalt catch men. . . . they forsook all and followed HIM" (Luke 5:10-11).

Today many people are in the depths of despair, discouragement, and despondency. The Lord challenges us to "launch out into the deep and let down your nets where the people are." We are to reach them with the message of hope in Jesus Christ.

His command to us may be to launch out into some new place. Or, He may send us back to the same place. Wherever He places us, when we reply, "Nevertheless at Thy Word," launch out and let down our nets, there will be results in the lives of people.

As we launch out into the depths of His purpose for our lives, we launch out into the depths of His resources, His power, His promises, His provisions. The limitless supplies from God's inexhaustible storehouse will provide every need under the most severe trial. Appropriating the resources of God is the secret of abundant living and service.

Is something holding you to the shore line today? Your own desires? Personal plans? Family? Pleasures? Business? Friends? May we "cut every shore line," launch out, and "catch" people for Him.

Stephen, a man full of faith and of the Holy Ghost . . . . And Stephen, full of faith and power, did great wonders and miracles among the people (Acts 6:5,8).

Stephen, a deacon in the early church, was a great man of God, full of faith and the power of the Holy Spirit. He could be called "The Man with the Shining Face."

Some Jewish leaders began to falsely accuse him. "And all that sat in the council, looking steadfastly on him, saw his face as it had been the face of an angel" (Acts 6:15). As these men looked at him, there was no anger or hatred on his face, only the outer radiance on the face of a man who was in close touch with God, "a man with the heavenly glory." Someone has called it "A Fluorescent Face."

Stephen, standing before them, gave a great defense of his Christian faith. They were furious as they listened to him. "But he, being full of the Holy Ghost, looked up steadfastly into heaven, and saw the glory of God, and Jesus standing on the right hand of God" (Acts 7:55).

They took him out of the city. "And they stoned Stephen." Stephen prayed, "Lord, lay not this sin to their charge" (v. 60). What a spirit of love and forgiveness he had for them!

A man named Saul, later called Paul, watched the stoning. In Stephen he saw a life touched by God, a face reflecting the presence of God. He heard Stephen talk about God. He heard him pray. Could he ever forget a man who could pray for his enemies, asking God to forgive them? Stephen's spirit-filled life must have made an impact upon Saul that day.

Today what effect do our lives have on others? Do people see the reflection of God's presence on our faces? Do people hear us talk about the Lord as Stephen did? Do our attitudes show a loving and forgiving spirit?

As people watch our lives what do they see and hear? It is not just what we do, but what we are, what we say, and what our attitudes are that can have a great influence on those about us.

Is the shine of God on your life?

April
24

For which cause we faint not; but though our outward man perish, yet the inward man is renewed day by day (2 Cor. 4:16).

Paul's life was filled with hardships. He underwent great persecutions; he was beaten: he was shipwrecked. He wrote, "We are pressed on every side by troubles, but not crushed and broken. We are perplexed because we don't know why things happen as they do, but we don't give up and quit. We are hunted down, but God never abandons us. We get knocked down, but we get up again and keep going" (2 Cor. 4:8-9, LB).

Paul realized the strenuous years of service had taken their toll on his body. Yet none of his trials and persecutions had daunted his spirit. He said, "For which cause we faint not." "We do not become discouraged" (2 Cor. 4:16, *Amplified*). "We never give up" (LB). Outwardly he might be weakening, but inwardly he was being renewed constantly. "The outward man does indeed suffer wear and tear, but every day the inward man receives fresh strength" *(Phillips)*.

We, too, recognize the outward weakening in our bodies. Yet we can experience the inner renewing of the Lord day after day. The Lord invites us, "Come unto me, all ye that labour and are heavy laden, and I will give you rest" (Matt. 11:28). We go into His presence weary, discouraged, defeated. There we exchange our weakness for His power and strength. Our spirits are lifted, our weariness is gone. "I have strength for all things in Christ Who empowers me—I am ready for anything and equal to anything through Him Who infuses inner strength into me, [that is, I am self-sufficient in Christ's sufficiency]" (Phil. 4:13, *Amplified*). We can face life then with courage, saying as Paul did, "I faint not."

Throughout life our bodily strength decreases but our spiritual strength continues. "They go from strength to strength—increasing in victorious power" (Ps. 84:7, *Amplified*).

"They that wait upon the Lord shall renew their strength; they shall mount up with wings as eagles; they shall run, and not be weary; and they shall walk, and not faint" (Isa. 40:31).

For our light affliction, which is but for a moment, worketh for us a far more exceeding and eternal weight of glory (2 Cor. 4:17).

We are not promised a life of ease and comfort. Troubles come into our lives. Burdens build one upon another until we often feel we will go down under the weight of them.

Paul could easily identify with us, for his life was filled with afflictions. He knew what it was to suffer. He said, "Three times I was beaten with rods. Once I was stoned. Three times I was shipwrecked. Once I was in the open sea all night and the whole next day. I have traveled many weary miles and have been often in great danger from flooded rivers, . . . I have faced grave dangers from mobs in the cities and from death in the deserts and in the stormy seas and from men who claim to be brothers in Christ but are not. I have lived with weariness and pain and sleepless nights. Often I have been hungry and thirsty and have gone without food; often I have shivered with cold, without enough clothing to keep me warm" (2 Cor. 1:25-27, LB). Such a list should qualify him to speak. However, as he weighs his afflictions, he called them "light" and "but for a moment."

We may say, "Paul, your afflictions may have seemed light to you, but mine are SO heavy. Mine have been going for SO long." But Paul knew that afflictions "WORKETH FOR" us, not against us.

However, remember, the last chapter has not been written. We are looking at our troubles from our viewpoint, not God's.

James wrote, "Consider it wholly joyful, my brethren, whenever you are enveloped in or encounter trials of any sort" (James 1:2, *Amplified*).

Count it ALL JOY. The trial itself isn't joy, but its outworking in our lives results in eternal glory for God.

Affliction worketh glory if we look away from the seen to the unseen; from the immediate to the ultimate; from the visible to the invisible.

One day the trials will be forgotten when we see HIM face to face. It will be worth it all then.

April

26

While we look not at the things which are seen, but at the things which are not seen: for the things which are seen are temporal; but the things which are not seen are eternal (2 Cor. 4:18).

The sixteenth through the eighteenth verses of this chapter are dear to me, for my pastor used them at my husband's funeral.

At that time I reevaluated my life. I discovered material things were more deeply rooted than I realized. My home was very dear to me and it was hard to leave it. I knew I must focus my eyes, not on my home, my family, or friends, but on the LORD HIMSELF.

Paul had the proper spiritual perspective. In the midst of his light affliction, he saw all of his troubles and trials in the light of eternity. This removed the stress and strain of them. He looked away from the troubles to the Lord.

Where are you focusing your eyesight today? On material things? On problems? On heartaches and pain? If we constantly look at our afflictions, they become magnified and fill our vision. We need to look away from the things we can see and focus our spiritual eyes on the things we can't see.

We are told that after looking at something close for a time, we need to rest our eyes by looking away to the far horizon. At the time of my husband's death, I spent some time at the ocean. I discovered that when I kept my eyes on the shore line all I could see were the large waves breaking on it. However, if I lifted my eyes to the distant horizon, the water appeared calm.

I realized I had been concentrating so on the waves breaking in my life, the problems close at hand, that I had failed to see the Lord in the midst of them. As I looked away from my problems, I experienced the joy then of being assured He was bringing out of my trouble an eternal weight of glory.

One moment of glory will outweigh a life time of suffering. It will be worth it all when we see Jesus.

Rejoice in the Lord alway: and again I say, Rejoice (Phil. 4:4).

Joy is one of the characteristics of a Christian. This joy is not displayed by a grin on the face, but a radiance reflecting the peace and confidence of a heart at rest in the Lord.

Paul's writings are full of joy and rejoicing. It was real to him, for he experienced it in circumstances which were not conducive to joy. He wrote Philippians while in prison, yet even there his life was filled with a joy whose source was in the Lord.

Joy is more than laughter. Laughter can conceal a sad heart, but the Holy Spirit reflects joy from the life of the one who has found Christ to be his sufficiency. Joy is more than happiness. Happiness may depend on what happens; joy is dependent, not on our circumstances or people, but on Him.

We can rejoice whatever our situation may be, for our joy is IN THE LORD. We may try to excuse ourselves by saying, "If you worked with the person I do, you couldn't rejoice;" or "If you had my heartache you couldn't rejoice." You may not be able to rejoice in your environment, or with the people with whom you work, or with your particular problem, but you can rejoice in HIM who is the source of this victorious rejoicing. Real joy doesn't mean the absence of trials and sorrow, but the joy of the Lord in the midst of them.

It is possible to rejoice in the Lord at all times and in all places. It can be a constant rejoicing; not just some of the time, not just when we feel like it, not just when the days are bright and sunny, but ALWAYS. Even when our eyes are flooded with tears, His joy can fill our hearts.

Today is your life filled with heartaches and pain? Are the tears falling? As you seek HIM, you can experience the deep inner joy that He gives. He will fill your life with His joy.

"Delight yourselves in the Lord, yes, find YOUR JOY IN HIM at all times" (Phil. 4:4, *Phillips*).

April
28

And he said to them all, If any man will come after me, let him deny himself, and take up his cross daily, and follow me (Luke 9:23).

When the Lord Jesus issues an invitation to "Follow Me," it is accompanied by certain conditions. First, it requires a total commitment of our lives to Him. He said, "IF any man will come after ME." Committal has the meaning of deposit. When we deposit money in a bank, we leave it there for safe keeping. In committing (depositing) our lives to Him, we give them to Him unreservedly.

Jesus said that we must deny self to follow Him. We must give up all rights to our lives, relinquishing our interests, ambitions, goals, desires, even our own ability.

As we deny self, we must take up the cross of submission to His will for our lives. Paul wrote, "I am crucified with Christ: nevertheless I live; yet not I, but Christ liveth in me: and the life which I now live in the flesh I live by the faith of the Son of God, who loved me, and gave himself for me" (Gal. 2:20).

Jesus said there must be consistency in following Him. We must follow Him daily; not just when we want to, or when we feel like it.

It costs something to deny self, take up our cross, and follow Him. However, he doesn't force this commitment on us, the choice is ours.

One day George Mueller was asked the secret of the power of God working in his life. He replied, "There was a day when George Mueller died, died to George Mueller, his opinions, preferences, tastes, and will; died to the world, its approval or censure, died to the approval or blame even of my brethren and friends. Since then I have studied only to show my self approved to God."

Jesus' invitation is to all. "Then He spoke to them ALL: If anyone wants to follow in my footsteps, he must give up all right to himself, carry his cross every day and keep close behind me" (Luke 9:23, *Phillips*). God can use anyone who is willing to do this.

The secret of the Lord is with them that fear him (Ps. 25:14).

Someone has translated this Scripture verse as, "The friendship of Jehovah is with them that fear Him."

A friend has been defined as, "One who knows all about you and still loves you." I have some close friendships which I cherish very much. These friends have endeared themselves to me. They have shown expressions of their love and friendship. They have been understanding. They have been dependable. They know my faults, yet, because they love me, they overlook them.

What an awesome, humbling truth this—I can have the friendship of Jehovah. All that characterizes a true friendship is exemplified in God's relationship with each of us. "There is a friend that sticketh closer than a brother" (Prov. 18:24). How deeply He loves us. He knows all about us. He loves us just as we are. His love never changes. "Yea, I have loved thee with an everlasting love" (Jer. 31:3). He is always faithful. "Great is THY faithfulness" (Lam. 3:23).

True friends enjoy each other's company and want to spend time together. There are things you confide to your dearest friend, things you couldn't share with anyone else. It is an honor to have a secret entrusted to you.

Our dearest Friend, the Lord Jesus, has special secrets to share with us from His Word and in our times of prayer. This means we must spend time with Him. As our friendship deepens, He can entrust more secrets to us.

Some of His secrets may come in rough wrappings, but within are secret gems from His heart of love.

There must be a response on the part of both parties to keep up a friendship. The Lord is ready to be our "Dearest Friend." Are we responding to His friendship?

We often sing, "What a friend we have in Jesus, all our sins and griefs to bear." WHAT A FRIEND! God desires our friendship, undeserving and unlovely as we are. As we ponder the privilege of friendship with Him, we bow in humbleness. As our heart fills with love for Him, it overflows with His love for us.

"We love Him, because He first loved us" (1 John 4:19).

For me to live is Christ (Phil. 1:21).

One day a very personable young man was making an installation in a home where I was visiting. During a conversation with him, I asked, "Do you have a purpose for your life?" "Yes," he replied, "but I don't know what it is."

Someone has said, "The reason so many people don't get anywhere is because they weren't going anywhere when they started." Many people today have not discovered the real purpose for living.

After Paul met the Lord Jesus Christ on the road to Damascus, life was never the same for him again. He had a real purpose for living. "For me, to live is Christ—His life in me" (Phil. 1:21, *Amplified*). The LORD was the OBJECT of his love and devotion; his goal was to know Him; his ambition was to please Him.

Life is a challenging experience when we live with Christ, and He with us. In our times of joy, we live Christ; if we are having material success, we live Christ; if we are experiencing sorrow, we live Christ; if we live through financial disaster, we live Christ; during a time of family heartache, we live Christ.

When we live Christ, He becomes the center and circumference of our lives. We have "His ears for hearing, His eyes for seeing, His face for reflecting, His lips for speaking, His feet for walking, His life for living."

The story is told of a couple who bought a beautiful, expensive painting of Christ. When it was delivered, they went from room to room, studying the best place to hang it. However, they couldn't find a place in their home where it seemed to fit. Finally they decided the only solution was to remodel their home around the picture.

This may only be a story, but it is illustrative of what God may have to do in our lives. If He is to have preeminence, some remodeling and redecorating may be necessary. It is not living LIKE Christ or FOR Christ, but it is CHRIST living in us. Then we can say as Paul said, "For to ME to live IS CHRIST."

And when they had lifted up their eyes, they saw no man, save Jesus only (Matt. 17:8).

One day Jesus took Peter, James, and John up into a high mountain. Suddenly a bright cloud overshadowed them. A voice said, "This is my beloved Son, in whom I am well pleased; hear ye him. . . . And Jesus came and touched them, and said, Arise, and be not afraid. And when they had lifted up their eyes, they saw no man, save JESUS ONLY" (Matt. 17:5,7,8).

Fear and frustration may fill our lives instead of the peace and joy we once knew. We may have turned from God's will for our lives, walking in ways of our own choosing. We may be focusing our eyes in the wrong direction. We need to lift up our eyes and "See no man, save JESUS ONLY."

One day a group of people were attending an auction in London. The auctioneer brought out a dirty looking violin. He said, "I am offering you a genuine Cremona made by Stradavarius. It is very valuable. What am I bid?" The people, however, examined it critically, questioning its authenticity. Five guineas was the highest bid.

Just then a man entered the shop. He walked over and picked up the violin. After carefully tuning it, he placed it in position. A murmur spread over the crowd—"The great Paganini." As the bow touched the strings, such beautiful music filled the room the people were spellbound. When he finished, there was a moment's hush. Then everyone began clamoring for the violin.

Fifty guineas! Sixty! Seventy! Eighty! At last Paganini himself received it for one hundred guineas. Whenever he played it audiences were breathless at the music that came forth under the touch of the master's hand.

Today has the song gone out of your life? Are the tears falling? Are you dissatisfied with your life? Lift your eyes to Him. Let Him fill your vision. See JESUS ONLY.

The touch of the Master on your life can bring peace of heart and mind. He will bring forth the beautiful melody of His life, on the chords of your life. In turn, your life will be a blessing to others wherever you go.

May
2

God hath said, Ye shall not eat of it, neither shall ye touch it, lest ye die (Gen. 3:3).

There is much discussion on the relevancy of the Word of God to life today. Is it for us? Does it work? Does it meet the needs of people today? Many find it difficult to accept the "Thus saith the Lord," and the "It is written." They read into it what they want it to say.

In the Garden of Eden Satan appeared to Eve, saying, ". . . hath God said, Ye shall not eat of every tree of the garden?" (Gen. 3:1). There was only one tree which they were forbidden to eat. But Satan was trying to cast doubt into her mind concerning God's Word.

Then Satan contradicted God, saying, "Ye shall not surely die." God said! Satan said! Whom would Eve believe and obey? She chose to believe Satan, thus transferring her obedience from God to Satan.

God speaks to us today through the Bible. It is His Guidebook, revealing to us His plan for our lives. "But he answered and said, It is written, Man shall not live by bread alone, but by every word that proceedeth out of the mouth of God" (Matt. 4:4).

Satan is still trying to cast doubt in people's mind concerning the Word of God. He attempts to confuse its real meaning to us. He misquotes it, adds to it, takes away from it, or tries to change its meaning.

Sometimes when problems arise, temptations come, or decisions have to be made, we attempt to interpret God's Word to our own situation, giving it the meaning we want it to have. Satan can bring confusion to our mind at such times by whispering such things as, "But your situation is different; God doesn't expect it to apply to your case; this is not an important decision." Thus he tries to lessen the authority of what God says in His Word.

May we, with an open heart and mind, search His Word, asking the Holy Spirit to reveal to us the authority of it for our particular need and give a willingness to be obedient to God's "It is written," "Thus saith the Lord."

And Moses said unto the people, Fear ye not, stand still, and see the salvation of the Lord, which he will shew you to day (Exod. 14:13).

As the children of Israel left Egypt, they found themselves in a dangerous situation. In front was the Red Sea; advancing from the rear was the enemy.

They were frightened, for their eyes were focused in the wrong direction—upon the Egyptians instead of upon the Lord. "The children of Israel lifted up their eyes, and, behold, the Egyptians marched after them" (Exod. 14:10).

What could they do? Nothing. Trapped, they were looking for a way of escape. But Moses said, "Fear ye not, stand still." God was in control and they could trust Him to open a way where there was no way.

Moses continued, ". . . and see the salvation of the Lord." They were to be still and with their spiritual eyes look to the only One who could bring deliverance. "THE LORD shall fight for you, and you shall hold your peace."

"Red Sea" experiences come into each of our lives. We are hedged in, with no visible way of escape. God's words, "FEAR NOT," are for us today. We may be trapped as the children of Israel were, but we need not fear. God's power is limitless. He will open a way for us where there is none.

Our part is to stand still and wait upon God. Only God knows and can lead us in the way that is best. Only God is strong enough to deliver us from the attacks of the enemy. In our walk of faith there is no place for human activity. Trying to fight our battles with earthly weapons is wasted energy. We must stand by and let the Lord do the fighting. Hezekiah said of his enemy, "With him is an arm of flesh; but with us is the Lord our God to help us, and to fight our battles."

It doesn't require faith to begin a journey when we can see the way through.

Faith is taking the next step when we can't see beyond it.

May

4

And the Lord said unto Moses. . . . speak unto the children of Israel, that they go forward (Exod. 14:15).

Now was the time for action—GO FORWARD. God gave them their marching orders as He said to Moses, "Speak unto the children of Israel, that they go forward." The Israelites might have said, "But the Sea is before us." "Yes, I know, but I will make a path." There was only one way to go—forward. Their only way THROUGH was UP. They must trust God completely. Although their physical eyes were on the water, their spiritual eyes must see the One who would make a path for them through the sea.

Self effort is not sufficient. It shuts God out. Faith enables us to stand still and let God into our needs. Then the need becomes His to solve. He can and will do for us what we cannot do for ourselves. Someone has said, "When you let God in, the supernatural becomes the normal."

At His command we can move forward even when it is not reasonable or logical, even when we are fearful, even when we are weak. God doesn't show us the complete blueprint but leads us step by step. Progress is dependent on our obedience to Him. The way of victory is the way of faith. Faith expects from God what is beyond all expectation.

As we face our needs of today we must be reminded to "stand still" until God says "go forward." Then we will go forward in His power and strength, knowing He will lead us safely through. There comes a time when God tells us to move forward. Our part is to obey; His part is to remove the obstacle.

It doesn't require faith to begin a journey when we can see the way through. But to begin when we can only see the next step requires faith. Victory comes as we move forward.

"This is the victory that overcometh the world, even our faith" (1 John 5:4).

I cried unto the Lord with my voice, and he heard me out of his holy hill. Selah (Ps. 3:4).

Throughout the Psalms we find the word "Selah." One day I discovered a meaning that brought new appreciation and understanding of its use in Scripture.

"Selah" is a musical word, meaning in the Hebrew "rest," "pause," "a lifting up." In the temple music there would be a rest for the singers while the instruments continued playing. In the *Amplified Bible* "Selah" is translated "pause, and calmly think of that."

God put rests in David's life that he might "pause and calmly think" that—God helps, God hears, and God blesses. David said, "Many are saying of me, There is no help for him in God" (Ps. 3:2, *Amplified*). In the rest stops of his life David had learned by experience that "God has helped ME. Selah—pause and calmly think of that."

Not only did God help David, but He heard his cries in time of need. David could say, "God heard ME. Selah—pause and calmly think of that."

David recognized God's blessing on his life. "Your blessing be upon Your people" (v. 8, *Amplified*). He could say, "God has blessed ME. Selah—pause and calmly think of that."

What God did for David, He will do for us. At times, we too, need to experience a "Selah" in our lives, a time when we pause and rest. To be still and rest is good therapy for today's fast pace of living. The heart strings may be taut, even on the verge of snapping. Suddenly, God inserts a "Selah," a rest, that we might pause and calmly think of Him. As we lift our souls to Him, we are refreshed. The tension lessens, we gain a deeper view of God's goodness, and He becomes more real.

May we not miss the blessing God has for us in our "Selahs"—the times of rest and refreshing in our lives. Someone has said, "There is no music in a rest, but there is the making of music in it."

Today we can pause and calmly think—God helps ME, God hears ME, and God blesses ME.

May
6

My flesh and my heart faileth: but God is the strength of my heart, and my portion for ever (Ps. 73:26).

Today many people are living in circumstances for which there is no way out humanly speaking—BUT GOD. Some are experiencing storms so severe they are almost sinking—BUT GOD. Others have hearts almost breaking with sorrow and pain—BUT GOD.

In this Psalm the writer was confused and troubled. As he looked about him, there were many things he couldn't understand. Why were some people better off materially than he? Why did others seem to have less trouble than he? Yet he had tried to live for God.

The more he pondered this, the more he was bewildered at the seeming injustice he saw about him. Why didn't God do something?

His feeling of frustration continued UNTIL—he went into the sanctuary of God (Ps. 73:17). In God's presence the answer came. He discovered he had been looking at the problem from his own viewpoint. BUT GOD completely changed his attitude. He discovered God knew what was going on but God wasn't through with the wicked yet.

His problem was that his eyes were focused in the wrong direction. He had been looking at people and circumstances instead of the Lord. He had left God out of his thinking.

When he went into the sanctuary he saw things from God's viewpoint. He had been looking at the immediate, but God could see the ultimate. He realized God was still in control.

He said, "Whom have I in heaven but Thee? And there is none upon earth that I desire beside Thee. MY flesh and MY heart FAILETH: BUT GOD is the strength of my heart, and my portion for ever" (vv. 25-26). He realized that God was all he needed. "Whom have I but thee?"

Burdens may press; disappointments may come. We may feel deserted. Family may fail us, friends may forsake. We may cry out, "My heart faileth." All may seem wrong BUT GOD is the One we need. "He is the strength of MY heart and MY portion forever." He is never unfaithful. He can turn our sorrows to joy, our distresses to deliverances, our trials to triumphs, our problems to praise.

In every thing give thanks; for this is the will of God in Christ Jesus concerning you (1 Thess. 5:18).

There is a legend about two angels—Angel Requests and Angel Thanks. Each morning they come from heaven and go on errands all day. At the close of the day Angel Requests has his basket full, but Angel Thanks only has a few in his basket. Have you ever stopped to consider how many "Thank You" messages you send up to God in comparison to the number of requests?

Thanksgiving is not an arbitrary choice we have, but it is a command from God. "In EVERYTHING GIVE THANKS." It is not difficult to give thanks when life is going along smoothly and we have what we want.

But what about the times when everything goes wrong? When we are sick? Discouraged? In despair? Heartbroken?

Regardless of our circumstances, we are told to give thanks; give thanks IN everything, not FOR everything. "Thank [God] in everything—no matter what the circumstances may be, be thankful and give thanks; for this is the will of God for you [who are] in Christ Jesus [the Revealer and Mediator of that will]" (1 Thess. 5:18, *Amplified*).

This Scripture verse tells us we are to give thanks, for it is the WILL OF GOD FOR US. Paul reminds us, "We are assured and know that [God being a partner in their labor], all things work together and are [fitting into a plan] for good to those who love God and are called according to [His] design and purpose" (Rom. 8:28, *Amplified*). It must be personal—"concerning YOU."

We may be going through testings and trials today. We can be thankful that God loves us enough to trust us with testings. We can thank Him for the necessary lessons we are learning. We can thank Him for the assurance of knowing that He has the answer for our need.

As we thank Him for all the happenings in our life, the unpleasant ones as well as the pleasant, He can turn them into blessings. Thanksgiving can lift us above our circumstances.

Have you been thanking Him in everything? Take time to do so today.

May

8

But be ye doers of the word, and not hearers only, deceiving your own selves (James 1:22).

As people entered the chapel on a certain military base, they would pass a signboard listing the services of the day and their hour. Leaving the chapel, again they passed this signboard. Usually there is nothing on the back of such a sign, but this one was different. Painted on the back, facing you as you left, were these words, "But be ye doers of the Word, and not hearers only."

Although knowledge of the Word is essential, knowledge alone is not the measure of our spirituality. We must go beyond our knowledge of it and appropriate it into our lives.

One who listens to God's Word but does nothing about it is likened to a man who hastily glances in a mirror, then turns away, forgetful of what he has seen.

"For if a person just listens and doesn't obey, he is like a man looking at his face in a mirror; as soon as he walks away, he can't see himself anymore or remember what he looks like" (James 1:23-24, LB).

Dr. Erdman says, "What a magic mirror the Word of God provides. It shows a man exactly what he is with all his faults and failures. Yet as he gazes, he beholds another image, that of Christ, and he sees what he himself should be. Most marvelous of all, as he gazes steadfastly at Him, he is 'transformed into the same image from glory to glory.'"

It is not enough to hear what God has to say to us in His Word. We need to take action as it is revealed to us. We need to become doers of His Word. Words are empty without lives that back them up.

Jesus said, "But if anyone keeps looking steadily into God's law for free men, he will not only remember it but he will do what it says, and God will greatly bless him in everything he does" (v. 25, LB).

"We only know as much Scripture as we put into practice."

For I know whom I have believed, and am persuaded that he is able to keep that which I have committed unto him against that day (2 Tim. 1:12).

May and June are special family months. During these two months we celebrate Mother's Day, Father's Day, and Children's Day. This includes each one of us, for we are a member of a family unit—a father, mother, son, or daughter. However, more important than being a member of a human family is having the assurance we are a member of God's family.

Paul wrote, "I KNOW whom I have believed"; not "I hope I believe," "I think I believe," "I may believe," or "I am trying to believe," but "I KNOW." This was complete assurance. Paul had more than just an intellectual knowledge of Christianity; he had a personal relationship with a Person, Jesus Christ. His faith was not just based on WHAT he believed, but in WHOM He believed.

Today, do you have the assurance of knowing you are a member of God's family? Can you say as Paul did, "I know WHOM I have believed; I know He is living in my life"?

Also we can KNOW His safekeeping as we commit our lives completely to Him. ". . . and am persuaded that HE IS ABLE TO KEEP THAT which I have COMMITTED unto Him."

In the Greek, the word "commit" in this verse has the meaning of deposit. If we desire to open a savings account, we select a bank in which we have confidence. Then we deposit our money in it for safe keeping. Suppose we decide it is not safe and withdraw it from the bank. Then we decide it is safer in the bank than in our care. We return to the bank with our money and re-deposit it. You would say, "That is silly." It is. Yet how many times we do that with our needs. We deposit ourselves, our loved ones, our problems with God. Then we pick them up and carry them back with us.

You can KNOW that you and everything touching your life is safe in His keeping. "I know WHOM I have believed, and am persuaded that HE IS (today) able to keep that which I have COMMITTED unto Him against that day."

May
10

Where is God my maker, who giveth songs in the night (Job 35:10).

Is there a song in your life today? Or has it ceased? It is easy to sing in the daytime when all is going well, but the test is the ability to sing when there is no ray of light. It is in the nighttime a special song is needed. It is then that God, the Composer of "songs in the night," gives a special song of faith and joy, to encourage and comfort us. No night is too dark for His song.

Are you passing through a night experience that has stilled the song in your life? It may be sickness, depression, sorrow, discouragement, or defeat. We spend the night hours tossing and turning, trying to solve our problem. It is then that God gives a special song to cheer us, one we can't compose, a gift from Him. As we wait before Him, He floods our whole being with His melodious song. It isn't a song for the future, or after the burden lifts, but for our present dark night.

As I write this, I am going through one of the darkest times of my life. The night after I had first written this, I sat by the side of my sister all night long trying to quiet her. What a sweet song He gave me that night. This song included a time of counting the many blessings He had given me in the past. His promises were a part of my song as I repeated many of them, claiming them for my need. There were musical notes of new lessons I was learning in my night watch experience.

The world's supply of attar of roses used to come from the Balkan mountains. The workers started picking the petals at 1:00 at night, stopping before dawn. Scientific tests had proven that forty percent of the fragrance of the roses disappear in the daylight.

"When the clouds of affliction have gathered, and hidden each star from my night, I know if I turn to my Father, sweetest songs He will give in the night."

Blessed is the man whom thou choosest, and causest to approach unto thee, that he may dwell in thy courts: we shall be satisfied with the goodness of thy house, even of thy holy temple (Ps. 65:4).

Are there times when you feel no one appreciates you? No one really needs you? At such times, just remember, Someone does love you with a special love. There is Someone to whom you are very special—God Himself.

God has chosen us for Himself. "Blessed is the man whom thou choosest." We are accepted in the Beloved; we are very precious to Him. "While we were yet sinners, Christ died for us" (Rom. 5:8). God paid a great price for us. "But you are not like that, for you have been chosen by God Himself—you are priests of the King, you are holy and pure, you are God's VERY OWN—all this so that you may show to others how God called you out of the darkness into his wonderful light" (1 Peter 2:9, LB).

There are many important people today with whom we could never have an appointment. There are other people with whom we could have an appointment but it must be arranged far in advance. Yet the God of the universe has given us access into His presence. Through Jesus Christ we can come before Him at any time. We don't have to wait for a special appointment. We don't have to reach a certain spiritual level. The way is always open. ". . . and causest to approach unto thee. . . ."

What a privilege that He will make our lives His home. "As God hath said, I will dwell in them" (2 Cor. 6:16). Do we treat Him as a guest or is He at home in our lives?

Many seek satisfaction in material possessions. But these are only transitory. We can know what it is to be abundantly satisfied with His goodness. The Lord Jesus Christ is the only source of complete satisfaction. "He satisfieth the longing soul, and filleth the hungry soul with goodness" (Ps. 107:9).

He has chosen YOU that He might bring complete fulfillment to your life. Do you not realize how valuable you are to Him? Pause and praise Him for this.

May
12

Except the Lord build the house, they labour in vain that build it: except the Lord keep the city, the watchman waketh but in vain (Ps. 127:1).

As we celebrate Mother's Day, many times we will be reminded of the importance of the home and the mother in the home. We often hear it said, "The strength of a nation is in the home."

Homes are made up of individuals, and the strength of the home depends on the strength of the individuals living in the home. So it is important that our lives be built on principles given by God Himself.

The building of our lives can be compared with the building of a house. In the building industry certain builders have gained a reputation for trustworthiness. People have learned that their houses are well built and give satisfaction.

We have the best "Builder" for our lives, God Himself. "Except the Lord build the house." His blueprints are "custom planned" for each individual life. His materials are top quality. He never makes a mistake in His building.

The foundation of the life He builds is Jesus Christ. "For other foundation can no man lay than that is laid, which is Jesus Christ" (1 Cor. 3:11).

As we commit and trust ourselves to Him, He builds our lives in the image of His Son. "We are his workmanship, created in Christ Jesus unto good works, which God hath before ordained that we should walk in them" (Eph. 2:10).

At the time the construction of the Brooklyn Bridge was to begin, the engineer in charge became very ill. Each day he sent his wife with the blueprints. She checked to see that the construction was done according to specifications. At night she gave her husband a complete report, getting his orders for the following day. At last the bridge was finished. The engineer was sufficiently better that he was permitted to be taken on a cot to see the bridge. As he looked at it, tears streamed down his cheeks. "Oh," he said, "it is just as I planned it."

Are we allowing God to build our lives just as He has planned them?

But of him are ye in Christ Jesus, who of God is made unto us wisdom, and righteousness, and sanctification, and redemption (1 Cor. 1:30).

The world today is striving to acquire knowledge. Yet knowledge alone does not give wisdom. Wisdom is defined as, "The quality of being wise; good judgment based on knowledge." Real wisdom is God-given. "But God hath chosen the foolish things of the world to confound the wise; and God hath chosen the weak things of the world to confound the things which are mighty" (1 Cor. 1:27).

In the 24th verse God's wisdom is defined, "Christ . . . the wisdom of God." Wisdom is the ability to meet each situation with discernment and good judgment. When Christ becomes our wisdom, He guides us in making right decisions. He becomes our wisdom for solving our problems.

God requires a righteousness we do not have. But in His great love He provided His righteousness for us in Christ Jesus. "For he hath made him to be sin for us, who knew no sin; that we might be made the righteousness of God in Him" (2 Cor. 5:21). His righteousness makes us acceptable to God. "Making us upright and putting us in right standing with God" (1 Cor. 1:30, *Amplified*).

He is made sanctification to us, setting us apart for God's plan, to conform us to the image of His Son. Sanctification is said to be "Christ in you," the perfection of His life imparted to us and manifested through us. As His life is imparted to us, the Holy Spirit produces Christlikeness in us. It is nothing WE DO, but the outworking of His inworking.

As our redemption, He releases us from the bondage of sin's power over our lives. "Providing our ransom from eternal penalty for sin" (v. 30, *Amplified*). But it includes more than deliverance from the penalty of sin. It is our ultimate deliverance from the presence of sin, the completion of our salvation at Christ's return.

There is a chorus we sing which says, "Jesus Christ is made to be all I need, all I need." In Him we appropriate into our lives All He is made to be for us. Have you availed yourself of all that is yours in Him?

May

14

Epaphras, who is one of you, a servant of Christ, saluteth you, always labouring fervently for you in prayers, that ye may stand perfect and complete in all the will of God (Col. 4:12).

Little is known of Epaphras, but in the above Scripture verse, we learn several things which reveal his greatness before God. He was a servant of the Lord Jesus Christ. A servant yields his will completely to the one he serves. He serves his master with complete disregard for his own interests. His time and strength, his all, belong to his master. He owns nothing apart from the one he serves. This was true of the relationship of Epaphras with God. He had no desires, interests, or plans apart from God.

Then Epaphras believed in the power of prayer. Some people say they can't do very much—all they can do is pray. That is the most important thing anyone can do. "The effectual fervent prayer of a righteous man availeth much" (James 5:16). It has been said that the test of what we really are as Christians is what we are on our knees.

Not only did Epaphras pray but he considered prayer a part of his service. ". . . Always labouring fervently for you in prayers. . . ." In Luke 2:36 and 37 we read of Anna, one who served God in this way. "And there was one Anna, . . . (who) served God with fastings and prayers night and day."

Epaphras prayed for the spiritual maturity of his fellow believers, that they might be perfect and complete in the will of God.

Are we true servants of the Lord Jesus Christ? Are our wills yielded to Him? Do we have no desires, interests, or plans apart from God? Do we pray for the spiritual growth of believers? Can it be said of us, "I, _____ , a servant of Christ, . . . labouring fervently for you in prayers, that ye may stand perfect and complete in all the will of God."

"Epaphras . . . a real servant of Christ Jesus . . . works hard for you even here, for he prays constantly and earnestly for you, that you may become mature Christians, and may fulfill God's will for you" (Col. 4:12, *Phillips*).

And he arose, and rebuked the wind, and said unto the sea, Peace, be still. And the wind ceased, and there was a great calm (Mark 4:39).

While Jesus and His disciples were out on the Sea of Galilee, a violent storm suddenly overtook them. As it broke in fury upon them, the disciples realized their danger.

Turning to Jesus for help, they found Him asleep, undisturbed by the storm. Frantically they aroused Him, crying, "Master, carest thou not that we perish?" The storm didn't waken Him, but the cry of His children brought immediate aid. Jesus arose, rebuked the storm, saying, "Peace be still." The miracle was the immediate calming of the sea. Jesus said, "Why are ye so fearful? How is it that ye have no faith?" Perplexed, they said, "What manner of man is this that even the wind and the waves obey Him."

Storms can break suddenly in our lives, bringing winds of adversity and waves of trouble. Lack of faith results in fear. We may cry, "Carest thou not that we perish?" We are only a cry away from Him. As He looks at the storm in our life, He replies, "Peace, be still." This does not mean the outward circumstances may subside immediately, but He does calm the storm in our heart.

Need we fear when He is the Pilot of our lives? We are safer in the storm with Him than in the calm without Him. When the Titanic was built, it was called "the unsinkable ship." Yet the world soon learned that this was not true when it sank after hitting an iceberg.

With Him as our Pilot, no matter how severe the storm, we are "unsinkable" when He is in control.

Is He saying to us today as He did to His disciples, "Why are you timid and fearful? How is it that you have no faith—no firmly, relying trust?" (Mark 4:40, *Amplified*). Why are you afraid today? No faith? Faith is the answer to fear. Regardless of the fierceness of the storm, faith in Him is the answer for our fears.

Fear sees the storm; faith sees God in the storm. John Newton said, "With Christ in the vessel I smile at the storm."

May
16

Surely thou also art one of them; for thy speech bewrayeth thee (Matt. 26:73).

Often, as soon as a person begins to speak, we know the area of the country he is from. How? We detect it from his speech.

On the night Jesus was betrayed, someone said to Peter, "Thou art one of them; for thy speech betrayeth thee."

Our conversation, even the words we use, is very important.

People listen to us and form opinions of us by what we say. I discovered this from the following experience. I had a special interest and concern for the spiritual life of a young woman. One day I made a rather light remark to her. She looked at me and said, "That doesn't sound like you."

I realized she had been watching my life and listening to my conversation, and this remark didn't fit her standard for me. Later, I confessed it to God, asking Him to guard my conversation that it might always honor and glorify Him.

In the office, in the home, in the neighborhood, wherever we are, people are listening to what we say. One definition for betray is "reveal unknowingly." It is often in the unguarded moment that our talk reveals our inner life.

In Revelation 14:5 we read, "And in their mouth was found no guile: for they are without fault before the throne of God."

One evening we were having dinner with several friends in a restaurant. It was late; the restaurant was nearly empty and we were leisurely visiting over a delicious dinner. As we were leaving, the hostess said, "You must be Christians. Every time I passed your table you were talking about Christian things. I am a Christian, too."

We have the privilege of showing forth Christ by our speech each day. Can it be said of us, "And in their mouth was found no guile; for they are without fault before the throne of God"?

"Oh, that my tongue might so possess the accent of His tenderness; oh, that it might be said of me, 'Surely thy speech betrayeth thee.'"

For we are his workmanship, created in Christ Jesus unto good works, which God hath before ordained that we should walk in them (Eph. 2:10).

The manufacturers of a well-known silver plate were proud of the fine workmanship of their product. Then they decided to produce a silver polish that would preserve the luster of their silver. Their advertising read, "Trust the creator of fine finishes and delicate tracings to produce a polish that will preserve its mellow beauty."

When silverware is manufactured, lovely patterns requiring fine and intricate work are "traced" onto silver pieces to enhance their beauty. Then it requires polishing to give the mellow glow of the finished product.

God, the Creator, has made us a new creation in Christ Jesus. He, the Master Workman, wants to produce the mellow beauty of a radiant Christian life in us. He desires to perfect the fine tracings in our lives to bring out the beauty of His Son. "To be molded into the image of His Son [and share inwardly His likeness]" (Rom. 8:29 *Amplified*). As we yield our lives to Him He will trace His own special pattern in them to produce the inner beauty of Jesus Christ.

Chastening is a part of the process necessary to etch these delicate tracings, bringing out the inner radiance of His presence. Do you wonder why trouble strikes? Why misfortunes, heartache, or illness come? The Bible tells us, "For the Lord corrects and disciplines every one whom He loves" (Heb. 12:6, *Amplified*).

As His masterpiece we are not just to be put on display, but we are to fulfill His work for us. Thus, some of the delicate tracings and polishing are necessary to accomplish His pattern.

The advertising for silverware and polish said "Trusting the Creator." We must trust our lives to our Creator for He will spare nothing to complete His work in us. But we can know we are in the hands of an Artist who makes no mistake.

"Being punished isn't enjoyable while it is happening—it hurts! But afterwards we can see the result, a quiet growth in grace and character" (Heb. 12:11, LB).

Which is Christ in you, the hope of glory (Col. 1:27).

Paul wrote of our hope as believers which he called "the blessed hope." He said, "Looking for that blessed hope, and the glorious appearing of the great God and our Saviour Jesus Christ" (Titus 2:13).

At the Ascension of Jesus to heaven, two men in white apparel appeared to the disciples, saying, "This same Jesus, which is taken up from you into heaven, shall so come in like manner as ye have seen him go into heaven" (Acts 1:11).

Today we live in expectation of the promised return of Jesus Christ. We do not know when He will return but we look up in anticipation of it.

Not only is His return a living hope in a believer's life, but it has an effect on the way he lives. When we are expecting company, we make preparation for their arrival. We clean our homes, setting everything in order. As we await His return, we need some inner preparation. Our lives must be kept clean. There may be some things in them to be put in order. "And every man that hath this hope in him purifieth himself, even as he is pure" (1 John 3:3).

The return of Jesus Christ is our hope for the future, but what about hope for today? Many are without hope because they are without God. One definition of hope is "that in which we place our confidence." The Lord Jesus is the object of our hope, the One in whom we have placed our confidence. "Christ in you, the hope of glory."

With His presence within, we know that He is our hope for a consistent life of victory. Sometimes we try to live the Christian life; we struggle to achieve victory; and over and over we go down in defeat.

When a puppet is being manipulated, it moves in perfect harmony with the hand within. When the Lord Jesus lives within, and has complete control of our lives, we will move in perfect harmony with Him.

Our hope for the future—Christ will return. Our hope for today—the presence of the indwelling Christ giving victory in our lives.

And the Lord was with Joseph (Gen. 39:2).

Joseph had become the second highest ruler in Egypt. He attained this place of prominence by a difficult road of loneliness and injustice. His brothers, hating him intensely, sold him into slavery, and he was taken to Egypt. Separated from family and friends, he must have been lonely and homesick. But "the Lord was with Joseph."

Through a series of events over which he had no control, he was imprisoned. Who would consider taking educational courses in prison? Yet Joseph's imprisonment was a training period for God's future plan for him.

He learned patience while in prison. Authority given him over the prisoners developed his leadership ability. This was preparation for him later when he directed food distribution during a severe famine.

Joseph may have questioned why his brothers mistreated him; why he was sold into slavery; why he was imprisoned on a charge of which he was innocent. Yet he didn't let his prison experience embitter him. Although he didn't understand it, nor could he see what the future held, he was aware of God's presence with him in prison.

Today you may be in a prison. Perhaps you are misunderstood by your family. Or you may be far away from home, and lonely. Whatever your prison experience, humanly speaking, there may be no way out, no immediate solution. What is your reaction? Are you rebellious? Are you questioning God?

God knows the lessons we need to learn, lessons of patience, submission, and self-denial. Our faith may need strengthening. We may be so concerned that God remove us from prison that we miss the lessons He has for us in prison.

Our prison term may seem long, but the God who was with Joseph when he was taken into Egypt, and the God who was with him when he was put in prison, is the God who is with us today. He has promised, "I will never leave thee, nor forsake thee" (Heb. 13:5).

May
20

But as for you, ye thought evil against me; but God meant it unto good (Gen. 50:20).

Joseph had been placed in charge of a food program during a famine in Egypt.

Hearing that food was available there, Joseph's brothers came to purchase a supply. What mixed emotions Joseph must have had when he saw his brothers. This was his opportunity to retaliate. But Joseph had no spirit of revenge. He had no ill will toward them. He was aware that God was working through his afflictions to bring about good.

He said to his brothers, "For God did send me before you to preserve life. . . . So now it was not you that sent me hither, BUT GOD" (Gen. 45:5,8).

Although the brothers were afraid Joseph would take revenge on them, he assured them, "Fear not: for am I in the place of God? But as for you, ye thought evil against me: BUT GOD meant it unto good, to bring to pass, as it is this day, to save much people alive" (Gen. 50:19-20).

Joseph faced each difficulty in his life with two words, BUT GOD. He didn't know why he was sold into slavery—BUT GOD. He couldn't understand his prison term—BUT GOD. He couldn't explain why he had been lifted to such prominence—BUT GOD. "YOU thought evil against me, BUT GOD meant it for good."

He experienced the truth of what Paul wrote. "And we know that all things work together for good to them that love God, to them who are the called according to his purpose" (Rom. 8:28).

On a piece of embroidery, each stitch is necessary to complete the pattern. Even a few black threads enhance the beauty of the other colors. As God works out His pattern for our lives, He places each stitch carefully. It may hurt, but it is meant for our good. He knows where to weave in the dark threads to increase the beauty of our lives. WE do not see the completed pattern, BUT GOD does.

God is working in our lives today, even though we cannot see the completed pattern. We can say, however, "BUT GOD meant it unto good."

God has great confidence in you to place you where you are.

Is not the whole land before thee? separate thyself, I pray thee, from me: if thou wilt take the left hand, then I will go to the right; or if thou depart to the right hand, then I will go to the left (Gen. 13:9).

When Abraham journeyed into the promised land, Lot, his nephew, accompanied him. He and Lot accumulated so many flocks and herds, there wasn't room for both of them. Their herdsmen began to quarrel, each wanting the best pasture land for his flocks. Abraham realized they must separate.

Because Abraham was older and God had promised the land to him, he was entitled to first choice of the land. But he waived his rights, letting Lot choose first. Then he took what was left.

Lot looked about at the well-watered plain of Jordan. Knowing it would be advantageous for him and his flocks, he made what would appear the best choice. He did not realize the disastrous results his wrong choice would have on the life of his family. Later God destroyed Sodom where he lived; Lot escaped with his wife and daughters. Disobeying God's command, Lot's wife looked back, becoming a pillar of salt.

Lot had only considered his temporal advantages, not his spiritual welfare. He had put earthly possessions first and they failed. Ultimately, in grasping for material gain, he lost all.

By giving Lot first choice, Abraham was really leaving it up to God to choose for him. The one who gives in, rather than quarrel, even when right, is the one who really wins.

Throughout our lifetime we will have many choices to make. Unless we let the Lord choose for us, we too, may make wrong decisions. We may make a choice that brings material gain but ultimate spiritual loss. Many times in our life of faith we will waive our own rights as we follow His choice.

What motivates your choices? Do you seek the mind of the Lord or follow your own natural wisdom? If you let the Lord choose for you, you will have the best; you will always have the right choice.

"He always gets God's best who leaves the choice with Him."

May
22

But thanks be to God, which giveth us the victory through our Lord Jesus Christ (1 Cor. 15:57).

Many Christians are unsettled and unstable in their daily living. They are living short of God's standard for them. One day they are on the mountain top; the next in the valley. One day they are up, the next day down. Many accept such inconsistencies in Christian living as the normal. God's standard, however, for the Christian is moment by moment victory. "Nay, in all these things we are more than conquerors through him that loved us" (Rom. 8:37).

There can be a life of victory. It is assured, for its source is in God Himself. "Thanks be unto GOD." It is a gift from God. ". . . which GIVETH us the victory."

None of us can have this victorious life in his own strength. The secret of living victoriously is not in struggling to gain a hard-won victory, but living in the power of the victory provided in Christ. "This is the victory that overcometh the world, even our faith. Who is he that overcometh the world, but he that believeth that Jesus is the Son of God" (1 John 5:4-5). In Him, the victorious Christ, we can live in complete victory as a day by day experience.

This victory is ours potentially when we receive Christ as Savior. It becomes real in our daily experience as we appropriate it into our life situations and circumstances.

Today are you living a life of defeat? Or is it a life of victory part of the time and defeat part of the time? Are there some areas in your life where you need victory? What are they? Worry? Fear? Temper? Selfishness? Self-pity? Criticism? Perhaps you have been trying to fight the battle in your strength. It is time to quit fighting and claim victory by faith. We can commit our failures and defeats to Him and claim His victory. We can say, HE IS MY victory.

"Now thanks be unto God, which always causeth us to triumph in Christ, and maketh manifest the savour of his knowledge by us in every place" (2 Cor. 2:14).

He healeth the broken in heart, and binds up their wounds (Ps. 147:3).

For many years there was a company in Denver that had a fine reputation for mending china and glassware. They could restore it so perfectly you couldn't find where the break had been.

Life is filled with heartaches and sorrow today. Behind many a smile is a broken heart. Burdens come, one upon another, until we are almost crushed by their weight. Some beautiful dream you had looked forward to with such hope may have dissipated. You may be overcome with loneliness. Your heart may be broken and you cannot understand what has happened. We are not promised we will have an easy or comfortable life. Jesus said, "In the world ye shall have tribulation" (John 16:33).

But there is Someone who sees our broken hearts and lovingly understands. The Lord Jesus is the "Mender of Broken Hearts." He sees them and is ready to pour His healing balm into them and bind up our wounds.

A cathedral in Europe had a beautiful stained glass window. During a storm it was shattered, breaking into many small pieces. The pieces were carefully gathered up and packed away.

One day a stranger came to the village. He had heard of the broken window and asked if he might have the pieces. He said he could restore the window to its former beauty, but he must have all the pieces. Since the villagers had no use for them, they let him take them.

Nothing was heard from him for months. Then one day he returned with the window. After placing it in the cathedral, he invited the people to come and view it. They gazed in amazement at its loveliness. No one could tell it had been broken. In fact, it was even more beautiful than it had been before.

Today your heart may be broken. The Lord Jesus can restore it, bringing new beauty out of it, but you must give Him ALL the pieces.

"The Lord is nigh unto them that are of a broken heart" (Ps. 34:18).

In Revelation 21:4 we read, "And God shall wipe away all tears from their eyes."

May
24

And he hath put a new song in my mouth, even praise unto our God (Ps. 40:3).

One of the lovely gospel songs we sing is "Praise Him! Praise Him! Jesus our blessed redeemer. Sing O earth, His wonderful love proclaim." Praise is glorifying God; being occupied with His blessings. Many are the blessings for which we can praise Him.

Sometimes we think it takes pleasant, quiet surroundings in our lives to give us a song of praise. But David had learned the blessing of praising Him in the time of trouble and danger. When in a precarious position, completely helpless in a deep pit and struggling in the miry clay, he went into God's presence and poured out his heart. As he waited patiently and expectantly, God heard his cry and answered.

David said, "He drew me up out of a horrible pit—a pit of tumult and of destruction—out of the miry clay, froth and slime, and set my feet upon a rock, steadying my steps and establishing my goings" (Ps. 40:2, *Amplified*).

Then God gave him a "singing heart," a heart filled with praise. God had lifted him from his insecure and slippery position to a place of security on a rock. No wonder he could praise God. In Psalm 34:1 he said, "I will bless the Lord at all times: HIS PRAISE shall continually be in my mouth."

God has done this same thing for us. From the depths of sin, He lifted us and set us upon the Rock. The rock symbolizes Christ, the Rock of our salvation, our Source of security and strength.

Then He gave us a new song, one which continues throughout our lives. It is a song of praise for what He has done for us, and continues to do. Each new trial brings a new song of praise. Each new answer to prayer gives new opportunities to praise God, the One who is both the source and object of our song.

May we let God give us a NEW SONG of PRAISE today whatever our circumstances may be. "Many shall see it, and fear, and shall trust in the Lord" (Ps. 40:3).

But it is good for me to draw near to God: I have put my trust in the Lord God, that I may declare all thy works (Ps. 73:28).

Asaph was perplexed over the injustices of life. He became a "ruffled" personality as he considered the prosperity of the evil-doers. Was it worth trying to live an upright life as he did?

However, his answer came as he went into God's presence. He realized he had left God out of his thinking. God wasn't through with the people yet.

Some wonderful assurances came to him. First, he was assured of God's presence. "I am continually with thee" (Ps. 73:23). No matter where we are or what is happening, we are assured of His presence.

God's power was assured Asaph. "Thou hast holden me by my right hand" (v. 23). I remember well the last roller coaster ride I had. It was considered a "thriller." On previous ones we had always been strapped in. This one only had a bar in front of us. The operator instructed us to hold on to the bar and not let go. When we began going up and down and from side to side, I was sure I could never hold on. About that time I promised the Lord if He would get me back safely I would never ride again, and I never have.

In our Christian experience I am glad we don't have to hold on to God. We would not have sufficient power. He holds us and never lets go.

Asaph was assured of God's guidance. "Thou shalt guide me with thy counsel" (v. 24). When we do not know which way to go, or what decision to make, He does it for us.

Asaph came to a wonderful conclusion. "HE is the strength of my heart" (Ps. 73:26, LB). Our weakness becomes His strength. He is our portion forever, sufficient for each need each day of our lives. Asaph, a ruffled personality, became a restful personality, as He put his trust completely in God.

No wonder he could say, "But as for me, I get as close to Him as I can! I have chosen Him and I will tell everyone about the wonderful ways He rescues me" (v. 28, LB).

May

26

As ye have therefore received Christ Jesus the Lord, so walk ye in him; Rooted and built up in him, and stablished in the faith, as ye have been taught, abounding therein with thanksgiving (Col. 2:6-7).

Christianity is more than a creed; it is living in vital union with Christ, our lives centered in Him. There are several verbs in the above Scripture verses which characterize our relationship to God; walk—rooted—built up.

First, we are to walk as a Christan—"walk ye in Him." Walking in Him denotes motion and direction. It involves progress; one doesn't stand still in a walk. Then the Lord is our companion on our walk; we do not walk alone. Our walk is important; it should match our talk.

A Christian is likened to a tree, rooted in Him. If we are to grow upward, our roots must reach downward, nourished in Him. Strong, deep roots in our lives strengthen us against the storms that beat on our lives.

Next, we are to be built up in Him. As it takes time to complete a building, so it is a continuous process to be built up in Him. Stone by stone, brick by brick, our lives are built according to the blueprint God has designed for us.

Walking! Growing! Building! These are steps in our Christian development. Walking goes ON—indicating progress day by day. How far have we progressed in our walk with Him? Roots go DOWN—indicating inward growth as we reach downward and nourish ourselves in His Word. Are we being strengthened by feeding daily on His Word? Building goes UP—indicating outward growth into His likeness. Can others see Jesus in our lives?

Going forward—growing inwardly and revealing Him outwardly—this is our privilege. "As you have therefore received the Christ, [even] Jesus the Lord, [so] walk—REGULATE YOUR LIVES and conduct yourselves—in union with and conformity to Him. Have the roots [of your being] firmly and deeply planted [in Him]—fixed and founded in Him—being continually built up in Him, becoming increasingly more confirmed and established in the faith, just as you were taught, and abounding and overflowing in it with thanksgiving" (Col. 2:6-7, *Amplified*).

But none of these things move me, neither count I my life dear unto myself, so that I might finish my course with joy, and the ministry, which I have received of the Lord Jesus, to testify the gospel of the grace of God (Acts 20:24).

Paul gave a farewell message to the Ephesian elders. As he reviewed his ministry, he reminded them that it had been a call from God. He was serving them in Christ's stead. He gave his service in a spirit of humility, wanting no glory for himself.

Even then, as he told them good-by, he knew his life was in danger. Yet it didn't disturb him. He said, "Neither count I my life dear unto myself." Whether he lived or died didn't matter. Nothing could move him from the course God had set before him. To the Philippians (3:14) he had said, "I press toward the mark for the prize of the high calling of God in Christ Jesus." No price was too high, no obstacle too great, to keep him from completing his work. He was determined to finish it with joy.

What about the course of your life? Has trouble come? Are there obstacles in your way? Are things happening you can't understand? Are you uncertain what lies ahead? Can you say as Paul, "Neither count I my life dear to myself"?

God has given you a life plan, an aim, a goal. It fits into His overall plan of reaching the world for Jesus Christ. We do not all have the same plan. What do you count dear—the life plan God has given you, or one of your own devising?

As you press on toward the mark of the high calling of God through Christ Jesus in your life, there may be trouble, there may be failure, there may be heartache. With your eyes upon the Lord Jesus, you can say as Paul, "None of these things move me."

Do you count your life dear to yourself? Or to God? If your life is committed to Him completely, regardless of circumstances or environment, you can finish YOUR course with joy.

He giveth power to the faint; and to them that have no might he increaseth strength (Isa. 40:29).

Are you saying today, "I am so weary I wonder if I can get through the day"? We fortify ourselves with vitamins, minerals, and pep pills to help revitalize us and increase our energy. One day Julia Ward Howe slumped into a chair, saying, "I am tired—tired way down into the future."

With all the aids we take there is still something lacking. We have not made provision for strength for the inner person. We have failed to go to the source of real strength, God Himself.

God, who by His power created the universe and all that is in it, says, "Look up into the heavens! Who created all these stars? As a shepherd leads his sheep, calling each by its pet name, and counts them to see that none are lost or strayed, so God does with stars and planets" (Isa. 40:26, LB).

This same all-powerful God is the source of our strength. "Power belongeth unto God" (Ps. 62:11). He has an inexhaustible supply. "Don't you yet understand? Don't you know by now that the everlasting God, the Creator of the farthest parts of the earth, never grows faint or weary? No one can fathom the depths of His understanding" (Isa. 40:28, LB).

God knows how easily we faint and become discouraged when the storms beat upon our lives. It is not His purpose that we faint and grow weary. His promise of power and strength is for the weak; to those who are fainting; to those who have NO might. He comes with a constant supply. He has promised, "And your strength be equal to your days" (Deut. 33:25, *Berkeley*). He is adequate for our every need.

This power is a gift from God. "He GIVETH power to the faint." The condition for receiving it is waiting upon the Lord. "But they that wait upon the Lord shall renew their strength" (Isa. 40:31). The only power God can give is His own power. Since it is God-given power, it can do what human strength can never do. It has been said, "The power behind a Christian is greater than the problem before him."

This power of God is available today. Are you appropriating it?

But they that wait upon the Lord shall renew their strength; they shall mount up with wings as eagles; they shall run, and not be weary; and they shall walk, and not faint (Isa. 40:31).

The following fable relates how the birds are supposed to have received their wings. They were created without wings. They had lovely plumage, they could sing, but they could not fly. Then God made wings and placed them in front of the birds, saying, "Come, take up these burdens and bear them." At first the birds hesitated. Then they picked up the wings in their beaks and laid them on their shoulders. At first they were heavy and hard to bear. But soon, as they folded the burdens over their hearts, the wings grew to their bodies. Their burdens had become wings by which they could fly.

Often the burdens of life press upon us so heavily we feel we cannot carry them any longer. We ask God to remove them. But His plan is to use them to develop wing power in our lives.

When the eagle watches a storm approaching, he waits until it strikes. Then he faces it, spreads his wings, and rises upward through it. As storms break upon our lives, our wing power takes us through the storm and lifts us above it.

Sufficient strength to mount up on wings as eagles comes from "waiting on the Lord." It has been said, "Mounting wings have been fashioned for those who wait on the Lord."

The word "wait" in this Scripture verse has the meaning of "habitually trusting." Those who wait on the Lord will keep trusting in spite of their difficulties. When we bring our needs to Him and wait before Him, He gives strength to rise above them. It is an exchanged strength, exchanging our human strength for His divine strength. "For my strength is made perfect in weakness" (2 Cor. 12:9).

In our weakness we become strong. We say, "I can't do it." God says, "I can do it for you."

What are you waiting on today? Things? People? Money? Possessions? Waiting on HIM gives the quiet confidence of His presence upholding us moment by moment.

May
30

God is faithful–reliable, trustworthy and [*therefore*] *ever true to His promise, and He can be depended on" (1 Cor. 1:9, Amplified).*

Have you ever seen "Old Faithful" geyser in Yellowstone National Park? I remember our first visit there. Upon our arrival we were told the time of its next eruption. As the time drew near, we gathered with a large crowd to view this spectacular event. According to schedule, "Old Faithful" erupted just as they had said it would.

As I watched, I thought of the faithfulness of the One who made the geyser. In Psalm 89:8 (LB) we read, "O Jehovah, Commander of the heavenly armies, where is there any other Mighty One like you? Faithfulness is your very character."

God is faithful and we can depend on His faithfulness. "If we believe not, yet he abideth faithful: He cannot deny Himself" (2 Tim. 2:13). Not only is God faithful, but His faithfulness is great. "It is of the Lord's mercies that we are not consumed, because His compassions fail not. They are new every morning; GREAT is thy FAITHFULNESS" (Lam. 3:22-23).

To understand and appreciate His faithfulness, we need to know His promises for He is faithful to them. "Let us hold fast the profession of our faith without wavering; (for He is faithful that promised)" (Heb. 10:23). We can have assurance not only that God can but will do all He has promised. "Hear my prayer, O Lord; answer my plea, because you are faithful to your promises" (Ps. 143:1, LB). Hudson Taylor said, "We need a faith that rests on a great God and that expects Him to keep His own Word and do just as He promised."

Friends may fail us, our family may fail us, but we can depend on God's faithfulness to us. "Yet the Lord is faithful and He will strengthen [you] and set you on a firm foundation and guard you from the evil [one]" (2 Thess. 3:3, *Amplified*). Because God is faithful, we can come to Him in confidence with our needs.

"I will sing of the mercies of the Lord for ever: with my mouth will I make known THY FAITHFULNESS to all generations" (Ps. 89:1).

Finally, brethren, pray for us, that the word of the Lord may have free course, and be glorified, even as it is with you (2 Thess. 3:1).

When Paul became a Christian he asked, "Lord, what wilt thou have me to do?" (Acts 9:6). God's purpose for Paul is stated in Acts 9:15: "For he is a chosen vessel unto me, to bear my name before the Gentiles, and kings, and the children of Israel." Paul did not underestimate the power of prayer in service for the Lord. It was demonstrated in the ministry of the early Christians. "And when THEY HAD PRAYED, the place was shaken" (Acts 4:31). Things happen when we pray.

Paul asked the Christians to join him in prayer that God's Word might have free course. Free course is a figure of speech taken from the races held at the Gothic stadium. It has the meaning of "running without hindrance." Paul urged them to pray that God's Word would move rapidly to accomplish its purpose.

In Isaiah 59:16 we read, "And he . . . wondered that there was no intercessor." We talk a great deal about prayer, we read books about it, we attend seminars about it. We believe in the power of prayer. But that is not enough. It takes a life to intercede for a needy world.

To be an intercessor means giving time to prayer, it means giving ourselves to prayer. It means we come into God's presence to get His mind about the one for whom we are praying. It means living close to the heart of God.

God has promised that as His Word goes forth it will accomplish His purpose. "So shall my word be that goeth forth out of my mouth: it shall not return unto me void, but it shall accomplish that which I please, and it shall prosper in the thing whereto I sent it" (Isa. 55:11).

But it takes intercessory prayer for the Word as it goes forth. This is what Paul was asking for. In Psalm 126:6 we read, "He that goeth forth and weepeth (prayer), bearing precious seed (God's Word), shall doubtless come again with rejoicing, bringing his sheaves with Him."

"But I GIVE MYSELF unto PRAYER" (Ps. 109:4).

June

1

So my counsel is: Don't worry about things–food, drink, and clothes. For you already have life and a body–and they are far more important than what to eat and wear (Matt. 6:25, LB*).*

As I waken early in the morning, I enjoy the singing of the birds. Often one sits on a ledge outside my window warbling a beautiful morning concert for me. They are out early, searching for their daily provision, yet as I listen to them sing, I detect no fretting, frustration, or worry. The Bible says, "Your heavenly Father feedeth them" (Matt. 6:26).

Today it is easy to become so pressured in accumulating material things, we worry ourselves into a state of frenzy. Jesus spoke of the uselessness and futility of worry when he said, "Don't worry about THINGS—food, drink, and clothes. For you already have life and a body—and they are far more important than what to eat and wear."

Jesus used the birds as an illustration of freedom from worry. "Look at the birds! They don't worry about what to eat—they don't need to sow or reap or store up food—for your heavenly Father feeds them. And you are far more valuable to him than they are" (v. 26, LB).

Neither are we to worry about what we wear. "And why worry about your clothes? Look at the field lilies! They don't worry about theirs. And if God cares so wonderfully for flowers that are here today and gone tomorrow, won't he more surely care for you, O men of little faith?" (vv. 28-30, LB).

Jesus said to His disciples, "O ye of LITTLE FAITH." If we are worried and anxious, doesn't it reveal our lack of faith in God to care for us? The antidote for fear is putting our trust completely in Him.

Trust and worry do not dwell together. If we trust, we do not worry. If we worry, we do not trust.

In Psalm 86:2 *(Amplified)* we find a good definition of trust. "Preserve my life, for I am godly and dedicated; O my God, save Your servant for I trust in You, leaning and believing on You, committing [all] and confidently looking to You, without fear or doubt."

So don't be anxious about tomorrow. God will take care of your tomorrow too. Live one day at a time (Matt. 6:34, LB).

One day as I sat in a railroad station, a woman hurried in. As I watched her, I was aware that she was having difficulty with her reservations. Finally she came and sat beside me. She related all that had gone wrong. Finally she looked at me and said very seriously, "Can you think of anything I should be worrying about that I am not?" We smile at that, yet by the way we live do we display that attitude? I remember a time in my life when I thought I must be overlooking something if I wasn't worrying.

One of the greatest fears today is of the unknown, the uncertainty and insecurity of tomorrow. God's Word tells us we are not to be anxious about our tomorrows.

Worry accomplishes nothing. It can't add to the length of life; it can't change its course; it can't solve one problem. "Will all your worries add a single moment to your life?" (Matt. 6:27, LB).

Worry shows lack of trust in the Lord. It is saying in effect, "I don't believe God is big enough to handle my problem."

Worry adds tomorrow's cares to today's load. Someone has said, "What I have to do tomorrow has made a wreck of me today."

Worry is a useless expenditure of time. In Psalm 37:8 (LB) we read, "Don't fret and worry—it only leads to harm."

This does not mean we are not to plan for our future, making no provision for our needs. If He is mindful of the birds and flowers, will He not care for us? But our trust must be in HIM.

Our tomorrows are in God's hands. They are His tomorrows. As they become our todays, we can deposit them with Him, knowing our sufficiency for them is in Him.

Someone has said, "Anxiety does not empty tomorrow of its trials—it simply empties today of its joy. Anxiety does not empty tomorrow of its sorrow—it empties today of its strength."

June

3

You chart the path ahead of me, and tell me where to stop and rest. Every moment, you know where I am (Ps. 139:3, LB).

As we planned our vacation each year, we made careful preparations. After deciding where to go, a travel agency would chart our trip for us. It supplied us with maps of the area. Places of scenic and historical interest were marked. Included were suggestions for motels and restaurants, everything to provide for our needs on the trip. Having all this planned ahead made the trip easier and much more pleasant.

God has a planned path for each of us. In Jeremiah 29:11 *(Rotherham)* we read, "I know the plans which I am planning for you, plans of welfare and not of calamity to give you a future and a hope."

Not only does our heavenly Father know His plan for us, but He has it charted. "As thou goest step by step, the way shall be opened up before thee" (Prov. 4:12, *Free translation*).

Being an all-wise God, He knows the importance of "rest stops" along the way. Because He knows we may fail to take them ourselves, He includes them at the right places on our path for our benefit.

Not only does He give us rest stops to refresh us, but also to give us quiet times to think of Him and be aware of His personal love and care; to have a time of communion with Him. After Jesus' disciples had had a busy schedule, He charted a "rest stop" for them. "And he said unto them, Come ye yourselves apart into a desert place, and rest a while" (Mark 6:31).

Sometimes we feel God has forgotten all about us. But the psalmist had learned God never forgets. "Every moment you know where I am."

There is much instruction and encouragement in resting on God's Word. We can be assured there is rest for us today wherever we are, whatever our situation. This is not an outer rest of circumstances, but an inner rest of soul. "So then, there is still awaiting a full and complete Sabbath rest reserved for the [true] people of God" (Heb. 4:9, *Amplified*).

And he said unto them, Come ye yourselves apart into a desert place, and rest a while: for there were many coming and going, and they had no leisure so much as to eat (Mark 6:31).

What a busy schedule! You are probably saying, "It sounds like mine." When they were too busy to eat, it was time for a "rest break."

After a busy time of serving others, Jesus knew His disciples needed rest. He invited them to spend time alone with Him to refresh themselves.

God knows that we, too, need rest for our inner being, so He provides "Resting Places" along our way. In Isaiah 40:31 we learn the source of our rest. "They that wait upon the Lord." It is in His presence we are refreshed from the weariness of life's journey.

There is a PLACE of rest; it is "in the Lord" (Ps. 37:7). He gives us a personal invitation to "Come unto ME." He doesn't say, "Go," but "Come." Resting is always IN HIM.

Rest is a GIFT. Jesus said, "I will GIVE you rest" (Matt. 11:28). How often we are pressured and frustrated when He is inviting us to come and receive His rest.

Rest comes through our RELATIONSHIP with Him. "For only we who believe God can enter into His place of rest" (Heb. 4:3, LB). Our access to God is through the person of Jesus Christ.

He may move us occasionally to new resting places. He may move us to a place where we are alone, away from family and friends. But He can make it a resting place for us.

One year my resting place was upon a sick bed. Many days I could not lift my arms even an inch from the bed. It was a difficult year, but a good one, for the Lord and I had wonderful times together.

Jesus said, "But thou, when thou prayest, enter into thy closet (His special resting place for us), and when thou hast shut thy door, pray to thy Father which is in secret; and thy Father which seeth in secret shall reward thee openly" (Matt. 6:6).

His personal invitation to you is, "Come apart and rest with me." What is your answer?

June
5

The Lord is my shepherd; I shall not want (Ps. 23:1).

David wrote this Psalm out of his experience as a shepherd boy. He had learned many things about sheep and their need of a shepherd's care. Sheep are such helpless and foolish animals. They cannot defend themselves. They easily go astray. Without a shepherd, they soon become scattered.

In his relationship with God, David compared himself with a sheep in need of a shepherd. He said, "The LORD is my shepherd; I shall not want."

The shepherd loves his sheep, and regardless of how many he has, he knows each one by name. He makes himself responsible for caring for their needs. Many shepherds have even lost their lives caring for their sheep. So the sheep need have no worry—their trust is in their shepherd.

Through the years David had found his Good Shepherd to be his all-sufficient One. Because His resources are inexhaustible, he could write, "I shall not want." The *Amplified Bible* reads, "The Lord is my shepherd [to feed, guide and shield me]; I shall not lack." Having no wants gives a feeling of contentment.

Years later One came who said, "I AM the GOOD SHEPHERD, and know my sheep, and am known of mine" (John 10:14). Our Good Shepherd, the Lord Jesus Christ, has a personal interest in each one of us. We can have implicit trust in Him, for He does not overlook even one need.

Once a pastor confessed to a fellow pastor his lack of complete trust in the Lord for some personal needs. "Do you believe the Twenty-third Psalm?" asked the fellow pastor. "Of course," was the first pastor's reply. The fellow pastor continued, "Does the shepherd take care of all of the needs of his sheep, or some of them?" Suddenly the Scripture had new meaning for the first man. He realized that he had been SAYING he believed it, but now he REALLY believed it. The Lord is your shepherd and mine, and He meets all our needs, every one of them.

Do we merely SAY "I believe He is my shepherd," or do we really believe it and trust Him. This life of trust begins by personally knowing the Good Shepherd and committing our life to Him.

The Lord is my shepherd; I shall not want (Ps. 23:1).

Little words often have great significance. In the above verse the personal pronoun "MY" is important. The little two-letter word indicates a relationship between the Lord and David. David didn't say the Lord is "a" shepherd, but "my" shepherd.

Sheep easily go astray. It takes the shepherd's careful search to find them and restore them to the fold. "All we like sheep have gone astray; we have turned every one to his own way; and the Lord hath laid on him the iniquity of us all" (Isa. 53:6).

Jesus Christ came as the Good Shepherd to make possible a personal relationship between God and man. Jesus said, "I am the good shepherd; the good shepherd giveth his life for the sheep" (John 10:11).

One of England's leading actors was being honored at a banquet. After dinner the Master of Ceremonies asked the actor if he would recite for the guests. He consented, asking if there was something in particular someone would like to hear.

After a moment's pause, an old clergyman spoke up, saying, "Sir, could you recite the Twenty-third Psalm?"

For a moment the actor was speechless. Then he said, "Yes, I will be glad to, but on one condition; that is, that after I have recited it, you will do the same."

Impressively the great actor recited the Psalm, holding his audience spellbound. As he finished, a great burst of applause broke forth from the guests.

After the applause ceased, the clergyman quietly arose. The audience listened as the Psalm was given. When it was done, there was not a dry eye in the room.

After a moment of silence, the actor said, "I reached your ears, but this man reached your hearts. I know the Psalm, but he knows the Shepherd."

Do you only know the Psalm, or do you know the Shepherd? Can you say, "The Lord is MY Shepherd?" If not, would you like to invite Jesus Christ into your life to become your personal Savior and Good Shepherd?

"But as many as received him, to them gave he power to become the sons of God, even to them that believe on his name" (John 1:12).

June
7

He maketh me to lie down in green pastures: he leadeth me beside the still waters (Ps. 23:2).

The shepherd is at the very center of the life of the sheep. He provides for their every need, satisfying them completely.

Sheep will not lie down if they have cause to be fearful. They are easily frightened. However, as soon as the shepherd appears and moves in the midst of the restless flock, they become quiet.

The lives of many Christians are filled with fear, bringing restlessness and frustration. Our Good Shepherd appears, saying, "Fear THOU not; for I am with thee" (Isa. 41:10). His presence in the midst of our need removes fear and gives rest.

Sheep will not lie down if they are hungry. The shepherd searches for the best pasture land available for his sheep. Our Good Shepherd knows we need to be well nourished for inner satisfaction. He provides nourishment for us from the green pastures of His Word. Nourished by it, we can lie down in quiet contentment.

Occasionally He has to MAKE us lie down. It may take illness, loneliness, heartache, or sorrow to accomplish this.

Not only does the shepherd lead his sheep in the green meadows of nourishment and rest, but beside the still waters. We are refreshed at the waters of quietness. The word for "still" waters can be translated "stilled" waters. Sheep will not drink from a rushing stream. They instinctively know that if their coat of wool becomes wet, they could drown. Sometimes the shepherd builds a little dam in a rushing stream to enable the flock to drink from "stilled" waters.

At times the swift moving streams of life almost engulf us. God has to dam up a quiet stream where we can come and drink deeply of the Water of Life. We may discover that the very circumstances dreaded most bring spiritual refreshment.

Our Good Shepherd loves to see His sheep contented and relaxed, refreshed and satisfied with Him.

Today are you nourished and refreshed? Are you fully satisfied? "Blessed are they which do hunger and thirst after righteousness: for they shall be filled" (Matt. 5:6).

He restoreth my soul: he leadeth me in the paths of righteousness for his name's sake (Ps. 23:3).

Sheep stray easily. It is the shepherd's business to find the ones who have strayed and restore them to the fold.

Like sheep, we, too, go astray. At first we take one step away from the Good Shepherd, then another one. Before we realize what has happened, we have strayed from God's path of righteousness to a way of our own making.

Then we need the restoring touch of our Good Shepherd. The Hebrew word for restore means, "to turn about." We need to turn from our way to His.

David wrote from his own experience. He remembered a time when he had strayed and was out of fellowship with the Lord. He cried to God, "Restore unto me the joy of thy salvation" (Ps. 51:12). In His faithfulness, the Good Shepherd brought him back into fellowship with God.

In Isaiah 42:3 we read, "A bruised reed shall he not break." Shepherds in olden days played on reeds. They were easily broken and could not be mended. It was easy to make another, so the shepherd would snap it in two, throw it away, and make a new one. Our Shepherd does not do this. When the music is gone out of our soul, God does not snap us in two and throw us away—He mends and restores.

To guard against straying from His care, we need to spend time with Him, keeping close to His heart of love.

Some shepherds take time to be alone with each of their sheep every day. While grazing, one by one the sheep leave their pasture and go to the shepherd. He pats the sheep, rubs it, and lets it know it is very special to him.

If sheep have need of time alone with their shepherd daily, how much more important it is for us to spend time with our Shepherd. Keeping close TO Him keeps us from straying FROM Him. We are special to Him and He loves to have this close, intimate time with each of His children.

"I have loved thee with an everlasting love" (Jer. 31:3).

June
9

Yea, though I walk through the valley of the shadow of death, I will fear no evil: for thou art with me; thy rod and thy staff they comfort me (Ps. 23:4).

Sometimes the shepherd leads his sheep through dark, deep valleys where dangers lurk, where robbers and wild animals hide. Yet the sheep need not fear, for their shepherd watches over them.

The above Scripture verse does not say, "the valley of death," but "the valley of the shadow of death." Does this not include our entire earthly pilgrimage which finally leads to our heavenly home? On our way we may go through such valleys as fear and darkness.

We can walk through these valleys with confidence when we have the COMPANIONSHIP of the Shepherd; "I will fear no evil, for THOU art with me."

In Palestine when a shepherd moves his sheep to a higher pasture, often he has to take them through a valley. Our valley experiences lead us to "higher ground" in our spiritual experience.

Not only do the sheep have the companionship of the Shepherd, but the COMFORT of His rod and His staff. They are the weapons He uses as He leads them through the valley. The rod is used on the enemies, the staff on the sheep.

"Your rod [to protect] and Your staff [to guide], they comfort me" (Ps. 23:4, *Amplified*).

The rod is the symbol of His defending power. It is the weapon He uses to strike down the adversaries in our way. We need to transfer the responsibility of our safety to Him and stay close behind Him.

The shepherd uses the staff to keep his sheep from wandering, to draw them back into the way when they do, to lift them from places of danger into which they have fallen, and for correction.

There are many lessons we learn as we travel through the valley. Through them we have a greater appreciation and love for the Good Shepherd.

How we can thank Him for the companionship of His Presence and the Comfort of His rod and staff as we travel with Him!

Thou preparest a table before me in the presence of mine enemies (Ps. 23:5).

The psalmist has such an awareness of dependence upon his Good Shepherd. Through his life experiences he had learned that there is no want to the one who trusts his life to the Good Shepherd and walks close to Him.

As our Host, the Good Shepherd invites us to His table which He has provided and placed before us. He has taken utmost care to prepare His very best, amply providing for our every need. "And my God will liberally supply (fill to the full) your every need according to His riches in glory in Christ Jesus" (Phil. 4:19, *Amplified*).

The pastures where the sheep grazed in the Holy Land often had poisonous plants and dangerous animals. The shepherds would go before the sheep, digging out the dangerous plants and driving away animals that might harm the sheep.

Then the Good Shepherd prepares a table for us, with Himself as our Host. Because His meals are well-balanced, we are always satisfied at His table. "And Jesus said unto them, I am the bread of life: he that cometh to me shall never hunger; and he that believeth on me shall never thirst" (John 6:35). What a wonderful thought that daily we are His special care and that daily He is serving us.

We may be surrounded by enemies of doubt, fear, envy, self-pity, and rebellion. But in the midst of them our loving Host has prepared our daily provisions.

At His table there is a never-ending supply. His provisions never fail. "There is no want to them that fear him . . . they that seek the Lord shall not want any good thing" (Ps. 34:9-10).

God's banqueting table is set before us. It is a table for our spiritual nourishment and refreshment. The food is not prepared ahead of time so it becomes stale, but just when needed so it is fresh. All we need is provided for us in the person of His Son, Jesus Christ.

This table is placed before us for our benefit. If we are to be nourished by God and His Son, we must partake of them. Are you nourished by them?

June

11

Thou anointest my head with oil; my cup runneth over (Ps. 23:5).

In Eastern countries it was customary not only to bathe the feet of guests as they arrived, but to pour fragrant oil on their heads, as a gesture of love and welcome.

Throughout Scripture, oil is a symbol of the Holy Spirit. No service is fruitful unless done in the power of the Holy Spirit. The Holy Spirit not only reflects the presence of Christ from our lives, but emits the fragrance of Jesus Christ, the Rose of Sharon. Another work of the Holy Spirit is to counteract irritations in our lives.

At certain times of year, sheep are troubled by nose flies and parasites. The shepherd uses an ointment containing oil to rub on their noses and heads as a protection.

This is illustrated in our lives by the fact that we become annoyed by the irritations in our lives. The Spirit of God can counteract these aggravations of personality conflicts and other frustrations that torment us. He has the power to overcome such attitudes as jealousy, pride, and murmuring.

As David pondered on the blessings he had received from the Good Shepherd, he said, "My brimming cup runs over" (Ps. 23:5, *Amplified*). We have been provided such an abundant life through Jesus Christ. He said, "I came that they may have and enjoy life, and have it in abundance—to the full, till it overflows" (John 10:10, *Amplified*).

As we are fed at His banqueting table and controlled by His Holy Spirit, we are filled to the full until the cup of our lives overflows.

It is not the cup that is important. Cups are made of various kinds of material, some are ordinary earthenware cups, others of lovely china. They are various sizes and for various uses. It is important, however, what we are filled with. Only that with which we are filled overflows. It is important to be in the place of God's choosing that He can channel the overflow for His purpose.

The cup of our lives should be full to overflowing with the life of Jesus Christ Himself.

Someone has said, "Our cup may be small, but we can overflow. We may not hold much, but we can overflow a lot."

Surely goodness and mercy shall follow me all the days of my life: and I will dwell in the house of the Lord for ever (Ps. 23:6).

In David's daily walk with God he learned that his Good Shepherd was sufficient for every need. He could say from his personal experience, "Surely goodness and mercy shall follow me all the days of my life."

As we look ahead we cannot see "all the days of my life" that lie ahead. David said "ALL" the days, January through December; not just the bright days but the dark ones, not only the easy days but the difficult ones. He doesn't say months or years, but "days"—the "days of my life," each one of them.

Do we look ahead and wonder what next year or next week or tomorrow holds for us? Regardless of what comes, there will never be a day that God's choice guardians, goodness and mercy, will not follow us. They will accompany us every day on our earthly pilgrimage.

They are attributes of God. David wrote, "O taste and see that the Lord is GOOD" (Ps. 34:8). Paul wrote, "But God, who is rich in mercy" (Eph. 2:4).

Someone has said, "Goodness to supply every want, mercy to forgive every sin; goodness to provide, mercy to pardon."

David said, "SURELY goodness and mercy shall follow me." We can be assured of this because He has never failed in the past; because He has pledged His Word and it has never failed. We can have the assurance of knowing that His goodness and mercy are with us today.

It is personal, for us, as it was for David. We can say, "shall follow ME all the days of MY life."

When life comes to a close on earth, I can say, "I will dwell in the house of the Lord for ever." Jesus promised, "In my Father's house are many mansions: if it were not so, I would have told you. I go to prepare a place for you. And if I go and prepare a place for you, I will come again, and receive you unto myself; that where I am, there ye may be also" (John 14:2-3).

The Lord is my shepherd; I shall not want (Ps. 23:1).

"I shall not want" means "I shall not lack" (Ps. 23:1, *Amplified*).

I shall not lack REST—"He maketh me to lie down in green pastures."

I shall not lack REFRESHMENT—"He leadeth me beside the still waters."

I shall not lack REVIVING—"He restoreth my soul."

I shall not lack GUIDANCE—"He leadeth me in the paths of righteousness for his name's sake."

I shall not lack COMPANIONSHIP—"Yea, though I walk through the valley of the shadow of death, I will fear no evil: for thou art with me."

I shall not lack COMFORT—"Thy rod and thy staff they comfort me."

I shall not lack SUSTENANCE—"Thou preparest a table before me in the presence of mine enemies."

I shall not lack JOY—"Thou anointest my head with oil."

I shall not lack ANYTHING—"My cup runneth over."

I shall not lack ANYTHING IN THIS LIFE—"Surely goodness and mercy shall follow me all the days of my life."

I shall not lack ANYTHING IN ETERNITY—"and I will dwell in the house of the Lord forever."

Once a little boy was taught the first sentence of Psalm 23 by his uncle. The uncle said, "The Lord is my shepherd." The small child repeated it. Thinking this was as much as the boy could remember, the uncle said, "That's enough." The little fellow repeated, "That's 'nuff." From then on whenever asked to repeat the verse he would say, "The Lord is my shepherd—that's 'nuff."

The Lord is MY Shpeherd, all the days of MY LIFE.

And let the peace of God rule in your hearts, to the which also ye are called in one body; and be ye thankful (Col. 3:15).

On the boundary between Argentina and Chile is a famous bronze statue of Christ, called, "The Christ of the Andes." It was erected after a pact was made between these two countries in 1902 as a symbol of perpetual peace between them. The people said, "Sooner shall these mountains crumble into dust than Argentina and Chile break their peace, which at the feet of Christ they have sworn to maintain." It stands as a symbol of the only One who can bring peace to a world or to an individual.

There is much talk today of world peace. World rulers meet together to discuss ways of accomplishing this. Yet none of their plans have brought a lasting peace. In the midst of schedule-packed lives individuals are searching for inner peace as a defense against the stress and strain of today's living. There may not be peace in the world today, but there can be PEACE in the HEART.

The secret of inner peace is letting God's peace rule in our hearts. "Let the peace of heart which comes from Christ be always present in your heart and lives" (Col. 3:15, LB). God has provided peace for us through the person of Jesus Christ. "HE is our peace" (Eph. 2:14).

The word "rule" carries the thought of arbitrating or umpiring, the settling of differences where there is a conflict in thoughts, motives, and attitudes. When Christ controls our lives, He will settle our problems and differences, giving us inner quietness and calmness.

It doesn't mean we will be free from conflicts and disturbances. They will come; but the Lord Jesus will give quietness in the midst of them. When we encounter differences of opinions, irritations, and annoyances, He will give His peace. When frustrations build up, He will give calmness of spirit. Someone has said, "Let Him be the decider of all things within your heart."

There is peace in the heart for us today through the Lord Jesus Christ.

June
15

Let the word of Christ dwell in you richly in all wisdom; teaching and admonishing one another in psalms and hymns and spiritual songs, singing with grace in your hearts to the Lord (Col. 3:16).

Not only does God provide peace for the heart (Col. 3:15), but HIS TRUTH for the mind. "Let the word [spoken by] the Christ, the Messiah, have its home (in your HEARTS and MINDS) and dwell in you in [all its] richness" (Col. 3:16, *Amplified*).

It gives instruction for daily living, encouragement, comfort, and spiritual strength. It brings correction and reproof. "Every Scripture is God-breathed—given by His inspiration—and profitable for instruction, for reproof and conviction of sin, for correction of error and discipline in obedience, and for training in righteousness [that is, in holy living, in conformity to God's will in thought, purpose and action]" (2 Tim. 3:16, *Amplified*).

As we meditate on God's Word and assimilate it into our lives, it becomes such a part of us that we unconsciously let it direct our daily steps.

Saturating our minds with it produces right attitudes. It keeps our minds pure. "Fix your thoughts on what is true and good and right. Think about things that are pure and lovely, and dwell on the fine, good things in others. Think about all you can praise God for and be glad about" (Phil. 4:8, LB).

The person who lets the Word become a part of his life does not have the frenzied restlessness that we see in many people in this tension-filled day.

Are you spending time in the Word, letting Him speak to you through it? Are you living in accordance with His directions in it? "Remember what Christ taught and let His words enrich your lives and make you wise" (Col. 3:16, LB).

Someone has said, "A Word-filled life, one in which the Word dwells richly, is filled with song." "Teach them to each other and sing them out in psalms and hymns and spiritual songs, singing to the Lord with thankful hearts" (Col. 3:16, LB).

A heart filled with peace and a mind nourished by God's Word is a life filled with song. Do you possess a peaceful heart? A singing heart?

And whatsoever ye do in word or deed, do all in the name of the Lord Jesus, giving thanks to God and the Father by Him (Col. 3:17).

God has given us a guiding principle for our lives—doing everything as His representative. "And whatever you do or say, let it be as a representative of the Lord Jesus, and come with Him into the presence of God the Father to give Him your thanks" (Col. 3:17, LB). This covers every area of our daily living; in our homes, our business world, our neighborhoods, wherever we are, whatever we do. "And whatever you say or do, let it all be done with reference to the Lord Jesus" *(Williams).* Don't leave Him out of anything.

When we do all in His name, representing Him, our desire will be to please Him. "Make it our ambition, whether in our home or away, to please Him" (2 Cor. 5:9, *Weymouth*). Is this your ambition?

We will do everything for His glory. "Whether wherefore ye eat, or drink, or whatsoever ye do, do all to the glory of God" (1 Cor. 10:31). Everything in our lives, regardless of how small, ordinary, or insignificant, should be for His glory. Is this your desire?

All we do will be with the right motive. It has been said, "His name is our standard of perfection. When all is done in His name, there is never a mis-taken step, a mis-spoken word, or an act rescinded." Do you make periodic checks to see if your motives are right?

Sometimes we feel if we were taken out of our present environment, it would be easier. But the standard is, "WHATSOEVER ye DO (and that includes WHEREVER YOU ARE) through His strength and power you can do ALL in His name."

Does this seem an impossible attainment? It is. We can't do it in our own strength, but God enables and empowers us for it through the Holy Spirit.

"For God is at work within you, helping you want to obey Him, and then helping you do what He wants" (Phil. 2:13, LB).

June
17

For in him dwelleth all the fulness of the Godhead bodily. And ye are complete in him, which is the head of all principality and power (Col. 2:9-10).

Have you ever said to yourself, "I wonder what God is like? Can anyone really know Him?" So that you might know HIM and what He is like, God came to earth revealing Himself in the person of Jesus Christ. "It is true that no one has ever seen God at any time. Yet the divine and only Son, who lives in the closest intimacy with the Father, has made him known" (John 1:18, *Phillips*). Everything that makes God God is in Christ. "Because in Him there is continuously and permanently at home all the fulness of the Godhead in bodily fashion" (Col. 2:9, *Wuest* translation from the Greek).

To know what God is like we must know Christ, for the fulness of God is in Him. As Jesus spoke, it was the voice of God speaking; as He walked, it was the feet of God walking; as He saw the needs of people, it was the eyes of God seeing them as individuals whom He could help.

Not only did He come to reveal God, but to bring completion and fulfillment into our lives. Through our personal invitation to Christ to become our Savior, we are complete in Him. "Ye are complete IN HIM" (Col. 2:10). The word "complete" is the identical Greek word for "fulness" in verse 9. This means His completeness makes us complete and gives us fulfillment.

"And you are in Him, having been completely filled full, with the present result that you are in a state of fulness in Him who is the head of every principality and authority" (v. 10, *Wuest*).

We are often content to struggle alone with our weak resources when we have in Christ His all-sufficiency, enough to meet every need. If we need strength, He is our strength; if we need peace, He is our peace; if we need patience, He is our patience. In ourselves we are nothing; in Him, everything. Knowing it is available is not enough, however: we must appropriate it.

Someone has said, "Today's problems need hold no fears for us and tomorrow's uncertainties need cause us no worry, for His fulness is ours. We are complete in Him."

But Martha was cumbered about much serving, and came to him, and said, Lord, dost thou not care that my sister hath left me to serve alone? bid her therefore that she help me (Luke 10:40).

Care—just a word with four letters, yet encompassed in it is the weight of the world. Who has not felt the pressure and burden of care? Who has not at some time cried out, "Lord, don't you care? Have you forgotten me?"

Jesus was visiting in the home of Martha and Mary. "But Martha was the jittery type, and was worrying over the big dinner she was preparing" (Luke 10:40, LB).

Mary had learned the importance of taking time to rest at the feet of Jesus, listening to what He had to share.

But Martha was cumbered with serving. Left alone to prepare the meal, she felt sorry for herself. She was more occupied with WHAT she was doing for Him than with the One for WHOM she was doing it. Her motives were all right but her spirit was wrong.

She became upset with the preparation of the meal, came to Jesus, and said, "Lord, dost thou not care that my sister hath left me to serve alone?"

Jesus answered, "Martha, Martha, thou art careful and troubled about many things" (v. 41). He was not rebuking her for her desire to serve Him, but that she was filled with care and worry over the details of preparation. Her priorities were not in the right order.

Jesus said to Martha, "But one thing is needful! and Mary hath chosen that good part, which shall not be taken away." He was really saying to her, "You ask Me, 'Dost thou not care?' I do care. But I want your fellowship more than the food you are preparing. This is what Mary has chosen and put first in her life."

Most of us must confess there are times in our lives when we become so burdened with the cares of the world, that we feel alone and neglected as Martha did.

1 Peter 5:7 gives the Lord's answer to us. "Casting your care upon him, for he careth for you."

We must bring our cares to Him, casting them upon Him, not just some of them, not just a few, not many, but every one—ALL.

We can be "FULL OF CARE!" or "FREE FROM CARE!" WHICH?

June

19

Being confident of this very thing, that he which hath begun a good work in you will perform it until the day of Jesus Christ (Phil. 1:6).

Today is a day of short cuts and time savers. We use instant mixes, pre-cooked food, drip-dry materials—everything that will bring rapid results, thus saving time.

Sometimes we try short cuts in our Christian growth but discover this doesn't work. Paul, voicing his confidence that God will complete the work He has begun in His children, wrote, "And I am convinced and sure of this very thing, that He Who began a good work in you will continue until the day of Jesus Christ—right up to the time of His return—developing [that good work] and perfecting and bringing it to full completion in you" (Phil. 1:6, *Amplified*).

We are eager to reach maturity but there are no short cuts, no 'instant' formulas, to spiritual growth. Sometimes we become impatient with the process, but God knows what He is doing. It doesn't develop overnight. It is a continuing process throughout our entire lifetime. God isn't in a hurry, for He desires a life not just to be lived on this earth but to live with Him throughout all eternity.

In beginning a picture, an artist sketches the outline in first. Then the finer details are filled in. So it is in our Christian lives. When a person becomes a Christian, the outline of his Christian character is sketched in, but the details that bring maturity are filled in throughout his entire life.

The Greek word translated "will perform it" has the meaning of "will evermore put its finishing touches to it." Little finishing touches on a dress transform it into a work of art—finishing touches, but oh so important. There are many finishing touches that our Master Artist needs to put on our lives to complete them according to His plan. We may not see what He is doing but we can be confident that He will not leave undone what He has begun.

It has been aptly said, "Be patient with me. God isn't through with me yet."

I will instruct thee and teach thee in the way which thou shalt go: I will guide thee with mine eye (Ps. 32:8).

In preparation for daily living, we enter as a student in God's University. He promises to be our teacher. "I, the Lord" (Ps. 32:8, *Amplified*).

God promises three things in this verse. First, He says, "I will INSTRUCT thee." Instruct means to communicate knowledge, to inform. God will impart to us the knowledge we need to walk in the light of His will. He imparts this knowledge in such a way that we can know and understand. His Book of Instructions is the Bible. It has been said, "When all else fails, read the instructions." We will not always find specific directions, as, "do this" or "don't do that." It would be easier if we did. Yet as we read it regularly our hearts and minds are open to His instruction. He can reveal His will to us.

Next, He says, "I will TEACH you in the way you should go." "I will train you" *(Berkeley).* So God has provided a Practical Training Course and the Holy Spirit is our special Instructor for it. "But the Comforter, which is the Holy Ghost, whom the Father will send in my name, he shall teach you all things, and bring all things to your remembrance, whatsoever I have said unto you" (John 14:26).

Many schools have special counselors who give guidance and direction to the students. God gives special counseling, too. He says, "I will COUNSEL you with My eye upon you" *(Amplified).* God sees our "step by step" needs and gives "step by step" counseling, for He keeps His eye upon us at all times. "Behold, he that keepeth Israel shall neither slumber nor sleep" (Ps. 121:4).

What a wonderful promise for us in our daily living. Often problems arise that we do not know how to handle. There may be needs with no apparent solution. Situtations may be beyond human possibilities. God's promise for you, "I will instruct you—I will teach you—I will counsel you."

Someone has encouraged us by saying, "We are partners with God to do the impossible."

June

21

For God hath not given us the spirit of fear; but of power, and of love, and of a sound mind (2 Tim. 1:7).

Everywhere we turn today, in society, in the business world, and in the home, tensions and pressures are creating a spirit of fear in the lives of people.

We must confess that many situations arise in our lives that produce fear. It may be illness, failure, financial loss, loneliness, loss of job, or death. Sometimes fear is the result of trying to handle our situations ourselves instead of committing them to the Lord.

Fear is not from God but from Satan, and he is satisfied when he can cause us to push the panic button. Some people are more fearful than others, for that is their very nature.

However, God does not want us to fear. Throughout the Bible He has said, "FEAR NOT." He gives us His spirit of power to overcome our fears. It is available day by day to lift us above our circumstances, enabling us to face them victoriously. The secret of this power is the presence of the all-powerful One. David knew the reality of a life free from fear. "I will FEAR NO evil, for THOU art with ME" (Ps. 23:4).

God is love, and when He indwells us, His love fills our lives, leaving no place for fear. "Love contains no fear—indeed fully-developed love expels every particle of fear" (1 John 4:18, *Phillips*).

We need not fear, for God has given us a sound mind. A sound mind is a well-balanced mind; a disciplined mind; a mind that trusts in the Lord and rests in Him; a mind that believes and appropriates His promises into his life; a mind controlled by the Holy Spirit.

We need not fear, for in Christ we have His power. He said, "All power is given unto me in heaven and in earth" (Matt. 28:18).

We need not fear, for in Christ we have His love. "That the love wherewith thou hast loved me may be in them, and I in them" (John 17:26). We need not fear, for in Christ we have a sound mind. "But we have the mind of Christ" (1 Cor. 2:16).

For other foundation can no man lay than that is laid, which is Jesus Christ (1 Cor. 3:11).

One time I lived across from a large cathedral. It was a beautiful stone building with lovely stained glass windows. Each week organ recitals were held there in the late afternoon. As the late afternoon rays of the sun streamed in, it took on increased beauty.

Much planning and expense had gone into the construction of the cathedral. As I looked at it, I didn't see the foundation or the structural framework of the building. I saw its outward appearance which made it a cathedral of beauty and service to mankind. Yet a solid foundation supported the building. A strong superstructure had been built on the foundation.

This is an illustration of our lives. To stand against the stress and strain of life, we need a solid foundation. The foundation of our lives is not built on a human leader or on philosophies, but on the person of Jesus Christ. "For other foundation can no man lay than that is laid, which is Jesus Christ."

Materials used to build the superstructure of our lives must not be inferior or unworthy, but that which produce strong character and conduct. Someone has said, "We are to use only such materials and work as pass the building code of eternity."

Six types of building material are mentioned—three perishable materials—hay, wood, and stubble; and three imperishable materials—gold, silver, and precious stones.

When we build with our plans, ambition, and desires, we are building with hay, wood, and stubble. When the Holy Spirit builds, He uses gold, silver, and precious stones—that which conforms us to the image of Christ and brings glory to Himself.

One day we will stand before the Lord and our lives will pass His scrutiny. We will each have to give an account of what we have done with our life. As it goes through the test of fire, the hay, wood, and stubble will be burned, leaving the gold, silver, and precious stones.

What kind of superstructure are we building on our foundation? Hay, wood, and stubble? Or gold, silver, and precious stones? The choice is ours.

June
23

As the hart pants and longs for the water brooks, so I pant and long for you, O God. My inner self thirsts for God, for the living God. When shall I come and behold the face of God? (Ps. 42:1-2, Amplified).

The writer of this Psalm tells of the longing of his innermost being for God. He uses the illustration of a deer craving water to quench its thirst, perhaps after having been pursued almost to the point of exhaustion. As the deer craves water, so the soul thirsts after God.

Someone has called this Scripture passage, "The Pursuit of God." The heart of man is created in such a way by God that we are incomplete until He occupies His rightful place in our lives. Augustine said, "Thou hast made us for thyself, O God, and our hearts are restless till they find rest in thee." The desire of the writer of this Psalm was not for pleasures, people, or position, for they do not quench the inner thirst of the heart. Only God can do this. His desire was for a new and deeper awareness of the reality of God Himself in his life.

God allows circumstances to come that create a longing in our hearts for Him. The dark times and trials of life, when God seems so far away, can develop a greater hunger and thirst after His presence. As the longing of the heart is satisfied by God's presence, there will be the satisfaction of contentment in Him.

This cry was voiced in Psalm 73:25. "Whom have I in heaven but THEE? And there is none upon earth that I desire beside thee." His heart had complete satisfaction in the Lord.

What is the desire of your heart today? Are you longing for a closer walk with Him? Does your innermost being cry out for the reality of God Himself? Sometimes we stop at the blessings and experiences, so we miss the Blesser. The blessings and experiences should lead us to God Himself. As we drink deeply of the Water of Life, our thirst will be quenched and we will be completely satisfied with Him.

"There is NONE upon earth that I desire but THEE."

After these things the word of the Lord came unto Abram in a vision, saying, "Fear not, Abram: I am thy shield, and thy exceeding great reward (Gen. 15:1).

When Abraham's nephew, Lot, was captured, he and his band of armed servants delivered Lot. Abraham refused to take any of the reward from the king of Sodom, for his dependence was on God, and not on a human king.

It was "after these things" that God revealed Himself to Abraham in a special way. Perhaps he had become fearful. He had defeated King Chedorlaomer, making him a bitter foe. The king might decide to attack Abraham next. He may have had a feeling of discouragement. Sometimes this is a natural reaction after a time of victory. Also, God had promised him that he would have a son and that the land would become his. These promises had not been fulfilled. Had God forgotten? Didn't God care? Would God keep His promise?

God spoke to him, saying, "Fear not, Abram." It was God's promise of PEACE for Abraham. It was as if He were saying, "Don't let your heart be filled with fear. You can have peace, for I am your peace."

God also promised Abraham His POWER. "I am thy shield." Abraham didn't live within the security of a walled city. He was open to attacks of the enemy. God promised to be his shield, protecting him from danger.

God promised Abraham the sufficiency of His PRESENCE. "I am thy exceeding great reward." What a reward, to have fellowship with God Himself.

God knows that sometimes we, too, need an encouraging word. In time of anxiety He says, "Don't fear, I am YOUR peace; don't faint, I am YOUR power; I will protect you from danger and from the onslaughts of the enemy; don't falter, for MY presence is with YOU; I am your great reward."

What more can we want today, whatever our need, than to have His peace, His power, and His presence.

June

25

As the rain and snow come down from heaven and stay upon the ground to water the earth, and cause the grain to grow and to produce seed for the farmer and bread for the hungry, so also is my Word. I send it out and it always produces fruit. It shall accomplish all I want it to, and prosper everywhere I send it (Isa. 55:10-11, LB).

The going forth of the Word of God is compared to the rain and snow falling on the earth, watering it and making it fruitful. It will not return void, but will accomplish God's purpose for its going forth. It has been called "God's Guided Missile."

Dr. Malan of Geneva was taking a trip to Paris one day. He began a conversation with a man who started to reason with him about Christianity. Each time the man presented an argument, Dr. Malan used the Word itself in answer. The man would evade the Scripture but give another argument. Again Dr. Malan would answer with God's Word.

Years passed. One morning Dr. Malan received a letter from this man. He said, "Years ago you used God's Word with me and every time I answered, you again used the Word until I felt I was fighting not you, but God. Now I am a Christian."

When the seed of God's Word is sown in our lives, it accomplishes God's purpose as it produces the fruit of His Spirit within. It gives guidance and direction.

Not only has God promised a harvest from His Word planted in our hearts, but as we scatter it in the world about us it will accomplish all He had in mind. He will make it productive wherever He sends it.

One time a noted evangelist was to hold meetings in England. In testing the accoustics of the building, he quoted a verse of Scripture at the top of his voice. Later he learned that a workman on a scaffold high up near the ceiling had heard the verse and had become a Christian.

Are you one of God's seed sowers, sharing His Word with others? God has promised that as we sow, He will produce the harvest.

For I believe God, that it shall be even as it was told me (Acts. 27:25).

Paul was traveling by ship to Rome when a great storm arose. The ship was driven off course. The storm hid the sun during the day and the moon and stars at night. Everything possible was cast overboard, but to no avail. They said, "All hope that we should be saved was then taken away" (Acts 27:20).

Though all human effort had failed, Paul said, "Be of good cheer." Could they be of good cheer when they might lose their lives? Paul continued, "There shall be no loss of any man's life among you, but of the ship" (v. 22). Paul knew the "Great Encourager," the One who can keep our spirits up in the midst of the storm.

Then Paul gave the reason why he could be cheerful. He states his deep faith in God. "Wherefore, sirs, be of good cheer: for I BELIEVE GOD, that it shall be even as it was told me" (v. 25). He was in such close communication with God that God could reveal His will to Paul. God had promised Paul that their lives would be spared and Paul believed it, just as God had told him. Paul's belief was not in SOMETHING, but in SOMEONE, God Himself. It is easy to believe God when everything is going smoothly, but Paul could trust Him in the midst of a fierce storm. Paul's faith was based on God's Word to him—"even as it was told me."

There are storms that rage in the world today, not on oceans and seas, but in hearts and lives of people. Perhaps you are in a storm today. As you face it, you, too, can meet it with the same strong faith in God that Paul had. As we keep our communication line open with the Lord, He can share His words of promise we need in our time of storm.

Are you keeping close enough to the Lord in your storm that you can face it with complete assurance and trust as Paul did, saying, ". . . for I believe GOD, that it shall be even as it was told me"?

June
27

Speaking to yourselves in psalms and hymns and spiritual songs, singing and making melody in your heart to the Lord (Eph. 5:19).

Have you experienced a day when you had the "blues"? You seemed weighed down with the cares of life? Suddenly you heard someone singing or whistling and your spirits were lifted. What therapy music is!

When Jesus Christ enters a heart, along with a new relationship comes a new song. It may not be an outward song, but it is a song of joy that comes from the heart. Even though we may not be able to sing aloud, the inward song of the heart will lift our spirits and the melody of it will catch the ear of the listening God.

The hearts of the early Christians were full of song because the presence of the Savior was so real in their lives. Paul and Silas were able to sing this song when in prison. "And at midnight Paul and Silas prayed, and SANG PRAISES unto God: and the prisoners heard them" (Acts 16:25).

We are to make melody to the LORD. This turns the eyes of our heart on Him. It keeps us thinking of Him. One of the blessings of the Christian faith is that it enables Christians to sing under all circumstances. Our song of the heart comes from the confidence we have of knowing God is adequate in spite of outward circumstances and He is in control regardless of our situation.

Every Christian should have a song of joy overflowing from the heart as a fountain of joy.

Are you a member of the heavenly "singing company"? Is your heart singing and making melody to the Lord? If not, begin singing even though you may not feel like it. Soon His song will well up and overflow from your life, blessing those about you. "O for a thousand tongues to sing my great redeemer's praise; the glories of my God and King, the triumphs of His grace."

"Speak out to one another in psalms and hymns and spiritual songs, offering praise with voices [and instruments], making melody with ALL your HEART to the LORD" (Eph. 5:19, *Amplified*).

There hath no temptation taken you but such as is common to man: but God is faithful, who will not suffer you to be tempted above that ye are able; but will with the temptation also make a way to escape, that ye may be able to bear it (1 Cor. 10:13).

In the automobile industry, before new models of cars are put on the market, they must undergo rigid tests on proving grounds. The manufacturers want to be sure that changes made and new features added will stand up under all driving conditions. They are not tested to make them fail, but to prove their endurance and to discover weaknesses.

When I first became a Christian I was surprised that I continued to have problems and temptations. Then I discovered I was not alone in this. Other Christians had similar experiences. I learned that God had a way of victory for me in and through them.

There is a two-fold meaning of "temptation" in Scripture. The same Greek word is used for both temptation and testing. A definition often given for temptation is "yielding to that which is wrong and contrary to God's purpose," and it does have that meaning. Such temptations come from Satan, not from God. However, God allows testings and trials to come into our lives to prove us and to develop a strong Christian character.

We are not the only ones undergoing testings. Even though all our temptations are not the same, none is exempt from them.

Wuest has said, "God in His wisdom plans the test, and limits the temptation. God in His love sends the test, and permits the temptation. God in His grace meets the test and overcomes the temptation."

God has provided a way of escape in the person of Jesus Christ. In our weakness, He is strong; in our temptations He is all-powerful; in our testings He is victorious.

"For because He Himself [in His humanity] has suffered in being tempted (tested and tried), He is able (immediately) to run to the cry of (assist, relieve) those who are being tempted and tested and tried [and who therefore are being exposed to suffering]" (Heb. 2:18, *Amplified*).

June

29

Whereupon, O King Agrippa, I was not disobedient unto the heavenly vision (Acts 26:19).

Paul was on trial before King Agrippa, defending himself for the sake of the gospel. He recounts to King Agrippa how his life had been completely transformed; how he, Saul, the persecuter of Christians, became Paul, an apostle of Jesus Christ.

His "heavenly vision" of Christ came when he was traveling on the Damascus road. That day his personal experience with Him was so real that he committed his life completely to Jesus as Savior and Lord. "I know whom I have believed, and am persuaded that he is able to keep that which I have committed unto him against that day" (2 Tim. 1:12).

Then he had a "heavenly vision" of the ministry God had called him to. He said, "Lord, what wilt thou have me to do?" The Lord replied, "I am going to send you to the Gentiles to open their eyes to their true condition so that they may repent and live in the light of God instead of in Satan's darkness" (Acts 26:17-18, LB). The persecutor now became the defender of the very faith he had sought to destroy.

His life and ministry became centered in the Lord Jesus Christ. He said, "For to me to live is Christ" (Phil. 1:21). He had no aim or purpose but that which the Lord Jesus had for him.

Now, after long years of hardship, suffering, and danger, he was called before the king to give account of his life. As the result of a fruitful ministry for the LORD, he could say to the king, "I was not disobedient to the heavenly vision."

Have you had a heavenly vision of Christ? Only as He fills your vision can you have the heavenly vision of His ministry for your life. Paul said, "For I am determined not to know anything among you save Jesus, and Him crucified."

Oswald Chambers said, "It is essential to practice the walk of the feet in the light of the vision."

May each of us be able to say as Paul did, "I was not disobedient to the heavenly vision."

And he removed from thence unto a mountain on the east of Bethel, and pitched his tent, having Bethel on the west, and Hai on the east: and there he builded an altar unto the Lord, and called upon the name of the Lord (Gen. 12:8).

When God called Abraham to Canaan, he became a "pilgrim," living in a tent the rest of his life. He could not become too deeply attached to any place, for he had to be ready to move at God's command. "It was faith that kept him journeying like a foreigner through the land of promise, with no more HOME than the TENTS" (Heb. 11:9, *Phillips*).

Abraham was not concerned with earthly possessions, but by faith he looked to a life beyond. "For he was waiting expectantly and confidently, looking forward to the city which has fixed and firm foundations, whose Architect and Builder is God" (Heb. 11:10, *Amplified*).

Abraham built an altar wherever he pitched his tent. He was not only a pilgrim, but a worshiper. Worship and communion with God had priority in his life. He made room in his life for God.

We, too, are pilgrims on this journey of life. "For this world is not our home; we are looking forward to our everlasting home in heaven" (Heb. 13:14, LB).

As earthly pilgrims, we, too, must live "tent lives," ready to move at God's will. Sometimes He has to uproot us, moving us to a new place to prevent our becoming too attached to our present surroundings. He may move our "tent" to a new city, a new place of employment, a new neighborhood.

Not only are we pilgrims, but also worshipers. We must build an altar wherever we pitch our tents, giving God place in our lives. We must take time to worship Him. One definition of worship is "being occupied with God." It is easy to become so engrossed with earthly things we forget to take time to be occupied with Him. Wherever we live, we must give Him place in our lives. "That in all things he might have the preeminence" (Col. 1:18).

Does God have room in your life? In all of it? Or only part?

July

1

Then Jesus turned, and saw two following, and saith unto them, What seek ye? (John 1:38).

One day Jesus saw two men following Him. He turned to them, asking, "What seek ye?" It could have been to satisfy their curiosity. Or they may have wanted to know more about Him.

He invited them to spend the day with Him. We are not told what they talked about, but when they returned, Andrew said, "We have found the Messiah." His search was fulfilled in Jesus Christ.

If the Lord were to ask us today, "What seek ye?" what would our answer be? Are we seeking material things, a new home, new furniture, a new car, pleasures, fame, social position? Many of these things are attractive, many are good. Yet we have to confess they have not brought the satisfaction we expected. We are still longing for something more, something we do not have. Only inner peace and fulfillment, not material possessions, bring satisfaction.

There was once a young girl who had a strand of pearls which she treasured very much. One evening when her father came home, he asked her if she would give him her pearls. Although they were only imitation, she prized them highly. How could she part with them? As her father continued to hold out his hand, she quietly considered his request.

Finally she slowly went to her room for her pearls. As she returned, she dropped them into his hand. Then he reached his hand into his pocket, drawing out a box which he placed in her hand. As she opened it, she gazed on a beautiful strand of real pearls.

What are you seeking today? Satisfaction from material things? Satisfaction from that which is just an imitation? True satisfaction will never come from things that have only earthly value.

Only in Jesus Christ will you find that which has eternal value. Complete fulfillment comes not from possessions, but from a Person, Jesus Christ.

"What seek YE?" God promises, "And YE shall seek ME, and find me, when ye shall search for me with ALL your heart" (Jer. 29:13).

I will very gladly spend and be spent (2 Cor. 12:15).

The Lord Jesus had demonstrated His willingness to spend and be spent for a needy world while He was on earth. "Even as the Son of man came not to be ministered unto, but to minister, and to give His life a ransom for many" (Matt. 20:28). Jesus was interested in everyone from the learned Nicodemus to the most loathsome leper.

After Paul met Jesus Christ on the Damascus road, the love of Christ was so shed abroad in his heart that his one aim was to spend his life in service for Jesus Christ. "Whatever we do, it is certainly not for our own profit, but because Christ's love controls us now" (2 Cor. 5:14, LB).

Paul identified himself with Christ's concern for the spiritual needs of people. There were no limits to his expendability. "I am glad to give you MYSELF and all I have to help you grow." He longed to see them mature spiritually. Someone has said that Paul was saying in effect, "I live so that Jesus Christ can help Himself to my life at any moment for any purpose."

We do not become an isolated island when we become Christians. We do not box ourselves in, having no contact with the outside world. As the Spirit of God begins to move upon our hearts we have the same concern and compassion Jesus had for others.

What a goal—to be selfless, to be so expendable! Are we expendable for Christ in this day when there are so many people with needs? Are we willing to give ourselves to minister to them? Can we say as Paul did, "But I will most gladly spend and be utterly spent [myself] for your souls" (2 Cor. 12:15, *Amplified*)?

Perhaps some of our trials and heartaches have been allowed to bring us to the place of selflessness so that we might be more expendable for others.

It is not just giving money and material things to others, but ourselves, our love, our concern, our interest in them as individuals.

Can we say, "My time, strength, talent, my all, are available for God to use to expend on others"?

July

3

If my people, which are called by my name, shall humble themselves, and pray, and seek my face, and turn from their wicked ways; then will I hear from heaven, and will forgive their sin, and will heal their land" (2 Chron. 7:14).

We are living in a day when our world is on the brink of upheaval. World leaders are seeking solutions for the complex problems they face.

In the above Scripture verse we have a divine prescription for the remedy of international as well as personal needs.

God's prescription begins with God's people. "If MY people, which are called by MY name . . ." They hold the key to spiritual awakening in the world today.

Our lives are to be characterized by humility, prayer, seeking God's face, and repentance. This will bring God's attention to our cry, forgiveness of sin, and health for our land.

Throughout the history of our world, many times Christians have interceded with God in behalf of their country and its leaders. God heard and answered their prayers.

In the summer of 1776 the Founding Fathers of the United States were having difficulty in completing plans for forming the thirteen colonies into a nation. Although many plans were suggested, none seemed right. In the midst of their debate, Benjamin Franklin was asked his opinion. Hesitating a moment, he slowly arose and delivered a brief but powerful talk based on Psalm 127:1, "except the Lord build the house, they labour in vain that build it." Then he said, "Gentlemen, everything we have tried so far has failed. Why don't we try prayer?" They paused for a time of prayer. From then on a spirit of unity prevailed.

Prayer has changed the course of history in the past. It can do the same today. In Isaiah 1:9 we read, "Except the Lord of hosts had left unto us a very small remnant, we should have been as Sodom, and we should have been like unto Gomorrah."

Our greatest weapon against Satan is prayer. What a privilege God has entrusted to us, the privilege of bringing to Him the needs of our world, our communities, ourselves.

A small remnant of praying people can change the course of world history.

If the Son therefore shall make you free, ye shall be free indeed (John 8:36).

Freedom is a great heritage of our land. One of the great freedoms upon which our country was founded is the freedom of worshiping God according to our own desires. The famous Gettysburg Address includes, "that this nation, under God, shall have a new birth of freedom—and that government of the people, by the people, for the people, shall not perish from the earth."

However, it may be possible to accept our freedom—we may appreciate our freedom to worship and serve God—yet miss the reality of a personal freedom within.

What is true freedom? Some may answer, "Freedom of worship, freedom of speech, freedom from want, freedom from fear." Yet many people enjoy these blessings who have not experienced true freedom. True freedom is found in Jesus Christ. "And ye shall know the truth, and the truth shall make you free . . . . If the Son therefore shall make you free, ye shall be free indeed" (John 8:32,36).

True freedom is to be set free from the guilt of sin through the atoning work of Jesus Christ on the cross. "For God sent not his Son into the world to condemn the world; but that the world through him might be saved. . . . he that believeth not is condemned already, because he hath not believed in the name of the only begotten Son of God" (John 3:17-18).

Not only are we freed from the guilt of sin but from its very power in our lives. "In the same way look upon yourselves as dead to the appeal and power of sin but alive to God through Christ Jesus our Lord . . . . For sin can never be your master—you are no longer living under the Law, but under grace" (Rom. 6:13-14, *Phillips*).

We have the promise that if we let the Son make us free, we will be free indeed. Paul wrote, "Now the Lord is that Spirit: and where the Spirit of the Lord is, there is liberty" (2 Cor. 3:17). As we let the Spirit of God control our lives, we will have real liberty. We will be free—free indeed.

July
5

Commit thy works unto the Lord, and thy thoughts shall be established (Prov. 16:3).

Many times we face the uncertainty of knowing God's will for a particular need. It may be a decision we must make. It may be a solution to an impossible problem.

We may say, "If only someone could make the decision for me." "If someone could tell me what to do."

It is a relief, releasing the pressure and relaxing the tension in our lives, to know that we have Someone Who CAN make our decisions and solve our problems for us.

How wonderful it is to commit every detail of our lives to God; our plans, our needs, our problems, everything that touches us. As we commit them to Him, they become His details, His plans, His work. "Commit your way to the Lord—roll and repose [each care of] your load on Him; trust, lean on, rely on and be confident also in Him, and He will bring it to pass" (Ps. 37:5, *Amplified*).

As we commit ourselves and our plans for our day to Him, our thoughts are brought into agreement with His will and our plans become His plans. "Roll your works upon the Lord—commit and trust them wholly to Him; [He will cause your thoughts to become agreeable to His will, and] so shall your plans be established and succeed" (Prov. 16:3, *Amplified*).

As we commit our works to Him, we no longer choose the outcome, but leave it with Him. "We can make our plans, but the final outcome is in God's hands" (Prov. 16:1, LB). This means we must not try to get His approval of OUR plans, but accept HIS. In the *Living Bible* we read, "We can always 'prove' that we are right, but is the Lord convinced?" (v. 2).

He doesn't want our plans, but our lives, so He can work His plans through us. As our minds become agreeable to His, we experience peace. "Thou wilt keep Him in perfect peace, whose mind is stayed on thee: because He trusteth in thee" (Isa. 26:3).

"A man's mind plans his way, but the Lord directs his steps and makes them sure" (Prov. 16:9, *Amplified*).

I will sing to the Lord as long as I live. I will praise God to my last breath (Ps. 104:33, LB).

"Whistling in the Dark" was once a popular song. There is a real truth in the title. We have discovered from experience that "Whistling in the dark" can lift our spirits in our night watches. When discouraged and dejected, music can encourage and strengthen our hearts.

Music has an important place in the Christian life. In the Old Testament, singers were especially appointed to serve God in His sanctuary. In the New Testament, Paul wrote of a "singing company." "As you converse among yourselves in psalms and hymns and spiritual songs, heartily SINGING and making your music TO THE LORD" (Eph. 5:19, *Berkeley*).

When Jesus Christ becomes our personal Savior, He gives us a new song. "He has given me a new song to sing, of PRAISES to our God" (Ps. 40:3, LB).

Then the psalmist says, "I will sing as long as I live." On the bright days and the dark days, the sad and the happy days, the easy and the difficult days, we will sing to the Lord. In Job 35:10 we read, "Where is God my Maker, who giveth songs in the night?" We can have a lifetime of singing to Him.

Then the psalmist says, "I will praise God to my last breath." Today our hearts may be heavy. Our song may be gone. Praising God is an effective way of bringing back our song. The song of the heart, even though weak, catches the listening ear of God. Our spirits are lifted and our hearts overflow with joy. There can be a lifetime of praise to Him.

He says, "My meditation of him shall be sweet" (Ps. 104:34). Real meditation is thinking of HIM.

Then He says, "I will be glad in the Lord." The rest of our days, our lifetime, we can be glad in the Lord.

"I will bless the Lord at all times: His praise shall continually be in my mouth" (Ps. 34:1).

July 7

O how love I thy law! it is my meditation all the day" (Ps. 119:97).

What a privilege we have of being able to read the Word of God. Most of us have a number of copies of the Bible in our homes. We are reminded in the above verse that we are not only to read it but meditate on it.

One definition for the word "meditation" is "to think in view of doing." According to this definition, how much real meditation do we do? Do we hurriedly read the Bible as a habit, not thinking of what we are reading? Do we read it as a duty, because we think as a Christian we should? Or do we pause as we read it, meditating upon it with the view of appropriating it into our lives?

As we read and meditate on it, we need to assimilate it, digesting it that we may be nourished and grow by it. "As newborn babes, desire the sincere milk of the word, that ye may grow thereby" (1 Peter 2:2).

Not only are we to assimilate it for growth, but to practice it in our everyday lives. "But be ye DOERS of the Word, and not hearers only" (James 1:22).

David meditated on God's Word because he loved it, and he loved it because he meditated on it. He couldn't get enough of it. He meditated "all the day." It is important to be regular in spending time in His Word. We need to keep our minds saturated with it.

Paul challenged Timothy, "Meditate upon these things; give thyself wholly to them; that thy profiting may appear to all" (1 Tim. 4:15).

Meditation is not something we can do hurriedly. The Lord Jesus Christ is revealed to us from the pages of the Bible. Our meditation is to lead us from the Word of God to HIM. We are to consider HIM. Such meditation on Him brings us to our knees in humility and praise. Our hearts overflow with love.

With the psalmist we can say, "My meditation of HIM shall be sweet: I will be glad in the Lord " (Ps. 104:34).

He has enriched your whole life. He has helped you speak out for him and has given you a full understanding of the truth" (1 Cor. 1:5, LB).

How rich we are in Christ! As Christians, our whole lives are enriched in Him. "But God! So rich is He in His mercy!" (Eph. 2:4, *Amplified*). "He did this that He might clearly demonstrate through the ages to come the immeasurable (limitless, surpassing) riches of His free grace (His unmerited favor) in kindness and goodness of heart toward us in Christ Jesus" (v. 7).

Paul wrote, "In EVERYTHING ye are enriched by Him." We are enriched by Him not only through times of ease and prosperity, but in the dark days. We are enriched through each circumstance and experience of our lives.

But our lives are not enriched just for our own use. He has promised to "help us" speak out for Him. We are a vital part of His communication system which takes the Gospel to the entire world. We have a message, His message, to share with others. We have a life, His life, to live before others.

Our lives are enriched by His wisdom and understanding. The Holy Spirit has been given to us to reveal His truth to us. "But I will send you the Comforter—the Holy Spirit, the source of all truth. He will come to you from the Father and will tell you all about ME" (John 15:26, LB). What an enrichment that is—"will tell you all about ME." The Holy Spirit, the source of all truth, makes our Lord real to us. Through the Holy Spirit we "grow in grace, and in the knowledge of our Lord and Saviour Jesus Christ" (2 Peter 3:18).

How rich we are today! ALL of His resources are available for our use. He empowers us to speak for Him. He increases our knowledge of Himself. Each circumstance that has entered our lives has made us richer. "In everything ye are enriched by Him."

"Though he was rich, yet for your sakes he became poor, that ye through his poverty might be rich" (2 Cor. 8:9).

July
9

The Lord upholdeth all that fall, and raiseth up all those that be bowed down (Ps. 145:14).

David had known God for a long time. He had seen His handiwork in the world about him. David had often communed with God. Many times he had experienced His loving and protecting care.

In this Psalm, David's heart overflows in praise to God. "I will praise You, my God and King, and bless Your name each day and forever" (v. 1, LB). He cannot comprehend the greatness of God. He says, "Great is Jehovah! Greatly praise Him! His greatness is beyond discovery!" (v. 3).

He rejoices in the personal concern of this same God for His own children. "The Lord upholds all those [of His own] who are falling, and raises up all those who are bowed down" (v. 14, *Amplified*). "The Lord lifts the fallen and those bent beneath their loads" (v. 14, LB).

What an encouragement it is to us to know that the God whom David praises for His greatness and goodness is ever mindful of us. Today He is personally concerned for you and me. He feels with us the grief we are experiencing. When our burdens almost overwhelm us, He is waiting to uphold us, and raise us up. He is always near to comfort and strengthen.

From His open hand He provides for our needs. "The eyes of all wait for You—looking, watching, and expecting; and You give them their food in due season. You open Your hand, and satisfy every living thing with favor" (vv. 15-16, *Amplified*).

One day a little boy was in a grocery store. The owner told him to reach in the case and take a handful of candy. The little fellow hesitated. Then the man reached in, took a handful and gave it to the boy. Later, the boy said to his mother, "I knew his hand was bigger than mine."

David closed the Psalm with, "My mouth shall speak the praise of the Lord, and let all flesh bless—affectionately and gratefully praise—His holy name for ever and ever" (v. 21, *Amplified*).

Blessed are they which do hunger and thirst after righteousness: for they shall be filled (Matt. 5:6).

What do we do if we are hungry? We eat. What do we do when we are thirsty? We take a drink.

Jesus used the everyday experience of eating and drinking to illustrate a spiritual desire. Jesus said, "Blessed are they which do hunger and thirst after righteousness."

Very little happiness is registered on the faces of people today. An emptiness in their lives has not been filled, and they are hungering and thirsting for something more than what they have. The accumulation of things, material possessions, or attainment of position in society cannot satisfy the heart. "Happy are those who are hungry and thirsty for true goodness, for they will be FULLY SATISFIED!" (Matt. 5:6, *Phillips*).

This verse promises that our inner hunger and thirst can be filled, but only filled with the righteousness of God. Phillips calls it the "goodness of God." Righteousness is being right with God. It is being right with God through Jesus Christ. In 1 Corinthians 1:30 we read of Christ that "He is made unto us . . . righteousness."

Some fill their lives with possessions, homes, family, clothes, bank accounts, fame, talent. But none of these things satisfy. Satisfaction and fulfillment come to those who fill their lives with the righteousness (or goodness) that only God gives.

The psalmist wrote, "O God, thou art my God; early will I seek thee; my soul thirsteth for thee" (Ps. 63:1).

Paul reviewed his life, sharing that which gave it reality and satisfaction when he said, "Yea doubtless, and I count all things but loss for the excellency of the knowledge of Christ Jesus my Lord: for whom I have suffered the loss of all things, and do count them but dung, that I may win Christ" (Phil. 3:8).

Only in turning to Him can our lives be fully satisfied. Jesus said, "I am the Bread of life: he that cometh to ME shall never hunger; and he that believeth on ME shall never thirst" (John 6:35).

Are you hungering for peace and contentment? Are you longing for joy and satisfaction? Then let Him fill you with Himself today.

"O taste and see that the Lord is good" (Ps. 34:8).

July
11

Now as soon as it was day, there was no small stir among the soldiers, what was become of Peter (Acts 12:18).

Peter had been taken prisoner by King Herod. His time of execution had been set. There seemed no way out—but there was a way up. Peter's friends gathered in earnest, unceasing prayer for him.

Peter had been put under strong security guard. He was even chained to two of the guards. Humanly speaking, he was beyond help. "BUT GOD." Two small words, but what they can mean in a life! "BUT GOD." With Him all things are possible.

What was Peter doing that night in prison? Even though his execution was near, he was sleeping. Peter was trusting the Lord.

Suddenly, at almost the last moment, an angel of the Lord appeared to Peter to lead him safely out of prison. As Peter followed the angel, each door opened before them until they were past the iron gate leading to the city.

He made his way to the home where his friends were gathered in prayer for him. A young girl, Rhoda, went to the door in response to his knock. Hearing his voice, she hurried back to share the good news with the others. Only when they saw him with their own eyes could they believe his miraculous deliverance.

In the meantime, what was happening when Peter's escape was discovered? ". . . there was no small stir among the soldiers, what was become of Peter." How shocked they must have been to learn their prisoner had disappeared.

"No small stir"—as the result of prayer Peter was miraculously delivered. There was "no small stir" in the city because a group of believers met together in united prayer.

What is happening today as the result of your prayers and mine? Is there "no small stir" because we have prayed? Someone has said, "Earthshaking events are caused by heaven-moving prayers."

"The effectual fervent prayer of a righteous man availeth much" (James 5:16).

The Lord will give strength unto his people; the Lord will bless His people with peace (Ps. 29:11).

A popular song we used to sing is entitled "Stormy Weather." In Psalm 29 David reminds us that we may encounter "stormy weather" experiences in our lives.

During these turbulent times we need a security strong enough to carry us through.

Throughout Psalm 29 one phrase, "the voice of the Lord," is repeated several times. We are told the meaning of the name "Lord" in this Psalm is said to be, "He (Who) is."

As the storms come, we can be assured that "He Who is" is in them, going through them with us even though we may not see Him.

He allows the storm so that we may learn necessary lessons and so that He may give us opportunities to be brought into a closer walk with Him. Even our obedience to Him may lead us into a storm.

His resources are adequate and His promises sure. He has promised us a limitless supply of strength, a strength equal to our needs. It comes from waiting upon the Lord. "They that wait upon the Lord shall renew their strength" (Isa. 40:31). It is said that as a storm approaches, the eagle is the only bird that will not seek shelter. He faces the storm, and with wings spread, allows the storm to carry him to higher heights. So, as God draws near in the storm, He lifts us by His strength to higher spiritual heights.

Not only are we given strength to go through the storm, but a tranquil heart and mind in the fury of the storm. The peace He gives is a part of the fruit of the Spirit. It is a supernatural calm produced by the Holy Spirit.

The "God Who is" is with us today, with His provision of strength and peace. Why be weak when we have His strength? Why be troubled when we have His peace?

Someone has said, "The strength of the Lord enables us to bear the pressure of the storm; the peace of God keeps the disturbing elements of the outer storm from penetrating our inner being."

July
13

But as we were allowed of God to be put in trust with the gospel, even so we speak; not as pleasing men, but God, which trieth our hearts (1 Thess. 2:4).

One day a man came to the door asking the woman of the house for some food. She had little food on hand but told him if he would go to the store for her, she would feed him. She gave him a five dollar bill and sent him for some hamburger. Would he return? In a short time he was back with the meat and the change.

As he thanked her, he said, "It wasn't your feeding me that touched me most. It was your confidence in trusting me with the five dollar bill."

God has entrusted something very special to us, the Gospel. Have we accepted it as a sacred trust from Him to us? His trust in us is great, for He has no other plan for reaching people for Himself.

Paul laid down some qualifications for our lives if we are to fulfill our God-given trust. First, our desire must be to please God. "We do not aim to please men, but to please God who knows us through and through" (1 Thess. 2:4, *Phillips*).

The Word of God needs to be our Book of instructions and inspiration. "The Word of God, which is effectually at work in you who believe—exercising its (superhuman) power in those who adhere to and trust in and rely on it" (v. 13, *Amplified*).

Our walk must be worthy of the one Whom we serve. "To live lives worthy of God" (v. 12, *Amplified*).

We need love and concern for those with whom we serve. "But we behaved gently when we were among you, like a devoted mother nursing and cherishing her own children" (v. 7, *Amplified*).

Paul reminded them that his reward (and ours) will be the souls in heaven because we have been faithful to our trust of the Gospel.

"For what is our hope or happiness or our victor's wreath of exultant triumph when we stand in the presence of our Lord Jesus at His coming? Are not you? For you are [indeed] our glory and our joy!" (vv. 19-20, *Amplified*).

And they said, We saw certainly that the Lord was with thee (Gen. 26:28).

Isaac lived a quiet, rather uneventful life. During a time of famine he moved to Gerar. The scarcity of water made it a valuable commodity. Wells were essential for the flocks and herds.

Because Isaac had a real need for water for his flocks, he began opening up the wells his father had previously dug. However, the Philistines claimed them as fast as he had them opened. Instead of retaliating and fighting for them, he relinquished his rights and moved on. He became a peacemaker.

Later, Abimelech came to make a treaty with Isaac. He said, "We saw certainly that the Lord was with thee." What more wonderful thing could be said of a person than that the Lord could be seen in his life! Abimelech, his former enemy, wanted a peaceful relationship with Isaac because he could see God's blessing on his life.

What is the influence of your life in the world today? Can your friends and loved ones, your neighbors and those with whom you work, see the Lord in your life?

Isaac was an ordinary person, but he did not have an ordinary God. The Philistines were impressed with Isaac because they could see the God of Isaac in his life. We may feel we are just ordinary people, with no great influence for God. But our lives can become extraordinary as we allow God to reveal Himself to others through them.

Spurgeon said, "The best life of Christ is His living biography written out in the words and actions of His people, so that it is said of them, 'They have been with Jesus; they have been taught of Him; they are like Him.'"

Gordon Maxwell, a missionary to India, asked a Hindu Pundit to teach him the language. The Hindu replied, "No, sahib, I will not teach you the language. You would make me a Christian." "Oh, you misunderstand me," Mr. Maxwell answered. "I am only asking you to teach me your language." The Hindu replied, "No, sahib, I will not teach you. No one could live with you and not become a Christian."

July 15

Enlarge the place of thy tent, and let them stretch forth the curtains of thine habitations; spare not, lengthen thy cords, and strengthen thy stakes (Isa. 54:2).

Many people today are searching for something to fill the emptiness in their lives. They say, "I'm searching for an answer to life. I have tried everything." Not long ago at a large airport, a fine skycap helped me with my luggage. I handed him a little booklet, "Life Has an Answer," along with my tip. "Do you have that answer?" I questioned. "No," he replied, "but I am trying to find it."

It has been said, "The tragedy of this generation is that there are untold millions still untold." "Where there is no vision the people perish" (Prov. 29:18). Today God is giving us many opportunities to enlarge the "place of our tent" to reach many of these millions for Himself.

As we stretch forth the curtains of our habitation, our vision will include women who are frustrated, discouraged, defeated, feeling no one cares; men who are caught in the pressures and temptations of the business world; young people and children who are wanting something real.

We are told to lengthen the cords. Cords of love and compassion in our lives must be lengthened to dear people all about us for whom Christ died. We are to minister to them in Christ's stead.

Not only are cords to be lengthened from our lives, but the stakes of our lives must be strengthened. We need the strong stake of faith—taking God at His Word and believing He means just what He says. The stake of God's Word must be anchored deep within. Prayer must be a strong stake. There must be stakes of submission and obedience.

The challenge for us in today's verse is in two words, "SPARE NOT." God "spared not." It cost Him a great price to provide eternal life for a lost mankind. "He that SPARED NOT his own Son, but delivered him up for us all" (Rom. 8:32).

Today are we willing to "SPARE NOT" our time, our talent, our possessions, our lives, our all, in behalf of those who need Him?

Cause me to hear thy lovingkindness in the morning; for in thee do I trust: cause me to know the way wherein I should walk; for I lift up my soul unto thee" (Ps. 143:8).

In the morning, when you waken, what is your response to the day? Do you want to turn over and go back to sleep? Are you grumpy? Does everything seem to be wrong? Or do you jump out of bed, ready for the day?

The psalmist gave a wonderful formula for beginning a new day. He said, "Cause ME to hear thy lovingkindness in the MORNING." We are to turn our thoughts to God first—THY lovingkindness. Do we begin the day thinking of God and His goodness to us? Or do we rush into His presence and out without becoming quiet enough to hear Him speak to us?

How different a day can be when we begin it with Him. The day may be dark and dreary, we may not feel well, we may be facing great problems and needs. But our spirits are lifted as we pause to praise and thank Him for His lovingkindness.

The psalmist reflects this as he says, "For I lift up my soul unto THEE." We read in Lamentations 3:22 and 23, "It is of the Lord's mercies that we are not consumed, because His compassions fail not. They are new EVERY MORNING: Great is thy faithfulness."

As we quietly wait before Him until we become confidently aware of His presence, we will be assured of His guidance for the day. "Cause me to know the WAY wherein I should WALK." We can hear His voice saying, "This is the way, walk ye in it, when ye turn to the right hand, and when ye turn to the left" (Isa. 30:21).

What an encouragement to know that the day doesn't depend on us, but on Him—hear Him. Neither does the way depend on us—walk with Him. "Let me see Your kindness to me in the morning, for I am trusting You. Show me where to walk, for my prayer is sincere" (Ps. 143:8, LB).

July 17

That Christ may dwell in your hearts by faith (Eph. 3:17).

We give casual friends limited freedom in our homes. Close friends are permitted into every part of it. But family members have rights and privileges reserved only for them.

The word "dwell" in this verse means to settle down and be at home. When Christ comes into our life as Savior He wants access to every area of it. "I am crucified with Christ: nevertheless I live; yet not I, but Christ liveth in me: and the life which I now live in the flesh I live by the faith of the son of God, who loved me, and gave himself for me" (Gal. 2:20).

Since we are His purchased possession, we should give Him His rightful place in our lives, letting Him have control. Paul wrote, "Haven't you yet learned that your body is the home of the Holy Spirit God gave you, and that he lives within you? Your own body does not belong to you. For God has bought you with a great price. So use every part of your body to give glory back to God, because he owns it" (1 Cor. 6:19-20, LB).

As His purchased possession, He has a right to use our lives in the way He desires. He has a right to use our time for Himself, our strength, our money, our talents, our family, our home, our business, our all.

Queen Victoria once visited a widow who lived near her summer home. This widow had a radiant love for Jesus Christ which some of her neighbors resented. After the queen's visit, her neighbors asked her, "Who is the most honored guest you have ever had?" They expected her to say "Jesus," but to their surprise she replied, "Her gracious Majesty the Queen." "But what about Jesus, the one you talk about so much? Isn't He your most honored Guest?" "Oh, no," she replied. "He is not a guest; He lives here."

Today is Christ really at home in your life or is He just a guest? Does He have freedom or limited access? Is your life available for Him to use wherever and whenever He desires?

What time I am afraid, I will trust in thee (Ps. 56:3).

David was always honest in his reactions to the circumstances of his life. He was willing to admit his weaknesses but he didn't concentrate on them. He took them to God and let Him meet them for him.

Fear was very real in his life. He didn't try to cover it, but confessed it. "What time I am afraid."

Today many fears fill our lives. We fear poverty, sickness, loneliness, death. We fear the dangers of the night and the pressures of the day.

David learned that the only way to be released from fears was to TRUST in the Lord. "What time I am afraid, I will trust in thee." He changed the focus of his eyes from his situation to the Lord. Faith replaced fear. He PUT his trust in the Lord. This was an act of his will. "In God have I put my trust: I will not be afraid what man can do unto me" (Ps. 56:11).

Freedom from fear is the result of confidence and trust in God. We may be helpless against fear, but God is not. When trusting God, there is nothing to fear.

Faith is more than believing what God can do. It is trust in the Person of God Himself. "But without faith it is impossible to please him: for he that cometh to God must believe that He IS, and that He is a rewarder of them that diligently seek Him" (Heb. 11:6).

When a person trusts God, He will not be afraid. "I will trust and not be afraid, for the Lord is my strength and song; He is my salvation" (Isa. 12:2, LB).

One day a father discovered his little boy had climbed an old tree. The limbs were beginning to break under the boy's weight. The father held up his arms and called, "Jump! I'll catch you." The little son considered the offer for a moment. Then, as more limbs began to break, he said, "Shall I let go of everything, Daddy, and trust you?"

What a lesson for us. Our heavenly Father wants us to let go of everything and trust Him.

July

19

And why beholdest thou the mote that is in thy brother's eye, but considerest not the beam that is in thine own eye? (Matt. 7:3)

If we are to be effective ambassadors for Jesus Christ, there must be consistency in our daily living. Jesus used an exaggerated illustration to emphasize the importance of our attitude toward others. He uses the comparison of a mote and a beam, which is like comparing a small splinter to a telephone pole. He reminds us that it is easy to see the mote in another's life, but overlook the beam in our own.

This is an exaggeration, of course; but it is no more so than amplifying the shortcomings in the life of another and overlooking and excusing larger ones in our own lives.

Jesus always condemned the sin of judging. "Judge not, that ye be not judged" (Matt. 7:1). Sometimes we make ourselves self-appointed judges. What right do we have to criticize someone whose fault may not be as serious as ours? Our own faults impair our spiritual vision so we cannot criticize constructively.

The habit of faultfinding may develop without our being aware of it. We may attribute wrong motives to the actions of others and be judgmental without knowing all the facts of the case. Usually we have insufficient information and are not wise enough to make a correct judgment. We need to be careful, for people can be injured by being misjudged. Occasionally characters have been shattered by such unfair and incorrect criticism or judgment.

We must guard against becoming hypocritical. Jesus said, "Thou hypocrite, first cast out the beam out of thine own eye; and then shalt thou see clearly to cast out the mote out of thy brother's eye" (Matt. 7:5).

Before we can help others, we must examine our own lives and be sure they are right in the sight of the Lord. We may discover we have a beam in our life instead of a mote.

Oswald Chambers said, "God never gives us the gift of discernment that we may criticize, but that we may intercede."

"Therefore all things whatsoever ye would that men should do to you, do ye even so to them" (v. 12).

Not slothful in business; fervent in spirit; serving the Lord (Rom. 12:11).

Do you know people who conduct their business so efficiently they are said to have an "eye for business"? Others are so haphazard you wonder how they are able to remain in business.

As Christians, we are "in business," the "greatest business in the world." We are in partnership with God to share the gospel of Jesus Christ. Regardless of whether we are serving in Christian or secular fields of activity, whatever we do should be done for Him. "And whatsoever ye do, do it heartily, as to the Lord" (Col. 3:23). Whether we are operating a typewriter, making beds, studying in school, or whatever it is, we should do it diligently as unto Him.

We are not to be half-hearted, lukewarm, lacking zeal in our service for Him. The Spirit said of the Laodician church, "I know thy works, that thou art neither cold nor hot: I would thou wert cold or hot. So then because thou art lukewarm, and neither cold nor hot, I will spue thee out of my mouth" (Rev. 3:15-16).

We should be enthusiastic in all we do for Him. One day after I had finished speaking at a meeting, a young homemaker came to me, saying, "I am so glad to hear someone who is excited about Jesus Christ."

It has been said, "As a bondslave, whose heart is captivated by the loving-kindness of his master, will perform devoted service far beyond the call of duty, so the Christian with fervency of spirit will serve the Lord."

Are we ready to go beyond the call of duty for Him? Or are we apathetic in our service? Have we lost the enthusiasm and love we used to know? Occasionally we hear of an epidemic of sleeping sickness. Is it possible that we might have "spiritual sleeping sickness"? If so, we should ask God to restore to our lives the joy and fervency we once had.

It is time to awake. It is time to avail ourselves of the opportunities that are before us to serve the Lord with quiet earnestness and enthusiasm of spirit.

July
21

Thou shalt call his name JESUS: for he shall save his people from their sins (Matt. 1:21).

What a common thing a name is. Some names are more common than others. Check in the telephone directory and count the number of Jones and Smiths listed. But let a personal interest or love become attached to a name, then a common and ordinary name is transformed into a very special and important one.

We are told that the name "Jesus" was a common name in the Holy Land at the time He lived on earth. But as He began His earthly ministry, His name took on importance. Crowds began following Him, desiring to see the one Who was performing miracles wherever He went.

But there was a deeper meaning attached to His name. "Thou shalt call his name Jesus; for he shall save his people from their sins" (Matt. 1:21). He came to earth to become the Savior of the world.

It is a SOVEREIGN NAME: "Wherefore God also hath highly exalted him, and given him a name which is above every name: That at the name of Jesus every knee should bow, of things in heaven, and things in earth, and things under the earth" (Phil. 2:9-10).

It is a POWERFUL NAME: "Neither is there salvation in any other: for there is none other name under heaven given among men, whereby we must be saved" (Acts 4:12).

It is an EVERLASTING NAME: "Thy name, O Lord, endureth for ever; and thy memorial, O Lord, throughout all generations" (Ps. 135:13).

We are bearers of that name, and must be careful that we bring honor to it. In the Song of Solomon 1:3 we read, "Because of the savour of thy good ointments thy name is as ointment poured forth." We are bearers of the ointment of His name. We bear it not to be confined in our lives, but to be poured forth as a sweet fragrance.

Today He is only a name to many. But to us who know and love Him, He is as precious ointment in our lives, ointment to be poured forth from our lives as a sweet savour of His presence.

But he knoweth the way that I take: when he hath tried me, I shall come forth as gold (Job 23:10).

In His Word, God has given some answers to the question, "Why does He allow His children to suffer?" He reminds us that we can expect trials along the way, but He will never let us suffer needlessly. There is always a divine purpose to be accomplished when He permits trouble to come.

He knows our way from the beginning to the end. "But he knows every detail of what is happening to me" (Job 23:10, LB). He knows the trying experiences we face. He concerns Himself with our pathway. "He pays attention to it" *(Amplified).*

Sometimes the Lord uses suffering to chasten His children. "For whom the Lord loveth He chasteneth" (Heb. 12:6). He proves His love by allowing trouble to come. Trials can bring correction and reproof to our lives.

The Lord, our Great Refiner, sometimes uses the fire of trouble to refine our lives. Fire does not harm gold, it only separates the impurities. God is never in a hurry as He works in our lives, for it takes time to process pure gold. He never leaves us in the fire longer than necessary, but watches over us carefully and lovingly, ready to turn off the heat when He sees the perfect reflection of His face in us.

What is your reaction to your suffering today? Are you bitter? Are you rebellious? Or are you submissive? Are you rejoicing in the midst of trouble? Can the perfect image of Christ be seen in your life today? Trials do not come by accident. He is aware of every heartache and sorrow and "pays attention" to them. He can convert them into opportunities to draw us closer to Him if we let Him.

We may not understand the reason for our trouble, but He uses it to bring forth gold in our lives. "That the trial of your faith, being much more precious than of gold that perisheth, though it be tried with fire, might be found unto praise and honour and glory at the appearing of Jesus Christ" (1 Peter 1:7).

July
23

But watch thou in all things, endure afflictions, do the work of an evangelist, make full proof of thy ministry (2 Tim. 4:5).

As Paul's life was coming to a close, he encouraged Timothy to continue on in the ministry of serving Jesus Christ. "For yourself, keep your mind sane and balanced, meeting whatever suffering this may involve. Go on steadily preaching the gospel and carry out to the full the commission that God gave you" (2 Tim. 4:5, *Phillips*).

Paul outlined some guidelines for Timothy in fulfilling his ministry. These same principles can be directives for us as we serve as "workers together with God."

First, we are to "stand fast." We are to be stable, not to be swayed by people, opinions, ideas, or feelings. "Be calm and cool and steady" (2 Tim. 4:5, *Amplified*).

Then, we are to "do the work of an evangelist." Every person without Christ is a mission field. This gives us a large field in which to serve.

Lastly, we are to "fully perform all the duties of your ministry" *(Amplified).* We may feel insignificant and unimportant; we may think others better qualified; but God has a place for us to serve and He enables us to fulfill it.

It is easy to become weary and discouraged. We may want to quit. But God's Word says we are to "be instant in season, out of season" (v. 2). In Galatians 6:9 we are reminded, "And let us not be weary in well doing: for in due season we shall reap, if we faint not."

God's workers come and go but His work continues throughout the centuries. The plan and purpose of God will continue until the return of Jesus Christ.

May each of us "make full proof of the ministry," so that when we stand before Him, we will hear his "Well done, thou good and faithful servant" (Matt. 25:21).

Blessed are the pure in heart: for they shall see God" (Matt. 5:8).

In the Beatitudes Jesus gave some principles for real happiness. One of them is "Blessed (the word 'happy' is used in some translations) are the pure in heart: for they shall see God."

The heart refers to more than the physical organ. It includes the entire personality, the mind, will, and heart, the total person. Blessed is the person who is pure, not just on the surface, but at the very center of his being.

Purity of heart does not come through environment, education, or good thoughts. It is an inner miracle wrought in the heart by God. When we receive Jesus Christ as Savior, our hearts are made pure through the cleansing power of His blood.

The pure in heart are not pious, nor hypocritical. They are not perfect, but sincere and honest, genuine and real. Their motives, desires, and intentions are pure. They are submissive to God's will.

Purity of heart is essential to a vision of God. Jesus promised that the pure in heart would see God. Today we see Him through Jesus Christ. Jesus said, "He that hath seen me hath seen the Father" (John 14:9). What we see depends on what we are looking for. Hebrews 12:2 reads, "LOOKING unto JESUS the author and finisher of our faith." The pure in heart have a singleness of focus centered in Jesus Christ.

Many who deal with precious gems, judging and evaluating their worth and genuineness, keep a perfect gem close by. Often they pause and look at the genuine one. Only as their vision is filled with its beauty and perfection can they detect the counterfeit.

In our daily living, as we keep our eyes upon Him, He fills our vision and keeps our hearts pure.

One day we will see Jesus face to face. Paul said, "In the same way, we can see and understand only a little about God now, as if we were peering at His reflection in a poor mirror; but some day we are going to see Him in His completeness, face to face" (1 Cor. 13:12, LB). What a day that will be!

July
25

And when he putteth forth his own sheep, he goeth before them, and the sheep follow him: for they know his voice (John 10:4).

Jesus uses a familiar illustration of the shepherd and his sheep to explain His relationship to His own children.

For the sheep to follow they must hear and know the shepherd's voice. Eastern shepherds sometimes keep several flocks in one fold at night. In the morning each shepherd calls his own sheep and they respond to their own shepherd, not to another. To follow our Good Shepherd we must know and recognize His voice.

He puts us forth, sometimes in places we do not want to go, places of which we may be fearful, places of impossibility. However, we can follow Him trustingly, for He meets the circumstances of our way before they reach us. He is in our tomorrows, preparing them to become our todays.

He goes before, never asking us to go where He does not go Himself. He puts us forth; He goes before us and we follow Him.

To know and recognize His voice, we must be familiar with it, be close enough to hear it, and then listen to it. We must be quiet enough to be able to sort out His voice from the great bedlam of voices about us.

The result of hearing and knowing His voice is that the sheep FOLLOW HIM. Some sheep may follow closer than others, but a general characteristic of a sheep is to follow. As we follow our Good Shepherd, He will lead us out to reach those who do not know Him.

An Indian missionary had to make a trip through an unknown country at night. As his guide went ahead of him, the missionary looked down and could not see a road. Finally he said to the guide, "Where is the way?" The guide replied, "There is no path, but I am the way. Just follow me and you will reach the end of your trip safely."

So, we, too, should not keep our eyes down on an obscure way, but on our Guide, listen to His voice and then follow Him.

And he said unto them, How is it that ye sought me? wist ye not that I must be about my Father's business? (Luke 2:49).

As Mary and Joseph were returning home from the temple, they discovered that Jesus was missing. Returning to the temple, they found Him there. He said to them, "How is it that you had to look for Me? Did you not see and know that it is necessary (as a duty) for Me to be in My Father's house and [occupied] about My Father's business?" *(Amplified).*

His one interest—to accomplish His Father's plan for Him—the redemption of a lost humanity. This was to be accomplished through His death on the cross. One day He said, "I must work the works of him that sent me" (John 9:4). To His disciples He said, "My meat is to do the will of him that sent me, and to FINISH HIS WORK" (John 4:34).

When Jesus returned to heaven, He entrusted to us the responsibility of completing His Father's work. His Father is our Father, and His business is our business. He said, "As my Father hath sent me, even so send I you" (John 20:21). We sing, "I'm here on business for my king." Are we fulfilling the business He has assigned to us?

He felt an urgency about His work. "Wist ye not that I MUST be about my Father's business?" Do we have this same sense of urgency? We must work today. Our day of opportunity for sharing Christ is passing by. Tomorrow may be too late.

There is a story that one day an angel said to Jesus, "Now that you have returned to heaven, did you leave a plan for carrying on your work on earth?" "Yes," said Jesus, "I left a group of men whom I trained. I have given them the responsibility of carrying the gospel to the world." "But suppose they get tired and quit, or become discouraged, or lose interest, what other plan do you have?" "I have no other plan. My trust is in them to finish My work for Me."

The Father's business is Jesus' business, and our business.

July
27

And the whole congregation of the children of Israel murmured against Moses and Aaron in the wilderness (Exod. 16:2).

In crossing the desert area of our country occasionally, I see oases with a few trees, a limited water supply, and a filling station. These provide "rest stops" for the traveler on his journey.

As the Israelites started their march across the desert they soon began to experience the rigors of wilderness travel. After three days without water, they began to murmur and complain. Suddenly their spirits rose as they discovered water, only to be disappointed when they found the water to be bitter.

Instead of trusting God, they began to murmur against Moses and Aaron. Indirectly, they were murmuring against God, Who was their real Leader. However, in spite of their complaining and lack of trust, God sweetened the bitter water so they could drink it.

God may schedule a wilderness journey for our lives. We may encounter bitter waters. Possessions may be taken from us, dear ones forsake us, plans crumble in our hands. Disappointments may come, confidences be betrayed, cherished ideals shattered.

We, too, may begin to murmur and complain. Bitterness may creep into our lives. It is easy to be sweet when everything is going our way, but when it becomes difficult, we begin to complain. God's Word reminds us, "Neither murmur ye."

Murmuring and complaining can lead to self-pity or criticism. They show a lack of faith in the Lord.

He can sweeten the "bitter waters" of our lives. It is the Lord Jesus who sweetens them for us. He doesn't always remove them, but He gives us the sweetness of His presence and blessing in the midst of them.

We can expect "bitter waters" on our wilderness journey, for God uses them as a "proving ground" to test us. Through them we are brought to the end of ourselves and into a closer relationship of trust in the Lord.

May we not be like the children of Israel, guilty of ingratitude. Instead, may our hearts and lips be filled with praise. "I will praise Him with my whole being."

The Lord God is my strength, and he will make my feet like hinds' feet, and he will make me to walk upon mine high places (Hab. 3:19).

During the days of difficulty and discouragement Habakkuk had learned to walk by faith with God. He could say, "The Lord God is my strength."

He compared his feet to hinds' feet by which he was able to climb above discouraging circumstances and walk on higher spiritual levels.

A most thrilling sight in high mountain country is watching deer bound up the mountainside. They leap from one ledge to another, often from precarious positions. We marvel that they don't lose their footing and fall to their death.

The hind is the female red deer. Deer have the ability of being surefooted. Because of this, they can jump confidently from rock to rock without danger of slipping.

Also, the hind tracks perfectly. As the hinds move, their rear hooves step into the front hoof marks. This prevents them from slipping, for their rear feet rest securely in the prints made by their front hooves.

God plans our pathway through life. "You chart the path ahead of me" (Ps. 139:3, LB). His path is a perfect way. "As for God, his way is perfect" (Ps. 18:30). The psalmist uses the same illustration of the hinds' feet. "He maketh my feet like hinds' feet, and setteth me upon my high places" (v. 33).

God charts the path of His will before us. As the hinds' front feet mark the steps in which their rear feet follow, so God marks out the steps of His will before us. Our part is to place our feet in His steps. Sometimes His paths before us are steep; sometimes they are over rough and dangerous places. Yet we need not be afraid, as we place our feet securely in His steps. As we "track" in His marks, our feet will not slide. "My steps have held closely to Your paths—to the tracks of the One Who has gone on before; my feet have not slipped" (Ps. 17:5, *Amplified*).

As God's mountaineers, we can walk on the high places of spiritual victory in Him.

July
29

Bear ye one another's burdens, and so fulfil the law of Christ (Gal. 6:2).

One day I watched a small child piling up blocks, one on top of another. Finally the tower of blocks became so high it toppled over.

In many of our lives today "towers of burdens" are building up. The burdens pile one on top of another until we feel we can't bear another one without "toppling over."

God has given us the ministry of being Burden Bearers. He said, "Bear ye one another's burdens." Many are carrying heavy burdens, burdens of heartache, sorrow, disillusionment, frustration. Yet often we become so wrapped up in our own little world we forget that there are people about us who need a friend, someone with whom they can share their heartaches. The *Living Bible* (Gal. 6:2) says, "Share each other's troubles and problems, and so obey our Lord's command."

We need to put ourselves in their place, empathizing with them. "Rejoice with them that do rejoice, and weep with them that weep" (Rom. 12:15).

Such love and concern for others is motivated in the heart indwelt by Christ and controlled by the Holy Spirit. Paul wrote, "We then that are strong ought to bear the infirmities of the weak, and not to please ourselves" (Rom. 15:1).

Our great Burden Bearer, the Lord Jesus, invites us to bring our burdens to HIM. "Come to Me, all you who labor and are heavy-laden and OVER BURDENED, and I will cause you to rest—I will ease and relieve and refresh your souls" (Matt. 11:28, *Amplified*).

Even though we may enter into the burdens of others, we are not to carry them, but bring them along with our own burdens to the great Burden Bearer. "Casting the whole of your care—all your anxieties, all your worries, all your concerns, once and for all—on Him; for He cares for you affectionately, and cares about you watchfully" (1 Peter 5:7, *Amplified*).

We should ask ourselves today, "Is there some burden I can ease, some load I can lighten for someone?"

It has been said, "A bell is no bell, 'til you ring it. A song is no song, 'til you sing it. Love isn't love, 'til you give it away."

And it shall be, if he call thee, that thou shalt say, Speak, Lord; for thy servant heareth (1 Sam. 3:9).

Many people today are benefited by a small instrument known as the hearing aid. However, to be effective, it must be worn and tuned in.

Spiritual hearing aids are important for communication with God. But we must keep them turned on and tuned in to be able to hear Him speak.

The Bible tells of little Samuel who learned to use his "spiritual hearing aid." He served Eli in the temple, performing small tasks for him. Three times one night Samuel thought he heard Eli calling him. Finally Eli realized that it was the Lord speaking to Samuel. He said, "Go, lie down, and it shall be, if He call thee, that thou shalt say, 'Speak, Lord, for Thy servant heareth.'"

When Samuel heard God's call again, in simple childlike faith, he said, "Speak, for Thy servant is listening" *(Berkeley)*.

Today are our ears tuned in to His voice? Or are they so filled with the static of THINGS that we cannot hear HIM? The confusion of many voices is great today—the voices of pleasure, fame, business, self-desires, service. Being so taken up with things may hinder us from hearing HIM.

J. Allen Blair has said, "By our attitude we translate this verse, 'Listen, Lord, thy servant speaketh.'" We do all the talking, instead of listening.

God speaks to us in our quiet time with Him in the Word and in prayer. Sometimes He speaks to us through people. He often speaks to us through circumstances. Every time a circumstance presses against us, we need to pause and say, "Speak, Lord; what do you want me to discover through this experience?"

Anything that prevents our hearing Him speak should be tuned out.

Someone was asked why his preacher always had something new to tell them in his sermons. The reply was, "Why, you see, he lives so near to the God of heaven, he hears a great many things we don't get near enough to hear."

"God speaks loud enough for the willing soul to hear."

July
31

For thus saith the high and lofty One that inhabiteth eternity, whose name is Holy; I dwell in the high and holy place, with him also that is of a contrite and humble spirit, to revive the spirit of the humble and to revive the heart of the contrite ones (Isa. 57:15).

Since our astronauts have been traveling into outer space, we have become much more aware of the magnitude of the great universe. It is difficult to fathom its vastness. The earth is one of nine planets revolving around the sun. The galaxy of which our earth is a part is only one of millions of galaxies. As we consider God's handiwork, we recognize the majesty and omnipotence of the One who created the heavens and earth.

Isaiah recognized the greatness of God and His exalted position. "For thus saith the high and lofty One that inhabiteth eternity, whose name is Holy; I dwell in the high and holy place." In Isaiah 6:1 we read, "I saw also the Lord sitting upon a throne, high and lifted up." He is not limited to time and space as we are.

Not only is He ". . . high and lofty . . .," but He is eternal. ". . . that inhabiteth eternity . . ." Our lives seem to be controlled by clocks, calendars, and schedules. But God is not bound by time. Psalm 90:2 reads, "From everlasting to everlasting, thou art God."

Our God is a Holy God ". . . whose Name is holy . . ." Today there is a tendency toward a casual approach to God. Perhaps we need a new awareness of His Holiness, giving us an attitude of reverence as we come into His presence.

God speaks of two dwelling places; the throne of heaven and the throne of the human heart. He said, ". . . I dwell in the high and holy place, with him also that is of a contrite and humble spirit."

How big is God? He is the God of the universe, big enough to inhabit eternity. Yet the God of the universe is also the God of the individual, small enough to live in my heart.

With humbleness and adoration we can say, "My Lord and my God" (John 20:28).

For now I know that thou fearest God, seeing thou hast not withheld thy son, thine only son from me (Gen. 22:12).

The above Scripture verse became very real to me during a time of testing in my life, a time when I was at a low ebb physically and emotionally after a serious illness.

I was lonely, feeling that no one cared for me, loved me, or understood me. There were times when I couldn't pray words, only lift my heart to God, knowing He heard the cry of my heart. Although I couldn't understand what He was doing, I knew this experience was a part of His plan for me.

During this time, one thing kept my faith from wavering, I was assured of one fact and never doubted it—GOD cared for ME. Although I couldn't understand what was happening, I was sustained by His Word.

At that time I was studying Abraham's life of faith. Early one morning I was reading Genesis 22. "After these events, God TESTED and PROVED Abraham" (Gen. 22:1, *Amplified*). "For NOW I KNOW that thou fearest God, seeing thou hast not withheld thy son" (v. 12).

When I had totally committed my life to the Lord years before, I had asked Him to do whatever was necessary to conform my life to the image of Jesus Christ. I now realized He had been testing me, as part of the conforming process necessary to make me the person He wanted me to be.

It was as if God was saying to me, "I have been testing and proving you. NOW I KNOW that your life commitment was genuine and sincere."

From that experience came a greater knowledge of God Himself and a depth in my walk with Him I had not known before.

You may be wondering "why" your life is filled with trials and trouble. Perhaps God is testing your life to prove the reality of your commitment to Him.

Have you committed everything in your life to Him? Can He say to you, "NOW I KNOW you have not withheld any part of your life from Me"?

God-yielded wills produce God-planned lives.

August
2

A sower went forth to sow (Matt. 13:3).

As we drive through the country, we notice some of the fields are sown, and some are not. Some are producing a harvest, some are not. However, when we do see crops growing on the land, we are sure of one thing, there has been some sowing of seed.

Jesus said, "A sower went forth to sow." The seed to be sown is God's Word. "Being born again, not of corruptible seed, but of incorruptible, by the word of God, which liveth and abideth for ever" (1 Peter 1:23).

It has a world-wide scope. The field is the world. The fields are ripe unto harvest. "Lift up your eyes, and look on the fields; for they are white already to harvest" (John 4:35).

There is an urgency in seed-sowing today. "I must work the works of him that sent me, while it is day: the night cometh, when no man can work" (John 9:4).

Laborers are needed. "Pray ye therefore the Lord of the harvest, that he would send forth labourers" (Luke 10:2).

After the seed is sown it needs to be watered with the tears of our prayers from a heart of compassion. "He that goeth forth and weepeth, bearing precious seed, shall doubtless come again with rejoicing, bringing his sheaves with him" (Ps. 126:6).

The amount of reaping depends on the amount of sowing. "He which soweth sparingly shall reap also sparingly; and he which soweth bountifully shall reap also bountifully" (2 Cor. 9:6). Only a bountiful sowing brings forth a bountiful crop.

We read in Haggai 2:19, "Is the seed yet in the barn?" I heard a young man from one of the small countries in the Orient share from this verse. He was pleading with the audience to get the Word of God to his country before it was too late. He said, "Keeping the seed in your barn won't bring a harvest. It has to be planted." He closed by saying, "Is the seed yet in your barn or are you planting it?"

Are we hoarding the seed in our barns or are we planting it? Are we sowing sparingly or bountifully?

Seed in the barn doesn't bring forth a harvest.

A merry heart maketh a cheerful countenance (Prov. 15:13).

Have you ever sat where you could watch crowds of people and study their faces? I do this often, and I notice that very few of them register joy or cheer. Yet it takes less effort and fewer muscles to smile than to frown.

One of the television networks has produced a show based on smiling. "Smile! You're on Candid Camera!" In one of my former places of employment we were reminded so often of the importance of giving service with a SMILE.

A sunny, happy countenance should characterize the life of a Christian. God's Word gives us the recipe for a cheerful countenance. "A HAPPY heart makes the face look sunny" (Prov. 15:13, *Berkeley*). This is an inner cheerfulness which is not affected by circumstances. "A cheerful heart makes a good cure" (Prov. 17:22. *Berkeley*).

The reality of a cheerful countenance comes from a heart at peace with God. An inner joy and radiance from a heart resting in God is reflected on the face, giving it a special glow. Smiles are the outward expression of the inward joy.

Often when a cheery person with a bright smile on the face enters a room the entire atmosphere is changed. Spirits are lifted. Such a cheery disposition acts like a tonic. A smile is contagious.

One evening a sister-in-law called me. She said, "I saw you today. Is something the matter? You looked so sad. You looked as if you didn't have a friend on earth." Perhaps that was the way I felt. But I asked God to make His joy so real in my heart that it would always reflect in His smile on my face.

The happy people are those who are so filled with the peace of God that they can rejoice at all times, in every place, in every situation. Christ is not only their Savior, but their daily portion.

It has been said, "A smile is a light in the window of the face that shows that a happy heart is at home."

Be sure you have your brightest and cheeriest smile with you today.

August

4

If thou wilt . . . give unto thine handmaid a man child, then I will give him unto the Lord all the days of his life (1 Sam. 1:11).

Hannah was in deep distress because she had no children. This was a disgrace to Hebrew women. To make matters worse, she had to share her husband with another wife who taunted her about her barrenness. This brought frustration. "And her adversary also provoked her sore, for to make her fret" (1 Sam. 1:6). Even her husband's assurance of his love for her didn't bring comfort.

In bitterness of spirit, she cried to the Lord. As her tears fell, she poured out her heart to Him in prayer.

She had been praying for what SHE wanted. "Give ME a child." Now she prayed, ". . . Give me a son, then I will give him BACK to YOU, and he'll be yours for his entire lifetime" (1 Sam. 1:11, LB). Although she wanted a child more than anything else, she was willing to give him back to God for His service.

When Hannah exchanged her heart's desire for God's will, he answered and gave her a son, Samuel. As she remembered her promise to give him back to God, she recognized her responsibility for teaching him about God during the few short years she would have him at home. She instilled into his life spiritual principles that eventually made him the great man God could use.

Perhaps you have been praying for something and the answer has not come yet. It may be something you want very much, yet God has not given you your request. Ask yourself the question, "Am I asking for what I want or what God wants?"

The answer to Hannah's prayer didn't come until she let God give her the answer that was according to His will. God may be waiting for you to give back to Him that which you hold dear. You must let go of even your dearest treasure, placing it in His hand. Then as you open your empty hands to Him, He can fill them with His answers to your prayers, with His plans for your life, the ones He knows are best for you and will glorify Him.

Teach me to do thy will; for thou art my God: thy spirit is good; lead me into the land of uprightness (Ps. 143:10).

David was a man who lived in close companionship with God. God was very real to him. In the first part of Psalm 143 he brings his needs to God. He prays, "Hear my prayer, O Lord, give ear to my supplications" (v. 1). "Hear me speedily, O Lord: my spirit faileth" (v. 7).

David began his day with God, asking God to speak to him, "Cause me to hear thy lovingkindness in the morning" (v. 8). How eagerly he must have come into God's presence each morning to hear God's Word for him for that day. He had learned not to do all the talking. He said, "Cause me to HEAR." Do we take time each day to hear Him speak to us? Is our daily prayer, "Cause ME to hear?"

Then he asked God to guide his steps in the way he should go. "Cause me to know the way wherein I should walk; for I lift up my soul unto thee" (v. 8). There must be coordination between our ears and our feet. Not only should our ears be tuned to hear Him, but our feet should be obedient to follow His directions.

David's difficult experiences brought him to the place of complete dependence upon God. Not only did he pray to know God's will, but that he might walk in it. "Teach me to DO thy will; for thou art my God. . . ." He asked God not only to be his Teacher, but to be his Guide. "Lead me."

Because his confidence was in God, because he had assurance of knowing, "Thou art MY GOD," he could trust God to teach him and lead him in His ways.

Is our request of God for today, "TEACH ME—LEAD ME"? We should not only ask God to teach us to do His will, but also to lead us in conformity to it. It is more than KNOWING God's will; it is WALKING in obedience to His will.

Martin Luther said, "I may not know the way, but well do I know my Guide on the way."

August
6

Till we all come in the unity of the faith, and of the knowledge of the Son of God, unto a perfect man, unto the measure of the stature of the fulness of Christ (Eph. 4:13).

God has a place for each of us in the body of believers and a function for each of us to perform.

Believers are to be equipped for the two-fold work of reaching the world for Jesus Christ and strengthening the believers spiritually. "Why is it that he gives us these special abilities to do certain things best? It is that God's people will be equipped to do better work for Him, building up the church, the body of Christ, to a position of strength and maturity" (Eph. 4:12, LB).

This is an age of "instant mixes," "instant coffee," "instant telephone dialing," with everything geared to increase speed in today's living. However, we do not have "instant maturity" in the spiritual realm. Spiritual growth does not come overnight. It takes time—"Till we all come."

God's plan is to bring us in our spiritual growth into the "unity of the faith, and of the knowledge of the Son of God." We are to come to a oneness of faith that is built on a knowledge of Him. Acts 4 tells of the oneness of the early Christians. "And the multitude of them that believed were of one heart and of one soul" (Acts 4:32).

We are to mature "unto the perfect man." This does not mean to achieve perfection, but to become full grown. We are to mature into the design God has for our life. We are to be His workmanship.

There is one standard by which we are to measure our spiritual progress, the standard of Christ, "unto the measure of the stature of the fulness of Christ." As we mature in Him, He will be experienced in us and expressed through us.

Are you saying, "I can never attain this measurement"? We can't, but the Holy Spirit working within accomplishes it in us.

Our measurement is "the fulness of Christ." Measured against Him, how far along are we on the road to spiritual maturity?

And a book of remembrance was written before him for them that feared the Lord, and that thought upon his name (Mal. 3:16).

During a time of spiritual decline, a faithful group of believers loved God and remained true to Him. Four things are mentioned about them.

First, their hearts were filled with the "fear of the Lord." This term is an Old Testament description of the godly who live with an awareness of God's presence. To fear God meant they gave Him the reverence and honor due Him.

Then, when they met together they talked about HIM. What do we talk about when we get together with other believers? They were encouraged and strengthened as they shared what God meant in their lives and what He had done for them. "That which we have seen and heard declare we unto you, that ye also may have fellowship with us" (1 John 1:3).

The reason their conversation was full of Him was that they "thought upon His name." They filled their minds with Him.

Often as I leave a home where I have visited, my hostess will bring the guest book for me to sign. It is their Book of Remembrance of those who have been their guests.

God has a special Book of Remembrance in which He records the names of His children. "The Lord hearkened, and heard it, and a book of remembrance was written before him for them that feared the Lord."

The Lord said, "And they shall be mine . . . in that day when I make up my jewels" (Mal. 3:17). The Amplified reads, "My special possession, My peculiar treasure." We are His, His special treasure. Not one of us is forgotten by Him. He knows each of us by name.

He says, "YOU are mine." When we realize we were bought with so great a price, the life of His Son, can we doubt His love and care?

Our names may not be in the Who's Who of the world's great, but the names of God's own family are recorded in His Book of Remembrance.

Is your name there?

August
8

Set a watch, O Lord, before my mouth; keep the door of my lips (Ps. 141:3).

If we could carry a recorder with us for one entire day, recording every word we say, and the recording were played back at the end of the day, I am sure we would be surprised and perhaps even a little ashamed at some of our words.

Psalm 141 was very likely written by David when he was fleeing from Saul. Evil things were being said about him. He was being slandered by his enemies.

He recognized his weakness and knew if he weren't careful, he could speak angrily to his enemies. He might say things he would be sorry for later.

So he asked God to guard his speech, to set a watch before his mouth, and to keep the door of his lips.

We, too, need a sentinel for our mouth to be placed as a guard over each word before it leaves our lips. In unguarded moments we speak without thinking and say things we are sorry for later.

Failure to control our words is one of our greatest weaknesses, causing much harm. The moment we speak, others are affected. Words that go forth cannot be recalled.

The sentinel over our lips must guard carefully our hasty words, unkind words, untruthful words, impure words, harmful words, angry words.

Someone has given this good advice; "When we are hurt, keep still; when we are slandered, keep still; when we are impatient, keep still." If we wait a while before answering, our feelings may cool off and our attitude change.

Time brings a restraining effect, preventing a hasty answer.

Jesus gives us a good example. It was said of Him, ". . . neither was guile found in his mouth" (1 Peter 2:22).

We need to commit our lips to the Lord. They can become a blessing to God and to people. They can praise God and talk to Him in prayer. They can speak words of encouragement, kindness, and comfort to others to cheer them.

"Let your speech be alway with grace, seasoned with salt" (Col. 4:6).

I can do all things through Christ which strengtheneth me (Phil. 4:13).

Have you ever been asked to do something and your first response has been, "Oh, but I can't do that"? You give up before you ever try.

Once a small boy was struggling to lift a heavy rock. His father watched him struggle for a time, then asked, "Are you using all your strength?" "Of course I am," replied the boy impatiently. "No, you are not," answered his father. "You haven't asked me to help you." Like the little boy, how often we try to do things in our own strength. We have a source of strength beyond ourselves that is sufficient, a God-given strength.

Paul had learned the secret of this strength. He wrote, "I have strength for all things in Christ Who empowers me—I am ready for anything and equal to anything through Him Who infuses inner strength into me [that is, I am self-sufficient in Christ's sufficiency]" (Phil. 4:13, *Amplified*).

He made a very inclusive statement when he said, "I can do ALL things." His strength and power were not in himself but in Christ, ". . . HIM Who infuses inner strength in me." He could face prison, endure persecution, be content wherever he was, in the sufficiency of Christ.

Three times Paul asked the Lord to remove an infirmity—a thorn in the flesh. But the answer was not the one he sought. Instead God said, "For my STRENGTH is made perfect in weakness" (2 Cor. 12:9).

God's strength! Paul's weakness! "Made perfect" is the connecting phrase. It is the same word that Jesus used when He said, "It is finished," as He hung on the cross. So God's strength is "finished," "completely made perfect," in our weakness. It is not human strength or confidence God chooses to use, but human weakness.

It has been stated, "Into the hollows of our nothingness God fits the dynamos of His power." John Hunter has said, "Strength for all things; ready for anything; equal to everything."

"They that wait upon the Lord shall renew their strength" (Isa. 40:31). As we wait on Him, we exchange our weakness for His strength.

August
10

But ye, beloved, building up yourselves on your most holy faith, praying in the Holy Ghost, keep yourselves in the love of God, looking for the mercy of our Lord Jesus Christ unto eternal life (Jude 20,21).

The above Scripture verses outline some important principles for strengthening our Christian life. Our life in Christ is compared to a building. For a strong structure, a building must be constructed on a solid foundation. Our life, too, must have a strong foundation. "For other foundation can no man lay than that is laid, which is Jesus Christ" (1 Cor. 3:11).

Upon this strong foundation of Jesus Christ we are to build a life of faith. "But you, dear friends, must build up your lives ever more strongly upon the foundation of our holy faith" (Jude 20, LB).

Reading the Word of God and appropriating it into our lives is vitally important in the building up of our faith. "Faith cometh by hearing, and hearing by the Word of God" (Rom. 10:17).

Prayer is necessary for strengthening our faith. It is more than "saying" prayers. In our own inadequacy the Holy Spirit prays through us. "Learning to pray in the power and strength of the Holy Spirit" (Jude 20, LB).

We are to "keep ourselves in the love of God," a love that is steadfast and unchanging. We must never forget that He loves us just as we are, and just where we are. No matter what storm may enter our lives, no matter how contrary the wind, we live within the circle of His love and need never doubt His love for us.

People in the world today need to know that God loves them. We can be a channel through which His love can flow out of our lives to others. "Stay always within the boundaries where God's love can reach and bless you" (Jude 21, LB).

To keep ourselves in His love we must be obedient to Him. "When you obey me you are living in my love" (John 15:10).

Lastly, we are to keep "looking for the mercy of our Lord Jesus Christ unto eternal life." Keep looking up! He is coming again!

And as thy servant was busy here and there, he was gone (1 Kings 20:40).

"I am so busy" is the great American expression. We live by the calendar, the clock, and the appointment book. Our lives are like the servant mentioned in the above verse, we are busy here and there.

When God had a lesson to teach King Ahab, God sent the prophet to Ahab with a story. The prophet disguised himself as a soldier. He related that a prisoner had been trusted to his care. The responsibility should be his top priority. Yet he became so busy he failed in his responsibilities. He said, "As thy servant was busy here and there, he was gone." He was busy, but not with his special assignment.

The responsibility of the soldier was to look after the prisoner. Yet he became so engrossed in minor things that the real responsibility entrusted to him slipped away.

God has a lesson to teach us from this story. Life today is characterized by busyness. Activity seems to be our motto. God has commissioned us as ambassadors for Him, His representatives on earth today. We are here in His stead. We must be careful not to miss our opportunity by being too busy here and there. We must not let it slip away.

What special trust has God given to you? Is it someone in your family, a neighbor, a dear friend? Is it someone you don't even know whom He may put across your path? Is it a letter He wants you to write, or a telephone call you are to make? You must determine what God wants you to do. His assignments are to have top priority.

After the death of Cecil Rhoades, the millionaire statesman, a note was found among his papers to the effect that if God had something for him to do, the most important thing in life for him was to know what it was and to do it.

There is always time to do what God wants.

"Make the best use of your time, despite all the evils of these days" (Eph. 5:16, *Phillips*).

August 12

Continue in prayer, and watch in the same with thanksgiving (Col. 4:2).

Paul was in prison when he wrote his letter to the Colossians. What would have been your prayer request in a similar situation? To be delivered from prison, wouldn't it? But what did Paul ask them to pray for? He asked them to continue in prayer, "That God would open unto us a door of utterance" (Col. 4:3) to give forth the gospel.

Paul was a man of action, but he realized that if his service was to be effective, it must be empowered through prayer.

E. M. Bounds has said, "What is needed today is not more or better machinery, not new organizations or more and novel methods, but men (and women). The Holy Spirit does not flow through methods, but through men. He does not come on machinery, but on men. He does not anoint plans, but men—men of prayer."

We aren't told to "pray when it is convenient" or "pray when we have time," but to "continue in prayer." Continue comes from a word meaning "persevere earnestly." We are to live in constant communication with God.

We are not to become weary in our prayer life, but to persevere earnestly to be steadfast. "Be earnest and unwearied and steadfast in your prayer [life], being [both] alert and intent in [your praying] with thanksgiving" (Col. 4:2, *Amplified*).

One morning a woman came into a prayer group I was in. She was so excited as she shared her good news. She said, "I just received a letter from my brother telling me he has become a Christian. I have prayed for him for forty years."

Spurgeon was once asked the secret of his success. He replied, "My people pray for me." One time three young men went to hear Dr. Spurgeon preach. Since they arrived early, a man asked if they would like to see the heating plant. Because it was July, they were curious and went to see it. They were taken downstairs and there found seven hundred people praying for Dr. Spurgeon and for the Word of God as he gave it forth that day.

"The effectual fervent prayer of a righteous man availeth much" (James 5:16).

Blessed be the God and Father of our Lord Jesus Christ, who hath blessed us with all spiritual blessings in heavenly places in Christ (Eph. 1:3).

We live in a competitive world, a world in which there is a constant striving toward the accumulation of possessions. As God's children, we have all the vast resources of heaven's wealth at our disposal. We don't have to work for this wealth. It has been deposited for us "in Christ."

"In" is such a little word, only two letters, yet joined with the word "Christ," it reveals our privileged position as a believer—"IN CHRIST." These two words are the master key giving access to all the spiritual blessings available to us in the heavenlies. In Christ we have all the spiritual blessings needed for living a life "in Him," and all that is His becomes ours. "And since we are His children, we will share His treasures—for all God gives to His Son Jesus is now ours too" (Rom. 8:17, LB).

To be "in Christ" means a complete change of life. Without Him we are spiritually dead, but in Him we become spiritually alive. "That even though we are spiritually dead and doomed by our sins, He gave us back our lives again when He raised Christ from the dead . . . and lifted us up from the grave into glory along with Christ, where we sit with Him in the heavenly realms—all because of what Christ Jesus did" (Eph. 2:5-6, LB). Someone has said, "Our heart is in the heavenlies but our feet are on earth."

God has a vast deposit of resources for our use, in His Bank of Heaven, sufficient for any need, any time, even an emergency. From our position in Christ we can always draw on them.

All His resources are available in Christ, but we must take possession of them by faith and appropriate them into our lives.

Ruth Paxson has this helpful little outline:

IN CHRIST

denotes our position—where He is, we are
defines our privileges—what He is, we are
describes our possessions—what He has, we have
determines our practice—what He does, we do.

This is our position "In Christ." May we avail ourselves today of all the vast storehouse of riches He has for us.

August
14

Is there any word from the Lord? (Jer. 37:17).

One day I took some copy material to our Publications Department to be proofread. In a short time one of our staff called me. She was laughing as I answered the phone. One section of my material was entitled "Bible Reading Meditation." In error I had typed it "Bible Reading MEDICATION." I replied, "Bible Reading Medication should develop into a good idea for a devotional."

As we administer medication to bring relief to the body, so God's Word applied to our lives can bring relief for our spiritual ailments.

The Bible is relevant to the personal needs of our lives. Within its pages are prescriptions that bring spiritual health. It relieves the pain of the heart; it brings quietness to the disturbed mind; it supplies strength for the body.

As each day is a new day, filled with new needs, we should begin the day by asking, "Is there any word from the Lord for ME today?"

We can be assured that He does have a Word for us for each day. However, just reading it or even memorizing it is not enough. We must assimilate it and let it become a part of our lives.

Each day as I open His Word, I ask Him for something especially for me. Sometimes I stop at a single word or phrase. Other times I read an entire verse, several verses, or a chapter. Then I meditate on what He speaks to me from it. I consider how I need to apply it to my life. I make notes in a notebook on the thoughts He has given me. Then I pray over it for my life. It is with excitement that I go to Him for His Word for me.

He has something for you from His Word daily. Pray as you begin reading that the Holy Spirit will give you what you need.

Andrew Murray said, "The vigor of our spiritual life will be in exact proportion to the place held by the Word in your life and thoughts."

Has some verse or portion from His Word become yours today?

I will bless the Lord at all times: his praise shall continually be in my mouth. My soul shall make her boast in the Lord: the humble shall hear thereof, and be glad. O magnify the Lord with me, and let us exalt his name together (Ps. 34:1-3).

Many of the Psalms are filled with praise to God. This Psalm is no exception. Praise has been defined as, "The occupation of the soul with the blessings of God."

The psalmist's heart was filled with praise, but not because his life was easy. He said, "I will praise the Lord NO MATTER WHAT HAPPENS. I will constantly speak of his glories and grace" (Ps. 34:1, LB). In fact, when he said, "Many are the afflictions of the righteous" (v. 19), he was speaking of that which was true of his own life.

David could praise God at a time when his life was in danger. Although he had become a homeless exile, yet he could sing praises to God.

He said, "I will bless the Lord at ALL times; his praise shall CONTINUALLY be in my mouth." It was not just praise in his heart, but praise on his lips. It is easy to praise the Lord in days of prosperity, but David could praise Him in times of adversity. He could praise the Lord in EVERY circumstance. Such melodies of praise come from the lips of those whose hearts commune with God.

We, too, can join the choir of praise. We can praise Him at all times, in all circumstances, on good days and bad days, in health and in sickness, in sad times and glad times. Does this seem impossible to do? As we allow Him, the Holy Spirit will produce such a heart of constant praise to God.

George Matheson was a blind preacher of Scotland. One time, after he had become blind, he prayed, "My God, I have not thanked thee for my thorn. I have thanked Thee a thousand times for my roses. Teach me the value of my thorn."

"O magnify the Lord with me, and let us exalt His name together." Someone has said that "by so doing, we begin heaven beforehand."

I sought the Lord, and he heard me, and delivered me from all my fears. This poor man cried, and the Lord heard him, and saved him out of all his troubles. Many are the afflictions of the righteous: but the Lord delivereth him out of them all (Ps. 34:4,6,19).

Psalm 34 begins with David praising God. The above verses reveal the reason for his praise. Fear had filled his heart because of the trouble he had been experiencing. Knowing and believing in the power of prayer, he sought the Lord, his sure source of help.

God heard and delivered him out of ALL his fears, ALL his troubles, ALL his afflictions. No wonder his heart was so full of praise to God!

Fear! Trouble! Affliction! Who has not experienced them? Fear has filled our hearts, troubles have mounted, afflictions have crushed us. What God did for David, He can do for us. If we seek Him, He will hear and deliver. He has promised to deliver us from EVERY trouble, from EVERY affliction.

Deliverance may not come in the way we expect it, or at the time we want it. He may not deliver us out of them all, but He will deliver us in the midst of them all.

In his later years of life, George Frederick Handel lost his money. His health failed. His right side became paralyzed. His creditors were threatening him with imprisonment for non-payment of his debts. He had no place to go but to God. Putting his trust completely in Him to meet his needs, he decided to go into seclusion. There he spent much time in meditation and prayer. Out of this time spent with God came the greatest of all his oratorios, "THE MESSIAH."

Someone has said, "He who knows God and remembers that He has a father's heart and a mother's concern for His own, will never be panic-stricken even when all the heart considered stable and permanent comes down with a crash."

"The angel of the Lord encampeth round about them that fear him, and delivereth them" (v. 7).

They looked to Him, and were radiant (Ps. 34:5, Amplified).

Some people always seem to radiate joy from their lives. It sparkles from their eyes and bubbles from their lips. Just looking at them gives a lift to our spirits. Through observation we discover that their radiance comes from within. It is as though a light had been turned on in their lives.

The secret of this inner radiance is found in this verse: "They looked unto HIM, and were radiant." The Lord is the source of their radiance. A Chinese version of this verse reads, "All who look to the Lord have light on their faces."

The Lord Jesus said, "I am the light of the world" (John 8:12). As we invite Him into our lives, His light is turned on within us. The inner radiance of His light within reflects His beauty and loveliness. We become radiant Christians.

One morning I stood chatting with a waitress in a dining room where I was having an early morning breakfast meeting. She said to me, "Look at these women; how happy they are. Look at their smiling faces at eight o'clock in the morning." She was observing the radiance of the presence of Christ in their lives.

This does not mean that radiant Christians are free from trials. But they have taken God into their plans, committed their way to Him, and are looking to Him in restful confidence.

One time when Adoniram Judson was home on furlough, a boy, seeing him on the street, thought he had never seen such light on a human face. Finally he recognized him as a missionary whose picture he had once seen. The young boy was Henry Clay Trumbull who later became a famous minister himself and wrote a book of memories. One chapter he entitled "What a Boy Saw in the Face of Adoniram Judson."

"But we all, with open face beholding as in a glass the glory of the Lord, are changed into the same image from glory to glory, even as by the Spirit of the Lord" (2 Cor. 3:18).

"There will be more reflection of Jesus when there is more reflection on Him."

August
18

O taste and see that the Lord is good (Ps. 34:8).

When something wonderful happens to us, we say, "The Lord is so good." But what happens when trouble comes, when health fails, when we lose our job, when our homes fall apart? What about the times our hearts are crushed with sorrow, our bodies suffer pain, we are misunderstood? Do we still say, "The Lord is good?"

When difficulties come, the enemy of our soul will try to cause us to doubt the goodness of the Lord. But we must remember that He is always good. He is just as good in the dark times as when everything is going smoothly.

David speaks in Psalm 34, not from a problem-free life, but from one filled with trouble, with heartache, with sorrow. But through it all he had made a great discovery. "The LORD is good." He encourages us to make this same discovery: "Taste and see that HE IS good."

Taste is defined as "to sample, test, experience." David encourages us to "sample" or to "taste," that we might see that the Lord is good. As we begin "sampling" the Word of God, a desire is created for more of the Lord. Jeremiah wrote, "Thy words were found, and I did eat them; and thy word was unto me the joy and rejoicing of mine heart" (Jer. 15:16).

Taste also means "test." As we put His promises to the test, claiming them for our need, we learn that the Lord who keeps His promises is good.

Taste has another meaning, "experience." As we put Him to the test in our lives, He becomes increasingly real in our life experience. There we learn that God is good in every circumstance of our lives.

If David were here today, he would say, "Taste and see for yourself that the Lord is good." As we taste, sample, test, and experience Him, we discover that He is good. When we believe He is ALWAYS good, it gives us confidence and security.

"Oh that men would praise the Lord for his goodness, and for his wonderful works to the children of men" (Ps. 107:8).

Then Philip opened his mouth, and began at the same scripture, and preached unto him Jesus (Acts 8:35).

While Philip was preaching in Samaria, having wonderful results, an angel of the Lord appeared to him, saying, "ARISE, and GO toward the south unto the way that goeth down from Jerusalem unto Gaza, which is desert" (Acts. 8:26).

What a shock this must have been to Philip. Imagine leaving a successful meeting and going to the desert, without a reason given. But Philip was a man willing and ready to be led of the Spirit of God. "He arose and went" (v. 27). It was not necessary to know why he was being sent, but it was important to be obedient.

At this very time an Ethopian, the Minister of Finance to the Queen, was traveling across the desert. The Spirit of God said to Philip, "GO NEAR, and join thyself to this chariot" (v. 29). God's timing is always perfect.

The eunuch, knowing he had a spiritual need, was trying to find an answer from reading God's Word. Philip, discovering a seeking heart, told him about Jesus. ". . . began with the same Scripture and then used many others to tell him about Jesus" (Acts 8:35, LB).

God is looking today for people like Philip who are willing to be led by the Holy Spirit to share Christ with people who are searching. It may mean the Lord will move a person across the country to minister to someone searching for an answer to his need.

One day after sharing with a group how I became a Christian, a woman came to me, saying, "I'm so glad I came today. I have believed in God all my life. I have prayed. But I never knew how to become a Christian and no one could tell me. Today you told how. I invited Christ into my life and am going home a Christian."

God had directed me to that city because He knew a searching heart was ready to receive Christ.

Are we so open to the moving of God's Spirit that He can direct us to people with searching hearts? Lamentations 1:12 reads, "Is it nothing to you, all ye that pass by?" May it be "something" to us. May we be ready to answer God's call to minister to searching hearts.

August
20

But do thou for me, O God the Lord, for thy name's sake: because thy mercy is good, deliver thou me (Ps. 109:21).

Psalm 109 was written at a time when David was deeply disturbed. He was being falsely accused, apparently without cause as far as he could see.

David had learned not to tell God what to do for him. He prayed, "Do THOU for me." In effect He is saying, "Do whatever is best." Because he had confidence in God, he knew he could trust himself and his problems completely to God, for God would only do His best for him.

He knew that his extremity was God's opportunity. "But as for me, O Lord, deal with me as your child" (Ps. 109:21, LB). David was implying, "Lord, I am coming to You in my need. I don't know which way to turn, but I have implicit confidence in You; You choose what is best for me." David said, "But do THOU for me, O God, the Lord."

David confessed, "For I am poor and needy, and my heart is wounded within me" (v. 22). God, in His tender love, reaches down and applies His healing balm to broken hearts. "He healeth the broken in heart, and bindeth up their wounds" (Ps. 147:3).

Then he asked God to deliver him in such a way that everyone, even his enemies, would recognize God's power. "Help me, O Lord my God: O save me according to thy mercy: that they may know that this is thy hand; that thou, Lord, hast done it" (vv. 26-27).

David concluded with, ". . . He shall stand at the right hand of the poor. . . ." How comforting it is to have a friend stand by in time of trouble. The Lord is even more to us than an earthly friend. He is especially near in time of need.

Sometimes we say to a friend in whom we have confidence, "Do what you think best." We wouldn't say this to someone we didn't know intimately and trust implicitly. This is the confidence we can have in God. Today, are we saying to Him, "Do what YOU think best for me"? A trusting heart CAN say, "Do THOU for me."

Take heed therefore how ye hear (Luke 8:18).

How many times has someone spoken to you, yet when he or she finished, you couldn't remember what the person had said? You heard, but had not really listened. How many times have you read the Word and when you finished you could not remember what you had read?

Luke 8:18 says, "Take HEED therefore how ye hear . . ." It is important to take heed, to listen, in order to know what God wants to say to us, for it is His personal message to us.

When the Lord Jesus was on earth, crowds of people followed Him, listening to Him. If we had been alive then, would we have been part of the crowd listening to His every Word?

As He speaks to us from His Word by the power of His Spirit, we should not only hear Him but listen to what He is saying. "So be careful how you LISTEN" (LB). We need LISTENING HEARTS. "Her sister Mary sat on the floor, listening to Jesus as He talked" (Luke 10:39, LB). Seven times in Revelation we read, "He that hath an ear, let him hear."

We must come to the Word with an OPEN HEART, with a desire and willingness to receive what He has for us from His Word. He knows the areas of our lives that need to be changed and uses His Word to reveal and minister to our spiritual needs.

The Bible says, "Every Scripture is God-breathed—given by His inspiration—and profitable for instruction, for reproof and conviction of sin, for correction of error and discipline in obedience, and for training in righteousness [that is, in holy living, in conformity to God's will in thought, purpose and action], so that the man of God may be complete and proficient, well-fitted and thoroughly equipped for every good work" (2 Tim. 3:16-17, *Amplified*).

Then we need OBEDIENT HEARTS. "But be ye DOERS of the Word, and not hearers only" (James 1:22). To listen only is not enough. We must "take heed" to His Word, walking in the light of it. We must listen that we might hear Him say, "This is the way, walk ye in it" (Isa. 30:21). Then our listening hearts become obedient hearts.

August
22

God's laws are perfect. They protect us, make us wise, and give us joy and light (Ps. 19:7, LB).

As we see the beauty of the world about us, our thoughts turn to the God Who created it in all its glory and majesty. In the first six verses of Psalm 19 the greatness of God is revealed in the WORK of His creation. "The heavens declare the glory of God, and the firmament shows and proclaims His handiwork" (Ps. 19:1, *Amplified*). The heavens do not point to themselves, but to the work of another.

In verses 7 through 11, God is revealed in His WORD. Only in the Scriptures do we learn of His redemptive plan for mankind. In it is revealed the resources of God designed for the inner life of man.

As the psalmist considered God's Word, he enumerated some of the attributes of God's Word and some of its effects in our lives.

It is perfect—without flaw or defect. It is complete. It accomplishes everything it needs to. It convicts of sin, pointing to the Savior. It restores the soul, refreshing the inner life. "It restores the whole person" (Ps. 19:7, LB).

It is the sure Word of God, reliable, trustworthy to follow, giving us wisdom and direction.

His Word is right. It leads us in a straight path to our goal in Christ. It rejoices the heart, delighting those who obey it, bringing the joy of the Lord into each heart.

It is the pure Word, purifying us as we allow it to be personally applied to our lives. It enlightens, illuminating the dark for us, clarifying our vision as we walk in obedience to it.

It is clean, a cleansing agent for our lives. It has an enduring quality, preventing us from defiling ourselves.

It is true and righteous, ever faithful. It reveals His holiness and justice. It shows that He is right in all He does.

The Word of God has its proper place in our lives when we allow it to accomplish for us and in us what God intended it to. Are we giving it proper place in our lives?

More to be desired are they than gold, yea, than much fine gold: sweeter also than the honey and the honeycomb (Ps. 19:10).

It has been said, "We must know the Word of God to know the God of the Word." The universe reveals the handiwork of God, but the Bible reveals the heart of God. The Word has a great effect on our lives, enriching them as we read and meditate on it.

A great value is put on the teaching of the Bible. David said, "More to be desired are they than gold, yea, than much fine gold." If you were to list your valuable possessions, would you include your Bible? It's POSSESSION is better than gold.

His Word brings abiding PLEASURE to those who search its pages. ". . . sweeter also than honey and the honeycomb." Have you had a special need and when you opened the Bible and read from it, it was sweet to your taste as it met your need? It is a PROTECTION, warning us of temptations and pitfalls, and rewarding those who obey it. "Moreover by them is thy servant warned" (Ps. 19:11). There is PROFIT in keeping it. ". . . in keeping of them there is great reward."

Do you want to know more of God? Then turn to His Word. Let Him reveal Himself from its pages. The Holy Spirit will make the one revealed in His Word real in your life.

When Alexander Duff sailed for India as a missionary, he took a library of eight hundred books, much treasured by him. In a shipwreck he lost all of them. Looking back to the sea, he saw something small being washed ashore. Picking it up, he discovered it was his own Bible. He decided God was showing him that the Bible was worth more than all the other volumes of his library. Through his study of the Word, God became more real to him, and his life was a great blessing to the people of India.

The Bible is the only Book whose Author is always present when one reads it.

August 24

Let the words of my mouth, and the meditation of my heart, be acceptable in thy sight, O Lord, my strength, and my redeemer (Ps. 19:14).

In Psalm 19 David wrote of God's great and glorious power revealed in the heavens and the earth. What beauty we see displayed in His Creation! What power is demonstrated! David also wrote of the divinely revealed and inspired Word of God.

Then David closed the Psalm with a very familiar prayer. As he lifted his voice in worship to God, he asked God to control both his inner and outer life.

First, David prayed that the words of his mouth would be acceptable to God. Suppose we made a tape of all the words we speak each day and at night before retiring we would play the tape back. Would we be pleased with what we heard? Or would we be surprised to hear the words we had spoken during the day? Would they be gentle, kind, loving, comforting, encouraging? Or would they be harsh, bitter, unkind, critical?

But David continued to pray that not only his words but even the meditations of his heart be acceptable to God. He knew his words indicated the condition of his heart; that the outer expressions of a life in words and actions come from an inner attitude of heart and mind. Matthew 12:34 says, ". . . out of the abundance of the heart the mouth speaketh." The *Living Bible* reads, "For a man's heart determines his speech." If our heart is right with God, our words will be acceptable to God, and our conversation will please Him. David was more desirous of pleasing God than people.

He cried out to God, "Search me, O God, and know my heart: try me, and know my thoughts: and see if there be any wicked way in me, and lead me in the way everlasting" (Ps. 139:23-24).

What about our conversation today? Is it acceptable to God? Are our thoughts pleasing to Him? What are the meditations of our hearts?

May our prayer be that the words of our mouth—what we say; and the meditations of our hearts—what we do; reveal an inner and outer life that is acceptable and pleasing to God.

He that dwelleth in the secret place of the most High shall abide under the shadow of the Almighty (Ps. 91:1).

Insecurity is a characteristic of many people today. They are constantly searching for ways to give themselves greater security. They purchase insurance to cover every conceivable kind of hazard. They install various kinds of protective devices to give safety in their homes. Yet with all these precautions they are still fearful and worried.

The above verse is a favorite Scripture. Psalm 91 has been called the "Traveler's Psalm," for its blessings can be appropriated for our journey through life. It is a hymn of trust and assurance. The Berkeley translation calls it "Divine Security." It brings words of comfort, peace, and strength.

In the midst of our worry and fear-filled lives, God has a secret place where we can live with Him in perfect security. "Dwelleth" means to reside habitually with Him; it means to live in His presence. There we have a place of safety. No harm can touch us, we are protected from danger, and we are safe IN HIM.

"He who dwells in the secret place of the Most High shall remain stable and fixed under the shadow of the Almighty (Whose power no foe can withstand)" (Ps. 91:1, *Amplified*).

When the storms of life break on us we have a secret place where we can run for safety. When we are misunderstood, when false rumors are circulated about us, when we are deeply hurt by someone dear to us, we can hide under the shadow of our almighty God, and feel His comfort and understanding pour into our hearts. He can minister to us as no one else can.

There we find ourselves having heart to heart communion with God. In Song of Solomon 2:3 we read "I sat down under His shadow with great delight." "Sat down" indicates abiding there with no desire to leave His presence.

There in His presence we find protection, security, peace, and delight.

It has been said that "under the shadow of God's wing the little shadows of life are blended into His peace and thus lose their terror."

August
26

I will say of the Lord, He is my refuge and my fortress: my God; in him will I trust (Ps. 91:2).

Yesterday we considered the security there is for those who abide in the secret place of the Most High God.

The one who dwells in the secret place, "will say OF the Lord, He is MY refuge, a hiding place from danger, and MY fortress, a defense against my enemies."

A refuge is a safe retreat from a pursuing enemy. A fortress is a tower of defense, standing firm to meet the attacks of the enemy. We have no power or might of our own to resist the temptations and trials that come. They are too strong for us. But in our safe place of refuge there is safety.

The picture of a mother hen gathering her chicks under her wing illustrates this truth. During a storm how quickly the little chicks run to the mother hen and hide under her sheltering wings.

Under His wing is security, stability, and safety for us. "He shall cover thee with his feathers, and under his wings shalt thou trust; his truth shall be thy shield and buckler" (Ps. 91:4).

He has promised those dwelling in the secret place complete deliverance. "He shall deliver thee"; He will protect from every danger. "He will cover thee with His feathers"; He will free you from every fear; "Thou shalt not be afraid." He will keep you from harm; "No evil will befall you"; "No plague will come nigh thee."

God has promised some "I wills" for those abiding in Him, "I will deliver," "I will set him on high," "I will answer him," "I will be with him," "I will honor him," and "I will satisfy him."

When trouble comes and we run to Him, we will find Him our safe refuge. When opposition comes and we trust Him, we will find Him our fortress.

Spurgeon said, "We commune with Him, for He is the Most High God. We rest under the shadow of the Almighty God. We rejoice in Him as Jehovah, or Lord. We trust Him as El, the Mighty God."

This God is "MY GOD; IN HIM WILL I TRUST."

Abide in me, and I in you. As the branch cannot bear fruit of itself, except it abide in the vine; no more can ye, except ye abide in me (John 15:4).

When Jesus talked to His disciples about the fruitful life, He compared it to the union of the branch and the vine. It is the life of the vine flowing through the branch that produces fruit. This is the reason for the existence of the vine. Only as the fruit is produced is the purpose of the branch accomplished.

Jesus said, "I am the vine, ye are the branches." Only the branch bears the fruit. Fruit is the natural result of the life of the vine flowing through the branch. "Ye have not chosen me, but I have chosen you, and ordained you, that you should go and bring forth fruit, and that your fruit should remain" (John 15:16).

The branch does not have to struggle to produce fruit. All that the Vine is and has is available to the branch. Someone has said, "Christ is the source of this life; we are the channels to express it. He is the secret of our life; we are the natural manifestation of that life."

The condition for fruitbearing is abiding. Jesus said, "Yes, I am the Vine; you are the branches. Whoever lives in Me and I in him shall produce a large crop of fruit" (v. 5, LB). Jesus did not say "abide WITH me," but "IN me."

As we abide in Him, the fruit of the Spirit, the Spirit of Christlikeness, such as joy, peace, gentleness, is produced in our lives. Abiding in Him results in fruit in our service of sharing Jesus Christ with others.

As we abide in Him, we recognize our dependency upon Him. He said, "Without me ye can do nothing" (v. 5). Abiding in Him gives the branch constant communication with Him. As we live in Him and He in us, He becomes our close companion. From a life of abiding in Him comes a productive harvest of fruit—MUCH fruit.

Are you abiding in Him? Is your life producing much fruit?

August
28

Every branch in me that beareth not fruit he taketh away: and every branch that beareth fruit, he purgeth it, that it may bring forth more fruit (John 15:2).

As branches in God's Vine, we have only fulfilled His purpose for our lives when there is fruit. But God is not satisfied with "just" fruit. He desires more fruit—much fruit.

Growing roses was a special hobby of mine. I learned that to develop stronger branches and produce larger, more beautiful roses required drastic pruning each spring. Later, when the bushes were covered with lovely roses, the importance of earlier pruning was proven.

Just as pruning is necessary for bushes and trees, so pruning is necessary if our lives are to bring forth more fruit. "And He cleanses and repeatedly prunes every branch that continues to bear fruit, to make it bear more and richer and more excellent fruit" (John 15:2, *Amplified*). The Father does the pruning, and prunes away anything that hinders the production of fruit in us.

He may use circumstances such as adversity, affliction, heartache, sorrow, and loneliness in His pruning process. "Now no chastening for the present seemeth to be joyous, but grievous: nevertheless afterward it yieldeth the peaceable fruit of righteousness unto them which are exercised thereby" (Heb. 12:11). Circumstances may hurt, but God allows them to increase the fruit production in us.

He also uses His Word to cleanse and purify us. "Now ye are clean through the Word which I have spoken unto you" (John 15:3).

Two results of fruitfulness are mentioned. First, we will have an effective prayer life. "If ye abide in me, and my words abide in you, ye shall ask what ye will, and it shall be done unto you" (v. 7). If we abide in Him, and are obedient to His Word, and our requests are in accordance with His will, we can expect God to answer.

Then, a fruitful life glorifies the Father. "Herein is my Father glorified, that ye bear MUCH fruit; so shall ye be my disciples" (v. 8).

What kind of a harvest are we producing in our lives today? Is there fruit? More fruit? Much fruit? Is He being glorified by an abundant harvest in our lives?

These things I have spoken unto you, that in me ye might have peace. In the world ye shall have tribulation: but be of good cheer; I have overcome the world (John 16:33).

Jesus' earthly ministry was coming to a close. Just before His betrayal, He spent His last evening with His disciples. He knew they would enounter difficult days ahead, days filled with trouble and trials. He encouraged them by saying, "I have told you all this so that you will have peace of heart and mind. Here on earth you will have many trials and sorrows; but cheer up, for I have overcome the world" (John 16:33, LB).

Since those words were spoken nearly two thousand years ago, there have been few intervals of peace on earth. Many conferences have been held to draft plans for world peace, but none have resulted in a state of peace.

Since we have not been promised freedom from tribulation, we need not be surprised when trials overtake us. The Lord Jesus Christ told us to expect them. He said, "In the world you have tribulation and trials and distress and frustration" *(Amplified).*

We need not panic when tribulation comes, for we are promised peace. This peace is in a person. Jesus said, "IN ME you may have perfect peace and confidence. . . . be of good cheer—take courage, be confident, certain, undaunted—for I have overcome the world.—I have deprived it of power to harm, have conquered it [for you]" *(Amplified).*

"IN ME" ye shall have peace. The source of this peace is Jesus Christ Himself. We read in Ephesians 2:14, "He is our peace . . ." We can have His peace at all times; we can have it in times of conflict, confusion, and chaos; in the midst of insurmountable problems; in times of sickness; in times when our lives are filled with tension, turmoil, and trouble. Our peace is in HIM, not our circumstances.

In the midst of our trials we can "BE OF GOOD CHEER." Why? Because Jesus said, "I have overcome the world." He accomplished this by His death and resurrection. In Him we can be triumphant.

In the world — tribulation! !
In Me — Peace!

August
30

One thing have I desired of the Lord, that will I seek after; that I may dwell in the house of the Lord all the days of my life, to behold the beauty of the Lord, and to inquire in his temple (Ps. 27:4).

Late for an appointment, a man hurried out and hailed a cab. Jumping in, he said to the driver, "Get going and drive as quickly as you can." After a few blocks, he impatiently asked, "Are we almost there?" "Almost where?" replied the driver. In his hurry the passenger had failed to give the driver the address of his destination.

That may seem an unlikely story, yet today many people are so busy trying to keep up with the rapid pace of living, they haven't stopped to consider what their goal in life is.

David had a goal in his life, a goal that his heart was set on achieving. He said, "ONE THING have I asked of the Lord, that will I seek after" (Ps. 27:4, *Amplified*).

Since David was in danger, helpless, and friendless, he might have prayed for his safety, but that was not the primary desire of his heart.

First, his heart's desire was "that I may dwell in the house of the Lord—in His Presence—all the days of my life." He wanted to live in the presence of the Lord all the days of his life. He longed for the constant companionship of God.

Next, his desire was "to behold the beauty of the Lord." He wanted his vision filled with the Lord.

Then he wanted "to inquire in His temple." He wanted God's answers to his problems; to know God's will; to become better acquainted with God.

He had his priorities right. He longed for companionship with the Lord—to be occupied with God's Person; He wanted to seek His will—to be occupied with God's guidance.

Jesus Christ came that through Him we might have the constant companionship of God, see Him with our eyes of faith, and walk in obedience to His will.

How sweet are thy words unto my taste! yea, sweeter than honey to my mouth (Ps. 119:103).

Someone has said, "The Bible is God's Word to us. We are to read it to be wise, believe it to be safe, and study it to be approved. It is the traveler's map, the pilgrim's staff, the pilot's compass, the soldier's sword, and the Christian's charter. Christ is the grand subject, our good its design, and the glory of God its end. It should fill the memory, rule the heart, and guide the feet. Read it slowly, frequently, prayerfully. It involves the highest responsibility, will reward the greatest labor, and condemn all who trifle with its sacred contents."

How important is God's Word for our lives. Jesus said, "You search and investigate and pore over the Scriptures diligently, because you suppose and trust that you have eternal life through them. And these [very Scriptures] TESTIFY ABOUT ME!" (John 5:39, *Amplified*).

It is possible to read it and yet miss the personal application of it in our lives as they were doing. Jesus said, "They are they which testify of me" (John 5:39). They knew the Scriptures, but they had missed its most important purpose of revealing the Lord Jesus Christ as the Son of God, the Savior of the world.

Do you enjoy reading the Bible? Do you search for the many wonderful truths revealed in it about Jesus Christ? Are you becoming more like Him as you assimilate it into your life? Are you appropriating it into your daily living to meet your needs?

It is said that the silkworm grows to be similar to the colors of the leaves on which it feeds. Jeremiah 15:16 reads, "Thy words were found, and I did eat them; and thy word was unto me the joy and rejoicing of mine heart." George Mueller said, "The vigor of our spiritual life will be in exact proportion to the place held by the Word of God in our life and thoughts."

The psalmist said God's Word was sweet to this taste, even sweeter than honey. May our taste for God's Word never become dull.

September
1

O God, thou art my God; early will I seek thee: my soul thirsteth for thee, my flesh longeth for thee in a dry and thirsty land, where no water is (Ps. 63:1).

While David was alone in the wilderness he was evidently reminiscing of the time when God had been very real to him in the sanctuary. He still desired the reality of God's presence that he had known in the past. He said, "O God, thou art MY God." From the depths of his soul he cried out, "My soul thirsteth for THEE, my flesh longeth for THEE in a dry and thirsty land, where no water is."

The story is told of a Thai man who came to a Thailand mission station. They said to him, "Are you looking for some medicine?" "No," he replied, "I am looking for God."

There are many hungers and thirsts in the world today. Some people hunger for position; some for power. Others hunger for pleasure, love, or acceptance. People are searching everywhere for things that will satisfy. But inner satisfaction does not come through things. Jesus assures us that the hunger and thirst of our soul can be satisfied. "Blessed are they which do hunger and thirst after righteousness: for they shall be filled" (Matt. 5:6).

Inner fulfillment comes from HIM. David said, "Early will I seek HIM." When we read the Bible we must seek Him on its pages. When we enter the prayer closet we must become quiet enough to hear Him speak to us. We must not stop short of anything less than God Himself.

Today, are you seeking for inner peace? Are you longing for something to satisfy? You can be satisfied; you can have inner fulfillment as you seek and find it in Jesus Christ. He said, "If any man thirst, let him come unto me, and drink" (John 7:37).

Tell HIM today of the longing of your heart. Seek Him from the Word of God. Talk to Him, and let Him talk to you in prayer.

Your inner longing can be satisfied in Him today. "My soul shall be satisfied as with marrow and fatness" (Ps. 63:5).

To see thy power and thy glory, so as I have seen thee in the sanctuary (Ps. 63:2).

David was alone in the wilderness when he prayed this prayer. Yet even though he was lonely, he didn't feel sorry for himself. Someone has said that although he was in the wilderness, there was no wilderness in his heart. He let his thoughts wander back to the time when God had been real to Him in the sanctuary.

Now he wanted a fresh revelation of God. It is wonderful to remember what God has done in the past, but it should challenge us to experience God's power and glory in a fresh way today. What has He said to you TODAY? What is He doing for you NOW?

God's power is available for our every need. Paul wrote, "I pray that you will begin to understand how incredibly great HIS POWER is to help those who believe Him" (Eph. 1:19, LB).

His power to work in us goes beyond what we can ask or think. "Now to Him Who, by (in consequence of) the [action of His] power that is at work within us, is able to [carry out His purpose and] do superabundantly, far over and above all that we [dare] ask or think—infinitely beyond our highest prayers, desires, thoughts, hopes or dreams" (Eph. 3:20, *Amplified*).

Charles Ryrie has said, "The glory of God is displaying God to the world." This He did in His Son, Jesus Christ. "And the Word was made flesh, and dwelt among us, (and we beheld His glory, the glory as of the only begotten of the father,) full of grace and truth" (John 1:14).

Today we can see the glory of God revealed to us in Jesus Christ. "God, who first ordered light to shine in darkness, has flooded our hearts with His light, so that we can enlighten men with the knowledge of the glory of God, as we see it in the face of Christ" (2 Cor. 4:6, *Phillips*).

Then as our vision is filled with Him, we can reveal His glory to others wherever we may go.

September 3

When I remember thee upon my bed, and meditate on thee in the night watches (Ps. 63:6).

Often in the night time when we are wakeful, our minds go back to the past and memories flood our thinking. Our memory seems to work overtime at night.

David had remembered the wonderful things God had done for him, and pondered on God's wonderful kindness to him. "Because Your loving-kindness is better than life, my lips shall praise You" (Ps. 63:3, *Amplified*). How dear life is to us. We make every effort to prolong it and care for it. But David believed that the lovingkindness of God was better than life.

In the barren places of our lives, in times of helplessness, we, too, can experience God's loving-kindness. As we recognize all that God has and is doing for us, what joy it will bring into our lives.

When we can't sleep, how often we begin to think of all the things we have to do, or we worry about our problems. The more we try to sleep, the wider awake we become. But David had learned a wonderful way of spending his sleepless hours at night. He had a wonderful occupation, remembering God and meditating on Him. His experiences with God were real. Thinking of Him in the night watches brought joy. He said, "When I remember THEE upon my bed, and meditate on THEE in the night watches" (Ps. 63:6).

This is wonderful occupation for our sleepless nights. We can think of all that He has done for us and meditate upon Who He is. Instead of counting sheep, we can count our blessings, numbering them one by one. As we do this, our hearts will be filled with praise. What sweet times we can have with Him in the quietness of the night. What peace He will bring to us. It may be He has some special word to share with us for our encouragement and comfort. It may even be a gentle admonition.

Meditation is not dependent on books, methods, or on our own efforts. We are to meditate on HIM. "My meditation of HIM shall be sweet: I will be glad in the LORD" (Ps. 104:34).

Because thou hast been my help, therefore in the shadow of thy wings will I rejoice. My soul followeth hard after thee: thy right hand upholdeth me (Ps. 63:7-8).

David had much to thank God for. In the above verses he enumerates some of his blessings.

First, he had the SURETY of GOD'S PRESENCE. "Because THOU hast been MY help." Throughout his lifetime, David had experienced God's help. Not one of his needs had been too great for God's help. In Psalm 46:1 we are assured, "God is our refuge and strength, a very present help in trouble."

He often experienced the SAFETY of GOD'S PROTECTION. "Therefore in the shadow of THY wings." The overshadowing protection of God's wings of love and care constantly surrounded David. "He who dwells in the secret place of the Most High shall remain stable and fixed under the shadow of the Almighty (Whose power no foe can withstand)" (Ps. 91:1, *Amplified*). In our time of danger He is our Protector. "He shall cover THEE with his feathers, and under his wings shalt thou trust" (Ps. 91:4).

In his heart was a SONG of PRAISE. "Will I rejoice." One of the lessons we learn from David is his constant praise of the Lord. He didn't just praise Him on the bright sunny days, but on the dark and dreary days. God can give us "songs of praise," too, even in the night season. He can teach us to sing in our desert experiences.

He had SECURITY on GOD'S PATH. "My soul followeth hard after Thee." We are always secure as we cling to God through the difficult places of life. "My whole being follows hard after You and clings closely to You" (Ps. 63:8, *Amplified*). We are not to cling to things or people, but to God.

Then he knew the STRENGTH of GOD'S POWER. "Thy right hand holdeth me." The fear of falling is removed as we let God hold us by His powerful right hand. "For I, the Lord your God, hold your right hand; I, Who say to you, Fear not, I will help you" (Isa. 41:13, *Amplified*).

Surety, safety, songs, security, strength—these are all blessings from God for us today.

September

5

Then I come to them of the captivity at Telabib, that dwelt by the river of Chebar, and I sat where they sat, and remained there astonished among them seven days (Ezek. 3:15).

Ezekiel went to God's people in captivity with a warning from God. However, before he gave the warning, he sat with them seven days. It was as if God was saying to him, "Not yet, Ezekiel. Before you can minister to them, before you can give them My Word, you must sit with them and experience what they are going through, so that you may have a deeper spirit of compassion for them."

For seven days he sat where they sat. He could feel their needs with them. He could see their problems through their eyes. Then he was ready to share God's message for them.

Today many people have aching hearts. They need to know that someone loves and cares for them. God has called us to minister to them for Him. He has given us the privilege of identifying with them that they know that we care, and, even more, that He cares. But we are not really prepared to help them until we have felt their suffering with them.

Dr. Edman once said, "Compassion is a flame of fellow-feeling, a blaze that burns with desire for the welfare of others. It is embers of empathy that are warm with insight into the heart of another. It both anticipates and understands their problems and perplexities with the sensitivity that inquires indwardly, 'If my soul were in their soul's stead.'"

The Hebrew word for mercy means "to get inside one's skin so as to become completely identified with another." Empathy is identifying our lives with another until his needs become ours. We see the circumstances of another through his eyes, hear with his ears, and experience his feelings.

How we need such a spirit of empathy for our friends, our neighbors, our families. We need to sit in their place until we not only understand their problems, but experience their feelings. Then we are ready to share that Jesus Christ is their only answer.

"Is it nothing to you, all ye that pass by?" (Lam. 1:12).

By faith Moses, when he was born, was hid three months of his parents, because they saw he was a proper child; and they were not afraid of the king's commandments (Heb. 11:23).

When a baby boy was born to Jochebed and Amram, the joy of having him was overshadowed by a decree issued by Pharaoh that all Hebrew baby boys must be killed.

But Jochebed and Amram had a deep faith in God. They knew the God in whom they trusted was greater than the king who had issued the decree. BY FAITH they committed their little one to God's care.

When the baby could no longer be hidden, Jochebed placed him in a basket among the reeds at the river's edge. Miriam, his sister, hid nearby to watch him. Having done all she could to protect him, Jochebed trusted him to God for safekeeping. Someone has said, "Jochebed worked as though everything depended on her and trusted as though God must do it all."

Later, when the princess came to the river, she found the baby. Miriam offered to secure a nurse and went for the baby's mother. What joy filled the mother's heart as the princess placed him in her care until he grew older.

Jochebed realized her responsibility for teaching him about the living God in whom she and Amram believed. During the formative years he was in her care, she instilled into his little life a faith in God. Need we wonder at the faith of Moses after being reared in a home with parents who trusted God so completely.

Today the world is in need of homes built upon faith in the living God.

What strength there is in a home where the Bible is read, where prayer is a daily habit! What God can do in a home where He is given control! Who can measure the power and influence of such homes where their members trust God and have a close walk of faith with Him!

Even one person in a home who believes God and lives by faith, can have a great influence upon it.

May our lives be a great spiritual strength in our homes today.

September
7

He went out unto his brethren, and looked on their burdens (Exod. 2:11).

When God allows us to go through a time of testing and trial, He is, at the same time, working out His plan for our deliverance.

While the Israelites were oppressed slaves in Egypt, God was preparing Moses to be their deliverer. Moses must have remembered that his parents were slaves, and wondered what was happening to them. Very likely he knew God was going to use him to liberate the children of Israel from the power of the Egyptians.

One day he made an important decision as to his future. "By faith Moses, when he was come to years, refused to be called the son of Pharaoh's daughter; choosing rather to suffer affliction with the people of God, than to enjoy the pleasures of sin for a season" (Heb. 11:24-26).

One day when Moses went to visit his fellowmen, he saw an Egyptian mistreating one of the Israelites. After "he looked this way and that way" (Exod. 2:12), he killed him, hiding his body. Very likely Moses felt justified in trying to right their wrongs. However, his brethren rejected his help. He fled to the desert for safety, arriving there alone, discouraged, a failure.

What had happened? Wasn't he to be their deliverer? His problem was that, although he knew God's will for his life, he was doing it his way. He was working it out according to his schedule, not God's.

When he came to the end of himself in the desert, he became quiet enough to listen to God speak to him. He then began to learn that God's work must be done God's way.

We, too, may find ourselves in the desert, depressed, discouraged, a failure. We have to admit our plans have failed. When we get to the end of ourselves, we discover we have been doing God's will in our strength instead of in God's power. We must learn that God's ways are not our ways and His way is always best.

"Trust in the Lord with all thine heart; and lean not unto thine own understanding. In all thy ways acknowledge him, and he shall direct thy paths" (Prov. 3:5-6).

Not that we are in any way confident of doing anything by our own resources–our ability comes from God (2 Cor. 3:5, Phillips).

Moses had made himself the self-acclaimed deliverer of the children of Israel, only to find that his plans had failed. But God was not limited by Moses' failure. God was not through with him yet.

Moses may have felt he was qualified, for had he not received the best education and training for leadership in the courts of Egypt? "And Moses was learned in all the wisdom of the Egyptians, and was mighty in words and deeds" (Acts. 7:22).

We are told he had been trained for a top position in Egypt. Yet he had to realize that all his natural ability, education, and training did not qualify him for God's work. Moses had been too strong in his own strength for God to use. The desert is a wonderful place to lose self-sufficiency and self-will. In this place of obscurity he learned that neither he nor his abilities were indispensable to God.

Forty years may seem a long time to be in God's Preparatory Course for leadership, but God is never in a hurry. He is more interested in the individual than in his service.

Moses discovered that God's will must be done God's way. He learned lessons of dependence and complete trust in the Lord that he would need as he led the children of Israel out of Egypt.

Sometimes we, too, come to the end of ourselves, finding ourselves in a desert of our own making, thinking our lives are failures. Alone in the desert the self-life begins to die. Not only must we learn that God's will needs to be done God's way, but we must learn that God does not want our ability or inability, but our availability. God can only entrust His power to those emptied of self and conscious of their own helplessness.

As we yield our lives to Him we discover He exchanges our self-sufficiency for His all-sufficiency. He makes us the person He wants us to be and prepares us for the task He has for us to do.

September
9

And he looked, and, behold, the bush burned with fire, and the bush was not consumed (Exod. 3:2).

Moses had observed the cruelty of the Egyptians to his own Hebrew people. One day in a fit of anger he killed an Egyptian who was mistreating a Hebrew slave. His attempt to help his people had failed. Ian Thomas said, "Moses had committed himself to the task instead of to God."

He Who is to use the vessel must prepare it. God took Moses, a seeming failure, to the desert, a place of solitude and insignificance. There God was to do a work in Moses' life. In the desert Moses lost his self-sufficiency.

God knew Moses needed a greater awareness of His presence before he was ready for God's service. The person God uses can only accomplish God's purpose as God's presence fills his life and God's power works through him.

One day, just an ordinary day like any other, while Moses was on "the backside of the desert," he saw a strange sight. A common bush was on fire, but it was not consumed.

Moses decided, "I will NOW turn aside, and see this great sight" (Exod. 3:3). He took time to turn aside and found himself in God's presence. Do we take time to turn aside so that God can speak to us?

Then God spoke, "Moses, Moses." Immediately Moses answered, "Here am I." God said, "Draw not nigh hither: put off thy shoes from off thy feet, for the place whereon thou standest is holy ground" (v. 5). He is a holy God and His presence is always holy ground.

The bush ablaze was a picture or symbol to Moses of a life filled with the presence of God. It was the fire in the bush that made it extraordinary.

God was saying in effect to Moses, "Moses, you are to be My leader, but you are only a bush. Your greatness will depend on MY Presence indwelling you, possessing and controlling you."

Today God is looking for "bushes" who will be afire with His Presence. Ian Thomas has said, "Any old bush will do. We must come to the place where we present ourselves as we are—nothing—to be filled with what He is—everything."

Every day [with its new reasons] will I bless You—affectionately and gratefully praise You; yes, I will praise Your name for ever and ever (Ps. 145:2, Amplified).

This is a Psalm full of thanksgiving and praise, extolling the one Who alone is worthy of praise. David said, "I will bless YOU; I will praise YOU." His praise was not just for what God gave him or did for him, but for God Himself. He expressed his personal relationship to the one Whom he praises, "MY God, the king."

His praise to God is continual—"EVERY DAY will I bless YOU—affectionately and gratefully praise you." There is an interesting phrase in this verse—"Every day WITH ITS NEW REASONS." That includes today. Sometimes we feel that we have nothing to praise Him for. But if we look for them there will always be new reasons for praising Him.

The psalmist's heart was full of GREAT PRAISE to a GREAT GOD. "Great is the Lord and highly to be praised, and His greatness is [so vast and deep as to be] unsearchable" (Ps. 145:3, *Amplified*). He is so great that we cannot explain or fathom it. "How great he is! His power is absolute! His understanding is unlimited" (Ps. 147:5, LB).

Our praise is to be never ending. "I will bless Your name for ever and ever" (Ps. 145:1, *Amplified*).

Regardless of our circumstances, conditions, environment, or needs, we have new reasons each day for praising Him. We are assured of His unchanging love for us. "I have loved thee with an everlasting love" (Jer. 31:3). We are assured of His constant presence with us. "I will never leave thee, nor forsake thee" (Heb. 13:5). We are assured of His willingness to work out each circumstance in our lives for our good and His glory. "And we know that all things work together for good to them that love God, to them who are the called according to His purpose" (Rom. 8:28).

The psalmist ends Psalm 145 with a great finale of praise. "My mouth shall speak the praise of the Lord, and let all flesh bless—affectionately and gratefully praise—His holy name for ever and ever" (v. 21, *Amplified*). PRAISE YE THE LORD!

September
11

But when he saw the multitudes, he was moved with compassion on them, because they fainted, and were scattered abroad, as sheep having no shepherd (Matt. 9:36).

This past summer you may have been sightseeing in our beautiful world while on your vacation. Or you may have only been able to dream of such a vacation.

However, today, let us take a sightseeing trip, a trip with an eternal purpose in view. Jesus set the pattern for this kind of sightseeing when He was on earth. He was constantly aware of the needs of people and He had deep compassion for them.

As we begin our sightseeing trip with Him, we need to see people as He sees them through His eyes. "And what pity he felt for the crowds that came, because their problems were so great and they didn't know what to do or where to go for help. They were like sheep without a shepherd" (Matt. 9:36, LB).

First, we will travel with Him into the rural areas of the world, seeing them with Him. He said, "Say not ye, There are yet four months, and then cometh harvest? Behold, I say unto you, Lift up your eyes, and look on the fields; for they are white already to harvest" (John 4:35).

Then we will travel into the cities of the world, seeing them as He saw them. We read of Him, "And when he was come near, he beheld the city, and wept over it" (Luke 19:41).

As we travel with Him into our neighborhoods and communities, we will see them as He does.

However, if we are to have His vision of the world today our vision must be filled with Him.

One day Jesus took His disciples up into a mountain with Him. There He was transfigured before them. "And when they had lifted up their eyes, they saw no man, save JESUS ONLY" (Matt. 17:8).

As we see HIM ONLY, we will go out into the world, seeing it through His eyes.

"He that goeth forth and weepeth, bearing precious seed, shall doubtless come again with rejoicing, bringing his sheaves with him" (Ps. 126:6).

The battle is not yours, but God's (2 Chron. 20:15).

Abraham Lincoln once said, "I have been driven many times to my knees by the overwhelming conviction that I had nowhere else to go. My own wisdom, and that of those about me, seemed insufficient for the day."

Throughout the Bible, often the people of God were driven to their knees in prayer when they were powerless to withstand the onslaught of the enemy.

While Jehoshaphat was king of Judah, the land was being threatened by a strong aggressor. The natural plan would have been to recruit more men, step up production of ammunition, and improve their military strategy. But the king knew their resources were insufficient. Only God was powerful enough to conquer their foe. "Jehoshaphat feared, and set himself to seek the Lord" (2 Chron. 20:3).

In this national emergency he didn't rely on weapons, ammunition, or his army. What were they without God? He prayed; and not only did he pray, but all the people of Judah joined him. "And Judah gathered themselves together, to ask help of the Lord" (v. 4). A whole nation prayed. The king prayed, "We have NO MIGHT against this great company that cometh against us; NEITHER KNOW WE WHAT TO DO: BUT OUR EYES ARE UPON THEE" (v. 12). He did not have his eye on the problem, not on their weakness, but on almighty God.

The Spirit of the Lord came upon Jahaziel and God spoke through him, "The BATTLE IS NOT YOURS, BUT GOD'S" (v. 15). The people began to praise God for the victory which was to come, and soon the enemy was defeated.

We face an enemy, one who is too strong for us to conquer. We say, "We have no might against this great company that cometh against us." Then with assurance we continue, "The battle is not OURS, BUT GOD'S." Instead of focusing on the powerful enemy, we must look to the Lord—"OUR EYES ARE UPON THEE."

When a praying king and a praying nation waited upon God, He heard and answered. God will still hear and answer the prayers of praying nations and the prayers of praying people.

September 13

That he would grant you, according to the riches of his glory, to be strengthened with might by His Spirit in the inner man (Eph. 3:16).

Today not only are we caught up in the complexity of twentieth-century living, but in its conflicts and confusions. We question daily, "Where can I find help? To whom can I go?" We recognize our own human weakness.

What an intercessor Paul was. In Ephesians 3, we have one of his compassionate prayers as he pleads for believers. He knew we would experience not only times of physical weakness, but spiritual, as well.

His first request was that we build strong inner fortifications for daily living or we will fall before the power of the enemy. Christ, Himself, is our inner fortification, our inner strength. Paul wrote, "Be strong in the Lord, and in the power of his might" (Eph. 6:10). The Holy Spirit accomplishes this within us.

Our homes of today contain many electrical appliances. The power is available for their use, but they have to be plugged into the outlet before the power can operate them.

All the power of God is available for us; there is no limit to His supply. But we have to be "plugged in" to the source of power!

He gives us inner strength according to the riches of His glory. We cannot ask for too much, for it is inexhaustible. Once a man came to a king asking for something he needed. The king, in giving it to him, went beyond the request. The man said, "Your majesty, that is too much!" The king replied, "It may seem too much for you to take, but not for me to give."

Occasionally we hear of serious power failures. God's power for our lives will never fail. But it can be prevented from operating efficiently if we allow short circuits in our lives.

As His power is released within, He will give victory over every circumstance.

"That out of his glorious, unlimited resources he will give you the mighty inner strengthening of his Holy Spirit" (Eph. 3:16, LB).

And I pray that Christ will be more and more at home in your hearts, living within you as you trust in him (Eph. 3:17, LB*).*

Paul challenged the Ephesians to let Christ make His permanent home in their lives. "May Christ through your faith [actually] dwell—settle down, abide, make His permanent home—in your hearts" *(Amplified).*

When He lives within, He wants to control our entire personality, our emotions, our intellect, and our will. As we yield our emotions to Him, He can make a wonderful transformation. He can remove all our fears, giving us His peace. He can give victory over jealousy, envy, and quick temper if we let Him. His abiding presence is perhaps more clearly seen in our emotions than any other part of our lives.

The Bible says that we can have His mind. "Let this same attitude and purpose and [humble] mind be in you which was in Christ Jesus" (Phil. 2:5, *Amplified*). Someone has said, "Let His Spirit set a watch at the door of our minds so that all that enters will have His approval."

Perhaps the most difficult area to let Him control is our will. However, if Christ is to be at home in our lives, we must turn our wills over to Him. The psalmist said, "I delight to do thy will, O my God" (Ps. 40:8). Can we say that?

God dwelling in our lives means a whole heart relationship, emotions, mind, and will. As the self-life dies, the life of Christ fills us completely. "That in all things He might have the pre-eminence" (Col. 1:18).

Once a couple bought a beautiful large picture for their home. When it was delivered, they moved it from room to room, hanging it in different places, trying to decide upon the most appropriate place for it. No place seemed right, so they decided to remodel their home around the picture.

God may have to do a remodeling job in our lives before He can be at home in every part of our lives. He can make your life a beautiful home in which He dwells, as you enthrone Him at the center of your being.

September 15

That ye, being rooted and grounded in love, may be able to comprehend with all saints what is the breadth, and length . . . and to know the love of Christ (Eph. 3:17-19).

Paul reminds us that we are to be rooted and grounded in love. God IS love, so if we are rooted and grounded in love, we are rooted and grounded in God. This brings stability into our lives so that nothing can shake us.

Paul speaks of the four dimensions of love. First, the length of God's love is from everlasting to everlasting. "Yea, I have loved thee with an everlasting love" (Jer. 31:3). God is love and because He is, "He SO loves the world." As far back as you can think through the millenniums past, God loved. As far into the future as when time becomes eternity, God will still love. His love is eternal as God Himself. "Having loved his own which were in the world, he loved them unto the end" (John 13:1).

The breadth of His love is all-inclusive. He longs to draw all mankind to His heart of love. "For God so loved the WORLD." It's scope takes in everyone. Jesus had compassion for all segments of society. The lame and the blind were ministered to by Him. He was ready to meet the needs of such guilt-ridden adulteresses as Mary Magdalene and the religious intellectuals like Nicodemus. His love reached out to the loathsome lepers. It is as broad as the circumference of the world but only real in the lives of those who accept it through Jesus Christ.

The Duke of Wellington, the famous conqueror of Napoleon, was kneeling in a church one Sunday, ready to partake of communion. A private was also kneeling for communion. When the private discovered who was kneeling beside him, he was embarrassed. Quietly he arose, saying, "Pardon me, your grace." Wellington pulled him down beside him, saying, "In the presence of Jesus Christ there are no dukes." The breadth of His love takes in everyone.

Wrapped up in His love is His plan and purpose for His children. The length and breadth of His love is like the boundless ocean—there is no end to it.

May be able to comprehend with all the saints what is the . . . depth, and height; and to know the love of Christ, which passeth knowledge (Eph. 3:18-19).

Yesterday we considered the length and breadth of God's love. Today we will ponder its depth and height.

The death of Christ on the cross encompasses the depth of God's love. From heaven's glory, He came to earth to demonstrate God's love. "He humbled Himself, and became obedient unto death, even the death of the cross" (Phil. 2:8).

Fridtjof Nansen, the Norwegian explorer, attempted to measure the depth of the sea in a certain place. Unable to touch bottom with his instruments, he recorded the measurement, adding a note, "Deeper than that." Time after time he attempted to measure its depth in different places, but each time was unsuccessful. After his final entry in the book, again he wrote, "Deeper than that."

The depth of God's love touches the individual life, your life and mine. ". . . that he gave His only begotten Son." "But God showed his great love for us by sending Christ to die for us while we were still sinners" (Rom. 5:8, LB).

How high is His love? It is high enough to lift us up into a personal relationship with God through Jesus Christ. "That whosoever believeth in him should not perish but have everlasting life." It reaches up to the very heart of God and lifts us into His presence. "And hath raised us up together, and made us sit together in heavenly places in Christ Jesus" (Eph. 2:6).

Centuries ago in an underground dungeon was found the form of a cross on a rock wall. A prisoner had cut it into the rock with a sharp piece of metal. Above it, in Spanish, was the word for "height," below it the word for "depth," on one arm the word for "length," and on the other arm the word for "breadth." There in that lonely prison cell the prisoner had been meditating on the grace and love of God. The figure on the cross summed it up for him—the length, breadth, depth, and height of the love of God.

This is the love that passeth knowledge—the love of God.

September
17

Now unto him that is able to do exceeding abundantly above all that we ask or think, according to the power that worketh in us (Eph. 3:20).

Paul had an overwhelming awareness of the greatness and power of God beyond human expression. In Ephesians 3 he prayed that the Ephesian Christians might be strengthened in the inner man by God's Spirit, that they might know the love of God which comes from Christ's presence in their hearts by faith, and that they might be filled with the fulness of God. Through such a relationship with God, they could experience His power in their lives, a power to do far beyond their asking or even thinking.

"Now to Him Who, by (in consequence of) the [action of His] power that is at work within us, is able to [carry out His purpose and] do superabundantly, far over and above all that we [dare] ASK or THINK—infinitely beyond our highest prayers, desires, thoughts, hopes or dreams" (Eph. 3:20, *Amplified*).

God's resources are inexhaustible. Through prayer our needs and His resources are brought together.

God can do far beyond anything we can ask or think. "Where prayer focuses, power falls." When we focus on our needs and the needs of others in prayer, the power of God is channeled to meet those needs.

God is not measured by our asking or thinking. We often limit God by our meager asking. A legend says that one day there was great excitement in heaven. Several angels were wrapping a huge gift package. An angel passing by paused to inquire, "What are you so excited about?" "Oh," they replied, "at last someone has asked for something big."

Have we availed ourselves of the exceeding abundant resources of God? Our petitions can never exceed His ability to grant. "For with God all things are possible" (Mark 10:27).

There is no limit to what God is ABLE to do. There is no limit to His resources. His ability is beyond our prayers. His power and ability far surpass petitions. Someone has said, "Nothing is too great for His power, or too small for His care."

But grow in grace, and in the knowledge of our Lord and Saviour Jesus Christ (2 Peter 3:18).

Growth is defined as "to increase in size, quantity, or degree, and develop toward maturity."

If there is life, there is growth. If we have spiritual life, there should be evidence of spiritual growth. There should be progress along the road to spiritual maturity. Growth in two areas is emphasized here—growth in grace, and in the knowledge of Jesus Christ.

As we grow in grace, we reveal His love and humility in our lives. We are gentle and kind, giving preference to others. We will reflect His spirit of graciousness.

We are to grow in our knowledge of Him; not just in knowledge ABOUT Him, but in knowledge OF Him. "But grow in spiritual strength and become better acquainted with our Lord and Savior Jesus Christ" (2 Peter 3:18, LB).

Our Source Book for this knowledge of Him is the Word of God. "As newborn babes, desire the sincere milk of the Word, that ye may grow thereby" (2 Peter 2:2).

It is more than just knowledge, it is a knowledge that becomes real in our lives. The Holy Spirit takes our knowledge of Christ and makes HIM real within us. "But I will send you the Comforter—the Holy Spirit, the source of all truth. He will come to you from the Father and will tell you all about ME" (John 15:26, LB).

The process of spiritual maturity takes time. We are living in an age of "instant" living when we want things to happen fast, but this is not true in spiritual development.

Paul wrote, "UNTIL we all ATTAIN oneness in the faith and in the comprehension of the full and accurate knowledge of the Son of God; that [we might ARRIVE] at really MATURE manhood" (Eph. 4:13, *Amplified*).

Once when I was visiting in a home I found a place on the back of a door where the yearly measurements of their children were recorded, showing their growth over the previous year.

What is our measurement this year? Have we shown growth over last year? God wants us to grow from spiritual infancy to maturity.

September 19

But when the Holy Spirit controls our lives he will produce this kind of fruit in us (Gal. 5:22, LB).

The person controlled by the Holy Spirit is becoming the person God wants him to be, developing Christlike characteristics.

As the Holy Spirit produces God's LOVE in us, it will flow through us to others.

In Him we have a JOY that is not dependent on circumstances, a joy even in adversity.

Filled with His PEACE we are untroubled in times of trials. His peace gives a serenity of heart.

The Spirit produces LONGSUFFERING, or patience. Patience will then be our normal attitude toward others.

A Spirit of GENTLENESS gives us polite and gracious consideration of others.

GOODNESS has been defined as "being like God, filled with His goodness." It is living for others instead of self.

FAITH has the meaning of faithfulness, God's faithfulness. The Spirit will make us faithful and dependable.

MEEKNESS is submitting to God's will regardless of the situation, having His humility. The meek are the least conscious of it.

As the long distance runner learns TEMPERANCE, or self-control, in training for the race, so the Holy Spirit brings our lives under God's control.

The Fruit of the Spirit is a nine-fold variety of fruit. It cannot be tied on to our lives like ornaments on a Christmas tree. Neither can it be purchased at the supermarket. It is not the outward putting on of characteristics, nor is it produced by human ability. The genuine fruit of the Spirit comes from within. It is the life and character of Christ produced in us by the Holy Spirit. He produces in us the same qualities that are in Christ.

One day while making a purchase of perfume, I tried the perfume from several sampler bottles at the counter. After my purchase I went to another counter. The clerk said, "Are you wearing Chantilly perfume?" She had detected its fragrance, as it was one of the perfumes I had sampled.

When the Holy Spirit produces His fruit in our lives, we give forth the fragrance of the life of Jesus Christ wherever we go.

For this reason also we make it our ambition, whether in our home or away, to please Him (2 Cor. 5:9, Weymouth).

To please Him! What more wonderful ambition or desire could we have. This was the ambition of Enoch. "He had this testimony, that he pleased God" (Heb. 11:5). Jesus gave us the most perfect example of pleasing God. "For I do ALWAYS those things that please Him" (John 8:29). "My meat is to do the will of him that sent me, and finish his work" (John 4:34).

Paul was an ambitious man, but with one ambition—to please the Lord Jesus Christ. He wrote, "We do not aim to please men, but to please God who knows us through and through" (1 Thess. 2:4, *Phillips*).

Life is not easy. There are many difficulties to face, problems to solve, decisions to make, discouragements to bear, much work to be done. Yet through all and in spite of all our circumstances, our desire must be to please Him. "We are constantly ambitious and strive earnestly to be well pleasing to Him" (2 Cor. 5:9, *Amplified*).

This means we please Him in all we do and say, wherever we go. Our words will be pleasing to Him, our habits, friends, actions, thoughts, motives, priorities. It means we will be careful not to leave undone things that will please Him. The question of what is right and wrong is settled when our aim is to please Him.

Once a young man had been studying violin under a great master. At last, he was giving his first recital. The concert hall was crowded. After his first number he was given loud applause. He made a formal bow but seemed unaware of the great applause. After each number there was increased enthusiasm by the audience. After his final number they cheered loudly. Then they noticed the eyes of the violinist were fixed upon his master seated in the balcony. The master smiled and nodded his approval. Only then did the young man respond to the audience. His first concern had been to receive the approval of his master.

How we need to keep our eyes on our Master, with one aim, that of pleasing Him.

September
21

When thou goest, it shall lead thee; when thou sleepest, it shall keep thee; and when thou awakest, it shall talk with thee (Prov. 6:22).

In a day when we cannot depend upon the word of people, we can be certain that God's Word is dependable.

It will be our GUIDE for our pathway. "When thou goest it shall lead thee." When our way is dark, it becomes our light. "Thy Word is a lamp unto my feet, and a light unto my path" (Ps. 119:105). If our pathway has curves around which we cannot see, God promises, "And the crooked shall be made straight" (Isa. 40:4). For the steep climbs ahead, we read, "And I will make all my mountains a way" (Isa. 49:11).

His Word will be our GUARDIAN. "When thou sleepest it shall keep thee." In our unguarded moments it comes to us, keeping us from temptation, from wrong direction and decisions. "The law of his God is in his heart; none of his steps shall slide" (Ps. 37:31).

It will be our constant COMPANION. "When thou wakest it shall talk to thee." The Bible is the Living Word of God and it becomes alive to us as its messages become relevant to our personal needs. It is "The Word of God, which liveth and abideth for ever" (1 Peter 1:23). It is the voice of God speaking to us.

The Word speaks to us as it meets our needs, bringing comfort, enlightenment, instruction, peace, strength, and courage.

It talks to us through the promises of God. Someone has said that God has a promise for every need. It brings the right Word at the right time.

As I have been writing this devotional, I have had a deep heartache. "Why, Lord?" has kept creeping into my mind. I turned to God's Word for His answer. I took a card out of my Promise Box and there I read, "Commit thy way unto the Lord; trust also in Him; and He will bring it to pass" (Ps. 37:5). Peace came as God talked to me through His Word.

It is a Word for us personally. "It shall talk to THEE." Let it be your Guide, your Guardian, your Constant Companion day by day.

I am the Lord, I change not (Mal. 3:6).

Security is defined as "certainty, protection, freedom from fear." Most of us depend on things or people to give a sense of security. My home had always been dear to me. It represented a security I felt I needed. Although the Lord came first in my life, yet underneath, I still considered my home as my "security blanket."

Then one day in a few hours my way of living changed completely. As I went to the hospital on a Saturday afternoon to see my husband, little did I realize I would leave that hospital the next morning a widow. We had known we could expect this, yet we are never prepared when it comes.

In a few weeks I had to drop the "security blanket of my home" into God's hand and take from Him a new life style. I began a life of travel, living out of a suitcase and staying in different homes night after night. It is not the life I would have chosen, but I wouldn't want any other, for this is God's choice.

I have proved in experience what I had believed before. My security was not in my home or my possessions, but in my changeless Lord. I had to lift my eyes from MY life to HIM. He knew why I needed the experience I was going through. Even though my life changed, I discovered God was the same. He says, "I change not."

He wanted to prove Himself to me, for my trust and confidence must be completely in Him. This takes time. I learned then to "put" my trust in Him in a new way, letting Him become MY security for a new life.

Sometimes He removes things from our lives completely. Sometimes He removes them long enough to release us from them. Then He gives them back to us.

In a generation characterized by changes, God said, "I am THY God; I change not." Where is your security today? In possessions? In people? Or in God?

We have an unchanging security in a life controlled by the unchanging God.

September
23

What? know ye not that your body is the temple of the Holy Ghost which is in you, which ye have of God, and ye are not your own? For ye are bought with a price: therefore glorify God in your body, and in your spirit, which are God's (1 Cor. 6:19–20).

Dr. Timothy Richard asked a philanthropist from another country if he had read the New Testament. "Three times," he replied. "What impressed you most?" the doctor continued. Pausing, the other finally said, "I think the most wonderful thing to me in the whole Bible is this, that it is possible for men to become temples of the Holy Spirit of God."

We are God's possession, bought with a price, the death of Jesus on the cross. We are redeemed, "not . . . with corruptible things, as silver and gold, . . . but with the precious blood of Christ" (1 Peter 1:18–19). Then our bodies become the temple of the Spirit of God, a sanctuary for Him.

Since we are His purchased possession, He has a right to our lives. These Scripture verses remind us that we are not our own. Our bodies, with all their members—ears, eyes, hands, feet, lips, our all—belong to Christ. Therefore, we are to use them to glorify Him.

Several years ago I purchased some furniture. I paid cash for it and received a receipt for the payment. Then I said, "I have purchased the furniture, but for a few weeks I have no place for it. May I leave it here until the room is vacant where I am going to place it?" They agreed to this arrangement.

Later, I called and had them deliver it to me. It had been mine by purchase for several weeks. But it was not mine by possession until it was delivered to me.

Someone has said, "Consecration is a matter of letting God have what He has already paid for."

To whom does your life belong? Who do you want to please? In whom are your interests and desires centered? Your family? A friend? Yourself? Or Christ?

You are His purchased possession. Have you given Him complete possession of His property?

If a man wants to enter my service, he must follow my way; and where I am, my servant will also be. And my Father will honour every man who enters my service (John 12:26, Phillips).

September
24

When entering the service of our country, one must meet certain qualifications. Certain requirements are demanded of the recruit. Certain requirements are also expected of those who enter God's service. Jesus said, "IF any man serve me, let him FOLLOW me (John 12:26).

If we are to follow Him, we must keep in CLOSE CONTACT with Him. We must go His way. We must give up our plans for His, and let His interests become ours. If we are to know His directions for us and receive the daily supplies we will need, we must keep close to Him.

As we follow Him, we will go where He would go if He lived where we live. We will speak what He could speak if He met the people we meet each day. We will do what He would do if He were in touch with the lives of those we meet day by day.

If we are to follow Him, walking in His steps, speaking His Words, serving others for Him, we must have CONSTANT COMPANIONSHIP with Him. Jesus said, ". . . and where I am, My servant will be also." If we are to serve Him, companionship with Him is necessary. We must be careful not to become so involved with our service that we fail to take time to be with Him.

We may not know where He is leading us. All we need do is to follow Him.

It is fascinating to watch a puppeteer at work. The puppet follows perfectly the manipulation of the hand inside the puppet. For the person operating a puppet to accomplish all he wants to, his hand must be inside the puppet and the puppet must follow exactly.

May we place ourselves so at Jesus' disposal that we will follow Him, allowing Him to work perfectly through our lives. May we live in such close companionship that we won't miss one direction He has for us.

September

25

And this is life eternal, that they might know thee the only true God, and Jesus Christ, whom thou hast sent (John 17:3).

In John 17 we are privileged to listen to the Lord Jesus as He talks with His heavenly Father. His earthly ministry was nearly ended. Before Him lay the real work He had come to accomplish—the redemption of mankind through His death on the cross.

Even though He was facing His crucifixion, yet His prayer was not for His deliverance from it. He prayed for His disciples and for believers who down through the years would carry on the ministry of the gospel.

Lifting His eyes to heaven, Jesus said, "Father, the hour is come . . ." (John 17:1). This was the hour that He and His Father had planned—the completion of God's plan of salvation for a sinful world.

He continued, "And this is life eternal, that they might know thee the only true God, and Jesus Christ, whom thou hast sent" (v. 3). Eternal life is not imparted knowledge, but the reality of God in our lives through a personal relationship with Jesus Christ. Rainsford wrote, "The knowledge of which Christ speaks is not an intellectual, speculative, theoretical knowledge of doctrines; but an experimental, heart-affecting, life-influencing acquaintance with the only true God and Jesus Christ whom He has sent." We may know all about Him with our minds, and yet miss the personal knowledge of His presence in our lives.

Jesus Christ came to make possible eternal life. "The gift of God is eternal life through Jesus Christ our Lord" (Rom. 6:23).

Eternal life is not just endless existence. It is a quality of life, the life of God imparted to those who believe on Jesus Christ.

Through Christ all of the resources of God are available for our daily walk. He brings a new depth of meaning and purpose into our lives. We discover He is the one Who understands and sympathizes with us in every circumstance we experience. He is the one with whom we can share our joys and sorrows.

Is your knowledge of Him continually growing? Are you experiencing all the potential enrichment your life can have in Him?

I have glorified thee on the earth: I have finished the work which thou gavest me to do (John 17:4).

As Jesus approached the end of His earthly ministry, he lifted His eyes to heaven and prayed to His heavenly Father: "I have glorified thee on earth."

He never acted independently of God, but always did His Father's will. Earlier He had said to His disciples, "My meat is to do the will of him that sent me, and to finish His work" (John 4:34). He was not interested in building up a name for Himself, but in bringing glory to His Father.

Then He prayed, "I have finished the work which thou gavest me to do." He did not leave His work half done, but completed it to the last detail. "I have brought glory to you here on earth by doing everything you told me to" (John 17:4, LB). He had completed the work of revealing God on earth. His final work, His death and resurrection, was yet ahead of Him, but in His mind, He thought of it as already accomplished.

The Lord Jesus has asked us to continue His work for Him. ". . . even so send I you" (John 20:21). To do this, we must know the work He has personally called us to, and let nothing turn us aside from it. We must not quit because we are tired, bored, or discouraged. He is trusting us to finish the assignment He gave us to do.

One Christmas a father called his son to him. "Son, when you left school you came to work for me. I have trained you, I have watched your progress. Today, as a Christmas gift, I am taking you into the firm as my partner." Today, we are in partnership with the Lord Jesus Christ. He is expecting us to fulfill our part of this God-given trust.

Someone has said, "When I enter the beautiful City, and the saints all around me appear; I want to hear somebody tell me, 'It was you who invited me here.'"

May we finish the work we are to do for Him that one day each of us can say, "I have finished the work thou gavest ME to do."

September
27

I have manifested thy name unto the men which thou gavest me out of the world: thine they were, and thou gavest them me; and they have kept thy word (John 17:6).

In this Scripture verse, Jesus is praying specifically for His disciples and all those who would come to a personal faith in Him down through the ages. "Neither pray I for these alone, but for them also which shall believe on me through their word" (John 17:20).

"I have manifested thy name unto them." The word "name" has the meaning of person or character. Jesus came to show people Who God is and what He is like. "It is true that no one has seen God at any time. Yet the divine and only Son, who lives in the closest intimacy with the Father, has made him known" (John 1:18, *Phillips*).

He continued, "They have KEPT THY WORD." One time Jesus said to His disciples, "Will ye also go away?" Peter replied, "Lord, to whom shall we go? THOU HAST THE WORDS of eternal life. And we believe and are sure that thou art that Christ, the Son of the living God" (John 6:67-69).

God has given us His Word and it is His special message to us. One Christmas a little boy gave his grandmother a Bible for Christmas. He wanted to write something on the flyleaf. He remembered his father had a book with an inscription in it that he was proud of. He copied it carefully into the front of the Bible. Christmas morning when she opened her new Bible she found it inscribed, "To Grandma, with the compliments of the Author."

There must be a consistent reading of His Word day by day that we may know His message for us.

We must not only know His Word, but we must KEEP it. We must be obedient to it. "Blessed are they that hear the Word of God, and keep it" (Luke 11:28). "If a man love me, he will keep my words" (John 14:23).

What place does His Word have in your life today? Are you walking in obedience to it? Can the Lord Jesus say of us, "They have kept MY Word"?

And now I am no more in the world, but these are in the world, and I come to thee. Holy Father, keep through thine own name those thou hast given me, that they may be one, as we are one (John 17:11).

Knowing His disciples would not have an easy life in the days ahead, He prayed to His Father, ". . . keep through thine own name those thou hast given me." He had watched over them while He had been with them, but now He was handing them over to the keeping power of His Father. He didn't ask God to take them OUT of the world, but to keep them IN it.

He committed all believers to the safekeeping of God. "Holy Father, keep in Your name [in the knowledge of Yourself] them whom You have given Me" (John 17:11, *Amplified*).

The President of the United States, because of his importance to our nation, has a bodyguard of Secret Service agents for his personal protection. We are not in a position to be provided with Secret Service men as the President is, but we are so valuable to the Lord He has committed us to the keeping power of His Father. "Who are kept by the power of God" (1 Peter 1:5).

The Lord is our present keeper—"The Lord IS thy keeper" (Ps. 121:5). He is our personal keeper—"THY keeper." We are kept through the power of His name. There is authority and security in that name. "The name of the Lord is a strong tower: the righteous runneth into it, and is safe" (Prov. 18:10).

Paul's life was filled with hardships and dangers. He had learned from experience the keeping power of the Lord. He wrote, ". . . he is able to KEEP that which I have committed unto him against that day." Commit means to give something to Him for His safekeeping. It means bringing our loved ones, our problems, our life, our all to Him, taking our hands off completely and leaving them with Him. God is able to keep, but we must commit.

"Everything is safe which we commit to God, and nothing is really safe that is not committed" (A. W. Tozer).

September 29

If any man speak, let him speak as the oracles of God; if any man minister, let him do it as of the ability which God giveth (1 Peter 4:11).

Peter reminded believers that they are God's "stewards of the manifold grace of God." The *Living Bible* (1 Peter 4:10) says, "God has given each of you some special abilities; be sure to use them to help each other, passing on to others God's many kinds of blessings."

He calls us "good stewards." A steward is "one who has the responsibility of using something entrusted to his care."

As good stewards we are to speak as the oracles of God. We are God's mouthpiece to speak His Word. The *Living Bible* (1 Peter 4:11) says, "Are you called to preach? Then preach as though God Himself were speaking through you." Whether we share His Word in a public ministry or on a one to one basis, we are to speak it with boldness and certainty. We must know God's Word for we are speaking for God Himself.

Then we are to minister with God-given ability, for our own ability is not enough. Moses is a good example of such a one. It was after he had lost his self-sufficiency that God could use him. He discovered that the all-sufficiency of the Lord was available for Him.

As we speak, it is not our message but His; in ministering, it is not our ability but His.

Then he sums up the objective of our ministry. ". . . that God in all things may be glorified through Jesus Christ, to whom be praise and dominion for ever and ever. Amen" (1 Peter 4:11).

Peter reminds us of the importance of glorifying Him in ALL things. Not only are we to glorify Him in our service for Him but in every area of our lives. This includes not just our times of success, but our times of failure; not just in joy but in sorrow. Not just on the mountain top but in the valley. We are to glorify Him in every problem, every care, every joy—IN ALL THINGS.

A good steward speaks God's Word, ministers by His power, and glorifies Him in all things.

September 30

He maketh the storm a calm, so that the waves thereof are still. Then are they glad because they are quiet; so he bringeth them unto their desired haven (Ps. 107:29-30).

Occasionally I spend a few days at a motel close to the ocean. It is a beautiful spot, right on the beach, with a breathtaking view of the blue Pacific. Sometimes as I watch a storm raging out in the distance, I wonder about the ships that are being tossed about as the waves beat upon them.

The psalmist writes of the power of God that can control a great storm and can quiet the fears of those experiencing it. "For he commandeth, and raiseth the stormy wind, which lifteth up the waves thereof" (Ps. 107:25). In desperation they cried to the Lord and He brought them out of their distresses. He hushed the storm to a calm and stilled its waves. As He brought them to their destination, their hearts were full of joy. "Then the men were glad because of the calm, and He brings them to their desired haven" (Ps. 107:30, *Amplified*).

Today we may be in stormy waters tossed about by waves of trouble, heartache, doubt, or fear. We may have attempted our own methods of stilling the storm. We may have turned to people for help. Having found no human way of calming our storm, we may be almost ready to give up in despair.

However, there is a way of safety for us through the storm. Jesus Christ, our great Pilot, not only knows the way, but He can calm the storm and still the waves. W. Graham Scroggie said, "Storm-tossed seamen, needing tranquility, find a 'storm-stiller,' Jesus Christ."

Although our outward circumstances may be stormy, Jesus gives us that inner quietness of heart that steadies us in our storm-beaten lives. The psalmist said, "HE maketh the storm a calm, so that the waves thereof are still." Although the waves may beat against us, we have a God-given calm.

Is the storm raging in your life today? Are you almost sinking beneath its waves? HE will make YOUR storm a calm, bringing you to a desired haven.

October

1

And he said, What have they seen in thine house? (2 Kings 20:15).

One time we were informed that our apartment was to be redecorated. The painters would come in and complete the work in a day.

The larger pieces of furniture were moved into the hall. Other things were piled in the center of each room.

We had a Scripture calendar on our wall. Each morning after my husband and I had our devotional time, we read the Scripture reference for the day. This particular day, to our great amusement we read, "What have they seen in thine house?" As I looked about, I laughingly said, "It looks like a lot of junk."

When the decorating was completed and we began putting things away, I suggested we sort through personal things, throwing away the junk. I could see a great deal of junk in my husband's things. Yet later when I asked where his junk was, he said, "I didn't have any." He had put everything back in place.

When I sorted through my things, I discovered I couldn't find as much junk as I thought I had. I threw away very little.

The verse on the calendar came to mind. I wondered if this was the way God saw my life. Did He see much junk He wanted to remove, yet it seemed important to me?

One day God sent Hezekiah word that he would not live long. God said, "Set thine house in order" (Isa. 38:1).

Today is God saying to us, "Set thine house in order"? Does He see things He wants to remove? Are there things that need to be replaced?

Paul wrote of "junk" as hay, wood, and stubble that would be burned. Does God see hay, wood, and stubble which He desires to replace with gold, silver, and precious stones?

Paul said, "But any man who builds on the foundation using as his material gold, silver, precious stones, wood, hay or stubble, must know that each man's work will one day be shown for what it is. . . . If the work which a man has built upon the foundation stands this test, he will be rewarded. But if his work is burnt down, he loses it all" (1 Cor. 3:12-15, *Phillips*).

And God said unto Moses, I AM THAT I AM: and he said, Thus shalt thou say unto the children of Israel, I AM hath sent me unto you (Exod. 3:14).

What comes to your mind when you hear the word "God"? A right concept of God Himself greatly affects our spiritual life. In the Bible, the meaning of a person's name usually gives some indication of the character and work of that person. Throughout the Bible various names are used for God. As we study them, we discover a more complete unfolding of His character.

At the time Moses was to lead the Israelites out of Egypt, he said to God, when I come to the Israelites and they ask who sent me, ". . . What is his name? what shall I say unto them?" (Exod. 3:13).

In asking, "What is His name?" basically they were asking, "Who is He?" "What is His character?" God replied, "Thus shalt thou say unto the children of Israel, I AM hath sent me unto you" (Exod. 3:14).

God is the "Great I AM." In His vocabulary there is no past nor future tense; no "was," nor "will be," but always "now," "is," "I AM." His name indicates His self-existence and eternality. He has no beginning and no ending.

As we consider what His name "I AM" implies, we may ask, "I AM what?" for it is not complete. Hannah Smith has said, "This apparently unfinished name is the most comforting name the heart of man could devise, because it allows us to add to it without any limitations, whatever we feel the need of, and even exceeding abundantly above all we can ask or think."

It is as if God presented us with an unfailing supply of blank checks to be filled in with our need. If we need strength, He promises, "I AM your strength"; if wisdom, "I AM your wisdom"; if peace, "I AM your peace." Whatever our need may be, God becomes that which we need, and provides it for us through Jesus Christ.

"My God shall supply all your need according to his riches in glory by Christ Jesus" (Phil. 4:19).

October
3

If any of you lack wisdom, let him ask of God, that giveth to all men liberally, and upbraideth not; and it shall be given him (James 1:5).

In his short epistle, James has some principles for an effective prayer life.

Some people are afraid of bringing their requests to God, believing that they should not bother Him with their personal needs. They have failed to believe that God means it when He says, "Ask, and it shall be given you" (Matt. 7:7).

But the above verse reveals the fact that God is a God who delights to give, and give liberally. "He is always ready to give a bountiful supply." Our part is to ask, His to give.

The basis of our asking is faith. "Let him ask in faith" (James 1:6). Faith is trusting God to answer prayer, and to answer it His way, in His time.

In 1 Thessalonians 3:7 *(Amplified)* we find a definition of faith: "The leaning of your whole personality on God in complete trust and confidence."

We are warned against being indecisive. "He that wavereth is like a wave of the sea driven with the wind and tossed" (James 1:6). Instead, we are to ask in faith, nothing wavering, believing and waiting for God to answer. We are to expect His answer.

Next we must ask with the right motive in mind. We must ask in accordance with His will. "Ye ask, and receive not, because ye ask amiss" (James 4:3).

Prayer brings results. "The effectual fervent prayer of a righteous man availeth much" (5:16).

Through prayer Elijah controlled the weather. He prayed for the rain to cease and it did. He prayed for it to rain again, and it did.

There is power in prayer. "Ye have not, because ye ask not" (James 4:2). Prayer is dynamic; it is powerful; it works. It produces results, results that are specific.

James could write on prayer out of his own experience of a life of prayer. According to tradition, his knees were called "camel's knees." They were as hard as camel's knees, because he spent so much time kneeling in prayer.

How would our prayer life be described?

As for God, his way is perfect (Ps. 18:30).

Today our hearts can be encouraged as we recognize the truth of this verse. We may wonder about certain things that have happened to us. Our path may be dark ahead and we cannot see our way. It may be blocked by obstacles that we cannot see around. A sorrow may have clouded our sky. The plan of our life may have been completely changed. We may not know which way to turn. We may be wondering what is best for us.

When we commit our way to Him, it becomes His way. Then we can be sure that whether it is joy or sorrow, sunshine or clouds, health or sickness, plenty or want, His way for us IS perfect. We cannot doubt that. He sees the end from the beginning. He sees the pattern He is working out in our lives and will not make one mistake. We may not understand it, but He does. That is enough. Can we say, not with a sigh, but with a song—"perfect is His way" (Ps. 18:30, *Berkeley*).

Not only is God's way perfect, but He makes our way perfect. "It is God that . . . MAKETH MY way perfect" (v. 32). Perfect means "fulfill" or "complete." He completes or fulfills our life and brings it into conformity with His will. There is a making process necessary to perfect His way in us. It is the making process against which we often rebel.

A woman was complaining about the hardness of her life with all its trials and troubles. She said to someone, "I wish I had never been made." "My dear," replied her friend, "you are not yet made. You are only being made and you are quarreling with God's process."

He enables us to surmount our difficulties. As we yield ourselves to Him, He will complete the process of making our way perfect.

"For my thoughts are not your thoughts, neither are your ways my ways, saith the Lord. For as the heavens are higher than the earth, so are my ways higher than your ways, and my thoughts than your thoughts" (Isa. 55:8-9).

The joy of the Lord is your strength (Neh. 8:10).

Many physical fitness programs have been developed to produce strong bodies. There are programs for developing strong muscles, programs of exercise and diet, programs for taking a series of vitamins and minerals. This is done to increase the strength and energy needed for each day.

In God's Word we are given a prescription for increasing our strength. One ingredient of this prescription is joy; an inner joy produced by the Spirit of God.

Nehemiah and his people were observing the Feast of Tabernacles. As the law was read the people began to weep over their sins. But Nehemiah and Ezra said, "This day is holy to our Lord; and be not grieved and depressed, for the joy of the Lord is your strength and stronghold" (Neh. 8:10, *Amplified*).

Nehemiah encouraged them to rejoice in the Lord as they read the Word.

There is a special inner joy that overflows from the heart. It shines from the eyes. It gives special beauty to the lives of people. The secret of this joy is the Lord, for He is the source of this joy.

When we have the joy of the Lord we are strong in the midst of trials and tensions, fear and frustrations of life. Joy gives strength to our bodies and spirits.

The Amplified Bible reads, "Strength and stronghold." He who trusts and rejoices in the Lord has a strong fortress in which he is safe. The joy of the Lord transforms our weakness into His strength.

It is not every joy that brings strength, but the joy of the Lord. His joy is the joy of salvation, the joy of a yielded will, the joy of fellowship with Him, the joy of His steadfast love.

Do we know that inner joy that brings strength because we spend time with Him who is its source?

Someone has said, "The oil of gladness reduces friction and eases the wear and tear of living."

A joyful heart gives a joyful face.

"A merry heart doeth good like a medicine" (Prov. 17:22).

Jesus himself drew near, and went with them (Luke 24:15).

Cleopas and an unnamed companion were on their way home to Emmaus. As they trudged along, their hearts were sad. In the past few days, Jesus had been crucified and buried. Now startling news was spreading that He had risen from the dead.

While they were absorbed in talking of these recent events, "JESUS HIMSELF approached and walked along WITH THEM" (Luke 24:15, *Phillips*). But they were so busy talking ABOUT HIM they failed to recognize Him.

Jesus knew their bewilderment, but He questioned them concerning it. He said, "You seem to be in a deep discussion about something. What are you so concerned about?" (v. 17, LB).

They proceeded to tell Him of the recent happenings. They were troubled. Their faith had been shaken. They failed to understand what had taken place.

Jesus shared the Scriptures with them concerning Himself. What a Bible study it must have been, with Jesus as the Teacher! Later they remembered how their hearts were warmed as they listened to Him.

As we walk through life, we may be perplexed and disillusioned with things that have happened. Our hearts may be filled with sorrow, tears may be falling from our eyes. Jesus is always with us, but during such a time of need, He draws near in a special way. He asks, "What are you concerned about?" As He speaks, our hearts are warmed and the heavy load we carry is eased.

Perhaps we have been looking so intently at our problems and trying so hard to find an answer for them, we have failed to see Him walking with us in the midst of them. As He walks with us, He guides, protects, and provides for us.

We do not face our needs alone. He promises, "I will never leave thee, nor forsake thee" (Heb. 13:5).

Our road may be in the valley of discouragement and disappointment; the steep climb of heartache and sorrow; the rough path of pain. He knows each step of our way. He draws near to walk with us on it.

He is near to you today wherever you are, whatever your need, and walks with you as your close Companion and Friend.

October
7

And their eyes were opened, and they knew Him (Luke 24:31).

When they reached the village, Jesus started to go on. Perhaps He was testing them. Did they want more of His companionship? They invited Him to spend the night with them. They prepared a meal for Him and as they sat down together, He asked God's blessing on the food. As he passed the bread to them, "their eyes were opened, and they KNEW HIM; and he vanished out of their sight" (Luke 24:31).

What excitement and joy must have filled their hearts as they realized that Jesus had risen from the dead—HE WAS ALIVE. They had seen Him and walked with Him. Their hearts had been strangely warmed as He had opened the Scriptures to them. "And they said one to another, Did not our heart burn within us, while he talked with us by the way, and while he opened to us the scriptures?" (v. 32).

But Jesus did not want them to stop there in their spiritual experience. He wanted their spiritual eyes opened to see and know HIM. "And their EYES were opened and they KNEW HIM." It began with a revelation of the Scriptures to their hearts but led them on to a revelation of Jesus Christ as the living Savior.

If they had stopped with the experience of the burning heart, they would have missed the fulness of their experience, a personal revelation of Jesus Himself.

Today where are we on our spiritual walk? Are we still walking through the confusion of our lives, concentrating so intently on our trials, our discouragements and disillusionments, that we fail to recognize Jesus as He draws near? He joins us just where we are, at the level of our understanding and experience, and walks with us.

As we turn to God's Word, He opens our spiritual eyes.

Not only does He desire to open His Word to us, but He wants to reveal Himself to us from it. In John 5:39 we read, "Search the scriptures . . . and they are they which testify of ME." Don't stop short of letting Him reveal Himself to you from the pages of His Word.

Blessed be the Lord, who daily loadeth us with benefits, even the God of our salvation (Ps. 68:19).

A special day is set aside each fall to thank God for His blessings. However, as children of God, we should thank Him daily for His bountiful provisions. The psalmist wrote, ". . . who daily loadeth us with benefits. . . ."

One day as Jesus entered a village, ten lepers approached Him. Leprosy was a loathesome disease for which there was no cure at that time. Seeing Jesus, hope must have sprung up in their hearts. Perhaps they had heard reports of the miracles He had performed. They cried out, ". . . Jesus, Master, have mercy on us" (Luke 17:13). His heart was filled with compassion for them.

Jesus tested their faith. He said, ". . . Go show yourselves unto the priests . . ." (v. 14). According to law, a person cleansed of leprosy must go to the priest to be officially declared cleansed. As the ten lepers obeyed Jesus, they were cleansed.

What joy must have been theirs as they realized what had happened to them. Now they were free to go wherever they wished.

Suddenly one of them stopped. He remembered the One who had performed this miracle. Quickly he returned to Jesus and with a heart filled with gratitude he fell at Jesus' feet in worship. "And fell down on his face at his feet, giving HIM thanks" (v. 16).

Jesus said to him, "Were there not ten cleansed? But where are the other nine?" Nine had gone their way—happy—but forgetful and unthankful. Their interest was in what He had done for them, forgetting the One who had performed the miracle. Only one returned to Jesus to express his thanks and worship Him.

We say, "How ungrateful!" But how many times do we, too, fail to thank God for what He has done for us? Do we take time to worship Him?

Why not pause now and thank Him for all the blessings He has given you, for material possessions and spiritual blessings. Thank Him for the trials He has permitted that He might teach needful lessons to you. "It is a good thing to give thanks unto the Lord, and to sing praises unto thy name, O most High" (Ps. 92:1).

October
9

The righteous shall flourish like the palm tree: he shall grow like a cedar in Lebanon (Ps. 92:12).

In my early married life we moved to California. As we traveled across California at night, I remember the thrill of rousing from my sleep and seeing palm trees silhouetted against the sky in the moonlight. I had seen many pictures of them but this was my first view of a live palm tree. I still remember vividly my feeling of awe as I gazed at their stately beauty.

Someone has said, "The palm tree is God's portrait in nature of a Christian."

Certain characteristics of the palm tree picture the life and experience of a Christian. The palm tree stands above other trees, and is, by its nature, upright and stately. As Christians we are to manifest the righteousness and uprightness of God. "He that walketh uprightly walketh surely" (Prov. 10:9), How tall are we spiritually?

The palm tree is a tree of special beauty; it is one of the most graceful of trees. As Christians, our lives should reflect the beauty of Jesus Christ wherever we go. "And let the beauty of the Lord our God be upon us" (Ps. 90:17).

The psalmist said, "The righteous shall flourish." To flourish means to thrive, to prosper, to grow luxuriantly. We usually think conditions must be ideal for a luxuriant growth. However, the palm tree proves that this is not so. It grows in places not conducive to growth. They can grow in desert places where nothing else grows, providing oases for places of rest for travelers along the way. Where not much else grows we find the palm tree flourishing.

Christians can grow and flourish in the most trying conditions. Our present situation may not be ideal, but we can flourish there, for our Christian growth is not dependent on our environment but on the Lord.

The psalmist said, "And he shall be like a tree planted by the rivers of water, that bringeth forth his fruit in his season; his leaf also shall not wither; and whatsoever he doeth shall prosper" (Ps. 1:3).

Does your life show that you are a "palm tree" Christian?

The righteous shall flourish like the palm tree: he shall grow like a cedar in Lebanon (Ps. 92:12).

October
10

Yesterday we compared the Christian life to the palm tree. We considered its outward beauty as it flourishes. Today we will look at the inner characteristics of the tree which are an example of a Christian.

Most trees get their life through the sap that flows up the tree just under the bark. Not so with the palm tree. Its sap flows up the center of the tree, producing new life from the heart of the tree.

The life of the Christian comes from the life of Christ implanted in the heart. "That Christ may dwell in your hearts by faith" (Eph. 3:17).

We discover the palm tree not only grows but flourishes in the most unlikely places. Why? Because it has a hidden source of nourishment. Although no water may be visible, the tree sends down a large tap root with other roots deep into the earth, appropriating nourishment for the soil and searching out hidden springs of water.

We have hidden springs of Living Water from which we can draw nourishment. "If anyone is thirsty, let him come to me and drink. For the Scriptures declare that rivers of living water shall flow from the innermost being of anyone who believes in me. (He was speaking of the Holy Spirit, who would be given to everyone believing in Him)" (John 7:37-39, LB).

The palm tree can withstand winds and hurricanes better than any other tree, not because of greater resistance, but because they bend and yield. When the winds and storms beat upon our lives, we, too, can withstand their fury, as we bend and yield, submissive to God, allowing Him to bring good into our lives from them.

Many lives have been saved by finding water near the palm trees. God wants your life and mine to be the means of bringing others to the Water of Life.

When our lives are nourished at His hidden springs, they can flourish like the palm tree, displaying His beauty and uprightness. We will be able to live victoriously above our circumstances.

October
11

Now no chastening for the present seemeth to be joyous, but grievous; nevertheless afterward it yieldeth the peacable fruit of righteousness unto them which are exercised thereby (Heb. 12:11).

Often when the circumstances of life are seemingly against us, we feel God has forsaken us, or He is punishing us in some way. But this is not true. Chastening means discipline, training, instruction, and has a part in our Christian maturity.

We can expect discipline. It is a proof of His love. We read, "My son, don't be angry when the Lord punishes you. Don't be discouraged when he has to show you where you are wrong. For when he punishes you, it proves that he loves you. When he whips you it proves you are really his child" (Heb. 12:5-6, LB).

For a time divine chastening appears grievous. Being punished is not enjoyable while it is happening—it hurts. But God makes no mistake. We may not understand why He is thus dealing with us, but there is the "nevertheless afterward." In such times we can grow. Afterwards we can see how our heartache, sorrow, disappointment, whatever our trouble may be, were part of God's care for us. They had a purpose out of which ultimately blessing came.

"Now obviously no 'chastening' seems pleasant at the time: it is in fact most unpleasant. Yet when it is all over we can see that it has quietly produced the fruit of real goodness in the characters of those who have accepted it" *(Phillips).*

We must not waste our sorrow, pain, or loneliness, or whatever has come into our lives, by complaining and becoming bitter about it. We must look beyond the experience of discipline to the One who is allowing it and learn the lessons He has for us through it.

God wants us to trust Him even when we cannot understand. A faith that is not tried, not exercised, will not be strong.

Today you can rejoice, not for the trouble, but that God is proving His love for you and ultimately will accomplish His perfect work in your life for your good and His glory.

"A gem cannot be polished without friction, nor man perfected without the abrasive of trials."

Remembering without ceasing your work of faith, and labour of love, and patience of hope in our Lord Jesus Christ, in the sight of God and our Father (1 Thess. 1:3).

In his letter to the Thessalonians, Paul reminded them that he had been praying for them. He was a man of great activity, a busy person. He traveled many miles preaching the gospel. Yet he made time to intercede for believers.

Paul told the Thessalonians he remembered their work of faith. Faith is more than a mental assent. It begins with a relationship to God through Christ. "That Christ may dwell in your hearts by faith" (Eph. 3:17). "Without faith it is impossible to please . . . God" (Heb. 11:6).

The Thessalonians put feet to their faith. They worked by faith. Some people work for a paycheck, some as a duty, some for the desire of achievement. But the Thessalonians were more than "hearers of the Word," they were "doers of the Word" (see James 1:22).

Williams translates the work of faith in this verse as "energizing faith," a faith energized by actively believing and working. It is a faith that is vital and real.

Perhaps we should evaluate the motive of our work. Is it for the applause of people? The benefits we will receive? A feeling of accomplishing something? Or is our service a work of faith, a work we know has been God given?

Then Paul remembered their labor as one of love. Someone visited in a Bulgarian home once where one of the daughters was busily sewing on a dress. He said to her, "Don't you ever get tired of working on it?" "No," she replied. "It is my wedding dress."

Labor motivated by love is joyous. Williams translates it as "your toiling love." It is love in action.

The third mark of these Christians was their "patience of hope in our Lord Jesus Christ." This is endurance that is based on hope. As long as a person has hope, he can endure the trials of life. "Your enduring hope in our Lord Jesus Christ" (1 Thess. 1:3, *Williams*).

If Paul were writing of your faith, love, and hope, what could he say about it?

October
13

Thou art my hiding place; thou shalt preserve me from trouble; thou shalt compass me about with songs of deliverance. Selah (Ps. 32:7).

Songs! Music! What an effect music can have on us. Often when we are depressed or discouraged, the sound of music can lift our spirits, and drive away the feeling of despair. God is the Master Musician and gives songs an important place in our Christian experience.

God had filled David's life with song, giving him a "singing heart." The Psalms are filled with his praises and songs to God. As we study his life, we discover it was not an easy one. He experienced persecution. Several times the king tried to take David's life. Some of his family and close friends became his enemies. But through his trouble he learned to know God who could deliver him from them. In spite of all his heartaches, he could say, "I will bless the Lord at all times: His praise shall continually be in my mouth" (Ps. 34:1).

In Psalm 32:7 he wrote of his songs of deliverance. He could sing in the midst of trouble, for his security was in God who was the "source of his song." He said, "You are my hiding place from every storm of life" (LB). He was not spared from stormy trials, but he was assured of God's protection from the devastating effects of the storms. Sometimes he was protected IN storms; at other times he was protected FROM them. He said, "Thou shalt preserve me from trouble."

No wonder David could sing. He said, "You surround me with SONGS of victory" (LB). Encompassed with songs of deliverance and victory, why shouldn't he sing?

Is your heart a "singing heart" today? Regardless of present pressures, you can have a SONG—a song of deliverance. Someone has said, "It is easy to sing when we can read the notes by daylight. But God enables us to sing where there is not a ray of light to read by."

Our hearts are filled with joy and peace as we are surrounded with His songs of deliverance. "With jubilant songs of deliverance thou wilt surround me."

We are labourers together with God (1 Cor. 3:9).

As I watch sports on television, I am always interested in the teamwork involved in playing the game. Each player is carefully selected for a particular postion on the team. He then gives himself to play the game in that position with the one purpose of working together with the team to win the game.

God has chosen us to be "players" on His "team" in the supreme business of giving the gospel to a needy world.

He takes us into partnership with Himself, not because He has to (He could have worked out some other plan), but because this is His plan.

In partnership with Him all our possessions, our homes, cars, bank accounts, talents, all we are and have become His to use.

He places us where we are to labor together with Him. He has placed us wherever we are, in our city and in our neighborhood, to serve as a copartner with Him.

We are in partnership with God, not God in partnership with us. Sometimes we come to Him saying, "Dear Lord, I am going to work here today; I want to serve you here; come and help me." But He has the right to tell us where He wants us to serve. We should say, "Lord, where do you want to use me today? Place me there and use me." Only in this way will our labor bring glory to God.

F. B. Meyer has said, "Sometimes we want God to carry out our little plans, when He wants us to help Him accomplish His great plan."

Even the most efficient of us is only a tool in the hands of the Great Master Workman. There is a place for each of us and each of us should be in that place.

An ingenious little boy decided to start a business, promising God that he would share with Him the profits. He set up a lemonade stand on which he placed a sign that said, "Lemonade, Inc.; me and God, co-owners."

We are in partnership with Him in singleness of purpose and performance to finish the work He has given us to do.

October
15

When someone becomes a Christian he becomes a brand new person. He is not the same any more. A new life has begun! (2 Cor. 5:17, LB).

As I stand back and view my life, I find it filled with peace, quietness, calmness, and joy. This is the result of a great change that took place years ago. Since that day there has been one controlling purpose in my life. "For to me to live is Christ" (Phil. 1:21).

From early childhood I attended church. Yet as I grew older, I was aware of something missing in my life. There was an emptiness I could not understand. I longed for something to satisfy an inner yearning of my heart.

One day I turned on my radio and heard a pastor speaking about Jesus Christ. I listened intently to what he said and continued to listen each morning for about three months.

One Sunday evening when my heart was desperately reaching out for an answer to life, I went to the church where the program originated.

That night for the first time I realized that although I knew ABOUT Jesus Christ, I did not know HIM in a personal way. Although I believed with my mind that Jesus Christ came to earth to become the Savior of the world, I had never believed in Him and received Him as my personal Savior.

Alone at home that night I knelt down and confessed my need of a Savior and that I believed that Jesus had died and risen from the dead for me, personally. Then I invited Him into my life.

My life was filled with peace and joy. I knew for the first time that I had been accepted by God into His family. Based on the authority of God's Word, I knew I was a Christian. "I have written this to you who believe in the Son of God so that you may know you have eternal life" (1 John 5:13, LB).

I began to grow in my Christian life as I read the Bible and prayed each day. The Lord Jesus has become my dearest Friend as we have walked together through the years.

* * * * * * *

As you have read my story today, you may be saying, "I, too, am searching for an answer to life; for something real. I need a purpose for living."

Your life can change as mine did; you can become a new person through a personal transaction between yourself and Jesus Christ. If this is the desire of your heart, invite Jesus Christ into your life and become a member of God's family.

MY Commitment to JESUS CHRIST

I BELIEVE	that Jesus Christ, the Son of God, gave His life on the cross to free me from the penalty of sin and give me forgiveness.
I RECEIVE	Jesus Christ into my life as Savior and Lord through personal invitation.
I ACCEPT	God's gift of Eternal Life.

MY PRAYER

Dear Lord Jesus:

I CONFESS my need of you as a personal Savior.

I BELIEVE you died on the cross to pay the penalty for my sin.

I INVITE you into my life as my personal Savior and Lord.

Thank you for your gift of Eternal Life which I have just now received.

In Jesus' name, I pray. Amen.

Signed ______________________________

Date ______________

Your signature and date is a reminder of the moment you received Christ as your Savior and His gift of Eternal Life. It will indicate the sincerity of your transaction between you and God.

* * * * * * *

October
16

But we all, with open face beholding as in a glass the glory of the Lord, are changed into the same image from glory to glory, even as by the Spirit of the Lord (2 Cor. 3:18).

God's desire for our lives is that we be changed or transformed into the likeness of Jesus Christ.

His Word tells us that we are to behold as in a glass, or mirror, the glory of the Lord. The mirror we look into is the revelation of God found in the Bible. In it Jesus Christ is revealed to us as the glory of God.

As we behold Him in His Word, our lives begin to change into His likeness. "We all with unveiled faces reflecting as in a mirror the glory of God."

God wants the perfect revelation of Christ in His Word to become the perfect reflection of Christ in our lives.

The conforming process takes place as we behold with an open face. This requires that we take time to look into our mirror, the Word of God, and behold the glory of God as seen in the face of Jesus Christ. Beholding means to have a fixed gaze, not just a glance. "Simply fixing our gaze upon Jesus" (Heb. 12:2, *Weymouth*).

We are transformed into the same image from glory to glory by the Spirit of the Lord.

Then God wants the perfect reflection of Christ IN our lives to be reflected FROM our lives.

In the White Mountains of New Hampshire there is a granite cliff which resembles a face. It was told that one day a great man would come whose face would resemble the face on the mountain. A small boy, living close to the mountain, spent hours day after day looking at the face. After he reached manhood, one day the people realized he had become this man of the mountain. In the features of his face they saw the same profile as that etched on the mountain. Constant gazing on the Great Stone Face had imprinted its likeness on the boy's face.

Contemplation of Christ conforms us into His image. The likeness to Jesus will be reflected from our lives.

How excellent is thy lovingkindness, O God! therefore the children of men put their trust under the shadow of thy wings (Ps. 36:7).

In this Psalm, David shares a cluster of precious gems for those who have experienced the "steadfast love" of God (Ps. 36:5, LB).

Lovingkindness is described as "love in action." God's lovingkindness is His love put into action, which He demonstrated by sending the Lord Jesus to earth. "But God showed his great love for us by sending Christ to die for us while we were still sinners" (Rom. 5:8, LB).

First, there is safety for God's children. "Therefore the children of men put their trust under the shadow of thy wings." Even in times of great danger we are guaranteed a place of safety. He that "putteth his trust in the Lord shall be safe" (Prov. 29:25).

In Him we have adequate provisions. "They shall be abundantly satisfied with the fatness of thy house" (Ps. 36:8). Do we live meagerly when we could be partaking of His abundant supplies?

He not only gives us the capacity to drink "of the rivers of His pleasure," but causes us to drink. "I will make them to drink."

God is the source of our life, "with thee is the fountain of life" (v. 9). As we bring our needs and hold them under His unfailing fountain, He fills them from His resources.

Our way may be dark about us, but He is light, and "in thy light we see light."

One time a husband bought a match box for his wife. It was supposed to glow in the dark. But it didn't. The husband thought he had been cheated. Then he discovered some French words on the box. When translated it read, "If you want me to shine in the night, keep me in the sunlight through the day."

As we spend time in His presence, we absorb the rays of the Light of His Word. Then when our way is dark, the light of His presence shines on our path.

These precious gems from His Word reveal the lovingkindness of God. Are they yours?

October
18

Our father which art in heaven (Matt. 6:9).

Christians are to pray. In Matthew 6:6, Jesus said, "When thou prayest," not, "if thou prayest."

The disciples of Jesus came to Him one day with the request, "Lord, teach us to pray." He gave them a pattern for prayer. It was a simple, brief prayer, not just words to recite, but a guide to enable them to know the way to pray.

Prayer begins with an intimate relationship between a child of God and His Heavenly Father. Jesus instructed them to approach God, calling Him "Our Father."

Jesus warned them against hypocritical or repetitious prayers such as the hypocrites or heathen prayed.

Prayer is a line of communication between the child of God and His Heavenly Father. We are to begin our prayers with "Our Father," which gives God His rightful place. He is the object of our prayers. "Our Father" shows our family relationship. We place our trust and confidence in Him as a child does in his father.

Praying "Our Father" implies we are coming in the name of Jesus, for we can only come into God's presence through Jesus Christ. "No one cometh unto the Father, but by me" (John 14:6).

A child becomes a member of a family through birth into that family. So in our spiritual life. We become a member of God's family through the new birth. "You must all be born anew (from above)" (John 3:7, *Amplified*). Until we are in His family we are not entitled to use the term, "Our Father." Only as we acknowledge Him as our Father do we have the right to pray the rest of the prayer.

God, as our Father, is all you would desire in an ideal father. We can come to Him knowing He loves us. He is interested in our lives, and wants to involve Himself in them. He watches over us, ready to protect us. He provides for us bountifully from His great inexhaustible resources. He is near us, not far away.

We can come into His presence very simply, but in an attitude of reverence and respect. Someone has said, "Prayer involves the intimacy of speech without the absence of reverence."

Our Father which art in heaven, Hallowed be thy name (Matt. 6:9).

The basis of our prayer is our relationship to God through Jesus Christ. Through Him, we come into God's presence, recognizing Him as "Our Father." We begin our prayer in worship, "Hallowed be thy name." By hallowing His Name, we hallow God Himself, for His Name is an expression of His character in all its attributes, such as His holiness, righteousness, and truth.

To hallow His name, we must keep it holy and sacred. We must have respect and reverence for His character.

God revealed His holiness to Moses. Moses saw a bush on fire, but not being consumed. It was a symbol of the presence of God. God said to Moses, "Draw not nigh hither: put off thy shoes from off thy feet, for the place whereon thou standest is holy ground" (Exod. 3:5). Wherever God is, is holy ground.

God revealed His holiness to Isaiah. Isaiah saw the Lord high and lifted up and cried, "Holy, holy, holy is the Lord of Hosts."

The Old Testament scribes had such reverence for God that when they wrote His name, Yahweh, they bathed themselves, sharpened their quills, wrote the four Hebrew consonants, then wrapped the pen and put it aside. The pen had written the name of God and must not be used again. Do we show such reverence toward God? Although we can approach Him simply, may we never let it become casual.

Jesus said to pray, "Hallowed BE thy name," not "IS thy name." His name is holy, for HE is holy. His name is to BE kept holy in our lives by the way we live, what we look at, what we say, by our friendships, our pleasures, even by our reactions to the trials in our lives.

"Worship," it has been said, "is the soul being occupied with God." Is our attitude toward Him one of worship, acknowledging His Lordship and submitting to His will?

Calvin said, "That God's name should be hallowed is nothing other than to say that God should have his own honor, of which He is worthy, so that man should never think or speak of Him without the greatest veneration."

October
20

She hath done what she could: she is come aforehand to anoint my body to the burying (Mark 14:8).

Jesus was being entertained in the home of Simon the leper. As He sat there a woman came to Him, bringing an alabaster box of ointment of spikenard, very precious. This she broke and poured on His head. Judas was critical. It seemed such a waste, such an extravagance, accomplishing no useful purpose. He felt it should have been sold and the money given to the poor.

But Jesus could see into her heart. It was filled with love for Him and He was encouraged by her display of love. She had used her money to purchase the ointment. She used her time to pour it out on His head. He knew that her desire was to give Him that which was precious to her, so He said, "She hath done what she could."

It was not the value of her gift that was important, but her motive in giving. For this she received the praise of the Savior. "Wheresoever this gospel shall be preached throughout the whole world, this also that she hath done shall be spoken of for a memorial to her" (Mark 14:9). Nothing ever given to Jesus is wasted.

Years ago a young boy was leaving home to work in another city. His mother asked him to promise her that he would read the Bible and pray each day. Because of his love and respect for her, he made the promise and kept it as he grew older.

Later he became a salesman and as he traveled his territory, he still kept his promise to his mother. As an indirect outcome of this promise, the Gideon Association was founded and has been used of God to distribute Bibles around the world. This Christian mother, doing what she could, had a part in this world-wide ministry of giving out God's Word.

Do what we can, but do that much! Real consecration is considered a waste by those who are not truly consecrated.

What a commendation to have Jesus say of you and me: They have done what they could!

When thou passest through the waters, I will be with thee; and through the rivers, they shall not overflow thee: when thou walkest through the fire, thou shalt not be burned; neither shall the flame kindle upon thee (Isa. 43:2).

Have you ever experienced the devastating results of a flood or a fire? In a very short time that which had seemed so secure was completely swept away.

In today's tempestuous world, many Christians are feeling the fury of the storm and the fires of testing. In the midst of them, God speaks to us with the reassuring words, "The Lord . . . created thee . . . I have redeemed thee, I have called thee by thy name; THOU ART MINE" (Isa. 43:1). He has a deep interest in each one of us and we are precious to Him.

We are not promised immunity from going through deep waters of trouble; neither are we assured exemption from the furnace of affliction.

But we are assured His presence when the floods come and when the heat is turned on. He knows the depth and swiftness of the waters; He knows the temperature of the heat registered on the thermometer of our lives.

Storms may batter against us, the heat may be turned on, we may feel completely forsaken, we may say, "Has God forgotten about me?" But we don't go through them alone, for He has promised, "I will be with thee."

Today are the flood waters of trouble pouring over you? Are the waves rising higher and higher? The waters may be so swift and deep you may be almost sinking beneath them. But His comforting words come to us, "They will NOT overflow thee." The heat in your life may be increasing. You may long to draw away from its intensity. Yet he lovingly whispers ". . . thou shalt NOT be burned."

When we pass through the floods He is with us, so it will not be too deep. When we walk in the furnace we will not be burned, for we have the "asbestos" covering of His presence. He calls us by name, saying "Thou art mine—I will be with thee."

"God smiles on His child in the eye of the storm."

October
22

For he performeth the thing that is appointed for me (Job 23:14).

Most of us today find it necessary to keep appointment books in order to remember our daily appointments. With the full schedule I keep, I find it very important to keep an accurate appointment book and to check on it daily.

Job recognized that God kept an appointment of everything that was to be a part of his life. He knew that God would do all He had appointed for him. "So he will do to me all he has planned, and there is more ahead" (Job 23:14, LB).

Perhaps you do not understand what is happening in your life at this time. There may be no apparent reason for your trouble. But God has not promised that we will always understand the circumstances of our lives. We may never know why.

However, we can be assured that nothing comes into our lives without His permission. Paul wrote, "And we know that ALL THINGS work together for good to them that love God, to them who are the called according to his purpose" (Rom. 8:28).

When we believe that all He has appointed for our lives is for our good and His glory, and when we trust our lives to Him, then we can be assured He will do nothing short of His best for us. "No good thing will he withhold from them that walk uprightly" (Ps. 84:11).

Recently I have been working on a piece of needlepoint. As I look at the underneath side, it is a mass of knots and ends of yarn, with no distinct pattern visible. But it is different when it is turned over and viewed from the right side. There is a circle of flowers done in beautiful shades of yarn. The rest of the piece is filled in with a solid color, revealing a definite pattern.

This is an example of our lives. We see them from the wrong side, from our viewpoint, and all we see is the confusion of our circumstances. But God sees it from His viewpoint. He knows just where to put each stitch and shade to complete the pattern He has appointed for our lives.

"Lo, I am with you all the appointed days"
(Matt. 28:20, *Variorum Version*).

Maketh manifest the savour of his knowledge by us in every place. For we are unto God a sweet savour of Christ (2 Cor. 2:14-15).

Perfumes have a fascination for me. I cannot pass by the perfume counter without stopping to look at their displays. Once I read of a special one-million-dollar display of perfumes in the John Wanamaker store in Philadelphia. In the collection were perfumes from many countries. The highest priced bottle was marked one thousand dollars.

Paul wrote of the importance of fragrances. He said, ". . . and through us spreads and makes evident the fragrance of the knowledge of God everywhere. For we are the sweet fragrance of Christ. . . ." (2 Cor. 2:14-15, *Amplified*).

We are to be incense bearers carrying to those about us the fragrance of Christ wherever we go.

The source of our fragrance is Christ Himself. He is "the rose of Sharon, and the lily of the valleys" (Song of Sol. 2:1). He is the One "altogether lovely" (Song of Sol. 5:16).

As Christ indwells our life, the fragrance of His life permeates our life. As we linger in His presence He becomes so fragrant in us it is communicated through us to others wherever we go. ". . . and uses us to spread the sweet odour of the knowledge of Him in every place. For we are as the fragrance of Christ ascending to God."

The disciples diffused this spiritual charm. The members of the Sanhedrin took knowledge of Peter and John that "they had been with Jesus."

One day a gentleman went into a restaurant in Europe for lunch. Some workers were having lunch there. After they left he was conscious of a lovely odor of perfume in the restaurant. He asked the waitress about it. She said, "The people just in here are workers in a perfume factory. They are saturated with the odor of perfume which remains after they are gone."

Are we "always led in triumph in Christ"? Are we a savour or fragrance of the knowledge of Him wherever we go?

October
24

So, as much as in me is, I am ready to preach the gospel to you that are at Rome also (Rom. 1:15).

Today we hear people talking about what the world owes them. Some say, "I have something coming to me. The world owes it to me. I didn't ask to be born."

A debtor is "a person who owes something to another." Paul didn't feel that the world owed him a living, but he owed it a life. He carried the world on his heart. ". . . I have an obligation to discharge and a duty to perform and a debt to pay" (Rom. 1:14, *Amplified*). He felt in his entire lifetime he could never repay his debt. Someone said, "He was making past due payments."

Paul was eager to give himself unreservedly to His work. He said, "So, for my part, I am willing and eagerly ready to preach the Gospel. . . ." (v, 15, *Amplified*).

Paul said, "I am not ashamed of the Gospel . . . of Christ" (v. 16). He had confidence in the message he shared; he was confident it was the answer for the needs of the world. So he could say, "I am debtor; I am ready; I am not ashamed; I care about others; I am committed to their interests; I am confident in the power of the gospel."

One night we were traveling through a heavy snow storm. Suddenly, to our dismay, we slid off the road into a ditch. As we were trying to decide what to do, a car came by. As it stopped, several young men piled out and offered assistance. In a short time our car was back on the road.

In appreciation, we tried to pay them, but they refused to take anything. They said, "A few miles back we slid into the ditch, too. Someone stopped and helped us. They refused pay for it. This is our way of paying for what they did for us."

Today, we, too, are debtors—we have a debt to make Christ known to others. I am debtor! I am ready! I am not ashamed! Is this true of us today?

Trust in the Lord with all thine heart; and lean not unto thine own understanding. In all thy ways acknowledge him, and he shall direct thy paths (Prov. 3:5-6).

When I have need of direction and guidance for my life, I claim these verses more than any others as my assurance of God's promise to undertake for me.

How many times have we asked ourselves, "What am I to do? What is God's will for me?" God wants us to know His will for our lives. "Wherefore be ye not unwise, but understanding what the will of the Lord is" (Eph. 5:17).

We are promised God's guidance in this Scripture passage, but it has a conditional promise.

First, if we are to know and do His will, we must trust Him with all our heart. It has been said, "Faith consists of belief and trust. We believe with our mind but when it reaches the heart it becomes trust." We are to trust in the Lord with ALL our heart. In one language the word for trust means "leaning your whole weight upon Him."

Next, we are to put no confidence in ourselves, "Lean not unto thine own understanding." Instead of depending on human wisdom, we must seek the wisdom that comes from above. "If any of you lack wisdom, let him ask of God" (James 1:5). Then we are to acknowledge Him in ALL our ways, every area of our lives. This is to acknowledge that He has the right to be on the throne of our lives, in complete control.

We are to acknowledge Him in the affections of our heart, the thoughts of the mind, and the decisions of the will. To acknowledge God in all our ways is a committal of all our ways to Him in submissiveness. "In everything you do, put God first" (Prov. 3:6, LB). There is a two-fold relationship between God and man in these verses. Our part is to trust, lean on, and acknowledge Him. If we keep our part, God has promised to keep His part in directing our path. This is a never-failing promise to the one who meets its conditions.

October
26

And the Lord said, Behold, there is a place by me, and thou shalt stand upon a rock (Exod. 33:21).

One day I came into a meeting after it had begun. I sat down by myself on one side of the room. I was a little lonely that day. Someone sitting across the aisle made a place for me to come and sit by her. It gave me such a feeling of being wanted.

The Lord said to Moses, "There is a place by me." He is the God of the individual and we are very special to Him. He has a special place by Himself designed just for each of us. It is close BESIDE HIM in the heavenlies. No one else fits into our place.

From this special place of companionship with Him we can have conversation together, talking as friend to Friend. He will give us words of counsel, comfort, and guidance. At times He may have to chasten us, but He does it in love. From this special place beside Him we receive His directions for each day.

Then God said to Moses, "Thou shalt stand upon a rock." We are to be living stones, standing firmly on the Rock of Ages, Christ Jesus Himself. "He brought me up also out of an horrible pit, out of the miry clay, and set my feet upon a rock, and established my goings" (Ps. 40:2).

When the storms beat against our lives, when Satan attacks, we can stand steadfast and unmoveable because we are anchored in Him.

When we visited Washington Cathedral in Washington, D. C., we saw a large number of stones lying on the ground behind the Cathedral. They were of different sizes and shapes and each was numbered. I realized that each stone had a special place in the top of the Cathedral still under construction. Each had been shaped to fit into its exact place and numbered so the workmen would know where to place it.

We are being shaped and prepared on earth today for God's special place for us in Heaven. But until then He says to us, "Behold, there is a place by Me, and thou shalt stand upon a rock."

Dear brothers, is your life full of difficulties and temptations? Then be happy, for when the way is rough, your patience has a chance to grow (James 1:2-3, LB).

Today the world is full of people with lives full of trials. Our attitude and approach to trials has an important effect on our reaction to them. We can let them become problems, or we can let them become triumphs by lifting our sights above them to the Lord who is in complete control of them.

Christians can expect the PRESENCE of trials in their lives. They are not exempt. "Man is born unto trouble, as the sparks fly upward" (Job. 5:7). We would prefer another method than trials but we have no right to question God's method.

The presence of trials is a part of the refinishing and developing process of bringing us to a place of spiritual maturity. This should be our goal—reaching out to a life of maturity in the Lord.

Christians throughout the Roman Empire were noted for the joyful way they met problems. Paul is a good example. He and Silas could sing praises to God at midnight right in prison.

But God's Word assures us that in the midst of our trials joy can be real. "Is your life full of difficulties and temptations? Then be happy." The important thing is how we react to trials. As they come, count them one by one, and count them with JOY; not joy for them, but joy in the midst of them. We think it is joy when we escape trial, but not so in God's plan. As we accept and count them all joy, we mature and grow in patience as we learn the needed lessons. Adversity is a great teacher.

Our reaction to trials reveals the level of our maturity. What is our reaction when we are criticized? Our feelings hurt? When lonely, discouraged, or disappointed?

If we are growing, can we COUNT our testings with joy. We may not always be joyful, nor enjoy our trouble, but we can count it with joy.

Someone has said, "A trial is not something to be tolerated, but a trust to be treasured."

October
28

When the way is rough, your patience has a chance to grow (James 1:3, LB).

Yesterday we considered the fact that our reaction to the presence of trials should be counted as joy. Trials will come to us, we can be sure. But we are to count them as joy. Why? Because there is a PURPOSE for trials in our lives. Then "your patience has a chance to grow."

What do we do when the going gets rough? What is our reaction to trouble? God uses these difficulties as a process of development in our spiritual growth. In order to grow and mature in patience we need opportunities to develop it.

The diamond is the hardest natural substance known. Scientists believe diamonds were formed millions of years ago when carbon was subjected to intense heat and pressure.

The pressure and heat of trials is part of the process of developing the "diamond of patience." "The trying of your faith worketh patience" (James 1:3). It is a patience that is steadfast, a patience that endures, a patience that will not give up when the going is rough. "And patience develops strength of character in us and helps us trust God more each time we use it until finally our hope and faith are strong and steady" (Rom. 5:4, LB).

In our trials we discover what God can do. We experience His power and strength in weakness, His wisdom to solve problems. We learn to accept without murmuring the trials He permits.

Sometimes we think we are the only one going through trials. But we don't have to look very far until we find that most people are experiencing trials of some kind.

When adversity comes we can count it all joy for it develops patience.

Peter wrote, "And now, dear friends of mine, I beg you not to be unduly alarmed at the fiery ordeals which come to test your faith, as though this were some abnormal experience. You should be glad, because it means that you are sharing Christ's sufferings. One day, when he shows himself in full splendour, you will be filled with the most tremendous joy" (1 Peter 4:12, *Phillips*).

So let it grow, and don't try to squirm out of your problems. For when your patience is finally in full bloom, then you will be ready for anything, strong in character, full and complete (James 1:4, LB*).*

We can be certain of the presence of trials in our lives and assured that they have a purpose in developing patience, which builds steadfastness into our character. They are not a sign of God's displeasure. They prove the reality of our faith.

The PRODUCT of our trials is full growth and maturity in our Christian life. God's goal for our lives is a mature, well-balanced life. "When your patience is in full bloom, then you will be ready for anything, strong in character, full and complete."

God knows our need of patience. In Hebrews 10:36 we read, "For ye have need of patience." He knows when to send the trial and how severe it should be to finish its work in our lives.

The presence of trials in our lives, whether places, plans, or people, can be converted into strength and steadfastness of character as we commit them to the Holy Spirit.

This growth is not the work of a moment. It is the work of a lifetime. We become impatient, wanting things to happen right now.

"But you must let your endurance come to its perfect product, so that you may be fully developed and perfectly equipped, without any defects" (James 1:4, *Williams*). God desires completeness in our lives; as Williams says, "without any defects."

Our source for help in this process is prayer. "If you want to know what God wants you to do, ask him, and he will gladly tell you, for he is always ready to give a bountiful supply of wisdom to all who ask him; he will not resent it" (v. 5, LB).

Verse 12 sums up the matter of patient endurance under trial in that it provides a reward for all who endure it. "The man who patiently endures the temptations and trials that come to him is the truly happy man. For once his testing is complete he will receive the crown of life which the Lord has promised to all who love him" (v. 12, *Phillips*).

October
30

My power shows up best in weak people (2 Cor. 12:9, LB*).*

This verse has taken on new meaning for me recently. It was shared at my sister's funeral. Her life had been filled with much sadness, sorrow, and sickness. She had been a dialysis patient for a number of years. Three times a week she had to be on the kidney machine, six hours at a time. Many complications developed in her body as a result.

But to everyone who knew her she was a source of encouragement. Never did she complain, never did she indulge in self-pity, never did she become bitter toward God. If you called on her to encourage her, you would leave realizing she had encouraged you.

At the funeral the pastor shared that one day as he read the above Scripture to her he paused and said, "Does that remind you of anyone?" She looked up with a twinkle in her eyes and said, "I guess I'm a pretty good candidate." She had discovered the secret of experiencing the power of God in a weak body.

Paul had learned the sufficiency of the power of God for his life. He wrote, "My grace is sufficient for THEE." He continued, "Most gladly therefore (because I had discovered His sufficiency) will I glory in my infirmities (Paul spoke of one of his infirmities as a thorn), that the power of Christ may rest upon me. Therefore I TAKE PLEASURE (can we say that?) in infirmities . . . for Christ's sake: for when I am weak, then am I strong" (2 Cor. 12:9-10).

As we confess our weakness to God, He releases His power in us. In our human weakness we utilize His divine strength.

Not only is His grace sufficient for each trial, but for "THEE" in the midst of the trial.

Fannie Crosby has written many hymns that have strengthened Christians through the years. Blinded at a young age, she learned the sufficiency of God's power through her physical limitations. She once said, "If I had not lost my sight, I could not have written these hymns."

Someone has said, "Into the hollow of our nothingness, God fills the dynamos of His power."

Hast not thou made an hedge about him, and about his house, and about all that he hath on every side? (Job. 1:10).

One question asked through the ages is, "Why do the righteous suffer?" The Book of Job traces the perplexities of a man under severe suffering and trials. From his life we learn that some suffering is permitted to strengthen our faith, purify our lives, and give greater revelation of God.

God led him from one problem to another, eventually bringing him forth as pure gold (Job 23:10). Through the centuries he has been a comfort and inspiration to Christians in times of trouble, and an example of patience.

Job was a man greatly blessed with material possessions and a fine family. He was a righteous man who believed God.

One day Satan, the accuser of the brethren, appeared before God. God said, "Hast thou considered my servant Job, that there is none like him in the earth, a perfect and an upright man, one that feareth God, and escheweth evil?" (Job. 1:8). Satan said, "Doth Job fear God for naught? Hast not thou made an HEDGE about him, and about his house, and about all that he hath on every side?" Satan said, "You have given him everything he desires. Take them away and he will not serve you" (Job 1:9-10).

This was not a visible hedge, of course, but a hedge of God's protection and care of Job. Satan challenged God, "But put forth thine hand now, and touch all that he hath, and he will curse thee to thy face" (v. 11). But no one can break through the hedge surrounding our lives without God's consent.

God began to test Job to prove that he loved Him for Himself, not for what He gave him. He had confidence in Job. Immediately he opened His hedge about Job's life, and trouble poured in. Job lost his possessions, his family, everything.

What would have been our reaction to such trouble? Would we have blessed God? Or would we have questioned Him, asking, "Why?"

What was Job's reaction? Although he couldn't understand why his life was filled with such trouble, he "fell down upon the ground, and worshipped" (v. 20). Do we worship God in the midst of trouble? Job said, "The Lord gave, and the Lord hath taken away; blessed be the name of the Lord" (v. 21).

But Job's trouble was not over. Intensely painful sores covered his body. He wished he had never been born. Even his wife suggested he curse God and die. There seemed to be no adequate answer. Yet his faith lifted him above his circumstances, and he could say, "What? shall we receive good at the hand of God, and shall we not receive evil?" (2:10).

He was unaware of the agreement between God and Satan. However, he maintained a deep trust in God, although he couldn't understand.

What is your reaction to the trials of your life? Are you asking, "Why me, Lord? What have I done to deserve this?" Have you allowed yourself to become bitter? Or have you been able to say as Job, "Shall I receive the good, and not the evil; the pleasant, easy, comfortable things and not trouble, sorrow, or pain?" Do we serve Him only for the blessing we get from Him?

Suffering is a great school in which to learn trust. Job came to the end of himself and instead of trying to understand God's reason for the calamities in his life, he put his trust in God. As a result he came through his suffering with a triumphant faith in Him. He could say, "Though he slay me, yet will I trust Him."

Trouble develops patience in our lives. "Let patience have her perfect work" (James 1:4). God may chasten us through trials but He does it in love. "For whom the Lord loveth he chasteneth" (Heb. 12:6). He uses trouble to bring us back to Himself when we have strayed away.

God's ways may be perplexing and baffling, but one day when we stand before Him we will see clearly His purpose. Not only will we understand, but we will be able to thank Him and praise Him for the suffering He has permitted to strengthen our faith and to make us more like Him.

So when they had dined, Jesus saith to Simon Peter, Simon, son of Jonas, lovest thou me more than these? (John 21:15).

"Lovest thou me more than these?" How would you like to be asked that question by Jesus in front of others?

When Jesus asked Peter if he loved Him more than these, He may have meant more than fishing. Or He may have meant, "Do you love Me more than these others disciples do?" In the Greek it could refer to either things or persons.

A short time before, Peter had boasted he would never forsake the Lord though all the others did. Yet in a short time he had denied the Lord three times. Jesus may have been bringing Peter face to face with that boast. Regardless of His reason, Jesus wanted Peter to consider how genuine and deep was his love for Him. Did Peter love Him more than things, than people? Did he love Him more than anything or anyone else? Did he love Him without limitations or reservations?

As Peter considered Jesus' question, he was not as confident as he had once been. What could he answer? In the honesty of his heart he had to confess that he did not love Jesus with the highest love, in the spiritual sense. But he could say he loved Him with a deep affection. "Lord, you know all things, you know I love you."

I believe Peter's heart was stirred that day to the very depths of his being. I can hear him say, "Lord, I do love you, but I want to love you more."

The Lord Jesus re-commissioned Peter as His representative before the other disciples, saying, "Feed my lambs; feed my sheep."

If Jesus asked us today, "Lovest thou me more than these?" what would our answer be? Is there anyone or anything we love more than we love Him? It is more than saying it with our lips; it is loving Him with all our heart. It is the love of complete devotion to the Lord.

Can we say, "Lord, I do love you today, but I want to love you more. I want to love you with a love that is genuine, without pretense; with a love that is real."

November

2

Not that we are sufficient of ourselves to think any thing as of ourselves; but our sufficiency is of God (2 Cor. 3:5).

Paul had been writing the Corinthians about the privilege and responsibility of being a representative for Jesus Christ on earth. He said, "So that now wherever we go he uses us to tell others about the Lord and to spread the Gospel like a sweet perfume" (2 Cor. 2:14, LB),"Ye are our epistle written in our hearts, known and read of all men" (2 Cor. 3:2).

Paul knew that if his ministry was to be effective for God he must not rely on human resources but on the supernatural power of God. He realized that the ministry of sharing the gospel was not to be taken lightly.

He knew his inadequacy for his God-given work. He said, "But who is adequate for such a task as this?" (2 Cor. 2:16, LB). He confessed his lack of sufficiency in himself but recognized that his sufficiency was in God. He encouragingly said, "Not that we are sufficient of ourselves to think any thing of ourselves; but our sufficiency is of God" (2 Cor. 3:5).

Through the years God has used the weak things to confound the wise. He has used those with no ability to confound the mighty.

Any human capability we have, regardless of how great it is, is not sufficient for God's work. When he calls us, He calls us to a task beyond our human ability. He doesn't say, "Here is your do-it-yourself kit. You do it." Jesus said, "Without me ye can do nothing" (John 15:5).

Have you ever seen one of the brushes used by Leonardo da Vinci in his painting of "The Last Supper"? Suppose the brush had said, "When this picture is hung on display, hang me on the wall beside it." Would the artist have hung it there? Of course not! The brush was great in the hand of the artist, but that was all. The brush of itself could have done nothing.

Only as we are yielded tools in the hands of the Great Master, God Himself, are we sufficient for His use.

When my heart is overwhelmed: lead me to the rock that is higher than I (Ps. 61:2).

November

3

This Psalm was the cry of David's heart when he was fleeing from his son who was trying to usurp his throne.

His heart heavy with sorrow, he cried to the One who could meet his need. "Hear my cry, O God" (Ps. 61:1). Immediately he had an audience with the King of Kings. He continued, "Attend unto my prayer."

When he was almost overwhelmed, with the waves of trouble rolling over him, he said, "From the end of the earth will I cry unto thee, when my heart is overwhelmed: lead me to the rock that is higher than I" (v. 2).

This is the cry from many hearts today. As the storms of life sweep over us we cry, "Lord, hear me: Lord, lead me to the Great Rock of Safety, Jesus Christ Himself."

I recall a day when my life was overwhelmed in the midst of a storm. I felt myself almost sinking under the fury of it. I received a card from a friend that day. She related how she had felt constrained to send me a verse of Scripture. It arrived on the day I desperately needed it and it was this verse in the Psalms. God's timing was so perfect. He used it that day to remind me that He was with me in my storm and that He was allowing it to teach me some new lessons I needed to learn.

He gave me the assurance that He was lifting me above my circumstances to a place of safety and strength in Himself.

When troubles come, we can cry, "Lord, hear me! Lord, lead me." Our storms can become a time of victory as we let Him lift us up to the Rock that is above our storms, our Rock of Safety, Christ Jesus.

Is your heart overwhelmed today? Let Him lift you up to your place of security in that Rock, Christ Jesus.

November
4

And the Lord shall guide thee continually (Isa. 58:11).

One day a friend was taking me to the airport about fifteen miles from one of our large cities. The road was winding and not well marked. I said, "I am glad I am with someone who knows the way. I would never find it alone." She replied, "It isn't hard when you are with someone who knows the way." I was thankful for her guidance that day.

Many times we need guidance for our lives. We come to a fork in the road and do not know which way to go. We have to make an important decision and have no idea how to make it. We face a problem with no human solution.

There is a Heavenly Guide who is competent and qualified to lead us on our journey through life, the Lord Jesus. He knows the right way to take at each fork in our road. He can give the right counsel for each decision to be made. He has the power to solve each problem we face.

A guide not only gives directions but personally conducts the trip. Our Heavenly Guide not only gives directions for our journey, but He personally accompanies us on it. "Then spake Jesus again unto them, saying, I am the light of the world: he that FOLLOWETH ME shall not walk in darkness, but shall have the light of life" (John 8:12). Our way may not be easy. However, as we FOLLOW our Guide, He will lead us around or through each obstacle, and over every mountain of difficulty confronting us.

His guidance is CERTAIN. "The Lord SHALL guide thee." It is personal. "The Lord shall guide THEE." It is continual, enabling us to face each day with courage, unafraid of what lies before us. We must have confidence in our Guide, trusting ourselves completely to Him, keeping our eyes fixed upon Him.

An army officer was trying to train a squad of new recruits to keep step. It seemed utterly impossible. Finally, in desperation, the officer said, "Men! Take your eyes off your feet; look up; and your feet will follow your eyes."

The good man does not escape all troubles—he has them too. But the Lord helps him in each and every one (Ps. 34:19,LB).

Christians are not immune from trouble. The psalmist said, "Many are the afflictions of the righteous" (Ps. 34:19).

David experienced many afflictions in his lifetime but God delivered him from all of them. When he wrote this Psalm he was speaking out of his own experience.

We can expect afflictions to come into our lives, yet we are promised deliverance from each one of them.

In the dictionary "affliction" is defined as "suffering, distress, pain, calamity." But looking up the definition of a word in the dictionary does not give us the real understanding of that word. It needs the added interpretation of experience to make it real in our lives.

We may know the definition of the word, "affliction," in our mind but it only becomes real when the afflictions of sorrow, pain, failure, disappointment, or perplexity come into our lives.

Deliverance means to be freed from. But we only know the meaning of deliverance when we are freed from trouble, even in the midst of it.

Precious lessons are learned from our troubles and affliction. They cause us to pray. When we cry out to God, He hears our faintest heart cry and is right there to deliver us.

One time we were visiting an observation tower high up in the mountains. We saw the instruments the forest ranger kept focused on the mountains, constantly watching for fires. It reminded me that God keeps His eyes constantly focused on us, watching over our lives in loving concern.

Afflictions are certain, but deliverance is just as certain.

Paul writes so vividly of his many deliverances. "We are pressed on every side by troubles, but not crushed and broken. We are perplexed because we don't know why things happen as they do, but we don't give up and quit. We are hunted down, but God never abandons us. We get knocked down, but we get up again and keep going (2 Cor. 4:8-9, LB).

"Blessed is the man that trusteth in him" (Ps. 34:8).

November
6

Furthermore then we beseech you, brethren, and exhort you by the Lord Jesus, that as ye have received of us how ye ought to walk and please God, so ye would abound more and more (1 Thess. 4:1).

It has been said, "Our walk is what we are, translated into what we do." It is character expressed in conduct. It is made up of all of which our life consists, our business, our pleasures, our conversations, our trials, our problems.

Our spiritual walk begins at our new birth and continues to the end of our journey.

The National Bureau of Standards establishes accurate measurement standards. These perfect standards are maintained at the Bureau. All measurements made in the United States must measure perfectly with the standards at the Bureau.

The Lord has set certain standards for our daily walk. ". . . that as ye have received of us how ye ought to walk and to please God."

Following are enumerated some of God's standards. One standard is to please the Lord in our walk. "For this reason also we make it our ambition, whether at home or away, to please Him" (2 Cor. 5:9, *Weymouth*).

Our walk is to be worthy of God. "We told you from our own experience how to live lives worthy of . . . God" (2 Thess. 2:12, *Phillips*). To bring honor and glory to Him in our daily walk is to walk worthy.

Love should characterize our daily walk. "Live your lives in love" (Eph. 5:2, *Phillips*). Walking in love is to love as Christ loves.

We need wisdom on our walk. "Walk in wisdom toward them that are without" (Col. 4:5).

Our walk should be worthy of our vocation. ". . . to live and act in a way worthy of those who have been chosen for such wonderful blessings as these" (Eph. 4:1, LB).

Good works should accompany our walk. "For we are his workmanship, created in Christ Jesus unto good works, which God hath before ordained that we should walk in them" (Eph. 2:10).

As you check your spiritual walk today with God's Bureau of Standards, how does it measure up? God's standard for our walk is Jesus Christ. "As ye have therefore received Christ Jesus the Lord, so walk ye in him" (Col. 2:6).

And I sought for a man among them, that should make up the hedge, and stand in the gap before me for the land, that I should not destroy it; but I found none (Ezek. 22:30).

Israel had forsaken God and turned to idolatry and evil practices. God gave Ezekiel a message for His people. "I sought for a man . . . to stand in the gap; BUT I FOUND NONE."

Through the ages God has been seeking for people He could use, "I sought for a MAN." God is the God of the individual and He is searching for individuals who have committed themselves to live for and serve Jesus Christ.

He is looking for individuals who are willing to minister to the needs of people today, "I sought for a man AMONG THEM."

Wherever He has placed us, there we stand in the gap before God "for the land." We are to reach up to God with one hand and reach out into the world with the other hand, bringing God and man into relationship with each other through Christ Jesus.

When Jesus beheld Jerusalem, He saw the city and wept over it. Today we need to stand in the gap with seeing eyes, looking out on a lost world and with weeping hearts of compassion, longing to bring it back into relationship with God through Jesus Christ.

An evangelist told of a meeting he held in a Spanish church in New York City. A number of people responded to the invitation. They were to be taken to another room for further instruction.

One of the inquirers, a young woman, would not go. She had heard all she wanted to hear. The evangelist, very wisely, said, "May I pray for you? Then you may leave." As he prayed he was so moved by her spiritual need, his voice broke and tears came to his eyes. "I have prayed," he then said, "now you may leave." She said, "I will stay. If you cared enough to weep for me, you may talk to me."

God is looking for individuals today to stand in the gap who deeply care for the spiritual needs of those who need to know Jesus Christ.

November

8

And Jabez called on the God of Israel, saying, Oh that thou wouldest bless me indeed, and enlarge my coast, and that thine hand might be with me, and that thou wouldest keep me from evil, that it may not grieve me! And God granted him that which he requested (1 Chron. 4:10).

Jabez was a man who towered above his brethren. He "was more honourable than his brethren" (1 Chron. 4:9). He was born in an unhappy home. His mother even named him Jabez, which means sorrowful. What little we know of him reflects the fact that he lived in unpleasant surroundings.

In one short verse we discover that he was not defeated by any handicaps his environment may have produced. Instead, he had learned the power of prayer. "Jabez called on the God of Israel."

He didn't ask God to remove the difficulties in his life or to give him material blessings. He desired that his spiritual life be deepened.

From his innermost being he cried to God. "Oh that you would bless me." It expresses his dependence on God. Bless is a difficult word to define. Someone has said that blessing is "The working of God where there is nothing to account for His working."

He asked God to "enlarge my coast." Perhaps he was asking God to enlarge his capacity to receive the vast spiritual resources God had available. Perhaps he was praying for an enlarged outreach to others.

He asked for God's guidance upon his life, "that thine hand might be with me." What a request—to ask for God's hand to be upon his life to guide him and hold him steady in his daily walk.

Then he prayed, "Keep me from evil, that it may not grieve me." He knew his human weakness. He was not strong enough to withstand the attacks of the enemy. Perhaps he had known the grief of sinning and didn't want the experience to be repeated.

His prayer was filled with life-changing requests; and "God granted him that which he requested." He was known by his prayer life.

If a record of your prayer life were kept, what would others know of your life?

For God, who commanded the light to shine out of darkness, hath shined in our hearts, to give the light of the knowledge of the glory of God in the face of Jesus Christ (2 Cor. 4:6).

Glory is a difficult word to define. It has the meaning of "substance," or "worth." The glory of God is that which gives Him weight, substance, worth, reality.

God's glory has been revealed in all its perfection in Jesus Christ. He came to reveal what God is like. Jesus said to Philip, "He that hath seen me hath seen the Father" (John 14:9). As you look at Jesus, you see the glory of God revealed in His face. What we see of God and His glory, we see shining out in Jesus Christ.

Not only is the glory of God revealed in Him, but He reveals it in us. "God . . . has flooded our hearts with his light" (2 Cor. 4:6, *Phillips*). Jesus prayed to His Father, "And the glory which thou gavest me I have given them" (John 17:22).

But He has been revealed IN us that He might be revealed THROUGH us. "WE CAN enlighten men with the knowledge of the glory of God, as we see it in the face of Christ" (2 Cor. 4:6, *Phillips*). Others can see this glory of Jesus Christ in our lives.

It is the reality of Christ shining in our lives and filling us with the glory of His Presence that we can share with others. ". . . we can give them the knowledge of the glory of God as we see it in the face of Jesus Christ."

An English evangelist was to conduct meetings in a certain town. Preparations were being made in the home where he was to stay. One of the maids in the home, making a purchase at the market said, "You would think Jesus Christ was coming, such a fuss is being made." Later she returned to the market. "Remember I said you would think Jesus Christ was coming to our home," she said. "Well, He did."

This is the influence of a life from which the glory of God in the person of Jesus Christ shines forth.

November

10

But we have this treasure in earthen vessels, that the excellency of the power may be of God, and not of us (2 Cor. 4:7).

In the days of the early church, people had special earthen jars in which they put their jewels, gold, coins, and important papers for safekeeping. These pottery vessels were only of value because of the treasure hidden in them.

Our lives are compared to vessels. Not only are our lives referred to as vessels, but as earthen ones. There is nothing pretentious or of great value in earthen vessels. It is not the earthen vessel that is important but what it contains.

God's purpose in making us vessels is that we are to be containers for God's special treasure. The treasure in our earthen vessel is the knowledge of the glory of God which is seen in the face of Christ Jesus. The treasure, Jesus Christ, is reproduced in the lives of believers. God can take the most insignificant vessel and magnify and reflect the glory and beauty of Himself.

Through our human vessels the glory of God in Christ Jesus will be communicated to a needy world.

This treasure brings the power of God into our lives. It gives a life of power, a power that can change a life within. It is the power of the living Christ in our lives.

His power is sufficient for our daily needs. When we are exhausted, His power becomes our needed strength. When we are misunderstood or criticized it lifts us up above it. When we are unable to cope with home situations, His power can face them. Whatever our daily need, the power of God released in our life through Jesus Christ is sufficient for that need.

When I am in southern California, occasionally I visit Forest Lawn Cemetery to view the beautiful stained-glass reproduction of da Vinci's "The Last Supper." The lighting effects are so arranged that the light gradually fades from the faces of all the disciples, leaving only the face of Jesus.

The power of God reflects in our earthen vessel the treasure of the life of Jesus Christ in us.

But his delight is in the law of the Lord; and in his law doth he meditate day and night (Ps. 1:2).

Meditation is defined as "contemplation; reflection; contemplation on sacred matters as a devotional act."

The English word for meditation comes from the Latin word, "meditor," meaning to think over, consider, contemplate, reflect upon.

The source of our meditation is the Word of God. David said, "O how love I thy law! it is my meditation all the day" (Ps. 119:97).

Meditation is more than just Bible reading. It begins with the reading of it but continues in contemplating or considering the truth as revealed in it. "Thy testimonies are my meditation" (Ps. 119:99). "I will meditate in thy precepts, and have respect unto thy ways" (Ps. 119:15). "Thy servant did meditate in thy statutes" (Ps. 119:23).

The Bible gives a direct command to meditate. Paul said to Timothy, "Meditate upon these things. . . ." (1 Tim. 4:15).

Meditation on God's Word gives spiritual illumination. "The entrance of thy words giveth light" (Ps. 119:130). Meditation on God's Word allows the Heavenly light to break in upon our inner darkness. Only the light of the Word is strong enough to dispel spiritual darkness.

We need to gain knowledge from God's Word, but through meditation on it, it becomes a part of our life.

Meditation is essential for the person God can really use. When Joshua was to replace Moses as leader of the children of Israel, God said to him, "This book of the law shall not depart out of thy mouth; but thou shalt meditate therein day and night, that thou mayest observe to do according to all that is written therein" (Josh. 1:8).

George Mueller, the great man of God, said that at first he began his devotional time with prayer. Then he would read and meditate on God's Word. Later he discovered that his spiritual life deepened when he reversed the order. He opened his Bible first, asking God to give him illumination on it. Then he would read and meditate on it. And finally he would have his prayer time. This led him to a greater life in the power of God.

In meditation we bring ". . . into captivity every thought to the obedience of Christ" (2 Cor. 10:5).

My meditation of him shall be sweet (Ps. 104:34).

As we considered the subject of true meditation yesterday, we found its source is the Word of God.

Meditation on the written word leads us to meditation on the Living Word, Jesus Christ. God, in speaking of His Son, said, "This is my beloved Son, in whom I am well pleased" (Matt. 3:17). He is the object of our meditation. Only as we come into His presence, shutting out all other distractions and quietly consider HIM, will we know real meditation.

When we occupy our thoughts with Him we realize we cannot begin to fathom the depths of who He is. However, the Holy Spirit can reveal new and greater depths of knowledge of Jesus Christ Himself. "Christ is the exact likeness of the unseen God. He existed before God made anything at all" (Col. 1:15, LB). "In him dwelleth all the fulness of the Godhead bodily" (Col. 2:9).

As we meditate on Him, we contemplate who He is and why He came to earth. We reflect on what He did for us.

A dear Quaker lady used to spend a half hour each day sitting quietly. She called it her "still" lesson. God invites us to some "still" lessons. He says, "Be still, and know that I am God" (Ps. 46:10).

There are rich dividends from meditating on Him—such meditation will be sweet. Could anything compare with it? How real and personal His love for us! Solomon said, "HE is altogether lovely."

As we meditate on Him, we are released from pressure and tension, and our hearts are filled with peace and trust.

Meditation on Him shall be sweet, for He is our priceless possession. Paul said, "Yes, furthermore I count everything as loss compared to the possession of the priceless privilege—the overwhelming preciousness, the surpassing worth and supreme advantage—of knowing Christ Jesus my Lord" (Phil. 3:8, *Amplified*).

Such meditation on Him leads us to worship of Him. We bow and say as Thomas did, "My Lord and My God" (John 20:28).

Meditation of Jesus Christ is for each of us personally, "MY meditation of Him shall be sweet."

Do you take time to meditate? Is Jesus Christ the object of your meditation?

Dear friends, don't be bewildered or surprised when you go through the fiery trials ahead, for this is no strange, unusual thing that is going to happen to you (1 Peter 4:12, LB).

We are reminded in God's Word that we can expect trials. We are not to be surprised when they come. This doesn't mean God has forgotten us, forsaken us, or that He doesn't care.

We are to rejoice when they come, not just for the trials themselves, but for what they can accomplish in our lives.

In this portion of Scripture, Paul tells us two reasons why we can rejoice in them. First, "Instead, be really glad—because these trials will make you partners with Christ in his suffering" (1 Peter 4:13, LB). Next, "afterwards you will have the wonderful joy of sharing his glory in that coming day when it will be displayed" (v. 13).

Once a little piece of wood bitterly complained because its owner whittled away on it, cutting it and filling it with holes. The owner paid no attention to its complaining, but continued making a flute out of that piece of ebony.

Silently he was saying to the piece of wood, "Little piece of wood, without this cutting and trimming, you would only be a stick, of no use to anyone. It seems to you now that I am destroying you, but instead I am making you into a flute. Some day your sweet music will comfort many a sorrowing heart. My cutting is to make you a blessing in the world."

Through trials in our lives God is whittling and cutting us to make us a melodious instrument to be a great blessing to people and a praise and glory to Himself.

"These trials are only to test your faith, to see whether or not it is strong and pure. It is being tested as fire tests gold and purifies it—and your faith is far more precious to God than mere gold; so if your faith remains strong after being tried in the test tube of fiery trials, it will bring you much praise and glory and honor on the day of his return" (1 Peter 1:7, LB).

November 14

Even so the tongue is a little member, and boasteth great things. Behold, how great a matter a little fire kindleth (James 3:5).

If the words we speak each day were recorded, they would make a fair sized book. If all of our words were recorded in a book what kind of reading would it make?

The tongue is a small but important member of the body. James illustrated its power by some comparisons. "Men control the movements of a large animal like the horse with a tiny bit placed in its mouth. Ships, too, for all their size and the momentum they have with a strong wind behind them, are controlled by a very small rudder according to the course chosen by the helmsman.

"The human tongue is physically small, but what tremendous effects it can boast of! A whole forest can be set ablaze by a tiny spark of fire, and the tongue is a fire, a whole world of evil. It is set within our bodily members but it can poison the whole body, it can set the whole of life ablaze, fed with the fires of hell" (James 3:3-6, *Phillips*).

The tongue is small but powerful. How carefully we need to guard it. It is easy to make unkind remarks. We may repeat a bit of gossip without really knowing whether or not it is true. Characters and careers have been completely ruined from the circulation of false rumors. In unguarded moments, we may make a sharp or cutting remark which hinders our testimony. We may be critical of a person who needs encouragement, not criticism. Most of us have at some time regretted words too quickly spoken.

Have you shaken feathers from a pillow, then watched the wind take them into the air, scattering them in every direction? Have you then tried to collect them? It is impossible. So it is with words. Once spoken, they cannot be recalled.

The tongue has a great capacity for good or evil. "No one can tame the human tongue. Blessing and curses come out of the same mouth—surely, my brothers, this is the sort of thing that never ought to happen!" (James 3:8, 10, *Phillips*).

But the Lord said unto him, Go thy way: for he is a chosen vessel unto me, to bear my name before the Gentiles, and kings, and the children of Israel (Acts 9:15).

As I sit in airports, often I hear people being paged. No lengthy description is given to get their attention. The identifying mark by which they are contacted is their name. The name represents the person who bears it.

The name of Jesus represents Who He is, the Savior of the world. "Thou shalt call His name Jesus, for He shall save His people from their sins" (Matt. 1:21).

After Paul's conversion, God said of him, ". . . he is a chosen vessel to BEAR MY NAME before the Gentiles, and kings, and the children of Israel."

What a wonderful privilege was given to Paul, "a bearer of the name of the Lord Jesus Christ." The word "bear" is defined as "show" or "display." A beautiful diamond is often displayed on the background of dark velvet, enhancing its brilliance. Paul was chosen to be a vessel to display or show forth the beauty and loveliness of the person of Jesus Christ in his life.

We, too, have been given the privilege of being a "Bearer of His Name" in our corner of life.

It is a holy name, an exalted name. We must be careful not to dishonor it. His graciousness and majesty should reflect from our lives wherever we go.

A missionary was telling the people of a South Pacific Island about the Lord Jesus Christ. They said, "Oh, He used to live here." The missionary, wondering what they meant, discovered that a number of years before a missionary had come there to share the Gospel. He lived in their midst in such a way that when the Islanders were told of Jesus, they thought He must have been the former missionary.

Wherever we are today, whatever our circumstances, there we are to be "A Bearer of His Name." Can this be said of our lives?

What a high calling! A Bearer of HIS Name!

November
16

There is a lad here, which hath five barley loaves, and two small fishes: but what are they among so many? (John 6:9).

One day Jesus had been preaching to a large crowd. As evening approached, He was aware of their need for food. The disciples suggested, "Send them to find food." They were probably thinking, "Our means is insufficient. It is an impossible task. Where would we get enough food or enough money to buy food?"

But Jesus said, "Give ye them to eat." He asked what food was available. In the crowd was a little boy with a lunch of five loaves and two fish. When asked if Jesus could have it, he gave it all to Him, holding nothing back.

Jesus took the lunch of a boy whose name is not known, blessed it, broke it, gave it to the disciples to distribute and the people were satisfied.

We live in a world in need of spiritual food, food that will satisfy the inner hunger of people's lives. The Lord says, "Give ye THEM to EAT." He didn't say, "Form a committee or a commission." He said, "Give YE them to eat." His means of feeding a spiritually hungry world is through His own people. His command is for us today.

Sometimes we give God excuses why we cannot be involved in ministering to the spiritual needs of people. We feel we have nothing God can use, we say we are too busy, or we have too many home or business responsibilities.

We may feel we have little to offer Him, but little is much when God is in it. It is not what we have, but what we are doing with what we have. He uses what we have, but He must have all of it.

How often we limit what God wants to do in our lives. His power is at our disposal. When we give Him our all, He takes it and multiplies it by His power. Then what we do is not in our power but in His.

Do not understimate what God can do in and with a life that has been placed in His hands to use.

Be not afraid of sudden fear, neither of the desolation of the wicked, when it cometh. For the Lord shall be thy confidence, and shall keep thy foot from being taken (Prov. 3:25-26).

Many children have a "security blanket" which they have to take to bed with them. It may be a real blanket, a stuffed animal, or some toy. It is something they can tightly clutch in their arms to give a feeling of security and confidence.

As never before, fear is gripping the hearts of millions in the world today. It is a destructive force; one that can wreck homes and eat away at the hearts of people, bringing depression and despair.

In such an age when people's hearts are failing them for fear, many of us have "security blankets" to which we desperately clutch, something to give a sense of safety in a frightening world.

Some people turn to tranquilizers, alcohol, and drugs. But these do not bring a permanent peace of heart and mind. True peace comes from within. Only as our sins are forgiven and Christ dwells in our hearts can we have true peace, a peace the world cannot give or take away, a peace that endures.

The Bible often admonishes us not to fear. "Be not afraid of sudden fear."

A confidence that releases us from fear comes from peace of mind and heart and it comes from being at peace with God through Jesus Christ. Someone has said, "We think security brings peace—but real peace brings security."

Confidence has the meaning of "placing total trust in a person." To live a true Christian life, we must have a deep, unshakeable faith in the Lord. "It is better to trust in the Lord than to put confidence in man" (Ps. 118:8).

Man has a desperate need of security, but all the insurance policies available cannot give permanent security. Only when our confidence is in the Lord do we have nothing to fear and experience real security. "For the Lord shall be your confidence, firm and strong" (Prov. 3:26, *Amplified*).

"Now faith means that we have full CONFIDENCE in the things we hope for, it means being certain of things we cannot see" (Heb. 11:1, *Phillips*).

This thing is from me (1 Kings 12:24).

Through the years there have been Christians who have been put in prison because of their faith.

Today many Christians are in prisons, but not prisons confined within four walls. They are prisons of heartache, pain, loneliness, misunderstanding, or disappointment.

We look for some way to free ourselves from such prisons. We may even ask God to release us from them. But if we become quiet enough before the Lord to listen, we can hear Him say, "This thing is from Me."

Nothing comes into our lives but through Him. In 1 Samuel 3:18 we read, "It is the Lord: let him do what seemeth him good." Anything that concerns us, concerns Him. "He that toucheth you toucheth the apple of his eye" (Zech. 2:8).

When the enemy comes in like a flood with his attacks, when temptations assail, God reminds us: This thing is from Me. I have placed you there and have allowed it that you may learn to "be strong in the Lord, and the power of His might" (Eph. 6:10).

When we face sorrow, He says, "This thing is from Me. I am the God of all comfort." If the way is dark before us, He whispers, "This thing is from Me and I will give light for the next step." As we come to the crossroads, uncertain which way to take, He says, "This thing is from Me and I will teach you the way you shall go." When we have been hurt by someone, or something unkind has been said about us, He promises, "This thing is from Me and I will wipe away your tears and ease the heartache."

He has valuable lessons for us to learn from such experiences. Sometimes they are God's way of answering our prayers. Perhaps we have asked for His love, so He brings someone into our lives who is not easy to love. He promises, "This thing is from Me and I am giving opportunity for My love to become real in your life."

Wherever we are today, we are there, not by chance, but by choice—God's choice.

For God has said, I will never, never fail you nor forsake you (Heb. 13:5, LB).

The foundation of our faith is the Word of God. In this Scripture verse God Himself speaks, "For God has said." It is not what "they say," nor what "we say," but what "God says" that is important.

What did God say? He promised, "I will never leave thee, nor forsake thee." God always keeps His Word. He can be trusted.

The word "leave" usually means "to depart." In this verse it has a deeper meaning of "I will not let you go."

He is always near to come to our aid when we are in trouble. His promise gives us confidence. "That we may boldly say, The Lord is my helper."

Has there been a time in your life when you were overworked, when you had more to do than you could do? You were weary and discouraged almost to the breaking point. You were ready to give up. Suddenly a friend came, saying, "I have come to HELP you." How your spirits were lifted and the burden was eased.

The LORD is such a helper, One who is always near to give needed help. The Lord IS our helper. He is a present helper, even for today. "God is our refuge and strength, a very present help in trouble" (Ps. 46:1).

His help is for us personally. The Lord is MY helper. "MY help cometh from the Lord, which made heaven and earth" (Ps. 121:2).

There are times when friends cannot help, but the Lord can; when money cannot help, but the Lord can; when social position cannot help, but the Lord can.

We can depend on His help, for we have His promise that He will never leave us nor forsake us.

David Livingstone, when sailing for Africa the first time, was accompanied to the dock by some close friends. Concerned for his safety, they reminded him of the dangers, hoping he would yet turn back.

Livingstone quickly opened his Bible and read, "Lo, I am with you always." Then he said, "That is the word of a Gentleman. Let us be going."

November

20

Blessed be the King that cometh in the name of the Lord (Luke 19:38).

One day Jesus made a Royal Entry into Jerusalem, riding on a colt. Palm branches were waving! Garments were spread in the way! The people shouted in loud acclaim! "Blessed be the King that cometh in the name of the Lord."

The people had expected Him to set up a kingdom. When He refused the Kingship of an earthly kingdom, they went their own way again with lives unchanged.

True, He had come to set up a kingdom, but not the kind of kingdom they expected.

His kingdom was to be a spiritual one in the hearts of people. Instead of accepting the crown of an earthly kingdom, Jesus now faced a crown of thorns. He faced death on Calvary's cross so He could set up His kingdom in the lives of people.

A kingdom requires a king. In some kingdoms the king is one in name only, just a figurehead. In other kingdoms the king has ruling power. In the dictionary, a king is defined as, "One who rules for life."

Today the Lord Jesus wants to be the King of our lives, having His rightful place on the throne of our lives. There is just one throne in the human heart. We must determine who is to occupy that throne. Christ or self. It cannot be both. He does not want divided allegiance. One definition for kingdom is, "The realm in which God's will is fulfilled." As the King of our life He fulfills God's will in us.

When Raphael's picture, the "Sistine Madonna," was first brought to Dresden, it was displayed in the throne room of the castle. It was discovered that the best place to display it was the spot occupied by the throne itself. The king, taking in the situation, said, "Move the throne and make room for the immortal Raphael."

We sing, "King of my life, I crown Thee now." Have we allowed Him to be the King of our lives? Have we invited Him to occupy the throne of our lives? Have we crowned Him as our King?

By him therefore let us offer the sacrifice of praise to God continually, that is, the fruit of our lips giving thanks to his name (Heb. 13:15).

November

21

Hebrews 13 is filled with practical exhortations relevant to Christian living today. In verse 15 we are reminded to be full of praise.

If a record were kept, we might be surprised how little we praise the Lord. We sing, "Count your many blessings," but rush through the day without taking time to express our thanks to God for these blessings. We take the everyday things so for granted.

Praise should be our lifelong occupation—not occasionally, but continually. "Through him therefore let us constantly and at all times offer up to God a sacrifice of praise. . . ." *(Amplified).*

Praise to God ". . . is the fruit of lips that thankfully acknowledge and confess and glorify His name" *(Amplified).* Is this what God hears from our lips? Praise to His name? Or does He sometimes hear murmuring? Complaining? Gossip? Criticism? Praise to God is not just the verbal expression of our lips, but the reality of praise lived out from our lives.

We are to offer a "sacrifice of praise." A sacrifice is something offered to someone, usually at a cost. "A sacrifice of praise"—that is, praise that costs something.

During the last several years before my husband's death it cost me something to praise God. It was a sacrifice. My heart would be heavy, uncertain of the future. As I watched him suffer, I suffered along with him. It was not always easy to praise God. Yet as I lifted my eyes from my heartache to God, praise would not only fill my heart but my lips—a sacrifice of praise.

It is easy to say to God, "I will always trust you, no matter what happens." It is easy to praise Him when everything is going smoothly. But what about the time when we are suffering, when our hearts are breaking, when there seems to be no solution to our needs. To praise Him at such times is a "sacrifice of praise" that ascends as perfume to the throne of God.

November
22

Come now therefore, and I will send thee unto Pharaoh, that thou mayest bring forth my people the children of Israel out of Egypt (Exod. 3:10).

God called Moses to deliver the Israelites out of Egypt. He said, "Come NOW . . . and I will send thee." It was a simple, direct call. But Moses began enumerating excuses, one after another, why God couldn't use him. He gave such excuses as "Who am I, that I should go?" "What shall I say to them?" "They will not believe me." "I am not eloquent." "Lord, please! Send someone else."

God let Moses go through excuse after excuse, but each time He reminded Moses that it was not his ability or inability that would qualify or disqualify him for leadership. The same God who called him would enable him.

God asked Moses, "What is that in thine hand?" It was just a shepherd's rod, but God demonstrated to Moses that his shepherd's rod when given to God would become the rod of God, God's rod of power, in the hand of Moses as he became God's chosen leader of the Israelites.

Has God called you to a place of service that looks impossible to you? A place where you may not want to serve? Are you making excuses as Moses did?

God says to you as He did Moses, "What is that in thine hand?" You may answer, "All I have in my hand is a typewriter, some kitchen utensils, a pen or pencil, a tool, nothing of great value."

Whatever it is, when it is given to God to use, it becomes an instrument of power in your life for His use.

In the New Testament we read of Paul who in His weakness experienced the power of God in his life. He wrote, "I was nervous and rather shaky . . . but it was a demonstration of the power of the Spirit!" (1 Cor. 2:3-4, *Phillips*).

What is that in your hand? Place it in God's hand, for His use. God is not interested in whether you are capable or not. All He wants is your life afire with His presence, a life willing for Him to use in the power of His Spirit.

Enter into his gates with thanksgiving, and into his courts with praise: be thankful unto him, and bless his name. (Ps. 100:4).

November

23

The Thanksgiving season is a special time of giving praise and thanksgiving to God. Once a year, a day is set aside for expressing thankfulness, but for the children of God each day is a day of thanksgiving. The basis of our thanksgiving comes from a personal relationship with Jesus Christ. "Thanks be unto God for his unspeakable gift" (2 Cor. 9:15).

As we enter into His presence we are to "be thankful" and "bless His name." We are to come before Him with thank-filled and praise-filled hearts. God's mercies are new every morning but it is easy to forget to thank Him. A thankful heart is not dependent on the material things we possess but on the blessings that come from the Lord.

As we pause to thank Him for the blessings of the past year, we must not forget to thank Him for the lessons we have learned through our difficult times. We are not to be thankful for just the pleasant, easy things, but ALL things. "IN EVERY THING give thanks: for this is the will of God in Christ Jesus concerning you" (1 Thess. 5:18).

Our thanksgiving is to be continual, not just on Thanksgiving Day, but each day through the year. "Giving thanks ALWAYS for ALL things unto God and the Father in the name of our Lord Jesus Christ" (Eph. 5:20).

Thanksgiving expresses gratitude for what God does for us. Praise is our attitude toward God because of who and what He is.

Praise comes from a heart satisfied with the Lord. A satisfied customer is one of the greatest assets a business firm can have. "He satisfieth the longing soul" (Ps. 107:9). Does the Lord see us as "satisfied customers" with hearts overflowing with thankfulness?

It has been said, "We're so concerned about tomorrow that we fail to be thankful for today." As we praise and thank Him at all times and in everything, the minor notes of trouble in our lives become major chords of triumphant victory. May our lives be such a hymn of triumphant praise to HIM today.

November
24

Seek the Lord, and his strength: seek his face evermore (Ps. 105:4).

Today many are seeking for satisfaction and happiness. Some seek it in pleasure; others in fame; some in financial security; others in social position. But searching in these places is futile, for none of them bring the inner peace that people long for. Only in Christ do we find real peace, a peace the world cannot give, nor can it take away.

So often we seek for the things He gives us, but God's Word says we are to seek HIM, not His "presents" but His "PRESENCE." "Seek the Lord, and His strength; seek His face for evermore."

Today burdens weigh heavily upon us. Often we are so pressed in on every side that it seems all strength is gone. What a relief to know that when OUR strength is exhausted, we have HIS strength available. He is an unfailing source of supply.

Paul experienced the sufficiency of the strength which comes from God. God said to Paul, "For My strength and power are made perfect—fulfilled and completed and show themselves most effective—in [your] weakness" (2 Cor. 12:9, *Amplified*). Paul recognized the reality of it in his experience. "For when I am weak (in human strength), then am I [truly] strong—able, powerful in divine strength" (2 Cor. 12:10, *Amplified*). Sometimes God allows the pressures to come that we may discover how powerless and inadequate we are in ourselves, and that our dependence must be in HIM.

Not only are we to seek His strength, but His face. Many times our way is so dark we can't see ahead. At such times what comfort it is to seek HIM! "For God, who said, 'Let there be light in the darkness,' has made us understand that it is the brightness of his glory that is seen in the face of Jesus Christ" (2 Cor. 4:6, LB).

In order to see a person's face, we need to be close to that person. As we draw near to Him, the brightness of the glory of His face is reflected in our lives, and from our lives.

Be satisfied with nothing less today than seeking Him, His strength, and His face.

Speak out to one another in psalms and hymns and spiritual songs, offering praise with voices [and instruments], and making melody with all your heart to the Lord (Eph. 5:19, Amplified).

Have you experienced days filled with the "blues"? You seemed weighed down with cares of life. Suddenly you heard someone singing or whistling and your spirits were lifted. There is real therapy in music.

In the Old Testament, singers were appointed to serve God in His sanctuary. In the New Testament, Paul wrote of a "singing company." "As you converse among yourselves in psalms and spiritual songs, heartily singing and making your music to the Lord" (Eph. 5:19, *Berkeley*).

When Jesus Christ enters a life, with this new relationship comes a new song. "And he hath put a new song in my mouth, even praise unto our God: many shall see it, and fear, and shall trust in the Lord" (Ps. 40:3).

The hearts of the early Christians were full of song because the presence of the Lord was so real in their lives. They could sing regardless of their circumstances. Paul and Silas sang while in prison. "And at midnight Paul and Silas prayed, and sang praises unto God: and the prisoners heard them" (Acts 16:25).

This singing comes from the heart. Although we may not be able to sing aloud, the inward song of the heart catches the ear of our listening God.

We are told that the song of a man reflects his soul. Singing glorifies God when from our hearts we sing to Him. The secret of the singing heart is a spirit-filled life, controlled by the Holy Spirit, giving us heart songs in harmony with His purposes.

Are you a member of the heavenly "singing company"? Is your heart singing and making melody to the Lord? If not, why not begin to sing? You may think it only a joyful noise, but it will make you feel better, be a blessing to others, and rejoice the heart of your Heavenly Father.

"O for a thousand tongues to sing My great Redeemer's praise; the glories of my God and King, the triumphs of His grace."

November

26

And we know that all things work together for good to them that love God, to them who are the called according to his purpose (Rom. 8:28).

Has some friend quoted this verse to you in time of trouble? What was your reaction? Did you answer, "That is all right for you to quote to me, but you are not going through the trouble I am"? It is easy to share it with others but not so easy to apply it to the trouble we face ourselves.

Perhaps we should carefully consider each part of the verse to know what it really says.

First, Paul writes, ". . . all things WORK together for good." It is not by luck or by accident but by God "working" in our lives. In Philippians 2:13 *(Phillips)* Paul said, "For it is God who is at work within you."

It is not just some things that are working, or easy things, or pleasant things, but ALL things. It doesn't say they have worked or will work, but "work" now, today.

Paul continues, "All things work TOGETHER." When we view our experiences singly, often they are not good. Yet as we commit them to God, He will work them together for our good.

Perhaps today you are questioning the circumstances in your life. You may be asking God to remove them. But God desires to accomplish His purpose for your life. The pattern of His plan may not be clear to you yet, but you can be sure He is working and He wants to do nothing short of His best for you. God puts "signs of assurance" along the path of our lives, saying, "God at work."

Jeremiah 29:11 *(Rotherham)* says, "I know the plans I am planning for you, declareth Jehovah God, plans of welfare and not of calamity, to give you a future and a hope."

What assurance this is for us today! He doesn't say that we can hope or suppose that all things are working together for our good, but we can KNOW.

It has been said, "Those who leave everything in God's hand will eventually see God's hand in everything."

And we know that all things work together for good to them that love God, to them who are the called according to his purpose (Rom. 8:28).

Paul reminds us that not only do all our trials work together, but, ". . . all things work together for GOOD." Is tragedy good? Is sickness good? Is bereavement good? Usually we interpret good as comfort, ease, pleasure. We think of good as being free from pain, having a lovely home, the latest luxuries, such things. We measure good in terms of success, achievement of aims and goals in life.

But this is not God's way, necessarily, of demonstrating His goodness. Through the trials and troubles that come into our lives He is proving His goodness. The final results are good. The good which God has promised may not always seem good to us as we go through it. But we see only the immediate, while God knows the ultimate outworking of His plans for us.

It is important what we do in the difficult circumstances of our lives. As we let God fit them together He will bring good out of them. This is promised for those who love Him and are called according to His purpose. It is more than having a passive attitude of submitting to them, but it is letting God do the work.

He is not in a hurry as He works, but patiently waits for us to learn our lessons.

The Living Bible says, "We know that all that happens to us is working for our good if we love God and are fitting into His plans" (Rom. 8:28). Are we fitting into them?

When we work on a picture puzzle we put all its pieces out before us. At first we wonder where to start and how the pieces will fit together. As we begin to work, piece by piece, the picture begins to develop. Eventually the puzzle is completed with a picture just like the picture on the box.

God's plan for our lives is to conform us to the image of His Son. As we let Him fit every piece of our lives together, He transforms them more and more into the likeness of His Son.

November
28

To be molded into the image of His Son [and share inwardly His likeness] (Rom. 8:29, Amplified).

Someone once asked Rembrandt, the Dutch artist, "When is a picture completed?" He replied, "A picture is finished when it expresses the intent of the artist."

God is painting a picture on the canvas of our lives. ". . . to be molded into the image of His Son [and share inwardly His likeness]" (Rom. 8:29, *Amplified*).

This is God's plan for our lives. We are to be conformed to the family likeness of His Son.

In the beginning man was made in God's image. "And God said, 'Let us make man in our image . . .'" (Gen. 1:26). Through the entrance of sin this image was spoiled. In the person of Jesus Christ, God came to earth to restore this image. ". . . and He is the perfect imprint and very image of [God's] nature . . ." (Heb. 1:3, *Amplified*).

The image of Jesus Christ is to be formed in us. God takes our human nature and slowly and sometimes painfully begins to develop in us the likeness to Christ. "My little children, of whom I travail in birth again until Christ be formed in you" (Gal. 4:19).

God uses every circumstance, every problem, every trial in our lives in this transforming process. "We are assured and know that [God being a partner in their labor], all things work together and are [fitting into a plan] for good to those who love God and are called according to [His] design and purpose" (Rom. 8:28, *Amplified*). God's plan will be finished in our lives when we express the intent of the Master Artist.

One day I viewed some paintings in an art exhibit. As I glanced at one, my eyes were drawn to the frame. It was a beautiful, ornate frame. Finally I looked at the picture. It was beautiful, but overpowered by the frame. The purpose of the frame should be to enhance the beauty of the picture, drawing attention, not to the frame, but to the picture.

So our lives are to be a frame enhancing the beauty of Christ shining forth. May nothing in the "frame" of our lives detract or draw attention away from the picture of Jesus in our lives.

I am the God of thy father, the God of Abraham, the God of Isaac, and the God of Jacob (Exod. 3:6).

This year is drawing to a close. Soon we will begin a new year, one filled with new opportunities, new situations, new joys, new experiences of living.

With the uncertainty of these days, not knowing what the future holds, it is reassuring to know that the God of this past year will become our God of the new year.

In the above Scripture verse we note three aspects of God that will encourage us as we look into the new year. God said to Moses, "I am the God of thy father, the God of Abraham, the God of Isaac, and the God of Jacob." He is the GOD of the PAST. As He had been with Abraham, Isaac, and Jacob in the past, He promised to be with Moses.

As we look back in the past year, we recognize He has been our God of the past, meeting every need, even at times when we may not have understood how He was working. "Hitherto hath the Lord helped us" (1 Sam. 7:12).

He said to Moses, "I AM come down to deliver them" (Exod. 3:8). The God of the Past is the GOD of the PRESENT. He who has worked for us in the past will work for us in the new year. He promises, "I will be your God for the year before you." He is ready to come down and deliver us in the midst of each need next year. The psalmist said, "For thou art great, and DOEST (present tense, today) wondrous things: thou art God alone" (Ps. 86:10).

In Exodus 3:10 God said to Moses, "Come now therefore, and I will send thee." He is the GOD of the FUTURE. He invites us to come to Him in the future, so that He can continue to send us out to do His will and walk in the paths He has prepared for us, not only today, but in the days ahead.

He is the God of your past; the God of your future; the God of your present: the God of your today.

November

30

Behold, to obey is better than sacrifice (1 Sam. 15:22).

One day Samuel had to go to King Saul and tell him that he had disobeyed the Lord's command. Saul denied that he had been disobedient, yet Samuel had the evidence. When confronted with it, he confessed to it, but excused himself because he was afraid of the people.

Samuel said to him, "Behold, to obey is better than sacrifice."

Earlier in his life King Saul had been humble. Samuel said to him, "When thou wast little in thine own sight" (1 Sam. 15:17). But he had become self-sufficient. He had become disobedient to the Word of the Lord, interpreting God's instructions in his own way.

The Bible reminds us of the importance of being obedient to God's Word. "And remember, it is a message to OBEY, not just to listen to. So don't fool yourselves. For if a person just listens and doesn't obey, he is like a man looking at his face in a mirror; as soon as he walks away, he can't see himself anymore or remember what he looks like. But if anyone keeps looking steadily into God's law for free men, he will not only remember it but he will DO what it says, and God will greatly bless him in everything he does" (James 1:22-25, LB).

When we honestly face our lives in the light of His Word, the Holy Spirit will bring conviction in areas that need to be brought back into obedience to it.

"For the Word that God speaks is alive and active; it cuts more keenly than any two-edged sword: it strikes through to the place where soul and spirit meet, to the innermost intimacies of a man's being: it examines the very thoughts and motives of a man's heart" (Heb. 4:12, *Phillips*).

The enemy is hard at work to draw us away from walking in obedience to the Lord in the light of His Word. He is subtle in his working to lessen our love for the Lord Jesus Christ.

The Word of God at work in our lives keeps us obedient. "Thy word have I hid in mine heart, that I might not sin against thee" (Ps. 119:11).

Whatsoever things are true, whatsoever things are honest, whatsoever things are just, whatsoever things are pure, whatsoever things are lovely, whatsoever things are of good report; if there be any virtue, and if there be any praise, think on these things (Phil. 4:8).

It has been said that the thought life is the gateway to the soul.

Each thought that approaches the mind for entrance should pass inspection. Before we board a plane, each passenger has to pass through a security inspection. Either security officers must check the on-board luggage, or it is put under an x-ray machine before the passenger can carry it on the plane.

As thoughts come to the door of our minds they need to pass inspection before being allowed to enter.

Paul enumerates some inspection standards for our thoughts: "Whatsoever things are true." Jesus said, "I am the truth." In Him is revealed the truth about God. God has made the truth available to us in the Bible. As we fill our minds with Bible truths, our thoughts are centered upon that which is true, genuine, and real.

We need to open our minds to "whatsoever things are honest," those things that claim respect. We need to think on "whatsoever things are just," that which is right.

Thinking on "whatsoever things are pure" gives purity to our thought life. We are to fill our minds with "whatsoever things are lovely," things that give beauty of character.

"Whatsoever things are of good report" are the things that are worth talking about.

It is important to saturate our minds with the Word of God. We should fix our thoughts on these God-given standards which motivate us to a more Christ-like living. Our inner attitudes affect our outer actions. "For as he thinketh in his heart, so is he" (Prov. 23:7).

Today if we were to take the thoughts of our minds to God's inspection center, would they pass inspection, or would some of them need to be removed?

"Search me, O God, and know my heart; test my thoughts. Point out anything you find in me that makes you sad, and lead me along the path of everlasting life" (Ps. 139:23-24, LB).

December

2

Blessed be the God and Father of our Lord Jesus Christ, who hath blessed us with all spiritual blessings in heavenly places in Christ (Eph. 1:3).

As Paul began his letter to the Ephesians his heart was overflowing with praise to God, the source of all spiritual blessings. As we ponder WHO God is, and WHAT He has done for us, our hearts, too, are filled with praise.

God has a vast storehouse of riches reserved for us, His family. They are sufficient for every need, available at any time. Ruth Paxson said, "A Christian becomes the possessor of a heaven-born nature, so he needs heaven-sent supplies to nourish and develop it." From our "position" in the heavenlies with Christ we have access to them. We are blessed with ALL spiritual blessings.

What are some of our spiritual blessings? We have forgiveness: "It is through Him, at the cost of His own blood, that we are redeemed, freely forgiven through that full and generous grace which has overflowed into our lives and given us wisdom and insight" (Eph. 1:7, *Phillips*). From Him comes strength: "For I can do everything God asks me to with the help of Christ who gives me the strength and power" (Phil. 4:13, LB). Prayer is another spiritual blessing: "If ye shall ask any thing in My name, I will do it" (John 14:14). These are just a few of our spiritual blessings we have in Christ.

There used to be a program called "Missing Heirs." Inheritances had been left to heirs who could not be found. Every effort was made to locate these "missing heirs." Today are we "missing heirs" to God's inheritance because we failed to claim all that He has for us? Or have we "possessed" all blessings He has provided for us?

In Christ we have access to His storehouse of riches. All that is His becomes ours. "And since we are his children, we will share his treasures—for all God gives to his Son Jesus is now ours too" (Rom. 8:17, LB).

A "missing heir"? A "possessor of all spiritual blessings"? Which are we?

Teach us to number our days and recognize how few they are; help us to spend them as we should (Ps. 90:12, LB).

Our lives are like a jewel case in which God has placed our days as jewels. From our jewel case He draws out a day, one at a time, and presents it to us to use.

As we begin a new day we accept the finality of our yesterdays. They are past. Paul wrote, "Forgetting the past" (Phil. 3:13, LB). We face the uncertainty of our tomorrows. "For the length of your lives is as uncertain as the morning fog—now you see it; soon it is gone" (James 4:14, LB).

But we have the reality of our present moment, our today. How will we use it? We can spend it on ourselves, on some cherished plan or desire of our own. Or we can present it to our heavenly Father to use in a way that will bring joy to His heart and glory to His name.

With the privilege of using God's today, why waste time brooding or longing over the past? It is gone. Why be fearful of tomorrow? It may never come.

Today, now, this present moment, is a special gift from God. As we listen to His still small voice He will reveal how we are to spend it.

The psalmist said, "TEACH us to number our days." Someone asked Will Rogers how he would spend his days if he knew he only had a few left to live. He replied, "One at a time."

David wrote, "Lord, help me to realize how brief my time on earth will be. Help me to know that I am here for but a moment more. My life is no longer than my hand! My whole lifetime is but a moment to you. Proud man! Frail as breath! A shadow! And all his busy rushing ends in nothing. He heaps up riches for someone else to spend. And so, Lord, my only hope is in you" (Ps. 39:4-7, LB).

It has been said, "Tomorrow is God's secret, but today is yours to live. This is God's today; live it for Him."

December
4

I beseech you therefore, brethren, by the mercies of God, that ye present your bodies a living sacrifice, holy, acceptable unto God, which is your reasonable service (Rom. 12:1).

People are constantly asking the question, "How can I know God's will for my life?" In this chapter of Romans, Paul gives some principles to follow in knowing and doing God's will.

In 2 Corinthians 8:5 we read, ". . . but first gave their own selves to the Lord." God is more interested in our lives than He is in our service. Paul challenged the Romans to present their bodies to God. "Presenting" means to put something at the disposal of another to do with as he pleases. As we make a total commitment to Him, we present our bodies to Him, including our eyes, ears, lips, hands, feet, our all. We recognize His Lordship over our lives. We make our bodies available for His use at any time, in any way.

By such an act of commitment we give Him our wills, our ambitions, interests, our all, and in exchange we accept His will for our lives.

He has a right to be the Lord of our lives. Paul wrote, "When you think of what He has done for you, is this too much to ask?" (Rom. 12:1, LB). He purchased us at a great price, His death on the cross. Paul wrote, "Ye are not your own . . . ye are bought with a price" (1 Cor. 6:19-20).

When we present our bodies a living sacrifice, we become an instrument in which His will can be accomplished. As long as we keep self on the throne, our bodies respond to our will. When we yield completely to Him, and turn the control of our lives over to Him, He becomes our Lord. Paul summed it up in this way, "For to me to live is Christ" (Phil. 1:21).

We continually lay down our will and accept His. This exchange of wills becomes our altar of sacrifice.

Is your life totally committed to Him? Who occupies the throne of your life? Have you presented your body a living sacrifice, saying, "Here is my body for Your use; I'm available"?

And be not conformed to this world: but be ye transformed by the renewing of your mind, that ye may prove what is that good, and acceptable, and perfect, will of God (Rom. 12:2).

If we are to know and do the will of God we must first let Jesus Christ be the Lord of our lives.

We must not conform to this world with all its materialistic philosophy, nor to the thinking and behavior of those who do not know God. Paul said, "Don't let the world around you squeeze you into its own mould" (Rom. 12:2, *Phillips*). We are not to be squeezed into the superficial set of values and standards by which the world measures success and achieves its goals. "Don't copy the behavior and customs of this world" (LB).

The only way to keep from being squeezed into the world's mold is to be transformed into a new person.

As we saturate ourselves with God's Word, His Spirit begins this work of transformation. Paul wrote, ". . . but let God re-mold your minds from within, so that you may prove IN PRACTICE that the plan of God for you is good, meets all its demands, and moves towards the goal of true maturity."

Michelangelo always said that within every block of granite was a person waiting to be released. When he sculptored his famous statue of David, he used a piece of marble that had been discarded as worthless by another sculptor. But he could see the potential of a great statue in that discarded piece of marble. The stone was given another chance, and out of it came the great statue of David.

As we allow God to transform our lives, gradually we begin to emerge more and more the person God intends us to be. Then our lives will prove in practice that His will is good, acceptable, and perfect.

Fenelon said, "All that is in you, all that you are, is only loaned to you. Make use of it according to the will of Him that lends it. Never regard it for a moment as your own."

"God-yielded wills produce God-planned lives."

December
6

What is that to thee? follow thou me (John 21:22).

One morning soon after the Resurrection, Jesus was with some of His disciples. He challenged Peter with some important issues he must settle if he was to be an effective representative of Jesus Christ. Jesus recommissioned him to service, saying, "Feed my lambs"; "Feed my sheep." Then He commanded Peter, "Follow thou ME."

As Peter turned about, he saw John and said to Jesus, "Lord, and what shall this man do?" (John 21:21). Jesus, looking at Peter, perhaps with eyes that penetrated Peter's innermost being, said, "If I will that he tarry till I come, what is that to thee? Follow thou Me."

Jesus was saying, "Peter, what is to happen to John is not your concern. He is My concern. You will have all you can take care of if you follow the path I have set before you." How human Peter was! How much of Peter was yet in Peter!

There may be some of Peter in each of us today. How often we have complained to the Lord about those who do not seem to be as faithful in their service for Him, as we are. They seem to be willing for others to carry the responsibility, but we complain to Jesus, saying, "What about them, Lord?"

He replies, "What is that to thee—FOLLOW THOU ME." He is saying to us, "I will take care of the others. You are answerable only for yourself." We are not to concern ourselves with others, for they, too, are answerable to the Lord.

As we follow Him in complete obedience there will be "lambs" for us to lead to the Shepherd; there will be "sheep" to bring into the fold. We can be an instrument to bring someone closer to Christ. We can be an encouragement by a helpful word spoken. Because we have prayed, a need in someone's life may be met.

Instead of praying, "Lord, and what shall this man do?" instead of being concerned about others, may we earnestly say, "Lord, what wilt thou have ME to do?" (Acts 9:6).

"FOLLOW THOU ME !"

Then took Mary a pound of ointment of spikenard, very costly, and anointed the feet of Jesus, and wiped his feet with her hair: and the house was filled with the odour of the ointment (John 12:3).

One day Jesus was being entertained in a home in Bethany. A meal was prepared, with Him as the honored guest. Lazarus, Martha, and Mary were among those present.

Perhaps Mary wished she could do something for Jesus to show her love. Then she remembered her alabaster box. It was very costly, estimated at about a year's earnings. What had been her plans for this precious ointment?

She decided to anoint Jesus with it. There was only one way it could be opened. It had to be broken. After it was broken, it had to be used all at once and it could not be used again for anything else. In one act of love she broke the box and poured it all out on Jesus. She gave her best, not her second best. She not only GAVE to Jesus, she gave that which was costly and she gave it all. She held nothing back.

Mary loved; therefore, she gave. Out of the fullness of her heart she gave Him her most precious possession. The entire house was filled then with the odor of the ointment. It spilled over on others.

Do you have an alabaster box which has not yet been broken? Our alabaster box may be some cherished plan, some precious possession, some person, some resentment, or our own will. It has to be broken before we can pour our treasure out on Him. After it is broken the fragrance of the life of Jesus Christ is released from our lives, spilling over on others. Only then do we get God's best.

Mary poured out the perfume without measure, without limit. She poured out her all. Have you and I?

There is a fragrance surrounding the person who has held nothing back but given Him their all.

Someone has defined service as, "A life broken and poured out on Jesus." Jesus said, "She hath wrought a good work on ME" (Mark 14:6).

December

8

But despite all this, overwhelming victory is ours through Christ who loved us enough to die for us (Rom. 8:37, LB*).*

Sometimes we are tempted to think we have more than our share of trouble and heartaches. We begin to feel sorry for ourselves. We look at them with an attitude of defeat.

Paul was one of the greatest Christians, yet he endured great trials. He experienced extreme opposition and persecution in the ministry for Jesus Christ. When he wrote of having victory in the midst of trials, he was writing out of personal experience.

He wrote, "Who then can ever keep Christ's love from us? When we have trouble or calamity, when we are hunted down or destroyed, is it because He doesn't love us anymore? And if we are hungry, or penniless, or in danger, or threatened with death, has God deserted us?" (Rom. 8:35, LB). His answer was "No!"

He wrote that in the midst of and in spite of all these circumstances, "We are more than conquerors" (Rom. 8:37). It is encouraging just to know we can be conquerors, but to be MORE THAN conquerors, this is victory plus.

Paul shares some of the adverse circumstances He had faced, and over which he had victory—tribulation, distress, persecution, hunger, threadbare clothes, peril, even the danger of losing his life. In the midst of them he could say, "Nay, but in ALL these things we are more than conquerors."

We can be a conqueror when we gain a victory over the situation. But we are more than a conqueror when we have learned lessons we could learn in no other way. For example, when we come through tribulation having learned patience, it is a "more than" victory.

We can be more than conquerors in every difficulty. We can have "overwhelming victory." God's power available for such victorious living is provided for us in Jesus Christ. God doesn't spare us trouble but brings us through, "more than" conquerors.

The "more than" conquerors take the stumbling blocks of life and transform them into stepping stones.

Don't hide your light! Let it shine for all; let your good deeds glow for all to see, so that they will praise your heavenly Father (Matt. 5:16, LB).

We are living in a dark world today, one darkened by pain, sorrow, loneliness, and heartache. Many people are searching for a way out of their darkness, looking for just a little ray of light.

An artist once drew a picture of a winter scene. The trees were heavily laden with snow. To one side of the picture was a dark, bleak-looking house. The picture gave a feeling of depression.

Suddenly the artist, with a quick stroke of yellow crayon, put a light in the window of the house. The effect was magical. Immediately the scene was transformed into one of cheer.

This is what happens when Christ is invited into a life. He turns on His Light and a life is transformed.

When His Light is turned on within it shines out to others. We are to be "rays" of light, shining His Light on the paths of those about us. "YOU are the world's light. . . . Don't hide your light" (Matt. 5:14-16, LB).

Paul wrote, "You are to live clean, innocent lives as children of God in a dark world full of people who are crooked and stubborn. Shine out among them like beacon lights, holding out to them the Word of Life" (Phil. 2:15-16, LB).

Rudyard Kipling and his wife purchased a farmhouse on a mountain slope in Vermont. One day they hiked down the mountain back of their house and up the next mountain. They came to a tiny house where a woman lived by herself. "Be you the windows across the valley?" she asked. When they said, "Yes," she told them how much comfort the lights of their home were to her.

Suddenly she said, almost fearfully, "Be you going to stay and keep your lights burning, or be you not?"

After that day the Kiplings always kept the lights in the back of their house burning for their neighbor across the valley.

Can people say of us, "Be you the window shining? Be you going to keep your light shining; or be you not?"

December
10

For ye are the temple of the living God; as God hath said, I will dwell in them, and walk in them; and I will be their God, and they shall be my people (2 Cor. 6:16).

An English gentleman owned a hunting lodge in southern Spain. One summer the Empress Elizabeth from Austria wanted to rent his place while he was to be in England. The Englishman said he would not rent his place to anyone, but would be honored to have her Majesty occupy it for the summer.

Later in the year, the Englishman received a note that the Empress was to pass through their town and desired to breakfast with them. Again she expressed her appreciation to them and asked if there was any way she could show her appreciation. The Englishman said, "If your Majesty would send me a small photograph with your autograph I would appreciate it."

Several months passed with no word about the photograph. He decided she had forgotten her promise.

Finally one day an enormous box arrived. It contained a beautifully framed full-length oil painting of the Empress, executed by one of the finest artists in Europe. The Englishman had received from her much more than he had asked for.

This is an illustration of what Christ does for us. When we invite Him into our lives as Savior, we discover it is just the beginning. He gives us not only Himself, but so much more than we expected.

When God created us He created a place within our lives where He could dwell. He said, "I will dwell in them and walk in them; and I will be their God and they shall be my people."

He reminds us who we are—"I will dwell in them—and THEY shall be MY PEOPLE."

When He enters our lives He makes available for us all He can be to us and all He can do for us.

He demonstrates through our lives how the life of God can be revealed to the world as He dwells and walks in the life of a person.

This is made possible in us through His Son, Jesus Christ.

Blessed are the peacemakers: for they shall be called the children of God (Matt. 5:9).

Down through history many people have assumed the role of peacemakers, attempting to bring a state of peace in a world filled with its greed, evil, and fighting.

God has peacemakers today, peacemakers to maintain His peace. Jesus said, "Peace I leave with you, my peace I give unto you: not as the world giveth, give I unto you" (John 14:27). Jesus Himself is our peace. "For he is our peace" (Eph. 2:14).

Jesus said, "Blessed, or happy, are the peacemakers." We may think of peacemakers as easygoing persons, quiet spoken, never in a hurry, never ruffling anyone. This is not necessarily true. Peacemakers, first of all, know personally the Peacemaker, Jesus Christ. Their lives are filled with the peace of His presence. They radiate the reality of His peace.

PEACEKEEPERS are passive. They try to smooth over situations; they ignore problems. They may be like the ostrich that puts its head in the sand, unwilling to face the issue at hand. Usually this does not solve the problem.

PEACEMAKERS are active. They face a situation when it is necessary but they do it in a spirit of love and understanding. They keep their own relationship with others right as far as possible. They don't repeat gossip, nor say unkind things. They don't retaliate.

Peacemakers face a situation as Jesus would. This approach can only come after much prayer.

Someone has said, "A peacemaker doesn't try to stop a fight between fighters, but tries to bring a reconciliation between them." When a discussion becomes heated, a peacemaker can often bring an issue into right focus and thus be responsible for a peaceful solution to the argument.

Today you may be in some situation in your family, your neighborhood, or with a friend, where there is a need of a peacemaker. God can use you in such a role, with your attitude and words controlled by the Spirit of Christ, to bring a restoration of peace.

God is looking for people today to be "peacemakers" for Him. Are you available? He can use you.

December
12

Behold, thy servants are ready to do whatsoever my lord the king shall appoint (2 Sam. 15:15).

Absalom, the son of David, through clever scheming was turning the hearts of the sons of Israel against King David. One day a messenger came to David, saying, "The hearts of the men of Israel are after Absalom." King David realized he must flee for safety. His servants were ready to go with him. They said, "Behold, thy servants are ready to do whatever my Lord, the king, shall appoint."

The servants of David were willing to do their king's choosing. Their loyalty was undivided. He came first in their plans.

It is easy to say, "I'll go where you want me to go, dear Lord; I'll do what you want me to do." We may say to our King of Kings that we are ready for whatever He chooses or appoints for us, but are we willing to be obedient to do it?

Are we as loyal to the Lord as David's servants were to him? Or have we let some Absalom come into our lives to draw our love and loyalty away from our King? Is busyness an Absalom in our lives? Lack of compassion? Indifference? Self-desire? Self-will?

The people in the church at Ephesus had been devoted to the Lord. Yet they let activity crowd into their church life until their love for the Lord had lost its warmth.

The Lord sent them word, saying, "I know thy works, and thy labour, and thy patience. . . . Nevertheless I have somewhat against thee, because thou hast left thy FIRST LOVE" (Rev. 2:2,4).

Their works, their labor, their patience, had become "Absaloms," drawing them away from their first love.

Today, has our love for the Lord lost any of its first warmth? Is the Lord saying to us, "Thou hast left thy first love"? Or are we ready to say as the servants, "I am ready to do whatsoever my Lord, the King, shall appoint"?

"If position I choose, or place I shun, my soul is satisfied with none; but when Thy will directs my way, 'tis equal joy to go or stay."

If I speak with the eloquence of men and of angels, but have no love, I become no more than blaring brass or crashing cymbal (1 Cor. 13:1, Phillips).

God is love and in this chapter Paul translates His love into action. He reminds us of the importance of lives filled with God's love.

In the next few days as we consider this chapter of Scripture, may we let God search our lives, showing us areas where we may lack His love.

Paul said we may be gifted orators, able to sway multitudes of people by our ability to speak, but if our words are not warmed by God's love we "would only be making noise" (1 Cor. 13:1, LB).

We may have a deep insight into the Word of God, but it is nothing if we lack His love. We may have the best education, possessing much human knowledge, but without His love it is cold. Our mountain-moving faith is worthless without the love of God.

If we give all we have to help the poor, but give from a sense of duty or obligation instead of motivated by love, it profits nothing. Occasionally there are those who give their lives for their convictions. Yet without love it achieves nothing.

Paul described it in this way. "If I have the gift of foretelling the future and hold in mind not only all human knowledge but the very secrets of God, and if I also have that absolute faith which can move mountains, but have no love, I amount to nothing at all. If I dispose of all that I possess, yes, even if I give my own body to be burned, but have no love, I achieve precisely nothing" (1 Cor. 13:2-3, *Phillips*).

We may have an eloquent way of expressing ourselves, a deep insight into God's Word, the attainment of much knowledge, a strong faith, a desire to help those in need. But all of these are ineffective unless we are empowered by God's love.

It has been said that God's love must be supreme in the heart, mind, and will. Is His love supreme in your entire personality, heart, mind, and will? Does His love fill every area of your life?

December

14

This love of which I speak is slow to lose patience—it looks for a way of being constructive. It is not possessive; it is neither anxious to impress nor does it cherish inflated ideas of its own importance (1 Cor. 13:4, Phillips).

In contemplating a life controlled by God's love we realize we cannot live such a life in our own strength. This kind of life has only been lived by one Person, Jesus Christ.

The Holy Spirit produces these characteristics of God's love in us. Because it is hard to define love in a way we can understand, it is easier described in terms of action.

The love produced by the Holy Spirit is slow to lose patience. It gives a quiet poise and a calm spirit when the frustrations come. It can endure criticism, disapproval, and misunderstanding patiently. It can bear slights without being resentful.

God's love is more than being passively patient. It is kind in its actions. "Love is kind." It looks for ways of being constructive. Sometimes we are so busy we fail to do the little kindnesses we could do for others. We fail to take time to be kind; occasionally we act hastily, hurting someone unintentionally. We are sorry, but it is too late. However, God's love makes us considerate of others at all times. His love is kind even to those who have wronged us. Someone has said, "Kindness puts shoes on our prayers."

His love knows no jealousy. It is not possessive. It does not begrudge success that comes to another but enables a person to be happy for him.

Humility characterizes persons controlled by His love. They do not seek the limelight, nor do they show off. They do not try to impress and are not puffed up with pride. They do not boast; nor are they smug or self-righteous.

John Flavel said, "They that know God will be humble and they that know themselves cannot be proud." When we see ourselves as God sees us we are humble.

Measuring yourself by God's standard, what is your rating in patience, kindness, jealousy, and humility?

Love has good manners and does not pursue selfish advantage. It is not touchy. It does not keep account of evil or gloat over the wickedness of other people. On the contrary, it shares the joy of those who live by the truth (1 Cor. 13:5-6, Phillips).

God's love must not only dwell in our hearts but operate in our daily lives.

His love is not rude or thoughtless, but it is courteous. It smooths the sharp, rough edges of our lives, making us considerate of others, gracious and well-mannered. "Love [God's love in us] does not insist on its own rights or its own way, for it is not self-seeking" (1 Cor. 13:5, *Amplified*).

Such love is unselfish. It does not seek its own rights, or strive for place or position. Sometimes we pull strings to get what we want or we use people to further our cause. But God's love always puts the interests of others above its own and doesn't care who gets the credit. "Stop acting from motives of selfish strife or petty ambition, but in humility practice treating one another as your superiors" (Phil. 2:3, *Williams*).

God's love is not provoked; it is not touchy; it does not fly off the handle. His love does not get upset or irritable when criticized or misjudged. His love does not resent a sudden change of plans. "It is not touchy or fretful or resentful" (1 Cor. 13:5, *Amplified*). Instead, His love gives a calm acceptance of each day's situations.

His love always looks for the best motives in people, always considers them in their best light. It gives an understanding attitude toward others. It never keeps a record of wrongs done; it never thinks of revenge. "Love keeps no score of wrong" (1 Cor. 13:5, NEB). His love forgets.

His love does not gloat over the failures or mistakes of others. It is sincerely concerned with their well-being.

God's love rejoices in the truth and goodness of another. It is glad when truth is seen in the life of another.

As you have considered the characteristics of God's love enumerated today, have you found them operating in your life?

December
16

Love knows no limit to its endurance, no end to its trust, no failing of its hope; it can outlast anything. Love never fails (1 Cor. 13:7-8, Phillips).

As burdens come, we often feel we have reached the end of our endurance. But God's "love knows no limit to its endurance" (1 Cor. 13:7, *Phillips*). His "love bears up under anything and everything that comes" (1 Cor. 13:7, *Amplified*). It continues to the end.

God's love believes the best about people; imputes the best motives to their actions. It gives them the benefit of the doubt, trusting them until evidence proves otherwise. "Is ever ready to believe the best of every person" (v. 7).

His love hopes for the best, even in the face of adversity. It hopes through disappointments, never giving up. It doesn't despair over anyone or anything. "Its hopes are fadeless under all circumstances" (v. 7).

What comfort and strength it is to our weary, trouble-filled hearts, even though we can't understand what God is doing, to know His love is steadfast and unchanging. It endures everything and outlasts anything. It never fails.

When you check your life according to God's standard of love in action, what is your rating? Are there areas where you need to let the Holy Spirit work? Do those about you want to know the Lord because they have seen Him operating in your life?

A chaplain came to a wounded soldier. "Shall I read to you from the Bible?" he asked. "I would rather have a drink of water," replied the soldier. The chaplain brought the water. Then the soldier said, "I need something under my head." The chaplain made a pillow of his overcoat. "Could I have something over me—I'm cold," said the soldier. The chaplain covered the boy with his jacket. The soldier then said, "If there's anything in that Book that makes a person do what you have done for me, please read it to me."

"In this life we have three great lasting qualities—faith, hope and love. But the greatest of them is love" (1 Cor. 13:13, *Phillips*).

The Holy Spirit gives unlimited power to love others with His love.

December

17

For ye know the grace of our Lord Jesus Christ, that, though he was rich, yet for your sakes he became poor, that ye through his poverty might be rich (2 Cor. 8:9).

Another Christmas is almost here. Although we are caught up in the multitudinous preparations for the gala season, we need to take time to meditate on the real meaning of Christmas—remembering the birth of Christ.

Once there was a king who wanted to really know his people. He wanted to know the conditions under which they lived, that he might better understand their problems. So he removed his kingly robes and crown and put on the dress of his people. He left the magnificence and splendor of his palace, traveling incognito across his kingdom. Although he had laid aside his riches, assuming the poverty of his people, this did not change his position as king.

This is a picture of what the Lord Jesus did for us. He had lived with His Father in heaven. All of the glory of heaven was His, and all the riches of heaven at His disposal. He, the Son of God, was willing to leave it to come to earth as a human being that He might identify with us and experience life as we do. "For we have not an high priest which cannot be touched with the feeling of our infirmities" (Heb. 4:15). Yet His real purpose was to become our Savior, making possible eternal life for us, and making available all the riches of heaven.

He became poor, that we might become rich. "Who, being in the form of God, thought it not robbery to be equal with God: but made himself of no reputation, and took upon him the form of a servant, and was made in the likeness of men: and being found in fashion as a man, He humbled Himself, and became obedient unto death, even the death of the cross" (Phil. 2:6-8).

Through our relationship with Him, all the riches of heaven are available for our use. May we not live in spiritual poverty today because we have failed to claim all He has provided for us!

December
18

For unto us a child is born, unto us a son is given: and the government shall be upon his shoulders (Isa. 9:6).

During a dark period in Israel's history, Isaiah looked across the centuries and prophesied of One who was coming to earth to bring hope. He foretold the advent of the Messiah.

"A CHILD IS BORN"—His humanity. "A SON IS GIVEN"—His deity. God in the person of His Son entered the world in human flesh. "The word was made flesh, and dwelt among us" (John 1:14—a child born. "The Father sent the Son to be the Saviour of the world" (1 John 4:14)—a Son given.

Someone has said, "Man saw the light of the glory in the face of the Bethlehem Babe, Who was God, with God's thoughts and purpose, swathed in mortality." Jesus said, "He that hath seen me hath seen the Father" (John 14:9).

He who said, "I am the light of the world" (John 8:12), was God SEEN. He who became the Word, "In the beginning was the Word, and the Word was with God, and the Word was God" (John 1:1), was God HEARD. He who said, "I am . . . the life" (John 14:6), was God FELT. As He walked the paths of earth, He was GOD'S FOOT-PRINTS. As He spoke He was the voice of God. The touch of His hand was the touch of God.

He never "began to be." He has always been from eternity. He BECAME a child born of the Virgin Mary. He IS the eternal Son from eternity to eternity.

Isaiah said, ". . . the government shall be upon His shoulder." His government is spiritual and personal. Some day He will return as King of Kings and Lord of Lords.

Once a King of England entered a room where some British noblemen were gathered. As they stood to show their respect, he said, "Sit down. You are my friends. I am not the Lord." One nobleman replied, "If you were the Lord, we would not rise to our feet. We would fall to our knees."

He desires to be King of your life. Is He?

And his name shall be called Wonderful, Counsellor, The mighty God, The everlasting Father, The Prince of Peace (Isa. 9:6).

Nearly twenty-six hundred years ago Isaiah came with a message of hope for a hopeless world. This hope was wrapped up in the person of Jesus Christ—the long-looked for Messiah, the Savior of mankind.

The greatness of His Person is revealed in His Name. Isaiah wrote, "his name shall be called WONDERFUL." He is wonderful in Himself, in His Word, in His works. He is wonderful for WHO HE is, the Son of God. God said, "This is my BELOVED SON, in whom I am well pleased" (Matt. 3:17). He is wonderful for what He DID for us. "Who loved me, and gave Himself for me" (Gal. 2:20).

He is wonderful in His counsel to us, for He is the source of all knowledge and wisdom. "In whom are hid all the treasures of wisdom and knowledge" (Col. 2:3). People sometimes give wrong counsel, but He, the wonderful Counselor, always gives the right guidance for each situation.

As the MIGHTY GOD all "power belongeth" unto Him (Ps. 62:11). No need is too great for Him. Not only does He feel our difficulties with us, but goes beyond and acts in our behalf. It has been said, "We have only proved the sufficiency of God when we have asked of Him the impossible." He who is wonderful is our Mighty God.

He, the EVERLASTING FATHER, is the Father of eternity whose plans and purposes are everlasting. As His child, we have a place in His eternal plan.

He is the PRINCE of PEACE, administering His peace to confused hearts in a confused world. "For He is our peace" (Eph. 2:14).

JESUS—What a Name! "And His name shall be called WONDERFUL." "Thou shalt call his NAME JESUS: for he shall save his people from their sins" (Matt. 1:21).

The more intimately we know Him, the deeper our trust in Him. "And they that know THY NAME will put their trust in thee" (Ps. 9:10).

May the living presence of the One whose name is wonderful, fill our hearts and minds with His peace and joy today.

December

20

Behold, I will do a new thing; now it shall spring forth; shall ye not know it? I will even make a way in the wilderness, and rivers in the desert(Isa. 43:19).

In a few days we will be saying, "Happy New Year!" The New Year will not be a repetition of the one just past, but a year of new beginnings, new resolves, new plans. It will be filled with new experiences, new challenges, new opportunities, new lessons to be learned. We may be transferred to new surroundings. New joys may overflow our hearts. New sorrows and heartaches may enter our lives. Regardless of what the year may hold, God promises, "I will do a new thing."

As you begin this new year, what do you want God to do in your personal life? Do you desire a greater knowledge of His Word? If so, He will gladly open new truths to you from it. Do you want a more effective prayer life? He will give you new opportunities to trust Him in prayer. Do you long to know Jesus Christ in a more real way? He will lead you into a deeper and closer walk with Him. He promises, "I will do a new thing in your life next year."

There may be new wilderness experiences for us in the unknown year ahead. We may find ourselves in the desert. But God assures us, "I will even make a way in the wilderness, and rivers in the desert. . . . I give waters in the wilderness, and rivers in the desert, to give drink to my people, my chosen" (Isa. 43:19-20). In the wilderness and desert we are brought to a place of complete helplessness, learning total dependence upon God.

We sing a little chorus that says, "The Lord knows the way through the wilderness; all I have to do is follow." In these wilderness and desert times, He will do a new thing, transforming them into fruitful ones for His glory.

As God does a "new thing" in our lives, it will bring praise to Him. "This people have I formed for myself; they shall show forth my praise" (v. 21).

And she brought forth her firstborn son, and wrapped him in swaddling clothes, and laid him in a manger; because there was no room for them in the inn (Luke 2:7).

When a news event takes place in a small unknown community, newscasters give the town and its people publicity they have never had before.

One time as we were driving cross country, a highway sign outside a small town informed us it was the home town of the former Astronaut John Glenn. It had taken on importance because of his accomplishments in space.

Ordinarily the birth of a baby in the small town of Bethlehem would not have seemed important. But one night a baby was born there who has had a far-reaching influence on the lives of people down through the ages. This was the birth of Jesus, the Son of God.

When Mary and Joseph arrived in Bethlehem, they discovered there was no room for them in the inn. The only place they could find to stay was a stable where animals were fed. But that night the Savior of the world, Jesus Christ, entered history in that stable and was placed in a manger.

In the meantime, what were the people of Bethlehem doing that night? Were they discussing the political situation? Were they complaining about taxes? Were they having a good time? Whatever they were doing, they were so engrossed in their own plans they were unaware of what was happening close by.

We may wonder at the indifference of people to Jesus then. Yet what about our own lives today? Have we room for Him in our lives? Or are we so involved in our own plans we have crowded Him out? Have we become so preoccupied with our lives we have forgotten Him?

He was crowded out of the inn as His birthplace. Today He is often crowded out of the very celebrations which honor His birthday. We need to ask ourselves, "Have I let Him be crowded out of My Christmas plans, or have I put Him at the center of them? Have I crowded Him out of my life plans, or have I given Him room?"

December
22

And God set them in the firmament of the heaven to give light upon the earth (Gen. 1:17).

The southwestern area of our country has a lovely custom for outdoor lighting at Christmas time. The people make luminarias by placing sand in large paper bags. Candles are then placed in the sand. When the candles are lighted, the sacks glow with a soft light, giving a beautiful effect as they are placed along sidewalks, doorways, and porches.

To fulfill their purpose, not only must the luminarias be placed where they are to shine; they must be lighted as well. Their beauty is not in the paper bag, the sand, or even the candle; but in the warm glow of the candle after it is lighted.

In Genesis 1:17 we read that the moon and stars had a special place in the heavenlies, for a special purpose. They were placed "in the firmament of the heavens to give light upon the earth."

Our lives are to be shining lights for the Lord, reflecting His glory upon the earth. The Bible compares us to candles. "For thou wilt light my candle: the Lord my God will enlighten my darkness" (Ps. 18:28).

There are many ways of letting our candle glow—a letter of encouragement, a friendly phone call, a cheery smile, a kindly deed. Perhaps we are missing opportunities to shine for Him because we are looking for big places of service instead of taking advantage of the ones He has placed about us. "Don't hide your light! Let it shine for all; let your good deeds glow for all to see, so that they will praise your heavenly Father" (Matt. 5:16, LB).

As you place Christmas candles around your home this Christmas season, take time to check the candle of your life. Is it shining brightly? Or has it become dim by busyness, indifference, carelessness, or self-will? Perhaps the wick needs to be cleaned and trimmed so our light will shine more brightly.

At this Christmas season, may the world not just be aglow with the lights of candles and Christmas lights, but with the heavenly Light of the Word, the Lord Jesus Christ, shining through each of our lives.

Fear not: for, behold, I bring you good tidings of great joy, which shall be to all people. For unto you is born this day in the city of David a Saviour, which is Christ the Lord (Luke 2:10-11).

Today we often hear the phrase, "Happiness is." People everywhere are searching for that which will bring happiness. One day recently on my way to a luncheon I saw a sign on a restaurant which said, "We sell happiness." How sad that there are those who think happiness can be bought and sold. Real joy comes from within.

Christmas is a special time for celebrating the birthday of the One who came to bring joy. We sing, "Joy to the world! The Lord is come." The greatest "birth announcement" the world has ever known contained a message of joy.

What excitement goes into the planning and preparation for Christmas! Yet underneath the glitter and glamour of the holiday season all is not happy and joyful. We acknowledge that happiness is not found in the packages we open, the cards we receive, or in the entertaining we do. Underneath all the wrappings of the joyful holiday season our lives may be filled with heartaches and sorrow. There may be emptiness and loneliness.

But there is a joy we can have, a joy within that completely satisfies. It is not dependent on outer circumstances, what we have or what we do.

This was the message of joy that God sent. "For unto YOU is born this day in the city of David a Saviour, which is Christ the Lord" (Luke 2:11). Real joy comes from knowing Jesus Christ. It is a personal message. The angel said, "I bring YOU." It is universal; "Which shall be to ALL people."

God's joy comes from within; the world's from without. God's joy has deep roots in Himself; the world's only on the surface. God's joy is unending; the world's soon fades away. God's joy fills us completely; the world's is on the outside. God's joy satisfies; the world's cannot.

"Whom having not seen, ye love; in whom, though now ye see Him not, yet believing, ye rejoice with JOY unspeakable and full of glory" (1 Peter 1:8).

December
24

Behold, a virgin shall be with child, and shall bring forth a son, and thou shalt call his name Emmanuel, which being interpreted is, God with us (Matt. 1:23).

As we listen to the beautiful strains of Christmas carols filling the air, we are reminded of the real meaning of Christmas. Jesus came to earth to become more than just the Babe of Bethlehem. He came to be "Emmanuel, God with us." Years before, Isaiah had foretold of His coming to earth. "Therefore the Lord Himself shall give you a sign; Behold, a virgin shall conceive, and bear a son, and shall call his name Immanuel" (Isa. 7:14).

At Jesus' birth the angel said to Joseph, "Thou shall call His name Emmanuel, which being interpreted is God with us." In the person of Jesus Christ, God came to earth that He might be "GOD WITH US." But He came to be more than "God with us." He came to be the Savior that He might be "GOD IN US." "I will dwell IN them, and walk IN them; and I will be their God, and they shall be my people" (2 Cor. 6:16). Through Christ we can know what God is like and what He can do for us.

With His presence in us, we are assured that He will enter into each of our needs with us.

What is your need today? Is it comfort? He, the God of all Comfort, is WITH YOU, bringing His comfort to your hearts. Are you lonely? He has promised "I will never leave thee, nor forsake thee" (Heb. 13:5). Are you fearful? He is with you, quieting your heart as He says, "Let not your heart be troubled, neither let it be afraid" (John 14:27). Are you weak, wondering how you will get through the day? He is with you to strengthen you. "It is God that girdeth me with strength, and maketh my way perfect" (Ps. 18:32).

The Christmas season will soon be over. But the Christ of Christmas is always available every day through the year to meet our needs. Emmanuel—GOD WITH US—in the person of Jesus Christ—DWELLS IN US—that He might LIVE HIS LIFE THROUGH US.

For God so loved the world, that He gave His only begotten Son, that whosoever believeth in him should not perish, but have everlasting life (John 3:16).

Christmas is a gala occasion, a festive time, a time of expressing our love to dear ones, both family and friends, in many ways.

It is a time of remembering God's love for the world. God is the greatest Lover the world has ever known. "For God SO loved the world." HIS love is boundless, limitless, and unchangeable. Its supply is inexhaustible. It includes not only the lovely but the unlovely.

He proved His love by giving His Son as the greatest love gift ever given. "The gift of God is eternal life through Jesus Christ our Lord" (Rom. 6:23).

God's love not only reached down to a world in need of divine love, but it also included each one of us personally. He loves YOU. He loves ME. Unworthy though we are, His personal love for us is assured.

Jesus Christ demonstrated the reality of this love by His willingness to give His life on the cross, making available the gift of eternal life for us. God's Word says, "Who loved me, and gave Himself for me" (Gal. 2:20).

King Cyrus of Persia took a prince and his wife prisoners. "What will you give me to set you free?" Cyrus asked the prince. The prince replied, "Half of what I possess." "What will you give me if I set your wife free?" "I will gladly give my life," said the prince. The King, deeply touched, liberated both of them.

That evening as the prince and his wife rejoiced together over their freedom, he said, "Was not Cyrus a handsome man?" She replied, "I really did not notice him. I had eyes only for the man who said he would lay down his life for me."

What love JESUS showed when He willingly laid down His life for us! Do not our hearts overflow in response to such love? May our prayer be, "Lord Jesus, may I have eyes only for THEE, the One who laid down His life for me."

December
26

In this was manifested the love of God toward us, because that God sent his only begotten Son into the world, that we might live through him. Herein is love, not that we loved God, but that he loved us, and sent his Son to be the propitiation for our sins (1 John 4:9-10).

Love begins with God. "God is love" (1 John 4:8). We cannot understand the depth of His love. There are not sufficient words to adequately explain it. But we can experience it.

Love needs an object. We are the object of God's love. "For God so loved THE WORLD. . . ." (John 3:16). God revealed His love to us by sending His Son to "the world, that we might live through Him" (1 John 4:9). Jesus came "to be the propitiation for our sins" (v. 10). "Propitiation" in this verse carries the idea that the holiness of God had to be satisfied. God was completely satisfied with the death of His Son for the penalty of our sins. "In this act we see what REAL LOVE is: it is not our love for God, but His love for us when He sent His Son to satisfy God's anger against our sins" (v. 10, LB). In 1 John 3:16 we read, "We know what REAL LOVE is from Christ's example in dying for us. . . ."

I remember when the reality of God's love first filled my life. I had not been able to realize the constancy of His love for me. Some days I felt He loved me. Other days I wasn't sure. I thought His love depended on what I did or didn't do.

Then I discovered that His love for me was steadfast, never changing. He not only loved me, but loved me as I was. I didn't have to put on any pretense with Him. As I experienced and accepted His great love, I discovered that my one desire was to please Him.

The publisher of Tennyson's poems once said that every time they printed his poems an extra supply of the letters "l," "o," "v," and "e" had to be ordered, for he used the word "love" so frequently.

God has a sufficient supply of His love, to reach to ALL the world, for He IS LOVE.

And when he had gathered all the chief priests and scribes of the people together, he demanded of them where Christ should be born (Matt. 2:4).

Many will be traveling during the holiday season, some by planes through the skyways, others by high powered cars over super-highways.

Long years ago the wise men made a journey, but not in today's modern mode of travel. Their slow and tedious journey was made on camel back.

One night they saw a special star in the sky, indicating the birth of a new king. This had been foretold in the Scriptures. They decided to go in search of Him.

They inquired in Jerusalem where they might find Him. The scribes there were well versed in the Scriptures and informed them, "In Bethlehem of Judaea: for thus it is written by the prophet" (Matt. 2:5).

Although they knew where to find the record of His birth in God's Word, they had made no personal investigation. They had knowledge of the mind, but not of the heart.

The search of the wise men ended when they found the Lord Jesus Christ and bowed in His presence.

Today are we like the scribes? Or are we like the wise men? Although the scribes knew the Scriptures, telling where Jesus was to be born, they had not sought Him out.

We, too, have access to God's Word, but do we search it to know what it says? Do we appropriate it into our lives?

The wise men were not satisfied until they found Him. May we be like them, satisfied with nothing short of the Lord Jesus Himself. May the Holy Spirit continue to make Him more real in our lives that we may become more like Him.

You may know all ABOUT Jesus Christ but have never personally invited Him into your life. In John 1:12 we read, "But as many as received him, to them gave he power to become the sons of God, even to them that believe on His name." He is God's love gift to you, eternal life through Jesus Christ.

December
28

Whom having not seen, ye love; in whom, though now ye see him not, yet believing, ye rejoice with joy unspeakable and full of glory (1 Peter 1:8).

The Christmas message is the message of God's love for the world. "FOR GOD SO LOVED THE WORLD . . ." (John 3:16). In the most wonderful way, He demonstrated His love. "To us, the greatest demonstration of God's love for us has been His sending His only Son into the world to give us life through Him" (1 John 4:9, *Phillips*).

"For God so loved the world." This includes you and me. When God's love reaches down and touches our lives, His love becomes real in us. It is natural, then, for our hearts to respond in love to Him. "We love him, because HE first loved us" (1 John 4:19).

God's love is a unique love, an extraordinary love, a love for Someone we have not seen. Human love is dependent on sight, but our love for the Lord is real, though we have never seen Him in person. "WHOM having NOT SEEN, ye love." Kenneth Wuest says of those to whom Peter was writing, "They never saw the Lord Jesus with the physical sense of sight, but what a vivid portrait of Him did the Holy Spirit paint for them on the canvas of their spiritual vision."

This love is the product of faith. The world says, "Seeing is believing." The child of God knows that "Believing is seeing." "Though now you see Him not, yet BELIEVING." By faith we come to know Him, and the better we know Him, the deeper our faith in Him, and the more REAL He becomes to us. This strong, confident trust in Him brings joy to our lives, a joy beyond words, a joy unspeakable and full of glory.

Today are you aware of the personal love of God for you? Is HE the object of YOUR love? Do you love HIM? How much?

Though we have not seen Him physically, yet as we believe on Him and love Him, our lives will be filled with unspeakable joy.

And being warned of God in a dream that they should not return to Herod, they departed into their own country another way (Matt. 2:12).

In Matthew, the second chapter, we read of the wise men making a long journey in search of the newborn King. Guided by a star, their search came to an end in Bethlehem. With great joy they bowed in worship of the Christ child, presenting Him with gifts.

Herod had asked them to return to Jerusalem to give Him a report on finding the Babe. Very likely this was their plan. However, their course of travel was completely changed. God warned them not to return to Jerusalem. They were to return to their home "another way." Although they may have wondered why, they obediently followed God's direction.

In a few days we will enter a new year. As God places it in our hands, we will have the privilege of using it for Him. Most of us already have plans for it. Yet we can never be sure of what lies before us. Next year's path may lead us in a completely different way, a new way we have never walked before. It may bring a sudden change in our life.

God may say to us, "I want you to go 'another way' this year." You may be comfortably situated in your home, everything going well for you. Suddenly a change comes and you are to be moved to a new area. This is not what you would choose, but God says, "This is 'another way' for you to take this year." You may have to walk "another way" as someone dear to you has been removed from your life. "Another way" for you may be a serious illness. We may not understand why we must go "another way," but God does, and He never makes a mistake.

We should be ready to accept changed plans as the wise men were. When God leads us "another way" we need to be ready to follow.

God says, "I will bring the blind by a way that they know not; I will lead them in paths that they have not known" (Isa. 42:16).

December 30

The Lord is good, a strong hold in the day of trouble; and he knoweth them that trust in Him (Nah. 1:7).

Occasionally I am in an area that has been devastated by some disaster, such as a flood, a tornado, or an earthquake. Not long ago as I saw the devastation caused by a flood, as I viewed it, I was told that some good had come as a result of it.

God may allow storms in our lives, but He has a purpose to be accomplished through them. Nahum wrote, "The Lord hath his way in the whirlwind and in the storm" (1:3).

Often we focus our eyes on the storm itself, failing to see God moving on the waves of the storm, bringing good to us.

Nahum said, "The Lord is good." No matter how severe the storm, how dark the day, how impossible the problem, the LORD IS good.

Because He is good, He has promised to be a stronghold for us in our time of trouble. His stronghold is always accessible and always secure.

And God knoweth THEM that trust in Him. We may not be exempt from trouble, but we can trust Him in trouble.

During war days in a remote area, no air raid shelters could be built in one city because water was too near the surface. When the siren sounded, the people had to flee to the open fields.

One day as the siren sounded, a man gathered his few possessions and hurried out to the field. Soon planes could be heard above him. "What do I do now to protect myself?" he thought. His possessions gave him no safety; neither the degrees he had from leading universities in Europe and America; neither his friends.

Having personal trust in Christ, he repeated "The Lord is my shepherd . . . I will fear no evil: for Thou art with me" (Ps. 23:1,4). In his day of trouble he found Christ to be his place of safety, his stronghold.

When the storms break on our lives, we can flee into our stronghold, Jesus Christ, finding in Him security, a security that is ours twenty-four hours a day, each day of the year, throughout our lifetime.

Brethren, I count not myself to have apprehended: but this one thing I do, forgetting those things which are behind, and reaching forth unto those things which are before, I press toward the mark for the prize of the high calling of God in Christ Jesus (Phil. 3:13-14).

Well do I remember the first time I visited Yosemite National Park. Its grandeur was breathtaking. I shall not forget the first view I had of El Capitan with its sheer granite wall reaching up 3,604 feet from the valley floor. Its southeast side has challenged the most skillful mountain climbers. Until a few years ago, no one had been able to scale its vertical face.

Then two men decided they would attempt to accomplish what had defied climbers of the past. They set a goal of twelve days to complete this hazardous ascent to the top of the mountain. With expectancy they began their climb. Often they were delayed. It was time-consuming to drive pitons into the cracks in the wall by which they climbed up its steep face. They found only two ledges on which they could sit or stand. Winds, rains, and freezing temperatures hindered them, prolonging their climb to thirty-one days.

At last their goal was reached. Imagine the excitement and thrill of their success as they took the last step—they were on top of the mountain! When asked to describe their feelings in reaching the top, they said that they found it "a tremendous emotional fulfillment."

The apostle Paul experienced the challenge of climbing onward and upward in his Christian life. His one burning heart's desire was to know Christ more personally and intimately. He said, "Yes, everything else is worthless when compared with the priceless gain of knowing Christ Jesus my Lord. I have put aside all else, counting it worth less than nothing, in order that I can have Christ" (Phil. 3:8, LB).

The set of his life was directed toward the fulfillment of this goal. Paul often compared the Christian life to the running of a race. With his eyes on the goal, he realized that he had not yet reached the finish line, he was still running the race. "Not that I have now attained [this ideal] or am already made perfect, but I press on to lay hold of (grasp) and make my own, that for which Christ Jesus, the Messiah, has laid hold of me and made me His own" (v. 12, *Amplified*). Paul's life had one all-absorbing purpose—"this one thing I do" (v. 13).

Recognizing his race was not finished, he knew he must strip off everything that would hinder him from accomplishing God's purpose for him. He aimed straight for the goal. "Forgetting what lies behind and straining forward to what lies ahead, I press on toward the goal to win the [supreme and heavenly prize] to which God in Christ Jesus is calling us upward" (vv. 13-14, *Amplified*). He must forget the past with its accomplishments and its failures and press on to the prize of knowing Christ and complete fulfillment in Him.

As we are about to enter a new year, we can look forward to it with great expectancy. Christ is our goal. God desires that we "grow in grace, and in the knowledge of our Lord and Saviour Jesus Christ" (2 Peter 3:18). There are always new experiences and new lessons ahead to bring us to a greater knowledge of our Lord, Jesus Christ.

We are to turn our eyes away from the past year and look forward with anticipation to a new year, fresh from God's hand to us.

The climbers of El Capitan could have quit many times and turned back, but they didn't. They pressed on until they achieved their goal. We, too, must press on toward our goal, day by day, even when the burdens weigh us down, when the tears fall, when we are exhausted. Through each of these experiences, we gain a fuller knowledge of the Lord Himself; we become more like Him and we draw closer to Him.

May our prayer for the new year be: "So I run straight to the goal with purpose in every step" (1 Cor. 9:26, LB).

Scripture Index

Scripture Index

PRINCE OF PEACE

Books by James Carroll

MADONNA RED
MORTAL FRIENDS
FAULT LINES
FAMILY TRADE
PRINCE OF PEACE
SUPPLY OF HEROES
FIREBIRD
MEMORIAL BRIDGE
THE CITY BELOW
AN AMERICAN REQUIEM

PRINCE OF PEACE

JAMES CARROLL

A Mariner Book
Houghton Mifflin Company
Boston · New York

First Mariner Books edition 1998

The author gratefully acknowledges the following for permission to reprint previously copyrighted material:
"Recuerdo" from *Collected Poems*, Harper & Row.
Copyright 1922, 1950 by Edna St. Vincent Millay. Reprinted by permission.
Excerpts from "The Waste Land" in *Collected Poems 1909–1962* by T. S. Eliot.
Copyright 1936 by Harcourt Brace Jovanovich, Inc.; Copyright © 1963, 1964 by T. S. Eliot. Reprinted by permission of Harcourt Brace Jovanovich, Inc. and Faber and Faber Publishers.

Library of Congress Cataloging-in-Publication Data is available.
ISBN 0-395-92619-X

Printed in the United States of America
QUM 10 9 8 7 6 5 4 3 2 1

For My Son Patrick

IN MEMORY OF
PATRICK HUGHES

PRINCE OF PEACE

ONE

NOT many miles from the hill on which I stood they were prying great chunks of concrete off the mangled bodies of children. They were picking up corpses from ditches but leaving severed limbs to rot in the vicious August sun. And suddenly they were dropping from the sky again in their flashing Phantoms, blowing balconies off tall buildings, twisting minarets and smokestacks apart and stripping the trees of branches. They were pumping rounds of fire at targets picked off maps at random; their long-range guns were almost never silent.

But I didn't hear them. And usually I did not think about Beirut. I had not concerned myself with Lebanon, though everyone in Israel, even the brothers there at our remote priory, had thought of little else all summer.

I pulled the hood of my cowl forward for shelter against the sun. The desert wind snapped at the worn gray fabric of my habit.

Yes, to my ever-increasing surprise, what those words — priory, cowl, habit — indicate is true. I was a monk.

As in monk's bread? you ask.

As in jam. We were a small herd of bull-nuns, though the canonical constitution preferred to call us English Benedictines. We were a teaching order, centered at Downside Abbey in England. My priory, Holy Cross, was our contemplative outpost in the Holy Land. Our angels' island, as it were. The monks came there from sister monasteries in Britain and the United States. They came for three months, six, a year; for retreat or sabbatical; to renew their vows or — and alas, these fellows were always better company — to finalize their decisions to breach them.

I was one of the seven brothers who were there permanently. As the monastic argot had it, I was a lay brother, which phrase had always called to mind, forgive me, the interrogatory — "Lay, brother?" — of a hustling Eighth Avenue pimp. You, of course, are thinking, since you know your Benedictine history, Ah, poor lame-brained bastard! Lay brothers were the enlisted men of monasticism, the serfs, the Little Johns, who praised the Lord in meniality — Scoop that slop! Knead that dough! Stomp those grapes! — while the tonsured, the clerical officer class, aired their manicures, thumbed their breviaries and their noses. In the new Church, lay brothers were to be treated with all the dignity due the sons of God, a return to Benedict who brought democracy to the West. Monks were all equal in the Lord, *n'est-ce pas?* Still, some were more equal than others. The shit-work always fell to us.

Myself, I did not complain. But then I didn't harvest olives in the sun or scrape the cistern free of algae on my knees. I served as librarian and sacristan; no heavy lifting, inside work, a desk of my own.

The care of books remained, in my opinion, a noble function. Even those books. The bulk of my library consisted of outdated tomes, manuals of Scholastic philosophy mainly, and commentaries on canon law. You would not believe the dry-rot, the trivia, the efflorescent casuistry. Dust rose off every page. Papa John flung open his famous *aggiornamento* window, I'm convinced, less to let fresh air in than to throw such volumes out. The Church was entombed in their heartless formulations.

We Benedictines did not believe in destroying books, any books; we invented them, after all, in our *scriptoria*. Books were our sacred totems, our sacraments. And so Brother Librarians in England and America, on the theory that desert monks would read any old shit, sent us their mush-spined copies of the *Codex,* the *Devotio Moderna,* the *Imitatio,* the *Summa,* the *Oxoniense,* the *Moralia* and the *Etcetera.* Monk librarians on two continents knew of Brother Francis, bibliophile, fool and scholar *manqué,* who would receive each book gratefully, wipe it carefully and fondle it for a moment, even if for all the monk's bread in the world, he would never read it.

My duties as sacristan were less sacred. In fact they were mainly a matter of laundry. In the civilized world the sacristy, which is in effect the department of props and costumes, was always entrusted to Brother Swish, some monastic Edith Head. Not there. Me, I was an aesthetic minimalist. It was the desert after all, not Canterbury, and not Fire Island either. My simple responsibility was to see that Father Prior and each visiting priest had what they needed to concelebrate the daily liturgies. I spent much of my time therefore — this seems like an admission and would once have humiliated me to make it — ironing linens and vestments like a putzfrau. It would have humiliated me even more to confess, as I do now, that I had come rather to like it. There was a certain visceral satisfaction, one I could never have imagined in my previous life, in folding a Purificator precisely in thirds and creasing it with half one's weight on the old iron, transforming a balled, wrinkled cloth into a sacramental crisp and white enough to be worthy of the Sacred Species. As every housewife of the old school knew, and every confessor too, nothing pleases like making what was filthy clean.

"Ah, Durkin, you old fart!" I could hear my former colleagues bleating from the poker table in the faculty lounge, "And you hadn't even booze to blame it on!"

To which I'd have replied, better break your elbow than your knee. Better waste your liver than your soul. Ah, dear reader, what you'd never believe is that over those years at Holy Cross my gratitude at being there moved me more than once to tears. Of course it wasn't the *laborare* that did that, the menial work. I had not lost my mind. It had been an act of profound self-preservation when I took a lifelong vow of Stability to the Priory of the Holy Cross near the village of Tantur on the West Bank of the Jordan River. Once I'd had a thousand problems. But there I had only three: poverty, chastity and obedience.

You see, all I have to do is begin to sketch this story and I resort to self-sealing irreverence, the fake cynicism we came to expect of each other when the subject at hand was serious. But it can't be helped. My story begins in that monastery, and my own impulse, now, to be chagrined by that, is absolute. Still, I refuse it.

To put it as forthrightly as I can, I, together with my brothers there, had accepted the call to build, day in and day out, a living edifice of prayer.

"Come, come, Durkin!"

Let me say it, for my sake if not yours. My life's meaning had become, despite itself — what else to call it? — holiness. Shrinks say "wholeness" but miss by a mile what I'm talking of: prayer, the desert life, spiritual existence, the Eucharist and a strict observance of the monastic hours, from Matins to Compline. How can I describe the life to you and not sound addled, inane or, worse, sincere? Words fail me perhaps because in that setting and throughout my years in it we didn't use them much. Except for Sundays and feast days we continually maintained the Great Silence. In *lingua* that's *Magnum Silentium*, which sounds like a weapon, and of course it is. *Silentium* is the great enemy of *Sardonius*.

So there I was, in a monastery. And, offered with some embarrassment but no apology, here is the meaning I began to uncover there, but only on that day which would be, though I didn't know it yet, my last.

It distracted enormously when events outside our enclosure intruded. Like, if you will, the war between Israel and the Palestinians. Not a week had passed that summer in which one monk or another hadn't homilized about it at liturgy, and every day someone prayed for peace with justice if he was for the Palestinians, or for the survival of God's Chosen People if he was for the Jews. I was known to pray for help in bearing with special burdens, by which my quibbling brothers no doubt knew I meant them.

A mere distraction? you say. That vicious, unending conflict? That slaughter? Yes. For me, I admit it, until then. But then, suddenly, for once it was not "distracting" me. It was obsessing me. I had the eye all at once of a worried parent in time of war, and I didn't miss a thing.

I saw, especially, Beirut. It was a city without windows. I imagined all that glass in shards, a crop of blades, sprouting underfoot. I imagined all those panicked sleepers running from their tin bungalows without sandals, slicing flesh from bone, dancing on the streets, not in them. In the howl of wind that afternoon, for a change, I did hear them, wailers, gunners, dive bombers. I saw children. I saw girls. I saw one in particular pressing her entrails back into her stomach, but her wound was like the mouth of a shrieking Arab. And whom should she have hated? That wily devil Arafat, hiding in his sewer until the river of babies' blood overspilled a gutter on cue for television? Or should she have hated our own beloved Begin, more popular than ever, leader at last of the cossack charge of his dreams? Would he have known a pogrom if he was the one who ordered it?

I lived in Israel, but I was not a Jew; among Englishmen, but I was an American; as a monk, but I was not ordained. Once a scholar of some repute, I was the custodian of cast-off books and I did laundry. Therefore my opinions were so much sand in the brain. I tried to live without them, but on that day the war had begun to frighten me, and I knew why.

The sun was setting. The shadow of evening had already fallen across the distant desert valley. Beyond, on a butte just visible in the east, was the ruin of Herod's palace — Antipas, the Herod who beheaded John because his daughter asked him to. The ruin sat on a lonely pinnacle from which its privilege was to bathe in the golden light some moments longer.

I understood Herod better than the celibate exigetes did because, before I was a laundress-monk hidden in Judea I'd had my measure of prominence too, and more to the point I'd had a daughter of my own. I'd held her in my arms before her mother did. Those few moments after her birth — a tough cesarean; I'd thought they both were dying — remained for me the very definition of happiness, wholeness, peace. As she'd grown older and of necessity away from me, my devotion to her had only intensified. If she had asked for some crazed prophet's head on a plate and I could have given it to her, I might have once. Why then, you might well ask, had I abandoned her more than a decade before when she was seven years old and needed me more than ever? It will take all these pages to explain, and in a way they are addressed, first, to her, the long and complicated confession of a parent who lost his way. Let me say now only that she was the last of my loves whom I betrayed.

I faced the thing itself, the sun, and stared at it, which one never did in the desert, even at that moment when its lower edge was slicing into the earth like a saw blade into pulp. I turned slightly and faced Bethlehem two miles to the south. Behind me, eight miles north of a line of hills, lay Jerusalem. I was desolate but still pompous, and made much of that geography; a monastery between Bethlehem and Jerusalem, between birth and death, between the beginning and the end. As if it were the vision Jesus had from a hill like that — or from *that* hill — I had seen in that plain a literal army massing during the Yom Kippur War; hundreds of tanks, thousands of soldiers and in the darkness the blinking light of countless campfires spread across the valley like a reflection of the stars. It had become every army to me, a permanent vision, as the Arabs had become the Jews, permanent victims, and I had become inured to every plight but Herod's — who couldn't refuse his daughter. *His* Salome wasn't a seven-year-old; all my child wanted was her Daddy.

The wind picked up and I tugged at my robe absently, as if it were a blanket under which I had been sleeping badly. I shivered. I had been there, where to you the virtue of detachment would have looked very much like the vice of indifference, for a fifth of my entire life, and all at once I was afraid. How did Eliot put it? I had seen birth and death, but had thought they were different.

I slid one hand inside its opposite sleeve and my fingers touched the paper I had hidden there. The note was folded neatly as it was when handed to me by Brother Porter just before Vespers. Once in the chapel, in my stall, I had opened it inside the psalter and while my brothers had chanted, "Praise is rightfully yours, O God in Zion, Vows to you must be fulfilled," I had read my contraband message in a swirl of happiness and terror that nearly toppled me. "Jerusalem," it said.

Jerusalem! Not the ancient heartbreak, secret or memory. Not the city Jesus would have gathered to himself like a mother her child. Another Jerusalem than these, a mundane one in which traffic gets snarled, taxi drivers grunt at the size of tips, and tourists check into hotels.

I pulled the folded paper out of my sleeve and in the wind prepared to open it again. My fingers were trembling.

I remembered taking her into my arms, no, hands; she was too small for arms. The doctor had barely wiped her clean of blood, Carolyn's blood. Carolyn was my wife whom I worshipped, considering my worship a higher form of love when, really, much later, it was what drove her away. If I had left too it was only when I understood that she would never be mine again. I must have traveled in a trance. I had come to that monastery. I had presented myself to Father Prior who must have taken my derangement for devotion. I had been completely disoriented, but for one thing. I knew enough right from the beginning not to tell him the truth. If I had told Father Prior the truth, he'd never have let me stay.

"Truth? What is truth?" said jesting Pilate — Bacon's line — as he washed his hands. And I wonder now, sitting here, rubbing at the skin of my own truth, was it the question of a sophist or was he really tormented?

My anguish was permanent, but I had long deflected it. But that afternoon I couldn't. I opened the square of paper and in the day's last light, with my back to the monastery, read it for the second time. "I must see you tonight. I am at the King David Hotel in Jerusalem. Your Molly."

I flagged the rattling Arab bus that shuttled between Bethlehem and Jerusalem. The bus stopped for me as if it picked up vagrant monks at twilight all the time. With apologetic shrugs and my few words of Arabic I made the driver understand that I had no money for the fare. He waved me on. Mendicant Christians! What were our bizarre abnegations to him? I was grateful not to have the language. How could I have explained that a man of fifty, not perceptibly retarded, was violating a sacred vow by going into town without permission? Sometimes I saw my situation from the outside and it made me dizzy.

The bus was moving slowly. The road, winding up into the hills on top of which the city sat, was crowded with traffic. I had forgotten that, since sunset, it was Tishah-b'Ab, the late summer feast which drew Jews to Jerusalem from all over, including the controversial West Bank settlements. But this bus was nearly empty because it was for Arabs. There were a pair of old women in black shawls, three slouching youths in Banlon shirts and jeans, and a thin, hawk-nosed man seated by the door wearing, defiantly it seemed to me, the flowing Arab headdress. West Bank Arabs tended not to show themselves on Jewish feast days, and for good reason. The fanatics on both sides came out like goblins. They were the sensitive ones who were like the rest of us, but with less tolerance for life's cowshit. They'd rather be up to their asses in blood.

And so Israeli security was even more rigorous than usual. In Jerusalem, particularly in the Old City near the shrines, body-searches would be aggressive. Even monks got their flesh pressed on holy days, but I would not complain that night.

From the bus window I watched as the bleak dark desert landscape gave way to clusters of tall concrete apartment buildings which monotonously but so effectively surrounded Jerusalem. These apartment houses, hundreds of them filled with immigrant Jews, were the "facts" which bolstered Israel's resolve never to return East Jerusalem to Jordan. Since their strategic purpose was clear and crucial — and justified, I'd say — it didn't matter that the housing blocks, even at night, were unbearably ugly. The gray half-light of television glowed eerily in countless windows, and as we passed I wondered why those Jews were not going up to the city for devotions too. Was it Beirut? Were they watching the siege of the PLO stronghold on their little Sonys? Or did each apartment have its guard, its volunteer who stayed behind to resist when the Arabs finally came? "Remember," they would whisper to each other on that holy night, "the dogs attacked the last time on the Day of Atonement."

Tishah-b'Ab commemorates the two destructions of Solomon's Temple, the first in 586 B.C. over which Jeremiah wept, and the second in A.D. 70 over which Jesus wept in advance. These events, of course, have new meaning in our century as emblems of that people's fear. On Tishah b'Ab Jews remember all their destructions and their fear gives way, rightly, to their rage. Israelis therefore by the thousand streamed into the city that night to approach the Western Wall, to place their prayers in its crevices and to stroke those ancient stones or, ritually, to strike them.

The bus driver let out a curse. The slouching boys sat bolt upright. The bus stopped and suddenly the glare of spotlights blinded us. Roadblock.

The door slapped open.

Uzi-toting soldiers clambered aboard, two, then three of them.

The first soldier barked at the driver a word I did not understand, but I heard it as "Goatfucker!" The driver cringed and appeared ready to throw himself at the soldier's feet.

Another soldier leveled his weapon at the man in the headdress. With great dignity the Arab turned his head slowly away to look out the window. The soldier forced him to stand and frisked him. As the Israeli jammed the snout of his gun into the Arab's neck, the man barely seemed to register his presence. I could see his grandfather turning that impassive face on a two-bit British overseer.

The third soldier was approaching me. I imagined him demanding to know by what authority I had left the monastery. Instead he shocked me by saying in a friendly voice and American-accented English, "Good evening, Father."

I couldn't bring myself to answer him at first. Was I afraid?

"You're from Holy Cross, I assume."

"I am indeed." I adopted a cocky tone that in no way corresponded to what I was feeling. "Very clever of you."

He smiled. He was proud of himself. "I grew up in Latrobe, Pennsylvania. There's a Benedictine monastery near my aunt's house. I recognized your habit. Of course, now I know the Franciscans', Trappists' and Dominicans' too."

"Someone as smart as you are should know better than to call me 'Father.' Don't assume all monks are priests. And don't assume all Arabs are terrorists."

"Believe me, we don't, Father. These searches are for everyone's protection. Especially tonight, we can't be too careful."

"But you've called me 'Father' again. You're not careful enough to listen." I was aware that the other two soldiers had moved together on the three formerly slouching youths. Would the fools resist? Would there be shooting? I looked sharply up at the soldier above me. "We understand that you have to do this, but still it affronts what dignity remains to us."

Us? Was I throwing in with Arabs?

He nodded. He had been trained to be patient with the likes of me. We were the ones — the clergy, the Americans — who could cause them trouble. Clearly his job on this bus was to occupy the field of my attention so that his comrades could jam the rods of their guns into the collarbones and ribs of the Arab scumbags. As long as they were not too obvious about it they knew I would not protest. Of course he would attempt to ingratiate himself with me and of course — "Father" indeed! — his ingratiation would insult me. My resentment of his pseudo-deference, I saw too late, served his purpose.

One of the other soldiers called back to him. They were getting off.

"Good luck, Father," the Israeli said to me, and he saluted informally.

I stared at him. To my annoyance I saw that he was waiting for me to speak. "Shalom," I said.

The King David Hotel, touted spa of the Middle East, but famous first for having been blown up by young Menachem Begin in 1946. Nearly a hundred people died, many of them Jews. But its glory days returned. Nixon, Kissinger and Sadat stayed there. Also Rockefellers, Toscanini, successful salesmen from the Bronx and my daughter. Would I know her?

Once, in the alley behind our house on Brooklyn Heights, we were playing catch with an old tennis ball. In her exuberance — she was perhaps six at the time — she turned our game into a contest, "running bases" the boys called it, she said. I, not an athlete, was uneasy with her burst of energy as she tore up and down the narrow pavement, dodging my feeble efforts to tag her. She laughed continually. At a certain point I sensed that I would never catch her. She had me and she knew it. Her fuddy-duddy father. What child wouldn't squeal with delight to so defeat a parent? She zigzagged in, then out, daring to come close, but only to show how easy it was to scoot away. I remember how impatient she made me feel until I realized what was happening. My impatience changed in a sorcerer's flash to awe: my child was more alive than I was. She had a grace and fire all her own. I stood there slack-jawed, thinking, She is so fast! Happiness as brief as it was sweet overwhelmed me. Later I found Carolyn reading in the corner of our book-lined living room. Without explaining, I sat on the floor next to her chair and put my head in her lap and gazed up at her, silent until she asked and I said, "We have made a kind of masterpiece."

The King David Hotel had its name marked on its entrance in English, Hebrew and Arabic, an ecumenical gesture, but the doorman in his martial red jacket looked at me suspiciously. A monk on the loose? *Apostata et fugitivus?* You might think my Benedictine habit was what put him off, but the eccentric dress of religion was ubiquitous in Jerusalem. I nodded at him and pushed through the oversized revolving door.

I was uneasy because of the war and because of my daughter,

but also because it was years since I had been in a city at night. It was all like a dream to me.

In the lobby, mammoth pillars of pink stone supported the massive beams of a blue ceiling which could have been the canopy of a Semite chieftain's throne room. King-sized chairs of cedar and leather spread across the lobby. Sitting in the chairs or strolling between them were impeccably tailored guests. The men were large but not portly. They were smoking. The women glittered. Everyone looked rich to me. At each pillar huge sunflowers, bunches of them in front of floor-to-ceiling swatches of damask, arched over us from antique pots. A group of American Jews clustered at the reception desk in front of me. Those men were wearing yarmulkes, those women sensible shoes. All seemed to clutch guidebooks and they nodded in unison while the concierge explained in accented English how the adjacent road snaked across the valley into the Old City. Even those tourists were going to the Wall to grieve.

Finally I caught the eye of the clerk behind the desk.

"You have a guest registered? A Miss Molly Durkin?"

He flipped through the file. He looked up blankly. "No, Father."

I resisted the urge to correct him. "Are you certain?"

"Quite, Father."

"Would you check again? I'm sure she's here."

The clerk made a show of fingering the registration cards. Suddenly, at a particular one, he stopped and looked up. "You said 'Molly . . .'?"

"Durkin."

He shook his head and continued through the cards.

"What was that one?"

He flipped back to it absently. "Maguire. Molly Maguire."

It must be that the color drained from my face because he was staring at me. Molly Maguire? I could not grasp it. Molly Maguire? As in the Irish equivalent to the Stern Gang? Her very name was an assault, a bomb.

Why had it never occurred to me that once Carolyn married him, Molly would have taken Michael's name? Michael Maguire. How long had it been since I'd thought of him? Did Molly call him "Daddy"? Had he legally adopted her? Involuntarily, my mind threw up a picture of his face, smiling with such fondness. Michael, you bastard! You fucking bastard! You always said you loved us *both!*

The clerk was looking at me wearily.

"That's her." I smiled. "Her married name. I knew her parents. I still think of her as Durkin."

"Room 722. You can call from the phone-bank there." He pointed to a shelf in a corner ten yards away.

I approached the phones slowly, knowing I would never use one. Because I could feel the clerk watching me, I went through the motions of calling her room, all the while depressing the engage button. If even clerks cast a disapproving eye upon me, how would my daughter look at me? She rejected my name?

As I crossed the broad sweep of marble floor toward the massive bronze elevator doors, it was like walking back in time. Memories tugged at me the way Arab boys did in the marketplace. I shook them off as I had ruthlessly now for ten years, but they clutched this time.

My daughter's four-year-old face was streaming with water. Her soaked hair framed her eyes. She had just climbed up to the float and now, arms spread, she was about to throw herself back into the lake where I waited to catch her. Her trust in me was absolute.

The elevator doors opened. The operator was short and obsequious. His bellhop's uniform looked wrong. Then I realized that his pitch-dark hair was cheaply dyed. His skin was not ruddy but flushed with age. He was too old to be dressed like that. I wanted suddenly to ask him, Were you here when Begin bombed the place? Were any young girls killed?

The elevator doors opened again, then closed behind me. I felt like a sleepwalker. How could my Molly have taken another name?

When I had last seen her she had pleaded with me not to go. Owing to the setting perhaps — she was sitting on the knee of the Hans Christian Andersen bronze in Central Park — she looked even younger than seven. Her hands fiddled in her lap with a twig. I was standing beside her. Her head was bent, but I could see that the stress of what had brought us to that moment had set its stamp on her face. With difficulty she said one last time, "Please don't go, Daddy."

"My darling Molly, I would give anything not to." I raised my eyes and saw Carolyn standing mutely, mournfully, a few dozen yards away, waiting for us to finish. I half expected Michael to be with her, but he couldn't have been.

Molly was sobbing then. I took both her hands in mine and I kissed her cheek. At once I turned and ran. Before I reached Fifth Avenue, I remember, it began to rain.

At Room 722 I stopped. I listened for sounds: music, water running, talking. There were no sounds. I looked down at myself. What would I say when she asked about my being a monk? What would I say when she asked me why I never contacted her?

I knocked at the door.

Immediately she opened it.

Her beauty was complete. She stood there in front of me, perfectly still, like an artifact, but with an expression of such human longing that it stunned me when I realized it was longing for me. In her face sadness showed, but as a resonance, a depth. Her loveliness was wonderfully familiar to me. I saw the fulfillment of the abundant promise that always set Molly apart as a child, but also I saw her mother as she was at nineteen. I wanted only to look at her, but my eyes were blinded suddenly by tears. While outside the hotel throngs mourned the destruction of the Temple, the fiercest grief I had ever felt took possession of me. I had spent twelve full years avoiding that emotion, though, and I simply, by an act of will, warded it off.

Neither of us spoke. She stepped aside for me. Finally when I was in the room and the door was shut and the moment had come when we might embrace, she said, "I am sorry for taking you from your monastery."

I searched her face for an indication of sarcasm, but found none. I couldn't think what to say to her.

She turned from me and walked efficiently to the window which opened onto a small balcony. She stood by a table with her back to me. In the distance, framing her dramatically, were the illuminated towers of the Jaffa Gate, and all too easily I imagined the red burst of an explosion, the chunks of stone over-ending through the air, the screams of wounded pilgrims. The enemy from Beirut had struck back at last. I could see that girl pressing her entrails back into the cavity of her stomach, only now I recognized her as my daughter.

"Molly, why are you here?"

"Mother sent me."

"Why?"

"She wants you to come home. She sent me to ask you."

What could I possibly say?

When I did not respond, she faced me. "Will you?"

The show of longing with which she greeted me was gone, replaced by a studied indifference, no, *detachment,* which seemed unbearably cruel to me. And, of course, familiar.

It was the perfect vengeance. I'd practiced it for years.

I approached her carefully. "Molly, you know, we've jumped into the middle of a conversation we're not prepared for. We haven't even said hello."

She averted her face. The water in her eyes glistened. "I wouldn't have come, but Mother asked me."

When I put my hands on her shoulders she did not resist.

In my *hands* I had held her, she was so small!

"What's wrong, darling? Tell me what's wrong?"

She nodded toward the adjacent table. A newspaper was open on it, the *International Herald-Tribune*. She touched it. "Did you see this today?"

"No."

I made no move to look at it. She picked it up and held the page for me to read.

"China Discards Maoist Vision."

My eyes fell several inches to a headline in the lower right-hand corner. The type was smaller, but I read it easily.

"Michael Maguire, Ex-Priest, War-Protester, Is Dead."

TWO

To recover the secrets of one's past and lay them bare in the inchoate hope that even disordered testimony reveals the wider meaning of those events that left us numb — one attempts it feeling a certain desperation. I have found it impossible to resist finally, this strange impulse to sit at my desk — lean to your ear — and speak. It is writing, I know, but it seems like speech to me. An unexpected faith enables me to think I am not talking to myself, for I believe despite the evidence of the blank wall above me that you exist, that you lean toward me, that these solitudes — the writer's in his study, the reader's in his chair — are one solitude. If I am telling you two stories, Michael's and mine, and how despite everything they became this one, can't I also hope I am telling yours?

Flaubert said the artist, the soldier and the priest face death every day. I say, bully for them! The rest of us face it once, maybe, and after that isn't everything just fucking awful? But also . . . aren't we aware only then that we're alive? How often can one glimpse that open secret? And how often is the structure of its story revealed? Pity the sacred trio — artist, soldier, priest — if they do this every day. They could not possibly sustain the grief, the awe or the understanding, so death, shorn of its intensity, must become like flossing, like brewing coffee, like mail falling through the slot. Death; the artist paints it. The soldier wears it with his ribbons. And the priest douses it with holy water.

But you and I watch death cross the land like a shadow once

or twice in a lifetime, changing everything, and then we withdraw to our studies, our chairs, or to our lubricating wakes to tell the raucous and irreverent stories that alone make us know that we survived. You survived. I survived. Even if they don't know it anymore, the artists, soldiers and priests survived. And by God because *story* outweighs *history* — if I didn't believe that would I even begin? — so did the dead survive.

But dear old Henry James says, Don't state! Render! Don't describe what happens, let it happen!

So, my friend, I catch myself. No fustian pronouncements here, no lecture on the salvific effect of narrative impulse, no discursis on Coleridgean *biographia*. Don't explain, create! *Ex nihilo?* Not quite. The events and the people are real. And the time was that stretch of years in which we both came of age and went to the edge. This is the beginning, like all good ones, which contains the end. *Eschaton,* therefore. It was August of 1982. I was in Israel. And Michael Maguire was dead.

And with Molly, riding from Jerusalem, I could barely speak. I was filled with grief for Michael, but also for what I had not had with her. An infinity of tender moments seemed to have been squandered. I watched Molly's sparkling eyes and saw her mother's, that finely formed face, but every memory of Carolyn was a rebuke and I turned from it as I had ruthlessly for a dozen years.

Molly waited in the taxi down on the public road. She assumed I would accompany her back to America that night. She thought we'd returned to the monastery so that I could change from my habit into lay clothes. But what lay clothes? My overalls? How could I have explained to my daughter that her once distinguished father had returned to Holy Cross to ask the old goat prior for permission? The crunch of gravel under my feet was the only sound and it filled the night. It was only midnight, but not a light showed as I approached the monastery. Surely they had noted my absence at Compline. In more than a decade I had never missed an exercise.

With the hem of my habit in hand I leapt the stone wall and circled furtively behind the building toward the prior's room. Once beyond the chapel corner I saw that his light was on. I imagined him talking on the telephone to the Israeli police. But they would have been too busy on that feast night to come out until the morning. A search of the wadis would have been impossible in the dark in any case. If I had just secretly gone off with Molly wouldn't they have assumed I'd wandered into the desert in a mystical trance like Bishop Pike? They would have revered my memory. Monks and prelates *should* disappear without a trace, like Elijah.

This train of thought stopped me. I was standing in the ludicrous arrangement of stone and cactus that the prior referred to as his Zen Garden. The door of his room stood open to the night, and I could see him, a small, frail figure. His bony shoulders protruded under his Benedictine robe. He was bent at his table, like an old man over the wheel of a car. He was not on the phone. A wedge of light fell toward me, inviting my entrance, but I could not bring myself to approach him because suddenly I realized there was every likelihood that this man for whom I had such disdain was praying for me. And all at once my impulse was to throw myself upon him and cry, "Michael is dead!"

Michael was on Nixon's enemy list. J. Edgar Hoover denounced him before Congress. He was the most famous priest in America for a time; the priest against Vietnam. You remember him surely as one of the leading opponents of the war. But there was a secret Michael whom many fewer knew. Despite his reputation as an activist, he was sought out as a Confessor by many Catholics throughout his years as a priest. The elegance of his sensitivity drew people, and not only from among the antiwar crowd. I never confessed to him myself, but Carolyn did. Certainly their encounters in the Sacrament sustained their intimacy and the irony in that, in hindsight, seems particularly poignant to me.

Once I admitted to him that I no longer believed in God. Such a statement seems entirely unmomentous now, but I remember trembling as I said it then. Our certainties had all flaked away like dried skin. Michael sat in silence for such a long time that I began to wonder if he'd heard me. I was unable to read his face. Finally he replied with a voice so sad as to be completely unfamiliar. "None of us believes in God, Durk, but we act as if we do because we love each other. Otherwise . . ." He checked himself, as if he'd said too much already. I never asked him, Otherwise what? But I must have known. We have to help each other cling to God while we can, because eventually we do each other in and then God is all there is.

What desolation I felt, standing there outside the prior's room, watching him. That old monk had been my spiritual father now for more than a decade. We had never overtly expressed affection for one another. I'd hidden from him in my wry irreverence; the trouble with religious superiors, I'd say to myself, is they think they are. He had shown me only his stern mask. His habitual expression had for years been a version of a desert shrub's. Yet, watching him at his psalter and imagining him praying for me, I felt a rush of, yes, love for the man and for the company of brothers who had received me as one not merely welcome but wanted. That I dared allow myself at last to feel such love for those men was how I knew that I was leaving them and their monastery forever. Leaving without a word. It would have been impossible for me to explain. What? That I had a daughter? That she was waiting in a taxi? That she'd come to take me to America? That I was going to my wife's side at her husband's grave? That he was my dearest friend, my enemy? How explain such riddles? What could I have said? Not so much to make the prior let me go — I was beyond permission — as to make him understand. But weren't we beyond understanding too? Hadn't we always been? When I'd arrived years before, a vagrant refugee in flight from dingy rented rooms where for months after Carolyn had left me I'd groped for a way to live and for the bottles of cheap booze that were always rolling under the bed. I'd told the prior nothing then. I could tell him nothing now. He would be shocked to find me gone, hurt perhaps, but not really surprised. What monk ever presumes to know in the dark shroud of his vocation what the old *Deus Absconditus* is up to now?

"On the river of tears," Picard says, "man travels into silence." That was what I had done, going there in the first place. And now, grief-struck, stunned at Molly's reappearance, at the summons she'd brought not from Carolyn, but from my own life, I was doing it again. I was leaving the silence in silence.

I stifled yet another urge to burst in on the prior to throw myself before him for his blessing. Instead I stepped back from his door into the shadows of the desert. Goodbye, dear father, I muttered. God keep you, I prayed, since I cannot. *Ad multos annos.*

I turned, faced Bethlehem for a moment. The stars were spread above me like a jovial throng, but like applause in church, affirmation from the night seemed wrong. This was loss, all loss. First Michael, my friend. Now Holy Cross, my only brothers. Gone, all gone. Already my years in the place were sliding away. I knew that I would someday account for myself to Father Prior and to my gracious confreres, but not then. In fact, of course, these pages are my accounting, and finally my mouth is at the grill of their cloister. Their ears are pressed against it and I am whispering, Oh my brothers, this is why I came to you and why I left.

I didn't need a blessing. I didn't need permission. What I needed were my passport — I was Frank Durkin now, not Brother Francis — and something to wear. I circled the monastery and entered it by the proper door. The halls were quiet. In a few hours, but long before daylight, the monks would rise and sing the nocturnal psalms and they would pray for an absent brother. I stopped in the chapel to pray for them.

And then, in the laundry room, I traded my habit for a denim shirt.

"Why did you stay there so long?" she asked.

I looked past Molly to the desert nightscape we were leaving behind. The taxi was halfway to Jerusalem, and the garish suburban settlements were coming into sight. "Because no one asked me things I had no answer for." I laughed modestly, just glad to be with her, and despite herself she laughed too. Such questions could only make fools of both of us, her for asking, me for never being able to respond. When I looked at her silhouetted against the window I wanted it to be that I'd just awakened and that she and I were two of a family which had survived the harshest winter without wood for a fire. We'd stayed together through awful times. Her mother was a spinner, and I was a miller and she was the girl the prince was wooing. We were going home now. My wife would be in the corner at her wheel, making clothes for me.

"I hate it," my daughter said, about the land we were passing through.

"Because it's barren?"

She looked at me. "Because it's had you all this time."

"It has and it hasn't, Molly. The best years of my life happened without me." I smiled again, trying to steer away from her mood and from my guilt. We weren't an inch from the fact of my having abandoned her. "Tell me about Mount Saint Vincent's. I'm surprised you wound up there."

"Why? Because bright young women don't go to Catholic colleges?"

"No, because it's where your mother went, and she wasn't . . . well . . . exactly happy there."

"She says she was. She says she loved it."

"Really?" I didn't disguise my amazement. So Carolyn had mellowed too. "Is she still working?"

"Better than ever. She has a major show on now, in fact, at a gallery in Princeton. A dozen new paintings. There was an article in *Time* magazine."

I was surprised again, but now I did disguise it because of the envy it implied. "Very colorful? Geometric forms?"

"Mostly whites. She works in whites and pastels."

"Color was her trademark. Great splashes of color."

"She's more subdued."

Weren't we all, I thought. I returned to the haven of silence. These exchanges with Molly exhausted me. There were a million things I wanted to know, but each of her answers was like the glass wall in the Marcel Marceau routine; I kept bumping into it until a kind of panic set it. When I stopped talking, so did she.

In a few minutes the taxi slowed down. There was less traffic on the road than earlier, but the roadblock was still there. The taxi driver stuck his head out the window. The three soldiers were standing mutely before a pair of black-suited, bearded Orthodox men who were wildly berating them. The driver joined in, adding his own sharp voice, a one man antichorus. He was a Jew and his curses, if that's what they were, were in Hebrew. The soldiers waved us through. As we entered the outskirts of the city the taxi picked up speed.

"Everyone seems angry here," Molly said.

"They're at war. . . ." I almost called her "sweetie," but my tongue stumbled and the endearment remained unspoken. "It isn't anger. Everyone's afraid."

"But why can't they just live together? Why can't they just leave each other alone?"

She looked like a woman, but she wasn't quite. "They both want the same thing, Molly. That's the trouble. They can't both have it."

"What, land? There's plenty of land."

"Not 'land,' Molly. *Holy* land. Do we have time to take a detour? I'll show you something that will help you understand."

She looked at her watch. "We're supposed to be at the airport at two o'clock. They said the security check takes a long time."

I leaned forward toward the driver. "Can we get to Lod by two if we go through the Old City? I'd like to see the Wall."

"You have time, sir. But you'll have to walk. I can't get you closer than two blocks."

"Fine." I faced Molly. "I'd like to see it one last time myself."

"The Wailing Wall?"

"The Western Wall. You can't have come to Jerusalem and not have seen it."

"I came to see you." She poked me. "The Wailing Monk."

"If you only knew." I seized her finger and held it.

A few moments later we were walking hand in hand down the broad cobblestone ramp that led to the huge open plaza. We had been frisked by soldiers twice. The streets of the Old City and this route in particular were mobbed, even at that hour. Well before we saw them we could hear the throng at the Wall, the hum of prayers hung in the air like an electric effect, an otherworldly moan. When we came around a last bend the sight leapt at us, stunningly. Floodlights illuminated everything, the plaza, the mammoth Wall, the sea of black-hatted men. But, dominating it all, suspended above the Jews and their shrine, dwarfing them, dwarfing even that block-long construction of hewn boulders were the Dome of the Rock and Al Aqsa, the great Mosque, which sat on the Temple Mount, occupied it, as if it was built at the beginning for Mohammed, not Moses.

Molly pressed my arm, her nails bit through my shirt. She had gasped and was not breathing yet. We stood where we were, straining to take in the spectacle. Thousands of bobbing Jews, beseeching not Yahweh but the stolid indifferent stone; the brilliant blue tile and the golden egg, the mammoth Fabergé, of the Arab shrine; and between them at intervals along the top edge of the Wall, like forged spikes, scores of Israeli soldiers at perfect attention with Uzis between their arms and breasts. Set in the blazing light against the pitch black of night, it was like a de Mille version of the apocalypse an instant before his "Action!"

"There is a rock under that dome, an ancient boulder. Moslems believe Mohammed ascended into heaven from it, and that makes this shrine second only to Mecca. Jews believe that Abraham offered to sacrifice Isaac on the same rock, Molly. When God spared Isaac their religion was born. That's what they're fighting over."

"What are all these people doing?"

"They are reciting the antiphon of Tishah-b'Ab. 'Every generation in which the Temple is not rebuilt is guilty of its destruction.' They'll be here all night, praying for the restoration of Solomon's Temple, which implies the destruction of the Dome and Al Aqsa. The Arabs are right to be afraid of piety like this."

"Are you against the Jews?"

"No. I am afraid for them. And I am afraid of them. Many Jews feel the same way. What I wanted you to see was that *this* land is different. Step over here." She followed me up a set of stairs that led to a narrow alley winding back into the Jewish Quarter. From the top of the stairs was another view of another dome. This one was not illuminated, but even from several blocks away, its black unornamented form stood out sharply against the sky. "That is the Holy Sepulchre. Christians revere it both as the site of Calvary and of the tomb from which Jesus was raised. This patch of earth is less than half a square mile in size; the three great religions of the world all believe it to have been touched directly by God."

"And so they fight over it?"

"Yes. It's absurd, isn't it? What does God think, do you suppose?"

"I don't believe in God," Molly said. "I never understood why until now."

"You can't blame God for the madness of his people."

"He made them, didn't he?"

I poked her. "Not if he doesn't exist."

But she refused to treat this lightly. She turned from me. "I didn't say he doesn't exist. I said I don't believe in him."

"It is not easy here to believe in God. You're right about that." I was speaking softly. Molly gave no sign that she even heard me. "When I first came to Jerusalem I was put off by the shrines, even by the Holy Sepulchre. Bad art, contentious monks, superstitious tourists. The tomb of Jesus isn't even empty; a Greek priest with bad breath and no teeth waits in there to sell you candles. I hated the decadent religiosity of this place."

"But you stayed." She faced me. Her eyes were full.

I touched her cheek and I nodded. "There's an excavation cave I wish I could show you. It's being dug under a Russian convent not far from here. You go down, down, down, like into a mine, and you stoop through a tunnel to come out into a great, spacious cavern which is lit by naked bulbs. You stand before a large stone slab about nine feet long and three feet wide. It is unremarkable, an ordinary hewn piece of rock at your feet. You look down at it in silence for a long time, and finally you kneel and touch it and kiss it."

"Why?"

"Because it was the threshold stone of the city gate in the time of Herod. Only recently have archaeologists uncovered that section of the ancient city wall. They say it is certain that, only a few years before the threshold stone was covered by the rubble of the Roman destruction, Jesus of Nazareth stepped on it with his feet when he left the city to die."

Molly let her gaze drift across the city. "It's hard to picture Jesus here."

"Why?"

"Everyone's so mean," she answered sharply. She was dangerously close to losing her poise. What was she afraid of?

"The world is mean, Molly. And it makes us mean. In his own way Jesus was mean too. The Incarnation wasn't puppy love, you know. Jesus was one of us, that's all. It could have been the Bronx, but it was here. God came *here*. That's the curse of this place."

Molly was silent. In her face the immobile nightscape showed. Her eyes seemed to look out from one of the city's tombs, and I saw how very sad she was. Not fear, but grief was what undid her. I saw for the first time that she was a young woman profoundly in mourning.

"Michael was a good friend to you, wasn't he?" I touched her.

She nodded shyly. Now the tears came. She stood erect, ignoring them. The breeze feathered her hair. "He was more than that. Forgive me for saying this, but he became like a father to me."

"I'm glad, sweetie. He was the best man I ever knew."

"You don't hate him?"

"I did. You've been asking me why I stayed here so long. It was to purge myself of that, to recover from it. No, Molly, I don't hate him. I haven't in a long time. That's why I'm coming back with you. I have to say goodbye to Michael. He was more than a friend to me too. And when I failed you as a father, I thank God he was there to take my place."

Molly lowered her head and whispered now, "You didn't fail me."

And I could think of nothing to say to her, or of any way to touch her, because we both knew that she was lying.

After a long time I said, "We should go." I took her arm and led her back along the cobblestone ramp toward the street where the taxi was waiting.

After the glare of the floodlit plaza the narrow arched-over passageway was too dark to negotiate hurriedly. As we passed them I could make out the corrugated shutters that covered the stalls and alcoves of merchants. In the cramped Jewish Quarter the stale air with its unfamiliar odor, whether of food or waste, pressed on us. Three Hasidic men on their way to vigil at the Wall brushed by us, and I sensed Molly stiffen, as if modern women knew instinctively of their contempt. At a corner a machine-gun-toting soldier looked up from a match with which he had just lit a cigarette. "Hi ya, Father," he said. It was the young American who'd stopped the Arab bus. There was a snicker in his greeting, and I realized that he thought he had caught me, a monk out of habit, with a beautiful girl in the middle of the night. I winked at him.

And at that very moment from behind us came the explosion, like the sustained clap of hailstones on a metal roof, and instantly it seemed to me that since I first laid eyes on the army in the Judean desert valley ten years before I had been waiting for that outbreak. Without thinking I pushed Molly to the ground. I had no way of knowing how close the bomb or shell or grenade was to us, though I felt a blast of heat and I was sure the ground under us had been jolted. The noise of the explosion hung in the air, and then, as it faded, other sounds grew to fill the night. First, of human screams, a great roar of screaming that was coming from the plaza by the Wall. And then, more immediate to us, the clomp-

clomp of runners. When I opened my eyes to look, I saw squads of soldiers barreling past us. The American was gone.

Molly was pressed into the corner of a shuttered merchant's stall and I was on top of her. When I looked, I thought at first she was pushing her entrails back into the wound in her abdomen. But she was not. Neither of us was hurt. The explosion, it was only now certain, took place some distance away. At the Wall, or at the Dome of the Rock, or in the Holy Sepulchre. I pictured the night sky full of flaming debris. What had they blown to bits now, and whom?

Just as Molly and I were struggling to our feet the roar of the coming wave reached us. By the time we faced it, the wave of panicked, fleeing Jews was on us. Hundreds of the thousands from the Wall had squeezed into the narrow alley and were running blindly through it, screaming. Only the yard-square alcove we were pressed in saved Molly and me from being crushed in the stampede. We clung to each other as the throng's edge ripped at us. Molly had buried her face in my shoulder. Her eyes were tightly shut, but mine were open. I couldn't help but stare at the terror in the faces of those Jews. For that instant they were in flight from every pogrom, every massacre, every slaughter, every crucifixion men had ever inflicted on the creation of God. And I, in my corner, holding my grown child, watched with the eyes of a guilty bystander through which, unfortunately, I had seen everything.

THREE

MICHAEL MAGUIRE was mobbed by a throng of panicked fugitives too, but he was not free to watch from the edge of the road as I would be years later. The old men, women and children coursing past him were as desperate to escape as those I would see, but they pressed against each other, always forward, forward, with greater restraint. They were less an avalanche of terror than a glacier, and it was about to become Maguire's job to stop it.

It was January 4, 1951, the first of his fighting days. He was eighteen years old, had been in the army only since August and in Korea less than a month. Almost from the day of his arrival as a member of the 27th U.S. Infantry Regiment, the American forces had been falling back, withdrawing southward, collapsing around Seoul — not "retreating," the officers insisted — in the face of the shocking onslaught of Chinese troops. Maguire's company had been doing garrison duty in the Korean capital, but now it too had begun its move south. Maguire's platoon, consisting of seven GIs of whom he was one, a corporal, a staff sergeant and commanded by a second lieutenant, had been sent ahead the day before to guard the railroad bridge over the Han River a few miles below Seoul. But in twenty-four hours almost the entire U.N. force of soldiers and equipment had been evacuated across the Han, and now Maguire's platoon was one of only a few U.N. units remaining on the north side of the river.

The platoon's problem was the mass of refugees. Whenever the radio crackled its warning that a train approached they had to halt the flow of civilians long enough for the train to cross. But there hadn't been a train now for nearly two hours, and it was difficult to imagine that the stunned, inexorable mob would obey them if they ordered a halt again.

The river at that point was half a mile wide, but it seemed narrower because ice, white shoulders of it stretching from each bank, had begun to close on the center channel where the current ran most swiftly. It was so cold that Lieutenant Barrett gave permission to keep the jeep running so that the GIs could take turns sitting on its radiator to keep warm. The bridge was a rigid, solid multispan suspension structure, a quilt of pig-iron girders on top of concrete pilings, that the Japanese had built during their wartime occupation. Ice floes had begun to jam up at the pilings. The retreating ROK Army had demolished the center span of the bridge the previous July when the North Koreans overran the south. American engineers had rebuilt it in October after the U.N. breakout and the recapture of Seoul. And now Seoul was about to fall once more, this time to the Chinese, and its population was once more fleeing south. Maguire and his buddies knew that the bridge would have to be dropped again, but if it wasn't done soon, the river was going to be frozen clear across anyway, and no one would need a bridge. "If the Chinks don't catch us," they complained to each other, slapping their sides, "the fucking cold will."

Later Maguire would grasp the chronology of the seesaw victories and defeats that characterized the first phase of the war, but that day he did not understand what was happening. MacArthur's autumn assurance that his army would be home by Christmas was repeated now as a bitter joke. In the previous summer the North Koreans had conquered most of the peninsula, but that was before the Americans came. After the great assault at Inchon, the GIs took the peninsula back almost easily. When Maguire got his orders for Korea as one of the tens of thousands of quickly drafted relief troops the war — the "police action" as the president called it — was supposed to be over. Draftees like him expected ninety-day turnarounds. Now he and his regiment and, as far as he knew, the whole U.S. Army were running for their lives, just like the expressionless, sullen refugees passing stoically by him.

To tell the truth Michael Maguire understood very little of what had happened to him in the six months since he'd graduated from Good Shepherd High School in Inwood. He was one of only three boys in our class to be drafted. The rest of us pretended to envy them and, though we worshipped our older brothers for having fought in World War Two, I can recall no one of our group who went downtown and enlisted. It was as if, instinctively, we knew that Korea was not the war we wanted. As to why Michael should have been drafted, no one knew. His fame as a schoolboy athlete had carried around the city, leading some to think the Selective Service only picked those most likely to make good soldiers. But Tubby McGaw was drafted too. More confusing still was the fact that Michael's long-deceased father had been a New York City cop. None of us remembered him but it was neighborhood legend how he'd been killed in the line of duty, thwarting a holdup in Pop Mahoney's Variety Store. It was as if the draftboard, instead of exempting the only sons of widows, went out of the way to call them. Maguire's father a dead hero? Then the army would give him the chance to be one too. By rules we were all familiar with, it was a chance Michael was compelled to take, for it was unthinkable that he should apply for a hardship exemption. He'd have been a shoe-in for it, but he felt bound by an honor code of which his father was the mythic exemplar. We were far from cynical about such things, but that honor code of Michael's seemed anachronistic to some of us even then. His willingness to be conscripted by events would set Michael apart, for good and for ill, for the rest of his life.

The war in Korea was not the war against Hitler, and aspects of it troubled right from the start, but it was morally compelling nonetheless. However difficult it is to imagine now, America seemed as invincible as upright then, and we were sure that our mission in Asia was thrust upon us by a pleading world. When Michael left Inwood, even those of us who thought he was a sap to go were proud of him. I was also grief-stricken. Already the bond between us was stronger than blood. He was my best friend and I was his. For a long time I felt his absence as a bodily pain, and I came to hate the war that took him from me, even if I believed in it.

Forgive me if I homilize about it for a moment, but Korea serves as the first bracket not only for this story — for Michael's life —

but for the story of the tragic decline of America, which is of course our larger subject. It is only the failure of Communism to realize its own rhetoric that makes that first reflexive effort to oppose it seem naive. And it is only the recent collapse of belief in our own rhetoric about ourselves as free people defending freedom that makes our intervention in behalf of an invaded people seem militaristic. Contrary to present opinion, it is not that people were stupid in those days or prisoners of univocal thinking that draws all conflicts in black and white. They were neither morally nor politically shallower than we are. On the contrary they had a perception of one of the century's great facts, a perception since lost in the fog of our social, personal and political narcissism — that Communism is an inhuman system comparable to Nazism in every way but one: it works as a system of repression and conquest, but it cannot feed its people, and so eventually must fail whether opposed from without or not. The generation that fought Communism and contained it in Greece and Korea did not know that yet. I was an aware young man launched on a Greenwich Village phase of Camusian *engagement,* yet I did not know it. Communism, we believed, was capable of taking over the world. It is superficial therefore merely to fault Americans of that period for their paranoia, despite its dreadful domestic and international consequences. They moved — I should say "we" moved — in Eliot's phrase, "in the time between sleep and waking."

The point is that there were reasons, regarded as good ones then, and still so regarded by some of us, to perceive the Communists as monstrous. Every GI in Korea could have given them to you. Graphic stories of Red atrocities were a feature of basic training. What pimply-faced draftee could benignly contemplate the prospect of dying in a ditch with his balls in his mouth?

Later in life Michael Maguire would express the opinion that basic training was itself a kind of atrocity — a systematic numbing of individual conscience and will. His preoccupation by then would be not with how we were right about the Communists, but how we were wrong about ourselves. It would become his position that even a graced, generous society like America can be corrupted — will be corrupted — when its major effort is turned to the prolonged conduct of war. Basic training, his own experience of it, would therefore become a basic point of reference and a basic metaphor for the inhumanity into which America slipped. But that came later.

At the time, though, he knew something was dreadfully wrong with a system that celebrated and sought to nurture the sadistic in men. In a letter he wrote to me just before shipping out to Korea, he described with suppressed rage how his company's drill instructor had presented them on their arrival at Fort Dix with the gift of a pet rabbit, and how he had encouraged them to feed it and care for it and grow fond of it. Through the rigors of the training that rabbit — its childishly derived name was Thumper — sustained in Maguire and others the capacity for gentleness and warmth, feelings for which there were simply no other outlets. Maguire described how attached they became to Thumper. They fed the animal on scraps smuggled out of the mess hall. He described how on the day that basic finally ended and they were shipping out to various regiments bound for Korea, the DI gathered the company for his farewell talk. He took Thumper and, after fondling him and nuzzling him, he suddenly snapped the rabbit's neck with his bare hands and then threw it on the table and in quick order produced a gleaming bayonet with which he skinned and disemboweled it. Then he splashed on his men its blood, Thumper's blood, an unconscious mockery of the *Asperges Me*. And he swore that that was what the Commie bastards would do to any GI they caught alive, and so GIs just fucking well better do it to the Commie bastards first. Michael said in his letter that he was horrified by that drill instructor, but also by his own reaction to him, for in fact he accepted despite himself the slaughter of that rabbit as an image of Communists' skinning their prisoners alive, and it terrified him.

And now the ultimate Commie Bastards — Chicoms — had swept down on Seoul, whose citizens needed no Thumper lessons to be afraid.

Maguire watched as the Koreans funneled onto the bridge. They hauled ladened carts or carried their possessions on their backs, boxes and even pieces of furniture strapped to the large Korean A-frames made of tree branches. Some women carried loads on their heads, like Africans, and they alone managed a stately pace in the otherwise jerking crowd. Progress was too sporadic and the press of bodies too close to ride bicycles, so those who owned bicycles pushed them. Babies rode in bicycle baskets or on smaller versions of the A-frame on their mothers' backs, wrapped like papooses. The faces of the men and women were so lacking in animation of any sort that it was possible, by virtue of that lack, to imagine the oppression under which they'd lived. If one had only their faces to go by, they'd have seemed sullen, not afraid. Their fear was communicated through the ferocious concentration of their energy on movement.

The faces of the children, though, seemed alive, despite their being wrapped against the cold so that only their eyes, noses and mouths were visible. They reminded Maguire of the Hummel figurines his mother collected, with little dashes of color for features and an air of porcelain fragility, as if just looking at them would make them break.

As they moved by, Michael waited for someone to look at him, but their eyes were fixed on the heels of those immediately ahead. Even when they were shoved into each other, as happened increasingly, no one protested. Maguire felt sorry for them. Only the eyes of the papoose children snagged on him. Well over six feet tall, thin, cigarette dangling from his lips, M-1 slung on his shoulder, he was the embodiment of the fantasy Asians had of good-looking, friendly but also somehow frightening Americans. When he waved or otherwise acknowledged that he saw them, the children looked away. Alone of everything he'd seen in weeks, their shy glances made Maguire feel that there was something in that frigging country to protect. What would Chicoms do to enemy children? Maguire didn't believe it, but the Koreans said they ate them.

"Maguire!" Sergeant Stone's harsh voice cut through the cold. "On the double!"

The ten men of the platoon circled the jeep, drawing as close as they could to its radiator. Their breath rose in white puffs, a winter flower that bloomed and faded above them magically. Lieutenant Barrett was standing with one foot on the jeep bumper. When the men were assembled he said, nodding at the radio on Tucci's back, "Okay, boys, we got the word. We get one more train through, then we move out."

"Across the river?" O'Hara asked.

"Hell, yes. You think they'd leave without us?"

"Fucking-A!" O'Hara slapped Bean's helmet with relief. Bean just looked at him.

Lieutenant Barrett went on. "It's time to be on our toes." Something in the lieutenant's voice frightened the men. Maguire had been afraid since arriving in Korea, not acutely and certainly not in any acknowledged way, but in a dull, constant mortification of all his senses, as depressing as it was secret. Now he felt his fear quicken. He shifted his glance to the others. They were all staring at Lieutenant Barrett, riveted, waiting. Despite the cold a thin line of perspiration could be seen on the young officer's lip.

"The next train only has one car, get it? It'll be a big tender, only instead of coal it has a load of dynamite in it."

"Oh fuck," Lennie Pace said. He was the big Italian kid who admitted that he was only sixteen years old, but he was so brawny he passed for eighteen easily. Everyone mispronounced his name — it was "pa-chay," not "pace" — but he'd grown accustomed to that in basic. He'd only been in Korea a week. His fright was palpable.

Sergeant Stone gave him a look. Its thinly veiled contempt seemed lost on Pace, but it unsettled Maguire. He remembered that the sergeant was a veteran of World War Two.

So was Lieutenant Barrett, who made no secret of his resentment at having been called up from the reserves. He seemed young but had been in combat in the Philippines, though not as an officer. That he was new to command accounted perhaps for his stifled uneasiness. "When the train passes, we hop aboard, get it?"

"Even though it's moving?" Sully asked.

Maguire saw that the other men were at least as afraid as he was.

"Falling off the train is the least of your worries, believe me." Lieutenant Barrett looked nervously across at the mobbed bridge and he wiped his lip. "So we're on the train, okay? The engineer's going to stop it right in the middle. Then we get off, okay? We cover the crew. They get a jump on us."

"You mean everybody gets off the train?"

"The train is stopped, Sully. After the crew, we hightail the rest of the way off the bridge on foot. On the other side we hook up with Captain Ray. Get it?"

"So what about the dynamite?" Pace asked.

"Pace, you're a stupid Wop, you know that?" Sergeant Stone belted the kid's helmet.

"No, it's a good question," the officer said. "Usually, they'd string the charges out all along the bridge. They'd put them on the pilings. But there's no time. They're going to just blow it right there in the middle. Right there in the train."

"What about the jeep?"

"Fuck the jeep," Sergeant Stone barked. "Shut up."

Maguire thought the sergeant was right. The men were only asking questions out of nervousness. Obviously Lieutenant Barrett knew barely more than they did.

"Our job," he said, "is to clear the bridge." He looked at his watch. "We have half an hour. The train just left the depot. The lucky people who are already on the bridge will have just enough time to get to the other side. Nobody else gets on, so let's stop these folks. We'll only use what force is necessary, but we'll use it. Any more questions?"

"Yeah." Sully raised his hand like a schoolboy. "What about the Chinese?"

"They're on the way, Sully. Listen."

The men listened to the dull roar of artillery from Seoul. For the first time they realized that it was closer.

"The engineers have already taken the other bridges down, fellows. This is the last one left across the Han. The Chinese want it. It's up to us to see they don't get it. If we don't clear it right now so that train can move out fast, we're going to have to stay here and fight them for it. About thirty thousand of them."

"Oh fuck," O'Hara said.

The men took up their positions. There were two roadblocks, one at the entrance to the bridge itself and one about fifty yards up the railroad bed. At each the makeshift gate was in the raised position, letting people through. Sergeant Stone, Sully, Bean and Jones manned the outer one while Maguire, Brown, Pace and O'Hara manned the one at the bridge itself. Lieutenant Barrett and Tucci remained at the jeep. When everyone was in position Stone fired his weapon into the air and barked repeatedly the Korean phrase which meant "Stay back!" Both teams began to lower the gates.

Previously the effect of the gunshot and the order had been immediate compliance. The refugees, once halted, waited submissively for permission to resume. They'd thought nothing of waiting several hours. But now, as if they knew the score, their reaction was the opposite one. They surged forward en masse. Women, old men, even children threw themselves against those in front. They ripped the logs of the blockades from their leather hinges and tossed them aside like matchsticks. The people crushed each other to get onto the bridge. A-frames and carts were thrown into the river. Those who stumbled were trampled. Refugees farther back on the road pressed forward even harder. The knowledge of what was happening rippled back; thousands perceived it at once. Their escape was being cut off.

Cries went up: first of pain of those being crushed; then of protest at the prospect of being left behind. Sergeant Stone fired his weapon into the air again, and then the GIs did too. But the barrage only increased the panic in the crowd. The force of its surge doubled.

Maguire sensed that there was no stopping them, and he could feel their panic seizing him and the others of his platoon. What could they do? He for one was being swept onto the bridge, like so much flotsam in a surf. Even if he'd wanted to use his rifle he couldn't have raised it. He, Eddie Brown, the colored kid, and Lennie Pace were each several heads taller than the swarming Koreans, but they were powerless.

Maguire could see that the four soldiers at the forward roadblock had linked arms and were pushing against the tide of people. But then Sullivan's helmet was knocked off when someone clubbed him, and Bean simply disappeared as the crowd overwhelmed him.

Later Maguire would realize that Lieutenant Barrett had seen Bean drop too, because it was at that moment that he hopped behind the wheel of the idling jeep, popped it into gear, and gunned it right at the mob. He was still picking up speed when he hit the line of people midway between the two roadblocks, midway between the positions his boys held. It was an instinctive act, but not an irrational one. Barrett never hit the brakes; the crunch of flesh and bone was what stopped the vehicle. Maguire would later swear he heard the thunk of steel against bodies and of bodies against each other, but the real sounds of impact were lost in the roar of the revving jeep engine.

Though he would not articulate it until much later, it was at this moment that Maguire understood for the first time that judgments about right or wrong can be completely irrelevant. War presents men with certain circumstances and they act. That's all.

Not quite all. Also they perceive; perhaps they perceive, despite their numbness, with special clarity. Maguire saw the heads of Koreans cracked open like melons, gray matter spurting out like vegetable pulp and seeds, as if a pumpkin truck spilled right in front of him. He saw bodies flung through the air jerkily, limbs flailing like swingles, faces crushed against chests or against backs; bodies sprawling on top of each other, then being hideously bulldozed as the momentum of the jeep carried it fully through the line. A score of people were mauled, a dozen horribly killed, but the shock of violence — the wave it made — was felt, could be seen to be felt, all through the dense crowd. The grotesque sight of those split skulls was fixed in Maguire's mind and would always dominate his memory of that day. The memory would make him sick. But he would also always remember that it worked. Lieutenant Barrett had stormed the glacier and stopped it.

Tucci was standing in the jeep firing the submachine gun above the heads of the people. The staccato of his weapon gave perfect expression to the violent fury that always follows the release from danger. The Koreans, hunched over, protecting their heads, had lost their impetus. The GIs were in charge again. Maguire and the others formed ranks in front of and alongside the jeep. They stood with their weapons cocked, a more formidable blockade than ever.

"Cease fire, Tucci!" Lieutenant Barrett called.

When Tucci released the trigger a shocking silence fell. The groans of the wounded Koreans could be heard and also the distant booming of artillery, but still there was silence.

"Sergeant! Is everyone accounted for?"

"Yes, sir!"

"What about Bean?"

"Here, sir!"

"Tell these people anyone who moves will be shot!"

Sergeant Stone rattled off a few words in the strange language. The Koreans gave no sign they knew they were being addressed.

"That's you, Tucci," Lieutenant Barrett ordered. "Shoot them if they move. Don't wait for me to tell you."

"Yes, sir." Tucci, poised above the scene like the statue of a hero, was not as cool as he looked. He had never fired the submachine gun in action before.

Barrett shut the jeep engine off and hopped down. "Maguire! Brown! Let's help these people!"

They laid their rifles aside and knelt, trying to pull the tangled bodies out from under the front bumper of the jeep. Bodies were piled there three and four deep, like, Maguire thought, in a concentration camp. At first none seemed alive, but as they pulled, some victims began to move. The cries grew louder. The vehicle had come to rest right on the railroad tracks. One poor bastard's head was crushed against the rail.

Maguire retched, but he only turned his head aside. He, Brown and the lieutenant worked steadily to free the people, to drag the corpses away and to try to comfort the ones who were alive.

One little girl, a shattered but howling figurine, was strapped to her dead mother's back. Her mother's neck was broken, and her expressionless face was perversely askew on her shoulders. Maguire freed the girl, who was barely more than an infant. When he stood up with her he found himself facing Lieutenant Barrett. The officer seemed suddenly horrified. "Jesus Christ," he whispered while staring at the bawling child in Maguire's arms. "What have I done?"

Maguire buried the baby's face against his chest. It was how he'd held that rabbit. He wanted to say, "We all did it, Lieutenant," but he couldn't.

The crowd was still at bay and the bridge was clear when the train arrived. It pulled into view behind the scolding sound of its own engine and Maguire wanted to feel relief, but he had maintained his nerve up to then only by blanking out his ability to feel anything. He had spent the time trying to comfort the injured civilians, applying first aid, wrapping them in GI blankets, clearing stones from under them, wiping their faces. He realized that he'd begun to imitate their stoicism.

He had to remind himself that now he was going to leave. The train had come, in a way, for him.

"Move that jeep!"

Maguire looked around to see who Lieutenant Barrett was addressing, but he was nearer to the jeep than anyone. It was still blocking the track, and the engine was steaming steadily closer.

He hopped aboard the jeep, pushed the ignition button, and fiddled with the gear stick until he found reverse. He had to gas the engine to get the wheels over the iron rail. As he backed away from the track he continued to gun it instead of stopping; suddenly he knew that he wanted only to get away. He saw what he had in common with those Koreans, not stoicism, but heart only for escape. He careened backward in that jeep toward the riverbank, as if escape was waiting for him there.

Maguire would hear it said later that some men were made more acutely conscious by the bleak experiences of war, and it was true that his ability to see and smell and hear the minutiae of violence was heightened. But his ability to organize his perceptions into a coherent whole in which he was more than a detached observer abandoned him utterly. As far as he could recall he was barely aware throughout that episode of his own choices or even of his own reactions. It was a mad thing to do, for example, to send that jeep shooting off the edge of the cliff. It tumbled down the hundred feet of rocky incline and burst into flames just before it plunged through the ice. The gasoline fire was extinguished as quickly as it had ignited.

And Maguire, as if he'd practiced for a stunt show, had leapt free at the last instant, landed in a crouch facing the river, and watched until the jeep disappeared under a plume of steam. "Fucking thing," he said.

"Maguire! Maguire!"

The engine and tender were just crossing onto the bridge. The platoon was scrambling aboard. Sergeant Stone was waving Maguire's M-1 and calling his name, alarmed that he was being left behind.

Maguire had to run. The train was moving at a clip and he would not have made it if Brown and Pace hadn't pulled him aboard. He collapsed on the iron platform and then at last, leaving that nightmare behind, felt the first hint of relief.

But it was premature.

"Oh fuck!" O'Hara cried. "Oh Jesus! Fuck!"

The others saw what he saw. The wall of refugees had broken and they were rushing onto the bridge behind the train. Their grim stoicism was gone. The crowd of old men, women, boys and girls which had not moved for most of an hour was now a charging infantry, bellowing insanely as it stormed after them. Fatalistic

Orientals? Shock victims? A defeated populace? Resigned to wait for its new masters? None of these. They were like the notorious primitive armies of Sun Tsu, which depended less on weapons than on dreadful masks and frightening noises. But a mob is not an army. It is moved not by discipline but by emotion. The Koreans were one creature now, an incarnation of feeling that went beyond fear or rage into something wholly other, something infinite. Even from a distance Maguire could sense that now their energy was going to overwhelm any obstacle they met, and to their horror the GIs realized that the refugees were catching up with them.

"Fix bayonets!" Lieutenant Barrett ordered.

It was difficult to do it on the jolting train, but no one hesitated. In a moment all seven riflemen had the long blades fixed to the barrels of their guns, and Tucci had the safety off the Browning. No one, not Maguire certainly, allowed qualms to surface. The Koreans were no longer old men and women, no longer children. They were an enemy whom the odds favored.

A boy of about twelve was the first to catch the train. He was reaching for the rail when Pace poised to harpoon him, but at that moment the train picked up speed and a gap opened between the boy and Pace's bayonet.

The crowd kept coming even though the train was leaving them behind.

But just as it seemed safe again, the train slowed. Maguire had forgotten that it was going to stop in the middle of the bridge.

The iron wheels began to screech, and steam hissed out from the undercarriage.

And the refugees began to close the distance. The train jolted to a stop.

"Get ready!" Lieutenant Barrett ordered.

Maguire couldn't believe what they were about to do. Tucci raised his submachine gun, and the other soldiers aimed their rifles. Maguire tried to find a middle-aged man to aim at, but all he saw were Pappa-sans and children. "Go back!" he screamed suddenly. "Go back!" Sergeant Stone started screaming at them in Korean, and the other GIs chorused, "Go back! Go back!"

Tucci fired into the crowd, and the front rank fell. Immediately there was a pileup as the onrush continued. The bodies of the

Koreans, even the fallen ones, writhed as Tucci's bullets pumped into them.

Maguire couldn't tell whether the other soldiers were firing. He assumed later that he was himself firing, but he was never certain that he hadn't simply frozen while the merciless staccato went on around him. He wished desperately that the rabble-refugees had been a cavalry charging so that he could have aimed his gun at horses.

By the time Lieutenant Barrett gave the order to fall back, the engineers had already abandoned the train. Stringing detonating wire behind them, they were rapidly crossing toward the shore, and it was with infinite relief that the platoon took out after them.

It was impossible to run efficiently on the railroad ties, and the men stumbled constantly.

When Sully fell ahead of him, Maguire assumed he'd only tripped. He stopped to help him. Sully looked up with blood gushing out of a hole below his ear, then he collapsed, obviously dead.

Bullets pinged off the ironwork of the bridge.

Maguire was the first to see the flotilla of small boats in the river below. The channel between the iced margins was clotted with vessels. Scores of soldiers in mustard-colored uniforms were shooting at the Americans from the decks and superstructures of dozens of fishing boats and junks. "Chinese!" he screamed. "Chinese!" Some of the boats were already alongside the pilings of the bridge. The Chinese were grappling their way up.

The GIs ran even faster. The railroad ties were suddenly no obstacle.

Bean was shot. Lieutenant Barrett stopped for him, but then he fell too, clutching his chest.

Eddie Brown and Maguire scooped the officer up and, each taking an arm, carried him along. O'Hara and Pace started to pick up Bean, but he waved them off and they left him.

Tucci fired his submachine gun in a frenzy, and only then did Maguire realize that a pair of Chinese soldiers had just climbed over the railing right in front of them. The Chinese fell dead.

Tucci, Pace and O'Hara ran swiftly ahead. Fifty yards from the riverbank Maguire and Brown with the lieutenant between them came upon the corpses of the two engineers who had been stringing the detonation wire. One of them had his arms around the black plunger-box. The other members of the platoon mustn't have realized what it was because they'd run right by.

"Get it!" Lieutenant Barrett ordered. "Leave me and get that plunger!"

"No, sir," Maguire said. "We're getting you out of here."

"Fuck you, Maguire!" The lieutenant wrenched himself out of their arms and fell violently to the track. His blood had soaked even through the heavy winter jacket, turning the olive-green to black. He looked desperately at Maguire. "You've got to get off the bridge and blow it!"

Maguire looked behind him expecting to see the Chinese soldiers, but the wave of Korean refugees, having swarmed over and around the halted train, was rushing at them again. The fucking refugees! They'd overrun the Chinese too!

Eddie Brown picked up the wire-wheel and began to string it out, moving backward toward the shore. Maguire picked up the plunger-box with one hand and with the other hoisted Barrett over his shoulder. He ran as well as he could. He and Brown reached the far end of the bridge at the same time. Tucci was there and once his buddies were clear he began firing back into the onrushing refugees again.

It took several moments for Brown to cut and attach the electrical wire to the terminal in the detonator. When it was ready he looked up at Maguire. "Okay!"

Maguire reached over and grabbed Tucci. "Stop firing! Stop firing!"

There was no need now. Let the poor bastards make it, a few of them anyway.

Tucci obeyed Maguire. He stared at him dumbly. Tears stained his face. He'd been weeping all the while. He'd also wet himself.

Maguire felt a shocking sense of control. It had all somehow come down to him. When the first set of refugees rushed past him off the bridge, a token quota of survivors, he pushed the plunger without hesitating.

For an instant, long enough to turn toward the bridge but not to see the faces, thank God, of the Koreans who hadn't quite made it, there was no explosion. Then it came as a simple loud clap, followed by a muffled dull roar. The earth of the riverbank registered the shock. It moved.

The iron girders of the bridge's three central spans were tossed into the air, along with mammoth fragments of the locomotive and millions of splinters of metal and wood. The dust of tons of enginecinder and the smoke from the huge combustion billowed. Yet through that chaos of debris and noise Maguire swore that he saw severed limbs arching through the air and heard the cries of babies.

"Hey, hey, LBJ! . . ." At his side in demonstrations years later I was always aware of Michael's refusal to utter such taunts. ". . . how many kids did you kill today?"

FOUR

WHILE Michael went to Korea, I went to college. I hastily set about putting away, in Saint Paul's phrase, the things of a child, including, I'd have said with worldly relish, the phrases of Saint Paul. The idea — and it is the perennial idea of freshmen, one of the few they can be counted on to grasp — was to reinvent one's personality. For a punk from Inwood newly arrived at NYU in Greenwich Village, the quickest way to do that was to claim the fiercely romantic identity of the fallen-away Catholic. That meant having to learn at once to disdain above all others the figure of the Roman Catholic priest, that embodiment of smug sterility and intellectual vacuity.

And then, of course, almost immediately, I fell under the spell of Gerard Manley Hopkins. My attraction to him would be permanent and his aesthetic would even be the subject years later of my dissertation — "Instress and Inscape; the Diction of G. M. Hopkins." In those days it embarrassed me, as I was sure it did his Balliol friends, that he'd become a Catholic and a priest. I agreed with critics who asserted that his religious vocation had come at the expense of his literary one. What a waste! we said as if we were horny schoolgirls discussing the handsome curate. If Hopkins hadn't been a priest, we agreed in every seminar, he'd have been a lesser great poet instead of — how these distinctions mattered! — a great lesser one. When he called himself "Time's eunuch" we knew he was bewailing the mistake he'd made, the trick God played on him.

Now I understand that of course his priesthood was precisely what drew me to him. For my kind the priest is the linchpin of belief. In all my religious phases — whether I was fallen away, newly found or only, in current argot, user-friendly — priests have been at the center of my consciousness, and that's part of what's made me Catholic.

And priests, as you know already, will be at the center of this narrative.

None more so, beginning in Korea, than Tim O'Shea.

Father Timothy O'Shea — he answered neither to "Padre" nor to "Major" — was born in Tipperary. His parents emigrated when he was a child and he grew up to become a priest of the Archdiocese of New York. He was trained in philosophy to be a seminary professor. Though overage he had entered the army with Cardinal Spellman's blessing when his brother Ned was killed at the Battle of the Bulge. It was an impulse born of grief and patriotism and also of guilt at his exemption, but he never served with a combat unit during World War Two. Perhaps that's why he felt obliged to stay in even when the war ended. After two tours at stateside VA hospitals he'd hated to admit it but he welcomed this new war, and he'd had Spellman pull strings for his assignment to the 27th Infantry in Korea.

Father O'Shea wanted to be with lads in their extremity, the way he hoped someone had been with Ned in his. He wasn't prepared to find that at the front most GIs ignored him and what the commanders expected of him was help with the USO tours. Still, he had not adopted that ingratiating and implicitly apologetic manner typical of military clergymen, as if they were by virtue of their calling not quite manly enough to keep company with soldiers. Father O'Shea knew what contribution he had to make, even if the men didn't. An army's effectiveness depends most on the ability of its members to believe in the justice of its cause. Since Augustine and Thomas, the Church had considered every implication of each question concerned with that very element of warfare. Once the morality of going to war *(jus ad bellum)* had been established, then participation in war *(jus in bello)* could be encouraged. Once the criteria of the Just War Principle had been met, in other words, it was important that the warriors knew it. Father O'Shea would hold your hand if you wanted, but mostly he wanted to help you think about what you were doing on a bleak spit of land between the Yellow Sea and the Sea of Japan. He wanted to help you do your grim work there as well as possible, and he wanted you to be proud of yourself for doing it. He resented the commanders who required him to arrange the USO events, but in fact he epitomized what they wanted from their chaplains. He was the best goddamn morale officer in Korea.

"God," he said, quoting Emerson's line as a motto, "will not have His work made manifest by cowards."

Most vocations to the priesthood are inspired ultimately by the example of another priest. The priests of Good Shepherd parish in Inwood had a reputation, as a group, for kindness, and the junior curate was widely considered to be terrific with kids, but the parish clergy had made no more overt impression on Michael than they had on me. Priests had certainly been a fixed part of his world — his mother was a volunteer at the rectory — but they were far less central to it than, for example, coaches had been. He was very young when his father was killed, or it might have been different. Until Korea he'd never needed a priest for more than encouragement from the bench at basketball games.

Father O'Shea found him sitting on a campstool outside the quartermaster's tent, futilely trying to warm himself by a small portable kerosine stove. It was late in the afternoon and the crisp blue of the sky was softening. The 3rd Battalion, Maguire's unit, was holding a perimeter position of the makeshift encampment. The regiment, about a thousand men, was dispersed on the four peaks of a hill mass that dominated the main road south. Its mission was to cover the 24th Division's flank while it dug in at Osan. The four hills overlooked the rugged valley that had been cut over eons by the Han, and the regimental patrols were on the alert for signs of enemy activity. Word, though, was that the Chinese had stopped at the river.

What remained of Maguire's platoon had been split up. He, Brown and Pace were assigned to Second Platoon in B-Company, and it was scheduled to go on patrol at dusk. The other members were sleeping or playing cards in their tents. Maguire wanted the fresh air more than he wanted the rest or the warmth.

"Soldier, how are you doing?"

"Fine, Father." Maguire stood up and saluted, but it was clear from the priest's abbreviated return that he needn't have. Father O'Shea's bearing was lackadaisical. Not even his imposing uniform — the helmet with its white cross, the silver cross on his lapels, the major's gold leaves on his shoulders — overcame his air of informality. He pulled up another canvas stool and sat. He extended his gloved hand toward the stove.

Maguire stood awkwardly over him.

"Take your stool, soldier."

"Yes, sir." He sat.

"Cut the 'sir' crap with me, son. You're an Irish lad who ought to know better."

"Sorry, Father." Michael grinned. It came as a strange relief that this priest rejected martial despotism in favor of ecclesiastical.

"Where do you come from?"

"New York, New York, Father. Same as you."

"What parish?"

"Good Shepherd."

"Inwood? Is that right? Monsignor Riordan is an old friend of mine."

"Monsignor Riordan baptized me."

"No wonder you're good." The priest slugged Maguire's shoulder. "I hear you've been working on the railroad."

Maguire didn't react. At mess that noon some of the GIs sang the old folk song when he joined the tray-line, an indirect acknowledgment of what he'd done. It had made him uncomfortable.

When Maguire said nothing the priest was silent too for some moments. Then he said, "Lieutenant Barrett told me about it."

"How is he?"

"He needs to be evacuated. They're hoping for a chopper before we have to move."

"Is he . . . ?"

"He'll pull through. He's one tough soldier."

"I know. We'd still be over there if it wasn't for him. They mobbed us."

"I heard."

Maguire looked up sharply. "Did you hear what he did?"

The chaplain nodded.

Maguire wanted suddenly for the priest to say that what the

lieutenant had done, ramming that crowd with the jeep, was all right. But he veered away from that. "How's Jones?"

"He died this morning."

"Oh." Maguire exhaled slowly. It troubled him that he didn't feel more than a vague disappointment at that news. He'd liked Jones, though they'd never talked. He resolved to write his mother. "That's three," he said. "Plus the engineers; how many of them bought it?"

"Four. But Bean's okay. Just a flab-stab. Two other men have wounds that need more attention than they can get out here. Once the chopper comes . . ."

Maguire grunted and forced the mandatory irreverence of tone into his voice. "Tickets home."

"I guess those Chinese just showed up out of nowhere. Nobody thought they'd be in boats. You did damn well to get that bridge. Otherwise they'd be on us now. They could have eaten the whole division for lunch yesterday."

Maguire leaned forward to fiddle with the flame lever. He was grateful to have the chaplain's company, but he didn't feel like talking. That was why he'd left the tent.

Father O'Shea removed his gloves and offered him a cigarette. When they were both smoking he said, "I just wanted to be sure it wasn't bothering you."

Maguire stared at the cinder of his cigarette. "Shouldn't it?"

"It's got to bother a man some, a thing like that, but not so it gets in his way. I wanted to tell you about the principle of double-effect, in case you're interested." He waited for a reaction from Maguire. Emotional numbness was a sign of shock. The lad just worked his cigarette. "Lieutenant Barrett said it was pretty rough."

Maguire nodded.

"In many actions there's the intended good effect and the unintended bad effect. If the intended good effect — say, the blowing up of a strategic bridge — is justifiable, then the unintended bad effect — say, the deaths of civilians — can be considered moral."

Maguire looked directly at the chaplain for the first time. "That's it in a nutshell, eh?"

"You don't seem convinced."

"To tell you the truth, Father, I didn't think about it. Any of it. And I wasn't thinking about it now."

"Just a fighting machine, eh? A burp-gun with legs?"

"Isn't that the point?"

"Hell no! We're Americans, soldier." Father O'Shea instinctively adopted a brisk authority as he spoke now. Nothing irked him more than the kill-and-masturbate mentality of drill instructors, as if that was all soldiering was. He was "one of the guys" until a moment like this, but now he was an oracle. His authority was what rescued men from their confusion. "Americans, you hear me? We *think* about what we do. We know right from wrong and we stake our lives on the difference. Goddamnit, we bury men in the difference. That's what this war is all about. You want to be a burp-gun with legs, you join the other side. You want to be responsible for your actions, make humane decisions even in the heat of battle, always looking out for your buddies, then stay right where you are."

"I see what you're saying, Father. But I don't think it matters much to the people who got blown up."

"We pray for the dead, son. But we watch out for the living. It sure matters to Lieutenant Barrett. He's damn grateful to you for not leaving him out there."

"I didn't think about that either."

"No blame, no credit, eh?" The chaplain surprised Maguire by grinning at him and putting his hand on his shoulder. "What's your name?"

"Maguire."

"I mean your first name, son."

"Michael."

"The Archangel. The leader of God's army against Lucifer."

Maguire laughed.

"Monsignor Riordan christened you with that name? He'll be damn proud when I tell him what you did. And when he tells your folks, imagine how they'll feel."

Michael didn't say that his father was dead. The thought of that unknown ghost filled him, for a change, with calm. He'd scored every basket and lined every outside pitch and caught every buttonhook of his life with one eye on the man who wasn't there, and in our own small world where the legend of his hero father loomed we all knew it. "Go, Michael! Go!" we would cry from the stands as he led our teams to victory, but everyone knew that Michael drove so hard not because of our support but because of his father's absence. How could he earn that long-gone love? That was the void into which O'Shea stepped with his simple affirmation. For the first time in his life, Michael felt his father's presence.

When the priest stood up Maguire asked, "Hey, did you just give me absolution or something?"

"Maybe I did, Michael." The priest muttered a quick blessing and waved his hand over him. And then he reached inside his field jacket and pulled out what Maguire assumed was a pack of cigarettes. Weren't chaplains always giving out cigarettes to people? But it was a book with blue covers, small enough to close inside one hand. The chaplain handed it to him. "Here," he said. "This was my brother's. He was killed at the Battle of the Bulge. I'd like you to have it."

Instinctively Michael removed his gloves. It was the New Testament. He looked up at the priest. Years later, in describing this moment he would take refuge from its emotion in a Woody Allen line: I always carry a bullet in my shirt pocket in case someone throws a Bible at me. But at the time he was too moved to speak. The relief he felt came as a shock because he'd had no explicit idea how distressed he'd been. The priest had soothed the orphan-pain in him that was far older than a day. What had happened on the bridge had only uncovered it, and now, with this gift evoking so much — the New Testament, a dead brother, the Battle of the Bulge — he experienced a sense of embrace he'd never felt before. And at last he understood — how he needed this! — why we call them "Father."

That midnight an artillery bombardment began that veterans said was as bad as anything the Germans had ever thrown at the Allies in France. The Americans were pinned by the fire and even the patrols had to stay in their ditches. The frozen earth had resisted their efforts to dig out proper foxholes, but now the men wished they'd stayed with it. The ground on which they flattened themselves reverberated continually as it registered every shell that exploded on those hills. Some soldiers made fists of themselves in their shallow holes. Chunks of dirt and stone-chippings bounced off them endlessly. The noise of the heavy-caliber explosions coming after the piercing approach-whistles was so loud that their ears hurt, and they took to blocking them with the heels of their hands while their fingers pressed the cold metal rims of their helmets. Periodically, even through their gloves, they had to warm their hands, though, by stuffing them into their armpits. But quickly the noise of the bombardment was a worse pain again than frozen fingers. Now and then even that din was surpassed by the shrieking of a man who was hit. It was dangerous to look, for the popping of debris and shrapnel was constant.

It didn't take an Omar Bradley to deduce that the Chinese were advancing across the river valley during the barrage. Every man in the regiment knew that. But the bombardment went on so long — nonstop, all night — that they began to understand its purpose was not merely to cover that advance or even to neutralize their ability through shock, fear and disorientation to resist it when it reached them. The purpose of the aimed fire was to kill them.

The 27th Regiment was under orders to hold its ground, but only long enough to delay the onslaught. The American stand wasn't going to be made in the hills around Suwon, but at Osan. The regiment therefore was to withdraw before actually engaging the Chinese, and it was to link up with the main body of forces twenty miles to the south. But an orderly withdrawal was out of the question until the artillery fire stopped. Even panicked flight would have been impossible. And the artillery fire wasn't going to stop until the Chinese were ready to attack. By then what would anyone be able to do but run?

The terror of that night unhinged more than one man. Lennie Pace was crouched next to Maguire in the same ditch, and when a round landed close enough to singe their clothing, he tried to get out. Maguire and another GI grabbed him just as he was scrambling over the lip of the hole. "Let me go, you fuckers! Let me go!" Because of his size and toughness Pace threw the second soldier aside effortlessly. Maguire slugged him, but the punch seemed only to quicken his belligerence. Pace began to pummel Maguire, but Maguire clung to him. Pace tried to get away and he dragged Maguire with him. "You fucker!" he screamed. "I'll kill you!" Maguire held on until Pace fell into the fresh crater of a 175. It was still warm, but it was deeper and more secure than the ditches the men had dug, which were like shallow graves.

Even in the crater the hysterical soldier continued to slug away. Maguire covered his face and let Pace hit him. Most of the blows were lost in his heavy clothing or against his helmet. Eventually the Italian kid collapsed on top of Maguire. He was weeping. Maguire made no effort to get out from under him, but only closed his arms around Pace and held him. At first he envied him the catharsis, but then he realized that he'd shared it. They both felt purged. The terror of that night, Maguire saw, would be a bond forever.

In the release, the evaporation of tension that followed Pace's outburst, both men settled into a kind of sleep. One hears it said that such a drifting off is not uncommon during prolonged sieges. The psyche has its ways of escape even when the body doesn't. Some Londoners never slept well again after the Blitz ended, but during it, even in the rank discomfort of sewer tunnels, they slept like children. Neither the noise nor the cold, extreme as both were, penetrated the consciousness of either soldier for several hours.

Maguire woke first and he was amazed to realize he had slept. He actually felt a kind of refreshment. The artillery fire was still on, merciless as ever, but he wasn't cold. Pace was still on him, like a blanket. He was snoring lightly.

Maguire didn't move. Beyond Pace's collar, like a dream, he saw the morning star, Venus, hanging in the east above the notch in the hills where the sun would rise soon. Automatically Maguire's hand went to his breast pocket, to touch Father O'Shea's New Testament, as if it was going to save him or already had.

On the roof of his apartment house on Cooper Street, Michael and I had slept out through countless summer nights, though not in each other's arms. Imagine the cries resounding through Inwood of "Fairies! You fucking fairies!" It would have been disgrace enough to have it known that we called the roof our "lone prairie" and pretended that the straining barrel-staved water tank was our Conestoga wagon. When Venus appeared — it was the last star to fade because of course it wasn't really a star but a planet which reflected the coming sun's light instead of getting washed out by it — he always woke up and nudged me. We New York City boys did not take our heavenly bodies for granted. In our pale night sky only the luminaries shone because the dispersed light of the city screened all the ordinary stars and planets out. New York was that way with people too, although we didn't know it yet. Shining in that firmament meant, fortunately, as we would learn much later and separately, either burning to extinction or reflecting the light of some other star.

Venus seemed closer than ever that morning in Korea, and even though the barrage was still on, it seemed to Michael he had already survived it. His lucky star. The night was almost over. And what better omen for the day than the worn little book in his pocket.

The good book. The Bible. The glad tidings of Jesus Christ. Michael was no more religious than any of us, but like us he'd gone to religion class, however automatically, every day of his school life for twelve years. He'd heard the Scriptures read every Sunday and most first Fridays for eighteen. Surely he could remember some proverb, some parable, some saying of Jesus that would help him now.

He squinted at the morning star and a line popped open in his mind like the "Bang" on the flag out of a fake pistol. "He was the light of men, a light that shines in the dark, a light that darkness could not overpower." He had read those words a million times while the priest recited them in Latin; they were from the Last Gospel with which every Mass ended. "A man came, sent by God."

Michael told me over Scotch whiskey many years later that at that moment, half frozen, paralyzed under the weight of a shell-shocked soldier in a bomb crater on a desolate hilltop in Korea, he discovered for the first time that he did believe in God. He believed in the Resurrection. "What can I say? I saw His glory." He shrugged and drained his Scotch. "With Him on my side, who can be against me?" In other words, while fifteen thousand Chinese were steadily creeping toward him and his one thousand terrified frozen comrades, Michael Maguire accepted in advance whatever was going to happen to him, not only, as pious assholes were always doing, during the remainder of his life, but — much more difficult — during that very day. It was as if he knew how decisive it would be. I would wish many years later that he'd been killed.

The withdrawal began at dawn. Because artillery shells were still falling, though intermittently now, it was a retreat through a nightmare landscape, but the men of the 27th Infantry Regiment were so relieved to have their dreamless terror over that they pushed out energetically. Who wanted to wait for the Chinese charge?

It was impossible to assemble a proper convoy. The regiment's vehicles, marshaled along the main road, had been sitting ducks all night and the artillery had knocked most of them out. That meant forced march, which posed a heart-wrenching problem for the colonel in command: the wounded would have to be left behind. As of dawn, counting the casualties of the night shelling and those from the incident at the bridge two days before, there were fourteen of them. Two Medevac choppers had been promised the day before, but they couldn't come in during the heaviest bombardment. Though now it had eased, there was still no sign of them. It made no sense to leave behind a unit of healthy soldiers to defend the wounded until the helicopters arrived, because each aircraft could carry out only seven men. The fourteen, plus the medic, was stretching it already, and when the chaplain volunteered to stay behind, the colonel could not refuse. He said, "Take off your insignia, Father, and make sure Lieutenant Barrett isn't wearing his bars either."

Father O'Shea wasn't stupid. He wasn't going to fall into Chinese hands with gold leafs on his lapels. But he kept his crosses, on his helmet and his breast.

Word passed through the regiment quickly both that the wounded were being left behind and that the chaplain was staying with them. When Maguire heard it, he was just tying the flaps of the radio case that he and Pace had been assigned to carry. He looked up at the GI who'd told him, but he was gone already, scurrying down the side of the hill. He looked at Pace. "We can't just leave them here!"

"What the fuck, Maguire! What can we do?"

Maguire snatched up his M-1 and climbed quickly to the top of the hill. The wounded men were huddled on a level spot near the top of the next hill. Even without binoculars he could see Father O'Shea holding a man in his arms. They knew what was happening. Maguire searched the sky above the windswept hills, looking for the choppers. No sign of them. In the distance of the valley below, the figures of men jammed the roads, but these were not refugees. It was the massing army of the Chinese peasant-riflemen. He scanned the spiny terrain of the nearby slopes, but there was no sign of the enemy there yet.

A round landed in the gully between the hill on which he stood and the one where the wounded lay. Maguire didn't flinch. After the night, the occasional shell now seemed benign. He squinted, trying to make out Lieutenant Barrett.

Pace was at his elbow. "Sarge says to move it, Mac!"

Maguire looked at Pace. "How can we just leave them?"

"Fast! That's how! Come on, Goddamnit!" Pace's agitation was intense. He'd survived the night, but it had left him manic and insecure. He'd clung to Maguire's side since they crawled out of the crater. He was terrified of being alone, but he was also terrified of being left behind. Their company had been detailed to take up the rear, but most of it had moved out already. He and Maguire were the last ones left except for the lieutenant, the sergeant and the radio operator. Their job was to get the radio gear down to the jeep waiting on the road. It was one of the few vehicles still running, and Pace hoped to get on it. "Come on, you shit!" His voice cracked with panic.

But Maguire said suddenly, "What's that moving? Do you see that? Is something moving there?" He pointed to the lower slope of the opposite hill.

The urgency in his voice cut through Pace's agitation and he too fixed his stare on the brush and boulders across the way. Bushes were moving and he saw it too. Both men stared, motionless, not breathing. Bushes were moving up the hill, toward the party of wounded.

"Fuck!" Pace said, "It's them!"

The Chinese had brush fixed to their helmets and their backs, and they were steadily creeping up the hillside.

Pace whispered, "I thought they charged, whistling, screaming, banging cymbals and throwing grenades."

"Maybe they're just the advance patrol. I don't think there are that many of them." Maguire threw the bolt on his rifle.

"Hey, man, come on! Let's go!" Pace started to back off. He was eyeing Maguire as if he'd lost his mind.

Maguire raised his arm and pointed to a spot in the sky above the farthest ridge. "Look, Whirlybird!" He felt a rush of happiness, as if the helicopter was coming for him. But the rescue wasn't going to succeed, he saw suddenly. The Chinese patrol was closing on the hilltop. They'd drive the chopper off or down it. Locks snapped open in Maguire's mind, and he saw what had to happen. There was no experience of decision, only of insight; his response seemed no more the product of choice than a sunrise is. The second helicopter appeared as a dot moving behind but in sync with the first. "Lennie!" Pace was already fifty yards down the hill, clambering backward. "Lennie!" Maguire went after him. He caught up to him easily and grabbed him. "Lennie, we've got to slow them down! We've got to give our guys some time!"

"No, Maguire! Let me go!"

"I can't do it without you, Lennie!"

"Fuck you, man. I'm gone. Get your hands off me or I'll tear your fucking eyes out!"

Maguire released Pace roughly. "You chickenshit!"

Pace whined abruptly. "Don't call me that." Suddenly he looked like the adolescent he was, at the mercy less of his fright now than of his buddy's contempt.

Maguire turned and started up the hill.

Pace called him and Maguire stopped.

"You think we can help?"

"We can get them five minutes maybe. It might be enough. But we have to make the Reds think there's a bunch of us at them. That's why I need you."

Pace caught up with Maguire. "Okay. Okay. But don't let the fuckers kill me, will you?"

Maguire smiled. "No, I won't." He said this soberly, as if he meant it, as if it was his to mean. "You got a grenade?"

"Yeh. A deuce."

"Me too. We have to get close enough to throw them. Then we pin them down with rifles, get it? You take the left flank through that crevice. I'll slip across here. Keep an eye on me. Don't do anything until I do."

"Not too close, okay?"

"Just watch the bushes, Lennie." Maguire slapped his friend's shoulder. "We can do it. Those wounded guys would do it for us." He felt responsible for the boy suddenly, Maguire's first experience of that sensation, and it seemed to him that his affection for Pace at that moment was strong enough to protect him.

As they set off Maguire had to stifle a whoop, as if they were boys at play. His flash of exhilaration did not cancel his anxiety but matched it. He was operating on instinct, like a natural driving for the basket. He didn't know from one instant to the next what the moves would be, but he was in such perfect control of himself that even Pace, sensing Maguire's innate competence, was able to come back from the edge of panic.

They were crouched low, descending the slope easily, each with his rifle and his pair of grenades slapping against his field jacket. The morning light was bright already, but the sun was not above the hills yet and a broad shadow stretched across the ravine that separated the two hilltops. Pace followed the contour line toward an outcropping of rock that would give him shelter, while Maguire plunged directly across the undulations of the rough terrain. When he reached a thatch of waist-high brush in the crease of the gully, he stopped and hid. He could count the Chinese, even in their crude camouflage — more than twenty — but he could no longer see the plateau where the wounded GIs lay. He couldn't see the helicopters either, but he could hear them approaching from beyond the hilltop. All at once he felt he'd made a terrible mistake. He'd surrendered his position on high ground and now was below the enemy. They had every advantage. But the high ground hadn't been in rifle range. He caught Pace's eye and waved him on. Pace's reluctance to leave his cover was obvious, but Maguire stared at him until he set out again. They angled up the hill behind the Chinese as the yapping sounds of the choppers grew louder. The Chinese heard the helicopters too, of course, and, obviously hoping to snare one or both of them, they began climbing toward the pinnacle with abandon, no longer creeping stealthily or taking care to crouch. Instead of slaughtering a few wounded, their glory could be the destruction of the dreaded American machines.

Maguire and Pace threw their grenades within seconds of each other. The explosions, coming out of nowhere and without the prelude of the artillery whine, stunned the rearmost Chinese, as if the earth itself had burst against them. The two Americans threw again, and by the time that second pair of grenades exploded, every Red on the hill had stopped. They never expected the enemy from behind.

The grenades killed or wounded a handful and the nearest

Chinese took cover. Only those approaching the crest of the hill resumed running and, silhouetted against the sky, they were the ones Maguire and Pace chose as targets. The GIs were riflemen. This was what they'd trained to do, and they concentrated on lining up their sights and squeezing their triggers. They fired successive volleys, and the frontline Chinese began to fall.

A cloud of dust spilled over the ridge; the choppers were landing.

The Chinese patrol was under cover now, and some of its members had begun to fire back at Maguire and Pace, but against the shadow of the valley they presented obscure targets. Nevertheless Maguire fell prone behind a mound of dirt. He replaced the magazine of his carbine and pressed off several quick rounds. When he looked over at Pace it was like seeing a man about to walk off a cliff. Pace was still standing bolt upright and shooting his weapon efficiently, aiming carefully each time he pulled the trigger, as if he were on the firing range. Maguire wanted to yell "Get down!" but Pace wouldn't have heard him. Maguire resumed firing too; it was all he could do. Had Pace snapped? Or was it only his determination to show Maguire that he was not chickenshit? Maguire knew already that the big lunk was going to be hit, and that filled him with nausea and with guilt.

Like an apparition in a cloud the first chopper appeared above the lip of the ridge, lifting off unsteadily in a great roar, but instead of gaining altitude it jerked down along the curve of the hill toward Maguire. The second helicopter swooped up and immediately away.

Now the Chinese all over the hill began firing at the chopper instead of at Maguire and Pace, but the wash from the rotors kicked up a screen of dirt, and the peasant-riflemen were too agitated to fire accurately.

At first Maguire thought the helicopter, erratically dropping toward him from the hilltop, had been hit and was about to crash. But then he realized that its jerkiness was evasion, and that it was coming down to snatch Pace and him up.

Pace was still lost in another time. He had not been hit, though he continued to stand exposed, like a statue. But he was pressing off shot after shot. Maguire took his cue from him. All over the hill the Chinese too were upright, in the open, firing madly in the air, trying to bring down that helicopter. Pace and Maguire picked off one after the other of them. By now more than twenty Reds had been shot and still the brown hill was dotted with them. Maguire's estimate had been off by dozens.

The helicopter swerved and bounced in midair, as if it were being swung on a cable. A soldier was in the open door braced against the hatch frame, clinging with one hand to the lurching machine and, with the other, firing an automatic pistol down at the Chinese.

The chopper dropped dangerously and then hovered right above Pace. Pace reacted to it with shock, as if he'd just awakened. The noise and dust were infernal. Only an act of mind made it possible to see the thing as a rescuer, not monster. The skid-railing was just above his head and he could have grabbed it, but at that moment his back snapped in a sharp arc as he took a bullet. His body jerked again as it took another.

Maguire ran to him.

Unbelievably, gallantly, the helicopter waited.

Pace collapsed in Maguire's arms. That was it.

Maguire looked helplessly up at the man straddling the doorway. Wind tore at him. He was bareheaded and half-bald, naked without his helmet. Perhaps that was why Maguire had not recognized him. He was frantically gesturing with his pistol for Maguire to grab the skid. Only yards separated them.

Maguire's mind slowed down. Why didn't the man in the chopper jump down and help him save Pace? But that was impossible. Still he stared pleadingly up at him. Don't leave us here! He focused on the soldier's breast insignia off which light glanced. The silver cross. The man who'd been firing from the doorway was Father O'Shea.

The irony that his violation — his violence — should have so embodied his dedication stunned Michael. This priest would kill for me!

Michael shook his head and waved them off.

O'Shea was screaming at him, having dropped the gun and cupped his hands around his mouth, as the helicopter began to ascend. In the noise it was impossible to hear what he was saying, but then O'Shea, priest again, blessed him. Absolution. For an instant Maguire's eyes and the priest's met.

Michael told me years later that he felt in Father O'Shea's look an absolute affirmation, what he'd come to call, with Rogers, an unconditional positive regard. Michael might have called it by its other name — love — but his history with Father O'Shea was complicated by then. At that moment, though, he experienced the priest's gaze as if it were his dead father's or God's. The transcendence of that sensation, more than the violence around him, made him certain that he was about to die.

The helicopter swooped away, leaving behind in the relative silence only the popping of the Chinese guns.

Even that fell off to nothing as the last echo of the chopper engine faded.

Maguire listened and listened, but to Pace, not the enemy as it closed on him. He pressed the Italian kid against his own breast, the way he had that baby at the bridge, that rabbit in basic. He listened and listened.

He could have sworn he heard Pace speak: "You said you wouldn't let them kill me and I believed you."

But Pace was silence itself.

When his captors jerked Pace's body out of Maguire's arms, he saw a red mark on Pace's face, the impress of Maguire's own dog tag. He had crushed his buddy's face against it, stamping on the poor bastard's forehead for all eternity the negative of the ID number, rank, name, blood type and religious preference of the man who had led him to his death.

When the interrogators asked him their questions over the next thirty-three months, he answered as if he were reading from above the left eye of Lennie Pace: "Private First Class Michael Maguire, U.S. Army 73822094, O-positive, Catholic."

FIVE

THE Korean war could have saved us.

Forgive me that fustian pronouncement. The Korean war could have saved us? Saved us from precisely what, pray tell? What a wad of fibrous padding for cracks in the mind that statement is! Indeed. And I apologize. Unfortunately the statement is also true. If we'd learned from it, Korea could have saved us from the moral and political suicide we committed in Vietnam. Will future generations remotely understand what led America to squander her glory, wealth, moral position and the cream of her youth on distant conflicts of no true international significance, and to do so not once but twice? It is stunning to realize that a mere decade separated the ignominious end of the conflict in Korea and the launching of the doomed American effort in Vietnam. Were we asleep all that time?

In a way, yes. My friends and I, like the entire budding intelligentsia, were spellbound by the hocus-pocus of Cold War bombast. We believed that the transcendent political event of the era was the discovery that our leaders had "lost" China. Imagine. Congressmen, senators, diplomats, generals and presidents were regarded as having lost a nation of five hundred million people. As if it were a parking stub. Which of them, after that, would willingly be perceived as participating in the "losing" of anything else? Even Indochina, wherever that was? The nations of the world were like a hoard of marbles. For twenty-five years every president, military man and senior civilian to grace a table in Georgetown had his aggies to protect, his steelies, his walleyes, and his balls.

Now balls we understand about. We males are required, whether by nature or culture, to establish for ourselves and others that we have them. Rites of passage, journeys through the dark forest, Sacraments of Confirmation, Bar Mitzvahs, Eagle Scout ceremonies, fraternity hazing, panty raids, beerblasts — showcases all for two things. Balls. But it isn't enough to demonstrate potency, virility, once, at the beginning of one's manhood. Most of us have to do it again and again. Having established that we have balls, we have to regularly prove that we haven't "lost" them. Like we lost our parking stub or China or the war in Korea.

Unfortunately, by definition, the circumstances in which we must establish such a thing are rarely subject to our control. A bully shoves us in the corridor. A stranger asks our girl to dance. An army crosses a parallel of latitude. The process that ensues — ballbusting — is irrational and often degrading of others, humiliating for oneself and implicitly — here is the irony — emasculating. Like Korea was. Like Vietnam was. Like the behavior of boys on the prowl almost always is. But I am ahead of myself.

What I knew about balls in the autumn of 1953 was that Michael Maguire had them. Jesus, did he have them! He was a goddamn war hero, a repatriated POW, still tall, more erect than ever, as if he'd survived by holding himself rigidly at attention. His picture was in the papers and he was one of a group interviewed on television by Edward R. Murrow. Murrow had approved the Korean war and introduced his guests that night as "young men who had drawn a line not across a peninsula, but across the world."

Michael was thinner than he'd ever been, but not malnourished. He was gaunt, but like an ascetic poet. He had the lean visage everyone wanted in Greenwich Village. My friends there regarded the experience of the veterans as cavalierly as they regarded their own. I knew better. In the Village all experience was artifice, at the service of impressions to be made, whether on oneself — the Beats — or on others — the College Joes, of whom I was one. But men who'd been at war, men who'd seen violence and awful death at first hand, men who'd killed other men, nobly — these were creatures set apart, young gods to me. And none more so than Michael.

Having distinguished himself in combat he had then withstood pressures of what a phrase of the day tagged the "Red Hell." Unlike others he had not compromised himself before his captors. Only on his return did he learn that he had been, while imprisoned, promoted to sergeant and awarded for actions taken at the Han River bridge the Silver Star, and for actions taken in the hills outside Suwon the Distinguished Service Cross. For conduct while in prison he was awarded the Legion of Merit and two Presidential Unit Citations. He received this news as one chastened. I remember that on the Murrow show, in contrast to his comrades, he displayed a lively graciousness toward the Chinese and generosity toward the Americans whom imprisonment broke. When Murrow asked how he survived the brainwashing he replied that though he was interrogated regularly he was never tortured, and that his impression was that attempts to brainwash footsoldiers like himself were rare. He said that airmen and officers who resisted were the ones who deserved respect because they were the ones the Chinese singled out. When Murrow pressed him, he allowed that he did depend for solace on his Catholic faith and, yes, he supposed that POWs with strongly held beliefs might have had some advantage. Far from torturing him, he said, his captors had permitted him to keep the one possession that mattered to him, a small copy of the New Testament. Murrow asked him to hold it up for the TV audience, but Michael politely refused.

Michael Maguire was one of those celebrated in news stories and sermons as proof that Americans, even in that imbecile defeat, had conducted themselves with virtue and manliness. If we hadn't beaten Communism, we'd stood up to it. We'd contained it. Maguire and his kind enabled us to believe that we were still good guys with balls.

I was more awed by his status than anyone, more admiring, more moved to have him back. Yet weeks went by and I didn't see him. I rarely visited Cooper Street anymore since I'd moved to the Village and my parents had moved to Queens. But it wasn't just a question of not having run into him. How does one presume to kick the can with young Hector? How does one bridge the gulf between the infinitely mundane experience of a mere student — even one in the throes of Village liberation — and that of a returned warrior, a champion, a hero? We were both twenty-one years old, but he was an archetype of manhood. I was an Honors senior in Modern Literature and had the swagger for it.

Literature, after all, more than the life of license in Greenwich Village, had rescued me from the cramped sullenness of Inwood. My world had come to seem huge, bright and full of language, language even the great Michael Maguire could not have appreciated in its subtleties. But suddenly I wasn't sure. Who had left whom behind? I ruthlessly compared myself to my old chum and became to myself more a kid than ever. I "had gone back and forth all night on the ferry" with my Millay, but what was that? Michael had confronted the Waste Land itself, and "had bred lilacs" out of it. I assumed really that I would never see him again, except from a distance. The war — my exemption from it as much as his achievement in it — had changed, or so I thought, the very ontology of our relationship, as if one of us had been ordained or canonized or had undergone, as Christine Jorgensen soon would, a sex-change operation. What would he say to me? What would he think? His years in prison, his terrible time in combat — what a rebuke each reference to his experience was to me. When I'd heard that he was captured, I'd known at once that he and I would never have the most important things in common again.

During the long hiatus of the Panmunjom negotiations — they lasted two years, even while operations named Wolfhound, Thunderbolt, Round-up, Ratkiller, Ripper, Rugged and Piledriver failed at places named Bloody Ridge and Heartbreak — I thought of him continually. But would he believe that? When the prisoners came home, college boys felt more guilt than joy. Wouldn't Michael think I did too? I'd been gloriously freed from Inwood, that *parochia* we'd ruled together as boys, and had made a place for myself in the downtown world toward which we'd looked with longing. Michael had dreamed of college and digs in the Village too, a life of ideas, literature, liquor and sex. I'd plunged far enough into each to say I'd been there, and also enough to know the dream of such things can never be surpassed. But would Michael look at me now and see if not a hedonist and a coward, a frivolous aesthete? Would he see a weakling of the sort who went berserk in foxholes or who signed confessions in Chinese prisons? Later when I confided these insecurities of mine to Michael he laughed, though not cruelly. We were chums, he said, and would be always. Differences between us? Don't be a dope, Durkin! He didn't deny the differences but he dismissed them and therefore so did I. Now I see that perhaps we were wrong to. Michael Maguire was an anointed man. I would never be. We knew it then, but ducked. What we regarded later as the true beginning of our friendship was, after all, the beginning of the end of it.

Even before the sun was up that Sunday morning I was on the uptown A-train, headed for Good Shepherd and the 7:15 Mass. I hadn't been to church in a year, but this was a way to see Michael and perhaps, finally, talk to him. He was to be the main speaker at the annual Father and Son Communion Breakfast. Looking back on it, even given the insecurities I've described, it seems a curious choice of circumstances for our reunion, even if I'd wanted to make it seem a reunion of chance. Was I moved by an impulse I've forgotten? Did I in fact want to pray? The likelier explanation is that I wanted, first, to see him at remove, to see him before he saw me, to see him on the turf we'd had in common. We'd been altar boys together in that church and we'd roamed the parish hall as if we were proprietors of the place during bazaars and bingo and bake sales and talent shows and a dozen previous communion breakfasts. The first time either of us was made giddy by drink had been inside the huge sacristy closet where the deadly sweet altar wine was stored. The cheap but blessed sauterne was like cough medicine and we loved it.

The A-train clicked along like the Ellington tune, snaking under midtown, Central Park, Harlem, and Upper Broadway. There were few other passengers at that hour and so I found myself looking unselfconsciously into the black mirror of the windows. I worried that Michael would see what I saw. When the train periodically pulled into stations my eye was drawn to the bright posters and billboards on which were portrayed ruby-lipped women in calf-length skirts and pipe-smoking men in absurdly creased fedoras. It was a Sunday in December and there were scenes of couples under mistletoe and families at Christmas dinner which only heightened my sweet melancholy. A boy like me believed more firmly than he believed in God that he couldn't go home again.

At NYU I was regarded as something of a dazzler, I don't know why. I lived alone in a dark room below ground on Horatio Street, and in looking back it seems to me I spent an eternity at my table writing poems, whole afternoons walking the city alone or seeing Russian films in dingy movie houses. But I mustn't have been the recluse I fancied myself. In my junior year I was elected editor of the literary magazine and chairman of the Cellar Theater, a campus coffeehouse where we smoked and read our poems to one another. In public I was extroverted and humorous. I hit it off with the brightest of my classmates, and by my last year I found myself at the center of a lively intellectual crowd, mostly Jews, on whom the exotic airs of Bohemia seemed utterly natural. We gathered at night at the Cedar Tavern on University Place where we imagined ourselves hobnobbing with Jackson Pollock, Mark Rothko and their disciples. As would-be writers we fairly basked in the sporadic presence of Dwight MacDonald, Norman Mailer, Philip Rahv, Mary McCarthy, Delmore Schwartz and the old *Partisan Review* crowd. I had friends who insisted my poems were as good as anything that magazine was publishing and they were always threatening to go over to Rahv's table on my behalf. What a mortification it would have been. I could never bring myself to tell them how many times that magazine and a dozen others had already rejected my work. My fellow undergraduates thought of me as one of the two or three among them with *real* promise. I let them. I suspected the truth, however, that my flare for poesy would not outlast my adolescence. I would be a teacher like the rest of them.

My oh so worldly fellow students would not have recognized me by the feelings I was having on my way to Good Shepherd. The closer I came to the Irish neighborhood in which I'd been raised, the more inhibited I felt. By the time I got off at 207th Street and climbed out of the subway I had my overcoat tightly belted, my shoulders hunched against the cold and my head lowered, eyes on the sidewalk, like some bookish introvert come back to attend Mass with his mother.

The sun was up and Broadway, so domesticated there on the far tip of Manhattan, was yawning and stretching like the family collie. Terry Behan the baker who claimed then to be a cousin of Brendan's, but later when the writer was dissolute would deny ever having heard of him, was winding down the awning on his shop window. It was of pink canvas and carried the legend "Baking on Premises." He didn't look at me as I passed him and I did not greet him. I saw the church at the end of the block. But for its size it was an unremarkable structure of gray stone set back from the street by a stunted plaza and above the street by eighteen stairs. Many people were going in for Mass, and most of them were familiar to me. Automatically I took the stairs two at a time as I had done since high school, which was when I discovered that the steps were too shallow for a grown man to take in stride. The steps, I had decided one bold day in my sixteenth year, were made for children and old ladies, like the religion was.

I noticed in fact that the people approaching the church with me seemed mostly to be women, which one would expect at the early Mass. But this was Father-and-Son Sunday. Where were the men and boys? I'd expected to see a dozen of my schoolmates. Did I have the wrong weekend?

Even in my agnostic phase — never atheist; it was a distinction we made much of — I was a sucker for the silence of churches. When I traveled in Europe during graduate school I could never enter a cathedral without matching its hush with a piquant inner one which was like a voice rebutting my sophistication; God whispering, "Oh really?" The compelling atmosphere of the sacred depended in my case at least on certain visceral feelings of guilt, and no place ever evoked those more satisfactorily than Good Shepherd. The guilt I felt that day was so pleasantly familiar it was easy to think of it as an element of the holy. Even the obnoxious bustle of the old women with their satchel-sized purses staking out their favorite pews could not dispel the old *mysterium,* and I welcomed the sensation even as it welcomed me. The silence, the unctuous odor of votive candles, the warped sheen of the linoleum aisles and the hissing of the car-sized radiators touched off such warm feelings of belonging that I could have exclaimed, "Of course you can't go home again, but you can always go back to church!" I thought it was an original insight of mine when I understood that the church's main function is to be there to go back to.

This feeling of poignancy at Good Shepherd was as unexpected as sharp, and it filled me with a sudden sense of loss, not for belief or religion or Catholicism but for the neighborhood, the parish. I regretted not so much my own move away from it, but my parents', because as long as this was theirs it would have been mine. How could they have abandoned Good Shepherd? And for what? Queen of Queens? I resented my parents' move for the first time. So what that at last they had a little bungalow now and their own patch of grass. So what that they finally had a car. Wasn't it their job to keep my past intact so that I could wander through it now and then, nostalgically? It came as a surprise that my parents' choices, their lives really, could still impinge on mine. In the Village we thought parents counted for nothing. The best people, the ones we emulated, had never had them.

But at least the church of Good Shepherd was not like our apartment on Cooper Street. Those five rooms were someone else's now, with new wallpaper in the bathroom and pictures of different snow scenes on the walls. It was a relief that Good Shepherd, with its silence, odor, sheeny floors and hissing pipes was still mine. And if it was still mine after NYU, it always would be. Good Shepherd with its nuns, priests, old ladies, pamphlet racks, banks of red and blue votive lights, holy water fonts, pointed windows and mammoth electric lanterns under which I'd made a point since fourth grade never to sit was indelibly stamped on my soul, like grace. I did not realize until that moment how at sea I'd felt downtown, and how lonely. If I was at my desk too much or at the movies it was because no one I knew down there was an Inwood kid.

Like Michael. No wonder I'd come to see him here. In a park, a tavern or an Automat downtown I'd have been reduced to imitating Edward R. Murrow interviewing him. But here . . . I understood in a flash and for the first time that it was this place that had made us friends. That alone would have made it sacred.

I entered, dipping my hand, blessed myself, genuflected — right knee to left heel — and slid automatically into the corner by the confessionals.

"Msgr. Riordan," a lettered sign said over one, and I shuddered. He'd caught me smoking in the schoolyard and his mere stare had injected me with a terror I still felt five years later. I took up a place by Father Walsh's booth. He was a soft touch. The line of penitants waiting for him on Saturdays could run for an hour after the monsignor had returned to the rectory. You could confess to Father Walsh having been sinfully aroused and he wouldn't ask you if it was with yourself or with others.

I looked from worshipper to worshipper for Michael but didn't see him. He was taller than I was from the age of twelve and so all through high school had sat behind me, so I might not have recognized the back of his head, but there were almost no men or boys in the church anyway. Why weren't they standing in the right rear corner where I was? Even when the pews were three-fourths empty, my father and his cronies always heard Mass from there because at sermon time, but before the priest turned around to face the congregation, they could slip out the side door for a smoke. When my generation stood there it was to arrive late and leave early. But that morning in the last moments before Mass I was alone in the men's corner and it took me a moment to remember why. Holy Name Sunday was the one Sunday on which the male hangers-back joined the congregation. They would be wearing their funeral suits today and, having gathered in the choir room behind the sacristy, they would any minute now be entering the sanctuary in procession ahead of the priest. They would file out onto the laity's side of the communion rail and into the first dozen pews on both sides of the aisle. Even from the back of the church I would know their bright faces. The fathers would be red from the flush of weather, age and drink, and the sons would be red from embarrassment, unnecessarily since no one whose opinion they valued would see them in their obeisance.

Except me, of course.

I was famous among my old friends for having lapsed. In my rare summer forays into Inwood taverns I had, in the drunken company of mates who now worked as apprentices to their fathers in the Irish trades and on the waterfront, sworn with Jefferson upon the altar of God eternal hostility against every form of tyranny over the mind of man. "Including if needs be," I loudly added, "the tyranny of God Himself."

Now what would they make of me, timidly hanging back in my dark corner among the purple draperies of the confessional booths? "Monsignor Riordan." The very name frightened me and I moved away from his confessional again, as if an arm was going to reach out from behind the curtain and grab me. It was the pastor's whisper I'd imagined, not God's; "Oh, really, Mr. Durkin? Eternal hostility?"

A stirring in the sanctuary rescued me.

I focused on the sacristy door. The bell tingled and the pair of acolytes entered. The congregation coughed once and rose. The silent procession of the Holy Name Society began and I held my breath, straining every faculty of perception, not for the monsignor or my father's cronies or my old school chums but one. It was he I wanted, he I was afraid to see.

Two hours later, after the Mass during which I'd wanted only to chat with my solemn neighbors, and the breakfast banquet during which I'd ignored their openings, I was nearly out of patience because I'd yet to make contact of any kind with him. In the shrilly lit cavernous parish hall below the church he was being introduced by Monsignor Riordan. We had eaten our scrambled eggs and toast and now were smoking and sipping coffee, carefully not clinking the cup and saucer. The pastor's legendary ability to unsettle his parishioners was related in part to the rude disproportion of size between his head, which was huge and topped off by a bush of gray hair, and his body, which was slope-shouldered, waistless and too small. Physically he was graceless and disjointed, but he was a cultivated man and an accomplished orator of the Bishop Sheen school. When he spoke, even in conversation, he commanded absolute attention. "And Father O'Shea told me that even at the last moment, Sergeant Maguire could still have saved himself. That helicopter was right above his head. All he had to do was reach up and seize it. They were calling for him to do that. But did he? We know he didn't and we know what he suffered as a result. But why? Why didn't he latch on to that helicopter and hold on to it for dear life, and let it bring him safely home? Well, I'll tell you why. Because he wouldn't leave his brother to the mercy of those atheistic Communists, that's why. Father O'Shea said Sergeant Maguire was holding his mortally wounded comrade the way our Blessed Lady held her dear Son down from the cross. 'A Battlefield Pietà,' he called it. Sergeant Maguire preferred the final comfort of his compatriot to the solace of his own safety. Father O'Shea told me that there were tears in his eyes as that helicopter pulled away — and Father O'Shea, I'll tell you, men, is one tough Irishman — yet there were tears in his eyes as he watched the Reds closing in on Sergeant Maguire and his wounded *amicus*. And Father O'Shea said running through his mind over and over was that great line from Scripture, 'Greater love than this hath no man . . .'

"And do you know what I said to Father O'Shea, men? I said, 'You're damn right. Because he's his father's son and a Good Shepherd boy, and that's how we grow them here.' You know our motto: *Deus et Patria*. We teach our boys to give their all to God and Country, because God and Country have given all to us. Men, I want you all to stand up and welcome home Sergeant Michael Maguire of the United States Army."

We stood and clapped for a long time, and more than one of those men had tears in his eyes as Michael, resplendent in his brown uniform with its simple row of colored bars pinned to its breast, took his place at the podium. He was blushing so fiercely and he was so thin and his hair was so short and he stood so rigidly at attention that he seemed altogether unlike himself. It was my first unobstructed view of him, and I can't for the life of me tell you what I thought. I suspect I was hoping rather desperately that he was not about to say some version of "Aw, shucks, a man just does what he has to do." But also I hoped he wouldn't second the monsignor's saccharine canonization of him. I was not unmoved by the facts of his heroism or by the monsignor's reference to his long-dead father, but there were no tears in my eyes. I was afraid for Michael, having seen for the first time the new peril he had to deal with. Having survived the war as a hero, he had to survive the peace as one.

Finally the audience stopped clapping and sat again. When the last scraping of chairs had faded and quiet had settled over the men and their transfixed sons, Michael began to speak while staring at his hands, which were at rest on the podium. "I guess you're hoping to hear about the war, but I can't tell you much about it because I was only in combat a month."

He looked up and grinned and a few men laughed.

"It ended for me a long time ago." Michael let his eyes drift across the hall and I braced myself, thinking he would see me any minute.

"You probably want to hear about the Chinese prison camp I was in, but to tell you the truth there's not much to say about it. Two and a half years of nothing happening, nothing at all. What can you say about that?" He grinned again, but more awkwardly. He knew the audience expected some momentous statement and he was saying right off that he didn't have one to make.

"But Monsignor Riordan mentioned his good friend Father O'Shea, and I did want to say a word or two about him. Father O'Shea was in that helicopter because *he* had stayed behind with the wounded when it seemed certain the Chinese would take them. What struck me about that, and I think other GIs too, was that it seemed, well, not that surprising that the chaplain would do that. I mean he volunteered and all, and he didn't have to, and any other guy who volunteered to stay behind when the enemy is just down the hill, well we would have just thought he was nuts, you know?"

We laughed hard, all relieved at his lack of pompousness.

"But, well, Father O'Shea was a priest and I guess what I'm trying to say is that when the average Joe does something like that, he gets treated like a hero because the average Joe isn't supposed to stick his neck out. But well, if a guy happens to be a priest, then we change what we expect. A priest stays behind with the wounded and everybody says, Well, of course. He's a priest. That's what he's here for. And I guess that just makes me feel real proud to be a Catholic. I know I felt that way in Korea. See, in the army the Catholic guys feel sort of defensive about the priests, and when they're good ones, we're proud of them. Father O'Shea, well he was the best and everybody knew that. And it didn't matter if you were Jewish or even an atheist. He was with you no matter what you were. Of course if you were Catholic, he was *really* with you."

He stopped while we laughed warmly. Monsignor Riordan was nodding dramatically at his place, feeding the laughter. It faded and Michael resumed, more solemnly. "And I know that if Father O'Shea could have, he would have taken my place on that hill and later in the POW camp. He would have taken my place for any of it. And I'll tell you something, there were a lot of days when I'd have let him."

We laughed again, but quietly. That audience of three hundred plumbers, cops, carpenters and telephone repairmen was beaming at Michael. Eyes glistened everywhere in the hall. Pride, admiration, gratitude filled the spaces above us, like angels. But the sons, teenaged boys mostly, had reason to squirm. Each of them at that moment, by virtue of not being Michael Maguire, was a disappointment to his father.

"People have told me I was pretty special because I was lucky enough to pull through the time in the camp in pretty good shape. It sort of embarrasses me because I know I shouldn't be getting any credit for it." Michael stopped and for an instant he looked right at me, but there wasn't a flicker of recognition in his eyes. Finally he said, "I have to give credit where it's due and that's with God. This is the first talk I agreed to give since I got home. You can probably tell I don't do this much. I didn't do it at all in China."

We liked him needling himself, and were edified by his testimony. This was an audience of devout men, but they had no patience for overt expressions of piety and would tolerate sermons only from the clergy, if that. But this kid had earned the right. They liked him for his reticence. He was still a blue-collar guy and knew it.

"When Monsignor Riordan asked me to talk to you I thought about it and I said I would because Good Shepherd gave me my faith. The monsignor knocked it into me."

Laughs again and coughing, nods all around. Monsignor Riordan had been known to clip altar boys on the ear right in the sanctuary. Once, during Mass, when I gave him a finger towel that was wet he threw it in my face.

"And I figured this would be a good chance for me to thank God sort of publicly, which is something I promised myself I'd do. Or maybe I should say I promised Him. So anyway, that's what I'm doing up here. Not that God needs it particularly, but, well, I do."

And suddenly Michael stopped talking and bowed his head. We realized he was going to pray now, and we all automatically made some shift in posture, uncrossing our legs, scooting to the edge of our chairs, dropping our heads onto our hands so that we wouldn't have to watch. We snuffed out our cigarettes and as always we coughed.

Michael said so softly one had to strain to hear him, "Thank you, Almighty God, for getting me through and for bringing me home." He paused, then for a long moment was utterly still. I looked up at him. He resembled a statue, a GI at prayer. And I realized there was not an ounce of swagger in him, no artfulness or conceit. I don't know that I'd ever had the experience of seeing a person for exactly what he was. He was not a pretender of any sort, and he had come before us to claim nothing. Therefore we'd have given him anything. My anxieties in relation to our reunion dropped away. He was unlike anyone I knew. Straight as an arrow. Square as a die. A profoundly good man. I thought him beautiful.

"And . . . ," he continued softly, ". . . may the souls of the departed rest in peace, amen."

I made the sign of the cross too. Who was I kidding? Agnostic Fosdick! At that moment, because Michael Maguire believed in

God I did. I was only the first of many people to react to him that way.

He looked up at us now, somewhat helplessly. We looked back at him.

Finally, Monsignor Riordan stood up and began to clap, and so did we. But I sensed a reluctance all around me. Applause was off the mark. Not even a standing ovation was what the moment wanted. The young sergeant had touched us all and had made every category we might have applied to him — hero, leader, saint — irrelevant. We just would like to have sat there for a moment longer and looked at him.

Before the applause stopped, Monsignor Riordan shook Michael's hand and smoothly drew him back to his place at the head table. He picked up his napkin and pulled his chair out. He nodded once at the audience, his first acknowledgment of the ovation, and then, only then, he looked directly at me and his eyes held mine, held me. His look made me feel caressed.

SIX

"HE is a tower unleaning," I said to myself, that opening line of John Crowe Ransom's, as I watched Michael greet the others. After the breakfast broke up a reception line had formed spontaneously. The men and their sons waited decorously to shake his hand, but I hung back. How could I possibly have greeted him that way, as if he were a politician I wanted favors from? On the other hand how could I presume to set myself apart? Maybe I was just one of the gang. From Olympus didn't all mortals look alike?

"Good morning, Frank," Monsignor Riordan said, startling me.

"Hello, Monsignor." I shook his hand manfully enough, but he'd set my insides to quivering, as always.

"What do you think of your old friend?"

We both looked across the hall at Michael, who was graciously, patiently saying hello to each man, not with poise exactly, but with an utterly engaging awkwardness that served both to underscore his virtuousness and to put the Society members at ease. "I think he looks good, Monsignor. Real good."

"So do you, all decked out . . ." With a judging glance he took in my double-breasted suit, my starched shirt and tie, my polished wing tips. I had my overcoat over my arm, and my wide-banded felt hat hung at the end of my fingers. Like all college boys of the day I dressed the part of a bank teller or an FBI agent.

". . . We don't see enough of you around here. You shouldn't forget your old friends, Frank."

"I don't get back much, Monsignor."

"I gather that. And you didn't go to Communion either."

I blushed despite myself. In the old days when we all went to Confession on Saturday, if you didn't go to Communion on Sunday, it meant you'd masturbated Saturday night or, if you'd had a date, you'd copped a feel. I remembered our all-purpose if unconvincing cover: "I broke my fast, Monsignor."

He grunted. "How are Mom and Dad? We miss them since they moved to Queens."

"They're fine."

"Your father talking to you yet?"

My father hadn't spoken to me for a year after I'd chosen NYU over Fordham. My objection to the latter wasn't the Jesuits or that it was Catholic, but that it was only across the river from Inwood. It meant I'd have had to live at home, and not even my father's wrath was enough to make me do that. My father eventually softened toward me, but my family would never recover from the wound of our breach. It mortified me that the pastor knew about it. His hostile pressing made me feel deprived of oxygen. "My dad and I get along fine, Monsignor."

"Good. Glad to hear it. I know your mother was brokenhearted."

I forced a smile. "She's fine too."

We laid off each other and let our gazes drift back to Michael. After a moment the monsignor said, "Father O'Shea told me he was simply the bravest soldier anyone had ever seen over there. He saved a lot of lives I guess, but you wouldn't know it from him."

It occurred to me that Michael's greatest achievement was to have forced this bitter old fart to suspend his mordant disdain. I'd never heard him speak admiringly of anyone.

"And Father O'Shea knows what he's talking about. He's the head army chaplain in Germany now." The monsignor looked at me. "A colonel."

"Is that right?"

He stared at the bridge of my nose — for every Michael Maguire there are a thousand bums like you.

The last thing I'd imagined for our reunion was that when Michael and I finally met again our old priest-nemesis would be standing between us, but that is what happened. Michael was crossing toward us. When our eyes locked together I raised my hand to wave at him, but it seemed a wholly stilted gesture. Monsignor Riordan's presence? No, something else.

Now that I was facing my friend at last a new question had popped open in my mind. How would he take it that I'd created a personality around an imitation of him? Michael had always served me as a kind of compass of perception. With him what-was-what had always been obvious, and the things and styles that seemed good to him had by virtue of that seemed wonderful to me. He had been, and I gathered from his talk still was, both funny and solemn. They had seemed the perfect modes to me and I'd consciously tried to duplicate them in my own responses. I did not succeed, of course, but I became what I remain, ironic and pessimistic, the Greenwich Village versions of Michael's attitudes.

The closer Michael came the taller he seemed. He wore his nervousness quite loosely, as a given of the moment, as if awkwardness between us was the most natural thing in the world. He was the first to speak. "Welcome home," he said when he grasped my hand.

I had to smile; the son of a bitch welcoming *me* home! "Thanks," I said feebly.

"It must have been rough," he said. I realized what he was doing, turning all the shit they'd just been giving him on its ear by giving it to me. He was dodging the embarrassment of our reunion by making a joke on the leering Monsignor Riordan. Michael was proposing an improvisation. I caught it instantly, as if I was his drummer, as if this was Birdland.

"It wasn't that bad," I said. "You do what you have to do."

"I guess so. But I doubt if I could have."

"You never know . . ." I matched his grieving tone exactly. We were picking up where we'd left off. ". . . until you're in the situation how you'll react."

"Some men just have what it takes, I guess."

"Though really," I offered modestly, "I can't claim any credit."

"Well, you may not believe this, but . . ." Michael gave me his most meaningful look. ". . . I wish I'd been there with you."

"Where?" Monsignor Riordan asked, bewildered.

It was time to turn the scat around. I answered him, "Korea. I just wish I'd been with Michael, that's all. He has what it takes, Monsignor. Don't you think?"

The old coot blinked at me.

"I appreciate it, Frank," Michael said.

Monsignor Riordan eyed us both, then muttered, "I misunderstood. . . ." He turned and took several steps, then stopped and said to Michael, as if he were a schoolboy after all, "Tell your mother I have some envelopes that need addressing."

"Yes, Monsignor."

We watched the priest leave the hall. He seemed stoop-shouldered and weary, and I felt a twinge of guilt, as if we'd been tossing lit matches at a derelict.

The hall was nearly empty. The Holy Name Society volunteers were noisily clearing the tables. Michael and I stood in awkward silence until I realized that he was waiting for me to speak. It would have been wrong to be sarcastic, but the prank with Monsignor Riordan had been such a relief that I wanted to prolong it. "As I was about to say before I was so rudely interrupted by Kim Il Sung . . ." I grinned cockily, proud to have remembered the North Korean's name. ". . . it's great to see you're back." I slapped his back to underscore the hackneyed pun.

"Did you miss me?" he asked somewhat mockingly, as if to deflect the banality of my welcome the way he had the others.

But I met him head on. "Hell yes, I missed you. What do you think?"

"I think you're a turd," he said.

"Who's a turd?" I punched his shoulder. It was rock hard, and he cocked his fist to punch me back.

He held the pose for a long minute, hooding his eyes like a boxer posing for a photo. Then he straightened up and laughed. "God, we were punks, weren't we?"

"Some of us still are, Mike."

"I thought when I saw you in church, That can't be Durkin! You moved. Even your folks moved. I couldn't believe it when I heard they moved."

"Yes, they live in Queens. I never get up here anymore. I came up today to see you."

"Oh yeah? Not for the plenary indulgence?"

"Well, that too, naturally."

He looked away, as if our needling had run its course and he wasn't sure where that left us. After a moment he said, "How are they?"

"Who?"

"Your mom and dad. Mo."

"They're great. They love it out there. A yard, grass, their own tree, the whole bit. They flipping love it. Mo's in a nice Catholic high school. She calls herself Maureen now. My mother can still walk to Mass every morning and my old man has a clunker of his own. Everything's a dream but me. Me, I've lost my soul."

"Because you live in the Village?"

I shrugged. " 'N.Y.Jew' my father calls it. Famous for its urban campus, its liberal curriculum, its heterogeneous student body, but also for its atheists, Commies, dope fiends and transvestites. Professors stand in line to take whacks at Irish kids, to prove that there is no God but Sartre and Simone is his *savant*."

Michael said nothing. I realized that my blasé references would be lost on him, and I resolved not to show him up. The deprivation of his having not read a book in years only then struck me. The New Testament didn't count. "What about you?" I asked. "You get the GI Bill, right?"

"Rights."

Cracks, I thought. Everything is cracks. "I mean, are you going to use it, or what?"

"I don't know yet."

"When do you get out of the army?"

"I could be out now. My leave is up January first. I have to let them know by then."

"You wouldn't stay in?"

He looked at me sharply. "I wouldn't? Why not?"

I blushed. "Well, you know. Christ! It's the army!"

"And you civilians think the army is shit, right?"

His defensiveness stunned me. "I'm no civilian," I said inanely. I meant that the very notion requires a military point of reference.

"It's one of the things they say, you know. That civilians hate us. After the wars are over they just want soldiers to flush themselves down the toilet."

"You think the Holy Name Society hates you?"

He shrugged, pulled out a pack of Camels and lit one.

"If you did stay in, what would . . . ?"

"I'd apply for OCS. I guess they'd take me."

"You guess? Jesus Christ, of course they'd take you, after what you did."

He flicked the match, as if we were outside, and he said fiercely, "Let's cover that right now, Durk. I didn't do shit! Get it? Not shit! I don't want that what-I-did crap from you!"

"What crap?" I asked helplessly.

Michael's face was inflamed and his mouth had tightened in the way it always had when he was angry. His chin had a way of turning white, even while the skin from his neck up burned. I had a fresh ear now on the pitch of his emotions. He was puffing at his cigarette compulsively and his hand trembled. He was more tightly wired than I'd realized. I chided myself. What did I expect? It wasn't the Adirondacks he'd returned from that fall.

"I'm sorry," he said. "I think I'm on edge. I mean I know I'm on edge. I don't know what I'm going to do."

He stared at me. I remember how starkly I perceived his despair then. It was the despair of youth, the absolute conviction to which only the young are capable of clinging that the pattern of a lifetime is already set, and that never would zest, affection or spontaneity form part of his experience again. "Downward to darkness," is the feeling, "on extended wings." I was as young as he was, of course, and did not recognize the illusion for what it was, having not learned yet that despair overpowers us not once but repeatedly through life. Only in looking back on them are we capable of seeing how little true damage those fits have done us. At that moment, though, I felt only a bleak sweet kinship with Michael; I was as convinced as he was that the joy that had made us friends was irretrievably lost. But no real matter. Our despair would make us friends again.

"Maybe I'll do some coaching," he said after a moment. "Monsignor said I could lend a hand with the CYO league."

"Would they pay you?"

"I'm loaded. I've got two years' back pay piled up. Sergeant's pay."

"Wow. Well, maybe coaching's just the thing. You kept in shape, I guess, huh?"

"How many pushups do you want?"

"How high'd you get?"

"Five hundred."

"Jesus Christ, Mike! Every day?"

He smiled. "Morning, noon and night."

It was as if a bird had taken off from behind a bush by my feet, scaring me, but also giving me my first real inkling of what he'd been through. Fifteen hundred pushups a day? That was something I could understand. I'd never done fifty. All at once I realized that what seemed like strength to everyone else — the quality that pulled him through — was to Michael himself the most acute desperation. And I realized too that his ordeal had not ended. Now instead of Chicoms tormenting him he had us. We were punishing him with our distance from his experience, from the sickness of soul it left him with. The vicious routines required by mere survival had been suspended everywhere but inside him. A vacancy, willfully displayed, had come over him. A hero to the world, I saw at last, but a basket case to himself.

To my horror I found myself using the line he'd used on me in our shtick for the monsignor. "It must have been rough, Mike."

"Where the fuck have you been, Durk? I've been home on leave for weeks."

I had to look away, I was so ashamed. I'd been afraid to face him for fear of what he'd think of me. Yet I hadn't thought of him. It had never occurred to me that Sergeant Michael Maguire, D.S.C., Silver Star, could stand in need of me. "Mike, I'm sorry." I found his eyes. "I should have come up sooner. I was afraid to. You're a fucking war hero, you know. I'm a chump, a saphead."

He laughed. "That's true." He lowered his eyes bashfully. He regretted his outburst.

"But I'm here now. I came all the way up for you, and I want the credit. I even went to fucking Mass."

"Hey, come on."

"Sorry. But I mean I did, you know."

"Aren't you a Catholic anymore, or what?"

"I guess I'm not."

"Jesus!" he exhaled dramatically, as if he'd never met one of us.

I nudged him. "No atheists in foxholes, eh?"

"Do you know who said that?"

"No idea. Robert Service?"

"A priest said it. A priest said it on Bataan, a chaplain name of Father Cummings. You might like to know that he was killed later when the Jap ship carrying him and hundreds of other prisoners from the Philippines to Japan was sunk by an American submarine."

"God."

"Yeah, God. We had our own version in Korea: 'No atheists in foxholes, only assholes. The atheists are in college.' "

"Oh, fuck, Mike. Come on."

"Nothing personal, Durk. Hey, nothing personal."

"You said we civilians hate you, but that isn't it, is it? You hate us."

"Wouldn't you?"

"What, hate the people I was supposed to be defending? I wouldn't think so, no."

" 'A tidy foxhole,' we used to say . . ." He stared at his cigarette. ". . . 'and a tight asshole.' " He looked up at me. "I knew guys who shit their pants." He waited for me to react. When I didn't he said, "Hey, Durk, *I* shit my pants."

"Because you were afraid?"

"No. It was in the camp. I had the runs the whole time. Sometimes it just flowed out of me without my even knowing it, like I was a retard or something. Of course, there's nothing to clean yourself off with and you can't wash your pants. You know what happens? Do you?"

"No, I don't."

"You get used to it. You get used to the smell and to the crud in your pants and to the rash on your butt. And you don't have to be embarrassed because everybody else has shit in his pants too. At first I would pray for a solid bowel movement. I mean, can you believe it? Praying for that, Durk? But then I stopped praying about it because it stopped being important." Michael looked back at the Holy Name members who were stacking dishes onto a stainless-steel cart. "What do you think my fans would say if they knew their hero went around with shit in his pants for two years and nine months?"

"Hey, Mike, everybody shits, you know? Even the pope." As I said this I knew how off the point it was. Michael's caustic reminiscence seemed to fill a profound inner need of his, a declaration of the real, a rejection of the Hollywood fantasy people had of what he'd been through. Shit is real, no doubt about it. No wonder he was troubled: why should an experience of such prolonged and utter degradation have resulted in his glorification?

We were both, I think, aware of the irony that Michael's bitter remarks implicitly invited me into a new intimacy with him. Would I be the person to whom he could confide his experience? His true experience? Already I had some sense of how heroically he was fending off the reduction of his identity *into* heroism, and I saw how a willing friend — one to whom he could be everything but a hero — could help him. But for the life of me I could not think of a way to express my sympathy. Why couldn't I have said, simply, "You can tell me what it was like"? Perhaps because one cannot presume that such secrets as he had could be shared. Did I in fact want to be entrusted with them? If, as I have said, there was an invitation to intimacy in his show of bitterness, it was not enough. We were not ready for each other yet, that's what I felt. Suddenly I wanted to get away from him. I imagined myself saying, "Well, it's been cool. See you around." But that was equally impossible. I was paralyzed, neither here nor there with him.

"Anyway," he said. He dropped his cigarette on the floor. As he ground it out I wondered if it would do damage, but the floor was terrazzo.

He made no move to leave.

Since clearly we'd have each welcomed a way to prolong if not our conversation our time together, neither of us moved to end it. So we stood there stupidly in the corner of the parish hall. A long few moments of awkwardness passed before it was apparent that no one was going to rescue us.

"Want to walk me to the subway?"

"Sure thing," he said with counterfeit enthusiasm.

"You got a coat?"

He smiled. "No. Remember? I'm one tough s.o.b."

We left the hall and took the stairs in stride together. Outside I put my overcoat and hat on, but it didn't seem that cold and I felt citified. Michael didn't even turn his collar up. We walked with a studied casualness down Isham Street toward Broadway and the front entrance of the church. The sidewalk was deserted though the ten o'clock Mass was going on inside. It was that brief period when it was too late to arrive and too soon to leave.

Michael paused, and I thought he was reading the names of the clergy on the sham-Gothic sign nestled among measly shrubs off to the side of the main stairs. But he was staring at the weathered bronze plaque below the sign: a Celtic cross above the inscription "That Those Who Perished Shall Not Have Died in Vain," and then, "Catholic War Veterans, Shamrock Post 120, 1940."

Nineteen forty was the year the subway was completed from midtown Manhattan up to Inwood. The neighborhood celebrated that event, but it shouldn't have. That subway was what enabled my generation to escape.

I wasn't interested in Maguire's mordant preoccupation with the war or the dead. I turned and began to walk down Broadway toward the subway at 207th Street. Michael followed me, but I could sense his reluctance. I did not slow down for him. I passed the bakery, the shoe repair, the baby carriage store, the cavernous entrances to apartment buildings in which dozens of our schoolmates had lived. I passed the Green Acres Bar, the A&P, Connor's Funeral Home and two liquor stores. Not even the makeshift rack of Christmas trees in front of Manning's Fruit Stand stimulated my nostalgia. My earlier affection for the old neighborhood was gone without a trace, replaced by a much more familiar repugnance. I wanted out of Inwood, that cramped, small-minded enclave of dreary apartment houses and drearier people, the women forever pregnant, the men cheered not by home life or by work but only by the morose company of tavern-hounds and by the booze, the children eternally poked, pinched and chastised by mothers and nuns, and the whole throng of them cowed by priests to whom the great enemy was the world south of Dyckman Street where, notoriously, men and women read books and discussed ideas that had never been referred to in the seminary.

By the time Maguire and I reached the corner I knew that if I went down into that subway, leaving him behind, our friendship was over. I was furious at him. What the fuck was he doing back here? This was worse even than Queens! And what was this shit about the CYO, coaching Catholic kids for the monsignor? I faced him. "You know something, Mike, you ought to check out college. You ought to get a load of the Village."

"You love it, I guess, huh?"

"I'm the loneliest bastard you ever saw. If I died in my room tonight, nobody'd find me until the stench got to the landlord. But I'll tell you something, nobody steps on my hand down there." I was certain that he'd remember the time we were both altar boys, serving Monsignor Riordan's Mass. At Communion, the monsignor dropped a Host and it fell onto the floor at my feet, missing completely the gold paten I held beneath the chins of communicants just to catch the invisible crumbs. But this was the whole Host! the Body of Christ! — "Species" we called it, having our own words for such things — and on the cold, unconsecrated linoleum tile, and it was through my fault! Through my fault! Through my most grievous fault! Automatically, instantly, I bent to pick it up. I was going to put it on that golden plate, to save it, to rescue it, like Christopher did the Christ Child from the raging river. Alas, also I was going to touch it, and thereby compound the sacrilege, turn it into blasphemy. And so at the last moment, whump! Monsignor Riordan stomped on my profane hand with his hard black clerical boot.

Michael was staring at his feet.

"Mike, I have the feeling that if we just say goodbye now, then, well . . ." I couldn't finish the sentence. Direct expression on such a thing as the loss of one's oldest friendship was utterly beyond me. I felt an ominous wave of depression riding in.

"Then we've said goodbye," he offered with brutal matter-of-factness.

"Yes."

"And you don't want to do that."

"You do?"

" 'If such things as these are done when the wood is green what will it be like when it is dry?' "

I guessed his statement was biblical, or rather hoped it was, it seemed so weird. I didn't know what to make of it then, but now I see that epigram as the perfect comment on the situation. At twenty-one years of age were we going to behave like a pair of defeated old men whose choices had been worn down to nubs by a long streak of dead years? If we lacked boldness and vitality in our relationships then would we ever have had the qualities of youth? But in fact, then, Michael lacked both. He had been overwhelmed by the death of time itself, and now that he'd dropped the false front of his noble cheer it was obvious to both of us that time had yet to come to life again. The poor bastard had no capacity for the present tense. Later I would understand that, in that passivity and detachment from the here and now, he was like the survivors of many kinds of large trauma. He could have just returned from an icy peak in the Andes where he'd had to eat the flesh of his fellow plane-wreck victims. He could have just returned from a season on a raft at sea or from a year inside the embassy in Teheran. What he'd endured had ended, but it remained still more compelling than the "reality" he'd returned to. Not even familiar old Good Shepherd was real to Michael. Not even — I saw this suddenly — I was.

I punched his shoulder. "Hey, come on, keed. What say? Come downtown with me? We can ride the ferry. I'll read you Edna St. Vincent Millay."

He shook his head. When he looked up there were tears in his eyes. I'd never known him to cry. He said, "I'd like to do something with you, but not that."

"Okay, buddy. Anything you want."

He raised his eyes, as if to heaven. "I want to go up there."

I turned, facing down Broadway. Just beyond Dyckman Street, overshadowing Inwood, was the majestic wooded hill of Fort Tryon Park, and on top of it was the stone tower of the Cloisters, the museum that housed the Rockefeller collection of medieval art in stark monastic splendor.

"It's where I go," he said.

SEVEN

IN Europe Benedictines built their monasteries on mountaintops, and the hill in Fort Tryon Park overlooking the Hudson River was the perfect site for one. The Cloisters, of course, was not a true monastery or even an authentic imitation. It was a fantasy building, an ensemble of Gothic and Romanesque, constructed to display the pillars, doorways, arcades, stairways, frescoes, altars, holy water fonts, stained-glass windows, sculpted figures and tapestries that wealthy and cultivated American Protestants prized so highly in the early part of this century.

By and large the only Catholics who strolled the Cloisters' hallways in the forties and early fifties — the museum opened in 1938 — tended to be the Irish who were employed to do so. Many Inwood men worked there as uniformed guards, including for a time, on Sundays, my father. Despite the fact that the museum was a stunning monument to the aesthetic achievement of Catholic culture, the Catholics of Inwood knew better than to consider it theirs. What were a bunch of moth-eaten old wall hangings or limestone statues with smashed faces anyway? Everyone knew that what counted in monasteries and convents were the monks and nuns and their spiritual works of mercy. And as for religious art, my people liked their statues painted and their crucifixes in good repair. The Cloisters seemed a peculiar, empty, haunted place to the parishioners of Good Shepherd, and they were content to ignore it.

Beginning in the mid-fifties the Cloisters would, however, enjoy a vogue among a new type of Catholic, that first sizable generation of intellectuals and aesthetes, mostly laymen, who considered themselves disciples of Thomas Merton.

Merton had haunted the Cloisters while a student at Columbia and credited it with prompting his conversion. He was the first of many young Catholics to embrace the spiritual aesthetic of French monks and the humanist theology of French intellectual laymen. The Cloisters' connection with Merton's conversion made it the object of pilgrimage — was all the consecration the museum needed — for Merton was the prophet of aesthetic Catholicism. Even I was aware of Merton, and if I held myself aloof in those days from the religious movement he represented, still I watched it, sensing perhaps that eventually it would claim me. I always understood what, at bottom, such Catholics were doing. I should count myself among them because finally, in the sixties, I did succumb. I played a small part in the New York version of aesthetic Catholicism as an editor with the liberal journal *Jubilee,* and as a *Commonweal* savant. I liked having a desk between me and my movements, but even that didn't keep me from coming dangerously close for a time to something like commitment. My knack for detached — some said smug — analysis rescued me, although not before I'd been dubbed the Bill Buckley of the left. I was devastated by that, of course, though Buckley, I heard, was flattered.

Catholics like me had tried and failed to liberate ourselves from the stifling parochialism of Irish American Catholicism by rejecting it outright. When we found we couldn't shake that complex of guilt, nostalgia, conviction and belief, we rejected our early experience of Catholicism by embracing a truer, higher form of the Church, an older one, a more rigorous one, which was at once beautiful and intelligent. How did we know? Eminent converts as different as Clare Boothe Luce, Heywood Broun, Hugh Kenner, Robert Lowell, Allen Tate and Tennessee Williams told us so. And, most importantly, the American Protestant elite, the Berensons and Eliots and Cramms and Mrs. Gardners and even Rockefellers (whom to our shame we secretly admired and envied) had told us so. It was they, after all, who'd given us our Cloisters. Only bigots accused the Protestant collectors of plundering the Middle Ages; they had rescued it from the crass Enlightenment and the profaning Revolution.

We could go up to the Cloisters, listen to the recorded Gregorian, stroll the ambulatories, gaze out on the wild Palisades from ancient arcades, thumb our laymen's breviaries and claim our place not only in religion or culture, but in the very cosmos. We indulged our highly sensitive souls and never feared for a moment that we were like our cousins in the Bronx whom we referred to contemptuously as "BICs," Bronx Irish Catholics. Certainly we were not like our parents, hustling up to Good Shepherd in the shadow of this very place. Good Shepherd was the only Catholic church on all of Broadway, they boasted, as if it was a glitzy show palace for the soul. It was the center of their impoverished lives, and they were always going to novena or to Benediction or to bingo, or, if it was morning, to a crudely gabbled Mass in which no one sang and in which the priest, vested in the laughable fiddleback chasuble, spouted from the kitsch-filled sanctuary his gibberish about the Building Fund. We preferred, in sum, our curators to our curates. We loved everything about the Church except its people.

But the Cloisters was still new to me when I went up there that day with Michael. How was I to know it would become a haunt of mine and a central symbol of my life, of what was right about it and — though it would take two decades for me to understand this — what was wrong? I think it fitting now that Michael who never embraced the pretensions of intellectual Catholicism should have introduced me to the place and that it should have been the scene of the rescue of our friendship.

We were sitting on an oak bench in the garden with our backs to the Hudson River. Naked quince bushes clutched the air grotesquely with fingerlike branches, and in the spaces between the sham buttresses of the Gothic chapel I saw my first espaliered pear and apple trees. It was nearly midday by now, but the gray winter light was still diffuse, as in the early morning, and if anything the day was colder. The arches of the portico and the terra-cotta tiles of the sharply sloping roofs so suggested balmier weather that the unreality of the monastic setting was heightened. It was like being inside the wallpaper in someone's bathroom.

A choir of monks was singing a Gregorian melody, which I could identify now as *Gaudete in Domini Semper* but which at the time seemed too mysterious to be enchanting. It was, naturally, a record, but the loudspeakers were hidden and I kept picturing stalls full of robed figures in the chapels through which we had just walked. I was certain those rooms were deserted, but still . . .

The walls of the large pseudo-refectory had been covered with The Hunt of the Unicorn tapestries. For some moments Michael had stood in front of "The Unicorn in Captivity," that exquisite and poignant portrait of the mystic animal in its corral. Its white coat was stained with red liquid. Michael said, "I thought at first it was blood. But it's not. Look, it's juice dripping from the pomegranates in the tree." He smiled. "See? Captivity's not so bad."

In another room were the faded, patched-together but still stunning Heroes Tapestries, three of them; the pagan heroes, the Hebrew heroes and the Christian heroes, all portrayed alike on thrones with an abundance of crowns, shields, pikes and drums. The faces of the men were unyieldingly fierce, and it was possible to see them rallying throngs. Michael pointed out to me that King Arthur and Charlemagne were attended by cardinals and bishops; Joshua and David by courtiers and warriors; but Alexander and Caesar were attended by entertainers and women. "I'll take pagan," he cracked, surprising me.

He stopped in front of a small alabaster bas-relief that might once have adorned the front panel of an altar. The figures were worn and unlovely and the scene represented was too cluttered with horses, riders and anonymous attendants to make much sense of. But Michael pointed to the central figure, a helmeted man brandishing a sword, and he said jokingly, "That's me." When I looked again I saw that it was Saint Michael the Archangel. He was standing on a dragon whose face was smashed, whether by the sculptor or by time I could not tell.

The disembodied Gregorian music floating over the garden unsettled me. My eye traced the cruciform brick walks to the center of the garden, which was marked by a weathered white fountain, dry now. An adjacent plaque read "FROM THE REGION OF THE VOSGES, FRENCH (LORRAINE), LATE XV CENTURY. THE SHAFT AND PEDESTAL ARE MODERN."

"The shaft is modern," I said dryly.

Michael ignored me.

What shaft? I wondered. I couldn't see what the plaque referred to.

"So what do you think?" I asked vaguely. It was Michael and

his mordant silence that was unsettling me, not the goddamn pseudo-monastery.

He shrugged. " 'To one man he gives the ability to speak with strange sounds; to another he gives the ability to explain what these sounds mean.' "

"What the hell does that mean, Mike? You're acting weird, honest to God you are."

He laughed abruptly and slapped my knee. "You know my problem?" He withdrew a small book from inside his army jacket. "I have this thing memorized, and phrases from it keep popping into my mind."

"What is it?" But I knew what it was from the Murrow show.

"A pocket New Testament. It's all I had with me."

"You mean in China?"

"Yes. That priest gave it to me. That chaplain." He handed me the small book.

I opened it at random, automatically. But the impulse frightened me, as if there would be messages, and I refused to read. Instead I fingered the worn pages. "I see what you mean, Mike. Damn, no wonder you went religious on me."

"I didn't 'go religious.' " He took it back and opened it as if he knew the exact page he wanted. When he read it was in a voice so full of animation, so much his own, that I heard the words as a personal statement. " 'Make room for us in your hearts. We have done wrong to no one, we have ruined no one, nor tried to take advantage of anyone. I do not say this to condemn you, for as I have said before, you are so dear to us that we are together always, whether we live or die. I am so sure of you, I take such pride in you! In all our troubles I am still full of courage. I am running over with joy.' "

"Don't stop."

"He just goes on about Macedonia. Who gives a shit about Macedonia?"

I wanted to touch his sleeve or something. "Hey, I'm the one who takes pride in you," I said.

"Durk, let me be the one to say it for once, okay? I meant that about whether I lived or died. You were somebody I thought of."

"I appreciate that, Mike. I really do. But mainly I'm just glad that . . . you lived."

He nodded somberly. "I keep slipping into moods. I can't forget some of it."

"What?"

"Not everybody lived." He opened his book again, had his place in an instant and read, " 'I saw another angel coming up from the east with the seal of the living God. He called out in a loud voice to the four angels to whom God had given the power to damage the earth and the sea. The angel said, "Do not harm the earth or the sea or the trees until we mark the servants of our God with a seal on their foreheads." ' " Michael stopped reading and looked at me as if he'd proved something. My blank return look seemed to confuse him. He resumed reading. " 'And I was told the number of those who were marked with God's seal on their foreheads; it was a hundred and forty-four thousand, from every tribe of the people of Israel. There were twelve thousand from the tribe of Judah marked with the seal; twelve thousand from the tribe of Reuben; twelve thousand . . .' "

"Mike."

" '. . . from the tribe of Gad . . .' "

"Mike!"

He looked at me, then dropped his head into his hands. The New Testament fell to the ground. "There was a guy named Pace in my platoon. Lennie Pace. He died in my arms. When I released him he had a mark on his forehead." Michael loosened his collar and pulled his dog-tag out of his shirt. "This," he said, "like a stamp, right on his forehead, only reversed. Michael Maguire. O-positive. Catholic. Do you know why?"

"Why what?"

"Why my name was on his head?"

"Because you pressed him so hard. You cared about him."

"I got him killed. He would never have come with me, but I called him 'chickenshit.' He was a kid, he'd lied about his age. I mean he was like sixteen. I made him go someplace he didn't want to go, and then I let him down."

"Jeez, Mike, you feel lousy about it, eh?"

"I mean, I didn't kill him, I know that. But it seems . . . I just feel very, very guilty, like I did something wrong." He looked up at me. "I survived."

"That's not wrong."

"It feels wrong though."

"But it's not! It just isn't wrong, Mike."

"I keep saying that to myself, Durk. I even think it was by God's grace. I say He spared me for a reason. 'But God in His grace chose me even before I was born, and called me to serve Him.' "

"Maybe He didn't have a reason. Maybe He just likes you. And what's this 'serve Him' stuff? I mean, hell, if it was me I wouldn't have some condition on the thing, like you owed me your life or something."

"I guess we owe it to Him anyway. I mean, at first I thought that the rest of my life was like a bonus. You wouldn't believe what Korea was like, Durk. I never thought I'd live through it. And then the camp . . . I never, never thought I'd live through it. But I did. And then I realized that my whole damn life was a bonus to begin with. You know? I mean we didn't have to be here at all. Or anywhere. The whole frigging thing is, like, extra. You know?"

"It's not how I usually think about it."

"Me either."

"But you sound kind of . . ."

"What?"

"I don't think you have to feel guilty because you survived something other guys didn't. And I don't think it leaves you with all this huge debt to God. You sound kind of beaten down by the whole thing, Mike. I think it's too bad the chaplain didn't give you a copy of *Catcher in the Rye* and let it go at that."

"No, no. You're not getting it. This book saved my fucking life, Durk! It didn't beat me down! It's what let me beat them! 'Do not be afraid of anything you are about to suffer. Listen! The Devil will put you to the test by having some of you thrown into prison; your troubles will last ten days. Be faithful until death, and I will give you the crown of life.' "

"Ten days, eh?" I poked him.

"Give or take two and a half years." He laughed, and I realized it was his laugh that I had always loved most about him. His proud, dark-eyed, serious face became for a moment almost jaunty. Despite all of his anxiety, his edginess, it was apparent that his old self-acceptance undergirded him still. His laughter relieved me and made me feel bold.

"Tell me about the bridge," I said. "The papers always make it sound like a movie."

He shook his head and his genial countenance became severe again. "I can hardly think about it."

"Why? I thought it was the good stuff. Right out of *Gung Ho.*"

"The papers never mention the women and children." He stopped as if his statement explained itself. After a moment he added, half wistfully, "Whom I blew up."

"Chinese soldiers, I thought."

"You don't expect the army to give a medal to a man for killing refugees, do you? The bridge was jammed with refugees. We couldn't keep them back." He took out his cigarettes. "You think we can smoke out here?"

We both lit up. He stood and leaned on the wall facing the river. At first I thought he didn't want to be seen smoking by the monks. Or rather guards. Then I realized his gaze was fixed on the George Washington Bridge.

"It looked something like that," he said, "smaller, of course, and there were several spans instead of one big one. But from the hills it gave you the same feeling. A bridge, you know? There's nothing like a bridge."

We stared at the George Washington Bridge and smoked in silence. From that vantage the bridge seemed nestled in trees. A second hill, the promontory of the park, the site, in fact, of the original fort, rose up between us and the rest of the island. One would never have known we were in one of the largest cities in the world or that the bridge below us carried more traffic, practically, than any other bridge ever built. I tried to imagine it blowing up, cars, trucks, buses, girders and people falling into the river. Women and children, he'd said. I could not picture it.

"The thing is," he said slowly, "I can't figure out how to get going with normal life."

"That's why you want to stay in the army?"

"Oh God, Durk, you think I want that? The army? The fucking army? I just don't know what else there is." He flicked his cigarette and watched it arc into the shrubbery below. "It's like Paul says. To some men He gives the ability to explain. But not to me."

"You were going to explain about the bridge."

"What really knocks me out is how it didn't matter that much about the refugees. I mean we tried to keep them back and everything. That was my platoon's job. But it was like trying to keep back the wind or something. They just kept coming at us. At one point the lieutenant drove his jeep right into a bunch of them. Fucking creamed them! Right in front of me! Must have killed a dozen right there." He fell silent for a time, then resumed. "After the bridge blew we watched from the hill. I could see the people in the water. It was a fast current. It was freezing. They didn't have a chance. There were a bunch of Chicoms in little boats, a force that had been trying to take the bridge by sneaking up from the river. We expected them to beat the people down or shoot them. I mean those people were their enemy, but you know what? The Chicoms helped them. They pulled people in until those boats nearly swamped. I remember thinking, Jesus! The Reds are rescuing people, and we're blowing them up! How do you figure that? I mean the Reds were so ruthless, ruthless! But we just blew those poor people up! We just drove our jeeps right through them. How do you figure it, Durk?"

"You know the answer as well as I do, Mike."

"Sure. War is hell; you got to break some eggs to make breakfast, right. You know something? In the camp where I was, Chung Kang Djin, just across the Yalu, seven guys confessed. They were pilots. They said they were dropping germ bombs, trying to get the plague going in Asia; we wanted to spread cholera, cholera! The Reds put them on a platform and they made the whole camp listen to them, about five hundred guys. It was shit, just pure shit! Insect bombs! Plague bombs! Christ! Who'd believe that? But you know what? If they'd picked me, it would have been a snap for them. They wouldn't have had to ream my ass out at all. I'd have confessed. I'd have said we blew up a bridge full of toothless old ladies. We drove our jeeps into them. And we didn't give a shit. I mean nobody gave it a fucking thought."

"You did."

"Not at the time I didn't. At the time I just went from one minute to the next. I mean I was scared, Durk! I thought I was going to die. I don't know half of what I did. You get into like a trance. I got home and they gave me these medals and there was stuff in the citations I never heard of. Like it wasn't even me. You'd think they were talking about a different fucking bridge. The citation doesn't even mention the refugees. I mean I remember what happened to them. I can't forget! We were kicking these pathetic old people off the train. Bayonets! We had our fucking bayonets fixed,

Durk! God knows what I did forget! I know I had the bayonet on my rifle. I don't know what I did with it though."

"You didn't do anything with it, Mike. Come on."

"I did enough. I just wish the Reds asked me to confess."

"No, you don't."

"I do too, Durk. I mean I really do."

"That's what priests are for."

Michael grunted cynically, and frankly I was relieved. The confessionals at Good Shepherd were made for whimpering admissions about masturbation and neglected night prayers. What Michael was doing right then with me was confession enough. But he said, "I wish Father O'Shea was around."

I picked up the pocket New Testament from the ground. "For your penance he'd give you the Old Testament."

Michael laughed and slipped the book into his tunic. " ' "Go back home to your family and tell them how much the Lord has done for you and how kind he has been to you!" So the man left and went all through the ten towns telling what Jesus had done for him; and all who heard it were filled with wonder.' "

"What had Jesus done?"

"He cast the man's demons out." The tale amused him and his eyes brightened as he told it. "He drove them into a herd of pigs and the pigs went crazy — two thousand in all, it says — and ran off a cliff into the lake and drowned. Of course everybody thought Jesus was great, but some poor bastard owned those pigs, and he was wiped out!" Michael laughed heartily. "Get it?"

"No matter what good thing you try to do, somebody gets the shaft."

"And you said the shaft is modern!"

We laughed hysterically then, in that delicious, unpredictable way of which only adolescents are capable. Some of our worst moments in Good Shepherd had been our best ones when we'd cracked up and completely lost control of ourselves, bringing on the wrath of nuns and priests, laughing until our bellies and our faces ached. There'd been a time when we hadn't been allowed to serve Mass together because all one of us had to do was clink the cruets to destroy the other. One time the priest farted and Michael laughed so hard he had to leave the church before Communion was even served. I managed to stay but I had an open wound inside my cheek for days.

So laughing in the Cloisters' garden like that rescued us. Only when we stopped did it seem awkward that we had thrown our arms around each other's shoulders. Michael withdrew his first. "Want to see something eerie?"

I surveyed the garden with dramatic eyes. "Eerier than this?"

He nodded and set off. I followed.

Inside the museum it was no warmer. A guard watched us coming in and I was careful to close the heavy oak door softly. If it had banged, Michael and I would have begun laughing again.

Despite our mutual inarticulateness, Michael had successfully indicated his plight to me, its range between fear and regret, but I was too young — the field of my concentration was cluttered with poses and insecurities — to understand that what he was in fact showing me was a crisis of conscience.

Catholics are schooled to make much of conscience from an early age, although even our notion of it as the one faculty that sets the individual apart from the community derives from Luther. We learn at first to treat conscience like a domesticated animal, a house pet always ready to bark a warning but also slightly underfoot and often damned inconvenient. But there comes a time when conscience turns on us, clawing, and we are perhaps more shocked when that happens than our neighbors who never regarded conscience as a friend. That shock, of course, serves the Church's purpose, for likely as not we seek refuge from the attack in the Sacraments, and for a time the ritual of Confession rescues us, renewing the very world and reestablishing our cozy place in it. But eventually even the Sacrament of Penance falls short of what we need, and that crisp joy at being part of a total system that works — an answer for every question, a word of absolution for every sin — begins to fade. Some of us begin our serious drinking then: "Booze ain't my problem, Father. It's my solution." And some seek new shoulders or bosoms on which to lay their heads: "No one's ever really understood me, darling, until you." And some rededicate themselves to the old ways. They continue to confess, but as an act no longer of renewal, but of nostalgia. Catholicism is the progression of conscience experienced first as childhood chum, then as irascible boss, then as the invincible enemy, then as the familiar adversary who loses to us now and again, and finally as the old acquaintance rarely brought to mind.

I knew already that Michael was not going to be like the rest of us, accommodators, arrangers, moral amnesiacs. His conscience was no leprechaun on his shoulder or prick at the base of his spine; no fog of guilt rolling in after drink or sex or a particularly snide crack about the Jews. Conscience defined his capacity for grappling directly with life itself, including but not limited to what was flawed about it. Saint Thomas says that we are drawn instinctively toward the Good, like plants to light, and it was that trait, more than a dark moralism, though he had streaks of that too, that set Michael apart. At a certain point, later in his life for a brief moment, he became the compass rose for America herself because he could make the right thing known as the only thing.

Even as a kid in Korea he made his moves like the natural he was. He had the moral equivalent to the acute physical coordination that made him an exceptional athlete. Grace; he was a man of grace. It was impossible not to follow him — "Go, Michael, go!" — whether on a fast break toward the basket or, despite all one's inhibitions, into an act of civil disobedience. But that came later.

Once in a heated argument I demanded to know how he could be so cocksure as to what was right and what was wrong. He said, "I'm sure because I breathe." Yes, his conscience was like his breath or the circulation of his blood. Despite what it cost him and others who were influenced by it, nothing could ever impede its steady rhythmic insistence. At various times he would be ignored — he was dismissed once by the exquisitely condescending *New York Times* as "a man of good conscience but bad judgment" — and even condemned. But for some of us the effect of his example was permanent. A compass rose? Perhaps he was more like Polaris itself. We understood what I sensed inchoately at the Cloisters that day. I glimpsed his determined struggle not to justify what he'd been part of or to excuse it or to condemn it even, but simply to shape it into the great point of reference — his own Polaris — by which he would steer for the rest of his life. Conscience? That cauldron into which he poured his considerable knowledge of killing and torture and despair and loneliness. Conscience? It overwhelmed every other faculty of his: intelligence, memory and feeling. It stripped him of his ability to moderate, as I learned both happily and not so happily, either his rage or his love. Conscience? We knew that Michael Maguire did not have a conscience. A conscience had him.

It was the book of course, the small volume of tissue pages, that rooted him. At first I took his feat of memorization as mere memorization, the mind's equivalent of his fifteen hundred push-ups every day. But it was far more than that. Over the two and a half years, he had copied the Gospel line for line, in Paul's phrase, on the fleshy tablets of his heart. As meaning is present in the word, so that book became present in him. It provided margins within which war and death and deprivation and the destruction of his own innocence could all be faced and, finally, used. It was an instance of what had happened to Israel herself when all at once, within a generation of Moses, its Book occupied, like an army occupies terrain, the center of her awareness. From then on every political, religious, aesthetic and personal judgment was submitted to what-was-written. Naturally writing implies the writer whom Michael was as reluctant as Israel to name.

It was a long time before he spoke to me of his crisis in Korea as a religious conversion — who'd have thought a Catholic could be converted? I assumed at first the aura I sensed that day in the Cloisters was an effect of the piped-in Gregorian chant or the medieval art. But it wasn't. As I followed him into the Gothic Chapel I realized the aura I was aware of came from him. I sensed for the first time the presence in him to which he rarely referred but to which, to my knowledge save once, he habitually and absolutely deferred.

There was no sanctuary lamp in that chapel and instinctively I registered the absence of the Blessed Sacrament. So despite the magnificent windows and the marble high altar below the barrel-vaulted ceiling and the statues of the saints, the chamber seemed sterile to me. Despite my sophistication I'd have still preferred the BVM side altar at Good Shepherd, holy card art and all.

I drew close to Michael, who was standing between the laid-out tomb-effigies of a knight and a lady, the one encased in armor and the other reposed with hands folded on a great pair of breasts. But he was ignoring the breasts and the effigies. "Something eerie," he'd said.

At that moment, profiled against a small arched window with clear glass, *he* seemed eerie. A fucking saint? My old buddy? It was bad enough he was a hero.

My mind fled the thought. My eyes went to the window and out to the grassy slope of the promontory of Fort Tryon Park. Maybe Michael would see it as a mountain in Korea now, or as a hill in Galilee. But I didn't. From the south side of that peak one could look out on the most seductive city in the world. As teenagers Michael and I, like other rakes of Inwood, had brought girls up there. Furtively, without swagger, we'd coaxed them into bushes, and we considered ourselves wild as pagans when we pushed our tongues against the gates of their teeth and pressed the heels of our hands against their wire-mesh bras. The truth was that our inborn inhibitions were near infinite, yet made worse by the looming Cloisters. We knew it was a museum, but it looked like a tower from which nuns were watching, if not God.

It seemed to me that Michael was still in the grip of those inhibitions, as it seemed to me that I was free of them. That freedom was what I'd gone to Greenwich Village to obtain. Three and a half years of the life at NYU had confirmed what I'd gleaned from the fierce denials of the priests and nuns at Good Shepherd — that sex is all. Though it would have mortified me to admit it, my sexual experience in the Village was episodic and unsatisfactory, but the illusion of my liberation was in place. I had an image of myself as one who knew what was what between the sheets. It was an image I would lose, of course; having discovered that sex is all, one discovers later that all is chaos. But at the time I considered myself an initiate, and that was enough to make me feel like a man.

I was more a man in that regard, I thought suddenly, than the famous Michael Maguire. Hell, he wasn't a hero or even a saint. He was just a virgin. What Michael needed was to get laid.

He was staring at a gray tomb-slab attached to the wall of the chapel just there. I could discern on it the scratched outline of a monk — the cowl, the tonsure, the steeple of his hands; the smug posture.

"Look at that," he said. "It's eerie."

I read the Latin inscription. "*Hic pacet venerand Pater Michel.*"

"Here lies the venerable Father Michael."

EIGHT

"SOMEBODY I've never forgotten or forgiven myself for," Michael said to me many years later, "is Mary Ellen Divine. Do you remember her?"

I did vaguely, but I didn't answer him. He was in a confessing mood and I wanted to hear his story. I didn't want to short-circuit it with one of my cynical cracks. We'd been discussing an article of mine called "Sex and the Single God" in which I'd suggested that priestly celibacy was not only an aberration but a practical heresy since it implicitly denied the essentially sexual dynamic at work between the Persons of the Trinity. What claptrap! And I knew it at the time. I insist now that I was being at least partially ironic, although also, I admit, I'd allowed myself to think for a while that it mattered both whether priests got laid with permission or not and whether the Father, Son and Holy Ghost were real folks or just names we put on *Ipsum Esse.* I was happily married then, or thought so, and in the first throes of paternal bliss, and was inclined to reify both my family as the ultimate symbol of the tri-une God and fucking — "intercourse," we called it — as the great symbol of the divine interaction. "In His own image created He them; male and female He made them." It was a ludicrous twisting of traditional notions. In my scheme the Son became the feminine principle in the Trinity. But Michael took it seriously — he could be so fucking earnest — and it led to his impulse to tell me about his experience with Mary Ellen. My impulse to pile high the theological bullshit fell at once before an intense, slightly prurient curiosity. I'd have made an unworthy confessor because I wanted to hear the good stuff in detail and at the top. What had he done to her? And when? I would not realize until much later that what he really wanted to confess to me that night but couldn't was his love for Carolyn.

In our time Mary Ellen Divine was considered the most sophisticated girl in Inwood. She was a flat-chested, spidery girl, and this was well before the type was fashionable. But her dark eyes and bony face gave her a look of such intensity that other, more conventionally attractive girls seemed uninteresting by comparison. After high school she got a job downtown in Macy's. Her looks were so striking that eventually they put her behind the makeup and perfume counter. With artfully arranged hair and applied eye shadow and rouge she was like something out of a magazine. During high school she and Michael had been friendly but they'd never dated. I assumed that they didn't see each other again after he went in the army. Not so. Michael didn't tell me at the time, but he went down to Macy's not long after our encounter in the Cloisters hoping to find her.

It was the week before Christmas, and he went into the store on the pretense of buying a gift for his mother. He approached the perfume counter obliquely, one of the throng, as if he didn't know she would be there.

"Michael? Is that you?"

He feigned surprise. In truth he was not prepared for the sight of the glamorous woman, not girl, she'd become. He noticed her lips first, how red they were, opened in surprise as she stared at him. She wore a formal black dress that emphasized her slimness, and jewelry at her wrists and throat that flashed like the seasonal lights against the department store glare. At first Michael thought he'd made a terrible mistake. He felt she'd left him far behind. He stood there, surrounded by women, staring back at her, unable to remember what he was going to say. His speechlessness reinforced the impression that he was completely startled.

"My God!" she said, moving toward him along her side of the counter. "It *is* you!"

"Mary Ellen Divine!" he said, and he grinned.

They shook hands across the counter.

"What are you doing here?" she asked.

Suddenly it seemed juvenile to him to say he was shopping for his mother. It rankled that his mother expected him to go on living with her on Cooper Street after he got out of the army, which was one good reason for staying in. "I was just doing a little shopping."

She smiled at him. "For someone special?"

He nodded.

She gave him a look, as if she wanted to read his secrets, and then she asked casually, "Want suggestions?"

"Sure. Why not?"

She led him along the length of the counter. He had to weave between other shoppers to keep up with her. Finally she stopped. The display case featured small dark bottles of exotic fluids. Michael made a show of studying them.

"What's she like?"

"I don't know."

"You don't know what she's like?"

He looked up sharply, blushing. "Oh. No. I misunderstood. I don't know what she likes."

"If you tell me something about her perhaps I can make a suggestion."

"Well, she's . . . hard to describe." Michael lowered his eyes. He knew that he seemed smitten and he regretted the deception he'd stumbled into, but he was simply overcome by inarticulateness. Once he'd charmed girls with his talk, but that was before.

"Should I tell you what I like?"

"Sure."

"I like this." She reached down for a small bottle and brought it up to the counter top. She placed it carefully, as if it was fragile. "It's by Elizabeth Arden. It's called 'Garden of Delights.' It seems French, but it doesn't cost so much. It's cologne."

"That's nice."

"You haven't smelled it yet." She opened the bottle and briskly upended it on the inside of her wrist, then held her wrist for him to sniff.

He bent toward her. The sensuality of her pose, more even than the scent, was what struck him. He had never had the offer before of the inside of a woman's wrist. Her flesh there was whiter, and the veins were visible. It made him think of the inside of her thighs.

"It's what I'm wearing already, actually."

" 'Garden of Delights'?"

"Yes. Silly name, isn't it? But it's rather nice for seven dollars, don't you think?"

"Yes, indeed." In fact the last thing he felt prepared to comment on were the olfactory mysteries of women. His mother smelled of talcum powder, that was all he knew about it. He would never buy her cologne.

"Do you think she'd like it?"

"Is it . . . ? Gee, Mary Ellen, you've got me." He took the cologne from her. Its shape and feel resembled a Vitalis bottle, but the liquid was green. "I was thinking of something a little more . . . But if you like it . . ."

"I do like it, but there are other more special things." She smiled. "Things I can't afford."

"Like what?"

"Imported perfumes. From France."

"Could you show me some?"

"She *is* special."

He could only bring himself to nod. This deceit seemed ludicrous to him, and it was mortifying. He'd only wanted to conceal how foolish he felt, and how at sea. He was sick of the worship of his mother's circle of Good Shepherd biddies. He was sick of the goggle-eyed deference of the nuns and the chipper camaraderie of the priests who hailed him as if he was one of them. Upon his release from the Chinese prison he'd felt a great exhilaration, but that had faded and the confines of Inwood had been pressing in on him. Was the army his only way out? No wonder he was depressed. If anything, his rediscovery of our friendship only heightened this feeling because, after all, I was gone. Other people our age, even including the few old friends who were still around the parish, were uniformly stiff and uneasy in his presence. When he dared go into the neighborhood tavern, men bought him drinks and waited for his war stories. He'd bought his mother a television set when he'd first come home so that she could watch him on Edward R. Murrow, but in the weeks since his leave began, he'd watched it continually from the time it went on the air in the afternoon. He'd gone to Macy's looking for Mary Ellen partly out of his desperate but unadmitted loneliness, but more because he couldn't stay at home another day watching the antics of Kukla, Fran and Ollie.

"Here's one." Mary Ellen placed a tiny green vial in front of him. "It's called *Je Reviens.* That means 'I remember.' "

"It's French?"

"Parisian."

"Not a whole lot of it, is there?"

"She would just use a wee bit. It's the most wonderful perfume we sell. You'd know what I mean if you could smell it, but we don't open these. The assumption is, anyone who can afford it knows what it smells like."

"How much?"

"Forty dollars."

"For that little bottle?"

She nodded and laughed, and then started to put it away.

"I'll take it."

Mary Ellen looked up at him. "You're kidding."

"No, I'll take it. You convinced me."

"I wasn't trying to."

"You're a good salesgirl." Michael reached for his wallet. "Very good."

"You'll take her breath away, I promise you. My goodness."

He saw that he'd taken hers away. He handed her a fifty-dollar bill. "Can I get it gift-wrapped someplace?"

"Downstairs, beside the credit desk, just bring your receipt."

Mary Ellen turned away to write up the sale. She put the boxed perfume in a bag and brought it back to Michael. By then he'd had a chance to think of what to say. "Listen, Mary Ellen, I see how busy you are and everything, but I think it would be nice to shoot the breeze a bit, don't you? I mean, what a coincidence, running into each other like this."

"You look good, Michael. I'm glad. I'm glad things worked out for you." She handed him his bag, then lowered her eyes. "I prayed for you." She looked up quickly. "We all did."

"I know. I think that's why I made it."

They stared at each other and for a moment the bustle around them faded and they were aware only of each other. Michael felt both that they'd been very close friends once, which was not the case, and that he'd never seen her before. Her beauty seemed unreal to him, as if she were one of the store's perfect manikins. But for that instant her feeling, that worry, tinged perhaps with grief and also with the awe he'd grown accustomed to by then, communicated powerfully. She too saw him as a hero, and he sensed that she was drawn to him.

"Anyway, I was wondering how I could see you? Or when?"

Her eyes fell to the bag she'd just given him; what about his girlfriend?

He lowered the bag and deflected the problem it implied. "Or do you work around the clock?"

She laughed. "Not today. I work till six."

"Do you live in Inwood still?"

She nodded. He knew that she still lived with her parents on Isham Street.

"Well, I could ride the train home with you. I'm staying with my mother for a few weeks."

"I'd heard that."

"I have some other shopping to do. I could wait until you got off."

"That would be lovely, Michael."

"Maybe I could buy you dinner."

She stared at him, trying to read his expression, and she said nothing.

He spent the rest of the afternoon sipping coffee in an Automat. He watched the food-windows as if they were television sets.

At a few minutes before six he was back, but Mary Ellen was no longer behind the counter. For a moment he panicked, thinking she'd changed her mind and had slipped away. But then someone touched his elbow.

When he turned he was surprised to find not the glamorous woman with ruby lips, rouged cheeks and shaded eyes, and high-fashion dress, but the Inwood girl, in sweater and skirt, he'd known since they were children. She wore no makeup and her hair was in a ponytail. This second transformation stunned him even more than the first, and now he saw for the first time how truly beautiful she was. And also how familiar. Anxiety drained out of him. "My goodness," he said.

"You didn't think I go around like that, did you?"

"You didn't dress down for me?" He asked this ingenuously. He thought that if she had any appetite for him at all, it would be due to his uniform. It was why he'd worn it.

She shook her head. "Do you mind?"

"Heavens no!" He took her coat out of her arms and helped her into it. "Now I don't have to take you to the Rainbow Room."

It was dark and cold outside, but the sidewalks of Herald Square were crowded with shoppers. Men and women were holding each other and children were craning to see the scenes of Santa's Village in Macy's windows. A Salvation Army lady was ringing her bell, and from loudspeakers hidden above the elf-ridden window displays Bing Crosby was singing, "I'll be home for Christmas."

Michael had an impulse to take Mary Ellen's arm, but he checked it. He was nearly overwhelmed with the feeling that this was a moment he'd have dreamed of if he'd dared. A deep need of which he'd been inchoately aware was for that instant filled, and he felt suddenly free of his morose listlessness. It was possible for him to be inside such a scene, however contingently, a man with a woman on the streets of New York at Christmas. And not a mere man, but a soldier. For our generation the epitome of romance was the GI with his girl, and in our fantasies they were always either at the docks saying farewell or on those streets with snows falling and Christmas coming.

He bent toward her. "I meant what I said about dinner."

"I think that would be nice. I've already called my mother."

He laughed. What a pair they were! Sophisticated Manhattanites? Inwood Irish Catholics checking in with Ma. He was relieved, though, because she wasn't checking in with a man.

"Where would you like to go?" he asked.

"I'd like to walk first, wouldn't you? Have you walked up Fifth Avenue? Have you seen the decorations?"

"No."

"Michael, really! And you call yourself a New Yorker!"

"And I've never been to the Statue of Liberty either."

They kept their distance from each other as they cut across Broadway toward Fifth Avenue. They knew they were enacting a classic scene. The Christmas carols that wafted magically above them might have been the film score. They passed Santa Clauses and more bellringers. The laden shoppers were good-humored for a change and the mounted policemen at each intersection seemed a very emblem of the benign and joyous season. At Saks Mary Ellen pressed against the windows which displayed animated scenes of life in an Alpine village. "I think ours are better, don't you?"

Michael had barely noticed the Macy's windows, but it was his impression that they had nothing to compare with these lifelike mechanical figures that chopped wood and drove sleighs and toted baskets. Still he agreed with her vigorously.

At Fifty-second Street they crossed into Rockefeller Center to see the tree. They stood on the parapet above the skating rink, aware of the gliding couples and the smooth music, but their gazes were fixed upon the huge spruce decked so abundantly in gaudy lights that the tree itself, its limbs and needles and cones, had no substance. They had been raised to think of this scene, the tree and the rink, as enshrining Christmas every bit as much as the parish nativity, and it would fall short to say that they gave themselves over utterly to the prescribed sentimental enchantment.

"You know something?" Michael said.

She looked up at him. Lo and behold the first snowflakes began to fall at that moment. The film score swelled. Not even in his imagination would he have dared conjure an effect like that.

"I'll never look at this tree again," he said, his voice lowered, "without thinking of you."

Michael could read her. She was a young woman who had left other girls her age in the dust. She was smarter and more ambitious and not prepared for a moment to settle for the hemmed-in life of the old neighborhood. But she hadn't left it yet. She was like the princess of Inwood, but that had brought with it a grave problem: where were the princes? If they had energy or ambition of their own, they were gone. Michael knew that the boys who remained and with whom she might have been expected to make a life were nice enough. They were her friends and the sons of her parents' friends. But they had already settled for a world she found too small. She didn't know what she wanted, but she knew what she didn't want. And now here was Michael Maguire whom she'd always liked and who had always been so accessible. But he had become a legend, having shown such largeness of soul, such nobility, that it shamed her for having all those years taken his friendship for granted. He was like an apparition, a reincarnation, like one resurrected. And he had just said the most wonderful thing that anyone had ever said to her. The feeling was so unexpected, so poignant and sharp that she could hardly breathe, and this is what it was: here is my prince. She didn't forget for a moment that he had a girlfriend already, but that only sharpened her reaction to him.

At dinner in the Rockefeller Center Café just off the ice-skating rink, intermittently watching the pairs coast by in their languid ovals beyond the glass wall, they found their tongues. Each discovered in the other the all-too-familiar sense of hesitation, poised as both were on the very threshold of life. "I feel," she said passionately, "as if the world is about to open up for me and give me everything I've ever wanted. Only the secret word needs to be said, and I know what it is!"

"But you haven't said it."

She shook her head and sipped her beer. "Not yet."

"What are you waiting for?" He was ingenuous. She answered him with her stare. Michael knew, and he was taken aback by the knowledge. He said, "You are a bold girl."

"So I'm told. It's regarded as my failing."

"Not by me."

"But what if I was truly bold?"

"And did what?"

"Asked you to tell me about your time away."

"In prison?"

"Yes."

After a moment he said, "A Chinese government official came to our camp once and told us that World War Three had begun, and that the Russians had blown up New York with an atom bomb."

Mary Ellen was aghast. "Why did they do that?"

Michael shrugged. "Just to knock us down some more. He said the U.S. had surrendered."

"Did you believe it?"

"Do you believe things that happen to you in nightmares? After a while, when we didn't hear any more about it, I guess I decided it was just another turn of the screw. But by then I knew that it *could* happen and that was pretty awful too. The Reds do have the bomb. And they believe the ends justify the means. I think they're capable of anything." Michael checked himself. He had no interest in sounding like Senator McCarthy. He picked up the bowl of sugar cubes. "There was a period when they kept me alone, although mostly I was with other guys. But the time they kept me alone nearly did me in. I had to think of things to keep my mind occupied, like keeping track of the days. My cell had a dirt floor, and so every morning under a corner of my mat I'd scratch the date. I kept it up for seven months and eleven days when they put me back in the camp. And you know what? I had the date right!" He laughed, and his elation came back to him. What a triumph that had been. "And another thing I did was to try to memorize the squares and cubes of the numbers up to a hundred."

"Did you do it?"

He laughed again and nodded. "The square of your age is 441, and the cube is 9,261. What I wanted to do was figure out a system, like a table or a formula that would simplify the multiplication. But I never could."

"But you just did that all in your head?"

"Yep." He dropped the sugar cube into his coffee, then tapped his forehead. "You wouldn't believe the gobbledygook I've got up there."

"Monsignor Riordan told my mother you read the Bible a lot."

He shrugged and said, defending himself from the implicit charge of piety, "It was all I had. The New Testament, actually." He smiled. "That's not what I mean by gobbledygook."

"I'm surprised they let you keep it."

"They took it away during my time in solitary. You never knew what was coming with those guys. When they gave it back, I was afraid they would take it again, so I memorized a lot of it."

"But they let you keep it."

"Naturally. I think once you've protected yourself from something, it doesn't happen."

She thought about that. "You had to protect yourself against so many things . . ."

"Yes," he said easily enough, but she had spoken straight to his heart. Her simple statement seemed full of connotation, as if at last someone understood what he'd been through. It wasn't that they'd tortured him but that on the merest whim and at any moment they could have. "The question always was, How can this or that serve their purposes? An extra ration of rice or an unexpected move to another camp or a doctor showing up with malaria pills; no matter what they did, even if it was an improvement, you knew it wasn't for you. It was for them. Even when it came time for my release I found myself wondering, How will they use my freedom against me? Even now sometimes I wake up in the middle of the night and I can't believe there isn't a guard outside my door."

"That's just your mother," Mary Ellen said.

They both laughed hard. Inwood mothers *are* like guards. Mary Ellen's crack punctured his melancholy and he was grateful to her. He felt more and more exposed to her and more and more relaxed.

"You know what I learned?" he asked intensely. He felt as though he was shaking off the lethargy of three years. "I learned how tough we can be, how defiant."

She responded with a slight movement of her brow. What did he mean?

"I thought that we were raised by the nuns and priests, by our parents, to be good little boys and girls, obedient and unquestioning. I mean, wasn't that the point of all the stuff at Good Shepherd, the demerits and the stars, the rewards and punishments, the indulgences and the years in purgatory? I thought the whole system was to keep us in line. But you know what? We've been raised to a standard, and they held us to it so that when the time came we could hold ourselves to it. We weren't raised to be deferential and obsequious at all. We were raised to make judgments and live by them. 'Don't you know that God's people will judge the world? Do you not know that we shall judge the angels?' We're Catholics, Mary Ellen. We stand for something. And it makes us stronger than other people. It really does. I saw it with my own eyes. And the Communists know it too. That's why they hate us. But they also respect us. Catholics have to lead the fight against Communism."

"Like Senator McCarthy."

This was six months before Joseph Welch said, "Have you no sense of decency, sir, at long last? Have you no sense of decency?" And Michael was not equipped to evaluate the performance of the senator, but he wasn't enthralled by him. Unlike Mary Ellen and Inwood Catholics generally, he did not take his virtue for granted. No, the senator from Wisconsin wasn't what he meant at all. But he had a point. It was important to keep your eye on the ball, Michael would have said, and the ball was Communism, and how to lick it. He said as much to Mary Ellen.

Then they both fell silent, having lost the poignant, personal note of their talk in what must always seem by comparison the banality of politics.

After the waiter cleared their dishes and they were smoking their second cigarettes, Michael said, "So they think you're bold."

She nodded and looked at him through the smoke, touching her cigarette to her lips artfully. She *was* sophisticated, and he guessed that she'd had experiences with men that her mother didn't know of.

"Why exactly?"

"Because I don't believe that all the dreams have already come true. I don't believe that all the fabulous new worlds have already been discovered or that all the great ideas have already been thought up."

"I don't believe any of that either."

"I know you don't. It's obvious. You've got your hat set on something special."

"It shows?"

"I'll say."

"I wish you could tell me on what. I'm kind of at sea."

"You should go to college."

"I'm going to, one way or the other."

"And become what?"

Michael had not declared himself even to this extent before, and suddenly it seemed to him the conversation had taken a dangerous turn. "A lawyer maybe," he said. "I'd become a cop like my old man was, but to tell you the truth I've had my fill of guns. I'd like to do something that makes the world better, you know? You don't think that sounds hokey, do you?"

"I like hokey."

He trailed the cinder of his cigarette through the ashes in the ashtray. "Lawyer's work can be kind of dull though. Searching through the fat law books for legal precedents and all that. In the law I think they *do* believe that all the great ideas have already been thought up. I'm not sure."

"What does your friend think?"

Michael looked up sharply. He confessed to me that his first thought was, "Who, Durkin?" Then he realized what she meant. A coy thrust. He said, "She leaves it up to me."

"Smart girl."

"Yeah."

They could see through the windows that the snow was falling heavily now and they agreed it was time to head uptown.

On Fifth Avenue in front of Saint Patrick's Cathedral they paused. A service of some kind — carols perhaps or an Advent Mission — was in progress inside the Gothic church, and the snow was luminous against the brilliant blue windows. Michael and Mary Ellen stood there staring at the cathedral as if, magically, it would reveal its secrets to them. Was this the shrine of an Alpine village? Was it the insides of a spherical glass paperweight? In what way, exactly, was this real? To them at that moment Saint Patrick's was the most beautiful structure in the world and, sophisticates though they were, they shared a swell of pride that Fifth Avenue's masterpiece was their cathedral. Could Michael have imagined that only seven years after that moment he would prostrate himself on the floor of that very sanctuary to be ordained to the holy priesthood, and only seven years after that he would in its offices scandalously refuse to obey the explicit command of Cardinal Spellman? As if he had imagined not only these things but a whole life of heroic loneliness, he abruptly turned his back on Saint Patrick's and took Mary Ellen's shoulders in his hands. He intended to tell her the truth, that there was no other girl, that these hours with her had been his first truly happy ones since coming home, and that for the first time it seemed possible to him that he could do something with his life. Something worthy of his father's memory, worthy of his own having been spared in battle and in prison, worthy even of her!

"Mary Ellen," he began. But words failed him once more. Instinctively he veered into phrases he knew by heart. He spoke them passionately, loudly, his voice rising above the noises of the avenue. " 'Then a great sign appeared in heaven . . . a woman clothed in the sun . . . and . . . the moon under her feet and a crown of twelve stars on her head.' But the dragon was angry with the woman and went off to make war on her offspring. 'Then war broke out in heaven! Michael and his angels fought against the dragon who fought back with his angels, but the dragon was defeated. . . . Then I heard a loud voice in heaven saying, ". . . Now God has shown his power as king! Now his Messiah has shown his authority!" ' "

"Michael, you're making me nervous."

He checked himself and released her shoulders. The intensity of his emotion had him shaking. "I'm sorry," he said. "It was the woman, the idea of the woman. I saw you."

She shook her head. "You said everything they did served their purposes. Maybe the Communists let you keep that Bible to . . ."

"Make me nutty?"

She dropped her eyes. She had a Catholic's distrust of a Bible quoter.

But he crooked his finger under her chin and lifted her face. "I'm not nutty, Mary Ellen. I know I'm not the archangel and I know I'm not the Messiah. But I do feel like I was spared to do God's work. I think they let me keep that New Testament because He wanted them to. It was His way of introducing Himself to me. I know how strange it seems. It's strange to me. But also very real. I mean, I'm here. That's the basic thing. And why should I be when fifty thousand other fellows didn't make it? Well the answer is obvious to me. Something very important won't get done unless I do it. I know it sounds conceited or pompous, but I have the feeling that the world needs me."

"Maybe not the world, Michael. Maybe just a little part of it."

It was as if he didn't hear her. He said, "It's such an awesome feeling that, well, it's kind of paralyzed me. I haven't known how to get going. But now after talking with you I see that the way to start is just to start. For me it was a start just to walk into Macy's this afternoon."

"What do you mean?"

He reached inside his coat and took out the small gift-wrapped box. "This is for you. I bought it for you. *Je Reviens;* is that how you say it?"

"You mean . . . ?" She stared at the gift, not daring to touch it.

"I don't have a girl, Mary Ellen. Only the dream of one." Michael would say to me later that that was the first moment in his life when he'd stood on the near edge of love. He would stand there again, even more painfully, more happily. He saw her eyes fill. He said, "And she is a woman clothed in snow."

"This city," E. B. White said, "which not to look upon would be like death."

Michael and Mary Ellen looked upon it from the second hill in

Fort Tryon Park. They looked upon it regularly. As the days lengthened they would meet at Dyckman Street and follow the pathway up the wooded slope and around the peak on which the Cloisters sat. Michael never took her into the museum, never showed its treasures to her as he had to me, and that fact alone would have tipped me off to what was coming.

He and Mary Ellen went up the hill to watch the sun set behind the George Washington Bridge. They held hands but only once they were inside the park, as if the streets of Inwood would whistle at them. Often, once the golden mist of evening had faded to black, they would sit on a favorite bench and kiss. As the weather grew warmer and the color returned to the tips of the trees and the smell of forsythia hung above the hillside and the earth underfoot grew dry again, they sat on patches of grass to be alone. They stared out at New York, talking, held in place by the sight of the city that embodied their longing.

One balmy evening in May he took her hand and led her, unopposed, to a remote grove. He took her into his arms and they held each other. Her strong, narrow body matched his, pressed against him. Her hair was against his face and through strands of it, as through the wispy young leaves, he looked out upon the city. It was time for them to be lovers.

They had begun this before and stopped. Michael had discovered her breasts and explored her waist, the curve of flesh at her hip and the patch of rough hair between her legs. Mary Ellen had rubbed herself against him purposefully, to the point of his ejaculation, mortifying and stunning, inside his trousers. They courted, in other words, like what they were, children of another age, taking for granted their inhibition as well as their acute sense of sin, and paradoxically taking extreme delight, one lost to the present generation, in both. They were in no hurry, as if they knew that in sex anticipation is sweeter by far than what follows. They would take possession of each other as lovers, in other words, only when the rites of passion, longing and trespass had been fulfilled.

Tonight.

He undressed her even as they remained standing. She shivered when he drew her sweater back and off her shoulders. She let him find the clip of her bra. That his hands shook pleased her. She would never have permitted a man of experience to do this to her. When her skirt fell and she bent to remove her pants, then straightened, naked, he stepped back to look at her. This body, he felt, which not to look upon would be like death.

And she closed the distance between them. She fixed her eyes on the buttons of his shirt as she undid them. And she spoke. Her voice seemed distant, disembodied. "Michael, you have to tell me one thing." He waited. When she had his shirt unbuttoned she stopped and looked in his eyes. "My mother told me you're going to be a priest."

He nearly fell. "Oh, Mary Ellen, that's not true. That's not true at all."

"Monsignor Riordan told her. He told her I should leave you alone."

Mary Ellen laughed awkwardly, as if she'd brought the subject up against her will. She was only trying to dispel the ghosts of Inwood, ghosts she was sure could never claim Michael Maguire.

He took her into his arms and pressed her. Her breasts flattened against his chest. But suddenly she was wooden. She sensed that he'd drawn her into his embrace so that he would not have to look at her. "Oh, darling, you know how I feel about you. I love you. Everything else is far away and unimportant."

It stunned her that he hadn't denied what they were saying. His deflection seemed like an admission, and it panicked her. "He said you've applied for the seminary, that they've accepted you, that you begin in the fall. He said he's been tutoring you in Latin. Is it true?" Her voice was a whisper. Her weight was on him and her mouth was by his ear.

He did not answer. He could have said, "I haven't quite made up my mind to do it." Or he could have said, "What else can I do with my life?" Or he could have attacked the monsignor and her mother; why can't Catholics leave their bright young men alone? Why do they fold us in, corral us, ruin all our options but one? Of course he knew why; it was the genius of the system. His generation would be the last of which it was true, but the best, smartest and bravest boys were tracked inexorably toward one thing. The Great Vocation. Even angels bent their knees to priests. No one ever asked, Since when do angels have knees?

"Help me," he could have said, "to tell them no." But say no to God? He said nothing. He could not answer her.

She dressed herself. He watched her. It was as if a door closed slowly on a room. He would always think of it as the best room in the house.

Before she turned away she said, "I'm the one who helped you make your mind up, aren't I?"

He nodded. She had given him not the courage, but the will.

Tears overflowed her eyes. She was so hurt.

She said, "And you wanted to make love to me so that you'd have done it once. Right?"

He didn't answer.

"Right?" she insisted. Her voice rose sharply, and all at once her anger swept her hurt aside.

He stepped toward her.

"Don't touch me! Just answer me! You wanted to make love to me so that you'd have done it once! Right? Right?"

"Mary Ellen . . ." Of course, what she said was true, but he only saw it now. He'd never meant to hurt her.

"You goddamn saint!" she screamed. "You goddamn saint!" And then she turned, broke through the virgin branches that enclosed them and was gone.

Michael's hands trembled as he buttoned his shirt.

When he left the grove he walked to the peak of the hill and looked down on the city. The Cloisters loomed, a shadowy fortress, behind him. He told me that he wanted to concentrate on Mary Ellen, to memorize what they had had and what she'd looked like and what the touch of her flesh did to him. But he couldn't because, despite himself, his mind reeled off what he'd memorized before. "After this I saw an angel coming down from heaven. He had great authority and his splendor brightened the whole earth. He cried out in a loud voice . . . 'Whoever is meant to be captured will surely be captured. This calls for endurance and faith on the part of God's people.' "

NINE

EVEN if I had been able to imagine being a priest myself — they lived well, after all, did good things, had in their spheres great power and a leg up in getting their poetry published — I couldn't have stomached the thought of burying myself alive for six or seven years in a seminary. A seed bed, literally, from the same root as semen; often referred to accidentally by Catholics as the cemetery.

Most American seminaries, like Dunwoodie in Westchester County where Michael did part of his training, would have reminded you of the eccentric lavish country estates of extremely wealthy Protestants of the sort whose art collections wound up at the Cloisters. In fact many began as the estates of such people and came into the Church's possession only when the great fortunes began to fade under the burden of taxation in the period after World War One. It is an irony of American Church history that the leaders of the immigrant Church were financially in the position to ape the fabulous style of the WASP elite just at the moment when the WASP elite could no longer afford it. Of course, bishops were exempt from the other great tragedy, besides taxes, that befell the aristocracy about that time too — the shortage of good servants. And so Carnegies and Mellons and Lawrences and Biddles and Fricks retrenched somewhat, while Catholic orders and dioceses converted their splashy mansions into novitiates and seminaries. Now in the Berkshires of Massachusetts and on the Main Line of Philadelphia and on the fashionable North Shore of

Lake Michigan and in the hills overlooking the Hudson Valley the great prince archbishops — Spellman of New York, O'Connell of Boston, Mundelein of Chicago and Dougherty of Philadelphia — realized their poor boy dreams for country places of their own.

These seminaries had their acres of rolling lawn and their formal gardens with trellised rosebushes and clipped boxwoods, their lakes and ponds stocked with bass and their nine-hole golf courses complete with practice ranges and winter greens, all meticulously tended by legions of immigrant — though not Irish, who were above such work now — or colored gardeners. Now part of the grounds, however, were given over to football fields and baseball diamonds. To the tennis courts were added bunkerlike handball courts, but the swimming pools, with their threatening air of sensuality, were covered over for basketball. Amid cultivated groves of spruce and cedar loomed artificial grottoes, evoking Fatima and Lourdes, but also the cement-over-mesh "mountainside" in the zoo. To these shrines the boys were expected to come daily, pacing along the winding tidy pathways from one Bavarian-style "station" to another to tell their beads. Tell them what, you ask? No doubt how grateful they were, as the sons of the low and foreign born, to have been admitted to the world — for this was the delusion of that generation of ecclesiastics — of the American aristocracy.

Those places are mostly empty now. Despite their tax exemptions they cost too much to run. Even as conference centers or Job Corps training sites or retreat houses or old folks homes they turned out to be simply too drafty, too impersonal, too much the depressing relics not of one age, but of two. That the Catholics are stuck now with those lumbering white elephants in the Berkshires and the hills above the Hudson is the last revenge of the WASP elite who built them in the first place.

And of course the main reason they are empty is that today there are only a tenth the number of boys presenting themselves as candidates for the priesthood. In Michael's day the seminaries were jammed. Thousands of young men, beginning at the end of World War Two and continuing through the Catholic heyday of the fifties, entered every year. A huge expansion of facilities was required and the edifice-complex bishops built thousands of schools, churches and hospitals everywhere in America. It is both an achievement and a revelation that they did so without constructing a single architecturally distinguished building, adding sham-Gothic wings to the gracious old mansions or replacing them altogether with the sterile brick and poured-concrete of fifties "modern." One order sent off its plans for a new seminary building to the Vatican for review. The Vatican office wouldn't think of faulting the architect for his mundane design, but it did note that he had failed to include toilets and baths for the seminarians. It responded with the question, *Suntne angeli?* Are they angels?

They weren't angels. The seminarians were robust young men, talented, smart, well groomed, aggressively American, lovers of ball games. Their talk was full of slang and they were jazz buffs and devotees of Broadway musicals. But the life they led in the seminary derived from a fierce European regimen that hadn't changed in its essentials since the Reformation. Every Catholic seminarian in the world had his daily schedule, his course of studies, his style of dress, the length of his siesta and even his right to toilet facilities supervised by one curial office in Rome. The most minor detail of daily life (the Latin words, for example, with which seminarians awakened each other in the morning: *Benedicamus Domino! Deo Gratias!*) was considered as sacrosanct as the most major — that, say, the seminarian had slept alone that night. Every such detail, minor and major, was codified and had been for centuries.

The young men had such vitality, such abundant goodwill, and the Church herself enjoyed such a cheerful burst of energy in the period of her "arrival" in America that no one seemed to notice that the ideology underpinning all this building was fossilized. The classroom method of seminary education was intended to be a confrontation with the mind of Saint Thomas. But, first, it was conducted in Latin, a language which few professors, much less students, truly mastered. And, second, the structure of Thomas's thought was misunderstood. His masterpiece, the *Summa Theologiae,* has its origin as a record of a vital dialectic, a Socratic conversation that was supple and dynamic. Instead of teaching his method, most professors simply recited the record of it, so that Thomism was taken to be a kind of catechism for clerics. The monotony of the rote review of *Quaestio, Sed Contra* and *Responsio* was relieved only on those rare occasions when the class penetrated, as if by accident, to the genius of Thomas, glimpsing his still revolutionary insight, for example, that faith is not opposed to reason, but dependent on it, and vice versa. More often, the monotony was relieved not by understanding but by youthful snickers when the bland meaninglessness of the endless text-bound consideration was interrupted by a line made wonderfully ludicrous by loss of context, as in "Man in sexual intercourse is an animal," or "No part of a foot is a foot," or "The whiteness of a man's teeth primarily belongs not to him but to his teeth."

As undergraduates in philosophy, seminarians were expected to divine what Thomas, citing Aristotle, meant by potency and act. As graduate students in theology they were flogged with his distinction, also derived from "the Philosopher," between the *esse* and the essence of God. They were told that their vocations hinged on their successfully grasping such material, but no priest they knew, often including the professors themselves, showed the slightest sign outside the classroom that any of it mattered. Even the Five Proofs of God's Existence, which few remembered beyond the exam, would be of little use in the parish where priests weren't famous for arguing with atheists.

What counted for success in the seminary was mastering that peculiar mode of high-toned mediocrity — to be devout but not pious, savvy but not intellectual, athletic but not physical, self-confident but not arrogant, deferential but not insecure, jocular but not sarcastic, friendly but not intimate with anyone — that developed as the dominant personality type of the American Catholic priest.

Thomism was not taught in seminaries as a way of opening the minds of students to great ideas at all, and it did not matter for the life of the Church that the long, arduous academic program of the priestly formation system was a complete sham. The *Summa Theologiae* was one of history's few works of true genius but by the twentieth century its function as the base document of Catholic thought was merely metaphorical, and in fact the dry, static, constricted framework of the professors served that symbolic purpose better than a vital appreciation of the original theology would have. The *Summa* fit perfectly with the culture of immigrant Catholicism because, as presented in the seminaries, it embodied that sense Catholics had that there are only so many questions and in the symmetry of God's creation there are just that many answers. Perfect happiness — what we called "beatitude" — was possible to Catholics because we participated in a divinely ordained system in which the one set, *quaestio,* could be matched with the other, *responsio*. Even if a particular professor or priest didn't know the answer, someone did. The rector maybe, or the bishop. Certainly Saint Thomas did, or God. The rigid authority of Catholicism derived not, as Protestant critics particularly in America held, from the archaic monarchism of the papacy or a perverse vestigial love of feudal aristocracy, but from a deliberately sustained and unabashedly premodern philosophy that put hierarchy at the dead center of existence. And of course this *philosophia perennis* was not regarded as a system of thought, but as an expression of the Truth Itself. As long as they subscribed to it, what others experienced as the absurd, alienating pressures of life in the twentieth century had no discernible effect on those young men. The seminary discipline that we outsiders would wince to hear described kept seminarians, as an expression of the day had it, on the beam. Or as their motto had it, in all things, they kept the Rule and the Rule kept them. It was an ordered life on the way to Orders.

No wonder they loved America. It had given them their castle-seminaries where they could, on feast days at least, listen to Ella Fitzgerald and Duke Ellington in their music rooms, but where, also, they could pretend to enjoy not as remote historical figures but as present masters Aristotle, Augustine, Anselm, Abelard and Aquinas. They could be in the world but not of it, or was it of but not in? We never knew. The totalitarian quality of seminary life and its cultivated anachrony alerted them to the dangers of materialism and license that so infected their age. Or, as they might have put it about their *horae* if they'd known Robert Penn Warren to quote, "It is not dead. It is simply weighty with wisdom." All they knew finally was that how they lived made them feel so much a part of the most important project they could imagine that their responses, despite all the Jansenist gloom of centuries of Catholic moral teaching, were instinctively optimistic. During their golden age, seminaries of the Catholic Church in this country, in sum, took a huge crop of gifted boys, nurtured an irresistible camaraderie that made their common rooms and refectories puerile, discouraged true distinction among them, yet enabled them to lay a near permanent — though as it turned out years later, a merely apparent — hold on a rare American happiness.

One of the ways to prevent the emergence of an intellectual or personal spirit of true excellence in seminaries was to segregate the smartest and generally most promising young men from the rest. Among the diocesan clergy, as opposed to the religious orders like the Jesuits or Paulists, this actually occurred when top prospects from all over the country were sent for their theological education either to the North American College in Rome or to the Theological College at Catholic University in Washington, D.C. These two theologates produced the ecclesiastical elite from which future American theologians, canon lawyers and bishops were invariably taken, and that fact alone is enough to make one wonder about those places, but that's my prejudice, isn't it? Of course it is. Prejudice is my starting point on the subject of the American Catholic hierarchy. In fairness I should rein it, but, hell, fairness was excommunicated from the Church some time ago, and not by me. Let me make my simple point about these seminaries. Training of the leadership was the stated intention of the system, but perhaps its more telling effect on the Church at large was to remove from diocesan institutions the very element, the "leaven" in the metaphor of Scripture, that might have raised the standard of the whole American parish clergy through the period of its greatest prestige when, ironically, it was about to be put to its greatest test. But maybe not. I'm an opinionated cynic on the subject, but it seems evident nevertheless that even the flower of American Catholic manhood lost its bloom in those places too. Not to say its virginity.

But let me tell you about Michael's school because it's important for our story to understand what happened to him there. It happened to everyone who went through the place.

The Catholic University was founded with papal approbation in the late nineteenth century by bishops who were moved by the booming American embrace of higher education, and they encouraged their fellow bishops to send students and faculty, and religious orders to locate houses of study there. These bishops were enlightened enough to foresee the importance of professionally trained clergy and an educated laity, even though the immigrant poor who made up the bulk of the Church's members at the time did not seem to require intellectual sophistication either of themselves or of their leaders. But those bishops who look like giants, in Newton's image, only because they were succeeded by dwarfs, were not enlightened enough to imagine, nor were the structures of American society yet fluid enough to permit, that large numbers of Catholics could be educated in the great American secular institutions of higher learning. The impulse to establish the Catholic University of America was thus part of a larger pattern of duplicating the prevailing social structures, which led to the founding of such venerable institutions as the Catholic Boy Scouts, a Catholic Forestry Association, a Catholic Lawyers Guild, a Catholic War Veterans and a Catholic Philatelist's Club. By the time a fellow name of Francis Spellman was archbishop of New York it seemed the most natural thing in the world for him to preside over a Catholic debutante ball at the Waldorf Astoria. Spellman himself aspired to be the Catholic Frances Parkinson Keyes. He wrote a little-known novel called *The Foundling* which fell short, frankly, of her *Came a Cavalier*.

In short, the Catholic University of America became the centerpiece of a great Catholic subculture. It was an authentic monument to the aspirations of the simple people who built it. It was endowed not by a few bequests of wealthy people but by annual collections proudly taken up in every Catholic parish in America, as if this university was an extension — and of course it was — of the parish school. But it was supposed to be more. The dream was that it would embody in the New World the great tradition of Saint Thomas's Paris. Weren't universities invented by clerics, after all, under the sponsorship of popes? But CUA failed to distinguish itself and never made it to the first rank even of Catholic universities like Georgetown and Notre Dame and dear old Fordham where, having been launched on the seas of academe with my doctorate for a sail and my bluster for ballast, I pulled quickly in. Not much of a journey, you say, from Washington Square to Fordham Road, but the idea was to stay in New York. I dropped my heavy-duty anchor on a lightweight teaching job. The Jesuits loved my work on Hopkins for its anticlerical tone and thought of themselves as open-minded for hiring an Irish agnostic from NYU. I was better than a Jew. I didn't tell them about Inwood or that my best friend was a seminarian or that finally ending up at Fordham felt like coming home.

It was the perfect time to come to Fordham. In the next decade even an out-of-fashion ideo-Socratic like me — I hated the seminar method and only asked questions of my beloved imbeciles to wake them up — became a campus fixture, one might almost say a campus light. It helped that as we moved to a shiny new campus in mid-Manhattan, my Jesuit competition on the faculty — those bright would-be sons of my own Hopkins — began dropping like flies in the priest-exodus of the sixties. And lo! To keep me from an assistant's slot at Columbia, they would make me the youngest full professor in the place! They even would give me my whack at running the department just as Marshall McLuhan came on board with his barrels of bullshit about Swedish massage. He made me look unoriginal and unopinionated. I didn't mind the former — it is not a teacher's job to be original. But I couldn't forgive him for the latter. What does a teacher have but his opinions? Nor could I forgive him for earning so much more money than I. He couldn't touch me in the classroom, but his books on the end of books sold wonderfully. I used to wink at him in the corridor to let him know that I knew, but wouldn't tell. I seriously intended to challenge him to debate, but before I could the war hit us, made all the talk about McLuhan seem absurd — which was its one good effect — and made, eventually, the ground open up beneath my feet and swallow me.

But my failure is another subject. I was talking about Catholic University's. Even the Methodists, whose equivalent nineteenth-century movement resulted in Boston University, Northwestern, SMU, Emory, Southern Cal and my own NYU, outshone the Catholic bishops. Still, CU became and remains the center of the effort to educate American priests and nuns. Perhaps it was handicapped impossibly by its clerical orientation, though some of its priest-faculty, Fulton Sheen for example, or John Tracy Ellis, had left enduring marks. Of course CU has had its achieving laymen too. Among the alumni of its famous drama department are Jon Voight, the midnight cowboy, and Ed McMahon, the midnight card.

The site chosen for the university in the 1880s was on a hill just northeast of Washington, and over the next seventy-five years, around a first modest hall of lecture rooms and a primitive observatory where presumably the priest-astronomers asked forgiveness of Galileo, there clustered the monasteries, convents, postulates, juniorates, theologates and colleges of Paulists, Benedictines, Redemptorists, Oblates of Mary Immaculate, Claretians, Capuchins, Christian Brothers, Xaverians, Salesians, Oblates of Francis de Sales, Carmelites, Carthusians and half a dozen competing factions of Franciscans. Each of these places housed students who attended the university or faculty who taught at it. By Michael Maguire's time there, Catholic University and its religious satellites so dominated the growing new section of Washington known as Brookland that it was referred to as "Little Rome." It was the perfect setting, that genteel but modest neighborhood with its quiet tidy streets and small tract houses on quarter-acres of grass, each with its garage; the little tudor shopping centers with ample parking; the sprawling parks where Little League and Pop Warner flourished. Brookland was an early suburb and as such a type of the world into which the entire postwar generation of American Catholics was moving. The fifties boom was for the Church too a suburban phenomenon. Newly ordained clergy weren't going to serve in the gloomy parishes — "Saint Paul's," "Saint Mary's" — of the decaying cities, but in the bright new all-purpose parishes — "Our Lady of Hope," "Holy Innocents" — of the sparkling child-dominated suburbs. The knotty-pine cheer of such places already paneled their lives.

Thousands of young religious were at large in Brookland. On its streets monks, friars and cassocked seminarians could stroll in their medieval robes without the least self-consciousness. The officials deferred to them and the merchants gave them discounts. On the class-free mornings of Holy Days they could attend en masse in a local moviehouse special gratis screenings of features in which Bing Crosby was forever paying off the mortgage of the new church and Ingrid Bergman was perpetually taking her final vows. Brookland was an enclave like Vatican City itself, complete and entire, and across its boundaries the junior clergy were forbidden to go, except in the afternoons of those same Holy Days when they might hike across the city to Arlington for the Tomb of the Unknown Soldier or down to the Smithsonian, wondrously cluttered with the wax figures of Indian chiefs and the original Spirit of St. Louis. Not that larger Washington was regarded as wilderness or that the institutions of government weren't prized by those highly patriotic Catholics, but that, for all their success, the last vestige of that old alien feeling had yet to be removed. In truth it wasn't the *world* they were in but not quite of, but their beloved America.

In the fall of 1958 Michael Maguire began his second year at Catholic University's Theological College. Washington was continually abuzz with news; events that would shape the future followed each other in quick sequence that year. The president, acting on his own authority and with no particular regard for the precedent set, sent the U.S. Marines into Lebanon to restore order and bolster a friendly government. The Supreme Court, applying its own four-year-old principle, affirmed the right of embattled black children to attend a segregated school in Little Rock, Arkansas. "Here come the niggers!" the rednecks cried, and they were right. The first American satellite was successfully shot into space. Nikita Khrushchev became the premier of the USSR. A grand jury found that quiz-show winner Charles Van Doren, the son of my own literary idol, was a fake. The U.S. Food and Drug Administration was sponsoring tests on an oral contraceptive that would free women from the fear of pregnancy. Ché Guevara and Fidel Castro routed the last of Batista's troops to complete the liberation of Cuba. Stereophonic recording was developed and among young people outside the seminary the hits of the year were Buddy Holly's "Maybe Baby" and the Kingston Trio's "Tom Dooley." 1958 finished Elvis as a musical innovator — he went into the army — but it launched a trio of Liverpool teenagers who called themselves "The Silver Beatles." Any one of these events would have justified Eldridge Cleaver's comment made about Rosa Park's refusal to relinquish her seat to a white man on a Montgomery bus: "Somewhere in the universe a gear in the machinery had shifted." Taken together they support the view that the era of tumultuous change we call "the Sixties" actually began in 1958.

But no event of that year was more fraught with significance for the young men studying for the Roman Catholic priesthood than the death of the man who had come to embody everything triumphant, timeless and secure about their Church, but also everything static, rigid, morose and moralistic. He was an Italian, born Eugenio Pacelli, but revered by two generations as Pope Pius XII. When he died that fall many Catholics reacted as if some law of nature had been transgressed. His Holiness dead? That was no gear shifting, but the machinery shutting down. A kind of tensing — that glandular "*Achtung!*" — swept the Church, and with it the unexpected visceral knowledge that the last of the ancient command societies, dating back one and a half millennia, was, like an old Roman, about to fall on its sword. Catholics sensed implicitly that the ecclesial structure that had enabled their achievement in postwar America could continue serene and unshaken, immutable as well as infallible, only if Pius, as some thought he might, lived forever.

Seminarians were ordinarily restricted in their ability to follow the news. It wouldn't do to have them distracted by the man-chasing sensations of Jayne Mansfield or Marilyn Monroe. Let me say, aside, that the wholesome movie stars like Doris Day and Grace Kelly were vastly more seductive as fantasy figures to such repressed young males. After all they, like the "innocent" actresses, were being taught the manipulative values of chastity. The most insightful actress of the day, by the way, was Jane Wyman, being the first American to see through Ronald Reagan. But actresses are not my subject, alas. If they were I'd pay homage to Brigitte Bardot, who rescued cinematic eros from the weirdos on Forty-second Street. It was a great day for us Puritans when we learned that sex was art. But seminarians, I was speaking of seminarians.

Reports of goings-on in "the world," whether sex-related or not, could only make it more difficult for the boys to keep their eyes on the ball, in Michael's phrase, which was not God but the thirteenth century. And so by and large newspapers, magazines, radio and television were forbidden unless there was a Catholic angle to the event reported, Edward R. Murrow interviewing Senator and Mrs. Kennedy, for example, or any Notre Dame football game. This restriction, of course, played its part in the larger strategy of seminary discipline, which was to reduce those young men, even those best ones, to the status of dependent children. Seminarians were being trained in subservience, and no one had embodied the totalitarian system in which obedience was synonymous with humiliation better than Pius XII. He had run the entire Church the way every rector ran his seminary. When the cardinals of the Church sequestered themselves in the Sistine Chapel to elect a new pope, their Consistory became the top news story of the day and seminarians across America were not only permitted to follow it but expected to.

The places of honor in the students' common room at Theological College belonged to two pool tables and a Ping-Pong table. The television was a small-screen floor model with a battered wood cabinet, the hand-me-down gift of some faculty member, and it was impossible, even after the head student and two others lifted it onto one of the pool tables, for more than a couple of dozen fellows to watch it at one time. There were a hundred and twenty-two soutaned theologians in the room, the entire student body not counting the eight who were in the kitchen washing dishes, a chore everyone took turns doing except the deacons. Deacons could smoke too, though not in front of the others. Theirs were the petty privileges of a petty elite; the last lesson in how to be a priest.

It was the free period after the evening meal. Ordinarily, during those thirty or forty minutes, they all donned sweaters over their cassocks and went out in raucous groups of three, always three because more was impossible on the neighborhood sidewalks and fewer was forbidden. For a seminarian to stroll alone was antisocial, and for a pair to go could indicate an incipient "particular friendship." For obvious reasons homophobia thrived in the seminary culture, and not only among the faculty. Seminarians were alert for any sign of intense feeling in themselves or others. Affection reaching to any depth at all set off alarms, and you can imagine what that did to their capacity for friendship. And so as trios they strolled along Michigan Avenue or down Fourth Street or onto the CU campus to check the progress of "the shrine," the National Shrine of the Immaculate Conception, the massive Romanesque basilica that after intermittent construction over thirty years was nearly finished. With its pencil-sharp K. of C. bell tower and its brilliant blue mosaic beach ball of a dome, it already dominated the northeast hill of Washington as completely — and wasn't this the point? — as the Episcopal National Cathedral dominated the northwest hill. Unfortunately the Protestant Church was a classic Gothic masterpiece while the National Shrine seemed garish even to the unaesthetic Catholic donors whose names were being chiseled on pillars in the vast crypt. There was a story, in fact, that on the morning of the day that the great dome was dedicated at last the Blessed Virgin Mary herself appeared on the massive shrine plaza and said to two humble seminarians, "Tell the bishops that I want them to honor me by building on this very spot a beautiful church."

But that evening, despite the mild late October weather, they weren't outside. They were attending as well as they could to the tiny television. A hush fell over the room when Walter Cronkite reported the amazing news that the Consistory had still not chosen the new pope. The smoke had risen black twice that day, indicating two more futile ballots. Speculation now, he said, was that the cardinals, divided between progressive and traditionalist factions, were deadlocked. Cronkite went on to other news, but the seminarians ignored him, bursting into heated conversation of their own. Many took offense at the newsman's implication that liberal versus conservative politics, not the guidance of the Holy Ghost, would determine the outcome of the papal election. Others, the more worldly ones, thought it naive in the extreme to expect a secular commentator not to impose some human analysis on the sacred process.

Gene O'Mally didn't care, frankly. He was worried about the game. The next day Theological College was playing the Paulists, and on the Paulists' court. O'Mally was the captain. He was a type and I know all about him. They came through Fordham by the gross. Even as I remember what Michael told me of him I can read his mind. He'd played basketball for Notre Dame, and he knew better than anyone that his team didn't have it. Hell, it was embarrassing. They'd lost six in a row now. Even the Capuchins in their fruity beards beat them, and the Paulists had won the league the year before.

Some people thought the seminary basketball league was frivolous, the litniks and the eggheads, but O'Mally's opinion was that God was as glorified by a nice lay-up as He was by the *Tantum Ergo*. But he also thought it was a disgrace to have all these effete religious orders trouncing the diocesan guys of TC, and he was going to do something about it. If he didn't, the Paulists, who could be vicious bastards, were going to run off a hundred points against them.

As the seminarians began to drift out of the common room — they had to be in their rooms in ten minutes for the night study period — he slid into line behind Mike Maguire. Oh, if he could just get the son of a bitch to play tomorrow, that would do it! Not that they'd win, but O'Mally just wanted to keep it from being a rout. Maguire, at six-three, was taller than anybody on the team, and the guys from Dunwoodie said he was good. In fact O'Mally had seen him shooting baskets by himself the previous spring, and he had the touch. The ball just floated off his fingers, like it had helium in it. He'd knocked off ten in a row from all over the court. But Maguire wouldn't play, and he didn't even shoot baskets by himself this fall. For sports all he did was swim laps in the CU pool. When O'Mally'd approached him in September he'd declined pleasantly enough, but firmly. He'd said he wanted to concentrate on studies and that b-ball wasn't his sport anyway. Maguire'd made a joke about being older and said his jock days were over. But O'Mally's theory was that Maguire was used to being the big shot. He never referred to the war-hero stuff himself, but everybody else was always aware of it. Hell, a lot of guys looked at him with a kind of awe. Maguire seemed oblivious to that, but probably he secretly lapped it up. He probably wouldn't play ball unless he was the captain. Well, O'Mally had decided during that miserable game against the Capuchins that if that was what it would take to get Maguire on the team, it was okay with him. He'd resign the damn captaincy and offer it to Mister Wonderful.

"Hey, Mike, how goes it?"

"Hi, Gene-o, how you doing?" Maguire was a year behind O'Mally, but at twenty-six, he was two years older. He'd gained weight since entering the seminary in New York four years before, and had lost the ascetic leanness and gray pallor he'd brought home from China. He was stoop-shouldered now, but no more than many tall men, and when he tired, his face took on a bony, haggard look. Still he was an imposing, robust man, devoid of boyishness, a handsome black Irishman in his prime. In the opinion of his superiors and most of his colleagues his physical stature was more than matched by other less tangible qualities of character. Once, on a bet, he skated out onto the freshly frozen lake at Dunwoodie. When the ice, which was too thin, began to crack he went faster and soon he was furiously skating across the lake, ahead of the crack. A gully of black water opened up behind him, but he never hesitated. He made it all the way across the lake, and the seminarians who saw what he'd done said to themselves, though not to each other, "Here is a man I want to be with."

Some of the fellows, however, could never master their ambivalent feelings about him. It was less a problem at TC than it had been at Dunwoodie, but even among the theology students in Washington there were men for whom Michael's background was an insufferable rebuke, as if he'd risked his life in combat and endured years as a POW precisely to make them feel inferior. What his fellows were not aware of, for Michael kept his feelings to himself, was the fact that he felt deprived of the very sense of manhood, of power, his years in Korea and China had given him. This man who'd survived war and withstood brainwashing had been cut down to size too by the chickenshit of seminary life. It had been like a return to the suffocating, child-pinching world of Inwood.

Once, the previous winter, he'd asked permission, as he was required to, of Father Farley, the gruff rector, to go ice skating on the Reflecting Pool at the Washington Monument. Father Farley said no, which so surprised Michael he involuntarily, for it was practically insubordinate to do so, asked why. The rector replied that it was dangerous. Dangerous! The water in that landscaped artificial pool was only three feet deep! At Dunwoodie Michael had skated across that cracking ice above twenty feet of water. "Go, Michael, go!" Michael Maguire had been a war hero! Had killed people! Had saved many lives! Stop, Michael, stop!

"Dangerous, Father?" he asked, his face reddening.

Father Farley stared at him.

After a long time, a critical time in Michael's life, he turned and left the rector's room, but not before saying, as he was required to even though he'd been refused, "Thank you, Father."

Michael worried, in other words, as much as any of them did about appeasing the great authority figures of rector and faculty, and he spent all of his energy, like the others, trying to dazzle not two parents but two dozen of them. If there was a difference between Michael and most of the others it was this: he was man enough to suspect what was happening to him. He was becoming what Saint Paul called a "eunuch for the Kingdom of God." And there's the key. He would never have tolerated it, but he had inherited a belief and had yet to question it that the emasculating shit of life in the Church was the absolute will of God.

Seminarians are inveterate nicknamers — they call each other "Fuzz" and "Spade" and "Champ" and "Wolfjaw" and "Bishop" and "Sleepy," always with a needle — and in Dunwoodie Michael had been tagged as "Mister Wonderful." Few had the nerve to call him that to his face, and it had evolved, as such handles do, first into "Won-ton," as if he was being ribbed for an interest in China, and then simply into "Won," pronounced "Juan." Michael knew better than to show how it insulted him, and he'd grown used to the complicated feelings his fellows had about him. But their bitterness, when it surfaced in a cold look or a snide crack, could depress him, and Michael had learned in Dunwoodie that nothing was served by outshining the others unnecessarily. That was, in point of fact, why he'd stopped playing basketball, a game at which since Good Shepherd no one he'd played with could touch him.

"What do you think, Won?" O'Mally asked. "Who's going to get it?"

There were Vatican-watchers among the seminarians who had all the leading candidates — the *papabili* — doped out. That crowd lived for Church gossip and it was them Michael kidded when he said, "Walter Cronkite, Gene-o. I think Walter Cronkite."

One of the wags would have come back with a Cronkitish, "*Et vos ibi!*" — "And you are there!" — but O'Mally wasn't famous for his wit and his Latin was far too workmanlike for cracks. He said, as they rounded a corner into one of the long dark corridors off which each man had his room, "But it's got to be an Italian."

At first Maguire thought that O'Mally was responding to his remark about Cronkite, but in fact he'd ignored it. Michael couldn't imagine that Gene-o really wanted to go on about this. There was nothing new to be said on the subject. In recreation and in every class for days now the Consistory had been the only topic. If they all talked about it compulsively it was surely because the interregnum was implicitly threatening. Where was Holy Mother the Church without her Father figure? "I hope it's Triozzi," Maguire said. "At least he knows the U.S. I think a lot of those Italians think we're all Baptists over here."

"He doesn't have a chance. Too young."

"That's true. Only sixty-three."

They both laughed.

"When we're sixty-three," Maguire said, "It'll be nineteen ninety-five."

"Speak for yourself, old man."

"That's right, I keep forgetting. I'm a delayed vocation."

They stopped at Maguire's door. The pause there should have

been the briefest possible, like one of them getting off a moving sidewalk. They were discouraged from talking at each other's doors, and absolutely forbidden, for the usual reason, to cross the threshold of another seminarian's room.

"Actually, Won," O'Mally said awkwardly, "I wanted to ask you something."

"What's that, Gene-o?" Michael waited. It could have been anything from switching a dishwashing assignment to help with his Canon Law notes.

"You probably know the team isn't doing that hot."

"Hey, the season's early, Gene-o. It'll pick up."

"It's a third over, Mike, and we haven't won a game. And we haven't played the toughest teams yet. Even the Capuchins beat us. Talk about mortification! Lord!" O'Mally fingered the row of cassock buttons that bisected him as neatly as a shrimp's vein.

Michael liked O'Mally. When he'd first come to TC, O'Mally had called on him somewhat formally to say welcome. It was a studied act of kindness — he repeated it for all the first-year men — but Michael appreciated it nonetheless. Later he understood about O'Mally's preoccupation with the basketball team and realized he was in fact scouting the new class, but that didn't seem to take from the gesture's sincerity. O'Mally was the kind who could talk with feeling and a pseudo-Freudian erudition about the importance of athletic competition as a sublimation of the sexual drive. Not that he would credit Freud, of course, who was still regarded as an enemy of religion, or for that matter, not that he would even know that the theory he was parroting originated with the notorious psychoanalyst.

"Losing is one thing," Michael sympathized, "but getting murdered is another. It's enough to make you want to quit, I'll bet."

"That's why I wanted to talk to you. We can't quit, of course. I mean, jeez, what a disgrace that would be. And imagine how that would look in my file. Farley would love it."

If seminarians were obsessed with Farley's opinion of them it was because no one got ordained without his recommendation. Students at TC were rarely fired, but the culture of seminary life required a constant insecurity. The rector and faculty nurtured it and students — remember, these were all men in their twenties — played into it. It was another of the ways in which the slave-master mentality of priests was inculcated. By the time a man makes bishop he has spent a lifetime cooperating in his own humiliation, and he can't understand, now that he's in a position to humiliate others, why they don't cooperate too.

"Anyway, quitting isn't what I wanted to talk to you about. I was hoping you might reconsider and come out." O'Mally leaned against the doorjam.

Maguire snapped on his desklamp, then sat on the edge of his perfectly made bed. "I know it's not easy for you to ask me, Gene-o."

O'Mally smiled. "It's not so bad."

"I'm not the easiest guy in the world to approach."

"That's true."

"I'd really like to help you out, but . . ."

"Hey, it's not me I'm asking for, Mike. It's the other guys. Jeez, talk about demoralized. You know what I'm saying to you? Your brothers need you. I mean it's that simple. Your brothers need you. Not because you're so terrific yourself." He smiled winningly. "But God happens to have given you certain gifts. You're taller than any of us. You can shoot. And you're tough. And why did God give you those gifts? Not so you could hang out with the litniks in the sacristy. God's favorite people are the jocks, everybody knows that. And you're a ten-talent guy if there ever was one. But you're just burying your talents like the fellow in the gospel."

" 'Well done, good and faithful servant,' " Maguire laughed. " 'You have been faithful over a little. I will put you over much.' "

"Just put me over tomorrow when we play the Paulists." O'Mally's face darkened. "You're probably better than I am, Mike. I think you probably ought to be captain."

"Don't be ridiculous. The guys elected you captain. What's my being captain have to do with it?"

"I thought maybe you'd come out if you were captain."

Michael stared at O'Mally. " 'You wicked and slothful servant'!" he said good-naturedly, disguising the insult he felt. Why didn't this son of a bitch take a hint? Michael simply didn't want to play. Think of it as an act of independence, one of the few he allowed himself in that world where conformity and dependence were the great virtues. It wasn't only the faculty you had to please, finally, but all your peers too. Everyone's opinion counted but your own. Here was O'Mally saying that in *his* opinion Maguire was a vain, arrogant showboat who could be bought off with the measly honor of being team captain.

"It would look good on your record if you were captain," O'Mally pressed.

"My record looks okay, Gene-o."

"Not if they think you're a loner, Mike. This is your chance to do something for the community."

How had such a small thing become so big? How could Michael's *not* playing basketball reflect badly on him? But O'Mally's thrust had struck home and Michael felt a moment's panic. Did they think him a loner? If his fellow seminarians so regarded him, wouldn't the faculty learn of it? Wouldn't Farley?

"Look, Gene-o, I'd appreciate it if you didn't press me on this." What Michael meant was, "Please don't tell on me." He knew that his act of autonomy was an offense, but there was little enough autonomy left to him and he had instinctively to protect it. How ironic that a last pathetic defense of his balls should have required the rejection of sport.

O'Mally shrugged and opened his hands. He was about to say a final word.

"Mister O'Mally!" a voice boomed down the corridor. It was Father Farley. "Get to your room!"

O'Mally flashed a stricken look, then disappeared.

The next morning Michael woke feeling a fresh insecurity about his status, and so he resolved that during theology class, at his first opportunity, he would dispel any possible impression that he considered himself apart from the others or, God forbid, better, by joining in the discussion with unusual energy. Class participation was one of the things you were judged on.

De Ecclesia, Ecclesiology; the subject of the class was the Church itself, and the ongoing Consistory had led the professor to focus for some weeks on the concept of Apostolic Succession. On that notion — that the bishops and popes of the Church are linked in an unbroken line to Peter and the Apostles themselves — rested both the legitimacy of Catholic Orders and the Catholic claim to spiritual and juridical superiority to the Protestant denominations. For days the professor had been displaying the charts of the historical record, the conclusive if mechanical evidence that Catholic claims were true. It was like an endless relay race with each bishop a runner taking the baton — God's Grace — and handing it on to the next. No matter that, far from sleek, ascetic athletes, most of them were like the characters Orson Welles portrays, pampered, self-indulgent, dictatorial and vain. The idea of Apostolic Succession was as central to the Church as the idea of the Balance of Powers was to the U.S. Constitution. From it derived the basic Catholic doctrine that the authority of bishops and pope came not from the people, but through the Apostles from Christ Himself.

"Any questions?" The professor blinked above his notes. He was an old man named Father James Ford, but because he'd always abbreviated his first name, "Jas.," and also, of course, because there was nothing modern about him, he'd been discreetly dubbed "Jazz" by seminarians years before.

Michael raised his hand and Father Ford nodded. "While there is no pope, Father, who can be said to hold the power of the Keys?"

"Why, the power rests with the whole Church."

"But then it reverts to the pope once he's elected?"

"Precisely."

"Thank you, Father."

Jazz blinked out at him.

Michael had hoped to get something going, but even he knew what a dustball his question had been.

"Anything else?" Jazz recognized another seminarian.

"In order to be in contact with the Apostles somebody has to be a member of the Church?"

"That's correct, although, as you know, the Holy Office distinguishes between *in re* membership and *in voto*. Who can tell me what this distinction means?"

No one moved.

Father Ford grimaced, as if their ignorance was a physical pain of his.

Michael raised his hand. "*In re* means 'in fact' and *in voto* means 'in desire.' "

Jazz nodded. "One can be incorporated as a member of the

Church *in fact,* as we are, or one can belong to it *in desire,* as in the case of a man who wishes to act in accord with the will of God. Why is this distinction important, Mister Maguire?"

"Because it's how we get around the doctrine that there's no salvation outside the Church."

The class gasped at Michael's phrase "get around," and braced itself. Michael realized it was a slip. He'd answered, stupidly, with what he really thought. He tried to bury it by going on. "Father Feeney was condemned for concluding that those outside the Church are *ipso facto* damned. That has never been the Catholic position. The Catholic position is only that there is no salvation outside the Church. And we can affirm that because *in voto* everyone is, in potency at least, even atheists whose 'desire' may be implicit, a member of the Church."

"Even Luther?"

"Yes, I would say so."

"Well, you're wrong. Membership *in voto* is available only to those who have had no opportunity to know the truth. Luther was a heretic and apostate." Father Ford was angry. To him Luther wasn't an obscure figure from centuries before but an enemy who still threatened, the embodiment of rebellion. If he had been squashed the first time he'd used a cocky tone with his professor the Reformation would never have happened.

Michael said nothing.

"Do you understand now?"

"Yes, Father," Michael answered.

"And is understanding Church doctrine our purpose, Mister Maguire, or is our purpose 'getting around it'?"

"Understanding, Father."

"I expect you to remember that, young man."

"I will, Father." Michael felt sick. He continued to stare back at the professor, but not defiantly. He was afraid to lower his eyes for fear it would seem coy.

Father Ford snapped his notebook shut and stood. The class stood. They recited the Latin prayer and, then, once the priest left, burst into muted conversation, a release of tension.

Michael walked from the room without talking to anyone, but when he saw O'Mally ahead of him in the corridor he grabbed his arm. "Hey, Gene-o!"

O'Mally faced Michael. "Boy, Maguire, you got the hot-foot that time, didn't you?"

Michael made a face, a quick intake of breath through gritted teeth. "And I was just trying to play the damn game. Speaking of games . . ." He paused. He knew what he was doing. One way out from under the awful feeling of having been slapped down would be to do what this kid had asked. Michael wanted to belong. He had felt a new blast of the old *voto* — the desire to appease. Finally it came to that, and the walls around the last small part of himself that he had not surrendered just collapsed. He felt like a child asking a harsh playmate, ". . . Do you still want me for this afternoon?"

"Pick!" the Paulist guard cried and moved toward the top of the key, driving O'Mally into the other Paulist who'd set himself.

"Switch!" Michael called, sliding away from his own man, the pick, to cover the guard. The guard went up for a jump-shot and Michael went with him. When the guard released the ball, it was still arching slowly upward when Michael slapped it away.

"Shit!" the Paulist said, but the play moved quickly away from him as O'Mally led yet another TC fast break. Approaching the key he drew one of the two defenders and dropped a short pass to Maguire who was coming in right behind him. Maguire drove into the left slot, drawing the other defender, then fired a pass across to Tommy Coogan, the second TC guard, who was open for an easy lay-up.

"Beautiful! Way to go, Coogs!"

Coogan crossed to Maguire on their way upcourt. "Mister Wonderful," he sang, "that's you."

Michael grinned. With less than ten minutes to go they were leading 74–70. TC hadn't beaten the Paulists in four years. Michael had already scored twenty-four points, but his real value to the team seemed to be the way in which his concentration and his hustle — his discipline — communicated to his teammates. He had a rare *esprit* and they caught it. On the basketball court his natural grace, his instinctive willingness to take risks, asserted themselves. It was the opposite of the inhibitions he felt throughout the rest of his life. He was a man of action again. Why had he denied himself this pleasure? So as not to show the others up?

To protect a little autonomy for himself? Or had he refused to play because he *was* a loner? No, not that. Suddenly he knew. He had denied himself this pleasure — driving, shooting, passing, scoring — because it *was* pleasure.

O'Mally had scored nineteen points, a personal high. Even if they couldn't quite hang on to win, although at last he believed they were going to, this was already the happiest day of his life. During his two years at Notre Dame, the truth was he'd been a substitute and he'd never really experienced until now the true ecstasy of the game. All he'd wanted was a ringer to keep the score respectable. It never occurred to him that what he'd get was everybody at his best together.

The Paulist forward took a bad shot. None of his teammates was in position for the rebound and Michael snagged it easily. He passed off to O'Mally for the run upcourt.

O'Mally's heart was in his throat. This would make it six, a lead of six!

But something happened.

The carillon in the Knights of Columbus bell tower at the shrine exploded with a loud peal of bells, and in quick succession bells began to ring loudly from the crenellated tower of the adjacent Paulist house and then from the Redemptorists' beyond the playing field and from TC across the wooded ravine behind the basketball court. The bells in the tower at the CU faculty residence began ringing too.

The players drifted. O'Mally started to throw a pass at Coogan, but Coogan wasn't paying attention. He was looking goofily up at the sky as if for a show of angels. Bells were coming from Trinity College across Fourth Street.

The referee blew his whistle; time out.

They all stood there listening as the bells from religious houses all over Brookland began to sound. It was the most extraordinary thing.

"*Habemus Papam!*" one of the Paulists cried. "We have a pope!"

And with that, the Paulists and the TC guys filed off the basketball court, some without picking up their sweatshirts. They were all dressed alike in tan workpants or old black cotton trousers and T-shirts. They didn't wear shorts. They crossed the driveway en masse and funneled quickly into the common room of the Paulist House. As a religious order, the Paulists took the vow of poverty, which meant that they had a new, expensive, large-screen television mounted nicely where everyone could see it. On the screen was a photograph of Saint Peter's Basilica and a correspondent on radio hookup was describing through static the white smoke that even then was pouring from the chimney above the Sistine Chapel. He said the cardinals burned their ballots without wet straw and that's why the smoke was white.

A few moments later the correspondent said that the first unconfirmed report was that the new pope was named Roncalli. Walter Cronkite came on then and awkwardly explained that Roncalli had not been mentioned as a possible pope. For the moment they knew nothing about him, not his first name, the see of which he was Ordinary, his age or the stripe of his politics. Nor did they have a photograph. The newsman flashed that twinkle of his, though, and said it was safe to assume that Roncalli was Italian.

The seminarians didn't laugh. A somber crowd, they pressed forward, listening, waiting to glimpse their future.

Michael looked out the window. O'Mally was still standing on the basketball court with the ball between his forearm and his hip, as if he expected the game to resume. "That guy," he thought, "doesn't have his priorities straight."

Later, by the time he told me this story, by the time he'd finally thrown off the pall of priestly subservience, long after the famous fresh air that blew into the Church with the election of John XXIII had grown stale, and after Eisenhower's Lebanon had become Johnson's Vietnam and Civil Rights had become Benign Neglect and birth control had become abortion and Lennon had become Lenin and the world had learned that at Auschwitz the smoke from the ovens was white because the victims' bones lacked fat enough to blacken it, Maguire had decided that O'Mally was the only guy of all who got it right that day.

TEN

THE breakfast dishes hopped when the monsignor slammed his hand down on the table. "The son of a bitch!" he said.

"Who?" Father Rice asked mildly without looking up from the *Times.*

"Moses! The son of a bitch!"

Father Rice raised his head and shook it once at Michael. "He doesn't mean the prophet."

Michael checked himself; Moses wasn't a prophet, but it wasn't a deacon's place to correct a priest, not even a vain, pompous one like Henry Rice.

The monsignor muttered under his breath while he read the article to its conclusion. Then he looked up at the table. Father Rice and Michael were the only ones left. Father Keegan was in the church already for the eight o'clock Mass, and Father Mahon was in the common room where he could have his morning drink in peace. Since Father Rice remained buried in his newspaper, Monsignor Ellis addressed himself to the new deacon. "He is one son of a bitch."

"Robert Moses?"

"He says this neighborhood is blighted. Blighted!"

Michael watched the pastor as he began to read the news story again. The Triborough Bridge and Tunnel Authority planned to demolish certain buildings on the West Side — "warehouses and dilapidated dock facilities" — to expand the access ramps for Lincoln Tunnel, an expansion made necessary by the in-town congestion resulting from the completion two years before of the third Lincoln Tunnel tube. The accompanying diagram indicated that one ramp would empty onto Forty-third Street, right in front of the parish school. Michael had only arrived at Holy Cross from Washington two days before, having been freshly ordained to the deaconate, which was, in effect, a kind of internship, the last phase of training before ordination to the priesthood. Michael would be working in the parish all summer and looked forward to his first experiences of pastoral ministry. But so far the talk had been of nothing but Moses's plan and the threat it posed to the safety of the schoolchildren. The old priest trembled visibly as he read. Michael looked in vain for signs of the bright, good-humored man he must have been in his prime. The first thing anyone ever said about Monsignor Ellis was that he had won the United States Amateur Golf Tournament in 1911, the year he entered the seminary. This was 1960; he was seventy years old, and his arthritis had kept him off the golf course for years.

He looked up again at last, fixing his stare in Michael's direction, but his eyes remained unfocused. "He won't get away with it, the goddamn child-hating Jew."

Neither Father Rice nor Michael commented.

Monsignor Ellis pushed his chair back from the table and stood up. His body creaked. "I'm going downtown."

In the argot of the New York clergy "downtown" meant the Chancery Office at Fiftieth Street right behind Saint Patrick's, and even priests for whom the trek was uptown referred to it that way. Holy Cross Church was on Forty-second Street at Ninth Avenue. The school was on Forty-third.

"The cardinal won't let this happen."

At the dining room door the pastor stopped and looked at Michael again. Now he did see him. "What'd you say your name was?"

"Maguire, Monsignor. Michael Maguire."

"What do I have you doing?"

"The hospital, Monsignor. I'm taking Communion to the hospital."

Monsignor Ellis nodded.

"And Father Mahon's going to take me over to the school this morning. He thought I could help the sisters get the children ready for the May Devotions."

"He would!" Monsignor Ellis said bitterly, and he left.

After a moment Michael said to Father Rice, "What did he mean by that?"

The priest turned the page of his newspaper, foppishly shooting a French cuff free of the black sleeve of his sharkskin clerical suit. He eyed the day's stock listings while he said, "The kiddies are the only ones left who can stomach Father Mahon's breath. They think he's funny. The nuns probably tell each other the poor dear's had a stroke. The school is the one parish duty, aside from the early Mass, that Monsignor hasn't had to take away from him. Of course, Father Mahon considers himself more overworked than ever. Hence his interest in you."

Rose came in from the kitchen and began to clear the dishes. She was even older than Monsignor Ellis; she limped just the way he did, as if her knee was arthritic too, though it wasn't. She'd been the housekeeper at Holy Cross almost as long as he'd been the pastor. Whenever he left the table she cleared it immediately, whether the curates were finished eating or not.

"Morning, Rose," Michael said.

She nodded at him and took his coffee cup.

Father Rice snapped his newspaper shut, stood noisily and left the room. As a rule he and Rose did not address each other unless the monsignor was present, in which case they were ingratiatingly courteous to one another.

Rose, mightily balancing a tray of dishes, left the room. From inside the kitchen she threw the switch that doused the dining room lights. Because the heavy curtains remained closed, it was as dark in there as it would be at night, though Michael knew that an April morning was shimmering outside. He sat at his place for a few moments longer thinking, What in God's name have I done to myself by coming here?

But he reminded himself it was only for the summer, and he knew he could bear anything until September when he'd return to Washington for his last year of theology. These two days at Holy Cross had given him his first taste of the ferocious chill inside which most American priests must make their lives, and it stunned him. But he refused to take it as more than an isolated instance. The priesthood was a lonely life, he knew that. But there was a consolation in the manly fellowship priests shared, and he was sure that in most rectories there was cheerful conversation at table and good-humored wisecracking around the television. Here, however, each priest had his own set in his room and apparently they were never together except to eat. A rectory full of loners, he thought. The seminary was right to discourage that tendency in the men. The evening meal the night before had taken a mere fifteen minutes from start to finish. Father Mahon might be a drunk, but he was the only one who'd showed even a mild interest in Michael. He decided to join him in the common room.

"What's on?" he asked, entering, surprised to find the television on.

"The *Today* show, my boy. Have a seat." Father Mahon slapped the leather hassock with his free hand. In the other he held a highball. He sat placidly in an easy chair, his legs slowly opening and closing. He grinned at Michael, then turned his attention back to the television show, sweeping a long strand of reddish-gray hair across his mostly bald pate.

"Monsignor went downtown to see Cardinal Spellman about the school," Michael began. "He said the archdiocese would never let the Triborough Authority get away with it."

Father Mahon grunted and sipped his drink. A large burly Irishman, it was easy to picture him behind an Inwood bar, serving drinks, or at an intersection waving traffic through, or, for that matter, in his undershirt operating a jackhammer.

"What do you think, Father?"

"It's not what I think. It's what I know."

When Michael realized the priest wasn't going to tell him, he pressed. "What would that be?"

Father Mahon looked at him. "Old man Moses and Spelly have a deal. No doubt about it. That ramp is going onto Forty-third Street and that's it. You watch."

"But the archdiocese would have a case. Imagine rush hour. How many cars use Lincoln Tunnel? Good Lord, the hazard would be enormous. I agree with the monsignor. It seems quite callous."

"Robert Moses? Callous?" Father Mahon laughed. He continued to laugh; inappropriately, Michael thought.

"They could route the ramp some other way," Michael offered.

"No need." The priest chuckled again, then stopped. He faced Michael. "Can't be any hazard to the children, can there, if there's no school?"

The two men stared at each other.

"What do you mean, Father?"

Dave Garroway was talking with Burt Lancaster about his new movie, *Elmer Gantry*.

"What do you mean, Father?" he repeated.

"Hey, Mike, call me Ed. You make me feel like an old fart. That what they call you? Mike?"

"Yes. Or Michael, either one."

"You're the war hero, right?"

"I was in Korea. Forgive me, Ed, but I don't follow what you said there, about there being no school."

Father Mahon lifted his shoulders dramatically, grimacing. "I've said too much already."

Michael stared at him.

"Let me put it to you this way, Deacon. Old man Moses and Spelly are like this." He held up a pair of crossed fingers. "Have been since the Saw Mill Parkway deal. Moses bought a corner of the property at Dunwoodie for two million dollars when he brought the Cross County into the Saw Mill. Same corner the real estate guys said was worth about fifty grand. He bought Spelly off, but good. And *for* good."

"How do you know about that?"

"I was procurator at Dunwoodie at the time. Nineteen forty-seven. They've been scratching each other's backs ever since. You think Moses would defy Spelly on something like this? You think Spelly would defy Moses?" He snorted. "Poor old Arthur. He's just the last to catch on."

"But you said . . ."

Father Mahon snapped his fingers at Michael. "It's gone! I said it's gone!" Father Mahon leveled his voice, and for a moment he seemed a different person, alert and sober, an Irish DA. "You go look at that diagram again, Mike. Notice two things. To bring that ramp out on Forty-fourth Street they'd have to reverse the direction of traffic going all the way across town, but that would screw up their fancy new alternating system completely. Second, to bring the ramp out on Forty-third, they've got to have twice as much street on both sides. They've got to take the school for that. You can bet Spelly got a pretty penny for it, not that we'll see a dull nickel."

"Well, they'd build a new school then, right?"

Father Mahon laughed.

"What about the children, Father?"

The priest tapped his head. "They will have thought of that. So happens old man Moses has just finished tearing down most of Clinton for that nice new Lincoln Center of his. Cut the heart right out of Saint Paul the Apostle two parishes up. You know the church on Fifty-ninth Street? Looks like an armory?"

Michael nodded.

"A thousand families evicted! Shipped out to Jersey or Bay Ridge or Flushing, like that!" He snapped his fingers. "So Saint Paul's has a school but no kids. Down here we got kids but no school. Just sixteen blocks away. A couple of used buses get donated and bingo! Problem solved! So what if it cuts the heart out of this parish. We're just 'blight' anyway. Relax, Deacon. All things come to him who takes it easy."

"Is this all . . . a surmise . . . of yours?"

Father Mahon seemed to think the question bordered on the insolent, but he decided, what the hell, not to take offense. "You mean has anyone taken me into his confidence? Or sought my advice?" He laughed. "I can figure it out, my boy, because I don't expect to be consulted. Poor old Arthur, on the other hand. His problem is he thinks he's the pastor of this parish, can't imagine he wouldn't be in on the planning. Ought to know better by now. There's only one pastor in New York, a roly-poly red-cheeked bowl of Jell-O, the Cardinal-Leprechaun. Only this Jell-O's got arsenic in it. This leprechaun has a rapier hidden in his shillelagh. I know it. Bob Moses knows it. And now even our wet-behind-the-ears war-hero deacon knows it. Want a drink?"

"No thanks. I'm on my way to the hospital."

"I used to have the hospital."

"Did you?"

Father Mahon stared at Michael, his eyes full of self-pity. "Yeah."

Here was a man, Michael sensed, who had tilted with Spellman and lost. He shuddered, as if he was seeing into the future, the shell of another man, the husk. He looked away. "I'll check in with you when I get back. We're going over to the school, right?"

"Sure. Got to show you around while it's still there." Father Mahon started. "Hey, don't say anything to the nuns, okay? Don't say anything about that to anybody. I'm just an old asshole breaking wind."

"I won't say anything."

The pastoral duties of the deacon include preaching, baptizing and bringing Holy Communion to the sick. As Michael went that morning from room to room in Saint Clare's Hospital, dressed in black suit and Roman collar, carrying the small ciborium and placing on the outstretched tongues of patients, young ones as well as old, men as well as women, the thin white wafer, the Blessed Sacrament, the Lord Himself, he realized that for a long time he'd carried a picture of a man doing exactly this. A picture of the priest who'd bent over his father at the end, a picture of Father O'Shea distributing Communion on a hillside in Korea the night of the barrage, a picture, he saw now, of the man he longed to be. It was to a hunger of his own that he brought the sacred food.

In one room there was a barely conscious man whose head was completely bandaged. Only two holes remained in the swaddling, one for breathing and one for an eye, which moved toward Michael when he touched the man's hand. Michael saw the eye register his collar, then settle on his face. Disembodied in that way, the man's eye flashed eerily, like an animal's in a cave. But then Michael sensed how it was pleading and he guessed the man was dying. He stood by him silently for a long time, holding his hand, returning his gaze. Then he said, "God bless you and keep you." All at once the man squeezed Michael's hand fiercely. Michael had never felt such an expression of gratitude before. He returned the pressure on the man's hand, not in mere sympathy, but with gratitude of his own. "I'll come back every day," he promised. For you, he thought, but also for me. This patient, like the others, was making possible for the first time in Michael's life — himself. That was what he felt. Until those first "priestly" moments — the patients all regarded him as a full-fledged priest; why wouldn't they? — it was as if he had always been someone else, and now at last, touching the bandaged man's hand, the pale cheek of an old lady, the arm of a teenager in traction, the bed of a burn victim, he touched himself with just that tenderness, just that acceptance. Ironically he knew that when they looked at him it was someone else they were seeing. He was an image of Christ now, a sign of His love; he was himself a sacrament. He'd become Michael Maguire by being more than the man of that name, and less. That was the point of the Roman collar, the point of the priesthood, and in fact it was the point of the rigorous abnegation one underwent in seminary. It was all worth it. He felt awed and humbled, profoundly unworthy. Yet, also, prouder and stronger than he'd ever been in his life. Thus, despite the glimpse he'd had that morning of the lifelong stalemate of rectory living and its effect on men who had begun every bit as hopefully as he did, and despite the premonitory chill Father Mahon gave him, Michael felt a surge of happiness to be in the ministry at last. Had he ever been happy before?

Father Mahon and Michael had lunch that day with the nuns in the teachers' dining room off the school cafeteria. The difference from the scene in the rectory was extraordinary. Father Mahon himself, free suddenly of bitterness and sarcasm, glowed pleasantly, and not only because of liquor. The women had an enlivening effect on him, and he conducted himself with an old-fashioned courtly flair that charmed the sisters. A dozen nuns and half a dozen lay women came and went, each with her tray, in a pleasant bustle. The talk was friendly and animated as they exchanged anecdotes about the morning. Three nuns had led a second-grade field trip by subway to the Central Park Zoo, and they recounted in hilarious detail each phase of it. One child had climbed into the Pulitzer Fountain at the Plaza Hotel, a younger Scott Fitzgerald.

Michael had trouble squaring these women with the image he carried of the grim crones of his childhood in Good Shepherd. In the seminary the only nuns he had encountered were the self-effacing Mexican sisters who prepared the meals and did the laundry. These women were Sisters of Charity and though their traditional black habits and stern Mother Seton bonnets, not veils, were grim enough, the nuns themselves were not. For one thing they seemed young, though in those days it was impossible to tell with precision. Sister Rita, the principal, reminded Michael of a Muriel Spark heroine, that witty liveliness and bright intellect not flaunted but definitely on display. She wasn't fifty, he was sure.

He'd expected them to defer to him and even to address him as "Father," but they didn't. Father Mahon introduced him as Michael and that was what they called him. Each woman he met found some way to make him feel welcome. After lunch Father Mahon excused himself to go back to the rectory — to say his breviary, he explained. No one winked, though Michael sensed that they all knew he was going back to drink himself to sleep.

Sister Rita showed Michael around the school. Holy Cross was a weary brick building dating back to the late nineteenth century. Only its arching, story-high paned windows distinguished it as a structure, but its corridors and classrooms were brightly plastered with drawings, cut-outs and the winners of poster contests. The floors were spotless and the windows were too. It was attended at that point by seven hundred and fifty boys and girls, a third of whom were Puerto Rican, a third Irish and a third Italian. "We should be called 'Unholy Trinity,' " Sister Rita said. The division was an accident of fluid demographics; a decade later the neighborhood would be almost entirely Puerto Rican and no one would call it "Hell's Kitchen" anymore. A decade after that the neighborhood would be full of affluent young professionals who thought their handsome brownstones, restored to perfection, were all the more wonderful for having stoically survived three generations of screaming filthy children. There would be few children by then, of course, anywhere in mid-Manhattan.

It didn't take years of pastoral experience to see right away that the school was the liveliest thing in the parish. The people came faithfully to church, but it was in the school, Michael realized, that the Church came faithfully to them. Take the matter of Spanish, for example. None of the parish clergy spoke a word of it. Sister Rita, her assistant and two other sisters were fluent. And the other nuns were all studying it in a special course at night run by the parents of children.

"Do you speak Spanish, Michael?"

"No, I don't," he admitted. In his embarrassment he offered the usual excuse. "Isn't it important to help the immigrants learn English?"

Sister Rita bristled somewhat. "Puerto Ricans aren't immigrants, are they? I mean of course they're American citizens, as you know. And many of them feel they have the right to maintain their Spanish heritage. And that enriches us as well, don't you think?"

"Yes, it does." He felt chastened but also chastised, and he had to stifle an old resentment.

"Some people feel that Puerto Ricans aren't quite as worthy of their attention as the Irish are."

" 'Some people' wouldn't by any chance be Irish, would they?"

Sister Rita laughed. "Father Mahon says you might be available to work with us."

"I'm looking forward to it."

The nun looked at him directly and said in a frank, unapologetic way, "We could use a man around here."

"I'm only here for the summer, Sister, and I assume the school year ends soon."

"Now is when we can really use you. This summer we're trying something new. We're going to have programs in the school that we hope will involve not just the students but their families as well. We'd like the school to be a real center of the community here. This neighborhood is full of life. We want to celebrate it. We want to bring it out into the open. The school gives us our entrée. The people cherish it. We want to help them cherish themselves. We could use your help if you're not busy elsewhere in the parish." She smiled; where else was there?

Michael felt like he'd walked out of a gloomy, unfriendly woods into a clearing that was splashed with sunlight, littered with flowers. "I'd very much like to be part of that, Sister, in any way I can. I'm at the hospital two mornings a week, but that's all."

"Good. I'll talk to the monsignor about it. Come into my office. I'll call him."

And just like that she did. Michael sat in a straight-backed chair opposite her desk. It was the chair, he realized, for mulish pupils. A saccharine portrait of the Sacred Heart hung on the wall behind her. Her approach to Monsignor Ellis was direct; she asked to have the deacon assigned to the school's Summer Outreach program, and she winked at Michael while listening to the pastor's response.

"Yes, Monsignor, we'll keep him busy, I promise you."

Her face changed and she listened again. Obviously the pastor had something else on his mind. Michael guessed that he was telling her about his meeting at the chancery. After a moment she said, "All right. I'm sorry. I'll talk to Sister Laurice about it. Thank you, Monsignor." When she hung up she looked at Michael and shook her head sadly. "He says the altar boys don't fold the finger towel properly. 'They just flop it in the dish,' he says."

"He didn't mention the Lincoln Tunnel ramp?"

Sister Rita reacted carefully, with a hint of the devious that suggested how the nuns and priests distrusted each other. "No, he didn't. Why should he have?"

"Well, it was in the paper this morning."

"I know."

"I would expect you two to be talking about it."

Sister Rita nodded. "Anyone would."

"But you don't?"

"The Lincoln Tunnel ramps have been in the works for months. Monsignor Ellis has insisted it would come to nothing. He refused to consider the possibility that they would actually run that traffic by our school. We decided we had to proceed without him."

"To?"

"To protect the children. We're going to take it to the parents. To the neighborhood."

Michael smiled. "The Summer Outreach program."

"That's right. It's called 'building community.' "

"It's called 'community organizing.' "

Sister Rita shrugged. "Public opinion; Robert Moses always needs to have public opinion on his side. That's how he operates. But he won't have it this time. Not when 'the good sisters' get through with him. We're going to get the ramp moved. It's our summer project, and you've just been assigned to it."

"Great!" Michael said, and he let his pleasure show.

"You haven't met my assistant principal."

"No."

Sister Rita looked at her watch. "She'll be back in twenty minutes. You should meet her. It's her show. Can you wait?"

"Sure," he said. "You're the boss."

Michael waited in the reception area outside the principal's office. Half an hour later a tall, slim nun breezed down the hallway. When she saw Michael she smiled at him but kept going. He stood and said awkwardly, "Hi."

She stopped. "Are you the new deacon?"

"Right. Michael Maguire." He put his hand out.

"I'm Sister Anne Edward." She had a striking aquiline nose and lively blue eyes, one of those nuns whose gift of presence was enhanced by the habit and whose face was made to seem radiant by the dark frame of the abstracting religious headgear. Michael guessed that she was younger than he was. When she took his hand he was struck by the force of her grip — it seemed unfeminine to him — and in some way he did not approve of in himself, he was put off by the forthright manner in which she returned his curious stare.

"I was just going in to see Sister Rita. I think she's waiting for me." She took a half-step toward the door, but paused like a girl on a porch who wasn't ready to say goodnight.

"I know. She wanted me to meet you."

"Oh." She smiled and blushed; you were waiting for me?

Michael gestured. "So lead on. I think she's waiting for both of us."

They went into Sister Rita's office. Even before the principal greeted her, Anne Edward said, "They wouldn't give them to me. They said the specific plans are not public documents. They were utterly condescending to me."

"What plans?" Michael asked. He hadn't noticed how agitated she was.

But now Sister Anne waited for the principal to nod before replying, "The tunnel ramp blueprints. We wanted to see exactly where on Forty-third Street the access will go."

Sister Rita said, "We can't start making an issue of it until we can show exactly what our problem is. We have to convict the planners with their own testimony. We need the documents. They've been very clever in keeping all the public talk vague and the diagrams sketchy, but we know they have detailed plans, and there have to be alternative plans too."

"Have you considered what the alternatives might be?" Michael asked.

"Forty-first Street," Sister Anne said. "They have to have considered it. They have to have drawn it up. It's what we'll be pushing for. That's why we need that plan too."

Michael realized it had never occurred to her that the school could go altogether; it hadn't occurred to either of them. He nearly blurted it — "The school is gone!" Father Mahon had said — but he checked himself instinctively. Already an incipient clerical loyalty inhibited him, despite his instinct that the initiative for the real welfare of the parish had fallen to these women. "Who has access to the blueprints?" he asked.

"Just officials," Sister Anne replied. "The Pharisees and the

Scribes. Aside from Triborough, only the City Construction Coordinator, who also happens to be a fellow named Moses, the Planning Commission, chaired by a fellow named Moses, and the Traffic Bureau."

"The Police Traffic Bureau?"

"Yes."

"Well, that's not run by Moses."

Sister Anne studied him. Her hand came lightly up to her lips and remained so for several moments. Her expression was both frankly interested and perfectly natural. Another woman, looking at a man like that, would have been thought perhaps somewhat overly personal. But Sister Anne Edward was clearly more interested in the subject under discussion than she was in this new young clergyman.

Michael felt himself begin to blush. He couldn't explain to her what he was thinking, and she would conclude that he was stupid. A mulish pupil after all. But he had just decided to find out before this went any farther just exactly what the threat to Holy Cross School was.

At police headquarters everyone nodded at Michael, and some officers even touched their hats. The shows of deference made him all the more self-conscious. He never for a moment was unaware of his Roman collar, and he felt vaguely guilty, as if despite his deaconate he was not truly eligible yet to wear it. The laity did not know about the distinctions of orders, major and minor, porter, acolyte, exorcist, subdeacon, deacon, priest, bishop. Were there stages of virginity? To the people you were a priest or you weren't. If you were, you wore a Roman collar, heard confessions, said the breviary, had Sunday dinner with your mother and never paid for tickets — concert, baseball or traffic.

On the sixth floor was the office of the Deputy Commissioner for Operations. Michael presented himself to the receptionist.

"Hello, Father," she said, a middle-aged woman with her dull hair in a bun. "What can I do for you?"

"I'd like to see Deputy Commissioner Kerr, if he's in."

She consulted the diary. "Do you have an appointment?"

"No, I'm sorry."

She stood up. "Whom shall I say . . . ?"

"Just say Joe Maguire's son Mike is here."

She studied him. "Father Maguire?"

He shook his head. "No, please. Just say Joe Maguire's son."

"Mike?" She pursed her lips disapprovingly, then disappeared into the adjoining office.

Michael focused on the oversized seal of the New York City Police Department that hung on the wall behind her desk. Its design — a pair of warriors flanking a shield below an eagle — was familiar to Michael because it dominated the Medal of Honor certificate displayed since his childhood in the living room of Cooper Street. Whenever Michael thought of his father, it wasn't the face of a man he conjured, but a place — the treeless hill in the Queens cemetery, bare except for the crowded rows of tombstones, from which one looked across the East River at the crowded rows of skyscrapers. As a boy, during those sad, pensive visits, it had been easy for him to think of the Chrysler and Empire State buildings as giant tombstones. What had been hard was having any specific sense at all of who his hero-father had been.

"Mike?" the voice called from the office, and then Ray Kerr, the deputy commissioner, who as a young cop was Joe Maguire's partner, came through the door. "My God, Mike!" Deputy Commissioner Kerr was so fixed on Michael as he approached him, hand extended, that the Roman collar didn't register. "Good to see you, Mike!" After shaking hands heartily, the two men stood back and looked at each other. The policeman's white shirt was resplendent at the shoulders with gold braid. They laughed at their costumes, but then Kerr said with alarm, "Hey, you're not ordained already?"

"I'm just a deacon, don't worry. Would I get ordained without you there? It's next year."

The commissioner flicked Michael's collar. "Well, you look wonderful. Christ, you must break the heart of every dame in New York City."

Michael smiled. "I would if they had hearts."

The receptionist had resumed her place at her desk.

"Right, Marie?" Kerr said, "Don't the best-looking guys always go in the priesthood?"

"Yes, sir."

"Come on in, Mike." They went into the deputy commissioner's office and sat in studded leather chairs. Marie brought coffee. Ray Kerr asked about Michael's mother and took obvious pleasure in hearing Michael describe her. She couldn't have been better, particularly now that Michael was in the city again. The commissioner told Michael about his own children; his daughter was in law school, but his son had quit high school to work in a garage. He shook his head, a bare hint of the disappointment he felt, then fell silent.

After a moment, Michael said, "Ray, I have a favor to ask."

"You name it, Mike. I'd paint the stripe on Fifth Avenue green for you."

Michael did not open the tube that held the blueprints until he was alone in his room at Holy Cross. The sun had begun its decline over New Jersey and the priests had already gathered in the rectory dining room for the evening meal, but he spread out on his bed the plans entitled "Manhattan Entrance Plaza, Expansion." It took him some moments to orient himself, and the first several sheets, while indicating other buildings on Forty-third Street, did not refer to the school. The width of the ramp entering Forty-third, however, was indicated as ninety feet, while the width of the street itself was indicated elsewhere as sixty. Thirty feet were going to have to come from somewhere. He found a sheet marked "Demolition," on which a wedge-shaped blue shadow angling intown from Forty-third Street and Tenth Avenue was superimposed on the plots of existing buildings. Holy Cross School clearly fell within it.

It was not as if he went down to dinner intending to keep it secret, but the mood at the dining room table derailed him. Monsignor Ellis had just rebuked either Father Rice or Father Keegan. Both men were flushed, bent over their food. Father Keegan, a frail priest of about fifty, had seemed timid before, but he was cowed now. Father Mahon smiled at Michael obliviously, his face still creased from sleep. Michael's entrance altered the silence, without ending it. The priests ate their soup daintily, but the sounds of spoons against dishes dominated. When Michael had taken his place and spread his napkin in his lap, the monsignor said coldly, "Nice of you to join us."

"I'm sorry," Michael said, automatically. Once he would have hated himself for his subservience, but by now it was ingrained. No one spoke. Rose served grossly overcooked lamb, and they went to work on that. It was going to be another fifteen-minute meal. Michael knew that it wasn't his place to speak, but he simply could not tolerate either the silence or the suspense.

"Monsignor Ellis," he began, "How'd it go this morning?"

It seemed to Michael that the three curates froze for an instant.

Monsignor Ellis, however, did not miss a beat. "Darn well!" he said. "Darn well!"

"How so?"

The pastor leaned toward Michael and gestured with his fork. "The cardinal gave me his personal assurance that there was no cause for concern. He's not going to let anything befall the children of Holy Cross." He resumed eating.

Michael looked quickly across at Father Mahon, but he was intent upon the bread he was spreading with oleo. After a moment, Michael asked, "So the ramp will be rerouted?"

Monsignor Ellis looked sharply at him. "Isn't that what I just said?"

Michael held the pastor's eyes for an instant longer than he should have, and that "insolence" — its implicit "No, that is not what you said, nor obviously what the cardinal said" — released the old man's fury. "Goddamnit! I will not have this at my own table! I will not have it! Do you understand?"

Michael thought it wasn't necessary to answer, but he was wrong.

"Well, do you?!" the priest shouted.

"Yes, Monsignor."

Nothing more was said.

Within five minutes the dreary meal was over and each of them had retired to his room.

Michael was shaken by the pastor's anger. He considered rolling the blueprints up and stashing the tube of them in the trash in the alley, but only for a moment.

"In for a penny," he said to himself, feeling something he hadn't allowed himself to feel in years. He picked up the phone and called the convent.

To his own surprise, when the phone was answered, he did not ask for Sister Rita, but for her assistant, Sister Anne Edward.

ELEVEN

THE next morning he found her in the schoolyard, a drab paved quadrangle that could have served as the exterior set for a prison film. She was supervising the ten o'clock recess, and the children were swarming like bees. Unlike the other nuns who had taken up their positions in the schoolyard and stood watching like sentries, Sister Anne Edward had joined in the games.

The game was kickball, and it was her turn to kick just as Michael arrived. She didn't see him. Otherwise she'd have been self-conscious when she hiked her skirts and charged the rolling ball, inadvertently displaying her old-fashioned ankle shoes, granny shoes, and a black-stockinged calf. She made contact with the ball — *thunk!* — and it sailed over the heads of the nearest children. But an eighth-grader in left field caught it in the air just as the nun rounded first base, and there was a resounding groan from her side.

Michael recognized her, of course, as the *Life* magazine cliché of the high-spirited young nun — "Good kick, Sister!" But her liveliness charmed him nonetheless and he was still applauding when she saw him. She laughed as she approached. "Were you watching?"

"Yes. You're good. The kid was lucky. That should have been a double."

"A double! That was a home run! I was robbed!" She grinned.

"Well . . ." Michael made a swatting gesture with the cardboard tube he was holding. "Try taking a crack with this."

"Are those the plans?" she asked, sobering.

"Yes."

"May I see them?"

"Out here?"

"I suppose not, but . . ." She looked around. "Wait a minute. I'll just tell Sister Laurice to cover for me." She ran across the schoolyard to another nun. She had to clutch the rosary beads hanging from her cincture. Returning to Michael she slowed to a walk because he was watching her, he realized, and so he looked away. Clothed in that particular habit — a black bonnet instead of a veil and wimple, a modestly waisted gown with flowing skirts instead of a scapular and multifolded robes — she looked more like a nineteenth-century New York Society widow than a medieval abbess, more like the Victorian Mrs. Seton, whose dress the habit memorialized, in fact, than like Eloise. Still, the effect of her clothing was the same. It made her another creature entirely, a mysterious otherworldly person who was unlike lay people or even priests. It made her a nun.

"We can go to the teachers' lunchroom off the cafeteria. Nobody will be there now. We can get some coffee."

"That would be great," he said, and they walked to the school side by side. Children waved and called her name, and some ran after her to clutch her hand for a moment before running back to their games. Each child she greeted or touched seemed special to her, and Michael sensed that each was.

She stood at the hot plate while the water heated, fussing with napkins and spooning Nescafé into cups. He listened to the faint swishing of her clothing, the rattling beads. Those subtle sounds were familiar to him from his boyhood, but at Good Shepherd School he had never watched nuns in the way he was watching her. Her body was lost in her habit and from behind not an inch of her skin was visible, not a wisp of hair. The vague outline of her slim figure, her efficient posture and carriage, suggested an unsensuous womanliness, but even that abstractly. Why then should her image have been the one to gnaw at the strange but necessary detachment he had cultivated over six years? But he knew why. She had given herself to God. She was a Bride of Christ. She was safe. He would never have allowed himself so blatantly to watch a real woman or think in this way about her. Sister Anne Edward was vivacious and pretty and smart, but what drew him to her finally — with a shock he realized that this was the first time he was in a room alone with a woman his own age since entering the seminary — was that she, like him, was, in one of the all-time fabulous phrases, a dedicated virgin. That meant not only that she too was trying to build a life around an inexplicable but compelling attraction to God, but also — and more importantly — that she was no threat. She was not automatically suspicious of him or condescending. He didn't have to prove to her that this choice was a worthy one. Outsiders would regard them as life's losers — who else became nuns and priests? — but they knew differently. Their vocation was a courageous rejection of the superficial and the sordid, a generous embrace of a life of service, the most ennobling calling there was. With anyone else of their own generation they'd have felt foolish and defensive. With each other, already, they felt better about themselves.

"Cream?"

"No, thanks. Nothing."

"No sugar?"

"No, thanks, Sister."

She served the coffee, then took a chair across the table from him. "You should call me Anne. I call you Michael."

"Okay." He smiled. "I never called a nun by her first name before."

"You still haven't."

"Anne."

"That wasn't so bad, was it?" She laughed and sipped her coffee. The sleeves of her habit fell back each time she raised the cup to her mouth, and he saw her forearms. She wore a man's watch. Her wrists were pale and he could see the faint blue lines of her veins. Other girls her age put perfume there.

"Like I said on the phone, it's bad news." Michael pushed his coffee aside and unrolled the Triborough plans. Anne Edward leaned forward. "Right there. See?" Michael planted his forefinger firmly. "The whole school is marked for demolition."

For a moment she said nothing. Then, exhaling dramatically, she leaned back in her chair. "And the monsignor says, 'Don't worry!' "

"Monsignor Ellis has his head in the trench, but that's because Moses is shooting live ammo. Obviously these plans are going through."

"No, they're not."

Michael shook his head. "Anne, if the cardinal has given the green light, and I'd say there's reason to think he has —"

"The cardinal doesn't understand the needs of this parish. If he did, he'd never permit the destruction of the school: The school is all there is at Holy Cross."

He said nothing.

"Don't you agree?"

Loyalty to his fellow clerics, whom she was criticizing — what did it require? He could say, No, there's also the hospital ministry, there are the daily Masses, there's the bingo. But those were rote exercises, and he already knew it. Only the school had life. He nodded, a small concession, but for him important. A break with clericalism. "Why else would I be here with you? I haven't shown these plans to the priests."

"They would say what you said, that it's all over. But do you know why they'd say that? Because the priests don't care about the school. They don't care about the children. Why should they fight for them? But if Robert Moses was coming through here taking away their liquor cabinet or their three days off a week or their free passes to fancy restaurants, *then* you'd hear a howl! *Then* they'd be on the cardinal's doorstep! And *then* Moses would think twice. But the priests are fatalistic now because all Moses wants to take away from the parish are its children."

When she sipped her coffee now her hands were trembling, and Michael saw that she herself wasn't nearly as bold as her speech was. When she looked at him across the rim of her cup, he saw that her eyes were full.

"I don't blame you for being angry," he said. She was right. It was an outrage. These nuns were right and the priests were not supporting them. Well, by God, he thought, I'll support them. Even if they're bound to lose. Now clerical loyalty *required* that Michael throw in with Anne Edward. Should he have let these nuns defend the parish alone? Should he have ignored what he saw in her eyes, what her speech revealed, what she was telling him? They needed the priests! They needed him! He said, "You love the children, that's obvious."

She put her cup down. "Of course we do. What sense does our life make if we don't love the children?"

Michael nodded. What a simple statement of the nun's vocation. Priests fall back on clerical privilege or on the transcendent function of administering sacraments or on the exercise of ecclesiastical power or on the superior social status they occupy in an immigrant community. Nuns fall back only on the people they serve, or on God. Michael was surprised by a wave of admiration he felt for her, and he wanted to express it. "Holy Cross is lucky it has you."

"Our order has been in this school for seventy years."

"And you?" Michael smiled.

"This is my second." She laughed and touched the corner of her eye. To purge a tear? "But I care about it as if I've always been here."

"Where were you before?"

"In the juniorate. In training. I came here right after I took vows. I felt so lucky to be assigned here. It's considered a privilege in our order because the people of this parish are so good."

"How'd you wind up in the convent, Anne?"

With a quick look she conveyed both that she did not take his right to ask such a question for granted, but also that she welcomed his interest. "The sisters in my high school; I thought, what fantastic women! They were so happy, their lives were full of meaning. I fell in love with them." She blushed but did not drop her eyes. "I fell in love with Christ." She laughed and added, self-mockingly, "Isn't that what girls in high school are supposed to do? Fall in love?" Despite her irony, however, Michael sensed the strength of her vocation. There was no equivalent for priests to the religious woman's fiercely romantic attraction to the mystical life. It was at root, of course, an attraction to the great dream figure of all time. Jesus was the ultimate Mister Goodbar.

"It's a great system, isn't it?" he said. "Now you're in a school impressing young girls with *your* happiness, with the meaning in *your* life."

"Yes," she said, but there was a hint of darkness in her that made him wonder, How happy?

She went on, "Maybe that's why the school is important to me. Schools are where we sisters do our work. Schools are where we sisters come from. We take care of our schools because they take care of us."

Michael nodded. He looked around at the corners of the room and suddenly realized that teaching nuns had been eating lunches in there for decades. Robert Moses was assaulting the ghosts of all those nuns too. A long line of fantastic women! Yes, Michael looked at her and thought that.

Perhaps she sensed these feelings in him because she continued to blush. When she didn't speak, the silence loomed between them. She picked her cup and saucer up and stood, but because her hand shook the cup rattled and she had to quiet it with her other hand. This was not like her, he sensed. She was ordinarily more self-possessed. Was he the cause of this tension? he wondered. Or was it only Robert Moses? She came to his side of the table and took his cup. She smelled of soap.

"Thanks," he said.

While she rinsed the cups and left them to drain, he rolled up the blueprints and put them into the tube.

She dried her hands while crossing to him, then dropped the towel on the table and reached for the cardboard tube just as he did. They picked it up together, each with a hand. The tube joined them. Their eyes met.

"I was going to take it," she said. "I have to show Rita."

"I have to get it back to the commissioner's office." Surely she understood that. "We can't keep it."

"But we need these plans, Michael. They prove our point. If we're going to rally the parish, they have to know what we're up against. They think it's just a widened street."

Michael felt sick suddenly. What was she asking him to do? What would the commissioner say if he didn't return the plans? What would the monsignor say if he found out? Or, good God, the cardinal!

He felt the pressure from her hand on the tube. She was pulling it toward herself. It was as if she was pulling him. They were physically close and no doubt since they were young and ripe, there was an erotic aspect to the charged field between them — they held each other's gaze after all for a long time — but it was not only that or even primarily. They were making a compact with each other, an alliance. And Michael didn't realize that that was what they'd done until, despite his inhibition, he let go of the tube, to let her take it.

Monsignor Ellis had assumed it would be the usual May procession from the schoolyard to the church front where the pale statue of Mary in its small grotto would be garlanded with roses as it had been every year since he put it there in memory of his mother. He hadn't presided himself in some years, but that hadn't mattered. Now it made him seem like a fool that he wasn't there, as if he didn't know what was what in his own parish. The first phone call was from a *New York Times* reporter, and the second was from the chancery.

An hour and a half after the end of the regular school day and well after such devotions were usually held, all seven hundred and fifty Holy Cross children filed down Forty-third Street, nuns herding them like collies. That block was little traveled for Manhattan, and as they always did when the pastor or the principal requested it, the police had closed the street. The girls were wearing their Communion and Confirmation dresses, and certain of them were carrying bouquets. The boys were wearing white shirts and blue ties, and their shoes were polished. As they marched along they sang, "O Mary, we crown thee with flowers today, Queen of the Angels, Queen of the May."

Neighborhood women leaned from their windows up and down the street to watch. One wiped a tear from her eye with the corner of her apron: such innocence! And what the world would do to it! It was a lovely spring afternoon befitting the ceremony, and the sky itself was blue as Our Lady's cloak. Father Mahon, looking stately and benign in his alb and gold-encrusted cope and attended by acolytes, each with his candle struggling in the breeze, stood on the top stair of the church entrance like a potentate reviewing his parade. He seemed indifferent to the implication when the nuns steered the cross-bearing eighth-grade boy and the garland-bearing eighth-grade girl at the head of the procession past the church, around the police barricade that closed the street and out onto the Ninth Avenue sidewalk, going downtown.

It was the height of rush hour, the sidewalks were crowded with the usual peddlers, but also with secretaries, shopgirls and clerks on their way home from work. The avenue was already jammed with automobiles heading for Lincoln Tunnel and buses for the Port Authority. Before the May procession intruded, the commuters had achieved, despite their numbers, the efficient, steady progress of their daily exodus. The alteration in the rhythm of that progress caused by the Holy Cross children was slight at first, but it was enough. Dozens of pedestrians slowed, then made room for the procession by spilling out into the street. Drivers cursed them, but they too slowed. At the intersections where the streets cut into the avenue, nuns raised their arms at the auto traffic as if it was Red Sea water. The commuters were amused at first, and they waited even if they had the light while the sisters waved the children through. ". . . Queen of the Angels . . ."

Policemen who saw it knew damn well what the effect of the disruption would be, but they had all been in such processions themselves, though not in midtown at rush hour. They weren't going to tell the nuns to beat it. They stopped traffic altogether and nodded at the sisters as they passed. One truck driver leaned out of his rig and joined in the chorus: ". . . Queen of the May . . ."

The decorum of the children was perfect. Those boys and girls, ordinarily the after-school bane of the fruit merchants and of the cops and of the newsstand hawkers, now went by with their eyes cast down and their hands in steeples.

But it was apparent on second glance, third at most, that this May procession was different. In every tenth rank of children was a pair of seventh- or eighth-graders carrying between them a large sign blazoned with the letters *S.O.S.* And trailing the procession were the ten tallest children carrying a large blue banner with white letters that read, "Save Our School From Robert Moses."

Michael had been walking behind Sister Anne Edward. He caught up with her. "You were right, Anne! You were right!" His exuberance overflowed. "You are *fantastic* women! Fantastic!"

She laughed. She was delighted with how it was going too. "You're not so bad yourself, Deacon!"

He fell into step with her. Taking the procession out onto Ninth Avenue had been her idea, but Sister Rita wasn't convinced until Michael had joined Anne in arguing for it. Without permits, which the police would never have granted, it was illegal to disregard traffic signals as they were doing, and the tie-up was building. "I think we have their attention," he said.

She gestured over the heads of the children at the line of automobiles. "They drive through here every day without a thought for the neighborhood and what they do to it. Maybe now they'll get the idea that people live here."

Michael waved at a glaring motorist, and through his grin he said, "They get it, Anne. They get it."

Under her breath she said, "They look mad, don't they? God, I hope nothing happens."

"Relax. Nothing will happen. It's a May procession! The folks who use Lincoln Tunnel will just get home late for dinner, that's all!"

Anne touched his arm. "I hope so, Michael. I wouldn't admit this to anyone else, but the whole thing makes me nervous. I can't believe we're doing this. Do you think it will really make a difference?"

"Hey, the parents and children of Holy Cross School have to be reckoned with, right? Now Moses will know it."

"And so will the cardinal."

Michael grimaced. "Let's leave him out of this." He clutched her arm, and they laughed like adolescents who had just defied a parent, although the parent didn't know it yet.

Her eyes flashed with delight. "Thanks, Michael." In that setting, despite her habit, she was the opposite of the churchly women enshrined by piety. The meek Bride of Christ? The Mother of Sorrows? The Woman Bathed in Tears? Her heart pierced seven times? Passive? Forbearing? Long-suffering? O Mary, we crown thee with flowers today? Not this woman. She was neither tough nor hard-boiled. On the contrary, she was caring and vulnerable. But threaten what she cared about and she became strength itself. She seemed more alive and more full of energy than any woman Michael had ever known. (What? All three of them?) It pleased him to think that his support had helped her to muster the nerve for this. She had helped him to muster his.

A stymied driver honked his horn angrily, and Michael waved at him. "Bless you, brother!" he called.

"Michael!" she said, half-teasing, but only half. "We shouldn't take pleasure in their discomfort."

"Yes, we should! It's them or us, Anne. And my money is on our side!" (What? All three dollars?)

She grinned at him happily. "We're doing it, aren't we?"

"Damn right. I'm going to run ahead. Try to keep the line up to pace here, Anne. I'll slow them a bit in the lead. And I want to make sure nobody bothers the kids when they make the turn at Thirty-ninth Street. Hell, I want to walk in front with them! This is great, Anne!" He clapped his hands and threw his fist in the air. Michael Maguire was a man of action again at last. Spontaneously he blew her a kiss as he turned and then, with an athlete's stride, ran out into the street and along the line of the procession. There were singing children on one side of him and irate motorists on the other. One could almost hear that young, smitten nun saying to herself, "Go, Michael! Go!"

By four-fifteen traffic all over midtown had slowed to a virtual halt, and the first radio reports were going out about what the WINS reporter dubbed "The SOS Parade." What was this anyway? Parochial school kids taking on Commissioner Robert Moses? What did he want with their school anyway? His Mid-Manhattan Expressway had been shelved, hadn't it? But you never knew. It was one thing for Moses to be blasted by Sutton Place matrons over his destruction of a playground above the East River or by the left-wing crowd who wanted Joe Papp to put on Shakespeare in what Moses called "my park," but Catholics? Nuns? The archdiocese? Was the commissioner taking on the cardinal? That would be the battle of Titans! *Find out what the hell is happening over there!*

By the time the procession had wound its way past the new Port Authority building at Forty-second Street, down to Thirty-ninth, across to Tenth Avenue and back up to Forty-third Street, bollixing traffic for an hour, the news organizations represented at Holy Cross included the *Herald-Tribune,* the *Post,* the *Daily News,* WMCA, WINS, WOR and a camera crew from WPIX-TV. The *New York Times* reporter who'd called the monsignor told his editor nothing newsworthy was occurring, and he would, after the storm broke that evening and the next day, be roundly rebuked.

After the last hymn was sung, Mary's head fittingly crowned and the throng of children dismissed with a blessing by Father Mahon, Monsignor Ellis appeared from inside the church vestibule. He had obviously been waiting for Father Mahon to finish. The pastor looked at the rheumy priest with contempt as the altar boys led him past, into the church. Then he faced the crowd. The children had begun to disperse, but many of their parents were there now, filling the street. They, together with the reporters, waited for Monsignor Ellis to speak. He fingered the row of red buttons on his cassock, but not nervously. These people didn't threaten him. Only phone calls from the chancery did that, and by God he was going to see that he got no more of those on this matter!

"I have a statement to make," he declared in his preaching voice. He waited, skillfully collecting their attention. Cameras ran. He said, or rather, proclaimed, "The May devotions of this parish have the sole purpose of honoring Our Blessed Lady. They have significance for the Church, but not for the world. Therefore some of you have wasted your time in coming here, unless of course you have been edified by the innocence of our children, which would be to the good. As for those of you who are parishioners: my dear people, I appreciate your concern. Rumors abound. Next we'll hear that our beloved church itself is marked for demolition! Nonsense!" He paused, then repeated that word, slamming his fist into his palm for emphasis. "I am authorized by the cardinal himself to say that nothing anyone does with Lincoln Tunnel is going to bother Holy Cross School one bit! You can rest assured, my dear people, that the cardinal would not permit it, and . . ." His finger shot up; this is the last word. ". . . neither would I!"

He turned away abruptly and disappeared into the church. The reporters murmured in protest, but no one went after him. This was another era. The press had yet to stumble upon the fact of its omnipotence, and newsmen hadn't begun to claim the right to ask anyone anything. They began to drift away, wondering what the hell had happened to the story.

When a camera crew from a TV station goes out, though, it's different. They *have* to get something whether it's used on air or not. The footage of the procession, of angry motorists shaking fists at altar boys, of the sweet girl on the ladder placing a little rosebud crown on the head of the statue, was all too good to waste. But there had to be some one-on-one with somebody in authority. The longshot of the monsignor on the steps wasn't enough. But he was gone. At first the TV crew foundered. Then, instinctively, they drifted toward Tenth Avenue instead of Ninth and found themselves in front of the convent. A tall young nun was standing there, as if waiting for them, in her stark, black, oh-so-photographable costume. She was holding oversized rolled papers — perfect visuals — and she said so sweetly, "May I help you?"

Michael watched the broadcast on the late news that night alone in the rectory common room. Father Mahon was already asleep and the other priests were still out. At first his solitude depressed him, but as the news segment came on he was profoundly relieved that he didn't have to watch it with the others. WPIX broadcast a first that night: a nun, without a hint of overt defiance but with a steely undertone all Catholic viewers recognized, apparently contradicted the pastor of her parish. The heart of the report was a dramatic juxtaposition of Monsignor Ellis's brisk denial that the school was threatened and Sister Anne's statement, buttressed by the set of blueprints she displayed, that the Triborough Bridge and Tunnel Authority intended to condemn the school the week after the term ended and to complete its demolition by the middle of July. When the reporter asked her why the archdiocese had not addressed the issue, she replied that the archdiocese had expected the matter to be resolved quietly, at the parish level. Unfortunately that didn't seem possible now. She and the principal and the parents of Holy Cross were confident that the archdiocese would now intervene and Monsignor Ellis would be shown to be right after all. There would be no problem about the destruction of the school because, the Sister of Charity said, the cardinal would not permit it. The news report concluded with the revelation that Robert Moses had been confronted by a reporter only moments before, coming out of a reception in his own honor at the Tavern-on-the-Green. He claimed never to have heard of Holy Cross School and said that, anyway, he was in the business of building things, not tearing them down. When the reporter told him the nun had Triborough blueprints that assumed the demolition of the school, he said, "If she has our blueprints, then the nun's a thief."

After the news, Michael changed his mind and decided that even the biting sarcasm of Father Rice or the cloistered murmurs of Father Keegan would have been preferable to what he had — the company only of an ominous dread so palpable that it might have been another person opposite him in the gloomy room. What the fuck had they done? What would happen now? He felt like that rebellious teenager again, but now his parents had been sent for by the headmaster. He snapped the television off, poured himself an inch of whiskey and sat again. The chair creaked, then the room filled with silence.

Within minutes restlessness overwhelmed him. He went to his

room, donned his rabat, collar and suitcoat and went out. On the street he turned automatically toward the convent. He stopped in front of it and stared up at the one room from which light shone. Hers? Had she seen the news? Did they even have television in there? With a shock he realized he didn't know. He'd known nuns all his life, but at what distance! Tonight he wanted to know how she was feeling. Was she afraid? But why should he know her innermost thoughts if he didn't know what color her hair was? He had watched her walking in that procession, watched the swish of her skirts, waiting for a glimpse of her flesh, a flash of white at the ankle or the nape of her neck, as if such meager sights would have opened to him her secrets. The arms and ankles and hair of certain premodern nuns were more alluring, vastly more erogenous, than the displayed pubes of vacuous movie stars are today. Michael was disgusted with himself. It's sexual, he thought. Only sexual! But he shook himself. Of course that wasn't so. It wasn't *only* anything.

He suddenly had the image of himself as a moonstruck courtier looking up at the window of the infinitely unattainable princess in her tower, and he laughed. Where was his mandolin? He laughed. Instead of long golden tresses up which he could climb, she had a shaved head. His life was a fairy tale on its ear. He was jealous of the charming prince for whom she was saving herself, but, alas, that was Jesus.

He realized for the first time that he had become in some way ridiculous. He was worried about her? But she was not the one who had, apparently, handed herself over to a piety of deference and submissiveness. Why wonder if she was afraid when, so much more to the point, he was. Afraid of Cardinal Spellman? Monsignor Ellis? Robert Moses? But Michael Maguire had medals to prove his courage. What were such old coots to him? What had happened to him over these years? But he knew. He had known all along.

It humiliated Michael to admit it, but what he was afraid of was the world outside the seminary, outside Orders, outside the Church. He was afraid of the world's dreary rootlessness, its shallowness, its paucity of transcendent meanings, what seemed to him a vast milieu of self-squandering. He equated it both with the shrill terror of the battlefield and with the devouring angst of his years in prison. The Church had saved him and had become his refuge, the rock on which he'd built a life for the sake of others. But somehow this fine, one might even say noble, choice had been trivialized, demeaned. He was no longer an honorable man whose strength of will was legendary; he'd been reduced by the process of "priestly formation" to a passive, dependent subject. Now that he had, almost despite himself, dared to defy the Great Parents — and hadn't he done even that out of the arrogant illusion that he was supposed to be in charge, at the head of parades? — he was terrified of getting slapped down. And for now at least he depended totally on the will of his superiors for his place in the snug, safe haven of the Church. So of course he was afraid of the cardinal and the monsignor. They were the ones who could force him out, exclaustrate him.

But wait! With startling clarity he saw that Sister Anne Edward was the one to be wary of, the one to fear. He saw that she was going to be the one to take the weight now, and that if he stood with her, he was gone. He would be kicked into the world, alone and with nothing. He would have kept faith with her, but he would have failed his vocation, his commitment and God. He would be cursed forever.

But how could he not stand with her? He had encouraged her, supported her, cheered her on. It was Lennie Pace all over again, but now his immunity from consequences, his own safety, wasn't up to luck or the bad marksmanship of the enemy. It was up to him.

Years later he told me that he walked to Greenwich Village that night, thinking to visit me. I was by then shackled by Freshman Composition to my junior post at Fordham. He realized at the last moment, rightly, I think, that I would have understood his anxiety less well even than one of the crusty priests he lived with. He was suffering a particular kind of panic, the discovery that beneath the illusion of clerical strength and altruism, he was utterly without direction, will or potency. Priests, he thought, could understand this, and that made him all the more afraid of not being one. He continued to walk all the way to the Battery, and then back. "In the dark night of the soul," Fitzgerald said, "it is always three o'clock in the morning." Michael did not know it, but it was a measure of his courage that he simply allowed himself to feel that desolation, even though he was years from understanding it. He was wrong to think it was just seminarians who panic when they finally see what they've become. Hell, every man has a night like that soon after the trajectory of his life suggests itself. That's when most of us get serious about drinking or sex or work or prayer. Michael walked, he told me later, just walked.

He followed Broadway up through Times Square. A derelict, sprawled against a building, spied his Roman collar and called out, "Hey, look at that! A fucking priest!"

Michael waved. "How'd you know?" And they both laughed.

At the newsstand on Forty-second he bought the morning papers. There was nothing on the *Times*'s front page or the *Trib*'s, but the *Daily News* blared, "Moses: 'The Nun's a Thief!' " and featured a photo of Sister Anne Edward above the caption, "Sister Mary Felony."

Michael studied the picture. Her eyes were large and, framed by the black headgear, emphatic, looking directly at the camera, directly at him. Her face seemed extraordinarily expressive, caught in a moment of intensity, and he could almost hear her describing what Holy Cross School meant to the children, to the families, to the nuns who'd given their lives to it and to the thousands of New Yorkers who'd learned to think and believe there. She was the defender of them all, and their rights had become the center of her life. Michael knew he was not like her in that.

He folded the papers under his arm and walked slowly through the last of night, aware of the sour air of the city in his nostrils and on his tongue. It seemed to him that the recognitions he had wearily come to finally, even those, were things he could find a way to live with. But here was another one, and it was impossible; he was not concerned with the school or the parish or even his own vocation as much as he was concerned with her.

From his room he telephoned as early as he dared. When the phone was answered Michael had a moment of panic in which he couldn't remember her name, and he felt very foolish. A nun answered brusquely, "Holy Cross Convent."

"May I speak to Sister Anne Edward, please?" He had an adolescent's dread of identifying himself. He didn't recognize the awkward boy his feelings had reduced him to. It was a mode he'd bypassed altogether.

"One moment," the nun said, and he was relieved.

When Sister Anne came on there was no animation in her voice.

"Sister Anne, it's me, Michael. Forgive me if I'm calling too early." He tried to picture her. Was she dressed? Was the phone pressed against her black bonnet? When they went down the hall for the telephone did they cover their heads?

"I've been up forever, Michael."

"Me too," he said. "I never went to bed." Walking away the night after years of monastic discipline had been, even in his mood, an adventure and his exhaustion pleased him. Indicating it was like bragging. "I couldn't sleep after the news show. I wanted to say you were magnificent. I almost called you right then. I was really proud of you."

Sister Anne was taken aback by what he said and for a moment couldn't speak. He would learn soon enough that his simple statement of support thrilled her, relieved her, enabled her once more to believe in what she'd done. She'd been expecting him to back away. "If you had called," she said, "you'd have found the line busy. Mother Superior called from Tarrytown."

"What did she say?"

"I'm transferred."

"What?"

"I'm leaving shortly, Michael. I'm glad you called. It's a chance to say goodbye."

"But why? Everything you said was perfect. You even gave the chancery its way out." He knew it wasn't true even as he said it, and in a part of himself he didn't approve of, he hoped they would get her out, that they'd make her disappear.

"I didn't have permission."

"For what?"

"For anything. The procession, which she called 'a profane use of the sacred'; the television interview, which she called 'the height of impudence.' "

"You weren't impudent."

"I *felt* impudent, Michael. I really did. It communicated. Mother said I was contemptuous. And do you know what?" Michael realized that she had begun to weep. "I am."

They were both silent for a moment, then Michael said, "But Sister Rita backed you up, didn't she? She's the local superior. She was in on everything."

"Mother gave it to her too. She 'deceived the pastor!' We're both . . . Oh, Michael, Mother said they're pressing charges. They're claiming the blueprints are stolen property."

"That's ridiculous, though. It's a red herring."

"Rita's frightened. It's not her fault. She's the one who said I didn't have permission."

"Oh, God."

"It's not her fault. You can't imagine what it feels like over here, like we've done something awful. Apparently the cardinal's very upset. He called Mother himself. He's furious. He says I put him on the spot."

Michael laughed. "I guess you did."

Sister Anne Edward laughed too. "I did, didn't I?"

"Wonderfully. I admire you enormously." He paused, to choose his next words carefully. This was thin ice but he wasn't flashing across it this time. "And I'd be proud to take my share of the blame with you."

"Michael, you can't! You're just a deacon. The cardinal would fire you in a minute. I'm telling you, he's furious."

"But, God, Anne, I led the parade! We all did it. You. Me. Sister Rita. Even Father Mahon."

"Well, I'm the one on record."

"But you shouldn't be alone."

"Michael, I can take it!" she said, suddenly impatient. "I knew what I was doing. Let me see it through."

His lungs clutched in his throat. He couldn't think what to say.

She said quietly, "I loved going down Ninth Avenue with you. It felt wonderful to me. I felt free and strong and was doing something I believed in. I still believe in it. And I'm grateful to you for that." He sensed her gratitude and her affection; once he'd have soared with happiness for either.

She was letting him off the hook. If he was going to stay on the hook with her, now was the time to say so. But he simply couldn't. It was a moment that he'd remember for the rest of his life.

"Where are they sending you?" That's it; a cool question, a little distance.

"The Mother House for now."

"In Tarrytown?"

"Yes."

"I'll call you."

The nun laughed, but not bitterly, as far as he could tell. "Not there you won't."

"I'll come and see you. I'll pass as your confessor."

"What I'll need is a lawyer. Michael?"

"Yes?"

"Be careful." And she hung up.

He stared at the phone, thinking, What is this? The Iron Curtain?

Michael found Father Mahon in the common room, drink in hand, though it wasn't nine yet. He was hunched over the *Herald-Tribune* spread on the hassock. When he looked up at Michael he was smiling. "He's dead," he said.

"Who?"

"Moses. Did you see what he said?"

"I did."

Father Mahon laughed and slapped the paper and leaned back, spilling his drink. "He's slipping. The old Bob Moses would have kept his mouth shut and won. He'd have said he was too busy planning the World's Fair, and then they'd have asked him about that. Now the son of a bitch thinks he can say whatever the hell pops into his head."

"I think they might be serious," Michael said. "I just talked to Sister Anne Edward and she said they're threatening to press charges."

The priest stared at him for a moment. "But the plans aren't stolen."

"It says 'Property of Triborough' all over them."

"But you got them from the cops."

"I did, that's right. But I don't —"

The phone rang. Father Mahon was the priest on duty and he immediately got up, composed himself and crossed to the wall phone outside the common room. "Guess what?" he said a moment later. "It's your cop friend."

Michael took the call. Then, obviously shaken, he went back in to sit by Father Mahon, and he indicated the priest's drink. "Maybe I should have a belt of that."

"I wouldn't recommend it. What did he say?"

"He had no idea the blueprints were controversial. He assumed I'd returned them two weeks ago."

"And he doesn't want his name associated . . ."

"That's right. I promised to keep him out of it."

Father Mahon sipped his drink and raked what hair he had nervously. He eyed Michael. The booze wasn't calming him the way it usually did. The first drink worked wonders most of the time. He said, "Damn. Now maybe she is a thief."

Michael lit a cigarette, but his hands shook.

Father Mahon was thinking out loud, not quite addressing himself to Michael. "These bastards would spike their mothers for the extra base. And, Jesus, maybe Moses didn't make such a dumb move after all. Suddenly the damn issue isn't the school anymore. It's the blueprints." He fell silent for a moment. When he looked up, his gaze had sharpened. "They can't press charges. Spelly can't let them rough up a nun. He and Moses will have talked already. Moses will agree to lay off. Spelly will agree to get the troublemakers out of here."

"She's gone already."

Father Mahon nodded. "No more processions, no more S.O.S. School year ends. Go ahead with plans. Moses gets his ramp. Spelly gets his cool million, or whatever. Holy Cross gets it in the eye. One, two, three." He drained his glass. "And you, my boy, will have learned a lesson."

"What if I called up the reporter and said I was the thief."

The priest grunted. "I knew you were a war hero. They didn't tell me you were a kamikaze pilot. You ask an easy question. The answer? One, you call up your reporter. Two, Spelly boots your ass out, making you just another schmuck layman for whom he has no responsibility. Three, they *do* press charges and, four, you go to jail." Father Mahon got up and crossed to the bar. "You'd just like to make it a little more difficult for them, wouldn't you?"

"Yes," Michael said. He wanted to find a way to stand by Anne. He wanted to find a way to live with himself.

As the priest poured his drink, he said, "Only one son of a bitch around here can do that."

Michael waited.

Father Mahon took a swallow, then faced him. "Me."

"You?"

He nodded, and he said gravely, without bravado, "I could stop the bastards in their tracks."

Michael waited.

"I was the presiding priest yesterday. I had the vestments on. I had the holy water. That was *my* procession, not some nun's!" His eyes flashed and suddenly there was a veteran preacher's energy in his voice, conviction, solemnity. A throng was before him now, a throng, Michael realized, of reporters. "I am the priest in charge of Holy Cross School. It is the duty and privilege assigned to me by the pastor of my parish. I am responsible for the welfare of that school, and the idea to save it from the expansion of Lincoln Tunnel was mine! *I* stole those blueprints! *I* told the nuns to make those signs. *I* told the kiddies to march down Ninth Avenue! And I regret none of it. And I come before you now to say that God won't let Robert Moses make a laughingstock out of one of my nuns! A thief indeed! The only thing that girl has ever stolen are the hearts of the countless children to whom she has dedicated her life. Robert Moses, for all his power — and yes, for all the good he has done — must not be allowed to demean the sacred vocation, the infinite sacrifice of every nun in this city! A thief? This Bride of Christ? This woman clothed in mystery? We do not expect those of other faiths to adopt our beliefs, but we insist that they respect them! Robert Moses has insulted every Catholic in New York. The man already controls every park, every bridge, every tunnel, every highway, every public works project! Does he also want to steal, like a *thief,* the archdiocese of New York? Is it his to decide which Catholic child shall have access to a parochial school? Is it his to decide which woman is worthy of the veil? Is it his to decide which Catholic parish lives or dies? I tell you it is not. And if you doubt my word, then I bid you, go downtown to that beautiful old cathedral, named for the patron of the humble Irish immigrants who have broken their backs and spilled their blood to build the great *public* monuments of this city for which Robert Moses, like a *thief,* steals all the credit. Ask the leaders of the great Irish building trades about that! And ask the Irish contractors if *they* think nuns are thieves! And at Saint Patrick's Cathedral, you ask His Eminence Francis Cardinal Spellman who *still* controls the archdiocese of New York and who alone has authority over its parishes and schools and who alone has the cherished responsibility to protect its children from the anti-Catholic assaults of the secular world and its women religious from the gratuitous insults of outsiders! You ask Cardinal Spellman who the thief is! I promise you he will neither repeat nor countenance the vile slander of Robert Moses!"

Father Mahon stopped. He put his drink down. His hand was steady. And then he looked at Michael.

Michael wanted to stand and throw his arms around the priest. Here was a spar to grab hold of! It could keep him from sinking! He said, "Do you think you could repeat that for the record?"

"You're damn right I could."

"You'd take a lot of heat."

Father Mahon laughed. "That's the difference between me and you. I'm 'a priest forever.' " He laughed again, as at his favorite joke. "Spelly would have fired me years ago if he could. He can't fire me now. Anyway, I'm going to make him a hero. The minute Moses thinks Spelly's on the way in, he'll back down."

"I think we should have it in the school cafeteria."

"Will you be with me?"

"Of course," Michael said, but once again he began to calculate the risk. And then, instantly, guilt overwhelmed him. First he'd hidden behind a nun, and now behind a whiskey-priest.

"Just nearby, son. I'd appreciate having you nearby." Father Mahon's eyes filled and he turned toward the bar where his drink was. Then he checked himself. "I better leave this alone for a while."

Michael stood and crossed to him, took his arm and pressed it. "You're a good man, Ed."

"I used to be." For a moment they were suspended in the silence of the room.

"I'll call the reporters," Michael said.

Father Mahon nodded. "I think I'll make a visit to the Blessed Sacrament; collect myself, you know?" He tugged at his collar, straightening it. A wily smile crossed his face. "Let old man Moses dump his shit now on a priest of the Roman Catholic Goddamn Church!"

TWELVE

"HE built all these roads, didn't he?"

Sister Anne Edward nodded, but remained silent.

Michael kept his eyes on his driving. He'd borrowed my car, an old Ford famous for not starting on rainy days, but that day was bright and hot. It was mid-July, and Michael had driven out to the Mother House in Tarrytown to pick the nun up. There was a block party at Holy Cross celebrating the victory and Sister Anne Edward, unknown to her, was going to be the guest of honor.

"Saw Mill River, Deegan, Taconic, Cross Bronx, Cross County, Henry Hudson. Incredible," Michael said. "And we beat him."

Sister Anne Edward harrumphed and repeated what Moses had said at his press conference the week before. " 'I planned to build the ramp on Eleventh Avenue at Forty-first Street all along. This confusion is what happens when the public intrudes itself on the planning process prematurely.' "

They both laughed.

And then they fell silent again and watched the gracefully cultivated knolls of the parkway passing by. Moses did build a hell of a lovely highway.

After a few moments Sister Anne Edward said, "My parents live here." She pointed to an exit sign. "Dobbs Ferry."

Michael glanced at her with surprise. Her family had money? He almost asked her; how rude. Instead he said, "They must like having you so close."

She gave him a look. "We don't go home, you know. I couldn't even attend my sister's wedding last year. My father was wild. He wishes I'd quit."

"Really? How about your mother?"

She shrugged. "She'd rather have the grandchildren, I think, than the Grace. She'd never say that, of course."

He looked at her again. Her parents' ambivalence about her vocation was a sure sign that they'd begun to make it in America. "What does your father do?"

"He's an importer."

"Successful?"

She nodded and smiled. "Diamonds."

Michael whistled dramatically, but perhaps he shouldn't have been surprised. Even if she was typical in her nun's romantic and self-denying attachment to the Lord and to the cloistered sorority, she was unusual in her capacity to muster self-assurance and will when the chips were down. She had not been your typical nun on TV, but that was Dobbs Ferry ego she had fallen back on. Marx was right: everything was a matter of class.

"Industrial diamonds," she said, "not ornamental. He's not Harry Winston." She paused.

Michael thought, Who is Harry Winston?

"He was going to sue the *Daily News* for calling me 'Sister Felony.' He was wild. They both were."

"But not at you?"

"Oh, no. They're not like that. They're on my side." She faced away. "Unlike some people I can think of."

"Has Mother Superior eased off?"

"She doesn't even talk to me."

"I was hoping she'd send you back to Holy Cross now that the dust is settling."

"I'm afraid not. I've been assigned to the library at Mount Saint Vincent's College in the Bronx. I'm going to be dusting books."

"Oh, God! How long will that last?"

"The sister whose place I'm taking was there seventeen years. She'd still be dusting but she died."

"Oh, Anne."

"I'll have all the time in the world, but she said I'm not to paint." She let him see how devastated she'd been made to feel.

"You paint?"

"Yes. It's the most important thing about me."

It seemed to Michael she was rebuking him for his ignorance, and he felt suddenly ill at ease. Why should he have known anything at all about her? They'd hardly ever talked about themselves. He'd visited her three times in June, but they had talked stiffly in the Mother House parlor, and only about the uproar at Holy Cross after Father Mahon's press conference. That he knew so little about her was an affront, perhaps, when compared to the charged air between them, the unexpressed but potent intimacy that he'd felt from her side since that first meeting in the teachers' lunchroom. She had communicated a certain affection, but he was sure she also felt disappointed in him. He had let her take the heat alone, after all, and now she was telling him in detail what that was like. Had she bristled because, really, she was angry at him? No. Not that. She had bristled, he sensed, because she had shared his intensity of feeling, and now his ignorance about her made it seem misplaced. Well, ignorance can be dispelled. "You grew up in Dobbs Ferry?"

"No, Bronxville. We moved when I was in high school. They have a fabulous swimming pool." Was she bragging? No. She was showing him that her parents' affluence had become as strange to her as it would be to him.

"A pool would be great on a day like this, wouldn't it?" He looked over at her, eyed her habit. "You guys must get hot in those things."

She smiled winningly. "They tell us to offer it up for the poor souls in Purgatory. But do you know what I think? In July we *are* the poor souls in Purgatory. I think I'm being punished for sins I committed in an earlier life."

"Maybe you were a thief."

"No, no, to deserve this?" She lifted a fold of her habit in her lap. "I must have been an ax-murderer."

"That explains everything. You're deadly."

Michael knew that she was desolate. He admired her for covering her grief but it wasn't working. If he'd been she it wouldn't have been the prospect of dusting shelves forever that would have depressed him, but the massive disapproval. The parish school's victory had been her defeat. If her superiors disliked her now, didn't that mean, finally, that Jesus did? Wasn't *that* what she'd be feeling? Michael wanted to touch her, to reassure her. Jesus had said, "Let the children come to me." Jesus would love Anne Edward more than ever. "Tell me about the painting you do. Have you been painting long?"

"I studied a year at the Art Students League after high school. They liked my stuff. I wanted to be an artist and a nun both."

"Why do you say 'wanted'?" The word made him nervous. Even if I hadn't pressed him into a study of Gerard Manley Hopkins, Michael knew how difficult it was to square artistic impulses with life in the Church. "Birds build," the poet groused, "but not I."

She did not answer him at first, but only stared out at the snaking road, the passing trees. She leaned into the wind at her window for the air, then faced him. She explained, pensively, "Until now the Order encouraged my work. My novice mistress was a sculptor who'd studied in Europe as a young woman, and she thinks I have real talent. She was the first one who enabled me to take myself seriously. She said I could glorify God with my gift. But now Mother tells me painting was a privilege, and it became the source of my vanity."

"Your vanity?"

"That's what she called it. Anyway, there was a problem even before this. Once I was assigned to Holy Cross my own work came last, just because there was always so much to do in the school. I love the children. I could never say no to them." She stopped talking. Michael thought she was finished. He looked at her. She was staring at him. She said, "I think to be an artist in the religious life, one would have to be in the cloister or in the novitiate or someplace. The only nuns I know of who are serious about art are Benedictines."

"It's hard to think of you as a contemplative. You're too good with people. It would be a waste."

"And dusting library books won't be?" She laughed, but at last her bitterness showed. She looked across at Michael and said, "If I was a contemplative I would have to talk to you through a grille."

"I'd hate that," Michael said quickly.

"Me too." She blushed and began to fuss with the rosary beads in her lap. "It's bad enough this way," she said, her voice barely above a whisper.

Michael knew what she meant. There *was* a grille between them. It thrilled him to think she hated it too.

She looked up brightly and said in a change-the-subject voice, "You know something about the contemplative life, I think."

He shook his head. "Not me."

"I mean the POW camp. I gather your vocation came from that."

"That's *my* previous life. It's like it happened to someone else. Whatever you've read about prison camps, remember this: writers always make life better and worse than it really is."

"But you came out of it wanting to be a priest."

"I did, yes."

"Why?"

This was the first time anyone had ever asked directly for an explanation, and Michael felt his face redden. He deflected her. "You tell me first. Why are you a nun? A rich girl, an artist, a rebel. How'd it happen?"

She shrugged. "I told you. High school. I fell in love." She looked right at him. "Jesus ravished me," she said blatantly. "He carried me away."

"And now?"

"I still love him. And of course, now I have my vow. But I haven't heard much from him lately. I think he's away on business." She grinned, then added, "I'm not a swooning teenager anymore, but I still believe. Now it's your turn."

Michael was in trouble. How could he possibly match her honesty? Or her feeling? Jesus was a compelling biblical figure to him, not a lover. "I want to serve the Church," he said automatically. It was a weak statement, and he knew it. He took refuge in lines from Maritain. "I want 'to celebrate the Eucharist, to assist the sick and dying, to console the afflicted, to instruct the Catholic people, to intercede for all and to bear witness to the truth.' "

"All that and golf on Wednesdays."

"Those are in fact the things I want to do. I didn't mean to sound pompous."

"Seminarians and young nuns have to sound pompous when they bare their souls."

"Are you baring your soul?"

"I would if I knew how. To you."

Michael was aware that the steering wheel was slick with perspiration. My hippo of a car lumbered along the serpentine parkway, and he found that he had let the speed drop to twenty-five. He gunned it back up to forty-five. Anne's simple statement unhinged him. What would happen if they put *those* feelings into words?

His reticence didn't stop her. "I'm having my problems, as you can tell. I have no one to talk to."

"You can talk to me, Anne," he said, not glibly. "I'd like to be your friend." It was a dangerous statement but still within bounds, he thought. Wasn't the ideal of such friendship held out to priests and nuns by hagiography that so emphasized the bonds between Saint Therese and John of the Cross, Saint Francis of Assisi and Saint Clare and, for that matter, Abelard and Eloise? Even Pius XII was known to have had for over forty years a special friendship with the nun who served as his secretary. But Michael was hip enough to know how easily such impulses between celibate men and women, who were poised on the brink of permanent adolescence, slipped over into puppy love, spiritual finger-fucking. He was right to be uptight.

Anne for her part veered away from the issue. She brought her hands together in front of her mouth, impishly.

"Can I tell you who I remind myself of? You won't laugh? Or think me 'vain'?"

"Of course I won't."

"Joan of Arc," she blurted; then added with mock solemnity, "She was condemned by the Church too."

"The judges of Rouen weren't the Church, Anne. Cardinal Spellman's not the Church and neither is your mother superior. They're wrong and they're unfair, but you mustn't think of them as the Church. The Church is the people of Holy Cross and they love you."

"They'll barely remember me, Michael."

"You saved their school and they know it." Michael almost told her of the plan to honor her at the block party, but checked himself. The secret — what joy it portended — was more precious than before. "They appreciate what you're putting up with."

"Will they appreciate it seventeen years from now?"

What could he say?

After a moment, she touched his arm. "I'm sorry. I'm having an authority problem."

"I don't blame you. You've been blasted by the very ones who should have supported you."

"You know something, Deacon? You're the only one who has. . . ." She stopped and leaned toward the window for a moment. ". . . You and my parents. I've been feeling somewhat bereft." She closed her eyes. Wisps of her hair tore free in the wind; blond, he thought. "The judges of Rouen may not have been the whole Church, but they sure were a part of it."

"They made Joan a saint, right?"

"I suspect she'd have settled for a few more years as an ordinary mortal." She faced him again. "Look, that's the point. I love Holy Cross. I love the Church. I love my Order. But I'm not going to give up my painting for any of them. I'm not going to be a martyr. If that's what the religious life requires, then I want no part of it."

"I wouldn't want part of it either, if I thought that's what it required."

"But you don't."

"No, not at all. You're right that authority is the problem here. We agree about that and we agree on what to do when authority is in the wrong. Hell, you take it on the best way you can. You rant against it." Was he really saying this? It was an act of his and he knew it. And she would know it. How had he ranted on her behalf? He felt nowhere near this brave, which of course was why he pretended to. "You try to change it. But you accept in principle its fundamental structure."

"Even if that means martyrdom?"

"Martyrdom is your metaphor, not mine. That's not how I feel about my life."

"Metaphor?!"

"I —"

"You don't feel this way because you're not the one who's on the spot!"

"I know that," he said quickly, guiltily. How he wished she wouldn't say it. "I've kept my head in the trench, and I don't feel right about it at all. You've really been out there by yourself." He glanced over at her and saw tears on her cheek. It happened that just ahead there was one of those rest area/picnic groves off the parkway and he swung into it and stopped the car. He leaned toward her and touched her shoulder while she wept as quietly as she could. She seemed so vulnerable. How he wanted to protect her, but he knew how he had failed her.

As if she read that in him she raised her hand to his and pressed it against her shoulder, and her body, until then a remote abstraction, took over the field of his perception. He felt suddenly through her habit the sharply defined bone of her left clavicle. He became aware of the clean odor of her skin, that nun's soap smell he'd noticed in the teachers' room. But now it seemed intensely erotic to him. She was more woman than nun and for a moment it was possible to forget all that kept them apart. He touched a tear at her cheek with the back of his free hand, then let his finger fall to her lips. She opened them and took his finger between her teeth and bit him just sharply enough to cause him pain.

He trembled. She was waiting. Ravished? Had she said ravished?

He pulled away.

She leaned against the door and turned her face from him. All he could see was the black of her habit.

When he resumed driving, he used his old trick, reciting Scripture, but to himself. "No one hates his own flesh," Paul said. What the fuck did Paul know? "He nourishes and takes care of it as Christ cares for the church." Right. Sure he does. Oh yeah.

Later, in a disembodied voice, he asked if it would be possible to see her paintings sometime, and she said yes, that very day, for there were several at the Holy Cross convent. She was polite about it. She'd love for him to see them. By the time they arrived at the parish they had their controls in place again. But it was different. Their shared embarrassment — they had a secret now — was what made them friends.

The block party was an ethnic bash: refried beans on soda bread; Italian ice in waffle cones. Children had their faces painted. The fire hydrant at the far end of the block was open, and boys in underpants wildly dashed in and out of the geyser. On the church steps an accordionist and a fiddler rendered Irish jigs while a couple of dozen elderly men and women with bright Irish faces and slightly glassy eyes kept each other company, nodding to the music. The gents kept threatening to ask the wizened colleens to dance, but never did. In the street, in the center of the block, several nuns had organized a game of Red Rover. Ten or fifteen children were arranged on a side, and every time the line held there were great cheers.

Michael felt that after years of pacing a room alone — for compared to this the seminary seemed that isolated, that pointless — he'd been released to the world. The festivity and the sun and the city itself all seemed to applaud not only him and not only Sister Anne at his side, but the two of them together. Now that they had their distance again, and in the context of the parish celebration, he dared to think that somehow they might yet find a way to ransom one another. He didn't leave her side. Not this time.

In the schoolyard the older kids had yet another game of kickball going. A man in a white shirt with bunched sleeves was rolling the big balloonlike ball at the kicker; it was Father Mahon. Michael and Sister Anne made their way toward him. When he saw them he pulled out of the game and came over to embrace Anne warmly. He tugged her back down the block toward the church. Parishioners greeted her, though the nuns kept their distance. Michael was looking for Sister Rita because he knew that Anne would be looking for her too.

A few moments later all the activity was suspended as the throng gathered at the foot of the church stairs. When Father Mahon had their attention he thanked the ladies who had prepared the food and the men who'd hung the decorations, and he said he hoped everyone would play games and dance in the street until dark. After that he hoped they wouldn't keep the fathers awake since everyone knew that priests in their rectories went to bed early and often. They all laughed, the more so because he was poking fun at himself. Then he introduced Mrs. Heaney, the president of the Mothers' Club. She could hardly be heard, but that didn't matter because everyone knew what she was saying. It was her job to present Sister Anne Edward with the felt banner the mothers had made. The young nun was quite moved, but she managed to unfold the gift and hold it up so that everyone could see it. "Sister Anne Edward," it read, "you S'd our S. Thank you. With Love from the Parents and Children of H.C." The people applauded loudly and Sister, for the barest moment, buried her face in the banner.

I was there. I stood on the edge of the crowd, utterly ignorant of the meaning of what had just happened, but nevertheless affected by it. That was the first time I'd laid eyes on Sister Anne Edward and I remember straining to see her because of the notoriety she'd received, and also because Michael had described the impression she'd made on him. As was arranged, I'd come uptown to pick up my car. Sister Anne was to return to Tarrytown with one of her fellow nuns that evening.

While I made my way through the crowd toward Michael, I was thinking what happy people those parishioners seemed to be, so unlike the sullen freshmen for whom I was endlessly diagraming compound, complex and simple sentences on blackboards in those days. I hadn't expected to find myself envying Michael, but as I saw the open fondness with which the people of that neighborhood engulfed him, I did.

I hooked up with him and his nun friend just as another nun did, the principal, Sister Rita. And so it was that I witnessed the awkward encounter between those two women, once so dear to each other. I could, of course, have had no idea how decisive that meeting would be not only for Sister Anne Edward, but for each of us.

"Oh Anne, it's so good to see you," Sister Rita said, but she made no move to embrace her or to shake her hand.

"Mother was kind to let me come," Anne Edward said stiffly, but even I sensed the power of her emotion. Was she afraid? Angry? Hurt? Was she going to cry?

"We managed to get Monsignor Ellis to call her." The principal smiled awkwardly. "What old nun can refuse the pastor?" She paused, then added, "I wanted to write you."

"I wish you had."

Rita lowered her eyes. "I was advised against it," she said miserably.

Then Michael noticed me, and he made the introductions. I knew I'd interrupted something, but it was clear even to me that the women needed more privacy than was available there for the talk they wanted to have. Michael described me as his oldest friend, and he draped his arm around my shoulder, but the tension between the nuns continued to dominate. They moved, as if to go off together. Sister Anne Edward said to Michael, "Thank you for coming for me. I enjoyed our talk."

God, they're formal with each other, I thought. Like Mennonites. What did I know?

Michael said, "Don't forget, before you go back, you're going to let me see your paintings."

"That's right," Anne said, with a relief that first displayed to me her desire to be with him, and that flash of warmth unaccountably filled me with relief too.

But the other nun interrupted. "I'm sorry, Sister, that's one of the things we have to talk about."

"What do you mean?"

"Your paintings are gone."

"Gone?"

"I had to send them to the Mother House. I sent all your things over a month ago."

"But they never gave them to me. Not my paintings! What did they do with them?"

"I don't know." Sister Rita lowered her eyes in exactly the way she had before. I realized it was a form of hers, an act of piety. There was even a name for it, I would learn: "custody of the eyes."

Not even I believed that she didn't know.

"You *do* know!" Sister Anne said, furious.

"I'll tell you later."

"Tell me now please, Sister."

"All right." The nun spoke as I imagined nuns spoke to their confessors, with more whine than penitence. "Mother told me at first to destroy your paintings. She said she should never have allowed you to pursue it. I pleaded with her. She relented and told me to send them to her instead."

"So that *she* could destroy them! Why didn't you call me? Oh Rita!"

Sister Rita looked up sharply. "You know why I didn't call you!"

"No I don't. I truly don't."

The women were suddenly at a standoff. Each had unfurled what she thought of as the truth. I glanced at Michael who hinted at his own frustration with a quick upturn of his eyes. I mistook his attitude at that point for clerical or at least masculine condescension.

Sister Rita abruptly turned away and cut through the crowd. Sister Anne Edward faced Michael. "Do you still want to see my work?" Her voice trembled with emotion. I recognized her defiance even without understanding it. And I sensed how large this moment was for her, without knowing why.

"Yes, of course."

"Can you drive me?"

Michael looked at me. I'd been counting on my car, but I said, "No problem, go ahead, I'll see you later."

Michael shook his head. "Come with us." He looked at her. "That would be okay, wouldn't it?"

I sensed her disappointment; how could Michael want me along? But she said, "Sure. The more the merrier."

And that is how it happened that I drove them that afternoon to her parents' house in Dobbs Ferry.

That town struck me as a place brimming with happiness, or is that how those of us raised and still living in the grim corners of the crowded city always felt in our rare forays out to the posh suburbs? Her family's house was large, set on a carefully landscaped knoll and surrounded by elm trees, which made it seem more private than it probably was. It certainly seemed less hot than Manhattan had, though we arrived in the middle of the afternoon and the temperature must have been near a hundred. The trees cast a benign pattern of moving shadow over the house, but that was no relief. I could not imagine how Michael managed in that collar and suit of his, much less his nun friend in her habit. The relevant heat had seemed, of course, to be in her, that plugged volcano, and I sensed her fury and her hurt despite the inconsequential chatter my presence imposed on them. Our ride up the Saw Mill River would have been less awkward if they had sat together in the back seat of my car. That arrangement at least would have reflected the reality of our relationships and allowed them perhaps a snatch or two of real talk about the inflamed decisions they were coming to. As it was, Michael had insisted on her riding in the front with me. I didn't understand yet how desperate he was to get his distance from her. I only knew that I felt entangled between them at once and I didn't like it.

The house, when we entered it, was cool. Sister Anne Edward ran ahead, calling for her parents. We followed as far as the entrance hallway which was dominated by an elaborately curving staircase with a gleaming mahogany banister. Michael grimaced at me and shrugged. We mirrored each other, slouching with our hands in our pockets, trying to seem casual, though obviously we felt like interlopers.

"I'm sorry to drag you out here," he whispered.

"No sweat." I pointedly ran a finger through the slick of perspiration on my forehead.

"Look at this." He crossed behind me to a large painting of a barn wall in winter. In it snow was falling in a keen wind; icicles hung from a wrecked gutter and the gleam of frost defined the grain of the unpainted wood. The painting captured perfectly the sparkle of winter. "Just looking at it cools me off."

"Is it signed?"

The name *C.P. Campbell* was carefully printed in the corner, and the year, 1956.

I stood back and said, "It's stunning."

"Thank you," Sister Anne said, from behind me.

We faced her. "It's yours?"

She nodded and looked at it wistfully, as if remembering flakes of snow whirling around her canvas. She grinned. "That's the north wall of our barn at our farm in Vermont. I painted it in each of the seasons. My father says he keeps this one out here because he can't afford to heat it." She approached the painting, resting her fingers on its frame for a moment, as if to reassure herself that it, at least, existed. Then she brightened. "I'll show you others, but first come meet my parents. They're outside."

We followed her through the narrow corridor that ran behind the staircase. The walls there were hung with several dozen family photographs, and I saw, displayed like treasures, the faces of children, a girl in a hammock, two boys clutching a dog, a man at the helm of a boat, a beautiful woman posed in a satin gown on the very staircase we had just left behind. They seemed creatures from a brighter world, and the flash of their smiles filled me with envy.

The corridor led to a solarium, and its french doors opened on a broad stone terrace. A lawn sloped gradually down over a distance of about fifty yards to a blue and white island in the green, a swimming pool. A man and woman were reclining on chaises longues and they remained oblivious to our approach until Sister Anne clutched her rosary and her hem and broke for them, crying out, "Mommy! Dad!"

"My God, it's Syr!" her father cried. "It's Syr!" He was up and running to meet her, a grinning, vigorous man in his fifties, tanned and muscular. When they embraced, I felt something of a jolt, as if the shock of their bodies colliding registered in me, but I think it was more the sight of that large, quite physical man clad only in his bathing suit taking that sternly garbed nun in his arms and whirling her around and around so that her black habit flew.

Her mother, knotting a terry robe, quickly joined them. When they hugged the two women burst into tears.

Michael and I stood oafishly by until her father noticed us. He approached Michael with his hand extended. "Hello, Father! Welcome! I'm Ed Campbell."

"I'm Michael Maguire, Ed. And this is Frank Durkin."

As Campbell shook hands with us he eyed his daughter. It was obvious something was wrong. She was sobbing against her mother's shoulder. When she realized we were watching she pulled herself together and brought her mother over to meet us.

Mrs. Campbell was a slim, tanned woman whose hair was partly blond and partly gray. She had the posture of a tower and her face, though lined, seemed young. When I took her hand I felt drawn in by her, and my unease left me. Her name was Anne.

Anne and Edward, I realized. Anne Edward. My first lesson in the naming of nuns.

Ed Campbell offered us beers, but then a better idea hit him. "How about a swim, fellows?" Before we could respond he led the way back to the house, saying that between him and his two sons they had suits galore. As we followed, Michael looked back at Anne who watched us smiling, as if the pleasure for her in seeing her strong-willed generous father override us was enough. I glanced back at her once more as we went in the house and was struck by — I could say *moved* by — the mammoth sacrifice nuns make. She had forsaken herself, and even there in the embrace of her home the stigma of her clothing, of her choice, set her apart. No swimming for Sister.

But I saw too, amazingly, why she'd done it. Only in that setting, heightening as it did the extremity of her situation, could I grasp its meaning. In her vowed life, in her hyperchaste body, in her loss of free will, she contradicted the world itself, its bondage to time and its steady quest for comfort. On that day in her merciless garments she contradicted the weather itself, and that act alone seemed transcendent. She was Crane's "wink of eternity," a spot of black in the glare on which it was possible for an instant to rest an eye. The great oppression is that things are what they seem and no more. Nuns deny it. How simple once one understands. And what fools they are unless the rest of us are wrong. Nuns teach us, if we let them, that we want to be wrong. If we don't let them, they're no bother unless your best friend gets involved with one.

In her presence so far that day I had been uncomfortable, and I hadn't fathomed Michael's apparent attraction to her, but now I saw her as an image less of rejection than invitation. In her radical straining against the flow of things was there some meaning for me? For my sense-ridden but senseless life as an aging boy-wonder whose zeal for literature had been swamped in the backwash of classroom drudge-work, and whose once cherished, oh-so-modern belief in "the dearest freshness deep down things," in the "shining shook foil" of "experience" had grown stale, like bread left out on the table overnight? What began in the Village as a permanent "liberty" in the sailor's sense had become for my generation, or my crowd at least, even as we drifted from the great promise of school into rather ordinary jobs, the lockstep, nose-to-tail of canine heat. Even as I gave my stirring early lectures on "The Wreck of the Deutschland" (which Hopkins dedicated by the way to five Franciscan nuns), I was always half thinking of the weekend and of getting laid. This nun made me uncomfortable, I realized, because her chastity-on-display seemed addressed to the likes of me, and I could admit it only when I'd met her parents whose lively bond with each other seemed not Manichean, as one like me would expect in the progenitors of the celibate, but downright voluptuous.

So Sister Anne Edward was straining against the flow of herself, as if her point wasn't at all that the world is evil, but that, even though it is good, it is far from enough. Life even in a loving family, even in a beautiful house, even as a promising artist, is not enough. How much less is it enough if life is among lonely Village girls who dream of Edna St. Vincent Millay and so believe us when we tell them that we part with our despair by parting our legs and whispering to each other like literary whores — give me "Baby, oh baby!" any day — "Death devours all lovely things," or "Love is not all; it is not meat or drink." After we have cheapened not only talk but good writing, no wonder the woman of silence reminds us that there is more, far more, not only than the worst, but than the best. That was why the radical denial implicit in Anne Edward's vocation had taken the form of a radical embrace. Had she been raised by lovers? Then she had to have for herself the Greatest Lover of them all. To my own surprise, I understood. In my last glimpse of her across the lawn I marked how she bent her head toward her mother and they laughed, and a rare affection fluttered above them.

When, suited, we went back out and across the lawn to the pool, they were gone.

Michael and I plunged into the water while Ed went back into the house for the beers. We rejoiced in the sheer release from the heat and I, for myself, felt momentarily freed of my Young Werther melancholy. The thrill of the wet cold enlivened me and I had, as it were, a brief foretaste of what was soon to come. Michael and I swam independently at first, then splashed one another boyishly, like a couple of Cooper Street kids away at camp for the first time.

Michael noticed before I did. He stood up in the pool abruptly, the water at his waist, his strong chest dripping, and his jaw suddenly slack. I turned to see what caused this shock in him.

She had just stepped off the terrace onto the lawn and was coming toward us in an unornamented, unskirted dark bathing suit of the sort competitors wore, but it registered as nudity, the simplified lines of her limbs, her long, elegant legs, her bare arms undulating sexually, as if to walk was an erotic act. Her cropped blond hair was short as a boy's, which made her long neck seem flaunted. Watching a lewd stranger coyly raise her nightgown at a window would not have been more electrifying than watching this virgin place one bare foot after the other in the grass. Her naked ankles! Her undraped thighs! She came not self-consciously but solemnly, as if taking possession of territory or enacting a rite of primitive religion. Drops of water clung to her. Had she just showered? To shave herself perhaps? Her skin was white as porcelain, cool, the Victorian ideal, but she seemed otherwise like a figment of the avant-garde, something out of Existentialist Paris, lacking only a cigarette and a hurt expression.

A faint smile and the barest color in her cheeks were the only hint of the bashfulness she surely felt. How long had it been since she'd so exposed herself? I pictured her before her childhood mirror, removing her anachronous garments, the black yardage, the linen at her throat, the constricting starched bodice, the layered underwear. And when she saw her parts whole, her breasts with nipples rising and her hips, her broad pelvis, the delta between her legs, her body in its prime come back to her, did her juice flow? Certainly she knew what an apparition of desire she would be to us.

In fact, I heard from Michael's lips a quick short cry, an "Oh!" that made me look at him.

His face was the face of a man who'd taken a severe blow. Without the water to float in I think he'd have been reeling. His disorientation was apparent, and his questions flashed in his eyes. Who was she? And what did anything he'd learned or vowed or prayed over have to do with the agony of this wanting? What were all those memorized verses of Writ to him now? He wanted her and his wanting trapped him. By then the choice was not between her and God or between her and the Church or between her and the priesthood, but between her and himself.

Because I cared for him as a friend my thought for an instant was how to help him. I knew right then of course that his pain would not be soothed until he took possession of her, and I think I knew also that eventually, no matter what promises to whom were broken, he would.

When I looked back at her I forgot him. As she approached the tile apron of the pool her step quickened, and she raised her arms together over her head, flaring her breasts, and then springing into the air, feet together, carving an arc through the heat with her flawless dive.

She swam underwater half the length of the pool, right at Michael, like a predator, and she surfaced two feet in front of him. "Hello," she said. But her meaning was, Here I am. What are you going to do?

"Venus Rising," Michael answered, but the rakish greeting had nothing to do with what he felt. I read his agony, though I didn't understand it yet. He was naked to himself for the first time. What was he going to do? Precisely nothing. Why? Because he *was* nothing. He would never know humiliation like that again.

She began to blush. Clearly she had planned her moves to this point, but no farther. She folded her arms across her breasts and let her face fall. Neither Michael nor I looked away from her. It would have been the merciful thing to do, for her counterfeit boldness had failed her utterly and she felt terribly exposed. But it was impossible to take one's eyes away. She was simply the most beautiful woman either of us had ever seen.

To my astonishment I was the one to steer us past that moment by saying simply, "Your father calls you 'Syr.' "

She nodded and laughed. "For 'Syrup.' Karo syrup." She laughed again. "My name is Carolyn."

Michael said sadly, quietly, "It's a lovely name, Carolyn."

And she raised her face to him exactly as she might have had he hooked a finger under her chin. I saw the worship in her eyes. For years I would try to forget that moment and its meaning. They beheld each other so steadily, so exclusively and for so long that I became embarrassed and dove under the water.

When I surfaced she had swum away. Her parents were approaching with refreshments. Michael called me, drew close and whispered, "As soon as we can you have to get me out of here."

Carolyn never returned to the convent. As Michael and I left that day, he took her aside for a moment. I saw them kiss, like a pair of figurines. Tears ran freely down her face when she followed him to the car, then stood waving as we drove away.

Michael didn't speak.

Finally, as we crossed into Manhattan, I had to ask him. "What did you say to her?"

"I said 'Goodbye.' I can't see her again."

"Why not?" I asked, though I knew the answer. I asked it calmly, though my heart soared with happiness. I cared not a whit for his agony then, and though I was in its debt, I did not for once admire his ruthless will.

"Because I love her," he said simply.

I nodded, as if my only meaning was that I understood.

THIRTEEN

OUR TWA flight from Tel Aviv arrived at Kennedy at 1:45 in the afternoon. My daughter and I took an hour to clear customs. Molly was carrying only a shoulder bag and I had nothing, save my toothbrush and passport, but that heightened the official's suspicion. When he asked me my occupation I wanted to say smuggler.

Then we were in a taxi sailing up the ramp of the Triborough Bridge. Ah, Moses! The cabbie cut dangerously in front of a truck. Molly and I exchanged a glance, then smiled; this was more dangerous than the terrorist-ridden road from Jerusalem.

New York was golden in the afternoon sun and my eyes feasted on the skyline, the most familiar sight there was. Only then, beholding the jagged frieze, did I realize how I had hungered for this city. I was nearly overwhelmed by a longing for the life I had denied myself.

The taxi took us directly to the cathedral.

Not Saint Patrick's; the funeral was to be held that night at the Anglican Cathedral of Saint John the Divine on Amsterdam Avenue near Columbia University, and that had loosed a flood of feelings that surprised me and disturbed me. At first I thought Carolyn had preferred the Episcopal Church and I was shocked. Had they converted? I asked Molly, and she said no. They had quietly continued to worship as Catholics all those years, mainly at the Jesuit parish not far from their apartment on West Seventieth Street. Since it was a church staffed by Order priests who had never known him personally — though perhaps some of them had played basketball against him — Michael had been able to go there with a certain, essential feeling of anonymity. Molly said that he and her mother had come to love the place.

But it hadn't mattered.

When, after Michael's death, Carolyn had called the Jesuit pastor, he had regretfully referred her to the chancery of the archdiocese. The chancellor had told her that Michael would not be allowed to be buried from a Catholic church. As an unlaicized but married priest he was an excommunicant, the archbishop had said. Canon law forbade him both a Church funeral and burial in sacred ground. The archbishop regretted it too, and he was sorry it came as a surprise. But, he'd said, he was sure Michael Maguire himself had understood the consequences of the decisions he'd made.

I was too stunned, when Molly told me, to realize how furious I was and how hurt, for myself as well as for Michael. What an obscenity such a last rejection was, even if, by Church standards, it was somehow defensible. I was confused by the fact that Molly seemed to have no particular reaction to the profound insult her mother had suffered. Was that because she expected no better from the Church? She didn't believe in God, she'd said. Wasn't it to her advantage to be free of those petty distinctions, as if, on any rational scale, it mattered, now that Michael was dead, which church he was buried from? Hell, from Molly's point of view Saint John the Divine *would* have been preferable. It at least was an authentic Gothic masterpiece, far more beautiful and, even unfinished, more imposing than the Fifth Avenue bauble, Saint Patrick's. And no mere museum like the Cloisters, Saint John the Divine had at least been the scene of vital human events of broad significance: huge ecumenical gatherings on the crisis of the city, on the meaning of the Holocaust, on ending racial conflict. Duke Ellington conducted his concerts of sacred music in that cathedral and was buried from it. Great festivals with jugglers and aerialists and minstrels, and countless productions of plays and chorales and symphonies reaffirmed the ancient connection of religion to art. And once, while FBI agents waited nervously to arrest him, Michael preached against the war from the cathedral's great pulpit.

Aside from Cardinal Spellman's famous sermon condemning — and therefore launching — the movie *Baby Doll,* and the funeral of Bobby Kennedy, what had ever happened of more than parochial interest at Saint Patrick's? Ironically, of course, Michael was ordained in its sanctuary, but that would be cited by the chancellor as the very reason his funeral could not happen there.

As the grotesque meaning of the archbishop's statement became fully apparent I involuntarily but graphically conjured an image of him, at once ingratiating and hostile: "The archdiocese regrets, the cardinal might wish otherwise, but the new pope, you see, has reinstated the traditional emphasis on the absolute and permanent character of priestly vows. After a regrettable period of laxity in the wake of the Vatican Council, the Church no longer contradicts herself in these matters." He smiled sadly, in my fantasy, shrugged, turned his hands out. What could one do?

And I was thinking, yes, the new pope. Not the Hamlet Paul VI was, but Shakespeare's Brutus, slayer of brothers. The new pope ran the Church the way the Party wanted to run Poland. Michael Maguire was for a time the Lech Walesa of American Catholicism, and he was not forgiven. It was my mistake, of course, to think he might have been.

So the taxi took us to Saint John the Divine. As we paid the cabbie and got out, the heat blasted us. It was as hot as the desert.

I stood looking up at the mammoth dark structure with its rose window, the tracery dominating the glass in daylight, its portal gargoyles leering down at me, its tympanum saints indifferent, and the carved stonework ribs of the entrance arches soaring to their crowns. The cathedral was too large, as if a mere human person was unworthy to enter alone. We should have gone in as members of a throng. But I reminded myself: *This* cathedral has welcomed outcasts. *This* cathedral has bent itself to Michael.

But I was immobile there before it.

It will be cooler inside, I told myself. The Gothic windows will be brilliantly illuminated by the fierce summer light. Saint John's was a perfect rendition of man's most magnificent expression, and, compared to it, all the box-forms of Manhattan's architecture, from the looming Behemoths downtown to the sterile dwellings across the avenue behind me seemed as impoverished as the thatched-roofed mud cottages in medieval villages, as if contemporary people too invested all their greatest treasure, skill and art, despite themselves, in the house of God.

Still, I did not want to go in there. Michael was laid out in some crypt chapel under the vaulting, tracery, clerestory, triforium, arcade; under buttresses, capitals, mullions, voussoirs, keystones and acres of leaded glass. A cruciform jewel.

But I knew Michael and knew then with a certainty infallible as the pope's that where he belonged that night was at the head of the aisle of even the most undistinguished Catholic church in New York. Good Shepherd, say, in Inwood, which I was sure he never ceased to love. "Durk!" I could hear him screaming at me. "Durk! Don't let them do this to me! Get me back where I belong!" And even in my imagination the panic in his voice was absolute.

In primitive religion the worst fate was to be a lost soul, a spirit improperly dispatched from the world and condemned therefore to an eternity of aimless wandering. And whose religion, when it comes to death, is not primitive? The new pope was right. My fury at him showed it. *These things do matter.* Scratch us and we are all primitives, desperate for the ancient rites done in the ancient way. The pope was only doing what he had to do to protect those rites. Michael Maguire was a priest forever, bound by vows he had renounced. Were we now to say his ordination in Saint Patrick's didn't matter? If that most solemn act of the Church did not matter, what did?

And who was I to judge the chancellor for pronouncing his anathemas? I had cut Michael off before the Church did. I had turned on him even more heartlessly. He had been bound by the implicit vow of our friendship and he had disregarded it. More than anyone he had known what Carolyn meant to me and he had been the only one who could have taken her and he had. Was I now to say his betrayal didn't matter? Hadn't Michael understood, as the chancellor put it, the consequences of his decisions?

What, that he should wander aimlessly forever? Could we mean it? Without the only blessing, the only forgiveness that he'd have wanted? Of course the Protestants could welcome him now, and the dean of the cathedral no doubt would asperge the coffin himself. But why not? Michael had not offended the Protestants. He had not betrayed them. To an entire generation he'd been a hero, the Prince of Peace. Only to the few of us who loved him most had he been the vilest enemy. I saw suddenly what I had in common with the cardinal. And also, since the Church had so resolutely condemned Michael, why Carolyn had needed me to come home. I was there, I understood finally, to pronounce the absolution that saves a soul from hell, and I knew, to my horror, that I could not do it.

Molly and I mounted the stairs and at the huge center portal — the lower of the pair of wrought-iron hinges was above the level of my eye — I found the ring handle that indicated which panel served as the quotidian door. But it didn't budge. I went to the side portal and tried its door, but it too was bolted. Only then did I recall that in the cities of America, God's house, even in the middle of the day, is locked from the inside.

Our path around the side of the cathedral took us through the garden which was elegantly laid out around a stunted steeple, a relic from some English town perhaps, which looked, when seen whimsically, like the topmost part of a church that was otherwise completely buried in the earth. An underground church, as it were. In fact the structure was an outdoor pulpit that hadn't been used in years, and I remembered being struck by its archaic beauty once before. I had been standing by it years ago when the agent of my destruction ambushed me.

"Molly!"

A boy of about eight, dressed nattily in a little blue blazer, had called her from a bench and was now running toward her. He was sobbing.

Molly dropped her bag and took a few steps toward him, and they embraced violently. He left the ground and for a long time she held him. I marveled at her strength, at the strength of her affection for the child, and I was filled with awe at that epiphany of her goodness. She was my daughter! And it ripped me anew that the degradation of my love for her mother had degraded in turn my fatherly love for her. Else would I have left? Else wouldn't I have fought Michael for at least my daughter's love? If I had been there she would never have taken his name. I was filled with regret, but also stern acknowledgment that opaque hardening is the only law that heartbreak knows.

When finally Molly turned to me with her arm around the boy's shoulder, I was in no way prepared for it when she said, "This is Eddie, my brother."

But I must have suspected it. Surely otherwise I'd have consciously entertained the possibility. Staring at the boy whose face, even wrecked with emotion, had the dark Irish charm peculiar to his father, I knew that I was looking at an extension — no, the consummation — of the adoration I'd seen in his parents' eyes that first day at the house in Dobbs Ferry. No wonder I hadn't wanted to contemplate this possibility. For the first time in many years I felt the full force of Carolyn and Michael's love for each other. It was glib of me to claim earlier that I had put my resentment behind me. Perhaps I could even have felt bitterness toward this child, but the intensity of his grief overcame me. Michael was his *father!* I knew what it was to feel bereft as he felt. And I knew what it was — though I had broken faith with this knowledge — to comfort a child who yearned for a father's touch. "The fathers of families . . ." Suddenly, I longed for Michael anew, to clap his back for what we had in common now, and quote Peguy: ". . . those great adventurers of the modern world."

"Eddie," I said, while he shyly avoided my gaze, "Are you named for your grandfather?"

The boy nodded and collapsed against Molly again, and I sensed that Carolyn's father had died at some point too. I looked at Molly with my question, and she flicked her eyes, yes.

When the boy pulled himself together I wanted to tell him I was sorry, but the words seemed cruelly glib, and I suddenly felt exhausted. Was I up to this? How many time zones had I crossed? I rolled down the sleeves of my shirt; that child was dressed the way I should have been. What was I doing there?

"Mommy's in the church." He indicated the doorway at the south transept. "I can't go in there because Daddy . . ."

Molly took him again. Without speaking we agreed that she would wait with him in the garden. He clung to her gratefully, and I crossed slowly to the stairs. At the threshold of the church I stopped. Inside the darkness beckoned, soothing and cool. I thought of the threshold stone of the ancient gate of Jerusalem, the one Jesus crossed. Then I entered the everlasting moment the cathedrals preserve for us.

It took some moments for my eyes to adjust to the dark, and at first all I could see were the brilliant blues and reds of the towering windows. There was not a sound in the vast church. As I moved to the center of the cruciform, my sight sharpened. Stairs to my right led into the sanctuary. The elaborately carved wooden stalls of the choir framed the space in which the high altar stood. Beams of sunlight filtered down upon it magically.

I did not presume to enter the sanctuary — lay brother, still — but crossed to the far aisle and followed it into the apse of the cathedral because I knew that in the classic plan the chapels are behind the choir in the alcoves formed by the easternmost buttresses. As I wound past the sanctuary and the altar and the bishop's throne, it wasn't Chartres I thought of but Saint Patrick's. For all their differences, those places inside were very much alike.

As I approached the chapels I instinctively slowed my pace, all at once conscious of the click of my sandals on the stone floor. I was aware of Carolyn's presence even before, as I passed a last column, she came into view. She was kneeling with her back to me before a subtly illuminated statue of the Virgin, and I froze. The sight of her, bent like that in prayer before the icon of Mary, that great sufferer, confounded me. An avalanche of emotion — love for her and infinite sympathy, grief for my friend, infinite loss — crashed down on me. I had no choice but to turn away and retrace my steps, back around the aisle to the choir. I could not breathe, and for an instant the dread phrase "Heart attack!" flashed before me. I slipped into a choir stall, a monk's stall, and collapsed, burying my head in my arms, weeping.

When I raised my eyes and beheld the sanctuary, it wasn't that moments had passed, but that years had fallen away.

Carolyn and I took places toward the rear of Saint Patrick's just as the great anthem of pipes and horns unleashed waves back and forth across the vault of the cathedral. The congregation rose to its feet and the flourish was followed by the grand processional antiphon, the ancient Gregorian *Ecce Sacerdos Magnus,* Behold the Great Priest! And the bobbing procession-cross flanked by candles led the long train of paired-up *ordinandi* vested in white albs with stoles slashing across their chests as deacons wear them, golden chasubles folded like large waiter's towels over their arms, into the body of the cathedral. The procession came nowhere near us but we were easily able to pick Michael out because he was the tallest deacon. He carried himself with a natural grace.

They wound through the nave and up the stairs into the sanctuary. Trailing them, between his chaplains, poking the floor with his crozier, was the diminutive figure of Francis Cardinal Spellman. It was the first time I'd ever laid eyes on him, and from where we stood, he seemed slightly ludicrous, that roly-poly cherub in miter and velvet slippers, like a newspaper cartoon of the time called "The Little King." It was the spring of 1961 and in fact Spellman's power was in decline. His worldwide influence had depended on his intimate relationship with the aristocratic Pius XII. He and the Peasant Pope, John XXIII, had not hit it off. John had raised Spellman's old rival, Cushing of Boston, to the College of Cardinals. As if that wasn't enough, the Kennedys had embraced Cushing too, and now after that winter's inaugural, the nation thought of the old coot from Boston as the preeminent American Catholic prelate. But here in New York, Spellman was still in command, and if New York was all that was left him, he would be more in command there than ever. Anyone who dismissed him, in other words, as a roly-poly cherub, made a big mistake. Spellman was the *Sacerdos Magnus,* and anyone who doubted it had only to watch this line of handsome, robust young men in their prime — men who'd have been the prizes of recruiters at firms all over Manhattan — kneel before him at his *cathedra* one by one to have their hands bound in linen cloth. In that consecration each made his obeisance in a ceremony derived from the feudal rite of fealty; obeisance not to God or to Jesus or to the Church, but to this man, to this — as the argot puts it with rare irony — Ordinary.

Spellman addressed his question in the Latin: "Do you solemnly promise to respect and obey me and my successors?" Michael like the others did not hesitate with his "I do." Years later he would openly break that vow and I would applaud him for it, thinking stupidly that he would keep his others. I would only wonder, not understanding yet how thoroughly that seminary meat grinder had chewed his ego up, what took him so long.

I remember the jolt with which he slammed his drink down on the table late one night. "Goddamnit, Durk, I *want* someone to obey! I *want* someone to respect! Authority is the basic principle of my life, and look what I've done to undermine it!" He had his finger on the irony of what he'd become. I said, cruelly perhaps, "You just want your daddy, Michael." He looked at me with shock in his face, as if he hadn't seen that elemental orphan's wish as a motivating force behind his vocation.

After making the vow of obedience, the *ordinandi,* in the metaphoric and dramatic climax of the ritual, prostrated themselves on the sanctuary floor, assuming the posture of the dead. Twenty or thirty corpses in white, utterly immobile for the transfiguring duration of the litany of the saints. Its strains, sung antiphonally between the schola, its precious falsetto, and the entire congregation, its ragged base, rose like incense to the vaulted reaches where the faded red hats of Spellman's predecessors hung rotting from the crown joint of the intersecting arches.

> *Kyrie Eleison!*
> *Christi Eleison!*
> *Kyrie Eleison!*
> *Sancta Maria, Mater Dei . . .*
> *Ora pro nobis.*
> *Sancta Michaeli Archangeli . . .*
> *Ora pro nobis.*

And so on through dozens of arcane names — Athanasius, Sebastian and Basil, Perpetua, Agatha and Felicity — men whose bodies were pierced like pin-cushions with Roman arrows and women whose breasts were crushed with Appian Way paving stones.

> All holy men and women, saints of God . . .
> Pray for us.
> Lord, be merciful . . .
> Lord, deliver us.
> Bless these chosen men . . .
> Lord, hear our prayer.

My true feeling surfaced even as I sang. Those poor sons of bitches! Chosen men? One can always tell God's chosen ones — Jesus, the Jews — when they get nailed or gassed. I rose up on the kneeler, straining to see Michael lying there, like a dead man, one of a massacred crowd. I could not tell which was him. Spellman knelt smugly above them, like Moses having laid low a band of Pharaoh's thugs.

Moses! I remembered Spellman's part in the humiliation of Carolyn less than a year before, and I was angry suddenly that Michael would bind himself to that petty tyrant. But my anger fell before my pity. Poor Michael! What was he doing to himself? At that moment surely he was in the grip of a vicious despair. Perhaps he was undergoing, victim of that liturgical enactment, a true foretaste of death. Or was he facing the facts about himself? That his touted bravery had driven him headlong from the world; he was dead to the world now! No human feelings in him from now on, no weakness, no vulnerability, and no autonomy. One of God's true heroes forever. Surely he saw the sham of it! Surely he knew that his priesthood was a blessed sleeve, a maniple, in which to hide the stump of his cowardice! Why else would an American male of my generation cooperate in the denigration of such a ceremony? I was utterly scandalized by it, and I think even now that I understood its radical character, therefore, far better than that edified throng awash in its ocean of sentiment. The ordination of a priest is an awesome, artful and affirming act only to those who buy the whole package, and I didn't.

Michael in fact was not seeing it my way at all. He told me later that he lay there on that cold stone floor in the grip not of despair but of euphoria. The Church to which he was giving himself, its theology, its liturgy, its discipline, was as seamless as the round of chanted music echoing above him, and he felt that the eyes of heaven — all those Felicities and Basils — *were* upon him. His clinging reservations, his shame at what he knew he'd become when he'd failed to stand with Carolyn, and the huge self-doubt I imagined as his burden had fallen away or had been lifted with the airy litany and incense to the shadowy cavern above. When he stood at last, it was no act of abnegation to kneel once more before the cardinal for the imposition of hands and the investiture. "Receive the yoke of the Lord, for his yoke is sweet and its burden light." As the cardinal crossed the stole on Michael's breast, he felt his heart lighten, for he believed fully for the first time that he was indeed called by God, no, seized by God, captured by him — he would almost have said "ravished" — to be held forever. The relief he felt came from the obliteration of his conflicts. There was no issue any longer of which choice to make, for with a clear-headed self-awareness, arrived at over seven arduous years, he had made his choice. That other human beings have to make their choices repeatedly, even their life-shaping ones — especially their life-shaping ones — was a fact without relevance for him.

The contradictions implicit in the Catholic priesthood — slavishly obedient men are expected to use mature judgment exercised with flair in their pastoral positions; men unconsciously in revolt against intimacy and domesticity are expected to nurture the family lives of others — simply did not exist for Michael Maguire at the moment of his ordination. He willingly suspended his disbelief so that Cardinal Spellman could seem a dignified figure of magnanimous authority, the congregation in Saint Patrick's a veritable choir of the moving spheres, and his own life stretching out before him an adventure of transcendent significance. The illusions were in place. Michael accepted with great joy the chasuble of charity upon his shoulders and the oil of kings upon his hands. He touched the chalice of gold and the paten with the sacred Host upon it. "Receive the power to offer sacrifice to God and to celebrate Mass for the living and the dead."

A priest undergoes, in the phrase of Saint Thomas, an ontological change, a change so fundamental that it reaches to the very core of his being, making him, according to this theology, a completely different creature. But Michael's happiness that day, he would tell me, derived from his experience that he became the man he always thought he was.

It was the previous September, only weeks after that day at Dobbs Ferry and after Michael had returned to Washington for his final year of seminary, that I had first called Carolyn at her parents' home. I talked to her on the telephone two or three times before I quashed the feeling that I was a thief and finally asked her out. We began in a tentative way "to see each other," a phrase then light years away from its present status as a euphemism for fucking. We first came together, in other words, the way porcupines, in the old joke, make love — very carefully.

Carolyn had suffered not one but two traumas, for she'd lost Michael and, even more shocking, the Church. If she'd been the Bride of Christ, now she was — and this was the feeling Catholics had about ex-nuns and the feeling Catholics expected ex-nuns to have about themselves — His unfaithful former wife. For a girl who'd been raised to expect affirmation and acceptance, it was a stunning blow to find herself in a situation of failure and rejection. Her parents stood by her, and no one openly derided her, but the shame hung over her nonetheless. It made her feel that she would never recover, would never know happiness, would never again bask in the easy love either of God or the Church, not to mention of a man. The greatest agony, of course, was in having had for a moment, then lost, the love of such a man as Michael. Hadn't it seemed in its intensity, its purity, the perfect gift from God?

Initially my company was a solace to her because I was Michael's friend. I could tell her stories about our boyhood, and she could describe the enthralling first discovery of her feelings and the pain she experienced at his rejection. She could describe her confusion; how could God's gift have become her sin? How could her urgent desire to serve the children have caused her disgrace? How could Michael have left her alone with such trouble? If she'd done nothing wrong, as I kept telling her, why was she consumed with sorrow? "Help me understand, Durk!" she'd cry. "Help me live with this!" And I did. She was no failure to me, no reject, no pariah, and eventually she knew it.

After a while she began to enjoy my company for its own sake, and she began to regard me in relationship to herself, not Michael. Only then, and most carefully, did I reveal my feelings to her, but still the effect of my admission was to make things more confused than ever. Now when I invited her to my somewhat shabby Village apartment, was it to make love to her? When she came to my apartment and I didn't make love to her, was she disappointed? I wanted her sexually more than I'd ever wanted any girl, but I had no intention of pressing her in any way. But, as a virgin, was she waiting for me to overcome her hesitancy? In order to have her, did I have to pretend that I was Michael? Looking back on it now, it seems a miracle that our relationship at last became clear, became *ours*.

We'd had dinner at the New Port Alba, a homey Italian restaurant just below Washington Square, and we headed out into the cold — it was February. We were going to Grand Central so that Carolyn could catch her train to Dobbs Ferry, but crossing the square we came upon an old lady who was trying without success to wrap herself in newspapers. She was blue with cold, wearing only a pair of sweaters and a wool knit hat. Without thinking, I took off my coat and draped her with it. It was a navy pea coat, easily replaced, and so it was not an act of great generosity. Still it was utterly unlike me. I crossed that square every day and hardly ever registered the derelicts. My impulse came from Carolyn, not that I was, grossly, out to impress her, but that, in her presence, such expansiveness came naturally to me. I not only loved Carolyn but loved myself as I was when I was with her.

The old lady cried, "God bless you!"

And as we walked away, Carolyn put her arm around me, to warm me. "You're good," she said.

She was looking at me with such affection that I replied, "Gee, maybe I'll go back and give her my shirt."

But now we had to stop at my apartment so that I could get my other coat, which meant we had to hurry to make her train. It *was* cold. We walked on as quickly as we could toward my place, Carolyn leaning on me, rubbing my arms, me reciting loudly Millay's "Recuerdo."

We were very tired, we were very merry,
We had gone back and forth all night
on the ferry.
We hailed "Good morrow, mother!"
to a shawl-covered head
And bought a morning paper, which
neither of us read;
And she wept, "God bless you!"
for the apples and pears,
And we gave her all our money
but our subway fares.

"Oh, Frank," she said excitedly, "could we do that?"

"What, give her all our money?"

"No. Ride all night on the ferry."

"Sure we can, kid. Stick with me."

"I mean it. I've never been on the ferry."

"Could we wait till August?"

"I didn't mean tonight." She pushed me, and I started to run. She followed, playfully. The truth was I didn't want to take her on the Staten Island Ferry. It was a cliché. It was where I'd gone with other girls, which was why I happened to know "Recuerdo." Reciting poetry into the wind worked wonders. I hadn't tried tricks like that on Carolyn. But, hell, the ferry didn't have to be a trick. It cost a nickel. It offered a great view of New York. It ran all night. And no one bothered kissing couples if they kept their clothes on.

"Hey, why not?" I said suddenly, stopping her. "Want to?"

"The ferry?"

"Sure! What the hell? It's a perfect night."

"It's freezing!" she laughed.

"You're telling me! What do you say?"

"Let's get your coat, then we'll flip a coin."

"Okay. That's a deal."

We ran the few blocks back to my apartment, holding hands, and my mind was filled with her image, how beautiful she was, how untamed, how untouched. It was the most I frankly hoped for, running, joined to her, like that, hands only, and such was my happiness that I thought it could be enough. By the time we got there we were both winded. Carolyn collapsed across my tattered overstuffed reading chair, while I caught my breath against the wall. We were grinning at each other like exhilarated kids. I took my topcoat from its hanger and put it on. She stood up. I produced a quarter and held it toward her on my thumb. "Still game?"

I saw a hint of insecurity in her eyes, but she nodded.

"Heads if by land, tails if by sea."

I flipped and it was tails. We both stared at the coin, stunned, as if that etched George Washington had just cried, "All aboard for Staten Island!"

"Oh," she said. When we looked at each other, I saw how vulnerable she felt. What was this anyway? And I resolved to leave my sure-fire poetry at home with all my hard-learned wiles and moves and savvy calculations. I was not on the make anymore. That, perhaps, was what she sensed, and what, as Frost said, made all the difference.

She said, "I'll have to call my folks."

"What will you say?"

"I'll say, 'We're very tired. We're very merry.' And not to wait up for me in Dobbs Ferry."

"You're good," I said and grinned. I was aware that those were the very words she'd said to me in the park. She'd made me feel not noble precisely, but, well, worthy. Worthy, I realized suddenly, of her.

She went to my phone. As she dialed, her hand shook slightly, but it wasn't her parents who made her nervous. When she told her mother that we were going to ride the ferry, it seemed ludicrous to me, but apparently her mother encouraged her, said it was just the thing for young people to do. It would mean missing the last train, Carolyn said; she'd stay in a hotel. It underscored the difference between our backgrounds when her mother did not object. In Inwood even that bright, self-assured young woman would have been scolded home by midnight.

When Carolyn hung up the phone she turned toward me. When our eyes met we realized together that we were in a completely new situation.

It was the first time an evening had passed in which Michael had not been mentioned. That told us.

It was unthinkable that we should have withdrawn from one another. That told us.

And now, by the same instinct, we knew that the Staten Island Ferry was nothing to us. We weren't going anywhere. And none of this was spoken or needed to be.

I let my coat fall from my shoulders. She started to unbutton hers but her hands could not manage it. She plunged them into her pockets and let her eyes fall instead. She couldn't look at me. She couldn't move. It was my place to cross to her, to take her hand, to show her what to do. But it was as if we both were virgins. I crossed without speaking. My arms went around her; I kissed her. But she was afraid, and I couldn't help but sense it.

"Shall we just go?" I asked.

"No. Durk, you're so good to me." When she looked up there were tears in her eyes. I must have been a blur to her. "I need you, Durk. Without you I'm nothing."

"Oh, that isn't so, Caro." I took her in my arms again, wanting to press into her what I thought. How wonderful you are! How beautiful! How good! But I saw too the other truth about her. She was bereft of any purpose in life, and of course she would be. She had been beloved of the Lord, and now she was His outcast. When her sisters, then Michael, had turned their faces from her, who was to say God had not? I knew her despair as if it was my own. She was nothing, nothing, nothing.

And therefore, ironically, at last, she was mine. To spare her the pain of her loss I'd have returned her at once to God or Michael. Having begun by wanting her, now I wanted only her happiness. My happiness was that neither God nor Michael seemed interested.

She wept quietly against my shoulder.

"I love you, Caro."

She shook her head. Yes? I know? Or could it have been, I love you too?

All at once her arms were around my neck and she was pressing her mouth against mine. I was opening her coat; she shrugged it off, barely pulling away; then I was undressing her while she kept coming at me with her mouth, as if finally the only pain she'd ever felt was hunger. I told myself it was hunger for me. Me, I said, she wants me! I nearly believed it. She was weeping all the while. Ungodly, frightening noises came from her. She pressed her fingernails into my neck, hurting me, and I had her by the hair, by the ears, by the bones in her face. I kept saying, "I love you, Caro," but she was the one who had us locked together. She was the one whose longing peaked first, who would not be denied. By the time we'd moved to my bed, naked, and had crashed down onto it, it was impossible to say who was taking whom. I knew that everything she had for a man who was not Michael was there for me. He was in my brain, whether in hers or not, but that didn't stop me from devouring her. Figments were nothing to me. Not even her body was a dream; it was the ultimate physical expression, those clasping legs, those curving breasts, the smell of perspiration, of crotch. And my body had never been so responsive, so alive to every sensation. We were weightless with each other.

I received what she could give gratefully. Her gift changed my life. Please don't think it pathetic of me, but because Carolyn found it possible to settle for who I was, I also could. If she had rejected me then I would never have accepted myself. So there's the great irony: because I knew she loved Michael more, that she loved me at all seemed miraculous. It was like *redemption* to me. I was the Earth after Copernicus, not wounded that I wasn't the center of the universe, but so awed by what that genius had revealed that I was glad to have a corner of the universe for my own. But metaphors fail me utterly. Copernicus indeed! I am simply saying that what peace with myself and what pride in myself I have ever known came from Carolyn that merry night.

I was for her the other thing, the lover absolute. It is a rare thing to act without reservation, without pretense; that was my virginity. Ineptitude, yes. Our timing was off, but who was clocking? There was awkwardness, but no mirror in the mind, no detachment, no dream of someone else. It was a simple, heartfelt cleaving. I felt the special weight it was to be initiating her, and sensed hovering beyond the ghost of Michael that other, holy ghost, her first chosen spouse, the Lord. But even His shadow seemed benign.

She embraced me — was this *my* suspension of disbelief? — as if I was quite enough for her.

Naturally, for a range of reasons, we felt somewhat awkward at Michael's ordination a few months later. As it happened, his ordination took place not long after we had become engaged. Carolyn, who had had no communication whatsoever with him and hadn't been invited, did not want to go. I insisted. I knew that I could not compete with a memory or a dream, whether hers of Michael or Michael's of her. My friendship and my love depended on their adjustment to what was real, and that would never be more apparent than at his ordination. But at the last minute Carolyn said she simply could not face it. She wasn't coming. We quarreled. It was a flashpoint, and she understood that if she did not come with me, then our relationship was at an end as well. It was the moment of her choice. The misery in her face made me think of Father Zossima's line — you understand by now that I take refuge in profane quotations the very way Michael did in sacred ones, and Dostoevsky remains a favorite — "Love in practice is a harsh and dreadful thing compared to love in dreams." Carolyn was looking up at me from the edge of my bed and as she said finally, "You're right," I was aware of her handing herself over to me in a way she hadn't yet. It was as if she had curled herself into a small wad and held it up between her fingers. I bent to her and put my hand under her head with a tentativeness that made my hand tremble, and I kissed her. She pulled me down onto the bed, on top of her, and with an abandon she had yet to demonstrate and I had scarcely suspected she was capable of, as if her acquiescence released all sexual restraint at last, she made love to me.

And made us late. I was acutely aware, not smugly so, that even while Michael, hands folded inside Spellman's, made his vow, my sperm was moistening the fold between Carolyn's legs.

At the end of the ceremony each of the newly ordained priests went to a section of the main communion rail or to a side altar to bestow on his family and friends his first priestly blessing. Carolyn and I approached with awe for what had just happened to our friend, but also with a more mundane fear that our appearance together at this moment would undermine each of us. As the line moved slowly forward I watched Michael raise his arms and eyes to heaven, smoothly and solemnly as if he'd always done it, and then cut the air in a cross and press his now consecrated hands onto the bent head of his mother. It moved me nearly to tears to see her. Michael took her by the elbow then and helped her up, and when he embraced her she almost disappeared in the wrap of his golden chasuble.

By the time Carolyn and I presented ourselves at the altar rail and knelt before him, he had blessed several dozen people. I couldn't help but grin up at him, and as he bent toward me with impressive solemnity I was afraid he would think me irreverent. But at the last moment he winked and my anxiety disappeared. Hell, after all that tossing and turning, it was Michael! My oldest friend, my friend for life! Ontological change or not this was still the man I'd grown up with. The distance between us and even the awkwardness I felt about Carolyn evaporated. No woman, no Church, no God, no meaningless observances or penances or humiliations were going to wreck our friendship.

Even my argument with his piety disappeared for the moment. In the case of Carolyn I had been the beneficiary of his self-denial, but otherwise I'd been depressed to watch the transformation of my strong-willed, active friend into a dependent, necessarily passive cleric. I thought the alleluiahs with which the Church propagated such abnegation — "I am a worm" was how the great Thomas à Kempis put it, "and no man" — was so much shit. But all at once I saw the thing differently. Now that he was a priest, perhaps I saw the other side of that self-surrender. Maybe it wasn't cowardice. Perhaps it wasn't mere masochism. Maybe that ancient impulse of religious men and women — "abandonment" — did express some kind of wisdom. Maybe even a sophist punk like me could understand it.

As I tell you this story now, looking back on that moment from a vantage two decades later, it is obvious to both of us that my suspicion of "holy obedience" — the ecclesial version of "wholly owned" — is intact. Still, even now, remembering how moved I was in that first encounter with him as a priest, I admit that something else was at work. Something else was in him. Hadn't it been superficial of me to dismiss Michael's experience, his choice? Wasn't it possible to see his self-surrender not as an act of feminine piety, but as a bold image of what we all do every day — this blind handing over of ourselves to the blank future? What if the cardinal *was* an authentic sign of God's presence, a proclamation exactly that God draws near to us in what is ordinary? What if Michael's belief in the Church, in other words, was true?

"Why do priests carry chocolate pudding in their wallets?" we Village anticlericals used to ask. "For identification. Har. Har. Har."

Why then was I weeping?

Michael loomed over me like an angel. He seemed a man of tremendous virtue and strength, and if I could have, I'd have put my hands in his and sworn fealty, not to God, to him. But with great sweep and priestly panache, he deflected my mind back to God, away from him. It was what he would always do to me. "*Benedicat Deus omnipotenti . . .*" And with his large athlete's hands he pressed down on the crown of my head, pressed so hard I imagined him praying like some fundy, "Believe, Durk! Believe!"

It had been six years since I'd discarded the faith and now, to put it simply, I took it back. Hell, even Wallace Stevens, the most eloquent agnostic of all — he wanted poetry to take the place of the God he couldn't believe in — became a Catholic on his deathbed. So did I have to wait until I was dying?

Oh, sure, you say, how they soften after college, once they have a job, when they fall in love and start thinking family. Can't send the kids to Sunday school if you don't believe in Sunday.

Maybe that's all I was doing, ending my adolescent apostate phase on schedule. But at that moment, with Michael pressing on my head, it seemed to me that God Himself — the Heavenly Condor — had swooped down, talons flashing, to seize me by the hair. I "had trod, had trod . . . bleared, smeared with toil." Not only that, "I had fled Him down the nights and down the days." But in Michael He had followed me. He was my "ransom, my rescue, my first, fast, last friend." Christ. Jesus Christ. He came back to me.

You see, what Michael did for me that day, pressing down, was to bring me back to myself. I was born like this. I am Catholic like I am freckled, like I am smart, like I am, under all this flippancy, afraid. Michael revealed to me how much I wanted to believe, and he reminded me that wanting belief is having it. That is the chief way in which belief differs from sex.

I felt defenseless. I wanted to tell Michael that I loved him. But my affection was swamped by tidal waves of guilt and remorse. How unworthy I was of this man, of his friendship, of his blessing. How unworthy I was of God. Those were the feelings I had. I wouldn't know how true they were until years later. I seized Michael's arm and like a self-loathing peasant — this gesture of subservience had always disgusted me, but it was the perfect primordial act — I pressed my mouth to his hand and kissed it.

If Carolyn's presence next to me upset him I did not see it. I was too ambushed by my own emotion — by my experience, for this is what it was, of conversion — to notice anything of their encounter, but when I looked at her as we both stood to leave the rail, I saw the black streaks of mascara beneath her eyes. She looked like she'd been beaten.

The reception for the *ordinandi* in the Cathedral Hall was jammed. Long tables were spread with sweet rolls and finger sandwiches. Hatted ladies were dispensing coffee from huge aluminum urns. The families of the new priests were crowding them. Flashbulbs, forbidden in the cathedral itself, were popping everywhere.

Priests' mothers were already laying claim to the linen bands in which their sons' hands had been wrapped during the anointing. It was the privilege of the mothers of priests to be buried with their own hands wrapped in the strip of white cloth that would still, years later, be stained with the sacred oil.

On smaller tables were displayed the priests' new chalices and patens which the laity could ogle but not touch. Also on those tables were tidy stacks of holy cards commemorating each man's elevation to the sacred state. I took one of Michael's. On one side was a Daliesque picture of Saint Paul, kneeling with a sword, looking up to heaven. For a holy card it was a manly pose, a dismounted warrior after all, exactly what I'd have expected from Michael. On the reverse side was a line of Paul's, a selection that frankly surprised me. "In my own flesh I fill up what is lacking in the sufferings of Christ for the sake of His Body, the Church." And beneath that verse were the words, "Reverend Michael Maguire, Ordained a Priest, May 22, 1961. Please Pray For Me."

I handed it to Carolyn and despite myself said, "I hadn't realized anything was lacking in Christ's suffering." Carolyn read the card and gave it back to me, apparently uninterested in what Reverend Michael did in his own flesh. Even in the flush of my "conversion" I thought the quotation smacked somewhat of smugness and self-pity, but I saved the card. Years later I would come across it in my Bible and see that it expressed perfectly what he'd done.

As we moved through the crowd, Carolyn clung to my arm as if the scene in the becolumned hall was foreign to her. She was afraid she would see someone she knew, someone from the Sisters of Charity. She was afraid those mothers of priests would point at her and snarl, "She used to be a nun." She didn't look it. She wore a trim tan linen suit with a bright blue silk blouse open at her throat. Her blond hair with which she'd lashed me that morning — she would never wear it short again — was in a perfect pageboy, and she wore a pillbox hat as becomingly as Mrs. Kennedy did. She had repaired her makeup and now held herself, despite the nervousness I could sense, with the poise of a movie star. Beautiful women have a right to feel ill at ease in the basements of cathedrals.

When Michael finally entered, his mother was on his arm. Her arthritis made it impossible for her to walk without help. He saw us, left his mother with his aunts and hurried across the large room. If space and decorum had permitted it, he'd have run. He arrived with his arms open and an expression of happiness I'd never seen in him before. He embraced us both, singly and with great feeling.

"Hello, Father!" I said, grinning again and abandoning for once everything but the pride and affection I felt for him.

" 'Call no man father,' you son of a bitch!" He laughed hilariously and clapped my shoulder. "Do it again and I'll break your arm." He was joking, but also making a point. Some priests are addressed as "Father" by everyone. If they were allowed to marry they'd be called "Father" by their wives.

To Carolyn he said more soberly, but with that broad smile, "I'm so glad you came." Obviously, he meant it. He took her hand.

"Congratulations, Michael," she said, then broke into a grin of her own. "Now they can't fire you."

"But I can't fire them either."

"What is all this about firing people?" I put in happily. His bondage was my freedom.

He turned her hand over in his own, fingering the modest diamond I'd given her.

He looked quickly at me and at last I saw a brief show of hurt in him. "My God!" he said, too stunned for the moment to veil his reaction.

All at once it seemed to me that every word Carolyn and I had said to each other and every tentative gesture of the flesh we'd shared were available to him as if now, ontologically indeed, he had mystic powers to penetrate our secrets. Could he know that not two hours before she'd ravished me?

I blushed and started to explain. "We'd have told you before . . ."

But he stopped me. He put an arm around each of us. His reaction was a denial of the visceral, an act of will and of generosity. But everything — particularly the solemn commitment he'd just made — required it. "I'm so pleased! I think it's wonderful! It makes me very happy." He crushed us together. "You can be my family."

For a moment we three held each other tightly. It was what I'd hoped for.

When we separated Carolyn brushed her pancake makeup from his cassock. She said to my utter amazement — we'd never discussed asking him — "Michael, we were hoping that you'd marry us."

"Of course I will," he said instantly. "I'd never forgive you if you didn't let me."

They stared at each other and for a moment they forgot that I was there. Carolyn had said in effect, "I came to your ordination; I want you at my wedding." I could sense the flow between them, the understanding, the effort to accept what was real, as well as the effort to transform their feelings into something new. But also I saw how they drew each other out of the world in which the rest of us lived, and I knew that I was forever banned from the deepest place in each of them. Of course I was wounded and jealous, but frankly I didn't know of whom. I wanted both of them the way they had each other.

"When are you planning it for?" he asked.

"August," Carolyn said.

Michael slapped his forehead. "August!"

"Why?"

"I haven't had a chance to tell you yet about my assignment."

What was to tell? Weren't priests always put in parishes? Our Lady of the Vouchsafe, Saints Maureen and Doreen, Saint Joseph by the Way. And weren't the new ones always put in charge of bingo and the altar boys and the annual picnic? But Michael's enthusiasm surprised me. Clearly the news of my engagement to Carolyn had not derailed him.

"What is it?" I asked.

"Do you remember Father O'Shea? That chaplain in Korea?"

The one whose life he'd saved, the one Michael had longed to talk to. Sure I did and said so.

"He's retired from the army. He's a monsignor now, and he's with the Catholic Relief Service here in New York; he runs the Far East Refugee Rescue operation. He's asked for me as his assistant. I'll be in a parish but only part-time. He and the cardinal are going over there this summer after the Eucharistic Congress in Manila. And I'm going with them."

"And you won't be back in August?" Carolyn asked.

"Not until September."

After a moment of rather awkward silence — Carolyn's mother had already begun making reservations, and Carolyn herself was prepared to take his unavailability as another rejection — I said, "We'll just do it in September then."

"Great!" Michael seemed to mean it, and it relieved me to see Carolyn's face soften toward him again.

At that moment people in the crowd behind Michael moved aside, opening an aisle. They fell silent, and craned to see the approaching figure. He was invisible to me because he was so short, but I knew it was Cardinal Spellman. It had to be. I exchanged a look with Carolyn. Who needed this? She was blushing, and I put my arm around her. I knew how vulnerable she felt. She'd been valiant, in my opinion, up to then.

Michael wore a stricken look too. It was for fear of this moment that he had not invited Carolyn to the ordination. He knew better than anyone what Spellman had done to her. And now he was sworn as Spellman's vassal. Or was it serf?

"Father Michael," Cardinal Spellman said, beaming up at him.

Michael bowed smoothly from his waist to kiss the prelate's ring, then said, stiffly, "Your Eminence, let me introduce you to some friends."

Carolyn and I each managed to kiss his ring. It was a gesture that couldn't have come less naturally to me, but Carolyn accomplished it smoothly, with a graceful half-curtsey. Still, she blushed furiously, and when Spellman, still holding her hand, said, "We've met before, dear, haven't we?" I thought she was going to faint.

What would have happened to Michael's new career if she'd said right then, "I'm Sister Mary Felony, Your Eminence. You saw my picture in the paper."

But she stammered, "You administered my Sacrament of Confirmation, Your Eminence." She forced a smile. "That was fourteen years ago."

Spellman put his hand on her forearm and asked, as if it was important to him, "What parish was that, dear?"

"Saint Peter's in Bronxville, Your Eminence."

He nodded. "And did I meet your parents?"

"Yes, you did, Your Eminence."

"And your mother is as beautiful as you are, if I recall." He smiled at her endearingly. He was like an old pol working the crowd, shuffling through what we all knew was his routine, but still we were affected, charmed even. His touch was light, and he held on to Carolyn's arm as if it was the most natural thing in the world for him to do so. He seemed benign, fatherly even, and I found myself softening toward him. I was nearly won over when he said to Carolyn with real feeling, "It is the great privilege of my position to administer sacraments to handsome young people like you. And then . . ." He grasped Michael's arm, while holding onto Carolyn's, an ironic if unintended linking. ". . . to think it is my honor to ordain God's new priests. Every night I get down on my knees to thank Him." He grinned suddenly. "Oh, but goodness, you don't want to hear an old priest boasting about being on his knees!" He looked at me. "And aren't you proud of Father Michael today!"

"Yes, I am," I said.

Spellman dropped Carolyn's arm to press Michael's with both hands. "We're proud of him too. It's not often the Church receives a man like Michael Maguire into her service." He was looking at me as he said that, but I sensed that Spellman was addressing Michael. He'd have been aware of Michael's war record, of course, and it would have carried great weight with a soldier-worshipper like Spellman. Now he was manifesting his attachment to Michael, though, of course, like all priests, he could only do so indirectly. "We expect great things from this young man."

Spellman still did not look at Michael, or else he might have witnessed the look Michael exchanged with Carolyn. There was apology in it, as well as misery, embarrassment. Michael's standing was considerable, obviously. But it had begun with his refusal to stand by her. With his standing, he felt, *on* her.

"And has he told you what we've planned for him?" the cardinal asked.

I nodded. "About relief work?" I couldn't remember the name of the agency.

"The most important work in the Church," Cardinal Spellman said. "Father Maguire is going to pick up where Doctor Tom Dooley left off, aren't you, Father?"

"It would be an honor to think so, Your Eminence."

I knew that the heroic doctor had died only months before. Spellman had been at his bedside. Spellman had pronounced him a saint.

The cardinal said, with a sudden fierceness, "Tom Dooley's people are suffering more than ever, aren't they, Father?"

Michael nodded.

"And Father Maguire is coming with me to see what can be done to help them."

"Where?" Carolyn asked, despite herself. Tom Dooley had worked in Laos or someplace. Hadn't Michael just said the Far East? But what was that to her?

Cardinal Spellman looked blankly at her. "Vietnam," he said.

FOURTEEN

It was one of those steaming mornings of the monsoon when the air over the lush terrain grew hot faster than the air over the bordering South China Sea. When the resulting massive thermal draft began to rise it sucked at the wet sea winds which then moved steadily inland, across the low coastal hills to the rugged mountains that formed the spine of the country and separated it from the Kingdom of Laos. And everywhere the rain fell.

The convoy of seven black Citroëns sped along the glistening paved road that would come to be called Route One when the Americans came, the only proper name for a north-south coastal highway. Affixed to the bumper of each automobile, although not to the escorting military vehicles, were two flags; the red-striped saffron flag of the Republic of Viet Nam, and the yellow-and-white flag, displaying the triple tiara and the keys of Saint Peter, of His Holiness the Pope. The tires of the automobiles hummed a steady sibilant, but the passengers for the most part remained silent.

They stared out the half-open windows and let the rain-soaked breeze refresh them, and they eyed the green blur of jungle, watching steadily. For wild animals? The spirits of ancestors? For friendly farmers? Every hundred or two hundred yards, even in the desolation of that countryside, a government soldier stood at present-arms, but with his back to the cars as they passed. No mere honor guard, those soldiers were outfitted for combat and charged with preventing an attack on that convoy. They had swept the highway for mines and booby traps. Now they were watching for signs of the guerrilla force that totally controlled the scummy swamp world in the delta region far to the south, around Saigon, making travel outside that city a nightmare. The guerrillas lived, as one of their slogans said, like owls in the night and foxes in the daylight, and they were known for striking, almost mystically, just when a traveler thought himself most safe. In addition to ambush those on foot had constantly to beware their punji traps, concealed pits with dung-encrusted bamboo spikes. Vehicles regularly tripped mines and hidden grenades, and once-innocent obstacles like fallen trees or collapsed culverts now certainly meant attack. In less than a year as an organized force the Communists had already assassinated more than four thousand village heads and district chiefs. But their random assaults were even more fearsome. On the road it didn't seem to matter whether their victims were women or children or even supporters of the Great Struggle, and that capriciousness only made the terror they inflicted more stunning. In Saigon in those days Americans were famous for refusing to leave the city. Government officials did so only with escorts, and the rich landlords who had to visit their holdings disguised themselves as peasants.

But here in the northernmost region between Hué and the border with North Vietnam, the population was loyal to the government and the guerrillas had yet to make an impact. But the three brothers who ruled South Vietnam, President Ngo Dinh Diem, his counselor, Ngo Dinh Nhu, and Ngo Dinh Can, the viceroy of Central Vietnam, were prudent men. The sentries they had posted all along the road from Hué to Quang Tri were members of their crack personal guard. The Ngos were taking no chances this morning, not on such a great occasion and not with such guests.

In the first car, but behind the military escort, Cardinal Spellman rode with his old friend, the fourth Ngo brother, Archbishop Thuc. Riding on the jump seat, facing them, was Monsignor Timothy O'Shea, and in the front seat, beside the driver, was Father Michael Maguire. The three Americans had arrived from Manila only the night before, and now they were speeding to Quang Tri, the northernmost city in South Vietnam, where Spellman and Thuc would preside at a ceremony attended by the elite of the country, marking the dedication of the huge new basilica of Our Lady of La Vang.

Archbishop Thuc, between puffs of his cigarette, said, "It will be like Lourdes, *Eminenza.*" He spoke with a pronounced French accent, though the title he used to address Spellman was the Italian. "La Vang will be the spiritual bastion of the country."

"All you'll need are the miracles," Cardinal Spellman replied. Michael caught a glimpse of him in the rearview mirror, and looked for signs that he was being facetious. There were none. Thuc nodded smugly. The miracles would come.

"We have built this shrine," Thuc said, leaning toward Spellman, "with the donations of all the people, even peasants. They gave their *sous* to thank Our Lady for the deliverance of her Catholic children."

Michael wondered, Would these "peasants" be at the dedication? Not likely. He had an American's distaste for the word, and it told him what he didn't like about the Vietnamese prelate. He carried himself like an Oriental Richelieu, and in his thin, ascetic visage, his dark, brooding eyes it seemed to Michael there was something merciless.

Thuc touched Spellman's hand familiarly. "Who would have been thinking fifteen years ago we would be together today, with my brothers serving the people? We owe our success to you, *Eminenza.*"

Michael strained to hear what Spellman said. In Manila, just days before, he had heard an Australian priest refer to Ngo Dinh Diem as "Spellman's seminarian." The priest explained that Diem had been forced into exile in the late forties. Ho Chi Minh had murdered one of his brothers, so Diem was fiercely anti-Communist, but he wouldn't support the French either. He'd had nowhere to go until his brother Thuc intervened with Cardinal Spellman. Spellman liked Diem's personal style — he was a pious, ascetic Catholic who attended Mass daily and who'd taken a private vow of chastity — and he took him under his wing. The Australian priest claimed that Diem had lived in one of Spellman's seminaries from 1950 until 1954. Michael was skeptical and said so. Hadn't he begun his own seminary course in 1954? And in Spellman's diocese? But the Australian insisted it was true, and in fact it was. Though Diem spent most of 1954 in a Belgian monastery, before that he had lived at Maryknoll, just a few miles from Dunwoodie. It amazed Michael that he hadn't heard of Spellman's connection with Diem before. The Australian had seemed to think there was something sinister in it, but, if it was true, Michael thought well of it. What should the Church use its influence for if not to bring to power worthy politicians who were inured to corruption and dedicated to Christian moral principles? Michael had said as much to the priest.

Spellman shook his head. "We are mere instruments, *n'est-ce pas?* We owe our success to Providence."

Thuc nodded, patting Spellman's hand. "And to Our Lady."

"With a little help from the U.S. Navy," Monsignor O'Shea put in gruffly. Spellman withdrew his hand from Thuc's and laughed, as O'Shea knew he would. As a cigar-chomping, tough-talking Irish ex-chaplain, O'Shea took more latitude with the cardinal than most priests, but that was why Spellman liked him. Frankly, Archbishop Thuc's deference bordered on the overweening and that never went far with Spellman. What O'Shea and Spellman knew was that if the Catholics of Vietnam had been delivered by Our Lady, she had made damn good use of the navy ships that brought a million of them from North to South after Dien Bien Phu. Tom Dooley, whose books had made that exodus famous, and had made the support of Catholics in Vietnam good politics in America, had begun as a navy doctor.

Spellman pointed to O'Shea. "And, I might add, a little help from Monsignor's Catholic Relief Service. How much do you calculate CRS put up for the early refugees, Monsignor?"

"Thirty-five million dollars, Your Eminence."

Spellman looked at Thuc. "And now the U.S. government has asked CRS to oversee the increased aid the president promised."

"Food, clothing and supplies," O'Shea said. "But also money. Some people aren't wild about the idea."

Thuc leaned toward O'Shea. "But we need those things. Our people *need* them."

"I know that, Your Excellency. But some people are a little nervous about our serving as a government channel. We've been raising our own funds up to now, as you know. In America we have this little thing called separation of Church and State."

Spellman grunted. "Forgive Monsignor O'Shea, Archbishop. He has an immigrant's zeal for American institutions." Spellman chuckled. "We natives understand there's a certain flexibility."

Thuc shrugged. "It is only sensible to use the Church for aid. In my country only the Church is everywhere."

"That's the point," O'Shea said. "That's why we've agreed."

"And I'm going to depend on you, Peter Martin . . ." The archbishop's Western name jarred Michael, but he realized at once it shouldn't have. It was his version of an Oriental's plastic surgery on his eyes. ". . . to see that all goes well. President Kennedy does not want any confusion, any scandal. He wants to make an impact on the problem, and fast. That's why they're not waiting until the aid distribution structures are established between the governments."

"You can depend on me, *Eminenza*. And on my family. You know that."

Spellman nodded. "I told our secretary of state that Vietnam would be the only country in the world where the ruling class didn't get rich off Uncle Sam. He said to me, 'How can you be so sure of that, Cardinal Spellman?' And I said, 'Because Diem and his supporters are my people.' I told him, 'The Ngos are a great and ancient Catholic family. They're not lackey converts who submitted to baptism to win favor from the French.' I said, 'The Ngos are real Catholics, Mister Secretary. They're incorruptible men of their word, absolutely trustworthy.' And do you know what he said to me? He said, 'Your Eminence, your endorsement carries a lot of weight in this office.' "

Monsignor O'Shea gestured with his unlit cigar. He was dying to smoke it, but Spellman wouldn't have it in the car. "Your Excellency," he said, "what the cardinal intends to emphasize, if I may speak . . ." O'Shea looked quickly at Spellman, who nodded. ". . . is the delicate position we are in. The new administration — a Catholic administration — has asked for assurance that the emergency aid program can efficiently and securely be administered through the structures of the Catholic Church. The last thing Jack Kennedy needs is a Church-related snafu, if you receive my meaning. And no black market. We want *your* personal assurance, Excellency. You should understand Cardinal Spellman's position with his own government. We are talking tens of millions of dollars here. Cardinal Spellman is depending on your government and on your family, Excellency. But first he is depending on you. Does that state the case fairly, Your Eminence?" O'Shea plugged his mouth with his cigar.

Spellman nodded briskly. "I go from here to Rome for Vatican approval. Caritas International will be the umbrella agency you'll relate to. It will be a Vatican-sponsored operation, but we'll all know where the relief is coming from. No one will mind the Church involvement if the hungry are fed and the naked clothed. Monsignor O'Shea will coordinate from our end. I have a meeting with Secretary Rusk as soon as I return. He wants my answer."

"By all means, *Eminenza*. I give you all assurance you ask. My brothers and I already discussed this. We had indications you might be speaking of such subjects. We are agreed. Aid will continue to be distributed through the Church, under my supervision."

Spellman stared at Thuc.

Until Thuc added, "Not through the party."

Spellman nodded. It was then Michael realized that this was the assurance the cardinal wanted. Michael didn't know it yet, but the party, the Revolutionary Personalist Labor Party of Vietnam, was the personal fiefdom of Diem's neurotic brother Nhu and already there were fears in Washington that he could not be controlled. The idea was to keep power tilted as much as possible away from him, even then. Thuc was seen to have a certain independence and they wanted to reinforce it.

Michael had assumed that at some point during that car ride he'd be introduced to Thuc, but he wasn't. He was just the junior ADC in the front seat, the guy with the chauffeur. He wasn't supposed to contribute to the conversation, and he wasn't expected to listen. But he had listened, carefully. This was the beginning of his education in new realities.

He felt somewhat awed when he realized what subtle brokering had been going on, and it excited him to see men like himself — *Church*men — in the thick of international power politics. Vietnam may have been a remote, backwater country, but it was a hell of a long way from Inwood. The more he saw of Spellman the more impressed he was. There was more to the man than the Saint Patrick's Day parades he presided over. If Diem had begun as his protégé, wasn't it admirable that Spellman was still working to get him what he needed to succeed? This maneuvering had been going on for a decade or more. While Americans, including Michael, had regarded Spellman as an affable but essentially parochial builder of schools and hospitals, he had been building a nation. And Spellman now was like an architect returning for a supervisory check on the structure he'd designed and which was nearly complete. A new nation, and its symbol, a basilica, in fact.

Yes, the architect, Michael saw. Tom Dooley was the patron saint. And because of the support generated by the cardinal and the doctor together, the guarantor of that Vietnamese triumph-in-the-making was now John Kennedy.

The worldwide defeat of Communism would follow quickly upon the heels of the eradication of poverty and hunger, and this generation of Americans and Churchmen had made that their priority. *That* was why Kennedy excited men like Michael; he represented a country and a Church reinvigorated and on the move. He was the world's equivalent of Pope John. Pope John's hope and John Kennedy's urbane optimism infected the age, and the two strains they represented came together no more elegantly than in one movement, Tom Dooley's movement, and in one man, Ngo Dinh Diem of South Vietnam. Michael remembered how, at his inauguration, just two days after Dooley's death, President Kennedy gave perfect expression to the ideals of the CRS and Medico and activist priests, he suddenly saw, like Spellman, O'Shea and even himself. They would go anywhere, to fight any foe, to pass on the torch of freedom, that God's work on earth might truly be their own.

The convoy slowed as it approached the outskirts of Quang Tri.

"Good Lord," Monsignor O'Shea said. The car had just rounded a curve leaving the thick green tangle of jungle behind. The land on either side of the road had been cleared for planting, but the fields were jammed with Vietnamese, thousands of them. The rain poured steadily off their conical hats, veiling their faces with sheets of water. The people waved and cheered, holding aloft rosaries and crucifixes, medals of the Virgin and rain-streaked pictures of the Sacred Heart. The closer the convoy drew to the city, the more solidly packed the crowd was and the louder their cheers became. Umbrellas began to appear as city-dwellers began to outnumber the peasants.

Monsignor O'Shea twisted in his jump seat to touch Michael's shoulder. He said, as if an emotion had taken him by surprise, as if the others were not there, as if he had the right to speak so intimately, "When those moments come, Michael, and come they will, when you wonder whether the life you've chosen is worth it . . ." Monsignor O'Shea paused to make the full weight of his feeling felt. His eyes were fixed on the grateful faces of the Vietnamese. ". . . remember this. Carry this scene, son, in your heart."

Michael nodded, though in fact he was embarrassed. He'd wanted to be included in the worldly talk before. He wasn't up for O'Shea's pieties. He said feebly, "It must have been like this going into Paris with Ike."

The monsignor snorted and turned to Spellman. "Don't you love him for that comparison, Your Eminence? He's comparing you to Ike."

"If I'm Ike, Tim, that makes you George Patton, and you remember what happened to him."

O'Shea winked and pointed his unlit cigar at Thuc. "And that makes your brother Charles de Gaulle."

Thuc grinned and shook his head. "No, thank you, Monsignor. One Charles de Gaulle is quite enough."

By the time the convoy pulled into the city proper, all four of the clergymen had fallen silent and were simply watching the mass display. Hundreds of thousands of people, more than the entire population of Quang Tri, were standing in the rain, cheering or clapping mahogany sticks together or waving their yellow-and-white papal — not American — flags. The din of the rain on the automobile roofs and the incessant roar of the crowd made conversation impossible, and in any case the members of the president's party were too moved for talk by the time they arrived at the basilica of Our Lady of La Vang, a huge structure made of cinder block or brick and faced with bright yellow stucco. However much the people loved their leaders, though, they weren't allowed anywhere near them. Rows of soldiers banked the entrance plaza, even though the only people admitted to the basilica grounds as such were appointed lay representatives of each of the country's two archdioceses, eleven dioceses, and eight hundred parishes.

Inside the church all was cool, dry and silent, though it too was packed. The elite of the nation were there, perhaps two thousand of them, sitting in their pews, facing forward, absolutely still. From behind they were a sea of heads. The women's were covered uniformly with black mantillas, as if the pope himself were coming. The men's heads were all uncovered, but the uniformity of their black gleaming hair, sharply parted, was striking too. Though Diem, Nhu, the archbishop, the cardinal and their attendants arrived amid considerable commotion, no one in the church turned to look at them. They would be signaled when to stand and when to look. Aside from that commotion the only sounds were the occasional rattle of rosary beads or the crackle of pages turning in prayer books. This congregation, in its recollection, its "custody" of the senses, was the fulfillment of a nun's dream.

Cardinal Spellman would preside over the dedication ceremony, though the celebrant of the accompanying Solemn Eucharist was to be Archbishop Thuc. Serving him as deacon and subdeacon were a pair of Vietnamese prelates. Michael and Monsignor O'Shea vested in surplices to serve as chaplains to the cardinal. Michael's job was to be sure that the missal was open to the proper page every time Spellman needed it, and Monsignor O'Shea was responsible for the relic.

"What's that?" Michael had asked, eyeing the black chalice case that O'Shea had brought on board the airplane in New York. They hadn't left the runway yet.

"You wouldn't believe it."

"What is it? Your chalice?"

The monsignor shook his head. "It's Saint Joan's toenail."

"What?"

"Joan of Arc, you've heard of her?" O'Shea began to laugh despite himself, and so did Michael.

"Her what?" The two priests were still laughing when the stewardess asked them to buckle up.

"It's Spelly's gift to the people of Vietnam."

"Jeanne d'Arc's toenail?"

"We shouldn't mock it, Michael. Stop laughing."

"I always wondered, did she paint them?"

"Come on, Michael."

"Where the hell did he get her toenail?"

"Saint Joan's in the Bronx. They had two."

"Oh, Jesus."

"Come on, Michael. Cut it out."

"But, Monsignor, she *had* to paint them! It's Joan of Arc, right? She had to paint them with asbestos nail polish!"

She'd been burned at the stake, cuticles and all. O'Shea had blushed and said defensively, "Don't you believe in miracles?"

And now at the basilica Michael watched as Monsignor O'Shea solemnly handed the gold reliquary the size of a cigarette pack to Cardinal Spellman. With like solemnity Spellman placed the relic in the aperture in the stone slab of the high altar. Then the clergy stepped back while the stonemason — an unlikely-looking Vietnamese worker in white gloves and tails — closed the aperture with a fitted stone, then troweled cement over it.

"The bodies of the saints lie buried in peace," Spellman intoned in Latin, "but their names will live on forever." And the choir sang the verses of a Psalm while he incensed the altar.

Michael and O'Shea exchanged a glance, and for a moment Michael felt like an impish altar boy controlling his giggles. How could they believe in this crap? he thought. The toenail of Saint Joan, Christ! It was to purge the Church of such mumbo-jumbo that Pope John had recently called the Council.

Everyone around Michael, though, was profoundly moved. Archbishop Thuc was weeping openly while the other Vietnamese clergy lined up to kiss the stone. Saint Joan was their patroness, the warrior-woman, the heroine of all that was good in France. And Vietnamese Catholics, Michael saw suddenly, were as French as Roman, and that came as a shock. How Vietnamese were they? he wondered suddenly. It was a reservation, a first, small one, he wasn't ready to deal with. He veered from it.

But his mind tricked him. Joan of Arc! He veered toward the image of that saint. He pictured her, saw her exactly, that warrior-woman. But Joan of Arc was someone else to Michael. Wouldn't he have pictured her walking toward him across a lawn? Wouldn't he have remembered her asking, "Can I tell you who I remind myself of?"

Anne. No, Carolyn. In her simple bathing suit, the simple perfect body of a saint. With her short blond hair, like Joan's, with her long, elegant limbs, her flaring breasts, walking toward him. Then, in the trick of his mind, she was raising his fingers to her mouth and biting him just sharply enough to cause him pain.

"The bodies of the saints," he'd have repeated to himself, "lie buried in peace, but their names — Oh, Carolyn!" He'd have considered himself free of this. He wouldn't have been able to think of her without feeling again the intense pain of his humiliation. ". . . live on forever."

By the time the Solemn Mass of Dedication was over the rain had stopped and the noon sun shimmered gloriously. The reception for dignitaries was held at the Governor's Palace, and it spilled out into the minutely designed Japanese garden. Steam rose from the broad green leaves and from the glassy surfaces of ponds. The white pebbles of the pathways glistened. The guests hovered in the shade of trees and gazebos.

Michael watched the Vietnamese with a certain detachment. By and large he was ignored, and that was fine with him. He was trying to decipher his feelings. He wanted to understand what he was seeing. The men were like mandarins, though dressed in dark Western suits and ties. They carried themselves with that combination of swagger and subservience characteristic of those who know their exact place in the structure of power. In Vietnam that place was determined, even for Christians, by the fates of heaven. But, like his equivalents everywhere, the mandarin lives to hold sway over many more people than hold it over him. They ignored Michael and even O'Shea because only Spellman of the Americans had a defined place in the structure of their world. He was its patron. Every male present owed his position and probably his life to the ruddy, bald, jovial prelate, and each one knew it. And now Michael knew it. The man who made princes of the Church made princes of the world as well! Michael felt like an initiate in secrets, and even to be a junior associate of the cardinal gave him a sense of power. His Roman collar had never seemed more magical.

Spellman was the one Westerner toward whom the Vietnamese elite felt none of their habitual ambivalence. They waited patiently in line to kiss his ring, a gesture that came more naturally to them, with their sweeping bow, than to Americans. It occurred to Michael that perhaps another reason they took so warmly to the archbishop of New York was that, unlike most Caucasians, he was as short and doll-like as they were.

Monsignor O'Shea caught Michael's eye. He raised a finger toward him, and Michael crossed the room promptly. O'Shea had just lit his cigar at last, and was standing by the doors to the garden, to blow the smoke outside so Spellman wouldn't whiff it. "So what do you think?" O'Shea asked.

"Of what?"

"Of our president."

Diem's toast had been a rambling monologue that made no sense, but Michael said, "Seems like a good man."

"We're damn lucky to have him. If it wasn't for him Ho Chi

Minh would have this whole country by now and where would these lovelies be?" He jerked his thumb at the elegant Vietnamese.

"At reeducation meetings."

"Well, you of all people should know what that means."

Michael lit a cigarette. Chain-smoking was something he had in common with Diem. He and the short man in the white suit both reeked of tobacco, but Diem's olive-skinned fingers didn't show the nicotine stain like Michael's did. Michael sensed that the president made O'Shea uneasy and he wondered why. What did O'Shea know? Obviously he knew a lot. Michael looked around the room at the prosperous Vietnamese. "Well, you have to give him credit. He feeds the sheep." Michael smiled at O'Shea. " 'If you love me, feed my sheep.' I guess that's what we help with, eh?"

"We'll have our work cut out for us when we get home."

"I gather. Thuc has his cut out for him too."

O'Shea nodded. "Now that he knows Spelly will be watching he'll perform. The man runs a very tight ship."

"But obviously he's dedicated to his brother."

"But these guys are old-fashioned Catholics, Michael. He's the bishop. In his area, they leave him alone. They want the people fed more than anyone. Nothing improves here until the people eat. Diem and Nhu know that. So does Kennedy. That's the point."

O'Shea stopped talking when he saw approaching a tall, thin American with angular features. He was wearing a white suit as were most of the Vietnamese. "Monsignor O'Shea?" he said. He seemed worried. He ignored Michael.

"Yes?"

"I'm John Howe."

"Mister Howe! Nice to meet you." They shook hands. O'Shea turned to Michael. "Mister Howe and I have had correspondence. Mister Howe is an AID officer at the embassy in Saigon. What, the 'Commercial Import Program,' is that what you call it?" O'Shea smiled, and then said to Michael, "He's been a big help." He said to the embassy man, "This is Father Michael Maguire, Mister Howe. Father Maguire is my new assistant in New York."

Michael and the man shook hands. There was something about him that Michael experienced as utterly new. He didn't know what it was but it drew him in. He watched carefully as Howe turned back to O'Shea. "Monsignor, I'm glad to have a chance to chat with you," he said smoothly. "When I heard the cardinal was coming I hoped you'd be with him."

O'Shea smiled. "It's nice to see you too."

Howe was holding a tall drink and he sipped it then, as he looked out across the crowd. For a moment Michael thought that was it — two men who'd exchanged letters but never met, greeting each other. Howe glanced at Michael and they nodded awkwardly. "How do you like Vietnam, Father?"

"I've only been here a day." Why did Michael feel wary? What was it about the man that unsettled him? He was almost as tall as Michael. He was fair, but he was no newcomer to the tropics and his skin was a tawny red. He was Michael's age, not quite thirty, but little lines, like spokes, creased his face, as if he worried a lot or grimaced.

Howe said to O'Shea, "When you're in Saigon, I'd love to show you around."

"Thanks, Mister Howe. I'm afraid our schedule is full up though."

Howe stared at him. "I was hoping you might have time to stop by the embassy."

Despite the suppliant statement, there was a hint of the imperial in it and Michael caught it whether O'Shea did or not.

O'Shea simply shook his head and smiled. "Sorry."

Howe glanced at some nearby Vietnamese, then let his eyes drift across the crowd again. Suddenly Michael recognized him as a figure out of a magazine, an advertisement. He should have been wearing a dinner jacket, and this should have been a country club dance. His handsomeness, his poise, his grace were part of a package and Michael realized it was one he himself, despite his kind of handsomeness and poise, did not possess. John Howe was a man from a different world. It was a world Michael's people only read about, or, if they gained access to it, it was as servants.

Howe said brusquely, "But you got the letter I sent you two weeks ago?"

"No," O'Shea answered. "We've been in Manila."

"Well, that's all the more reason I'd appreciate some time, Monsignor." Something in Howe's voice was familiar too.

"What's your problem, Mister Howe?" Good old Tim, right to the point, if gruffly.

But Michael noted that Howe didn't flinch. "I've been led to believe that once the new Vietnam assistance appropriation passes the Congress, Cardinal Spellman expects the major share of funds, food and supplies to be distributed through your agency."

O'Shea shrugged. "We've helped out here and there in the past."

"Indeed so. You've done wonderful work. CRS is the best private agency in Vietnam. But it's *private*. U.S. government relief should come under U.S. government auspices."

"Through *your* office."

"In point of fact, yes."

The two men stared at each other. Michael waited for one or the other to yield, but neither did. Michael sensed but did not understand the depth of their antagonism. This Irish priest. This highborn American diplomat. Unlike each other in every way, but at that moment they were twins in their disdain.

Michael sensed also, though, that Howe, unlike O'Shea, would never make his resentment explicit. Howe veered smoothly and said, "We share the same objective, Monsignor."

"That's right. But we don't share the same structure. There are nearly a thousand Catholic parishes in this country, all *over* this country, not just in cities. Those parishes are what the experts call 'indigenous institutions,' Mister Howe, and local people *already* look to them for assistance. What could your office possibly hope to set up to match that?"

"But Monsignor . . ." Howe reined something. Michael couldn't decide whether it was his impatience, his anger or his condescension. "The point of U.S. government relief is to help *all* the people of this country, not just the Catholics."

"Wait a minute, Mister Howe! Wait a damn minute! If you're saying the Catholic Relief Service and Caritas International benefit only Catholics, then I take strong exception, do you hear? Strong exception!"

Howe put his hand up. "I'm not saying that, Monsignor. I'm not talking about your agency. I'm talking about Vietnam." He smiled suddenly and said quite warmly, "You and I are on the same side. The last thing I want to do is offend you."

Michael believed him, and, despite himself, he was drawn to

him. For one thing, he'd recognized what was familiar in his voice. Howe had a subtler version of the New England–Harvard accent that made Jack Kennedy's speech so appealing. Michael wanted to hear him out. "What's your point, Mister Howe?"

Howe turned to Michael. "What percentage of people in this country are Catholic, do you think?"

"Quite a large percentage," O'Shea put in, but Howe ignored him.

Michael calculated. The population of South Vietnam was seventeen million. More than a million Catholics had fled the North. They must have joined at least three or four million others. The French were there a long time. He said, "A third. Thirty to forty percent."

Howe nodded dismissively. "Less than ten percent, Father. Including the refugees. Yet every governor of every province is a Catholic. Every senior officer in the army is a Catholic. The farmers who receive favored treatment in the land reform are Catholic. The students in the schools . . . the diplomats abroad, all Catholic. No offense, but where are the Buddhists? Where are the Confucians?"

"And where is the Church of England?" O'Shea asked bitterly. "Right, Mister Howe?"

"Hey, Tim." Michael took his elbow. O'Shea's tribal sensitivity embarrassed Michael.

But O'Shea didn't give a shit about embarrassment. He leaned toward Howe. "If your nice liberal American sensibilities are offended by the primitive practices of the natives here, perhaps you're in the wrong country. Why don't you put in for Italy? I'd be glad to ask the cardinal to say a word for you when he meets with Mister Rusk next week." O'Shea pulled on his cigar, satisfied with himself.

Howe smiled thinly. This immigrant shaman had no power over him, whatever his illusions. "Monsignor, you've taken what I said personally. That's not how I meant it."

"You've slurred the Catholic Church, Mister Howe. That may not be a 'personal' matter in your religion but it is in ours."

Howe nodded. His resignation was evident. He would withdraw now. His dignity, his self-esteem, would be intact. O'Shea, of course, and his assistant, would feel shabby. Howe said, "I look forward to cooperating with the relief effort however it is set up. Who will your representative in this country be?"

"Archbishop Thuc."

"I mean day to day, Monsignor. Who's going to handle logistics?"

"One of the archbishop's priests, Mister Howe. I'm sure you can find out from him."

"I assumed you'd have an American here."

"We don't work that way in the Catholic Church. We're a transnational institution." Unlike some I could name, was implied. "As I said, the structure is in place. And it's reliable."

"I'm sure it is." Howe shook hands with O'Shea. When he turned to Michael, wasn't there a hint of pleading in his eye? Can you help me with this character? Michael shook his hand noncommittally. Howe said, "Good luck, Father." Then he raised his drink in a mock toast and left.

O'Shea snorted and said to Michael under his breath, "Goddamn Prod! Typical! Trying to make religion the issue when it's just a run-of-the-mill turf fight. Shops all around him in that embassy are gearing up, military and agricultural development, health and sanitation. But he's just trickling along at the same old rate, surplus rice and CARE packages. He sees the boom coming and is afraid he'll be left out. He wants his hand on the spigot instead of mine. That's all."

O'Shea was ranting, it seemed to Michael. He'd rarely seemed so agitated. Michael said, mainly out of loyalty, "You stopped him cold when you said Spelly would be meeting with Rusk."

O'Shea nodded. "These guys are all alike. An eye forever cocked on that next promotion. I'll tell you something funny — he'd *love* to get shipped to Italy. Those Episcopalians just swoon for Italy." O'Shea slapped Michael's shoulder as if celebrating a victory over the old enemy, but Michael knew that Howe held them both in contempt. Michael was perplexed by his own inability to simply sweep the man aside, as O'Shea had. Was that because Howe was right? Or was it something else? Why did Howe appeal to him?

O'Shea was still jabbering. "It's people like him who worry that Kennedy's going to put holy water in White House commodes. If you ask him what a commode is, he looks down his Brahmin nose and says, 'I don't know. I'm not a Catholic.' "

"But he had a point, Tim."

O'Shea stiffened. "Is that so?"

"Only about wanting an American. It might make sense to have an American on the spot. You said yourself, Thuc has to know Spelly's watching. An American priest might keep him honest."

"Goddamnit, Michael. He's an archbishop of the Church. He *is* honest."

"He'll have pressures from his brothers, and you know it."

"Forget it. Spelly leaves Thuc alone. Once the stuff leaves New York it's their show. That's the way it's always been."

"Not with Dooley, it wasn't."

"Tom Dooley was special, Father. The people over here worshipped him. He saved this nation's hide. Anyway, the CRS has guidelines. We use local clergy where possible. You know that."

Michael nodded. He'd said enough. He looked across the room, blithely, hoping that O'Shea did not sense his surge of feeling. My God, he thought, an American! What an arena this would be. Not a desk in New York, not a parish in Queens. Not altar boys and Legion of Mary meetings. But a major role in what Kennedy called a "massive joint effort" to help democracy grow out of the ashes of conflict between colonialism and Communism. Here was a cause that mattered! How he wanted to alleviate suffering. Yes. But how, also, he wanted to leave behind the demeaning, petty restraints of the junior New York clergy! There was more, far more, to being a priest than the submissiveness of rectories, the banalities of parish life, and Michael Maguire, for one, was going to have it.

He told O'Shea he was going for a fresh drink, but instead went after John Howe. He found him in the spacious palace foyer, by the entrance. A servant had just handed him his hat.

"Mister Howe, just leaving? I was too." Michael fell into step with him. "Perhaps we could walk a bit." Howe eyed him for an instant, then nodded. The two men left the Governor's Palace together. Outside its gates the city was teeming. The press of the crowd made conversation difficult, so they moved through it in silence.

The dedication was the occasion of a great festival in Quang Tri. Farmers and their families from the surrounding countryside had come to town, and so had fishermen from the coastal villages. The narrow streets were crowded with food stalls at which the pilgrims vied for their midday meal. The foodstuffs were exotic — bird's eyes, fish heads, little heaps of slimy grubs harvested from inside palm trees, and piles of vermicelli, "little worms" indeed, which Michael mistook for pasta. The two Americans slowly moved through the crowd, towering over them. Those Vietnamese who acknowledged them addressed Michael in singsong French, *"Bonjour, mon père!"* Michael nodded, but Howe, as if addressed himself, returned their greeting in Vietnamese.

Soon the crowd began to thin as townspeople drifted inside for siesta. A few blocks from the basilica the neat whitewashed buildings of the central district gave way to rows of corrugated-roofed shanties. Tens of thousands of refugees had yet to be settled, and these were some of them. Children surrounded Maguire, tugging at his soutane. Their dark eyes implored, and Michael realized with a shock that the children were hoping for rice. He was a priest, wasn't he? He looked helplessly at Howe, whom the children had pushed aside and ignored. "You see," Michael wanted to say, "this is the difference between us. This is why I became a priest."

Michael pushed through the children, and he and Howe left them behind.

"Good Lord," Michael said.

"Shocking, isn't it, when you see it close."

"Yes. They're so desperate. It's why we should find a way to work together, don't you think? They're the ones we're working for."

"I couldn't agree more," Howe said. He looked at Michael with surprise. He hadn't expected conciliation.

Michael let his curiosity about Howe show itself. "Where were you before Vietnam?"

"The Congo two years. Before that Brazil."

"Always in relief work?"

Howe nodded.

"You speak Vietnamese, I noticed."

"Just a few words. I'm still learning."

"I admire that. I'm lousy at languages. Except Latin." Michael grinned self-mockingly. He saw that this was the assignment Howe wanted. O'Shea had been unfair.

At a hut farther along a family of six or seven hovered at the doorway. Two of the children, perhaps ten and twelve, each had a scar on one side of his head where there should have been an ear. Michael saw their parents in the shadows; their ears had been mutilated too. They watched from within their hovel with the peculiar, angled stance of the partially deaf. Michael had to look away. "Did you see that?"

"Yes," Howe said. "They're from Bao Lak, a province in the North next to China. The Viet Minh there were notorious. It's said they had a special penalty for anyone caught listening to 'evil words.' They ripped your ear off with pliers even if you were a baby in your mother's arms. Do you know what the 'evil words' were? The Catholic Mass."

"God."

"I'm not indifferent to what Catholics suffered in the North, Father."

"I know that," Michael said. "I saw the point you were trying to make to Monsignor O'Shea."

"I couldn't believe his reaction, frankly."

"I think he was trying to tell you that religion and politics don't mix."

Howe stopped and faced Michael. "Forgive me, Father, but that's quite fatuous, and I think you know it. Religion *is* politics here. Why do you think this basilica was built in Quang Tri? To anchor the Catholic population by the border with the North, to discourage Ho Chi Minh from crossing, that's why! The archbishop claimed in his sermon that the basilica was built by the donations of all the people. I couldn't believe no one laughed. The basilica was paid for by lottery tickets that Diem's police made the whole population buy. Everyone knows that here but Spellman. Hell, Spellman doesn't even know this is a Buddhist country."

"Yes, he does, Mister Howe." Michael reined his clerical defensiveness, which seemed banal compared to Howe's emotion.

"Well, Diem and his people don't know it. The U.S. government shouldn't be playing to their weakness. And their weakness, Father, frankly, is a shocking level of intolerance toward the majority of Vietnamese, and that has a religious aspect. That's all I'm saying." As abruptly as he'd stopped, Howe began walking again, leaving Michael to catch up with him.

Which accounted perhaps for the irritation he felt suddenly. Who the hell was Howe to lecture him? To club Spellman and O'Shea with his high-toned moral sensitivity? Wasn't his concern a bit overdelicate?

But Michael realized something about Howe then, trailing him by a pace, watching him move intently through the streets without seeing them. Howe was used to moving in a world of ideals and principles. Wasn't that the point of a Harvard education? Didn't men like Howe always know how other people, other nations, fell short of standards? Wasn't that — the moral shortfall of the other — their expertise? How angry it could make them, how impatient. "Hey, wait a minute!"

But Howe kept up his stride, ignoring Michael.

Maybe it was Howe's standards that appealed to Michael. Certainly his obvious dedication did. Michael admitted that the novelty of Howe's passionate idealism was stunning. So what that his own instincts, by nature and training, ran another way. Michael, like his kind, was pragmatic. The human condition was not a scandal to him, but a given. As far as Vietnam was concerned, in his opinion, religious pluralism could wait awhile. Democracy was the end, not the means. What mattered now was getting people fed. But Michael wasn't interested in debating his differences with the AID officer. What he was interested in, he admitted finally, was getting over here and playing on this team. Michael Maguire wanted off the bench.

He grabbed Howe's arm. They faced each other.

"You were also saying you could use an American priest."

"What?"

"As liaison between Archbishop Thuc and your office."

The two men stared at each other. Michael was aware of a current between them that had nothing to do with their positions. This could have been happening on a football field or in a school corridor or in a barracks. Michael recognized Howe as a man he wanted to be with. But Howe, perhaps sensing it, looked away. And Michael felt foolish.

"Yes," Howe said calmly. When he looked at Michael now it was with masterful detachment. "That would enable us to help with the relief effort."

"And to monitor it." Michael could be cool too. "You'd like to make sure the distribution is equitable, that *everyone* gets what they need. That's fair enough. I agree with you. And I agree that an American priest could help open up some lines of communication. I'd like to be that priest. . . ." Michael almost said "John" but he sensed that Howe would continue to call him "Father," and so he didn't use any address at all. "And you could help me get appointed."

Howe shook his head. "I don't understand."

"Cardinal Spellman and Monsignor O'Shea don't see the need as of yet. But I think if the suggestion originated at the upper levels of the State Department . . ."

"You've gathered, I think, that my influence there is limited. If I had my way His Eminence wouldn't be involved in Vietnamese affairs at all."

"Cardinal Spellman was involved in Vietnam when you and I were still in high school. It might help for both of us to keep that in mind. The point is, can't you make some recommendation? What if you compromised? What if you offered to support the distribution of relief through CRS, but with one condition. Wouldn't that carry weight?"

"The condition being . . . ?"

"Me."

"By name?"

Michael shrugged. "Why not? You could tell them you discussed it with me, at your initiative, of course. I'd report as much to Monsignor O'Shea. You could say my background would be a particular asset."

"What background?"

"I was a POW in China for nearly three years." Michael smiled. "I know the Oriental mind."

Howe stared at Michael, who read him. Hadn't he dismissed this priest only moments before? Now he was looking again, and for the first time he saw more than a Church functionary. There was a man here, with a history. Howe said with a certain deference, "That's the kind of thing they love at State."

Michael nodded. "Spellman loves it too. It proves his priests are real men, you know?" Michael grinned. He often mocked himself, but it wasn't like him to mock the cardinal. That he also mocked Howe for *his* nod to the mystique of war prisoners was inadvertent. "The point is, if you make an issue of it, there's a good chance they'll do it. His Eminence wants this operation to go smoothly, and he also wants his people in the middle of it."

Howe nodded. "All right. It could help, your being here." Howe hesitated, then added, "I think I could work with you."

Michael smiled. Was that supposed to be a compliment? For a Catholic priest, he was okay.

"May I ask you, Father, why you're interested?"

What could Michael say? To feed the hungry, clothe the naked, preach the good news to the poor? He too had *oblige,* if not *noblesse.* He checked his resentment and said what men in ward rooms and officers' clubs always say. "This is the action, isn't it?"

Howe's face broke into its first grin. For all their high-toned social concern, however differently expressed, this was the truth between them, what they had in common, and each saw it. "It sure is, Father. It sure is."

FIFTEEN

A MONTH later, Carolyn and I got married. I'd expected it to be awkward, having Michael as the priest, and so had Carolyn, I think, although we didn't talk about it.

But it wasn't at all, mainly because, lo and behold, Michael carried the ceremony off like an old smoothie. You wouldn't have believed how cool he was, how relaxed, witty, outgoing, affectionate. The ceremony was in the tailored yard of the house in Dobbs Ferry, so there was none of the anxiety that comes so naturally to wedding parties in churches, and Michael led us through our vows with such grace, such patent joy for us that even Carolyn, I thought, conquered her reservation. Oh that fucking reservation! For myself, holding her hand and pronouncing my promise, while feeling the weight of her gaze upon me, I never expected to be happier. Hell, I guess, as it turned out, I never was.

And what a relief it was to find Michael so excited about his own life. And with reason. As he described what he'd experienced — or rather discovered — in Vietnam, a great drama unfolding and a prospect that he would play an important role in it, I found myself thinking, God, Michael's world is going to be huge, so vastly larger than mine.

"So what do you think?" he asked.

"Sounds good," I said noncommittally. Was I just too much the cynic to respond to his enthusiasm? Was I jealous? Or was I simply unable to grasp what he was saying? What the hell did I know? Vietnam to me, as to almost everyone in 1961, was someplace near where Yul Brynner waltzed around with Deborah Kerr. Michael was whistling a happy tune, all right. And that was fine with me, though I suspect my eyes glazed over as he went on.

The weary nations of Europe, with their empires collapsed and their Enlightenment secularity bankrupt, could look now to a rejuvenated Catholicism and an America on the move. The pope and the president, the two Johns, all that shit; he was convinced of it. And he told me — how he would blush when I threw this back at him later — that Diem was an Asian Thomas More. So who was Cardinal Wolsey? I wanted to ask. That was Thuc, of course, though no one knew that yet. In Michael's view the Ngos' promise was enormous, and *that* was why it was crucial to go to their support. Ngo Dinh Diem, having been nurtured by American Catholicism and sponsored by it, now embodied its triumph.

Michael's triumph.

It is almost impossible now, given how badly that project turned out — which puts it rather mildly, doesn't it? — to imagine that Vietnam could ever have embodied such a dream. But it did. Still, even then I sensed that Michael's conviction was also a matter of something else. I didn't understand what he was really telling me until I looked across at Carolyn; she winked at me, and I realized that, of course, he had to go out now and save the world. Only the world itself, redeemed at last, could fill the hole that the loss of that woman had cut in him.

It was some months before Michael's assignment to Vietnam came through. Archbishop Thuc, of course, opposed having an American watchdog in his front yard, and he tried every way he could to get Spellman to change his mind. O'Shea had his reservations too. Was Michael seasoned enough? Would he walk with the roll of the place? But Spellman liked the idea and he liked having a priest who impressed the people at State. Michael arrived in Vietnam in January of 1962. He took up residence in the cathedral rectory in Saigon, but he had almost no contact with Archbishop Thuc from the very beginning. The first surprise was that the archbishop lived not at the cathedral but at Freedom Palace on Tu Do Street with his brothers. The second surprise was that his fellow priests had apparently been ordered to cooperate with Michael to the minimum, and beyond that to have nothing to do with him. He made the round of orphanages, refugee centers and hospitals that were being supported by the CRS. The European and American volunteers welcomed him, but Vietnamese relief workers, including nuns and priests, reacted as if he'd come to spy on them. In a way, he admitted to himself with a certain shame, it was true.

In Saigon he depended more than he'd have wanted on the Americans at the embassy for orientation. But, hell, the Vietnamese would hardly talk to him. And for some reason, John Howe didn't seem that anxious to school Michael in the local realities either. When they finally did get together, perhaps a month after Michael's arrival, it wasn't for a tour of AID projects or for briefings even. It was for tennis. Howe suggested it. Michael demurred. He didn't have a racket. It wasn't his game, really, he said. Howe insisted; he had two rackets. Michael knew the type. He liked to take on inferior partners now and then just to demonstrate the difference between pretty good and first rate, but what he said was, "If you're going to be in Saigon, you'll have to take it up. Everything important happens at the Cercle Sportif."

The Cercle Sportif was the high-walled colonial-era tennis and swimming club that the French planters had built for themselves. Its glory days were past, but it was still the nearest thing to an elegant spa in Saigon, and the remaining French elite now shared it with select Vietnamese, European and American diplomats and, lately, to everyone's chagrin, the news photographers and reporters who were coming to Saigon in ever greater numbers.

Michael met Howe at the front gate and was immediately embarrassed. Howe was decked out, scrupulously, in tennis whites. Michael was wearing black canvas basketball shoes, plaid Bermuda shorts and a blue sport shirt. He'd been afraid of this. Howe didn't flinch as they shook hands. Howe handed Michael his extra racket, and, as he followed him into the compound, Michael felt like Goofy the Dog.

To the right were the tennis courts, half a dozen of them, all clay, brilliant orange, and all in use. Other players sat at tables on the terraced lawn, watching. Everyone was dressed in white. To the left was a large swimming pool. Michael's eye went immediately to a pair of bikini-clad *colonistes* who sat on the near edge talking loudly in French. There were Vietnamese women, also in bikinis, less voluptuously endowed, but with long gleaming black hair that they displayed by tossing their heads. Beyond the pool was the awning-covered café leading into the *maison*. Men in white linen suits sat at tables with tall drinks in front of them, watching the *jeunes filles en fleur*.

Howe led the way toward the courts. "We're up," he said, as a doubles match ended. Michael felt a rush of anxiety as he unbolted the racket brace. Tennis was one of the games seminarians mastered, but he'd never played anyone in white before. Suddenly he realized he had no standards. How good had the guys in the sem been? How good was he? Michael had an athlete's pride. He did not want to be humiliated. It was bad enough that when he passed the players who were leaving the court they cast disapproving glances at his shoes. When he looked down he saw that the tread of his soles, a pattern of circles and triangles, was clearly imprinted in the clay. Oh, Christ!

During the warm-up hitting, when the spectators sized up newcomers, Michael's timing, naturally, was completely off. He missed shot after shot or sent them looping into adjoining courts. Howe had the smooth, steady stroke of someone who'd had his lessons early; by comparison Michael was a flailer. He knew he was already the perfect image of a fool. The perfect image, in *this* world, he thought, of a Catholic priest.

It took him most of the first set, which went all too quickly, to realize what was wrong. He'd played his tennis on all-purpose seminary courts, asphalt, never clay. On asphalt the ball sizzled, skipping across the surface, and Michael had developed a style that depended on speed and power. But the ball positively died on clay, and slow, careful moves, accurate placement and finesse were what counted. Michael consciously adjusted, and began to play better. He lost the second set, but not as badly. And by the third he realized that the spectators who'd dismissed their match earlier were watching intently. Michael matched Howe point for point and in the eighth game broke his serve. He won 6–4. When they shook hands at the net, Michael realized that Howe was shocked. Howe was embarrassed.

When they left the court, attendants had to come to repair the damage Michael's shoes had done.

They crossed the terraced lawn, went by the pool and took a table in the café under the awning. They complimented each other on the game. Howe said they were well matched and should play regularly. Michael promised to get the right shoes and they both laughed. They ordered drinks. Howe asked the waiter to bring them towels.

"So how has it been going, Father?"

Michael shrugged. "Pretty good. I've been learning my way around. We have a new center in Bien Hoa. I've been trying to help with that."

"Good." Howe smiled formally, then he wiped perspiration from his face and glanced around. Where were the damn towels?

Michael said, "I'm sorry I haven't been able to arrange your meeting with the archbishop. He hasn't even deigned to see me yet. I wouldn't say he's overjoyed at my being here."

Howe nodded. "He's no dummy. He knows you're one guy who could cause him trouble."

The waiter delivered the towels before Michael answered. He wanted to say, I didn't come here to cause anybody trouble. He didn't like the way Howe took it for granted that he shared his disdain for the archbishop.

They wiped their faces and their necks.

Michael said, "I visited an orphanage in Can Lo where the nuns and priests sleep on stone floors so that the children can have the beds."

Howe looked up at him sharply. "Why do you tell me that?"

Michael shrugged. "I was moved by it. There are dedicated priests and nuns in this country."

"I know that." Howe stared at Michael, making it obvious that he did not want his criticism of Thuc and Diem and Nhu reduced to primitive anti-Catholicism. "Hey, look," he said, "we can go around in circles, me saying the Catholics are bad, you saying they're good. So what? You know what my problem is. It's a Buddhist country."

The waiter interrupted again, this time with their drinks. Howe thanked him easily. Unlike Michael, he took the man's servility for granted.

When the waiter left, Michael leaned toward Howe. "Look, Catholics may be the minority here but they're in power not because of some conspiracy but because they're educated, they have Western values, and they appreciate what Communism can do to a country. I don't think it matters a damn how many province chiefs are Catholics. The question is, are they doing their job? The way I read recent history, I think they are."

Howe pushed the sugar bowl aside. "Can I give you a slightly different version of that history?"

Michael stared at him, sipped his lemonade, waited. He wanted Howe to quit beating around the bush with him. He knew they would never be friends until they could speak with each other frankly. And Michael admitted, he wanted to be friends with this man.

Howe nodded. "First, about this crap that Diem rescued the Catholics in the North from the Red Devil murders. Pure bull, Father."

"Wait a minute, Howe. What about that day in August, we saw those people with missing ears? You were the one who told me what their crime was, hearing Mass."

Howe waved his hand dismissively. "I was telling you what the people said, what they believed had happened. But it probably wasn't true."

"How do you know that?"

Howe worked at breaking up the sugar cubes in his tea. The ice was melted and he snapped his fingers at the Vietnamese waiter and barked several Vietnamese phrases at him. He waited for the boy to return with the ice. The interruption had the effect of defusing the challenge that had been implicit in Michael's question. While dropping a few cubes in Michael's drink as well, he said, "Because I know a guy who brags that he made that story up himself. An American. An Agency man who ran a string of 'black propaganda' agents whose job was to spread rumors like that among the Catholic population, to feed their panic. The Viet Minh were perfectly capable of mutilating people, but their targets were collaborators, not Catholics. There was no poetry to it — an ear because of the Mass you'd heard. That came from the CIA. I've heard that some of those agents carried out atrocities themselves, to frighten the people into running."

"But why? Who cared if the Catholics stayed or moved?"

"Think about it. Who was better known in the rectories of New York than in the villages of South Vietnam? Diem, the George Washington of Southeast Asia. But who the hell in this country ever heard of George Washington? When his people needed him most, fighting the French, he was living the high life in Spellman's seminary, giving tennis lessons to you guys." Howe grinned, but only for a moment. "Diem's power base was in Washington, not

Saigon. And only one group could change that for him. The Catholics in the North. They could become his base. So he had to attract them south, or drive them there, like cattle. Hence the U.S. Navy. Hence Doctor Dooley. Hence Cardinal Spellman, all portraying the Ngos as the rescuers of the refugees, when the case was just the opposite. That migration of a million people was the great CIA success of the decade, better even than the coups in Iran and Guatemala."

Michael sipped his drink. "I'm a little slow, John, aren't I? You're with the Agency, of course."

Howe shook his head. "Not on your life, Father. Their manipulation of your Church and your Churchmen is not only cynical but stupid, doomed to fail. Catholicism will never be anything here but a vestige of colonialism, and colonialism is dead. I don't think the CIA knows that yet."

Michael smiled awkwardly. The sweeping, and compelling, indictment of his Church embarrassed him, but he was not prepared to acknowledge this. "So remind me. Why was it you wanted yet another Catholic priest over here?"

Howe did not answer him.

Michael pressed. "You said, if I recall, that you wanted communication, but you haven't asked me anything about the local church. You said you wanted a meeting with Thuc, but obviously you regard him as one of the Borgias. What the hell do you want, John? Why am I here?"

Howe only stared back. Suddenly the man's inaccessibility infuriated Michael. Then he saw it. "Good God, you think I'll come around, don't you? I'll see it like you do, and I'll make my report to Spellman, whom you hold in contempt in every way but one. He's still the key to controlling Diem."

Howe laughed. " 'Controlling Diem!' Everybody is controlling Diem — Spellman, Kennedy, Nhu, Madame Nhu." He stopped abruptly and pointed to the far tennis court. "See that guy over there, playing doubles? That's our esteemed ambassador. His partner is the CIA chief of mission. They're playing against two guys out from Washington who are supposed 'to appraise the current situation.' Everything depends on what those men say. Oh, sure, Nhu makes them nervous, but he's paid to. He makes Diem look good by comparison. They never talk to anyone — forgive me, Father, for the theme! — but Catholics. And you know what else? They never leave Saigon. So Diem controls them. He controls Kennedy. He controls us."

"I leave Saigon, John," Michael said with bravado, "and no one controls me."

"Good for you." Howe stood up. Had he said that snidely? Michael thought so until he added somberly, "It is important that you see what's happening. That's all I wanted. That's why I hoped you'd come."

Howe gathered his rackets and turned to lead the way out.

At that moment a good-looking American woman approached him. She was wearing whites and carrying a racket of her own. "Jack," she called.

He opened his arms as she came to him, and without a thought they embraced and kissed blatantly. She might have been his lover, but, if so, Michael sensed, not his only one. Nor was he hers. She said, "Play with me. My partner didn't show."

Howe said, "Who was your partner?"

"Annie."

Howe winked at Michael. "Well, in that case . . ." As long as it wasn't a rival. He turned to Michael. "This is Sally Doubleday, Father. Sally writes for *Newsweek*. This is Father Maguire, Sally. He's with Church Relief."

Michael and the woman shook hands. She eyed him boldly, but he expected that. Now he was glad he wasn't wearing whites. He wasn't just another dashing correspondent or Foreign Service dandy. He never liked being different except when he saw how it piqued a pretty woman's interest. What really piqued that, of course, was her realization that he wasn't on the make.

She looked back at him once as Howe went off with her. Michael watched them both, but it was the change in Howe he was aware of. He was so much more relaxed suddenly, jovial, even, and high-spirited. Obviously Michael had an inhibiting effect on the man, and he regretted it. They would remain strangers. When Michael realized that Howe hadn't followed through on his suggestion that they play tennis again, he felt put down. Should he have let the bastard win? Was this a country club? Was Michael Maguire a ball boy?

He left the Cercle Sportif, knowing he wouldn't return, and angry because of it. But then he chastised himself. He wasn't in Vietnam to improve his social standing.

The month that Carolyn and I got married, September of 1961, the Communists took over a provincial capital just outside Saigon. They held it long enough to flaunt their impunity and underscored it by decapitating the Catholic province chief. Though we heard nothing about it in America, the raid was the beginning of a new level of terror. It frightened the people of Saigon, and the method of mutilation terrorized even the sophisticates and the Catholics. As Vietnamese they still believed that a decapitated person is condemned to an eternity of headless exile, the worst of all possible fates.

The Communists proceeded with their hit-and-run terror among the rural population and with their brutal assassinations of local officials. And it worked. The illusion of Diem's control collapsed. By the time Michael had arrived in Vietnam that winter it was obvious at once that the CRS estimates of the numbers of refugees, displaced persons and orphaned children were already outdated. The relief program he'd come to help administer, once seen as mammoth, would barely touch the surface of the problem. Michael assumed at first that that was the result of the new Communist-sponsored violence. Indirectly, it was. But the immediate cause of the people's misery was a tactic that had been adopted by the Diem government, the elaborate fortification of central villages, "agrovilles" or "strategic hamlets." It was a tactic that had worked against Communists in Malaya; in Vietnam the French had tried to hold every village and had failed. So now most villages were evacuated; it was a second mass-movement of Vietnamese under Diem. But these people were not Catholics and they were not willing, so their resettlement had to be forced. The Americans called it "Operation Sunrise," and Maxwell Taylor referred to the program as "a great national movement." But in practice it was violent and brutal, and the supposedly idyllic "agrovilles" were in fact concentration camps. By the end of 1962 ten million peasants had been confined to these heavily guarded centers, working their fields and paddies in the daytime and returning to the "hamlets" at night. Thousands of peasants who resisted this resettlement were thereby branded Communist and killed. Hundreds of thousands of others, terrified by the awful, alien crossfire they found themselves in, crowded into the cities, burdening them impossibly. Almost overnight Diem, as if ignorant of the sacrosanct character of the tie between the Vietnamese and his home village, the village of his ancestors, had created a grave crisis of personal and spiritual identity for his own people. He had made them into exiles in their own country. In the beginning his problem had been that they didn't know him. Now it was that they hated him. And exactly as he expected the American government to provide his army with weapons to enforce his policies, he expected the Church to provide his displaced and demoralized population with food, clothing and medical care.

It was an impossible job and Michael Maguire was one of the people who had it. The longer he was in Vietnam the more his focus narrowed. No longer did rhetoric about a new polity, a *via media* between right and left, appeal to him. His days were taken up with endless rounds of meetings with the various volunteer agencies and Church officials who were responsible for getting the supplies out to the countryside. In fact, Michael, whose duties had been only vaguely defined when he'd arrived, became a kind of troubleshooting dispatcher. He was the guy who ran from one logjam to the next, kicking them loose, from bureaucracy to ministry, from dockside to truck depot, from the American embassy to the offices of the archdiocese.

And most of the time, like all Americans, he was in Saigon. And from Saigon, as refugees poured in by the thousands with their horrible stories, it was impossible not to believe that the Communists had gone from their ruthless assassinations to a policy of mass murder. Ironically, when reasons began to appear for hedging his support of Diem, Michael, like the leaders in Washington, stiffened it. The more of the victims' suffering he saw, the more he accepted the arguments of the anti-Communists. And he accepted the government's position that until order was restored, even if that meant extreme defensive measures, like the "agrovilles," nothing else could happen. Given the urgency of the situation, concerns about Catholic predominance seemed irrelevant. It was just as well he wasn't seeing Howe. If the AID officer came at him about the Ngos' religious intolerance, Michael would have reacted as O'Shea had, spouting the old chestnut that anti-Catholicism is the anti-Semitism of liberal Episcopalians.

But then one day Howe showed up. He burst into Michael's

office without knocking. Michael was on the phone with a French warehouse owner who'd been looking the other way while his workers pilfered rice to sell on the black market. Obviously they'd done so at his behest.

Howe said, "Can you come with us, Father? I think you should."

Michael held his finger up and repeated his threat to the Frenchman, and promised a visit, then hung up. He looked at Howe. "What?"

Howe calmed himself by wiping the perspiration from his hands on his khaki trousers. He wore an open-necked short-sleeve white shirt and no coat. On his head was a baseball cap with a B on it, Boston. "Come with us. Right now," Howe said. He let his agitation show, an amplification of his abrupt demand.

"All right." Michael stood and buttoned the black soutane he wore most of the time, as the Vietnamese clerics did. He picked up the stiff linen collar from his desk and fitted it around his neck as he followed Howe out into the brutal midday heat.

Howe had an embassy car, a Ford or something, and Michael sat beside him in front. In the back was the striking figure of a saffron-robed Buddhist monk, an elderly man. His bronze skin was tight on his shaved skull and his eyes were fixed on a point beyond. Michael glanced back at him but the monk did not speak and Howe did not offer to introduce them. Throughout the time it took them to clear the city and drive well into the countryside, the three maintained their silence, and by then it had come to seem natural.

My Tho was a river settlement in the delta region south of Saigon, formerly a fishing center but now one of those towns that had been swamped by refugees. It took two hours of fast driving through unsafe country to reach its outskirts where they were impossibly slowed by the thick traffic of carts and staggering families. One never saw Americans in the smaller towns in those days; the American command was only about twelve thousand strong.

Michael said, "It reminds me of Korea," though for the first time he noticed that the Vietnamese had no equivalent of the Korean A-frames for carrying their loads. The people carried their bundles or their children in their arms, and seemed doubly burdened.

"I hate to do this, but . . ." Howe leaned on the horn and gunned the engine threateningly. The refugees made way.

Howe addressed the monk in Vietnamese. The monk responded and made a pointing gesture. The monk, Michael understood, was the one giving directions. After winding through several blocks' worth of crowded streets, they pulled into a broad, open square, and the scene they came upon disturbed Michael because of the suffering it implied, but it also filled him with pride.

An outdoor food line was in progress. Old men and women, children, the parents of families, refugees of all kinds were waiting patiently for their turn at the huge vats of rice from which Vietnamese Catholic nuns were scooping ample bowls full. Beyond the vats, small sacks of rice, enough to sustain a family for a week, were being distributed. The refugees had the blank look of the displaced, but that was normal. A nurse was moving among them, checking their sores and wounds.

Michael looked at Howe for his explanation.

Howe said, "Don't you notice something?"

Michael looked at the scene again. It was all as it should have been. There were government soldiers behind the rice vats with their weapons ready, but that was standard too. No one was being bullied. And food was being given indiscriminately to everyone.

"What am I missing?" Michael asked.

"Look at the line."

Michael traced the line as it snaked back and forth across the square. Hundreds of people were waiting. Then he saw it. The line of refugees, each with his personal bowl, was issuing from the open portal, like tape from a roll, of the church on the far side of the square. The Catholic church. Michael crossed toward it, with Howe and the monk behind him. And as he did he suddenly felt an ominous dread. What could he possibly find in there? He began pushing through the crowded square more roughly, though ordinarily he was most gentle with people in that situation. The closer he came to the church the faster he went. At the entrance he pushed a man aside. At first, because of the dark, he couldn't see. He felt the cool air rushing over him. Then his eyes adjusted. He saw that the line of refugees wound into the church through a door opposite and down the far side aisle to the sanctuary, then up the center aisle to where he was standing. In one way, out the other. Apart from a pair of crying children, the people were silent.

He walked into the church and crossed to the third aisle, which was not being used. As he walked forward he stared as hard as he could toward the sanctuary. What was happening up there? He saw a priest, no, two priests, one vested in cope and alb, the other in alb and stole. Acolytes stood by with candles, and candles flickered on the high altar. The priest was speaking to each refugee in turn, and the refugees were bowing. And then . . .

No! Michael stopped where he was. The refugees were not bowing. Each was in turn putting his head over a basin. A basin to catch the water which the priest was pouring over each one's head. The priest was baptizing them.

"No!" This time he said it aloud.

I simply must put in here what every kid in Good Shepherd grew up knowing, that the crime of the British against the Irish was embodied in the fact that the thin soup the government offered to the starving victims of the Great Hunger came at a price: only those who renounced their Catholicism were fed. As here only Buddhists who submitted to it were.

"No!" he cried. He was running down the aisle, then across the transept, pushing the Buddhist refugees aside to get at the priests. The acolytes scattered, splashing candle wax on themselves. Michael upended the table on which the basin sat, splashing water about, and he snatched the Sacramentary, the book from which the celebrant read the ritual words, out of the hands of the assistant priest. Then he took folds of the main priest's golden cope in his hands, and he shook the man, a frail, pathetic Vietnamese who tried to hide his face behind the stylized silver scallop shell he'd been using to scoop the water. The shell fell to the floor. When he released the priest, Michael had to clasp his hands together to keep from striking him.

Archbishop Thuc refused to give him an appointment. But Michael expected that. A few days later it was Ash Wednesday. Michael went into the cathedral well before dawn to pray, but not only to pray. He wanted to be kneeling, cassocked, in the front pew before the president's bodyguard arrived from the palace to secure the cathedral. The Ngos would be attending the early-morning Mass; they would wear their ashes on their foreheads, like flags, all day. And the archbishop would preside.

When the security people arrived, they ignored Michael, a priest at his breviary, an American. He was conscious of the movement behind him as the churchgoers who had to identify themselves with special passes began to arrive and fill up the pews. There was a stir about twenty minutes before the Mass was scheduled to begin. Michael turned and saw Madame Nhu striding down the center aisle, dressed in black, her head suitably veiled with the traditional mantilla. She clasped a white prayer book at her breast. Her long red fingernails shone like blood against the white book cover. Her eyes were downcast, as if she was approaching for Communion. Behind her were a pair of bodyguards. She'd have ridden over from the palace with Thuc. Diem and Nhu would come together at the last minute.

Michael closed his breviary, rose, genuflected, opened the communion rail and went into the sanctuary. He genuflected again, then crossed to the far left corner, to the sacristy door. He used his key on it, and went in.

Thuc was standing at the vestment case with the amice in his hands, a small white kerchief, the first of several pieces of ceremonial clothing the priest dons. Next to him was an assistant priest, holding the alb ready. In the corner beyond stood a mean-looking Vietnamese in a tan suit, the archbishop's bodyguard.

Before anyone could react, Michael crossed to Thuc and said, "Your Excellency, Cardinal Spellman has asked me to give you a message."

Thuc stared at him, frozen. Then abruptly he turned and addressed his assistant in Vietnamese. Michael thought at first that his ploy hadn't worked, but the assistant hung up the alb, turned and left the sacristy by the hallway door, followed by the bodyguard. Then Thuc looked Michael in the eye.

Michael said, "I was in My Tho three days ago. I was at the church of Sainte Hélène."

Thuc's expression was blank, though Michael was certain he'd been briefed.

"Refugees were being offered food and medical care on the condition that they accept baptism in the Catholic faith. By the time I arrived, hundreds had already been put through the form of the sacrament."

Thuc's eyes widened. "But that is a violation of canon law."

"Indeed so, Your Excellency. That's why I stopped it. And why I am talking to you about it today."

Thuc shook his head sadly. "The curé of Sainte Hélène is a man of no judgment. I shall, of course, remove him."

"Your Excellency, I am informed that churches at Long Xuyen, Can Tho, Dalat and Nha Trang are conducting similar mass baptisms in conjunction with the distribution of food."

Thuc looked shocked. "Impossible." He waited, perhaps to see if Michael could produce evidence, then reiterated. "No, impossible! Père Theiu at Sainte Hélène could perhaps behave in this way, thinking in his confused situation that we want this, but no one else. I'm sorry, Father. It is impossible."

"If you issued a statement guaranteeing the religious rights of the Buddhist population, your priests would be less likely to make such mistakes."

Thuc made a dismissive gesture. "The religion of the pagans is a *pot au feu*. Confucians one day, Taoists the next."

"They are Buddhists," Michael insisted. The archbishop's evident contempt made him angry, but it also stunned him to realize how ignorant he himself was. What were these distinctions? What was Buddhism based on?

"They are Confucians in good times and Buddhists in time of trouble. It is not serious religion."

"Leave that aside for a moment, Your Excellency. Clearly the ability of the government to control the country requires the loyalty of the Buddhist population but the Buddhist leaders feel —"

"Ah, the leaders, Father! They are Communists. The followers can be won over. But the leaders are Communists. That is well known." Thuc glared at Michael, satisfied with his statement of the decisive fact.

Michael saw there was no point in arguing about the rights of Buddhists. Error has no rights, *n'est-ce pas?* The point was to let him know that the baptism shit had to stop. It was sacrilege and it was bad politics.

"Cardinal Spellman's expectation, Your Excellency, is that the relief program will be kept apart from politics and also from religion. He wants me to emphasize that with you." Michael wanted Thuc to think he'd already heard back from Spellman. It didn't matter that he hadn't. He knew that Spellman would agree with him. Spellman would be furious at Thuc when he got Michael's report. "We are responding to simple human needs; we are not proselytizing."

Thuc nodded. "Of course not."

"Cardinal Spellman has asked me to be watching, Your Excellency. Just so you know."

Thuc did not respond. Michael knew that, in addition to the influence he could bring to bear on American policy, Spellman held the key to the realization of Thuc's great personal ambition, being elevated to the status of cardinal. Even as Spellman's mere agent, Michael felt the thrill of his power over the man and frankly relished it. Thuc tied the ends of his amice, and began reciting the prayers for vesting. Michael took the alb from its hook and handed it to him.

During the Mass, Michael knelt at the overstuffed prie-dieu in the sanctuary. He received his ashes from the archbishop — "Remember, man, you are dust, and unto dust you shall return" — then watched while the Ngos knelt at the communion rail: Diem, Nhu, Madame Nhu, and Ngo Dinh Can, the other brother, the shrewd governor of Hué. The archbishop smudged each of them, then each devoutly crossed himself. All at once their piety disgusted Michael. Whatever their political ambitions had been at the beginning, now they considered themselves the anointed of God with a sacred mission. Their arrogance was obscene.

After the Mass Michael hired a pedicab to take him to the Vinh Hoa Dao pagoda. Already the heat, the dirt and the noise of the overcrowded city made it unpleasant to be outside, and the jostling pedicab, with its crude wheels rattling over the cracked pavement, not to mention its association with class oppression, increased Michael's discomfort.

At the pagoda, one of the great temples of Vietnam, famous for its own beauty and for the exquisite ancient carvings and statues it was furnished with, Michael had to step gingerly up the broad sweeping staircase that led up from the avenue because refugees were all over it. Hundreds had made the steps of the pagoda home.

Michael entered the temple, and the tranquillity, the sweet incense, the soft light instantly soothed him, and the transcendent beauty of the large carved Buddha, which sat where in a church the altar would have been, made him want to kneel.

A young monk approached him and bowed. His head was shaven and his left shoulder was exposed. His feet were bare. Michael spoke the name of the monk who'd taken Howe and him to My Tho, Thic Nhat Than. The young monk bowed again and indicated that Michael should follow him.

They crossed the large, shadowy space and went through a series of smaller darker rooms until finally they came out into a garden, an exquisite, otherworldly enclosure with pools, plants of many kinds, glorious flowers and a maze of paths, brilliantly paved with round, smooth pebbles of white and black like stones of the Japanese *go*. It was impossible to think that the teeming desperate city was all around them. Even the sky above seemed bluer, less indifferent.

The young monk led Michael to the veranda at the far end of the garden and there he found Nhat Than, on his mat, robed in saffron, a calligraphy pen in hand.

Michael bowed. The monk looked at him stoically. He was at least seventy years old. Every pain, loss, every happiness, of each of his years had been transformed into that great, silent dignity.

Michael spoke to him in his halting French. "It will not happen again. If you hear any reports of it, tell me at once. I will stop it." He vowed to himself, this, if nothing else, would be his work here, however long he remained.

Still the old monk made no reply.

Michael said, "And if I may be so bold, Honored Teacher, I would like to ask your help. I would like to learn about your people. I would like to learn about your faith."

Thic Nhat Than eyed Michael carefully. Then, even while sitting, he bowed.

SIXTEEN

SOMEWHAT more than a year later, two men died a week apart from each other, one in a Renaissance palace in Italy and one at a crowded intersection in the center of Saigon. And after their deaths, everything was different.

Pope John XXIII died on June 3, 1963. No one knew it at the time, but his magnificent vision for the renewal of the Church, the humanizing of it, would be thwarted, not maliciously but nevertheless effectively, by his successors, the Self-doubting Pope who was obsessed by his own suffering, and the Commissar-Pope who is obsessed by his own power. John's instinctive embrace of the world and his belief in its goodness were replaced by the traditional suspicion. Though his Vatican Council continued without him — many Churchmen, like Spellman, had expected it would last weeks; it lasted years — and though certain superficial aspects of Catholicism did change, the Church's essential post-Reformation note — world-wariness — reasserted itself. Suddenly the Ecumenical Movement stalled, pluralism as a manifestation of vitality was rejected in favor of the former rigid orthodoxy; the introduction of democratic procedure into the structure of the Church was undone and the ancient disdain for women and for non-Christians and even for Protestants was quickened. Some Catholics remember John fondly, as a kind of miracle, but if you push them they will say he was the Pope of False Promises, and it would have been better if he hadn't started what he wouldn't be around to finish. You detect a hint of disillusionment in my tone, *n'est-ce pas?* And you think to yourself, How unlike him.

And then, the second death. On June 11, 1963, an old man climbed from an automobile and squatted on the pavement at a main Saigon streetcorner. He was a Buddhist monk named Quang Duc. He was surrounded by a thousand monks and nuns, and then by thousands of other people, including journalists, because everyone had heard what he intended to do. Quang Duc waited patiently, running an acorn rosary through his fingers, while two disciples doused his saffron robe with gasoline. The eerie sounds of chanting, but of nothing else, filled the square as the monks and nuns offered their prayer for him. Then Quang Duc said, "I return to the eternal Buddha." He struck the match himself. Instantly he was aflame. The plume of smoke, unlike the smoke over Auschwitz, was black with the lard of human flesh. And quickly the stench of the burning bonze, even more than the heat, drove the inner ring of monks back, though the farthest away pressed forward. Police tried to break through, but the holies prevented them. Witnesses shrieked in horror and bystanders wept. Quang Duc's devoted followers continued to chant, and all the while photographers and film cameramen took their pictures. After ten minutes the charred body of the old monk fell over. Nothing he had done in his long life had the effect his death would have. Within twenty-four hours the photograph of his body in flames would appall the world, stun the leaders of America and give the American public its first, though by no means last, shock of pure horror from Vietnam. Within weeks the leading Vietnamese poet and novelist Nguyen Tuong Tam would kill himself, perhaps a dozen other monks and nuns would publicly burn themselves to death, one nun would ritually hack her hand off before an altar, hundreds of Buddhists would begin a hunger strike, and tens of thousands would take to the streets, all to protest against the vicious despotism of Ngo Dinh Diem. Quang Duc had exposed it to the world for what it was.

Pope John had dreamed of eliminating from the Church once and for all the implicit intolerance, self-righteousness and triumphalism that periodically in its history had become explicit in tragically violent forms. But in the very season of John's death, a fanatical Catholic army whose generals mourned his passing was unleashed against a populace because of its religion, and it happened in Cardinal Spellman's protégé's Vietnam.

"They've lost their fucking minds, obviously." Howe threw the dispatch on his desk and looked across at Michael. "The esteemed governor of Hué, brother of our esteemed president, brother of our esteemed archbishop, brother of our esteemed chief of torture, brother-in-law of the Dragon Lady, has now issued a decree forbidding anyone from wearing Buddhist robes in a public place."

"Oh, God," Michael said. The police and Buddhist mobs had been skirmishing for days. "What will happen?"

"First reports are that now everyone in Hué, from taxi drivers to Catholic students, have declared themselves Buddhists and donned the robes."

"Good for them."

"Yeah." Howe turned in his chair to look out his window. His office occupied a corner in the rear of the embassy and its single window opened on the parking lot where the marines kept their jeeps. Beyond the lot was an iron picket fence and a side street, along which pedestrian and auto traffic moved as usual. The chaos in Hué had yet to break out in Saigon. "And all that shit is hitting the fan because of flags."

Howe didn't need to make his reference explicit. Archbishop Thuc had banned the display of the Buddhist flag, and the Buddhists had gone crazy.

"So what about the bombing? I heard there was a bombing up there." Michael had come to the embassy not to fence with Howe about the absurd denouement of Catholic-Buddhist conflict, but to learn if the rumors he'd been hearing about the violence were true. He had workers in Hué, and two American Maryknoll priests whom he'd befriended were there.

"A car blew up inside the old city," Howe said. "There were many casualties. We don't yet know how many dead, how many wounded. Governor Can issued a statement already saying it was the Viet Cong. He says the Viet Cong have taken over the Buddhist movement." Howe smirked. "As if they needed to. I think the V.C. are probably on vacation. Let the Buddhists and the Ngos finish each other off."

"When can I get a casualty list, John? I have friends up there."

Howe jotted something on a notepad. "I'll keep an eye on the wire for you. I'll call you."

"Thanks."

"So, can I ask you something?" He paused. Michael didn't bat an eye. He and Howe had had frequent if somewhat formal contact in the last year. They respected each other and kept each other posted but they had not become friends. Michael no longer felt that as a disappointment, and he no longer allowed himself to take Howe's aloofness as a personal or social rejection. Michael didn't know it, but he had drawn on his innate Irish knack for turning aside the snub. "What is Spellman saying now? What's he going to do?"

Michael had to look away. If they had become friends he might have admitted that Spellman never responded to his communiqués. At a certain point he'd begun describing in detail the mad behavior of Thuc and the other Ngos. At about that point the replies had begun to come, not even from O'Shea, but from O'Shea's assistant. The replies had a theme; keep the relief going. Separate it however you can from politics. And that's what he had done. Michael forced himself to smile at Howe. "You think the cardinal and I are on the phone each week? Come on, John. What do I know? Anyway, what does it matter at this point, what Spellman thinks?"

"When we've got the Asian version of the Inquisition going on here? We've got Frankenstein's monster; but you know who Doctor Frankenstein is, as well as I do."

Michael nodded. "But he's irrelevant to it now, John. These people wouldn't listen to the *pope.* I mean, Madame Nhu, Christ! She calls the monks who burn themselves the 'barbecued bonzes.' Nhu is hooked on opium. The archbishop thinks he's Torquemada. And Diem considers himself an Oriental El Cid taking on the Moors. The whole family thinks of itself as sent from God. This is their moment to come down from Olympus with thunderbolts. So who's going to listen to Spellman?"

"Kennedy," Howe said abruptly. "Kennedy has people telling him that when Diem wins this battle, everything else will fall into place. They're saying swallow your misgivings, look the other way while the monks burn themselves, and while the soldiers shoot the people in the streets. They're telling him that those are Communists in the streets and that the Buddhists are Russian agents. If Spellman broke with Diem, it would help Kennedy to."

Now Michael saw for the first time why Howe had cultivated him, even to the extent that he had. All along Michael had thought Howe wanted to influence events in Vietnam — to see that the aid was distributed equitably — but now he saw that Howe wanted to influence Washington. He said nothing.

Howe leaned forward across his desk. "The question, Father, has become, At what point does the Church proclaim its opposition to the regime it created? When every Buddhist in Vietnam is dead?"

"Wait a minute, John. Don't talk to me about the Church. This is the American embassy, where Diem's money comes from. You talk to me about distributing aid. Ninety-five percent of the aid coming into this country goes to Diem's army. That's *your* people doing that, not mine. Tell *them* about Hué, John. Not me. And not Spellman either. Just because the president's a Catholic doesn't mean he's waiting to be told by the hierarchy what to think. He's waiting to be told by you people, Goddamnit! Hawkins and Nolting are the ones he depends on. So get to them, John!"

"I can't," Howe said evenly, coldly. "People with my point of view have been shut out, and you know it."

"Maybe you shut yourself out, John. You look down your damn nose at everybody. You slug us with your offended sensibility. You're surrounded by moral pygmies, aren't you? Who isn't your inferior, John?"

Howe flinched, but that was all, and Michael regretted at once having cast the issue in terms of inferiority, or rather, having admitted that those were the terms that mattered. He regretted especially having so exposed his feelings, and therefore having underscored once more how they were different.

Howe sat at his desk, immobile, staring back at Michael. He wasn't going to speak.

Michael said, more to cover his embarrassment than to press the point, "If this was Africa and the Ngos were a clan of Ashanti chieftains at war with another tribe, you'd be much more tolerant. You'd still be horrified by the killing, but you wouldn't take it personally."

Howe said in a steely, cold voice, "How much more has to

happen in the streets and villages of this country, Father, before you take *that* personally instead of the petty slights you imagine having suffered from me?"

The answer would come soon enough. First, President Diem declared the nation's pagodas closed and he sent troops to surround them, though not just any troops. The raids on the pagodas in which dozens of monks were murdered and scores more wounded were carried out by the elite Catholic units modeled on the American Green Berets. Diem claimed that the pagodas had been taken over by Communists.

By the next morning, word spread through Saigon that thirty monks in the Xa Loi pagoda near Freedom Palace where the Ngos lived had been shot by government troops. When Michael heard of it he tried to call Howe, but he couldn't get through. Later he would learn that Nhu's agents had cut the embassy telephone lines. The Americans would know less than ordinary citizens, and they would not be able to protest until it was too late.

Michael went at once to the Vinh Hoa Dao pagoda across Saigon. It was easy to get there that day because for a change the streets of the city were empty. The Saigonese knew when to stay at home. The broad, sweeping staircase leading up to the temple, usually so crowded with refugees and knots of students, monks and nuns, was utterly deserted. As he ascended the stairs in the eerie quiet, he slowed his pace and resolved to take in every detail of what he was about to see. He knew before he saw it.

The magnificent pagoda had been ransacked and half-burned. The great gilded-wood figure of Buddha in the sanctuary had been toppled, and its face had crashed into the floor. Benches were splintered, shrines demolished. The charred heavy curtain along the far wall still smoldered, and the roof above that quarter of the pagoda had been consumed by the fire. Apparently a rainfall had doused the flames once the flames had opened the roof to the sky.

Michael walked through the far doorway, through the series of small rooms, into the familiar courtyard, as he had done dozens of times coming to see Thic Nhat Than. The garden had been wrecked too; plants were uprooted and strewn about, large palm trees had been felled and lay now like great timbers across the ruins. Statues had been smashed to bits. As he walked he expected to come across corpses, but he didn't, and that made the chaotic scene all the more bizarre, all the more ominous.

As he approached the veranda where he'd met Nhat Than, where they'd talked, each in his broken French, and where he'd allowed himself not only to share the Buddhist elder's dream for Vietnam, but also to feel the spell of his holiness, Michael was slowed by an awful stench. It was an odor unlike any he'd smelled before, and it made him feel sick. He thought of stopping, turning around and running away. I'd have gotten the hell out of there myself. But he didn't.

He mounted the three stairs and pushed a tottering rice-paper screen aside.

Thic Nhat Than, the Venerable, the Beloved, the Spiritual Master, was lying in two pieces before Michael. Only a foot-long deep purple river of coagulated blood joined his head to his body. On his severed face was frozen a look of pure horror.

"So he had John beheaded in prison . . ." Michael slammed his eyes shut against it. ". . . and the head was brought in on a plate."

Michael knelt. Instead of praying for the monk or uttering the Catholic words — he was instinctively respectful and would have observed only the Buddhist rubric if he'd known it — he stifled his infinite repugnance and picked up the old man's head and placed it against the trunk of his body. Instead of praying for him then, he began reciting the Act of Contrition for himself and for us, his people, for we had done this. But even that reciting he did automatically, a reaction in shock. In his mind other words replayed themselves, words he had not thought of in years, Tim O'Shea's words, in that faintly accented Irish voice saying, over and over, "God will not have his work made manifest by cowards."

When at last Michael stood, a man behind him said, "Amen."

It was Howe.

They stared at each other blankly. Michael just shook his head.

Howe said nothing, not "I told you so." Not, "Are you satisfied?" Not, "Now do you understand me?" Not, "This is why I wanted you here."

Michael said, "I'm going to New York. I'm going to tell them."

"Good."

"But first . . ." He looked down at the remains of Thic Nhat Than again, then around the garden. His voice cracked as he said,

"Do you think we should bury him?" There were no shovels but Michael realized that, given his emotion at that moment, he could have dug forever with his bare hands, through gravel, through stone. He wanted to rip out the hearts of Thuc and Nhu and Diem. He wanted to twist their heads off with his hands.

"No. His people will be back. They're the ones to look after him."

"Why did they leave?"

Howe shrugged. "They were afraid." He looked down at the corpse. "Not many men would have defied them by staying like this." He looked up sharply. "Would you have?"

Michael shook his head, no.

"Me either," Howe said. When he looked at Michael it was with an admission: I'm a man like you, just like you. All he said, though, or needed to say was, "Let's go."

They started across the ruined garden. Michael stopped and picked up a large fallen palm frond. He retraced his way to the veranda and placed it gently on Nhat Than's body, to cover him.

Michael had the airport cab drop him off at the Empire State Building, where the CRS offices were. But Monsignor O'Shea was not there.

Michael was exhausted. He'd been traveling, space available, on MATS flights for two and a half days. It would have made sense to sleep, but in his mind by then the situation in Vietnam had become even more anarchic, more violent, and his mission, therefore — for that is what it was to him — was urgent. He shaved in the office washroom, borrowed a fresh collar from one of the CRS priests, left his bag there and set out for the cardinal's house on Madison Avenue.

The walk took Michael up the best stretch of Fifth Avenue, and after a year and a half, it was a foreign world to him, one to which, in his state, he had no particular reaction. He passed mannequins and travel posters, windows full of books. He cut between secretaries and shoppers with painted toenails and high-heeled sandals, the girls in their summer dresses, as the early Irwin Shaw so exactly put it. Taxicabs gunned at him as he crossed the streets and pretzel-sellers hawked. But he was indifferent to it all. Even as he cut down Fiftieth Street, which runs between St. Patrick's and Saks, that cathedral for consumers, he remained mentally and emotionally clutched, as if a lump of dough had congealed in his lungs.

The cardinal's residence was a gray, neo-Gothic mansion, one of the city's great houses, but the fact that it abutted the cathedral on one side and on the other faced the Villard Mansions, one of the great houses in the world — though in those days a major publisher and the chancery of the archdiocese occupied its separate wings — made the cardinal's own four-story abode seem modest, though not particularly friendly. Michael tried to shake himself from his strange, almost panicky mood by taking its half-dozen stairs jauntily, and swinging the door open as if he did it every day. In fact, like the vast majority of New York priests, he had never been in the cardinal's house, and he had never expected to be. Even the cardinal's own staff lived down the block in another building, with the cathedral staff. For other prelates, dignitaries, grand marshals of parades, the cardinal's residence was the setting for receptions catered by the Waldorf Astoria; for would-be mayors, governors and even presidents, it was the source of an invaluable benediction. But for common clergy, the cardinal's house was trouble.

It was unheard of that a priest should go there unsummoned, and Michael hadn't even called ahead. After the bright morning sunshine, the dark, paneled entrance foyer closed on him like night, and it was only a voice from a room to his left that gave him a clue to protocol.

"Yes? May I help you?"

Michael pushed the door open. An elderly woman sat at a typewriter. The room was cluttered in a Victorian way, overcurtained, overfurnished, ill-lit. The woman herself, with pinned hair and a doily-lace collar, seemed musty, left behind by another time.

"I'm here to see the cardinal. I'm Father Maguire from the CRS."

"CRS?" She was not impressed by his collar.

"Catholic Relief Service."

"Oh." She picked up the phone and dialed. "Monsignor, there's a young priest here. He says he has an appointment, but not that I know of." She listened, then squinted at Michael. "What did you say your name was?"

"Father Maguire."

"Father Maguire, he says. From the CFM."

"CRS," Michael corrected, but she ignored him.

She hung up the phone. "Monsignor Dugan's office is on the second floor. You should take the elevator there. His office is right next to it."

"I'll just walk up. The stairs . . . ?"

"Take the elevator, if you please, Father. Monsignor said you should take the elevator."

They didn't want outsiders wandering around the building. The elevator would enable them to track him. He thanked the old lady, who only stared at him glumly.

The elevator was closet-sized, and the clunking of the manually operated doors reverberated through the walls of that part of the building. The engine thunked into gear when he pressed the number, and then whirred piercingly as the cubicle rose. A time machine, he thought, out of H. G. Wells. When it stopped, the doors opened. Monsignor Dugan, the cardinal's secretary, a man as short as Spellman but thin and sharp-featured, was standing opposite Michael with an open show of quizzical irritation. For a moment Michael thought he wasn't going to let him out. Michael recognized him as the priest who'd served as master of ceremonies at his ordination, where he'd proved himself a virtuoso of the profound bow and the obeisance. Michael felt suddenly like an altar boy who was about to be rebuked for his slothful genuflections.

"Father Maguire?"

"Hello, Monsignor." Michael put his hand out.

Monsignor Dugan shook it, not limply but not firmly either. His quizzical look made it clear he was trying to recall if anyone had told him that Father Maguire was returning from Vietnam. He cocked an eyebrow, waiting for an explanation.

Michael could not assess at first what he was up against, though Dugan had the reputation of being impossible to get by. Priests often said it would be easier to get in to see Mayor Wagner or Senator Javits or even Governor Rockefeller than the cardinal, not that any of them wanted to.

"Miss Leonard says you have an appointment?"

"Her mistake, Monsignor. I told her that I'd come to see the cardinal. She assumed I had an appointment. But I don't."

"Well, Father, surely you understand that it's impossible. I'd have had Miss Leonard say as much to you, but it would have embarrassed her to do so. We don't have priests coming in off the street and expecting His Eminence to drop everything to see them."

"I understand that, Monsignor. I would not think of doing such a thing myself, but I arrived within the hour from Vietnam. It is urgent that I see His Eminence at once."

"About what?" Dugan asked carefully.

"About Ngo Dinh Diem."

Dugan stared at Michael. What he knew about were parishes, the ones in hock, and priests, the ones who drank too much. He knew about the schools, the efforts of the lay teachers to unionize, and the seminaries, that certain professors were spouting the ultraliberalism of that Swiss heretic, Kung. He knew about the downtown bankers who could get broker's fees cut and city hall hacks who could get the building code waived and the Aqueduct regulars who tracked the big bettors. He didn't know about Vietnam. Suddenly he realized that this young priest occupied a square on which Spelly, against advice, had placed a stack of chips. He knew the stack was teetering. "Come with me," he said, leading the way into his office, "and I'll check the cardinal's calendar."

"I have to see him right now, Monsignor."

"That's impossible." Dugan faced Michael. He stood with his back to his desk.

"Would you ask him?"

Monsignor Dugan had been vaguely aware of the furor over recent events in Vietnam, but if there were implications for the archdiocese in that madness, he had missed them. "Are you here to discuss your work with the CRS? Is that the point?"

"Yes."

"Well, then . . ." He sat back on the edge of his desk. Only now that he saw how to deal with this did he allow himself a hint of kindliness. "Then the appropriate thing for you to do is to take it up with Monsignor O'Shea or Bishop Swanstrom. If need be, they will approach the cardinal."

Michael shook his head and said firmly, "I'm the one who's here, Monsignor. I'm the one who wants to talk to him. I've traveled for two and a half days to talk to him. If he won't see me, all right. But I'd like you to ask him."

Neither man would look away. Finally the secretary softened. "Shall I put it that a brother priest seeks a word of counsel?"

"If you like," Michael said, though inwardly he recoiled. These bastards always had to have the upper hand. You came to them as a subject or a suppliant, nothing else. Only the wackos caught Spelly's eye. But hell, maybe it was true; maybe Michael was like the alkies and the Casanovas, just another Father Fuck-up, a little younger than usual, and with his problem clothed in Asian intrigue. "Tell him I've just this moment arrived."

Monsignor Dugan nodded and left the room.

A few minutes later he reappeared, crooked a finger at Michael, then turned and led the way through a shadowy corridor to the cardinal's office.

The room was dominated by a large crystal chandelier which filled it with light, and after the gloom elsewhere that surprised Michael. Centered under the fixture was a long Catalonian refectory table with six ornately carved wooden chairs, and on the table were dozens of neatly stacked books and reports. On one wall was a portrait of the late pope, not John, but Pius. On another was the carved wooden crest of Spellman's cartouche, his coat of arms, which featured in elaborate serpentine the tassels of his red hat. On a third wall was a portrait of Spellman's predecessor, Cardinal Hayes; he was a stern-looking man who seemed to be glaring out at his successor's office disapprovingly. Below that painting was a leather wing chair arranged to face the cardinal's desk, which occupied the alcove of the bay window that overlooked Madison Avenue. The curtains were open and additional light poured in from the street, enveloping the cardinal himself who sat at his desk, back to the window, staring at Michael.

He was the sixth archbishop of New York, had occupied the chair since 1939 and had become for Catholics and most other Americans so much the epitome of a Roman Catholic archbishop that it was easy to forget that there had never been one like him before. His round smiling features were so familiar to New Yorkers because he loved to appear in public, at dedications and benefits, neighborhood festivals and civic celebrations. His commitments seemed wide-ranging and his presence to the life of the city seemed freewheeling, but in fact everything he did was calculated for effect. His purpose from the beginning had been to make an impact far beyond the confines of the Church and he did. His great accomplishment as archbishop was a subtle one: he had secured for himself a place of real influence among the power brokers and aristocrats of the nation in a way that no other Catholic prelate ever had, and he, more than any single figure, represented the arrival of the Catholic Church as a political and social force equal to any in America. He could be genial and friendly, but he never forgot his function for the Church, and that was to collect power, as much power as he could, not to aggrandise himself, but to reinforce the position of a community which even as recently as his own youth had been an oppressed, fragile collection of immigrant groups with little in common but their feelings of inferiority and their faith in the Church of Rome. His job had been to slam the door forever on the era when Catholic sensibilities could be ignored or violated or made mock of in this country. And so he had, from his position as archbishop of the greatest city in America, intruded himself into every area of the nation's life, from Cold War strategies as the Military Vicar to standards of popular entertainment as head of the Legion of Decency. Even if his patron, Pius XII, was gone, and even if his simple theology was being called into question by the Vatican Council, and even if, at seventy-five, he had lost a measure of vigor and had, for example, to lean on his chaplains to ascend the stairs of the high altar, he was still a man who knew what he was. He was authority itself. He was the cardinal.

"You know Father Maguire, Your Eminence," Dugan said.

Michael approached the desk as Spellman stood. He was wearing a red-trimmed black cassock with a broad silk sash. His short-cropped white hair framed his zucchetto, the red skull cap which, with its little center tab, Spellman adjusted, an absentminded gesture. When he offered Michael his hand, it was palm down, indicating that he expected, even across the expanse of desk, that the junior priest would kiss his ring. Michael did so gracefully, and he said, "Thank you for seeing me, Your Eminence."

"Father Maguire, are you all right?" Spellman looked at him intently, and Michael was surprised to sense his concern. "You weren't expected home, were you?"

Michael shook his head, but before he could speak Spellman turned to Dugan. "Did you offer him coffee?" He looked at Michael. "Have you eaten?"

"Yes, thank you," Michael said, though he didn't remember his last meal.

"Tell me what's been happening," Spellman said intently. "It must be chaos there."

Michael exhaled and felt his body relax into the chair. At last he was here, about to tell his story to the one man who could make it better, make everything better. He felt not only that he'd come home, but that he was with — though there was no personal justification for this feeling — his father. "Your Eminence, it's worse than chaos. For weeks there has been a well-organized, quite deliberate effort to destroy the Buddhists. All of the Buddhists. By now hundreds of monks and priests have been murdered. Thousands are in jail for no offense beyond their religion. And pagodas all over the country, small ones and great ones, have been ransacked and burned."

Spellman was shaking his head sadly. Light glinted off his rimless spectacles, making it seem for an instant that there were tears in his eyes, but not so. He said, "It must have been awful, seeing it up close, as you did."

Michael stared at him, perplexed for a moment until he realized that Spellman thought the trouble here was with his priest; poor Father Maguire, what terrible things he's been through. Michael sat forward. "Your Eminence, it is a religious vendetta. President Diem and his brothers have broken confidence with you. They are abusing the Catholic Faith terribly by conducting such operations in its name. A monk I knew personally was murdered in his sanctuary. His head was cut off."

Spellman continued to shake his head. "Inexcusable," he muttered.

Michael waited for him to say more, but he wasn't going to. "But, Your Eminence, my point is about Diem." *Your* Diem! he almost added.

"The *New York Times* thinks Diem is mad. They get all worked up because our nice pat American distinction between Church and State is not observed in Vietnam. But what about Israel?"

Israel? Michael couldn't comprehend this at all.

Spellman leaned forward. "There are religious groups in violent conflict in Israel too! What does Mr. Sulzberger say about that?"

"But in Vietnam, Your Eminence, we're talking about government violence against its own citizens."

Spellman's eyebrows went up. "Well, the main violence, of course, is against the Communists. It's a war, isn't it? You know what a war is like, Father. You know that better than I. Sometimes there are abuses. Obviously, those soldiers were on a rampage. But what did the Buddhists do to provoke them? A country at war can't have thousands of citizens in the streets trying to bring down the government, can it? We wouldn't have allowed that here during World War Two, I'll tell you."

Michael was stunned. Was Spellman offering a defense of the assault?

Monsignor Dugan appeared at Michael's elbow, surprising him, with a cup of coffee. Michael took it, though he thought the strong, black brew would make him sick. He thanked the monsignor, who withdrew.

After a moment the cardinal sat back, bridged his hands under his chin and asked, "What do you believe about Buddhism anyway, Father?"

"Theologically?"

The cardinal nodded.

Michael was instinctively wary. Was this the question of an Inquisitor? "I believe, as Pope John put it, that they are men of goodwill whose hearts have been imprinted with God's Law."

"But they are, whether culpably or not, prisoners of error."

Michael tried to sip the coffee. His hands shook and it spilled.

"Don't you agree?"

"I think that in Vietnam this week they're being treated as worse than that."

"Perhaps with reason, Father. Perhaps reasons you and I are not privy to. What if the Buddhist movement has been infiltrated? What if their leaders are Red sympathizers? What if their pagodas and temples were the sites of cell group meetings? What if they abused their sanctuaries by using them to stir up subversion? What if they are actively trying to bring Diem down so that the Communists can take over?"

Michael suddenly couldn't think of what to say. The gap between their points of view seemed infinite.

"Furthermore, Father, you have jumped to a conclusion that is completely unwarranted and, I might say, unjust."

"I have?"

"By holding Diem and Nhu responsible for this latest crisis. It is not their doing, whatever the justification or lack of it. Neither Diem nor Nhu ordered those troops against the pagodas."

"Your Eminence . . ." Michael felt as if he was humoring an hallucinator. ". . . Nhu's personal army did these things. I was there."

Spellman nodded and said calmly, "You've been traveling, Father. There have been developments. Certain of Diem's most trusted generals ordered the raids without authorization, conspirators who hoped to cause an uprising and the overthrow of democracy. Nhu revealed their names yesterday, after they were arrested. The Ngos are as upset about the excesses against civilians as you are."

Michael stared in disbelief. Was Spellman convinced of this fantasy?

"I have been in communication throughout the crisis with the Vietnamese ambassador in Washington."

"That's Madame Nhu's father! You can't believe him!"

Spellman looked sharply at Michael: Don't use the imperative with me, young man. He said, "I have his word that his government deplores the killings in the sanctuaries and I accept it. So, I gather, do President Kennedy and Secretaries Rusk and McNamara."

Michael saw suddenly what the Ngos were trying for — in one move to eliminate their Buddhist opposition *and* the dissident generals who threatened from within — and he realized that if they pulled it off they would be unstoppable. The *Times* was characterizing the entire family as mad, but this ploy was ingenious. Even at the moment of greatest outrage, they had given their sponsors in America an irresistible reason to stick by them — this "madness" was going to work! It would give them total control of their country. Weather this storm with us, they promised in effect, and *then* we'll unleash our evil genius on the Communists. You will have an invincible bastion — like Israel — in Southeast Asia.

"Your Eminence," Michael said slowly, "I bow to your more intimate knowledge, but, as you know, I have been there for a year and a half, and I feel it is my responsibility to report to you exactly what I have witnessed. Archbishop Thuc has delivered public diatribes on many occasions against the Buddhists. He has said again and again they have no rights. He has encouraged their slaughter. The crisis is a direct result of his fanatical speeches."

"But Archbishop Thuc is talking about the Communists, Father."
Michael nearly came out of his chair. He spilled coffee on the rug. "No, no, he's talking about the Buddhists! About *holy* men and women. About ninety percent of the population. The Ngos are bringing disaster to Vietnam and they must be stopped. *You* must stop them."

Spellman shook his head. "Your experience is valuable to me, Father. And I appreciate getting it firsthand from you. But you don't have the big picture. You're *too* close. *Too* involved. What you don't see is that the Communists are within an inch of taking over Vietnam. It would be their greatest victory since China. And the slaughter, of Catholics certainly, but also of Buddhists, would make what's going on now seem tame. In other words, the big picture suggests that now, more than ever, it is time to support President Diem and I do." He spoke with a finality that was intended to end this conversation, and it did.

Michael sank back into his chair, staring at his coffee.

"You've done a good job in Vietnam, Father. I've had nothing but positive reports. Even though it's been difficult, you can look back on your service there with pride."

Michael looked up sharply. What? Look back?

"And I think your experience will serve us in good stead. We're about to launch a new fund-raising drive called 'The Children's Relief Fund.' It's geared to assist the overburdened orphanages in Vietnam. You know about it." Michael nodded.

"I want you to head it up."

"But that would mean . . ."

"Coming back here."

"Your Eminence, I'm not ready to come back." Michael had to stifle the alarm he felt. "I can't leave Vietnam now."

"But your purpose is to help the victims of that war, isn't it? This is a chance to do something big for them. For the children, Father. For the orphans. I can sense your conviction, your passion, your concern, and so will the other bishops — so will the Catholic people. Your job will be to quicken the conscience of the entire American Church."

Spellman was right and knew it. Michael Maguire would be irresistible on the subject of what he'd seen in Vietnam. The money would pour in and new orphanages would go up all over that beleaguered country.

And, more to the point, Michael Maguire would be back in the States, in the bosom of the Church, where he belonged. Spellman wouldn't have considered for a second allowing such an angry, righteous young priest back into a situation of such moral and political complexity. But he would forbid and command only as a last resort. He liked his priests to feel honored by their assignments. He preferred their enthusiasm to their resentment. Spellman was nothing if not an inspired manipulator of his own men. "What do you say, Father?"

Michael only stared at him. There was a chamber in his brain in which the cardinal's words had not registered at all. There, images of what he'd seen in Vietnam continued to flash, but like a stark film with no soundtrack. A feeling of utter exhaustion came over him, and he wanted suddenly, irrationally, to lie down on the thick carpet of the cardinal's office. Perhaps then the tranquillity of that place would soothe him. He could close his eyes against everything he'd seen. When had he had such a feeling before? Such longing for peace, for escape, for quiet? He could have his rest if only he did what they wanted.

"You're one of my best men, Father," the cardinal said quietly. "I need you to do this for me. I'd consider it a personal favor."

It was in China, in the camp commandant's office. They'd refused to let him sleep for days. They'd wanted him to identify those of his fellow prisoners who were officers. He never did. It had seemed to him he'd learned to sleep even while standing up, even while they kept questioning him.

Michael snapped himself alert. This was not China. And he was not being asked to betray anyone. He was being asked to save the children of Vietnam. Yes. He was being asked to tell Americans what was happening there. Yes. He felt that peace coming over him. The peace of assent. Yes, he would do it. For the children. For the cardinal. For God whose Will it was, he thought, which then embraced him.

SEVENTEEN

Two months later Michael was in charge of arrangements for the press conference at which Cardinal Spellman was to announce the beginning drive of the Children's Relief Fund. The press conference was to be held at Idlewild Airport because the cardinal was leaving for Rome for the third session of the Vatican Council. His departure would give reporters a news angle that what they would surely take as just another Catholic appeal for money lacked.

Public interest in the council was growing, and not only among Catholics. Americans were beginning to sense what forces it was even then unleashing. Cardinal Spellman himself, however, did not yet understand its meaning. He was leaving for Rome as the senior prelate of the most fabulously successful national Church in the world. In the previous ten years the Catholic population in America had grown by 44 percent, and the number of children in Catholic schools by 65 percent. There were twelve thousand more priests in America than there had been in 1950, and in the same period the number of seminarians had doubled. And the prodigiously generous Catholic people of America contributed millions of dollars not only to their own parishes and schools, but to the offices of the Vatican and to the Church's worldwide works of mercy. To Spellman, those were the things that counted. He had expected in the first session the year before that the Council Fathers in Rome would want to know how American Catholics were doing it. But he was surprised. The Council Fathers, inspired by Pope John, if not the Holy Ghost, had so far shown no interest in wealth, in buildings, in numbers, or even in the kind of power represented by a Catholic in the White House. Their concern was simpler: had the Church become so obsessed with its own survival that it had forgotten its true mission — to proclaim the Gospel, to serve the poor, to work for peace and justice in the world?

But frankly that wasn't the question on anyone's mind at Idlewild that day. In the popular press the council was still treated as a kind of ecclesiastical Super Bowl, and the religious press was preoccupied with Church gossip. Several dozen reporters had shown up, including camera crews from two New York stations. When they had assembled in the makeshift auditorium, a rarely used waiting area off the main concourse, Michael went to the VIP lounge where the cardinal was waiting.

The room was lit like a cocktail lounge, and its walls were covered with a cheap version of the dark paneling salesmen might associate with rich men's clubs. The clergy dominated the place. Two auxiliary bishops, several monsignors and half a dozen priests were accompanying the cardinal to Rome. They and their clerical chums who'd come to see them off were standing in groups of three or four, talking softly. The cardinal was sitting in a corner. As he approached, Michael realized that one of the priests with His Eminence was Monsignor Ellis, the former golf champion and the pastor of Holy Cross. Michael had not seen him since his deacon summer.

Monsignor Ellis turned slightly in his upholstered swivel chair and fixed Michael with a stare. Spellman continued to talk to the priest on his other side. The monsignor sat rigidly upright, as if he wore a corset or a backbrace. Though he had to crane up at Michael, who towered over him, his expression achieved the familiar condescension. He looked more distinguished in his black suit with the tab of red at his throat than he had that summer in his cassock. A black fedora dangled from one hand, and he held a freshly lit cigar in the other. "Well, well, Mister Maguire. How are you?"

"Hello, Monsignor. Quite well, thanks. And you?" Michael put his hand out.

Monsignor Ellis transferred his cigar, and without rising, shook Michael's hand. "I guess it's 'Father' now, isn't it?"

Michael smiled. "For a couple of years, Monsignor."

When Spellman saw him, he stood up. Monsignor Ellis stood then too and took the cardinal's elbow. "I guess I was wrong about this one, eh?"

"You've been wrong about a lot of things, Arthur," Spellman said good-naturedly. Then to Michael, "Are you ready for me, Father?"

Michael said he was and led the cardinal back to the waiting reporters. But Ellis's comment preoccupied him. It was the first indication he'd had that the pastor had recommended against his ordination, and the realization stunned him. It wasn't simply that someone in authority had considered him unfit — though for a man who'd long been accustomed to the approval, even admiration, of his superiors that would have been blow enough. The shock he felt was more acute than that. Throughout the Holy Cross School controversy he had kept his head in the trench, and it still shamed him that Carolyn had taken the heat alone. Robert Moses and Cardinal Spellman may finally have yielded on the school, but they had blown Carolyn to Shanghai. The Church had made itself her enemy. And Michael had chosen the Church.

To discover now that Monsignor Ellis had disapproved of him anyway added to Michael's shame, multiplied it. He could imagine the old fart banging his table and saying, "Hell, if you'd had any guts you'd have stood up with that girl when she needed you! Then I'd have voted for you!" But of course he knew that Ellis's negative vote had been a simple effort to obliterate everything associated with what surely was the great embarrassment of his priesthood. He'd have voted against Jesus if he'd been the deacon that summer.

"Gentlemen, thank you for coming." Michael stood behind the microphones, but ignored them. They had been set at the cardinal's height, not his, and he'd have had to kneel to use them. "The cardinal will make a short announcement, then will entertain your questions for about fifteen minutes." Michael paused, looking over the audience. The Catholic press — the diocesan newspapers from New York, Rockville Centre, Brooklyn, Newark, Bridgeport and Hartford, the stringer from the Catholic News Service and writers from the Catholic magazines — was fully represented. Religion reporters from secular newspapers and wire services were there, and the TV crews from the pair of local stations. Michael didn't know them personally, but it was easy to imagine who they were. Uniformly middle-aged, gregarious men, smokers, drinkers, somewhat shabby in their old suits and frayed shirts. They'd begun their careers in journalism with the usual enthusiasm and perhaps more than the usual promise. They tended to be literate, liberally educated and, for journalists, reflective. But for one reason or another they'd slid from paper to paper — big-city daily to suburban weekly to diocesan — or from desk to desk — Metro to Obit to Religion. They were men who'd been shunted aside, and the news they covered was unimportant not only to their editors but to them. If the rare major story did break in their area — like the Vatican Council — these poor bastards were bumped by the first-stringers or the foreign guys. Except for a couple of them, they had not even been to Rome and weren't going now. Michael resolutely refused to make anything of it, but he knew full well that only failed reporters regularly covered the events that formed the core of his life.

But it wasn't the sight of the regulars that gave Michael pause. A young man in the third row had caught his eye. He wore heavy black-rimmed glasses, and his thick red hair was disheveled enough to suggest he rarely combed it. He looked nothing like the others. He was staring intently at Michael, and his air of expectation alone would have set him apart from his blasé colleagues. But there was something else. Suddenly Michael realized what had snagged his attention. The young man was not wearing a suitcoat; he sported an ill-knotted, gray knit tie on a faded brown workshirt. But it wasn't a workshirt. It was an old woolen army blouse like he had worn himself once.

Michael cleared his throat. "It is my honor to present the archbishop of New York, the Military Vicar for the United States Armed Forces, His Eminence, Francis Cardinal Spellman."

Spellman, so short and stout, so bald, so ruddy-faced, was in no way a figure of imposing physical presence. When garbed in the elaborate episcopal vestments he seemed slightly ludicrous. But when he wanted to, he could transcend his cherubic manner utterly, conveying more than a hint of his immense authority. He took his power for granted and so had no need to flaunt it. But when it was time to make a serious point, he knew how to do it. And nothing in his entire ministry was more serious than this. Oh, he wanted the funds to be raised and the orphans to be cared for, of course. The Children's Relief Fund was a fine idea, but not only for its own sake. He wanted Americans to remember that in the war against Communism their commitment had long since been made. Nothing reminded them so well, he knew from years of doing this, as the forlorn face of an orphaned child. He had that face in mind as he finished reading what Father Maguire had written for him. "In the last year alone more than a hundred thousand Vietnamese civilians have been killed and perhaps three times that many wounded. It is impossible to say with precision how many children have been left homeless and parentless by this violence, but surely the figure is many tens of thousands. The country and the cities are full of boys and girls, hungry, ill clothed and terribly afraid. In the chaos of the fighting no one will care for them if we do not. That is why the Catholic Relief Service of which I am episcopal director has launched this emergency effort, and why I call upon all Catholics and all Americans of goodwill to join us in it."

Spellman raised his eyes from the statement. "It should be emphasized in addition . . ." he began.

Michael studied his hands. He had been hoping the cardinal wouldn't ad-lib. It was impossible to predict what he would say.

". . . that these children are on the frontline of our war against Communism. It isn't a flood or an earthquake that rendered them homeless, motherless, fatherless. The Reds did that. They are doing it to the Vietnamese, but who they'd really like to do it to is us. Which is why we must stop them there. Otherwise, tomorrow it will be Australia and day after tomorrow it will be Hawaii. It is impossible to exaggerate what an evil force we are dealing with." Spellman stopped. Like an expert preacher he let the silence gather and build before going on. "Many of the children we want to help were forced to witness the beheading of their own parents." He paused again to let the men see how this moved him. "And we know for a certainty that the Reds would have murdered the children too, but they let them live because, alive, they are a drain on the resources of the struggling democratic government. But we are determined that not even such heinous tactics as these shall succeed! That is why we call upon Americans to do their part to see that democracy and freedom and Christian values survive in Vietnam. Only in that way will they survive here."

Spellman nodded at the reporters to indicate that he was finished.

Their hands went up. He pointed at an overweight gray-haired writer in the front row and said, "Hal?"

"Your Eminence . . ." The reporter struggled to his feet and had reference to his pad as he asked his question. "What do you think the chances are that the Vatican Council will allow some use of the vernacular in the Mass?"

Spellman flashed his famous twinkle. "If I have anything to do with it, none."

The reporters laughed.

"How much longer," another asked, "do you think the council will last?"

"I'd say we should wind it up this month. The bishops of the Church are busy men and have to get back to their dioceses." He smiled again. "I know I do."

"Will you be making your usual tour of army bases this Christmas?"

"Of course I will. This will be my twentieth year. I have to go; Bob Hope needs me. Besides, what would I do with all those Camels?"

The men laughed again. Spellman had been distributing packs of cigarettes to the GIs since the war. The tobacco company not only gave them to him to do so, but embossed each pack with his name and seal.

The cardinal swatted out answers to half a dozen like questions as if he was a coach drilling grounders to his infield. He was amusing and engaging, especially for an archbishop.

Then Spellman recognized the young man in the brown shirt. "Your Eminence," he began. His nervousness, apparent as he stood, set him apart from the regulars. "I'd like to ask about Vietnam." He paused. Cardinal Spellman stared at him, and the room grew utterly quiet, but for the whir of the TV cameras. The young man glanced over at one of the cameras, then went on. "We're supposed to be defending democracy there, right?"

"Yes," the prelate said carefully. "That's right."

"Why are you against elections then?"

One of the cameras stopped filming.

"I'm not against elections, son. Who said I was against elections?"

"You did, Your Eminence." He fumbled with a sheaf of papers. A notepad fell to the floor, but he found what he was looking for. "You said that the elections called for by the Geneva Convention would be, and I quote, 'taps for the buried hopes of freedom in Southeast Asia.' "

"Oh, you're talking about Geneva. That wasn't binding on anybody." Spellman glanced over at Michael, his irritation flared.

Michael raised his finger at the newsman from the second TV station, and in turn he whispered in the cameraman's ear. The cameraman straightened and snapped his camera off too.

"I respectfully disagree, Your Eminence," the young man continued. "The Geneva Convention called for elections in nineteen fifty-six. The government of South Vietnam has flagrantly violated —"

"The government of South Vietnam never signed that convention!" Spellman's face had turned crimson. Unconsciously he lifted himself on his toes. He gripped the podium, as if that pressure would spill off his tension. "And neither did the United States! Everybody knows you can't have fair elections with the Reds."

"So you are against elections."

"Rigged elections, yes."

"But when Ngo Dinh Diem held his own plebiscite in the South in nineteen fifty-six against the Head of State Bao Dai who had appointed him, he won by ninety-eight percent. Wouldn't you call that 'rigged'?"

Spellman answered with his fiercest stare. "Who are you, young man?" He asked finally. "I don't believe we've met."

"My name is Nicholas Wiley, Your Eminence. I'm with the *Catholic Worker*."

Spellman smiled. There was a stir in the room as the reporters nudged each other. The strained atmosphere eased. "Oh, the *Catholic Worker*." Spellman nodded sagely, then said, aside, "Some of my best friends are Catholic Workers."

The reporters laughed loudly. Several clapped. They were glad for the release of tension. They knew, of course, that the cardinal was referring to the controversy that ensued the year before when the *Catholic Worker* crowd publicly challenged him during the Archdiocesan Cemetery Workers' strike. But Spellman had crushed the gravediggers' union, and the *Catholic Worker*'s picket-line hadn't impressed anyone but kooks.

"I'm glad you people are taking an interest in Indochina. You tell Dorothy Day for me, will you, that she should preach her pacifism to the Reds."

The reporters chuckled, enjoying themselves now. This could have been embarrassing, but the cardinal was chewing the punk up.

"I go way back with Dorothy," Spellman said. And, again aside, with a showman's timing, "I'm the one who gave her permission to use the word 'Catholic' for her newspaper. I guess for 'Worker' she went to Joe Stalin."

Now the reporters were slapping their knees.

Nicholas Wiley took his glasses off and looked around. He was blushing and seemed disoriented. What could he do now but slink off? But suddenly he pointed his glasses at the cardinal. "You were talking about the children! You said the Communists were the assassins! But the International Control Commission reports that the South Vietnamese Secret Police are systematically murdering Buddhists even as we —"

Cardinal Spellman threw a glance at Maguire, who stood abruptly. "That's it," he said firmly. "Thanks very much, gentlemen."

Michael's crisp statement belied what he was feeling. Buddhists? Had the kid said Buddhists? But instead of welcoming Wiley's challenge as a version of the one he himself had tried to mount against Spellman, Michael resented it. The kid reeked of self-righteousness and was obviously a nut. His raising the issue like that would only confirm Spellman in his certainty that no one but kooks had questions about policy in Vietnam. It would have been pointless to admit the anger he felt toward the cardinal for his refusal to defend the Buddhists, and it would have been humiliating to acknowledge his peevish irritation at the punk who'd spoiled his press conference, so Michael channeled both feelings into the pretend authority with which he adjourned the session.

Before Wiley could protest, all the other reporters rose at once. He tried to say something, but his words were lost in the bustle.

The VIP lounge had been transformed by the clerics with their dominating black suits and flashing gold Chi-Rho-embossed cuff links, with their boisterous laughter and waving cigars, into a rectory common room. Even though it wasn't noon, there were drinks all around — the flow of booze was the great advantage of traveling.

It was a scene Michael had been relieved to return to after the loneliness of Vietnam. The camaraderie of priests, their great, if often biting, wit, their addiction to stories well told, their minds finely tuned to political nuance, their knack for deflating pomposity — these things made Michael glad to join their company. There'd been several rectory parties — *gaudeami* — in his honor since his return, and when the fathers sang, in reference to his old seminary nickname, the show tune "Mr. Wonderful," he was surprisingly moved.

When Michael walked in then, some moments after Spellman, the chancellor gestured at him and pointed toward the cardinal. Michael crossed to where he was sitting.

"I don't appreciate that one bit, Father. Not one bit."

"I'm sorry, Your Eminence. I should have checked him out. I have no idea how he heard about the press conference."

"There were television cameras present. Those people only want to embarrass me."

"It won't happen again, Your Eminence."

"And I didn't appreciate that statement I had to read either. Not one mention of what it's all about over there. I had to bring it in myself."

"My thought was to emphasize the children, Your Eminence. My thought was to leave politics aside, especially now that the situation there is so . . ."

"Well, you flatter yourself to call that thinking. It's not politics to speak out against Communism in season and out. It's faith and morals. And, Father, don't you forget it."

Michael had to look away. Everyone in the room was listening. He'd have felt abused and humiliated, perhaps, but his stronger feeling was one of embarrassment for the cardinal who, in Michael's opinion, was quite plainly making a fool of himself. But wasn't that Michael's way of deflecting his true reaction? He was deflection itself now.

The cardinal was finished with him. Michael took his leave, saying, "Good luck in Rome, Your Eminence." But Spellman ignored him.

When Michael had crossed the room, Don Duff, a priest who lived down the hall at Saint Gregory's, the Manhattan rectory he'd moved into, handed him a Bloody Mary. "That was rough, buddy," he said.

Michael nodded, "He's a little touchy, isn't he?"

"You'll get used to it." Duff smiled wanly. "And if he really takes to dumping on you, he'll make you a monsignor."

The two priests raised their glasses to each other.

Then Duff said, "You know what Adam said to Eve, don't you?"

"No. What?"

" 'Stand back! There's no telling how big this thing is going to get!' " Duff grinned.

If only all things were as simple as weather, Michael thought as he crossed the airport parking lot toward his car. In October, New York weather is either hateful or glorious and on that day it was quite the latter. The air, even over Long Island, had been scrubbed clean by the austere night, and now the late morning sunshine bathed everything it fell upon in warmth. The sky into which the airplanes climbed was cloudless, a perfect pale blue like the inside of a porcelain bowl.

One of the new passenger jets roared and Michael looked up at it. We marveled at aircraft in those days, the way we now do at microchips. Planes were still the great emblems of modern genius, and of course under Kennedy we had just launched the contest of all time — to build a better plane than the Russians and fly it to the moon. But Michael was neither an engineer nor an outer-space patriot. He automatically saw the silver fuselage and wings as a cross, then chided himself for piety. It was an old habit. In the prison camp a decade earlier he'd disciplined himself to look for crosses everywhere — in the plaster cracks, in the weave of his palm-leaf mat, in the shadows cast by the stockade grilles. Three trees on the low sky. Now he'd have said there were crosses enough in life without looking for them.

He was relieved that the press conference was over and that Spelly was gone, and he promised himself that he would not soon be in a position again to take such shit from anyone. After the autonomy of life in Vietnam it was a shock to be back in a position of such overt subservience. He hoped he could get used to it again.

As he pulled his car, a late-model black Chevrolet, out of the parking lot and onto the road that gave access to the expressway, he saw a hitchhiker. It would not have occurred to him to stop, but he recognized the young man's disheveled red hair, black-rimmed glasses and, obscured by a tattered lumberman's jacket, his army shirt.

Only after he'd begun to apply the brakes — after it was too late — did Michael realize that the sight of the kid pissed him off again. The last thing he wanted to do was ride into Manhattan with him. But he stifled his feeling with charity, the reflex-kindness priests were schooled in. Anger, resentment, bitterness they could show only to each other.

"Want a lift?"

"Oh, Father. Hi." Wiley was embarrassed and he hesitated.

"I'm headed for midtown," Michael offered.

"Oh. Well, I'm going to the *Worker*."

"Chrystie Street, right? Hop in. I'll drop you off."

"Oh, no," Wiley said, but he was getting in. "I'll just go to midtown with you. That would be great."

He carried an olive canvas satchel slung from his shoulder. It was stuffed with papers and books, but Michael recognized it as an army gas-mask bag. So the kid did his shopping in a surplus store. The shirt meant nothing.

Once he'd joined the flow of traffic Michael asked offhandedly, "Are you actually writing something about the cardinal's press conference?"

"I didn't mean to upset him."

"I don't think you did," Michael said automatically. If he instinctively denied the cardinal's anger, how much more readily would he disguise his own. "I doubt he's given you a further thought."

"He should give the point some thought, though."

"What, the Geneva Accords? Believe me, Cardinal Spellman has thought more about those than the diplomats who wrote them."

"You agree with him?"

Michael swallowed. "Sure I do." Who was Wiley after all? "The Geneva Accords were a French sell-out, my friend. They really were."

"De Gaulle says Vietnam should be neutral."

"Tell that to Comrade Ho."

"Did you ever read the Vietnamese Declaration of Independence? The one Ho wrote?"

"No."

The young man fumbled in his bag and pulled out a leaflet. "This is how it begins. 'All men are created equal; they are endowed by their Creator with certain inalienable rights; among these are Life, Liberty and the Pursuit of Happiness.' " He looked up from the page in triumph. Refute that, Your Holiness!

Michael remembered what Adam said to Eve: Stand back! Why should he rise to this kid's bait? "You said your name is Nicholas Wiley. I'm Father Michael Maguire, Nicholas. Good to meet you."

"Nice to meet you, Father." Nicholas leaned back against the seat. He put the pamphlet back in his bag, then took out a small cloth bundle. He put the canvas bag on the seat between them, and fell silent. Maybe he didn't want to talk about Vietnam either.

Wiley unwrapped the bundle in his lap. He spread the cloth, like a napkin, on his knees. There was a small block of wood the size of a cigarette pack, and a penknife. He opened the knife, then began to whittle. He looked across at Michael. "Do you mind? I'll watch the shavings."

Michael smiled. "No. Go right ahead. I like to watch an artist work."

Wiley sliced away at the wood. Michael drove in silence.

After a time, Michael, casting a glance at the canvas bag between them, said, "I like your bookbag."

Wiley looked at it, then went back to his carving. "Thanks."

"You know what they used it for?"

"It was for my gas mask."

"Yours?" Michael took his eyes from the road long enough to look at Wiley's face.

"I was in the army."

Michael tried to conceal his surprise. "So was I."

"What, as a chaplain?"

He shook his head. "GI."

Wiley seemed uncertain whether to believe it or not. "I don't think of priests as having been in the army."

Michael laughed. "My thought exactly about Catholic Workers."

"Well, I didn't last. I was only in for seven months. I'm a C.O."

"They let you out?" It was nearly impossible for Catholics to claim C.O. status because they could not base their pacifism on their religion. Everyone knew that Catholics were allowed to kill.

"I was discharged on medical grounds."

"Oh."

"I mean psychiatric. They decided I was loony."

"Are you?" Michael looked at him again.

"Depends on how you define it. Maybe. I know something snapped in me during basic. Maybe it was my mind."

"Or maybe your conscience?" Michael felt an inexplicable rush of sympathy for the kid, almost an attraction.

Wiley grimaced. "It's good of you to admit the possibility."

Michael thought of his own experience of basic, of that day when the DI took their pet rabbit and snapped its neck and disemboweled it with a bayonet. "I remember basic," he said, and for the first time he felt ashamed that he had not protested in Thumper's behalf. "They try to numb you, don't they?"

An expression of gratitude crossed Wiley's face. "Yes, that's right. That's exactly right. They want to turn you into a robot."

Michael nodded. Of course they did. How else could they get you to attack pagodas without hesitation? But that was someone else's army, not ours.

"If you think that," Wiley asked suddenly, "how come you're working for Cardinal Spellman?"

Michael shrugged. "I'm working for the Church, Nicholas. I'm working for the children of Vietnam."

"But the children of Vietnam are victims of their own government. Why isn't the cardinal opposing Diem by now? Why aren't you?"

But he was, wasn't he? Michael veered from the boy's question. "Perhaps because it's a little more complicated than you'd like to think. Ho Chi Minh may have plagiarized Thomas Jefferson, but he also heads an army of men who cut testicles off village chiefs and stuff them in their mouths until they choke to death."

Where had that come from? Michael realized at once and with horror that it was an image he had not from something he'd heard in Vietnam, but from one of the sadistic harangues of his basic training drill instructor, years before.

Nicholas stared at Michael, then energetically resumed his carving. After a few moments he asked, almost absently, "Were you drafted?"

"Yes. I was just out of high school."

Wiley calculated. "Were you in Korea?"

"Yes. I wasn't a C.O."

"I gathered that. Cardinal Spellman refuses to support C.O.s. As Military Vicar, he orders his chaplains not to write letters for them. Did you know that? He thinks we're cowards. Is that what you think?"

"That you're a coward? No. You seem to have the courage of your convictions. I know what guts it takes to buck the army. Cowards are people who go along with the crowd."

"You really think that?"

"Yes."

"Then why weren't you an objector?"

"Hey, look, Nicholas, I'll grant you your point of view. You grant me mine. Okay?"

Traffic slowed for a stoplight, which turned red just as they approached. Neither of them spoke until it turned green again and they were going. Michael knew that he had to be wary of his anger at the kid. The self-righteousness of purists always got to him. "I'll tell you, Nicholas, Korea was a bitch. We did stuff no human being should ever have to do, but there was no choice. Even in a Just War, you do what you have to do, number one, to survive and help your buddies to survive, and, number two, to get it over with quickly so the killing stops."

"What stuff?"

"What?"

"That human beings should never have to do?"

"Blow up bridges with people on them."

"You did that?"

"Yes."

"Is that why you became a priest? To atone?"

The question infuriated Michael, but he channeled his surge of feeling into his grip on the wheel. "Christ atones, Nicholas. We don't."

"But you're running the Children's Relief Fund. Was it children you blew up? Is there a connection?"

Michael drove mutely, but he knew the set of his mouth would give him away. No one had ever asked him questions like this before. What upset him was not the young man's effrontery, but the knowledge that these were questions he'd wanted to ask himself. Even to ask if there were connections between his past and his present was to see them. The orphans in Vietnam were, of course, the children of the Koreans he'd killed. It was a link he'd never allowed to come to consciousness while he'd been in Vietnam, but now, perhaps because that conflict had become somewhat remote and therefore manageable, it seemed obvious. But the orphans for whom he worked were something else too. They were the *anawim,* the least of God's children; they were the sheep whom Jesus said to feed.

"I guess I'm off base, asking that."

Michael shrugged. "Sure, there's a connection. Everything is connected to everything else." He looked at Wiley as he stopped the car for another light. "How old are you?"

"Twenty-two."

"I was twenty-two when I entered the seminary."

"Delayed vocation, eh?" Wiley grinned.

It struck Michael how young he'd been — as young as this kid — but he remembered feeling so old. Already the army and the war and the time in China and even Mary Ellen Divine had been behind him. Now it was ten years later and he felt much younger, as if that grim distant past belonged to someone else. When he looked at Wiley part of what seemed familiar was his premature weariness. Barely an adult, yet he solemnly carried, as Michael had, the weight of the world's great sins. Well, wasn't it that a certain kind of Catholic boy imagines at twenty-two that he is the Messiah come again? Whose shoulders wouldn't stoop under that burden? "So I went in the seminary, and you joined the *Catholic Worker.*" Michael put his car in gear. "Two sides of the same coin. 'Be ye perfect.' "

"I don't think so. I'm not trying to be perfect."

"You're trying to be pure."

"The difference between us . . ." Wiley had adopted the lecturing tone he'd used with Spellman. ". . . is that you're satisfied to pick up the victims of the violence. I'm trying to stop it. The Church has always served the State as a kind of ambulance service. It's like at an intersection where people keep getting run over. The Church will nurse their wounds. It will even build a hospital on the spot. But what it *should* do is go downtown and speak the truth to power until they put up a stoplight at that intersection so that people will stop getting run over. But that would be politics. And the Church doesn't involve itself in politics."

"It seems to me that Dorothy Day has picked up a few victims over the years. I didn't know she was opposed to that."

"She isn't. But Peter Maurin says that serving the poor has to lead to political action in behalf of the poor. The mission of the *Worker* is twofold. The soup kitchen is only half of it."

"And you're the other half?"

"You know, you're just like the cardinal. You people think the *Catholic Worker* is this weird bunch of zealots. You pat us on the head for the soup line, but you go 'tsk, tsk,' just like Wall Street when we push against the systems that keep our soup line crowded. You think our ideas are naive and you hold Dorothy Day in contempt."

"That's not true. I don't know a single priest in the archdiocese who holds her in contempt." Michael looked at the blade in Wiley's hand. He'd been cutting at the wood furiously, and now he was gesturing with it. Threateningly?

"Oh, yeah? Well, why hasn't a single priest in this archdiocese joined her on the picket line?"

"Because priests have other things to do, Nicholas. If you don't know what, ask Dorothy. She'd be the first to tell you that the members of the mystical body have different gifts and different responsibilities. Do you really think she would welcome priests on the picket line? I don't."

"Peter Maurin says priests belong in the world."

"Peter Maurin is a Frenchman, isn't he? He's a Personalist, right? The masses are saved by leaders who embrace renunciation and serve through the purity of their intentions. Et cetera."

"Personalism is the philosophy underlying the *Worker*. That's right. Peter Maurin is a disciple of Emmanuel Mounier's."

"Well, I'll tell you something funny, Nicholas. Ngo Dinh Diem is a Personalist too. Personalism underlies his regime. Ngo Dinh Nhu was a friend of Mounier's in Paris. The Ngos consider themselves moral exemplars, and that's their problem. Personalism is the root cause of the evil in Saigon."

"Evil? You think Saigon's evil?"

"How can I not think that after what they've done to the Buddhists and the students?"

Wiley stared at Michael. "I don't understand you, Father. I mean, you keep coming at me from different places."

"I just think it's ironic that Dorothy Day and Ngo Dinh Diem have something in common."

Wiley nearly gasped. "Diem's a dictator!"

But when Michael looked at him, Wiley burst into laughter. Dorothy Day in her sphere was a dictator too, and no one knew it better than the people who worked with her. The difference between her and Diem was that she imposed the Divine Truth she possessed on a small group of disciples and by force of her personality, while Diem imposed it by force of an ever-increasing American arsenal on an unconverted nation. Michael said, "I just think people should be a little less inclined to take their own virtue for granted. You know why I like Kennedy? Because he's not that great a Catholic. Good Catholics make me nervous." Who was he now, John Howe?

"But Kennedy backs Diem."

"Not for long. You watch. Diem's days are numbered."

"I hope so."

"Yeah, but you also hope for Ho Chi Minh, and I'll tell you something, that bastard is doing his best to see that that society collapses completely. And then he'll walk in and set up his utopian state in the rubble. Terrific. Maybe so. A humane socialist society out of what's left. Fabulous. But what about the kids whose parents have been killed? What about the kids who have to live like animals now, fighting over rat meat in back alleys, or selling their sisters to the highest bidder? I know of fifty thousand kids over there right now who are going to starve to death by the end of the year if I don't come through with something for them. Malnutrition, disease, famine, not to mention what the actual warfare is doing to them. You know what we're seeing now? Adolescent suicides! Unheard of in Asia! Children killing themselves because their lives are so horrible, or maybe because they figure their younger sisters and brothers will have a little more rice with one less mouth to feed. See, I think those kids matter, Nicholas. I doubt that your friend Ho does. To him, they're just more casualties of history on the bloody road to Revolution in the sky. Not me, though. I don't even care about Democracy, Nicholas. Or Land Reform, or elections, or the goddamn Geneva Accords. I care about the kids, that's all. And I'll tell you something. Their two best friends, maybe in the world, are fellows name of Spellman and Kennedy, who refuse just to brush off their clothes and walk away."

Wiley said nothing, and Michael's emotion receded behind the abrupt cloud of his embarrassment. He had not so exposed those feelings before, not to a layman and not to his fellow priests. In front of priests it was permitted, even expected, that he would display his surliness or his frustration, but not his exuberance, not his extravagant commitment. In front of lay people he was to display his moderation, his reserve. But about the children in Vietnam he had none.

They crossed Brooklyn in silence. When the towers of the bridge came into view, Michael's eye lifted. Being back in the city still exhilarated him, and his love of New York ambushed him regularly, the way it had when he'd come back from Korea. The sun glistened off the steel web of suspending girders, cables, stays, shrouds and wires. For a moment Manhattan was mere backdrop to this marvel, and the airy skyline only served to emphasize the gothic solidity of the stone towers. The achievement of engineering and imagination represented in the span took his breath away. It made him think of Saint Patrick's Cathedral, and indeed it had been built by the same Irish artisans, masons, stone-cutters, steelworkers and hod-carriers. Many of them died at their work.

Bridges! Michael and I grew up under their spell. Perhaps all island-folk do. From Inwood we'd climbed on dares up the parapets of the George Washington, and we'd dropped water-balloons on boat traffic from the New York Central Railroad Bridge and we'd smoked our first cigarettes in the dank riverbank shadow of the soaring arches of the Henry Hudson. New Yorkers never outgrow their enchantment with bridges. Carolyn and I, after our Village phase and when we'd had Molly, would buy a house we couldn't afford on Brooklyn Heights just because from its living room we could see the bridge, this one, Thomas Wolfe's bridge, Hart Crane's, Maxwell Anderson's and Arthur Miller's. Michael used to sit with me and watch the sun set behind it while I'd recite from Wolfe: "The Bridge made music and a kind of magic in me, it bound the earth together like a cry; and all of the earth seemed young and tender."

"Wonderful, isn't it?" I'd ask at last.

And he would tilt his glass like an old vaudevillian. "Hell of a lot of trouble to go to just to get to Brooklyn."

Crossing with Wiley that day, Michael went back in memory to that other bridge. With its pig-iron girders and stumpy pilings and its jury-rigged center span, it was nothing compared to this American masterpiece, not material for metaphors, poems or songs, no music, no magic.

His memory of that Korean bridge had come to him over the years with a certain regularity, and unconsciously he had ritualized it, had transformed it into the slow-motion climax of an arty war film. At the center of his memory was the explosion, the simple loud clap, the iron girders somersaulting through the air amid the millions of splinters and the dust of railroad cinders and the billowing smoke. He knew that there had been people on that bridge, and he had seen some of them in their particularity at the time — the Pappa-san, the shrieking old lady — but he never pictured them when he remembered the explosion.

But now as the car crossed with a bump the first metal-expansion joint — the threshold of the span itself — he remembered for the first time in years that other scene at the threshold of the Korean bridge. Lieutenant Barrett had just rammed his jeep into the throng. Michael had stooped to free a howling child from the straps tying it to the mangled body of its dead mother. He had taken that child in his arms, and he remembered that it refused to stop crying no matter how he jiggled it or cuddled it. Tears gushed out of its tiny almond eyes and oh what piercing shrieks that baby made. And suddenly the face he was seeing was an old man's face, its frozen look of horror, Thic Nhat Than's face, his severed head. Involuntarily he said out loud, "Oh, Christ!" And then he heard Barrett ask, "Oh, Christ, what have I done?"

"What?" Wiley asked.

"Nothing." The car rattled onto the iron grate, and the loss of solid roadway registered as a dangerous swaying, a drifting of the wheel in his hands, a loss of confidence in the car. He leaned forward over the wheel to concentrate on driving. Now it was the Manhattan skyline that dominated the field of his sight, Wall Street to the left, the Empire State Building and the Chrysler Building to the right. From Brooklyn the jagged magnificent row of skyscrapers always reminded Michael of the rows of gravestones in his father's cemetery, but that was an association he veered from, and he felt his control slip further.

Control; John Howe had said the question was how to control Diem.

But now Michael's question was how to control himself.

He tightened his grip and focused on the infinite detail of the great bridge as they went not over but through it. Finally his eye settled on the bright sky at the end of the tunnel the weave of girders made.

"Have you ever visited Chrystie Street?"

"In fact, I have."

"When you were a seminarian, right?" Wiley was folding his block, knife and the chips of wood back into their cloth. As he'd promised, he hadn't left so much as dust on the seat or floor.

Michael wanted to ask what he was carving, but it seemed, ironically, given their conversation, an overly personal question. He said, simply, "That's right."

"Funny thing, Father. You guys come like pilgrims to the *Worker* when you're in the seminary, but you never come back after ordination. Why don't you reverse the trend? Come on in and have lunch with us."

Michael looked at his watch. The car engine was still running and they were sitting outside the *Worker*. Derelicts had already begun to line up along the sidewalk. "I'm sorry, Nicholas, but I can't."

"Come tomorrow then. Come as our guest. You wouldn't have to work the line. I think Dorothy'd like to meet you."

"And I'd like to meet her, but . . ."

They stared at each other. Each was aware of the charged field between them. To his amazement Michael felt powerfully drawn to the kid. The strange energy that army psychiatrists had found pathological registered on Michael as vitality and eagerness. Nicholas Wiley was more alive, it seemed to him suddenly, than anyone in that crowd of urbane clergy he'd left behind. Wasn't that why in the kid's presence he had faced, if only briefly, the ragged feelings his time in Vietnam had left him with? No priest had yet asked him what it was really like there or how he felt about having left. If he'd gone into the *Worker,* it wouldn't have been to see Dorothy Day. There were domineering saints and mothers enough in every priest's life, and that was why they stayed away. It was Nicholas Wiley Michael wanted to be with. He had an impulse to confide in him right there. Confide what? He was aware that he hadn't even told Wiley explicitly that he'd been in Vietnam. Korea was easier to speak of, and that alone suggested how deep his feelings ran. Too deep, he thought, for a kid like this. But hell, even to himself he was boxes inside boxes, secrets inside secrets. All he knew was that when something shook him, he rattled.

"You're busy."

"I am. Yes."

"Okay." Wiley opened the door and got out. He leaned back into the car and flashed a winning grin. "But if you're ever down in the Bowery again, you know where to come, right? There's always room for one more when you're feeding two hundred and fifty."

"Thanks. I'll remember."

As Michael drove away an acute loneliness overwhelmed him and he thought, But if you're feeding thousands there's never room. He slammed the wheel with the palm of his hand. He was furious, but not with the *Catholic Worker* or the cardinal or the friendly but shallow priests he would now join for lunch. He was furious with himself.

EIGHTEEN

On All Souls' Day, the day of the damned, Jean-Baptiste Ngo Dinh Diem and his brother Nhu, both disguised — fittingly, though pathetically — in the cassocks of priests and cowering in the sanctuary alcove of a modest Catholic church in a Saigon suburb, were seized by rebel officers of their own army. The president and his first counselor were then shot and stabbed repeatedly, like victims of mad killers.

The people of Saigon knew that the Ngos were dead when radio stations played Chubby Checker's "Come on, Let's Twist!", a song that had been outlawed as lewd under the Law for the Protection of Morality. They poured into the streets and danced.

Archbishop Pierre Martin Ngo Dinh Thuc, the primate of all Vietnam, was in Rome for the fall session of the Vatican Council. He would not return to his native country. We would all forget him, and assume that he was dead until one stunning day we would read in a tiny paragraph on a back page of the *New York Times,* as I did not long ago, that he was at last formally excommunicated by John Paul II. But here's the hitch. He was drummed out of the Church not for having incited the slaughter of Buddhists, but for consecrating as bishop a mad Spaniard who claimed, comic-strip fashion, to be the pope. So much for the New Morality.

Madame Nhu would certainly have been killed alongside her husband and brother-in-law, but, as you may recall, she was in America on a lecture tour, angrily denouncing John Kennedy for having withdrawn support from Diem the month before. In October I had been present to hear her Dragon Lady diatribe at Fordham and to see our right-wing student body, to my intense shame, give her a standing ovation. When, a few days later, she was awakened in a fancy Beverly Hills hotel with the news of the coup and the murders, she ranted maniacally that God would swiftly punish those responsible.

Three weeks later, as she no doubt saw it, using the instrument of Lee Harvey Oswald, He did.

Now, looking back on it, one is tempted to see in President Kennedy's death meanings which at the time were irrelevant to it: if Kennedy's ascendance epitomized the triumph of American Catholicism, his assassination on the heels of Pope John's death and that of Spellman's protégé, Diem, revealed the hollowness of that triumph, nay, the utter vanity of it. If Kennedy's appeal to youthful idealism mobilized a generation to work for civil rights at home and the Peace Corps abroad, his absurd death made their disillusionment — their "days of rage" — inevitable. If Kennedy had in fact been the young god we considered him in our first grief, then he had been taken from us because we were mere mortals not worthy of him; worse, in the downward spiral of our self-doubt, we wondered, Weren't we all somehow guilty of his murder? And wasn't it therefore meet and just that after it, as after Diem's slaying in Vietnam, all the devils were loosed upon both lands? When the anointed king is killed, the law of nature is rent, the heavens open, the earth splits and the plagues come. Vietnam got "Big" Minh and the curse of a renewed American "friendship." We got Big Lyndon, whose own death would take place a decade later on the very day that the American phase of the Vietnam war — the fruit of that "friendship" — would end.

It was impossible at the time of Kennedy's assassination to arrange that avalanche of events and feelings in any intelligent pattern. All we could do was behold and ache, and marvel at the shock, the largest shock our generation would experience. We hadn't even known he was in Texas.

What were you doing when you heard the news? Even now, twenty years later, we ask that question and thereby reestablish for each other, for a moment, that bond. The loss we felt made us friends. A vast illusion of intimacy — we were a 190-million-member family — was what we got that day instead of meaning.

We ask each other what we were doing when we heard the news, but we don't have to ask what we did then, because we know. For three days we all did the same thing — sat groggily before our televisions and watched.

Me? When I heard, I was pacing ritually in the fathers' waiting room at Saint Vincent's Hospital in the Village. Carolyn and I had been married for two years. We'd moved to a small apartment on Cherry Lane, across from the theater. We considered ourselves very *avant,* me with my poetry, she with her painting. Sometimes I would pose for her in the nude, but only on two conditions, that she not paint my face and that she take off all *her* clothes too while standing at her easel. She never would, of course, being a "serious" artist, but sometimes we ended the session by making love. It was my reward. But however Bohemian we considered ourselves, Carolyn and I reacted to the discovery that she was pregnant like a pair of Micks from Inwood. What happiness! What a relief to think we could begin now to live the way we'd always really wanted to, the way, in truth, our parents had. Didn't we set about turning our ascetic, ill-furnished flat into a cozy nest, doilies, rockers, throw rugs and all! A nest to which we could bring our baby home.

I had intended to be with Carolyn throughout the birth, but her labor ended abruptly in an emergency cesarean, and I had been expelled from the operating room. I still find it nearly impossible to relate the two events, but our daughter was born less than an hour after the president was shot.

By the time the doctor came into the waiting room to tell me all was well, it was crowded with nurses, staffers and other doctors, all gathered around an old chocolate-colored Philco. It was still assumed that an elaborate plot had unfolded in Dallas, and there were reports that Lyndon Johnson had been shot too. No one seemed to know where he was.

"You have a beautiful daughter, Mister Durkin," he said. "And your wife is fine. I think they'd like to see you." He shook my hand, then moved toward the radio.

How can both of these things be true? I thought. But that was the extent of my reflection. I was tempted neither then nor later to see them as elements of one mystery, as a metaphor of the ambiguous, life out of death, that sort of thing. The events were completely separate, of totally other orders, yet each one left me numb.

The corridor was deserted. From inside the patients' rooms sounds of the morose narration wafted from radios and televisions, but the recovery room where Carolyn lay was unfurnished, empty except for her bed and medical paraphernalia.

Her eyes were closed. I approached and touched her arm and only then did a flood of relief and gratitude course through me.

But I had another, more powerful experience. It is like admitting to the foulest blasphemy to say now that I, alone of all Americans perhaps, thanked God that afternoon that He'd taken Kennedy. It could have been Carolyn, I thought, as if in the Divine economy — this was the irrefutable given of that moment — it had to be one or the other.

She opened her eyes and smiled at me. Then I wept.

"Have you seen her?" she asked finally.

I shook my head, trying to grasp both that there was this baby now, and that Carolyn knew nothing of Dallas.

"Go see her. She's beautiful."

We think of joy as the opposite of sadness, but it isn't. The sadness of that afternoon was monumental and, in a way already sensed, permanent. It did not yield to happiness, but neither did it make happiness impossible. The joy I discovered beholding my daughter was unexpected and unprecedented, but it seemed so natural that I gave myself over to it as if I'd always planned to.

Molly fit in the crook of my arm, a perfect loaf, and I loved her without limit from that first moment. I have referred already to the "ontological change" that traditional theology claims as an effect of ordination, a notion I had dismissed as meaningless. But to my amazement that arcane phrase described what had happened to me. The birth of that child made me a new person, a different sort of being altogether. She taught me in that first encounter that the most radical separation of all is between people who have brought children into the world and those who haven't; is between the way I was before that moment and the way I was after it. You probably think of me as an opinionated snob, but believe me I am humility itself compared to what I was before my daughter's birth. She called forth from me primordial hope such that even the president's death could not shake.

I returned to Carolyn's room. She was sleeping and so I stood above her and watched. She stirred and smiled and slept on. Her bliss, partly of the drugs, was total. When she awoke she squeezed my fingers and mouthed, "I love you."

I kissed her.

She said, "I dreamt that the president was killed."

"You didn't dream it, darling. He was."

"Is that why you were crying?" she asked. Disappointment dulled her eyes. She'd thought I was crying just for her. I knew I couldn't explain that, in fact, since I had thought she was going to die, I was.

Soon they moved her to the room she shared with another woman. The television, of course, was on. And we, like everyone, stared at it, as at shadows in the cave.

Carolyn drifted in and out of sleep. Periodically nurses brought Molly in, and Carolyn held her. Then, since sedation prevented Carolyn's breast-feeding her, I fed our baby until she slept. I took her back to the nursery because it was my wife, I thought, who needed my attention. Even when she was awake we hardly talked. I sensed that as the grim reality registered on her, Carolyn began to hate Oswald for what he'd done not just to Kennedy or to America, but to us. He had destroyed the purity of her joy. Was this a world into which a child should come? To her, the juxtaposition of the two events made them equally absurd, and by that night she was in the grip of a depression I could not penetrate.

When I returned the next day, that gloomy Saturday during which the rain fell everywhere in the East, she was withdrawn still. There were of course physiological reasons for her state. The ferocious labor alone would have sapped her strength, but the traumatic cesarean on top of it left her nothing with which to fend off the tidal wave of feeling. The spinal had caused an immobilizing headache and that, as well as her abdominal wound, required further sedation.

I knew what she'd been through and what she was on, but again and again I thought she was having such intense reactions to the assassination and to the birth that she simply couldn't share them with me. She seemed such a distant, passive stranger that I feared at first our baby would be affected by her detachment. But not so.

All day long we craned up at the television set while dignitaries filed past the flag-draped catafalque in the East Room. When Jackie appeared, Carolyn touched my hand and said, "She lost her baby in August." When I looked at my wife, she was biting her lip so fiercely I asked her to stop.

She brightened once, when Michael Maguire called to ask if he could visit. His call was a stunning surprise. We'd had no idea that he was back from Vietnam.

It was Sunday, early enough that no visitors were allowed, except fathers and, naturally, clergymen. After rapping softly on the door, he pushed it fully open and stood there. He had lost weight and his black suit hung on him. His Roman collar no longer fit and his eyes were like grottoes. I found the sight of him shocking. He looked unwell to me, haggard and nervous the way he had when he first came back from China.

Carolyn raised her arm toward him. He went to her, took her hand, then visibly checked his impulse to lean down to her. *Oh, kiss her!* I thought. *Kiss the poor woman!*

The blur had gone from her eyes. "We have the most beautiful baby," she said. In the vibrant timbre of her voice happiness at last displayed itself, and I was profoundly grateful to Michael for having come.

She looked at me. "Oh, Frank, take Michael to the nursery. Show him Molly."

"No," he said, still holding her hand. "First, let me look at you."

I turned to the window. It seemed unfair to watch them and, frankly, I did not want to see. The sun was shining that day, and I fixed upon a bright pigeon smoothing its tail-feathers on the ledge of the building opposite. The pigeon leapt into the air without warning, dipped, then rose, disappearing above the roof lines. Behind me David Brinkley was describing the riderless horse. I hugged myself and turned.

Michael and Carolyn were both watching the television. They had dropped each other's hands. Michael had lit a cigarette. The woman in the next bed, though her curtain was drawn, could be heard saying into the telephone, "They're bringing him now. Do you see it?"

To muffled drums, the cortege wound into view. The ceremony for which we had all been longing had begun, though this was only the transfer of his body from the White House to the Capitol. I remember the formation of soldiers ahead of the horse-drawn caisson. I remember that stallion, "Black Jack," with the empty saddle and the boots reversed in its stirrups. The military trappings were unfamiliar, but altogether the impression was one of a traditional, well-known ritual and it soothed us. The army band struck up the Death March as the formation turned onto Pennsylvania Avenue by the Treasury Building. Behind the caisson were the limousines. What could his wife possibly be thinking? What could she be saying to her children?

Michael said, "So many people went to Confession at Saint Patrick's yesterday that they set up confessional screens in the sanctuary. There were even more penitents than during the Cuban missile crisis."

"Why do people feel so guilty?" I asked, somewhat bitterly. I could have spouted my own theory. They're Catholics, aren't they? And isn't it easier to condemn yourself and endure any punishment than to believe that perhaps God cares nothing for the world? But that would have been my oh-so-worldly self speaking, the one who wasn't surprised when cruel things happened. My other self, the one into whom Michael had pressed belief at his ordination and to whom both Carolyn and now Molly were miracles of affirmation, knew that people feel guilty because they are not worthy of the gifts God gives.

"I don't think it's guilt, Durk. I think people are afraid to die. If it can happen to him . . ."

"That's how I feel," Carolyn said abruptly, surprising us both.

I expected Michael to respond with something perfectly consoling, but he didn't. He was as inarticulate as I was, which relieved me. I crossed to her side and took her hand. She looked up at me gratefully.

For some moments we simply watched, one man on either side of Carolyn, as the funeral cortege made its way down Pennsylvania Avenue, which was lined with throngs of silent, wounded people. It was like a dark parody of an Inaugural parade.

I resented it when the network switched us back to Dallas, the announcer explaining that Lee Harvey Oswald was being taken to another jail and promising us a glimpse of the man who had done this to us.

A crowded corridor; "There he is," the newsman said. I craned, despite myself, to see the piece of shit.

And then that moment of alarm, chaos, shouts and a wildly tilting camera. The reporter kept screaming, "They've shot him! They've shot him!" and all I could think was that by some mistake technicians had rerun, yet again, the awful sound from Friday.

A woman screamed in the corridor outside Carolyn's room, and then loud footsteps. Michael immediately went out, as if he knew someone needed the last rites. I remained with Carolyn and with that first-ever televised act of murder. I sat on the bed with her and she clung to me, and I thought, This is what it's like when we all go crazy.

"Is Molly all right?" she asked suddenly.

I'd forgotten her completely, and now the commotion in the corridor — an assassin loose in Saint Vincent's! — was a threat. I went out. Two orderlies were arranging a woman on a stretcher by the nurse's station. Michael was holding her hand.

Through the broad nursery window I saw that Molly was sleeping contentedly.

"She's perfect," I told Carolyn. "Sound asleep." I resumed my place on the edge of her bed, and she held on to me again, so fiercely it made me happy. The news reporter was more coherent, but he was still near hysteria and he kept repeating, "Oswald was just shot! Lee Harvey Oswald is lying on the floor! He's been shot! There are policemen everywhere here. I did not see who did it!"

I realized that only seconds had passed. I had apparently run to the nursery and back, and I was out of breath.

The confusion on the television screen continued. It was impossible to think of any image that crossed it as real, as it would have been impossible to anticipate that all the most devastating of those images would become clichés, these clichés. David Brinkley came on and stammered at us. And then we were watching the spirited riderless horse prancing its stately way up Capitol Hill.

When Michael came back into the room he said, "Did you hear her scream?"

"Yes. What happened?"

"She had a seizure of some kind, epileptic, I think. Did you hear what she said?"

"No."

"When she regained her senses she looked up and saw me kneeling over her and she screamed, 'A priest! Oh, God! Am I dying?' "

Michael's weary face broke into that familiar grin of his. "I'm the harbinger of death," he joked.

I felt a pang for him and opened an arm. He came into our embrace, more mine than Carolyn's. Once more the feeling we had for each other, that essence of friendship that would sustain us through nearly, but not quite, everything, asserted itself. While Lee Harvey Oswald breathed his last and while President Kennedy's remains approached the place from which he had said, "Let the word go forth . . . ," the three of us laughed quietly and shared thoughts, as Mrs. Kennedy would describe them, "that lie too deep for tears."

"She's beautiful," he said, though Molly was sleeping on her stomach and wrapped in the tight sleeve of blanket so that only the dark crown of her head was showing. We each leaned on the glass as if to draw as close to her as possible. "What a weekend to be born in. Durk, you should save the papers for her."

My impulse was the opposite, to shield her from those events, even to deny them. I changed the subject. "How long have you been back from Vietnam?"

"A few months."

"And you didn't call us?" I stared at him.

"I've been busy," he said, but he was blushing, looking at his feet.

"What have you been doing? You seem exhausted."

"I was in Los Angeles Friday. I took the Red Eye Special home. I could have stayed out there, but I wanted to be in New York. It was dawn when I got back. There was a message at the rectory from Mom about your baby. That news redeemed the other news. It made me very happy for you both. In fact it made me happy for the world. The Talmud says that when a funeral procession intersects with a wedding march, the mourners must give way."

"You've become ecumenical, Michael. I remember when you only quoted the New Testament."

He laughed. " 'Now war arose in Heaven, Michael and his angels fighting against the dragon.' " Facing me, he said soberly, "I was so glad they were both all right."

"It scared hell out of me, what Carolyn went through. Still does. Seems like that dragon has drawn close this week, waiting to snatch people we love."

"I felt that way. My first impulse yesterday was to go see my mother." He rolled his eyes self-mockingly, as if he of all people was a momma's boy. He was in fact a dutiful son. "Then I walked downtown from Good Shepherd."

"In the rain?"

"Yeah." He smiled. "The rain was good, purifying, cleansing, you know?"

"Yeah, like a carwash."

"I wound up at Saint Patrick's and went in to pray. That's when I saw all the folks at Confession. I went to Confession myself."

"I assumed you'd been hearing them."

"It's the first time I actually just went, you know? Like one of the people."

"I hope the priest gave you the same kind of shit he gives us."

"I chickened out." He smiled again and, leaning on the glass, cupped his hand to light his cigarette. "I figured I could either tell him I masturbate or tell him I'm a priest, but I couldn't tell him both."

"Let me guess."

"I said I'm a priest and confessed that four times I prayed the breviary without paying attention, and I genuflected twice without actually touching my knee to the floor. Oh, and that I've said Mass without wearing the maniple four hundred and seven times."

We laughed softly for a moment, but when he put his hand on my arm it was sadness we shared.

"So then you left the cathedral and found a phone booth and called us because it was the loneliness you felt that seemed sinful."

He met my eyes. "That's right."

"We've missed you, Michael. *Why* didn't you call us? And you never wrote. We were going to be your family."

"I don't know how to answer that, Durk."

"Just don't tell me how busy you are. I'll have one of those cigarettes. Thanks."

We stood in silence, smoking, looking at the baby. Finally he said, "You just never know what's going to happen, do you? I mean we all thought we had everything laid out. Kennedy was just hitting his stride. He was just getting control of things."

"Are you talking about Congress, or what?"

"I'm talking about Vietnam."

I stared at him, I'm sure blankly. I wanted to ask him what it was like there. Had he seen those monks burn themselves? I wanted to tell him that I'd been worried about him. But I didn't know how, thinking, still, in those days, that you didn't just say so.

"I don't know what his death will mean," he said. "Something terrible, I'm afraid."

I watched him smoke. He was already considering the consequences of Kennedy's assassination for the nation, for the world, for his own work. I saw how we were different. I was still in the grip of that present. Implications and consequences were nothing to me. Our brush with death — for what is childbirth but that, and what was Dallas? — had made the future an enemy to whom I was going, eventually, to lose my wife and daughter. Therefore I refused to think about it. I preferred to bask in the baby's presence — she was the present tense itself. Otherwise, like most Americans, I preferred the suspension of time in television that weekend; we knew instinctively that if we prolonged that awful moment, before it ended it would soothe us.

"What do they have you doing now?"

"Fund-raising." He smiled. "I'm a bingo-priest at last." He smoked his cigarette for a moment, then said, "I run something called the Children's Relief Fund. The idea was to build orphanages over there, but we can't keep up with the numbers. Since Diem's death, thousands of homeless Buddhist children are showing up. They were afraid before to show themselves to Catholic priests. Imagine."

I sensed the fury that filled him, but I barely understood it. Vietnam was more than I could think about.

We smoked and looked through the glass at the room full of babies. I remember thinking they looked like potatoes wrapped in foil.

"Molly. Carolyn said you're naming her Molly."

"Yes. Molly Saint Vincent Durkin." I laughed, but Michael missed my joke. "Edna Saint Vincent Millay was born here. Her parents named her for the hospital."

"You're kidding."

"No, really. Well, I'm kidding about naming Molly that. Carolyn and I laughed at the thought because Saint Vincent was a patron of Mother Seton; Mount Saint Vincent's was to be her exile. Just being here as a new mother is joke enough for her. Molly's middle name is Anne, for Carolyn's mother."

"And 'Molly'?"

"Snagged from the mists of our Irish past. We're lucky she was a girl. We hadn't agreed on a boy's name. I wanted 'Cornelius.' "

Michael laughed. "No wonder you didn't agree."

"Caro wanted 'Michael.' "

He froze with his cigarette halfway to his mouth.

"I'm kidding. She wanted 'Earl.' " I grinned at him.

He dropped his cigarette on the floor and stepped on it. I wanted him to admit that the reason we hadn't heard from him or seen him till now was that he still loved Carolyn. Now, of course, I understand that I wanted him to admit that as a way of punishing him. I wanted to see the pain he felt. I wanted to see the extreme of his loneliness. I'd have said at the time, though, thinking myself sincere, that I just wanted an honest conversation; I wanted the source of our awkwardness out in the open so we could deal with it. I'd convinced myself that since I loved him too, it was no big problem that he and Carolyn loved each other. I was custodian of Carolyn's love, not its proprietor, and I always knew it. But I'd have said that was more than enough for me. I was there day after day, and I was certain that over time familiarity alone would soften her heart to me.

Carolyn and I had not talked about Michael, and his absence since our marriage had made it impossible for any of us to normalize our feelings, to grow accustomed to them, to tame them. His being away kept the issue alive for both of us, kept him a figment, a dream, a threat, which now I see was why, whether innocently or not, he did it.

"It's the worst thing about celibacy," he said. The direct, abrupt reference to his condition surprised me. He lit another cigarette, and I realized he wasn't going to finish the thought, as if he'd begun it aloud inadvertently.

"What is?"

"Not having children."

Because of Molly, I saw that he was right, but I rushed to reassure him. "You have all those children whom you help."

He laughed. "Do you know who I spend my time with, almost all of it? Monsignors. Church bureaucrats. The heads of Catholic Charities or Offices for the Propagation of the Faith. In Sioux City one day and Mobile the next, and L.A. the day after that. Always in chanceries. You know what a chancery is in wrestling?

Any hold that imprisons the head." His bitterness surprised me.

"But you're building orphanages," I said. "You're taking care of children whose fathers are gone. You're a father, Michael, to thousands of them."

"But I never get to hold them." He looked at me. "Could I hold her, Durk?"

"Sure you can." Even if I'd known that one day Molly would have his name instead of mine, I'd have let him do it. He was my friend, and, having seen his pain, I wanted to take it away.

Saint Gregory's is a neo-Gothic church on East Seventy-ninth Street, and the rectory is a large stone building adjoining it. When Michael returned there late that afternoon, the steady rain and the shadows from the nearby buildings made the place even gloomier than usual, and it was with a shudder of reluctance that he mounted the stone stairs from the street and went in. He didn't go to his room, even to hang up his soaking coat, because he dreaded being alone, but also because he had no television. He went to the common room, and heard the reassuring hum of Walter Cronkite's commentary even as he pushed the door open. But his heart sank when he saw that, even though the television was on, none of the priests was there. Walter Cronkite had been describing the line of mourners passing the catafalque in the Capitol Rotunda to an empty room and that seemed to Michael, suddenly, the saddest moment of the weekend.

He poured himself two inches of Scotch and sat in the big armchair in the center of the room that the pastor reserved for himself. He hoped the whiskey would dull his sense of isolation, but if anything it only sharpened it. An hour passed.

A bell was ringing somewhere in the building. At first Michael ignored it. But it kept ringing. The doorbell, he realized. Why wasn't someone answering it? Weren't there staff people? Wasn't there a duty-priest? But then he realized that he not only felt alone in that building. He was alone.

The bell rang again.

He put his cigarette down and went to answer it.

When he opened the front door, there to his surprise was the kid from the airport press conference. What was his name? Wiley. Nicholas Wiley. It was dark by then but still raining. Wiley's coat was soaked and his hair matted, and Michael's first thought was, Where's your hat?

"Hi, Father."

"Nicholas . . ."

"I hope you don't mind my coming by. I've been thinking a lot about things. I mean, when something like this happens, you realize you better just go ahead and act on the impulses you have."

"Come on in."

"No, I can't." He looked up at the rectory. How unwelcoming it must have seemed to him.

"In out of the rain, anyway."

Wiley stepped past Michael, then Michael closed the door. They faced each other in the ill-lit foyer.

"This will just take a minute," Wiley said. He fumbled in his coat pocket, then pulled out a small packet wrapped in brown paper and handed it to Michael. "This is for you."

Michael took the package, but he was looking into Wiley's eyes. The boy seemed intense and alert, utterly in control of himself, but also brimming with feeling.

Wiley said, "You were nice to me, Father, and I liked you a lot. And I was hoping you'd visit us at the *Worker*. And then when the president . . ." He lowered his eyes, but only for a moment. "You were one of the people I felt close to. And I guess I thought, well, he'll never know unless I . . ." He shrugged and smiled shyly.

Michael felt ambushed, completely unprepared both for Wiley's expression and his own sudden, nearly overwhelming sense of need. Wiley had pierced it like the truest arrow. Michael channeled his feeling, his surprise, into the act of unwrapping the package.

It was a hand-carved wooden cross, two inches high, on a leather thong. It was stark and delicate. It was strong. Michael felt a rush of emotion. When he looked up at Wiley, their eyes met. When had he ever felt such a blast, like furnace heat, of another's affection? "Nicholas, it's beautiful."

"I made it."

Michael looked at it again. He remembered the kid whittling in the car that day. "It's just beautiful," he said. "I'm very touched."

"You were nice to me, Father," he repeated.

Michael looked into his eyes again. He wanted to say, I refused your invitation. I put you out of mind. I was afraid of what you wanted from me. He said nothing. Instead he put the cross around his neck. It hung at his breastbone. He fingered it. "I'll always wear it, Nicholas."

"You don't have to say that."

"No, I will. I really will. I want to."

"Well . . ." Nicholas smiled, he was so pleased. "I guess I better go."

"You won't stay? Have some coffee?"

"No." Of course not, and they both knew it.

They shook hands then, warmly.

At the door, watching Nicholas plunge out into the rain, the dark, Michael called, "Thank you. I really mean it. Thank you."

Nicholas waved. And Michael thought, This is what it's like when an angel comes and rescues us. No, not angel, he realized then. But son.

The cavernous Saint John the Divine seemed brighter then, but it was only that the pupils of my eyes had dilated. Our eyes, the "windows of our souls," in the nuns' phrase, can become accustomed to the most impenetrable dark.

I was kneeling still in the choir stall on the margin of the sanctuary, but the time had come for me to stand and go to her. Oh, Carolyn! How memory revived my worship! How magnificent you were! How bottomless your courage! It had been the great privilege of my life to be the awed man at your side on the day of our daughter's birth. Those were the things I wanted to say to you.

The sound of my sandals clicking on the floor seemed eerily distant, unrelated to the steps I was taking as I wound back toward the rearmost chapels. At the Lady Chapel I saw the Virgin Mary, hovering, suspended gravity, but Carolyn was gone, and I was filled with panic. Had I lost her again?

I turned and retraced my steps along the ambulatory. Just as I passed the arched entrance to a small room behind the choir, a sound stopped me,. a faint groan. After a moment's hesitation I crossed into a jewel-like baptistry. Windows high up in its tower admitted light, but transformed it, and the air itself seemed sacred there. The font was a carved marble masterpiece the size of a pulpit. Beyond it, against the far wall, was the casket, Michael's casket. I could hardly look at it. My eye gratefully came to Carolyn who was kneeling there with her back to me. She had a hand on the coffin, and that detail recalled a pose of Jacqueline Kennedy's. Grief choked me. There was no Walter Cronkite whispering here, and for once the comparison with the death of the president, which was the loss against which my generation measured all other losses, was inappropriate. This could have been the first death ever; that could have been Eve there, mourning Adam. But who would that have made me?

I approached slowly, as quietly as I could. Even from behind she was familiar enough to arouse a familiar ache. Had it really been a decade, a dozen years? Her blond hair, now riddled with gray, was pulled back and piled upon her head, exposing her neck. She was wearing a simple blue dress, belted at the waist. She was forty-four years old, but there was no thickness in her body yet. The sight of her curving flesh reminded me, though really I had never forgotten, of the dream it was to be inside her. Sunday afternoons, sex, the newspapers, Bloody Marys, cigarettes, Billie Holiday and complacencies without the peignoir. While pretending to idle through the *Times* I could watch her as she left our bed without covering herself to cross our bright bedroom — bleached floorboards, white walls and a ficus in the corner — to answer the telephone. Her nakedness from a distance was thrilling too, more exotically perhaps than up close, the thrill of the voyeur. I could study her body, her pert buttocks, her taut thighs, her ruddy breasts. When she had been aroused her breasts kept that lively piquant color for a long time. If the phone call was from someone she liked, she would whirl on the toes of both feet, a pirouette, and lift her hair from the nape of her neck and throw her head back with pleasure. She might signal me with a snap of her fingers, then put them to her mouth, meaning, "Cigarette, sweetie!" I would toss and she would catch. Her toned nudity was free of the extraneous and her movements were completely natural, musically natural, having neither flats nor sharps. She was as easy with herself in front of me as a model before her artist and perhaps, come to think of it, all the hours she had spent in studios with an eye on the nude was why. But there was nothing impersonal in my gaze, and I could study her for hours. I liked it when those phone calls lasted. When she finished and she came back to the bed I would spring out from behind the paper and take her. She would laugh and I would know that she had sensed my watching, that she had displayed herself coyly, foreplaying me.

Oh, Carolyn, I thought, without you I have been a man with no use for arms!

She was aware of me. I sensed the tension in her even before her head came up and her shoulders straightened. Once more my grief and longing took second and third place to panic; the panic of having found her. What would she say to me? And I to her? It was wrong, I felt all at once, my being there. I was no helper. I was no friend. I had not forgiven Michael. I had not forgiven her. I had tried to flee my hurt, but I had nursed it.

Slowly she stood and turned.

Her face was like wreckage, but her eyes did not falter. She looked at me directly, with that old resolve. Which then disappeared, and her will collapsed, and she shrieked, "Durk!"

She came at me with abandon, the way once she came at both of us, to hurl herself into that swimming pool.

Now she hurled herself into my arms. "Durk!" She had pronounced my name only once, but in that vaulted space, the sound hung over us like a canopy. And when her weight hit me, I absorbed it and held her. I was immovable at that moment, as a tree. "Durk!" She landed against my chest. My despair by hers was nothing. I had never taken such a blow before.

Her hair was at my mouth, but before I could look at her my eyes were caught by the sight of someone else, a figure in the shadows, standing just yards away, her mouth agape. Carolyn's shriek had frightened her, even as her appearance out of nowhere had frightened me. She was, I saw at once, a Vietnamese girl, about eight years old, and she was crying.

Light from a bank of candles flickered behind her. She was an apparition.

My mind leapt to what it recognized — that naked Vietnamese girl running down the road, fleeing blindly, running at her photographer with fresh American napalm bubbling her skin the way the sun bubbles tar, running at him as if his photograph would heal her. It did not, of course. Instead it scorched me and you, a branding iron, the fiery tool that told us and everyone who we had become.

And now I understood that this girl was Carolyn's other child and that in her Michael had found an orphan of his own for whom to make a home.

NINETEEN

It was the night of February 12, 1965. The Tonkin Gulf Resolution had passed Congress almost unanimously the previous August. Only the month before, on January 20, Lyndon Johnson began his own term as president, having won the office as the peace candidate. Less than three weeks after the inauguration, only five days ago that night, in retaliation for a bold Viet Cong attack against a U.S. Army barracks — a single barracks — Johnson ordered the first air bombardment of North Vietnam and decided to send two hundred thousand troops to the South.

But Michael was not thinking about those doomed efforts. That night his focus was narrower than the fate of Vietnam or the soul of America. As he watched the sky from the observation deck at the main terminal at JFK, he was thinking about the twenty-six children, all burn victims of napalm or white phosphorus bombs, whose plane was due in soon. This was the first attempt to bring Vietnamese victims of the war to America. It was sponsored by a Swiss humanitarian organization called Terre des Hommes which had already arranged for hospital beds and doctors' services in leading medical centers in Europe. In Vietnam doctors could do hardly more than wave flies away from the oozing skin of people unlucky enough to have been caught in a "hit" of napalm, and there were more and more "hits" every day. The gelatinous gasoline adheres to flesh absolutely and smolders indefinitely, leaving burns too deep to be treated in field hospitals and deformities too acute to be remedied without drastic and sophisticated medicine. Broken bones, ripped flesh, fractured skulls were one thing, but the little monsters with melted chins and no eyelids and charred blue skin and fused fingers were another. As the numbers of burned children increased and as more and more of them died agonizingly on the stone floors of the orphanages — cots, mats and sheets, which stuck to the wounds, only made their condition worse — even Catholic doctors took to administering merciful overdoses.

Now the Swiss had organized an effort to make that unnecessary. They hoped the initial evacuations would grow into a massive airlift of napalm victims, first of children, then of adults, to get them the treatment they needed. So, with no help from the U.S. government, Terre des Hommes was bringing its first flight of wounded children to the States on a chartered, specially fitted airplane. The Swiss organizers had gone through their Vatican contacts at Caritas International to find a coordinator of the effort in America. As you recall, Caritas was the parent organization of the Catholic Relief Service, and that was how Michael Maguire came to be standing on the deck at JFK that night.

Everything was ready. Seven ambulances were on the tarmac, nurses were standing by and units were prepared at Columbia-Presbyterian, Roosevelt and New York hospitals. Teams of some of the best surgeons in New York were scheduled to begin treatment of the children in the morning. At Michael's side were the Terre des Hommes representative in New York, a young plastic surgeon from Columbia-Presbyterian, and the former monsignor, now bishop-designate Timothy O'Shea, whom Cardinal Spellman had recently named as his auxiliary for the Military Ordinariate.

"Cold," O'Shea said. The four men stood with their shoulders bunched and their hands plunged in their coat pockets.

"What will the chill do to the kids, Doctor?"

"Same as it does to us. Nothing more."

"I'd think it would disorient them, their coming from the tropics."

"It disorients me," the doctor said, "and I'm from Jersey City." He shivered dramatically.

"They're late," the Terre des Hommes representative said. He was a Swiss diplomat, a middle-level administrator at UNICEF. "They would not be late if it was a government plane."

Michael leaned toward O'Shea. "Did you hear what Monsieur Hurot said, why the army wouldn't make a hospital plane available? The spokesman said it was inhumane to take an Asian child out of its native environment."

"Well, that spokesman should be fired," O'Shea said.

"No, just burned," the doctor said brashly, "and then taken to Vietnam so he could see what a humane environment it is."

"Worse were the airlines," the Swiss diplomat said. "If they transported burn victims, even the mildest cases, they said their other passengers would experience discomfort."

"Their *paying* passengers."

"Well," the doctor said, "I can see why the government wouldn't do it."

"Oh really? Why?" Monsieur Hurot asked.

"Simple. They can hardly ask the American people to support Johnson's new buildup if it's targeting children with napalm. This is their dirty little secret. They sure don't want it opened up in New York."

"Neither do we," Michael said. "If the press gets onto these children, Saigon will never let us bring out more."

"They certainly aren't targets anyway," O'Shea said.

The doctor gave O'Shea a quizzical look.

"It is not American policy to bomb civilians."

"Oh really? You think we're waiting here for military personnel, average age eleven?"

"Let's not turn these children into debating points, Doctor. They are tragic victims of war." O'Shea's voice was firm.

"I don't call it 'tragic,' Reverend. I call it criminal."

"Despite my collar," O'Shea said sharply, "I'm not quite so facile with moral judgments."

"I prefer to think of it as a medical judgment, Reverend. Napalm is medically contraindicated for human beings."

Michael interrupted them, placing an arm on each man. It was an argument he'd had his fill of. "Gentlemen, this is not the Fulbright Committee. Take it easy."

"The plane should be here," Monsieur Hurot said.

"Maybe it landed," Michael said. "Maybe it's making its way to the gate."

Monsieur Hurot turned and led the way into the terminal. The doctor followed him. As Michael started, O'Shea took his sleeve. "Why the hell is he here?"

"He pulled together the team of doctors, Tim. He's more important to this than any of us."

"He sounds like an SDS kid."

"In the operating room, his rhetoric won't offend."

"You just better hope he doesn't get quoted."

"He won't. He understands. He's in this for the long haul, Tim. He wants this flight to be repeated as much as we do."

"I'm sick and tired of our military people being maligned. Hell, you know as well as I do that Americans don't kill civilians."

Michael stopped abruptly. "No, I don't know that." He stared at O'Shea long enough for the older man to realize he was thinking of the bridge across the Han River. But Michael wasn't interested in talking about that either. He said, "What I do know is that Americans don't provide hospital planes."

"There's a war going on, Father!" O'Shea blew up. His face was the color of the monsignor's tab at his collar. "And American boys are dying in it. I would expect you to appreciate what that means." He swung away from Michael and stalked toward the long spiral of terrazzo stairs.

And Michael watched him, as sadness clutched his chest.

"Hello, Father."

Michael had been standing a little apart from the others. They were out on the tarmac now, near the ambulances. The plane had landed, but had yet to taxi into view. A light, cold drizzle had begun to fall. He turned toward the voice that had greeted him. It was Nicholas Wiley. "What are you doing here?" he blurted. They'd seen each other irregularly in the past year and a half, meeting for coffee, going for long walks in the park, and Michael had always been glad to see Wiley, but not then, even though it had been months since their last encounter.

Wiley sensed Michael's displeasure, but he grinned. "Waiting for the A-train?" Wiley's hair was long now, hiding his ears. He wore a floppy leather hat and an army field jacket on which was prominently displayed the chicken-foot peace symbol. A camera case was slung over one shoulder, and over the other the familiar canvas bag.

"I'm sorry, but you can't stay."

"Why not?"

"No press."

"What does that mean, Father? Where do you think we are? Russia?"

Michael looked nervously out at the airfield. The green-and-red wing-tip lights of half a dozen taxiing planes crossed in eerie patterns, and the sharp blue runway lights glistened in the rain like lapis beads. No plane seemed to be approaching yet. He faced the young man. "Are you still with the *Worker?*"

"Yes. I'm the managing editor now. Dorothy likes the way I stack bundles."

"I saw your name in the *Reporter* also, just a few weeks ago, wasn't it?"

"Yeah, I string for *NCR* sometimes."

Michael nodded. "Good for you," he said, but that decided him. The obtuse and obscure *Catholic Worker* was one thing, but the *National Catholic Reporter* was an ambitious and irreverent liberal weekly that would splash this story all over the country. The project would be finished before it started. He took Wiley by the arm and led him away from the ambulances, toward a nearby hangar building. Once they were under its eaves, out of the rain, he stopped. "Look, Nicholas, you can't stay here. You simply can't. I'm telling you to leave."

Michael's tone jarred Wiley. "Hey, Father, you can't talk to me like that."

"The hell I can't! You're unauthorized out here. This is off-limits to the public."

" 'Off-limits'!" A fierce expression crossed Wiley's face. "What is this, the army?"

"Yeah, it's the army, Nicholas." Michael pushed him once, firmly, toward the hangar door. "And I'm your son-of-a-bitch sergeant! Now move!" He pushed him again. In the back of his mind a voice said, This isn't the way to handle the kid; sweet-talk him, take him in. But Michael was angry, at the mercy of anger. He pushed him again.

But now Wiley pushed back. "Hey! Cut it out!"

The two men were squared off, and the next move had to be blows. They stared at each other, puffs of breath steaming from their mouths and nostrils.

This was a mistake, Michael saw. He hadn't anticipated Wiley's resistance, but he should have. The kid had taken on the army, after all. Michael raised his hands, palms out. "I'm sorry. I'm out of line."

Wiley eyed him carefully.

Michael backed off. "You do have a right to be here."

Michael's surrender disarmed Wiley. "Why don't you want me?"

"Because we can't have publicity. You know what we're waiting for?"

"Vietnamese children, burn cases. I have a friend at Columbia, in the medical school. He told me. I didn't know it was your project, though."

"Nicholas, if these kids become the focus of antiwar shit, then that's it. We won't get any more out. It's that simple."

Wiley did not react.

"Do you see my point?"

"But doesn't that play into the army's hands? Doesn't it serve their purpose to keep the outrage hidden?"

"Obviously, we can't debate this here." Michael looked past Wiley toward where the others were waiting. Still no sign of the airplane. He made a show of resignation, but in fact he'd had a new idea. "How about this? You can stay and watch the arrival, but you don't ask any questions of anybody, and you don't take any pictures. Then, tomorrow, come up to my office. I'll give you a full interview, an exclusive interview, and I'll get you into the hospitals."

Wiley agreed immediately.

But Michael intended to get in touch first with Dorothy Day. She believed in the primacy of meeting simple human needs. She was a master of publicity when she wanted it, but she would understand that sometimes it was deadly. He was sure he could convince her to call Wiley off.

"There is one thing I'd like to ask you, though, Father."

"Shoot."

"What's Monsignor O'Shea doing here? Didn't the cardinal just appoint him Military Vicar?"

"Yes, he did. Why should that disqualify him from being here?"

"These children are napalm victims, right? That's the U.S. Army, Father! The V.C. don't use napalm."

"The army wasn't aiming for these kids, Nicholas. You know that. Not even the fucking marines *try* to burn children." Michael realized that, like a coin that had been flipped, he had just changed sides. Discussions of the war were futile and infuriating for him because he could argue — he could feel — both positions.

Wiley smiled suddenly. "I never heard a priest say 'fuck.' "

"Did I say 'fuck'?"

Wiley nodded sagely and Michael laughed.

Wiley said, "At Berkeley someone hung a banner out that said, 'Fuck Communism,' and the John Birchers didn't know whether to rip it down or make one of their own."

Michael remembered what he liked about the kid, how his earnestness was tempered by humor. His guileless vulnerability was a relief after the habitual self-protecting calculation of Michael's own kind. "How've you been, Nicholas?" he asked suddenly.

"I'm in therapy now, Father." He looked away shyly and touched his hair. He could have been a hippie; Michael realized he *was* a hippie. "The army shrink told me I should get some help, but it took me a long time to see it. My doctor's a good man. He says I have a problem trusting people, but that maybe I can learn to trust him." He looked sharply at Michael, and a wave of insecurity crossed his face. "You think it's okay, don't you?"

"What, therapy? Sure I do."

"Some priests think it's a cop-out. I guess Freud had his problems with the Church, eh? Dorothy thinks we should just have Spiritual Directors, and let it go at that."

"I don't agree with her, Nicholas. I've known a Spiritual Director or two who could have used a shrink." Michael slapped Wiley's shoulder in a friendly way. He was aware that the ground had shifted under them. The young man's defiance had been replaced by the old deference of a Catholic seeking the approval of his priest. "I'm glad you're taking care of yourself."

"I guess I have some stuff to deal with."

"We all do."

"Could we talk about it sometime, Father? I mean, it's been a while since we got together."

"Sure, Nicholas," Michael said quickly, the pastoral reflex. But inwardly he was backpedaling. The kid seemed needy and unstable, prone like most radicals to politicizing his own insecurities. If they'd found it impossible to become friends the previous year it was because Michael could never quite relax with Wiley. Much as he wanted to he couldn't be himself. The kid was a little strange. "Though, you should check it out with your counselor. We wouldn't want to work at cross-purposes with your therapy, would we?"

"There are some religious angles, though, that my doctor can't help me with. Like, he doesn't agree with pacifism, but I think that's because he doesn't understand about the Crucifixion. Nonviolence always leads to the Cross. I know that. But the Cross leads to the Resurrection."

Michael looked toward the airfield. It seemed to him that one plane in particular had begun to make its way toward them, a four-engine Constellation. If so, that was it.

Wiley talked on as if he'd forgotten what they were doing there. "My therapist calls it 'passivism,' and he thinks Martin Luther King is a passive-aggressive. But, hell, so was Jesus! But what are we supposed to be, aggressive-aggressive? I mean, what's so bad about being passive-aggressive if it builds up the Kingdom of God? Or liberates God's people? Or ends the war? Gandhi says we have to be prepared to die for nonviolence, and that's what I think too."

"Nicholas . . ."

"But my therapist says Gandhi has nothing to do with me. That's what I mean, how can I —"

"Nicholas, I think the plane's here. We have a deal, right?"

Wiley's eyes went out of focus for a moment, strangely. Then, as if he'd snapped his own lapels, he seemed to remember where he was. He followed Michael's gaze out to the airfield, then assumed his earlier manner. "Right," he said. "No pictures."

"And don't talk to anybody."

"And I can see you tomorrow?"

"Yes, but only about the children." He resolved to call Dorothy Day, but had the feeling he should be calling the kid's doctor.

They walked out to the ambulances and joined the others. The rain was falling harder, and as the airplane closed in, the wash from its propellers swirled the ground puddles and whipped the air. The men had to hold their hats.

As Michael watched the plane porpoising slightly as it slowed and cut an exact arc behind the "Follow Me" truck, he knew very well what the moment meant. It had been more than a year and a half since his time in Vietnam, and since then the beleaguered country had become a mystical kingdom to him, a bewitched realm of the unreal with mad rulers and spiraling violence and a fairy-tale curse of reversals that turned every "improvement" into yet another unsolvable problem. He had been charged with relieving the suffering of Vietnamese children, and he had preached their cause with eloquence and feeling in pulpits and chanceries all over America. But in fact, however acutely he made others feel it, the suffering of those children had become a remote abstraction to him. Even the horror of napalm had until now generated a visceral reaction, but at the moral level more than the personal. It was the *idea* of its use that offended him, the *idea* of its effects that outraged him, the *idea* of burned children that made him afraid his country had lost its way. He could not tell you the name of any of its victims. He could not imagine what it was to hold one or love one or lose one. He was like the pilots who pressed their buttons in rarefied cockpits high above the earth. Whom the pilots injured Michael sought to heal, but from the same distance and with a like detachment. When he realized this about himself he shrank from the knowledge. Tonight, thank God, it was going to change. He wanted to take the first child he came upon into his arms, but even that image was wrong, a product of his quite American insensitivity, his sentimental abstraction, for burned flesh cannot be embraced without increasing the victim's agony infinitely. All one can do, really, for such children is to gaze upon them, find their eyes and not let them see you flinching. What they do for you, on the other hand, is obliterate your aloofness. Michael was ready for that, and he was smart enough to be afraid.

The Constellation stopped. Groundcrewmen ran under it with blocks for the wheels, while others pushed an aluminum staircase against the fuselage. A caterer's truck coasted forward to nestle inside the wing. Its hydraulic lift, holding wheeled stretchers instead of food containers, rose slowly. Finally the airplane's doors opened.

The Terre des Hommes representative was the first to mount the stairs, followed by the doctor, Monsignor O'Shea and Michael.

An air force steward saluted each of them inside the aircraft entrance, and that was the first sign — that he was military — that something was wrong.

Monsieur Hurot was speaking animatedly in French to a woman dressed in nurse's whites. The doctor squeezed by them toward the after-cabin where the children were. Michael followed him while O'Shea, who was fluent in French, remained with Hurot and the nurse.

It was Michael's first time in an airplane outfitted with pallets instead of chairs. It reminded him of those submarine movies, the walls lined with double-bunks, naked bulbs casting garish light, but only over the aisle. In the bunks all was shadow, and the children stirring under sheets were like creatures hiding in alcoves. No, it wasn't a submarine, he thought suddenly. It was a cave, a catacomb, and the bunks were the niches into which the martyrs were rolled. The Catholic tradition of embedding saints' relics in the altar began in that first generation when all Masses were said in secret and, because there was no other space in the tunnels under Rome, upon the tombs of the slain. In places, he thought, like this.

The doctor was leaning into a bunk, examining a child. He turned away abruptly and leaned into another to examine the child there.

Michael saw the face of a girl, her eyes hard upon him. To his relief, her face had not been burned, and though he sensed her fear and her discomfort he found it possible to smile at her. She was covered to her throat with a heavy woolen blanket, and belts strapped her in. The second sign that something was wrong.

The doctor went quickly down the aisle, bobbing from cot to cot. A pair of nurses stood aside for him, and a Vietnamese civilian, a man in a white shirt open at the throat, waited at the far end of the cabin. It was to him that the doctor finally blurted, "But they are not burn victims!"

Michael was right behind him. "What?"

"These children have not been burned. There isn't a burn case in here."

"What do you mean?" Michael's eyes fell to another child, a little boy perhaps eight years old whose ravaged face was so thin it seemed his cheek bones were devoid of flesh altogether. His eyes were lost in their sockets.

"They're sick, obviously. But they're not burned." He faced the Vietnamese. "What is this?"

The man seemed shocked. "Why, these are the children for Terre des Hommes. They are cardiac patients and victims of polio and leukemia. They are to receive treatment here."

Monsieur Hurot burst into the cabin behind them. "They have switched the children! There are no wounded children on board here at all!" He pushed past the nurses and past Michael and confronted the Vietnamese. "Are you Doctor Nguyen?"

"No. Doctor Nguyen was not able to come. I am Doctor Cao."

"I've never heard of you! You haven't been working with our people."

"Nevertheless —"

"But this is incredible! Where are the war-wounded? Our agreement with Doctor Ba Kha was quite explicit. We were not airlifting the chronically ill. This was not to be mere pediatrics! We were airlifting war-wounded children!"

"Doctor Ba Kha has been replaced."

"What?"

"Doctor Ba Kha is no longer minister of health." The Vietnamese doctor leaned toward Hurot and began to talk in French.

"Speak English!" Michael ordered. He understood already what had happened, and though his shock was total, he was not surprised. Neither Johnson nor Khanh, that month's ruler of Vietnam, could allow children mutilated by U.S. firebombs to come to New York. It had been naive to think they might. Still he had never felt so angry. His fists and jaw were clenched, his body rigid, as he held himself utterly in check. What? He should have hurled himself against those stricken children, as if it was wrong of them to have polio and not third-degree burns? Or against the nurses and the doctor who had cared for them? He was just learning what was truly maddening about the Vietnam war, both for those who fought it and those who fought against it: the real "enemy" was never there when you were ready to attack.

"My government approved this project," the Vietnamese said gravely, "because certain cases require treatment we cannot provide as well as hospitals in America." He gestured down the line of bunks. "These cases. Other illnesses and other conditions we handle adequately. Your organization wants to help our children. If you think these children do not need your help, examine them."

"But the napalm victims!" the young American doctor said. "Where are the napalm victims?"

"Napalm?" The reference seemed to mystify the Vietnamese doctor. "Napalm is used against the Communist soldiers."

Michael looked down at the boy beside him. From inside the caverns of his eyes he pleaded, as if he were a healthy child like any other, but only asking to be released from the tomb of his body. Michael touched him. "Lazarus," he thought. "Come out."

TWENTY

"YOU were there, Tim, damnit! You know what they pulled!"

O'Shea turned his chair slowly toward the window behind him. The view from his office on the sixty-fifth floor of the Empire State Building was hypnotizing, but the rain from the night before had continued and intensified. Sheets of it blurred New York. Queens was gone in the mist. He wondered if airplanes were flying at all. "We're lucky this isn't snow," he said in what remained of his smooth Tipperary accent.

"Tim!" Michael leaned across his desk. "Will you not talk to me about the weather!"

"Oh, Michael," O'Shea said mournfully. "I hate it when you go all earnest on me. It's how I know how young you are." He continued to look out the window, and his silence was absolute.

But this was a pretense of detachment on his part, one Michael saw through. He had a reaction of his own to what had happened the night before, but it certainly was not anger at the South Vietnamese government. He'd let Michael draw him into something he had no business with. He wouldn't have gone near that evacuation airplane if he had thought it was controversial. Whether knowingly or not, Michael had tossed him a hot potato, and O'Shea hadn't gotten to where he was — or, rather, where he'd be in a few weeks when he was consecrated bishop — by juggling those. But he wrapped his uneasiness in his tough-Irish-priest demeanor, as if the only issue that morning was his young assistant's emotionalism. He said, disarmingly, "Did you hear about the hippie liturgy they had at the Paulist church? They sang Negro spirituals and the priest gave a flower to everyone, along with rye bread Communion. God knows what they did at the kiss of peace. Probably passed around a — what do they call it? — fag."

Michael knew he was not expected to respond and he didn't.

"If they consecrate rye bread, what does transubstantiation do to the caraway seeds, do you suppose? You were good in theology." He continued to stare off vacantly.

Michael sat down in the chair facing the desk; all right, Monsignor, I'll wait until you're ready to talk to me.

Finally O'Shea faced him. "Your friends got their facts wrong. Something was lost in the translation."

"That's not it, Tim. The Vietnamese welshed. They fired the man who'd made the deal. Somebody got to them."

"And who would that be?"

"I'd like to know, Tim. Wouldn't you?"

O'Shea shook his head. "No. To what end? Michael, if the evacuation of children is a political problem, then we can't help with it, can we?"

"That wasn't my thought."

"Well, you'd better make it your thought."

"Why is it 'a political problem' to want to take care of wounded children?"

"It shouldn't be."

"It is, because their presence here would pose an obvious question, and there isn't a good answer for it."

"It is not your job to ask that question, Michael." O'Shea leaned toward him. "We talk about love and tolerance all the time around here, don't we? Maybe we've had it easy. I mean, love and tolerance toward refugees and children, that's a snap. But what about love and tolerance toward the men who are trying to keep Vietnam from sliding into the Communist pit?"

"These are the thoughts of a man who's preparing for a new job," Michael said.

"Don't insult me, Michael. It's how I feel regardless of my appointment."

"But as auxiliary bishop for the Ordinariate, you'll be paid not just to love and tolerate the military, but to bless it."

"That's right. And I'll do that with enthusiasm because I believe in the American military, and I accept the essential justice of our cause in Southeast Asia." After waiting for a comment from Michael, he leaned back in his chair and folded his hands at his chin. "Don't you?"

To Michael's surprise, it was not the interrogatory of a moral philosophy professor, nor even of an ecclesiastical superior, but the concerned question of a friend. No one had put it directly to Michael before, and he knew that his inability to answer with a simple yes was, in the arc of his life, literally momentous. He said carefully, "It's dawning on people that maybe the V.C. can win this thing. And if that's what they're thinking, well, you know what happens then. 'Justice' goes out the window, and what comes in are all the air strikes and artillery headquarters will give you."

"That's war, Michael. We've been through it."

"Not against guerrillas, we haven't. You're kidding yourself if you think the just-war categories still apply."

"But I think exactly that."

"And if what you call 'unintended side effects' have become the means?"

"Look, Michael, get off your high horse. Vietnamese civilians are getting mauled. I know that. But what can we do when the V.C. disguise themselves as peasants?"

Michael stood up. The older man's cool rationality seemed suddenly obscene to him. "We can admit that the rules of war simply don't apply. Obviously that has become policy. Why don't they say it instead of denying that it's happening?"

"You know why."

"Yes, because Americans don't want to be told they've become barbarians!"

O'Shea made a point of not responding to that.

Michael felt stupid suddenly. In 1965, even among the opponents of escalation, it was still unthinkable that we should simply abandon to the Communists the country we'd helped to create. (Of course, years later we did.) Michael sat again and tried to deflect the feeling that he'd made a fool of himself. It was a common experience of ours in those early convoluted conversations about the war, that what began as a clear instinctive revulsion at the endless escalation ended in a suspicion that one simply was not tough enough or pragmatic enough to see the thing through. We dreaded above everything the accusation that we suffered from, as the Bundys were always describing it, a failure of nerve. We were always eyeball to eyeball — not with the Russians; what did they care for the punji trap of Vietnam before we fell into it? — but with ourselves.

Michael forced a grin. "Maybe you were right. Let's talk about the weather."

But now O'Shea was serious. "You don't think I should take my new job, do you?"

"No, that isn't what I think." Michael was confused. What made this impossible was the way in which talk about right and wrong seemed increasingly out of place. Was that so in the thick of every war? Maybe the just-war theories were for the homefront folks, to spice their conversations. "I think it's a minor miracle that Spelly appointed you. I think you can make a difference, Tim. The chaplains will take their cues from you. They are the guys on the spot. You can help them remember what they're for besides saying Mass on jeeps."

"Maybe you can help me remember."

Michael leaned forward. "Everything I think about it, I learned from you."

The two men held each other's eyes, both aware of the strong, manly feeling that bound them. "So remind me," O'Shea said.

Michael nodded and responded as if elaborating the point of a dissertation. "Chaplains are for helping GIs and officers to do what's right. Right action, Tim. That's the main thing. Chaplains are for preaching a clear morality even in the middle of an ambiguous war." Michael smiled and raised a finger. "They should say, 'Don't fuck over innocent people. If you do, God fucks over you.' "

"So to speak."

"Keep the boys nervous about their immortal souls."

"You learned that from me?"

"Tim, I'll tell you, in Korea we were never nervous enough about that. You no doubt remember a lieutenant who drove his jeep right into a crowd of refugees. He had his reason. At the time I thought it was a good one. But we didn't think twice about it, and we should have, because the next time you don't think even once."

"The DI would say that thinking twice interferes with the soldier's job, and maybe makes it riskier for him."

"And he'd be right. In a firefight it might slow the soldier down just enough to make him lose. But that risk is worth it if other times it slows him down enough to prevent murder. It's a risk I'd take."

"Would you have fifteen years ago?"

"You tell me."

O'Shea nodded. "You were sensitive to this stuff. But frankly that's what set you apart."

"It's what you call 'going all earnest.' "

"It is, and I admit it. And it's why I keep you around, despite your fucking foul mouth." O'Shea grinned. "You're my barometer, Michael. You've always been. How will I know the weather without you? Maybe I should bring you along. Want to work in the Ordinariate?"

Michael shook his head.

"Of course not; silly thought."

"Actually, my next job is what I wanted to talk to you about, Tim."

"Good. Because it's on my mind too."

"I'm resigning from the Children's Relief Fund."

"What?" O'Shea was genuinely surprised.

"It's the right time, Tim. The Relief Fund's in good shape. Anybody can run it now. I want out." Something in O'Shea's expression startled Michael, a glimmer of hurt perhaps, a wound. Michael thought about the difference in their ages, more than twenty years. Once it had seemed an infinite stretch, but now Tim O'Shea seemed not all that much older. That meant both that Michael was getting up there — he was thirty-three — and that Tim, having begun as a surrogate father, had become a friend. This was going to be difficult. "And the man who takes your desk will want his own people."

"What if the man who takes my desk is you?"

"What?"

"You, Father." O'Shea smiled. "Bishop Swanstrom and Cardinal Spellman both agree. You're the man for the job, Head of the CRS Refugee Project. Spelly was going to tell you himself."

Michael was flabbergasted. After director, it was the most important job in the agency. He was far too junior. "God, Tim, you're not serious."

"Sure am. I expected an argument, but everybody agrees. You've done a hell of a job with the Fund. And the bishops you've dealt with are at Spellman all the time, how good you are. And I told Swanstrom frankly that if he didn't give you the Refugee desk I was going to ask Spelly to transfer you to the Ordinariate."

"And when was I going to be asked?"

"What?"

"Am I the pawn in your chess game, or what? You expect me to be grateful, don't you? I'm not surprised when the cardinal plays God with his priests' lives. I don't expect that from you. Why wasn't I the first person you talked to about this?"

"Well, because, of course, I knew you'd want it."

"But I don't, Tim."

"Oh, God!" O'Shea slapped his desk and pushed away from it, slamming back in his chair. His eyes went to the immaculate ceiling, and he muttered, "Give me patience." Then he bent forward and pulled a drawer open for a cigar. He calmed himself by trimming, licking and lighting it. "All right," he said through the smoke, "what's up?"

"I want you to send me back to Vietnam. While you still have the clout here, resurrect my old position or create a new one. On-site relief administrator, liaison with the local Church, liaison with AID, an appointment through Caritas, I don't care. But I want to go back to Vietnam, and I want a Church position."

"Good Lord, Michael! You know I can't do that. You've done your bit over there. And the last thing they need now is another American."

"But the buildup would justify it. If there are two hundred thousand military, there will be thousands of AID and State people. Nobody would think twice if you sent me back over."

"What for, Michael? What the hell for?"

"To find those children. The ones who were supposed to be on that airplane last night, and to get them out. And to get the others out."

"Don't be ridiculous. That's the most foolish thing I ever heard."

"You said I'm your barometer. I'm telling you the pressure is falling fast. Johnson has decided to wind it up, and it's going to be vicious. I'm not talking moral theology, Tim. I'm not talking right and wrong. That's for your chaplains to do. I just want to get those kids out. I want to get them to hospitals that can treat them. It's a goddamned outrage, what was pulled last night, and they're not getting away with it. Terre des Hommes says there have been a million child casualties since nineteen sixty-one, in just four years, and that was before LBJ decided to make the goddamned war . . ."

"You're a priest, Michael! Watch your language!"

"Oh, it's language that seems obscene, is it?"

"Your overreaction is what disturbs me. A million casualties? Where does that figure come from? What do a bunch of Swiss do-gooders know? Take it easy."

"So maybe it's *half* a million! Maybe it's only a hundred thousand! Okay? But why the hell are they sending us polio victims? Don't tell me to take it easy!"

"I *will* tell you to take it easy, Father. And I will tell you to remember who you're talking to."

"I'm talking to you, Tim." Michael checked himself. "You were there last night. You heard what the Vietnamese doctor said. They're going to hide what's happening now. They're going to deny it. Imagine what that will mean to the children. They'll have to bury them alive. They won't even get to field hospitals. They won't get first aid. Tim, somebody has to get over there. Somebody has to find those children and get them out."

"Monsieur Hurot is way ahead of you. Isn't that what Terre des Hommes is doing?"

"But to what effect? You said it yourself, a bunch of Swiss do-gooders. But I'm an American. I'm a decorated veteran; I'm a war hero, and I'm a Roman Catholic priest. I work for Francis Cardinal Spellman. Let the army try to flick me aside!"

O'Shea snorted and waved his cigar. "And let Francis Cardinal Spellman find out what you're up to."

"How can he be against saving children?"

"If they become a dove cause célèbre?"

"They won't. You know me better than that. I'm no dove."

"I was beginning to wonder."

"And my purpose is to help Vietnamese kids, not the SDS and not the Fulbright Committee."

"Don't be ingenuous, Michael. Suppose the army fights you. Suppose they make the not unreasonable case that the sovereignty of the Vietnamese government in caring for its own people has to be respected. Or suppose your worst suspicion is true and there's a conspiracy to keep the condition of wounded children secret and therefore out of treatment. You're telling me that at that point you wouldn't go to Fulbright about it? Or the press?"

"If that was the case, of course I would, and you'd help me, right? But you believe like I do that our military people are decent, and that all any of us need is a little moral clarity. Well, this is a way to get some."

"Don't be racist about it. Maybe Saigon cares about its own citizens too. Maybe the ARVN are decent too."

"I'd like to think that what happened last night was just a foul-up, some timid bureaucrat's decision. There's no set policy on evacuating victims yet, and I want to get there before there is one. If I can find out the facts — how many war-wounded children, where they are, what they get for treatment — and if I can take the facts to the right people, then we won't need a patched-together Swiss airlift. The army itself will get those kids out, on military aircraft and to military hospitals. Hell, Tim, I'm talking about something bigger and better than the Berlin Airlift!"

"But you're not the U.S. Air Force, Michael."

"That's right. I'm the Catholic Relief Service, and I know that people working in this office helped generate this war. By God, people working here now can at least get the wounded taken care of."

"You've just made the case for why you must stay here and take my job. CRS needs you at the top."

"I can't."

"Why?"

"Because half a dozen guys can do this job, and no one but me was on that plane last night. I made a promise to those children, Tim."

"You've made a prior promise, Michael. A solemn one, a vow."

" 'Obedience and respect.' "

"That's right."

"Tim, I'm asking you to help me keep that vow. You can do it. You know you can."

"You want to be the new Tom Dooley."

"Why not?"

"Actually, it's not a bad idea. There's only one problem with it. The brass won't let you in, not if they know what you're up to."

"That's why it has to be a Church job. We don't ask the brass, remember?"

"Spelly would. He wouldn't send you over there without checking it out with Washington."

Michael stared at O'Shea. "When the cardinal refused to let me go back before, he made it seem like the issue was how much more good I would do from here."

"And he was right."

Michael shook his head. "He slid one by me, Tim. He just didn't want me over there. He was afraid of what I'd see and what I'd do."

O'Shea thought for a moment, then nodded. "He still would be, Michael."

"That's why I need you, Tim. I'd like to slide one by him."

"What, I'm supposed to lie to him?"

Michael said nothing.

O'Shea turned away, swiveling toward the window. "Michael, God . . . I don't believe you're asking me to do this."

"Tim, I'm only asking you to let me go."

He swung back abruptly. "Rubbish! You're asking me to sponsor the next Don Quixote! You think you're Tom Dooley? Do you know who you'll be? Father Coughlin! It's always a disaster when priests involve themselves in politics, and that's what you'll be doing. You know it too, otherwise you wouldn't be asking me to cover for you with the cardinal. Good God, Michael! I'm about to be made a bishop!"

"I know that."

"Well, why are you putting me in this position then?"

Again Michael remained silent. He had to look away from his old friend.

O'Shea smoked his cigar. Finally he said quietly, "It's my first stack of real chips, and you want me to bet it all on you." He looked at Michael. "I owe you, don't I?"

"You owe me nothing, Tim."

"Except my life. You don't think I've forgotten that, do you? You've never asked me for anything before."

"I want you to let me go because you think it's the right thing to do."

"It's the most foolish damn thing I ever heard of. You have no business over there. And if you step on toes, it will reflect on CRS and embarrass me, and bring the cardinal down on both of us. Hell, I've just begun allowing myself to look forward to a nice career in the hierarchy. You could finish it before it gets off the ground."

"Tim, you're not responsible for what I do."

"The hell I'm not. At least give me credit for the risk I'm taking."

Michael smiled.

O'Shea said, "There's an opening on the Indochina Council of Volunteer Agencies. You'd represent Caritas. We could justify it by saying you're the only one with experience in the field. Actually, it's been a problem, trying to think of whom to send."

"Do you think I'm nuts?"

O'Shea answered carefully. "No, I think you're right, Michael. I think you're courageous and right and your feeling about it moves me. And I'm glad you pushed me. I can handle Spellman. But I'd appreciate it if he didn't read about you in the *Times*."

"He never reads the *Times*."

"I'm serious."

"I don't have an ax to grind, Tim."

As Michael stood up to go, O'Shea got off one last shot. "Are you sure you don't want to take twenty-four hours and think it over? Whoever takes this desk . . ." His cigar hand idled along the edge of it. ". . . gets made monsignor. You'd be the first in your class, Michael. A leg up."

"For my career in the hierarchy?" He grinned.

"It's priests in power who can do the most good. Don't forget that."

By the time they get there, though, Michael thought, after a lifetime of toeing the line for the sake of their next promotion, they've forgotten what "good" is. From many years before he heard O'Shea's lilting, Irish voice saying on that battlefield, "God will not have his work made manifest by cowards." But O'Shea was no coward. He'd just proved that once again. Michael said, "The sooner you come to power, the better, Tim."

"Monsignor Michael Maguire. I like the alliteration."

"Hell, Tim, a monsignor's a 'Domestic Prelate,' right? A former one yourself, you know what that is. He's the guy that makes the pope's bed."

"No, Father, that's the 'Papal Chamberlain.' The 'Domestic Prelate' makes the cardinal's bed."

TWENTY-ONE

NICHOLAS WILEY was waiting for Michael at his office.

Goddamnit! Michael thought, when he saw him. He hadn't called Dorothy Day yet. It was more important than ever to get Wiley off the story.

"How you doing, Nicholas?" They shook hands. The kid seemed nervous and ill at ease. "I'll be right with you."

Michael went into his office and closed the door. Now what? Damn!

He crossed to his desk, sat and picked up the phone. He got the *Worker* number from information, dialed it, asked for Dorothy Day and waited. When she came on the line he said, "Miss Day, this is Father Michael Maguire at the Catholic Relief Service."

"Yes, Father?"

"I'm a friend of Eileen Egan's, Miss Day."

"I know that, Father. She has spoken of you."

"She and I have often talked about the admiration we share for your work."

"Thank you, Father."

"Miss Day, I have a problem, and I need your help."

"Yes?" In her firm, quiet voice, the appropriate deference — no more — was implicit.

"I have Nicholas Wiley here. He wants an interview about a certain CRS project having to do with Vietnamese refugees."

"I know about it, Father. Nicholas told me. He didn't indicate there was any problem."

"I can't have him writing about it, Miss Day. Publicity will bring the government down on this. You understand about finessing authority."

"I understand about speaking the truth to power, not finessing it."

Michael told himself to be careful. With her "Yes, Father, no Father," it was easy to think of the woman as a Legion of Mary type. She was a Catholic Emma Goldman. "I can't give him the interview, Miss Day."

"But he said you promised it to him."

"I did, yes."

"Well then." She said nothing else. A silence fraught with sanctimony.

"I was hoping you'd take my word for it, my word as a priest, that right now publicity would destroy our ability to help these desperate people. I was hoping you would take him off the story."

"I can't do that, Father."

Oh, Christ, he thought, the principles! Which would it be, freedom of the press or the rights of laymen in the Church? "May I ask why, Miss Day?"

"I have no authority over Nicholas Wiley."

"If I can respectfully disagree, your authority over him is absolute."

"Nicholas Wiley doesn't work for me anymore, Father. He's no longer with the *Catholic Worker*."

"He told me you'd made him managing editor." Was the kid a liar? "He said that only last night."

"He was my managing editor, but he's not now."

"Well, when . . . ?"

"This morning, Father. As of this morning."

"Why?"

"I don't feel free to say. You'll have to ask Nicholas."

Michael was too surprised to respond, and Dorothy Day didn't help him. "Well then," he said finally, "I guess that answers my question."

"Was that all, Father?"

"Yes, Miss Day. Thank you very much."

"You're welcome, Father. And Father . . . ?"

"Yes, Miss Day?"

"Would you pray for us, please? Particularly today we could use your prayers."

"Certainly, Miss Day. I'll put you on the paten at noon." He looked at his watch. The archdiocesan seminarians were touring the U.N. that day, and he was scheduled to say Mass for them at the U.N. chapel. She'd think it an awfully establishment place for worship.

"Why, thank you, Father."

After he hung up, Michael had to stifle his dislike for her. Saints are great in heaven, as Cushing loved to say, but they're hell on earth.

How had Wiley crossed her? Sex? A girl in his bunk? That would get him kicked out on the spot, but he didn't seem the type.

Michael buzzed his secretary and asked her to send Wiley in.

"I guess I'm early, Father," he said, entering. He was holding his brimmed leather hat and still wearing his field jacket. His canvas bag hung from his shoulder.

Michael was aware now of what he'd missed before, the haggard, spent look, the red splotches on his skin, the disheveled clothing. Nicholas hadn't shaved and his long hair was matted at the ends. He'd been caught in the rain. Michael guessed he hadn't been to bed. "Take your jacket off, Nicholas. Have a seat." Michael felt sorry for him suddenly. Whatever he'd done, he hadn't deserved to be turned out in weather like this. The *Worker* had been his home since the army. "Do you want some coffee?"

Wiley shook his head. "I try to leave caffeine alone." He removed his jacket and let Michael take it. He remained standing.

"I used to have a field jacket like this. I should have kept it, eh? I'd be the counterculture priest." Michael smiled. While he hung up the jacket he asked, "Why do flower children love army clothes?"

"Because they're the color of the earth." Wiley answered as if he'd thought of it before. "When you take the militarist insignia off, the clothes are beautiful." Suddenly he grinned. "Just like soldiers. When you take our weapons away, we're just peaceniks and priests." He flashed a V-sign. "Peace, Brother. I mean, 'Father.' "

"You can call me brother if you want."

"I'd rather call you Mike."

"That's okay too, although Michael is what I go by."

"I've never called a priest by his first name before. I doubt if I could do it."

"My mother manages, and she's a lot more old-fashioned than you are. Why don't you sit down?" Michael pointed to the large vinyl couch, the room's only piece of furniture aside from the desk and chair. They both sat on it, in opposite corners. Michael hiked his leg up, taking his ankle in his hand and facing the young man. He was aware that his own clothing, his trim black suit and clerical collar, was the sartorial opposite of Wiley's jeans, workboots and blue shirt colorfully embroidered with, in point of fact, flowers.

"Nice office," Wiley said.

The office was smaller than O'Shea's, the linoleum floor was bare and the walls were unadorned except for a Mexican straw crucifix above the couch. But the window looked out on midtown, facing north. Even in the haze the great green patch of Central Park stretched before them like a carpet. There was definition to the clouds now, as if the storm was breaking. "I like it," Michael said.

"Great view."

They looked at the city in silence.

"You were wrong before, Father, about me being a flower child. Flower children have no politics."

"How would you describe your politics, Nicholas. As *Catholic Worker?*"

"I'm against the war. That's the main thing."

"That's not 'politics.' Everyone's against the war, especially the people who have to fight it."

"Our GIs throw prisoners out of helicopters when they refuse to talk. I'm against that."

"We don't have to argue about the war, Nicholas. Why don't you tell me about the *Worker?* What happened?"

For a moment Michael thought Wiley was going to cry, such a forlorn look crossed his face. But he said, "The *Worker*'s nowhere, Father. People dying in Vietnam, and on Chrystie Street nobody even talks about it." He reached into his canvas bag and pulled out a pair of tattered photographs that had been clipped from newspapers. He held them out to Michael who took them.

One showed a boy the trunk of whose body was mutilated by burns; the skin was gone and the bloody tissue was exposed. The other showed an old woman staring at the camera without affect, and holding in her arms a charred log. After a second look Michael recognized the log as an infant. "I've seen photographs like this, Nicholas."

"I can't get their pictures out of my head, Father. I go to sleep at night, their faces are in my head." His helplessness was unconcealed now. "I wake up and I wonder if I didn't dream up the war, my private nightmare. But then those pictures are still in my bag and the morning paper always says we're escalating. Sometimes I think it's making me nuts."

Michael hesitated. The kid was clearly asking for help, but he was already in therapy. Michael knew he should steer him back to the doctor. But it struck Michael that Wiley, in his emotion, was to him what he himself had been only minutes before to O'Shea. He remembered how touched he'd been when Wiley gave him the wooden cross he was wearing even then inside his shirt. "What's been going on with you?" he asked.

"A lot."

"I gather."

"It shows?" Wiley smiled thinly.

Michael nodded. "Mildly. But I just talked to Dorothy Day. She told me there'd been a problem, but she didn't say what it was."

Alarm crossed Wiley's face. "Why were you talking to her?"

"I'll tell you that in a minute, but why don't you tell me what happened first. I get the feeling you'd like to talk about it."

Wiley stared at his hands. They were large hands, and the flesh around both thumbnails had been gnawed. He did not speak.

Michael waited.

After a long time, Wiley whispered, "She kicked me out." When he raised his head to look at Michael, water spilled out of his eyes.

"Why?"

"Because . . ." His mouth twisted with a misery that throttled his capacity to speak. He continued to look at Michael as the tears came and then he began slowly at first, soon violently, to sob.

Michael slid next to him, to put his hand on his shoulder.

At last when he could speak he told his story. "Last night you wouldn't talk to me, but Doctor Levine did. He explained how those poor kids had been substituted for the wounded ones. I couldn't believe it. And I watched you and Monsignor O'Shea going around being polite to everybody and helping that Vietnamese doctor, I just couldn't believe it."

"We were trying to help those children, Nicholas. Even if they weren't the ones we expected, we couldn't just send them back."

"I know. But last night it just seemed to me like you were letting them get away with it. I kept thinking, what did they do to the kids who were *supposed* to be here?"

"I kept thinking that too."

"But it, like, made me crazy, Father." Wiley dropped his eyes to his hands.

Michael had to prod him. "How do you mean, Nicholas?"

"I walked into the city."

In the rain? Michael thought, From the airport?

"I guess I was in kind of a trance. What hit me last night was that when I became a C.O. I sort of washed my hands of the war, like Pontius Pilate. After I got out of the army, I thought I was home free, that all I had to do was, you know, keep my own nose clean. So I went to the *Worker* where, I mean, down there everybody's a saint, you know? Voluntary poverty, feeding the hungry, the brotherhood of man, all that stuff. And as for war, well, we're just against it period, you know? But so fucking what? We can feed the hungry until there's no food left, and that's just fine with the army. They don't even know the *Catholic Worker* exists. It just hit me last night that the *Worker* is completely irrelevant, because nobody down there is doing anything to *stop* it. God knows what the army is doing to those kids! But what are *we* doing to stop it?"

"Did you say these things to Dorothy Day?"

"I did, yes."

"And she didn't like it?"

"I walked all night. Finally I got back to the *Worker* this morning. It was later than I thought. I had no idea what time it was. I mean, that's stupid . . ." He laughed. "The sun was up, but I didn't even notice. When I showed up, the morning soup line was almost over. At seven we serve oatmeal and cornbread. I'd forgotten that it was my turn to work the line. Dorothy was there and she sort of criticized me. She said — right there in front of all these old derelicts — that I was thinking too much of myself lately and not enough of others."

"What did you say?"

"I asked her if I could talk to her in private. And she said no, that I should just get into the kitchen and do my job. But I didn't move. I think I just stood there looking at her. Everybody in the room got real quiet. And then I just said what I had to say about the *Worker.*"

"That it was irrelevant?"

"Yes, and that everybody who didn't work to stop the war was just as guilty of it as McNamara and Johnson." Suddenly Wiley started laughing bitterly. "What an asshole! Can you picture it? There I am surrounded by these poor old farts who only want to eat their cornbread so they'll have something in their bellies to soak up the shit-wine they drink, and I'm preaching a sermon to Dorothy Day about resistance! What an asshole!"

Michael didn't laugh. All this time his hand had rested on the kid's shoulder. Now he withdrew it. "But you had a point to make."

"Oh, and I made it. Do you know what Dorothy said when I finished? She said, 'Now go in the kitchen and do your job.' "

"And did you?"

"No." He stopped laughing. "There's the rub. I said I was going up to my room to write the story of the wounded children who couldn't get out of Vietnam. I told her that I was coming to see you about it. And I told her that from now on everything I did was going to have one aim — stopping the war. And she said that was fine, but it wasn't how things went at the *Catholic Worker.* And I said, 'You mean I'm out?' And she just nodded her head, her fucking head, like she was the queen of England. And I saw that as far as she was concerned I was just gone. I didn't even exist anymore. And you know what's funny? I thought she loved me."

Michael was stunned. "You know what, Nicholas? I felt after last night very much like you did. You called it 'crazy.' I don't think it's crazy at all."

Wiley raised his head sharply. "But you didn't take it out on some poor old bum."

"What do you mean?"

"There was a guy sitting there, just one of the street people, an alkie. I knew him. His name was Slate. He started yelling at me not to talk about America like that. I ignored him. Those old guys are all right-wing lunatics if they're anything. But he picked up his bowl and threw it at me. It hit me on the side of the head. It didn't hurt that much, but, well it made me snap, I guess. I don't even remember thinking. I just went across the table at the guy. I mean, an old wreck who can hardly climb stairs, and there I was pounding the shit out of him, as if he was McNamara. There I am, the great C.O., the pacifist, the would-be war resister, beating the shit out of the poor bastard. They couldn't pull me off him, and the next thing you know . . ." He lost control of himself for a moment, crying, then regained it. ". . . there's blood all over his face, and he looks like one of those people in my dream or in the pictures I carry, like a bomb has hit him. But it wasn't a bomb. It wasn't the army. It was me."

"You know what, Nicholas? I didn't pound somebody, but I might have. We both have strong reactions. You know who we remind me of? Peter. Saint Peter." Of all the characters in the New Testament, Michael was drawn to Peter. And in that way — for his contradictions, flaws, extremities, for his *brio* — he was drawn to this boy too.

Wiley snorted. "Speak for yourself, Father. I feel like Judas."

Michael shrugged. "Same difference. Judas and Peter both did the same thing. They both betrayed the Lord. The difference between them was in what happened next. Judas refused to let go of what he had done. Peter allowed Jesus to forgive him."

"Peter didn't beat the shit out of anybody."

"Oh, really? He cut the high priest's servant's ear off with a sword. Who are you, Nicholas? The worst son of a bitch to ever come down the pike? Come off it. So you lost your temper. So you beat somebody up. Hell, he asked for it. Obviously, who you wanted to pound was Dorothy. Maybe you did a pretty good job of redirecting your anger. I mean, I'd say she really let you down. I'd have been damn pissed if I was you. So you're capable of anger. Big deal. You're capable of violence. Welcome to the human race."

"I think maybe I broke Slate's nose. It was bleeding bad."

"He'll survive."

"I'll find him. I'll make it up to him."

"Good idea. And while you're at it, why not make it up to yourself?"

"What do you mean?"

"People like you and me, Nicholas, we tend to take the weight of the world on our shoulders. Like the wounded children; we have the same reaction. You carry your pictures around. In my own way so do I. As if we're the ones dropping napalm on them. Don't get me wrong. I think we have to feel it, and I think we have to do something about it. But we shouldn't beat ourselves for it. We're not burning those children. Look, I have a certain history, and so do you, and maybe we both feel some guilt about it — you for getting out of the army, me for not getting out. Bonhoeffer says guilt is an idol. We cling to our bad feelings and beat ourselves with the past when what we should do is let go of it, like Peter did. Once you let go of guilt, then you go out and change the world."

"But how?"

"By daring to live as a forgiven man."

"I don't know how to do that, Father."

"You start by listening to me when I forgive you. Would you like to call this 'confession'? Would you like absolution?"

"Yes. I'm really sorry for what I did."

"I know you are. Bow your head, Nicholas." Michael put his hand on the kid's head and pronounced the Latin words. He was thinking, It's the people who don't care about the war who are the sinners. The moderates, the balanced ones — they're the crazies. This kid, he thought, is decent and brave. I should be more like him.

After making the sign of the cross, the priest was silent and his usually churning mind became calm and then, as it were, empty.

Neither acknowledged it, but they were praying.

"What's my penance, Father?"

"Some breakfast, now, with me. Let's blow this place." They went down sixty-five floors to the coffee shop in the mezzanine. They took a booth. Michael insisted on Nicholas's eating, and to encourage him he ordered bacon and eggs himself, despite his obligation to fast before Mass. Nothing provoked the Lord's wrath more quickly than the heartless observance of ritual law. The people who'd left the wounded man in the ditch were on their way to church.

Nicholas touched a napkin to his mouth. "You were going to tell me why you called Dorothy."

"I wanted her to pull you off the story. I guess I didn't need to bother, huh?"

"I'm still on it, Father. I want to find out what happened to those other kids."

"You won't find out from me, Nicholas."

"I have an appointment with Monsieur Hurot this afternoon. He said last night he'd tell me everything he knew. I'm also meeting with Doctor Levine."

"They won't talk to you. They were stunned last night like I was. But they're still committed to the project. Publicity now will wreck it."

"Well, I'm committed too. I think America should know what's being done in its name. We have to get people's attention, and I think this will do it."

"But who would you write it for?"

"Don Thorman." The publisher of the *National Catholic Reporter*.

Michael calculated. He had met Thorman in Kansas City. In fact, Thorman was on the Midwest committee for the Children's Relief Fund. He was a gruff, amiable man, jealous of his prerogatives as a layman and a publisher, but also a responsible journalist and, beneath the irreverent mode, a traditional Catholic. Michael would talk to him. He smiled at Wiley. "You know you guys have been causing trouble since New Testament days."

Wiley looked at him quizzically.

" 'Jesus was speaking to the multitudes when his mother and his brothers appeared. They were anxious to have a word with him, but they could not draw near in that crowd, because of the press.' "

Wiley laughed, but only briefly.

They sipped their coffee in silence.

Nicholas said eventually, "I have to admit I'm disappointed. I thought we had a deal." He eyed Michael steadily, demonstrating, given what he'd been through, a remarkable resilience. Michael had not expected to be called to account for his broken promise.

"All deals were off after what happened."

"You mean because the army reneged on you, you could renege on me?"

"It wasn't the army, first of all. We were dealing with the government of South Vietnam."

"You're not responding to me, Father."

"Frankly, Nicholas, I'm not interested in a relationship with you that's defined in terms of an issue, even *this* issue. I'm aware that something personal has happened between us."

"I am too. And I'm grateful for it. You have me back on my feet. But now that I'm there, you've got to deal with me."

"Do you know what Jesus said to Peter after he forgave him?" Michael lit a cigarette, then gestured at the dishes on the table between them. "They'd just finished breakfast on the shore of the Sea of Galilee. Jesus said, 'If you love me, feed my sheep.' He said it three times, once for each time Peter'd denied him. 'Feed my sheep. Feed my sheep.' " Michael stared hard at Wiley. He wanted very much to win him over. "He didn't talk about issues or about saving the world or about converting Rome or about ending wars. He talked about a concrete, immediate, simple need. Someone's hungry, feed them. See, Nicholas, you and I can go on until we're blue in the face about the war. But meanwhile there are these kids with an immediate need for medical care, and I'm going to get it for them. And you know what? I've got three problems: I've got the government in Saigon, and I've got the U.S. Army, and I've got you. All three of you do the same thing. You put issues — whether it's stopping Communism or stopping the war — before people. Take those pictures out of your bag again. Look at those kids. Don't stop me from getting them to a doctor, Nicholas. Don't use them to make a name for yourself as an antiwar reporter."

"That's not it, Father."

"Are you sure?" Michael realized that now he was doing to the kid what Dorothy Day had done, accusing him of thinking only of himself. Michael knew, like Dorothy did, how vulnerable Wiley was. Before Michael had been urging him to let go of his guilt, but now Michael was using it against him. But he had to. At bottom, for all his Karl Rogers, he was just another Catholic priest controlling the behavior of a boy by undermining his belief in himself.

Wiley looked away. "Well, who does that make you, anyway? This isn't exactly the shore of the Sea of Galilee. And you're not Jesus."

"I know that."

"Am I the sheep you're feeding, is that it?"

"No."

"Well, you want me to act like one. You want me to just close my eyes and forget about the war."

"No, I don't. I want you to go after them, Nicholas, aggressively, responsibly. I think you're right to raise questions and to try to make people think about it. But find another way into it, that's all I'm saying."

"A way to make people pay attention, because it has to stop."

"You can do it. Write about your experience as a C.O. People need to hear that story."

"What are you going to do?"

Michael hesitated. He had to overcome an instinctive reluctance to tell him. "I'm going to Vietnam. I'm going to organize the rescue operation myself."

"Let me come with you," Wiley said instantly.

"No," Michael said. "You wouldn't help, Nicholas. I'm going to be dealing with the army. You'd have to get your hair cut."

"Why the army? I mean, Christ, they're the ones who are dropping the shit on them."

"Nicholas, I'm not coming back until it's army policy to care for the civilian casualties they cause."

"No way, Father."

Michael shrugged. "It's the only way we can fight a war like this and not lose our souls."

"Father, I don't believe you! A war like this can't be fought, period. What, first the U.S. spends a fortune dropping napalm on people, then it spends a fortune flying them back to the States for good old Blue Cross–Blue Shield? You're wacky! I thought I was wacky! The thing is to just stop it!"

"They won't just 'stop it,' Nicholas. Like it or not, that's the fact. Given that, what do we do? We have to conduct ourselves as humanely as we can."

"You'll be their window dressing. They might just latch on to your idea. It would be the perfect way to whitewash what they're doing. Jesus! At first I thought you were naive, but now I get it. You're right. They just might do it! A humanitarian airlift of wounded women and children. It would be brilliant!"

"That's right."

"But they'd be using you, Father."

"I'd be using them, Nicholas. I don't give a damn about anything but those wounded people."

"You're pretty sure of yourself, aren't you."

"I'm going at their jugulars, at their weak point. The commanders in Vietnam learned to think of themselves as soldiers in the war against Hitler. They're the original boys in white hats. They'll kill you, but only if they can think of it as an act of virtue. Honor, Nicholas. That's the deal with these guys. Honor, duty, country. And that's where you go after them. Honor, not guilt. Think of them as soldiers, not Catholics."

"You love soldiers."

"When I read about the V.C. assault at Bien Hoa, it was easy for me to imagine it: the shouts, the chaos, the absolute terror you feel at a burst of explosions right by your head, and guys you ate breakfast with falling over in front of you with their guts spilling out in the mud. At a moment like that the orders officers give don't mean shit. Soldiers just react, and you know what? They react for each other as much as for themselves. In a battle, soldiers have an instinctive generosity. Each man's own survival includes as the same thing the survival of his friend. The whole world should live that way. We should all be like soldiers in the heat of battle."

"But you're talking about killing."

Michael studied him. "Which makes it bullshit, doesn't it?"

"I guess. Except . . ." Wiley pushed crumbs with his little finger.

"Except what?"

"I wish I had friends to look out for, friends to look out for me."

Michael nodded. The kid wanted to go with him to Vietnam. But it was impossible. Nicholas Wiley belonged in Vietnam less than anyone. He had just been kicked out of his womb, the *Worker,* and now he was wandering around with his umbilical cord in his hand, looking for another to plug into. If not a womb, a cause.

Why then was Michael ambushed by the urge to take him along? Come with me, kid. Write the story. Be my partner. Let's take them on together.

But Michael knew. Through his shirt he fingered the cross that

Wiley had made for him, that had so soothed him once. Michael was going into combat of his own, and he could have used a buddy too, someone whose survival was intertwined with his. A Lennie Pace.

Lennie Pace. Michael hadn't thought of him in years. But Lennie, despite Michael's explicit promise — "I'll take care of you! Depend on me!" — had not survived. Was that when Michael had begun going his way alone?

He nearly asked Nicholas to come. What adventures they'd have shared! How different things would have been for both of them!

"Look," he said. "I'll tell you what. We can watch out for each other in another way." Michael grasped Nicholas's forearm across the table. "We can pray for each other. Let's pray for each other every day. You know that line of E. E. Cummings? I'll carry your heart, Nicholas. I'll carry it in my heart."

TWENTY-TWO

On the Vietnamese calendar, 1965 was the Year of the Snake. That year saw the first outbreak of racial violence in American cities and the beginning of the massive rejection by American young people of their parents' values and prejudices. It was one shock after another. In the spring the American embassy in Saigon was blown up and we saw in that flash the fate of the entire enterprise. In the summer James Meredith was shot on his walk through Mississippi; how familiar such fire from ambush would become. In the fall David Miller burned his draftcard at a demonstration in New York, and with it our traditional assumption that the Law was the friend of Justice. In the winter was held the first large, celebrity-studded antiwar rally in Washington; those pioneer marchers would not have believed — so momentous did the occasion seem to them — how little they and their millions of successors would affect the course of the war.

Nineteen sixty-five was the year in which Pope Paul VI visited the U.N., crying, "No more war! War never again!" But that year also, as if to remind us what else he stood for, he formally absolved the Jews of blame for the death of Jesus.

By the end of the year American troop strength in Vietnam would be approaching two hundred thousand, the air war — "Rolling Thunder" — against North Vietnam would have succeeded only in solidifying the resolve of Ho Chi Minh and his people, the underpinnings of the American economy would be destroyed, and it would be apparent to many that the Vietnamese

Communists' willingness to die ran far deeper, even, than the obvious American willingness to kill. Tragically, it would take eight years and the deaths of many hundreds of thousands, the destruction of the Indochinese environment and the obliteration of ancient Vietnamese and Cambodian culture before the American government saw that too. Nineteen sixty-five was the Year of the Snake all right; we didn't know it yet, but the snake was us.

"Ah, dear man," you say, "you sound like what you are, a fugitive monk in the throes of memory."

It is true. Once, at an earlier point in history, men like me came into their own, bewailing the disintegration of standards and blaming it ultimately on the unfettered human appetite for war. *They* were fugitive monks in the throes of memory exactly, Benedictines like myself in point of fact. And for a thousand years they made slaves of themselves to an idea, an ideal, a hope, that human beings can live with each other charitably, at the service of learning, art, a just society and God. They preserved the greatest of human thoughts — Aristotle's, Plato's, David's, and Saint Paul's; invented the most humane of social organizations — the jury, the monastery, the university and the modern city; sang the most exquisite music — chant; and created the most beautiful artifact of all — the Gothic cathedral. And when their era was over, their Enlightenment successors, the direct antecedents of the pragmatic humanists who brought us Vietnam, looked back upon it with disgust and called it — that time of fugitive monks in the throes of memory — the Dark Ages.

What Vietnam in 1965 reduced to for Michael Maguire was the noise of helicopters.

At first he found it frightening and disorienting, and if there'd been another way of getting around the country he'd have taken it. But he was a hitchhiker. He had to take what he could get. Having clambered aboard a command copter or an empty Medevac or one of the giant troop-carrying Chinooks, he could close his eyes and think he was in Korea. But in Korea helicopter use had been sporadic, limited to evacuation functions. In Vietnam, helicopters, massed in formations of dozens of aircraft, were at the heart of American strategy. The Air Mobile technique of swooping in from the sky while Cobra gunships covered and great clouds of dust rose above GIs leaping from their Chinooks like young gods reinforced their sense of being lost in a surreal world that had nothing to do with them. Michael didn't ride on *those* helicopters, of course, but still the machines disoriented him and came to embody everything sinister about the war, just as they did for GIs.

And oh, the fucking noise! Michael compared it to being inside a commercial clothes dryer, an analogy you'll find unhelpful unless you too have climbed into one of those giant tumblers, as he and I did in the basements of Inwood apartment houses. Once you braced yourself against the ribbed tank, you hollered, "Yo!" and your partner dropped in the penny and pushed the button. The trick was to hold yourself rigid at all points so that, as the tank revolved, you didn't bump. The game was to see if you could make it through the entire seven-minute cycle. Michael and I were a team because neither of us trusted anyone else to shut the machine off when through dizziness or fatigue we let go and began to bump. We called it "Niagara Falls."

"This is like going over Niagara Falls," he called to the machine gunner next to him, a perspiring black sergeant who was braced between his weapon and the steel frame of the lurching chopper, but half-leaning out of the open hatch. He nodded, but in the noise he hadn't heard what Michael'd said. He rode as if he'd been in helicopters all his life; he knew better than to try to make small talk.

Michael leaned into the wind a bit, to cool himself. He wore a short-sleeve white shirt, open at the neck, and black cotton pants. His face and arms were a deep red from four months of the fierce tropical sun. He'd arrived in Vietnam in March, at the beginning of the hottest season of the year. On his feet he wore the ubiquitous tire-rubber sandals of the Vietnamese. Soldiers, like the gunner, rarely saw mufti-clad Americans outside Saigon — even reporters were required to wear khaki in the field — and they assumed he was a CIA man. Despite his black pants, which Michael made a point of wearing as a vestige of the clerical, no one guessed he was a priest. Occasionally, in fact, he was chided for wearing the uniform trousers of the Viet Cong.

Despite the rigors of his itinerant, unsettled life and the wearing frustration of endless blind alleys and the numbing effect of what he saw when the alleys led somewhere, he looked and felt far healthier than he had when he arrived, a sallow-faced do-gooder, a citified stranger to physical exertion. Four months in Vietnam was long enough to make him feel that he hadn't left in the first place, but also long enough to dull the shock he'd felt at first at how different the country was now that an American army occupied it.

In four months he'd discovered only handfuls — hundreds, not thousands — of war-wounded children. He had encountered the maddening intransigence of GVN officials, the glib optimism of the American mission, the condescending detachment of journalists and the refusal of Vietnamese pacifists, the Buddhists and the students, to trust him. All the while he had watched as hoards of GIs poured into the country, and everywhere he went he saw bases and barracks under construction. And everywhere he heard rock'n'roll — "I can't get no . . . no, no, no . . . satis*fac*tion!" — blaring from AFN Radio.

One scene in particular stood out in his memory. After his first weeks of searching the countryside for the burned children, going from hospital to orphanage to refugee center and finding none, he'd become convinced that hundreds if not thousands of mutilated children were being kept hidden by the government. He'd returned to Saigon in a frenzy of anger and concern, as if the burn cases were prizes he was being cheated of. He could think of only one man who could help him find those children, John Howe, who by then was the deputy chief of AID at the American embassy. Without even stopping at the rectory where he was staying, Michael went to Howe's office, but Howe wasn't in. He was playing tennis at the Cercle Sportif. Michael went there.

He found Howe sitting at a table on the veranda with three other men in tennis whites. They'd obviously finished their match some time before, but their necks were still draped with towels. They were smoking and sipping drinks. As Michael approached, he saw that Howe looked thin and sickly. His gaunt, bony body contrasted with the healthy suburban look the others had. It was a shock to see Howe's decline. The country had worn him down.

When Howe saw Michael crossing toward them he stood up. "Father Maguire! My God! I'd heard you were back!" The warmth of Howe's greeting surprised Michael. What he'd remembered about the man was his aloofness.

"I'm sorry to come on you like this, Jack, but I have to talk to you."

"Sure. Sure." Howe looked at his partners, then said, "Fellows, this is Father Mike Maguire. He's, uh . . ." He looked at Michael. "Are you still with CRS?"

"Actually, I'm here for Caritas now. The Council of Volunteer Agencies."

"I thought you'd have come to see me before this."

"I've been in the countryside, Jack. That's why I want to talk to you."

"Are you the padre," one of the others asked, "who's been looking for the burned babies?" He was a lanky Southerner whose voice was implicitly disdainful.

Michael bristled, but controlled himself. "Burned babies?"

"Well, isn't that what you folks call them?"

"Father, this is Colonel Tom Vintner," Howe put in. "He's the chief public affairs officer for the air force here."

The colonel sipped his drink. Michael noticed now that it was straight whiskey and it was probably not his first. "That's right, padre. I'm the guy who reporters come to for their burned babies. Reporters just love burned babies."

"And what do you tell them, Colonel?"

"Why, the truth, padre." Vintner leered at Michael contemptuously.

Howe took Michael's arm. "Let's go, Father."

"Hold on, Jack," the colonel said. "You want the truth, padre, right? Even if it's unpleasant?"

Michael was aware that people near by, including the first Caucasian women he'd seen in many days, were watching them.

"Does the good padre have the stomach for the truth? That's the question."

Michael leaned down to him, placing his hands on the table, bringing his face close to the colonel's. "So what do you tell them about the napalmed children?"

"Why, that the only napalmed children in this country are the little thieves who burn themselves with pilfered gasoline when they try to cook with it, and those fuckers deserve anything that they get."

Michael reacted without thinking. He smashed the man in the face, knocking him backwards off his chair.

The bathing beauty on the diving board froze, the play of the doubles match at a nearby court stopped, the people at the surrounding tables fell silent. Everyone stared at Michael Maguire. Michael was more stunned than any of them.

Colonel Vintner struggled to his feet, dazed, and only the sight of his own blood flowing from his mouth, staining his shirt, seemed to make him realize what had happened. He lunged toward Michael, but Jack Howe stopped him.

"You were off base, Colonel," Howe said.

Vintner shook his fist at Michael across Howe. "You stay the hell away from me. I'll tear you apart."

Michael didn't move.

Finally the colonel's other friends coaxed him back to the table. Howe took Michael's elbow. "Come on. Let's go."

Outside the compound Michael faced the AID officer. "Christ, Jack, I didn't mean to put you on the spot."

"He had it coming. I've wanted to do that myself a dozen times." Howe grinned. "I don't have your flair or your right jab."

"Or my short fuse. It's the one thing I can't stomach cracks about. Jack, you've got to help me. I've been all over the damn country. I can't find those children. There have to be thousands of them. The government is hiding them, and I have to find them."

Howe shook his head. "Father, that's cockeyed. You're completely wrong."

"What, you think the only kids getting burned by napalm have stolen it to cook with?"

"Of course not." Howe looked away, and a pained expression unlike any Michael had seen from him before crossed his face. "I guess you don't know how bad it is here now." He looked fiercely back at Michael. "When the air force dumps its shit on a village, Father, nobody lives, get it? It's so fucking lethal that if it touches you, you're wasted. Women and children? Hey, *pas de problème!* Because we got a body-count going now, and it's how we know we're winning. That means every dead Asian, even a child, is tagged — literally on his toe — as a Communist. Get it? That's why there are no civilian casualties. Colonel Vintner will tell you all about it. I wish you'd killed that fucker."

Michael took a step back from Howe. Once he'd longed for an expression of feeling from this man, but now Howe's emotion frightened him. His eyes were distended and perspiration poured down his face. The buttoned-down, ever-cool aristocrat that Michael had known before was gone; in his place was this hothead.

Such anger seemed, in Howe, like madness. And it revealed as much as anything what the war was doing.

Howe took a handful of Michael's shirt. "Vintner will tell you! Because of our incredibly accurate targeting and our humane warn-and-clear techniques! No civilian casualties whatsoever! Because every dead Slope is *ipso facto* a dead Cong!" Howe was shaking Michael now, and Michael saw that it wasn't perspiration only on his face, but also tears. "And *that's* why there are no wounded children for you to rescue. Because they are all dead!"

The chopper dropped. Michael turned to look out the small window. The dramatic green mountain peaks past which they swooped seemed like the props of a boy's model railroad. Nestled at the base of one of them was a brilliant blue lake — an oval sheet of mirror — and on its shore Michael glimpsed the flat white roofs, each emblazoned with a red cross, of the hospital compound. The adjacent town, a collection of bamboo huts clustered around a large, twin-spired Spanish-looking church, was An Hoa, the Vale of Peace, an ironic name now since the fighting had recently come here too. An Hoa was only fifteen minutes by helicopter from the huge new air base at Da Nang, and the Americans had selected it as the site of a supply depot and light aircraft landing field, both of which were even then under construction on the shore of the lake opposite the hospital. It was toward the construction site that the chopper angled. Acres of jungle had been cleared and already a runway was being poured. Heavy green machinery — bulldozers, graders, dump trucks — crawled around on the rich dark earth like beetles. Still the region hadn't been cleared of Viet Cong, and Michael had been warned that the An Hoa Hospital — run by a group of German volunteers, not the government — was known to treat Communists.

"Here we are!" he shouted to the gunnery sergeant, and he jerked his thumb at the hatch.

The sergeant did not bother to watch as the helicopter landed.

Maguire was the only passenger. He hopped out. The rotor wash of air tore at his clothing. There was no reason to run, but he did, from habit. Everyone ran away from helicopters, in that familiar hunchback's crouch, as if they couldn't stand the noise or thought it was going to blow up or draw Charley's fire.

A dozen plastic bags, each with its yellow tag, were arranged neatly in three rows of four on the apron of the square of pavement. Marines began hauling them to the helicopter; American corpses were what it came for.

Michael watched from a distance until the chopper, still brisk despite its sad load, was airborne again. The gunnery sergeant stared at Michael from behind his weapon. Michael checked an impulse to wave at him. An eerie silence — though not really silence, since bulldozers worked near by — filled the air once the helicopter was gone.

A person whom he did not recognize as a woman until she spoke — she wore tan slacks and a loose tan shirt, dark glasses and a floppy white hat that obscured her face — approached and said, "Father Maguire?"

"Yes."

"Inge Holz. I am the nurse from Malta."

Malta was shorthand for the group that ran the hospital, the Aid Service of Malta, a Cologne-based organization of Catholics who did volunteer work in reparation for the crimes Germans inflicted on the Jews. "I come for you with our jeep." She smiled and put her hand out. Her brisk, one-pump German handshake surprised him. A pretty European woman was the last thing he had expected to see in An Hoa.

From the ground, looking up, the surrounding mountains were a rich blue, not green, and the lake along which they drove reflected the peaks against the cloudless pale sky. The near hills had been terraced by farmers, and the neatly hedged walls of piled stones, each defining plots of soil, which grew progressively larger according to the contour, lent the scene the tranquil, tidy air of a travel poster. At the foot of the hills drawing water from canals fed by the lake were rice paddies and at one point the road itself formed the dam between the body of water and the squared-off paddies. The nurse pointed to them and said, "The rice crop has fallen. Do you know why?" She looked at Michael. When he did not reply, she said, "Because it is here in the rice fields that the Buddhists have their dead buried. So many dead, so many killed, the seedlings choke."

Michael no longer reacted to such epiphanies with shock, and he knew why. The corpses were piled inside him too by now, choking feeling. He was afraid of his own numbness. "Around here?" he asked. He wanted to confront directly what she was telling him. He wanted to learn how the local horror was unique. "It's been that bad?"

"Since the marines, yes."

"They're trying to secure the area for their base, I guess."

"Always before the Viet Cong had left us alone. Now there is reason to come. They have something to attack. The marines have made the area less secure, not more. That is very bad, you understand."

"And your hospital treats mainly victims of the fighting?"

"Now, yes."

"And before?"

"Always leprosy."

Michael shuddered despite himself and fell silent.

He found himself thinking that the nurse's accent was wrong. The Europeans in Vietnam were French, not German. Germans were from that other war, that just one. He reminded himself that despite what the Ministry of Health official in Da Nang had said about her hospital, she was not the enemy. Sidelong, he looked at her. She had sharp features, and her face, what he could see of it for the hat and her glasses, was weathered brown. Premature lines at her mouth and eyes indicated the disregarded weariness that was habitual among volunteers. He watched her hands playing upon the wheel and gearshift. She drove with an *esprit* that bordered on the reckless, but which stimulated him almost erotically, even as he held on. The only flesh that he could see besides her face was that of her hand and forearm. He traced its outline until her skin was lost in the rolled sleeve. A perspiration stain emphasized the seam of her shirt. Now he saw the form of her breast. She raised her hand to tuck an elusive wisp of blond hair — how had he not noticed it? — up into her hat.

"How big is your hospital?" he asked, to rein his mind.

She shrugged, downshifted efficiently to take a curve, then speeded up again. "One hundred twenty beds, five nurses, one permanent doctor and two doctors from Da Nang. We have six clinics in surrounding villages, but since the marines it is impossible getting to three. Those clinics are, so to speak, closed."

"Have the Communists taken them over?"

She nodded. "That can be possible."

"I heard the NLF is strong everywhere out here."

She laughed. "Not in the daytime."

It was difficult to talk in the open jeep. His questions tripped over one another in his brain, but he waited. He wanted to see her face more clearly when she answered him. He sat back against the worn seat and enjoyed the wash of air. The scenery was stunning. The lake amid the mountains, like water in a cup, reminded him of the lake at Bear Mountain up the Hudson where the priests of Good Shepherd took altar boys on camping trips.

Soon they approached the hospital compound. "*Voilà,*" she said, turning in.

Michael saw four whitewashed stucco buildings, only one of which was two stories high. Huge overarching palms cast delicate shadows and a breeze off the lake cooled the air. Between the buildings were makeshift shelters, palm branches stretched across bamboo frames, and under them were the inert forms of dozens of Vietnamese men and women. At first Michael gasped, thinking they were corpses.

Fräulein Holz noticed his reaction. "They are the families of our patients."

"But they look dead, like a massacre."

She shook her head. "It is siesta, Father. Even during war the people need siesta." When she'd brought the jeep to a halt and shut the engine off, she said, "I told you one hundred twenty beds. What I have not said is in each bed two patients, and in children's ward, three."

"Do you see burns in your hospital?"

"Not often."

"When I came over I was very conscious of napalm."

She shrugged, callously. "If all weapons were like napalm, Father, people like us would not be needed."

"Forgive me, but there is a question I must ask you. I was told your hospital and dispensaries supply the Viet Cong with medicine."

She seemed amazed. She said, "They steal our medicine. We can do nothing."

"Do you lock it?"

"Of course we lock. Our medicine is precious. We have to ship it in from Germany."

"The government doesn't supply you because you are considered partisans."

She reached across from the driver's seat and took the cigarette he offered. While she lit it from his match she shook her head. "The government does not supply us because we will not black market with the district chief. He asks always a quarter of our drugs."

"You don't treat the Viet Cong?"

"We treat diseases and wounds."

"V.C. wounds?"

Inge Holz smiled at him through her smoke. "Is this *Beichte*, Father? Confession?"

"I think you ought to know what I've been told. Your hospital would be closed if you weren't German nationals."

"We treat all people who come to us."

Michael stared at her, then nodded. "Good. Then I'll stick up for you. The Council of Volunteer Agencies was asked to withdraw its certification from you."

But she wasn't grateful. "You collect evidence? Why should I believe you are a priest?"

Michael smiled. "I am, really."

"But perhaps a priest with the CIA. Priests in this country work for the government. What will you do with me, some head-shaving, no?" Now she smiled, but cynically.

He shook his head. "Nothing so exciting. Just what I said in my letter. Just a survey of hospital facilities for the Council." He paused. "When I first came, it was to lay the groundwork for an evacuation of wounded children to the States, but I've had no luck with that."

"Luck!" She laughed, then looked at him bitterly. "Why should you have luck here?"

She got out of the jeep, flicking the cigarette away. He followed her, for his tour of her hospital.

Children ranging in age from perhaps eight to twelve years old were gathered on their haunches around Michael in the shadow of a palm tree in the hospital yard. It was late afternoon of the next day, and the children, having overcome their bashfulness, were helping the tall American practice his Vietnamese.

In his time Michael had mastered not many more than a dozen rudimentary phrases. He had no gift for language. But he'd won the children over with his animation, his flamboyant gestures, his great-hearted but finally laughable rendition of words they took for granted.

"*Chào ong,*" he said earnestly.

The children laughed and clapped their hands at him because the phrase meant "good morning," and here it was afternoon. None of them dared correct him.

"*Tôi la, Père Michel.*" My name is Father Michael. "*Tên ông là gi?*" What is your name? He repeated the question until one of the children answered him, a boy who said his name was Tran. Michael bowed to him. The other children grew silent. Everyone waited for Tran to speak, as politeness required.

"*Ông sē ô lai bao lâu?*"

Michael made him repeat it very slowly until he understood; how long will you stay?

"*Thú-nam,*" he answered. Until Thursday.

Tran bowed, making it clear that the exchange satisfied what need he had to expose himself to the stranger. After that Michael found it impossible to draw out the children further. It was then, to prolong the encounter, that he began reciting all the phrases he could remember. He came to one that a boy in Pleiku had taught him. "*Doàn thanh niên ta Vung lòng tâm tri.*" We, the youth of the nation, must remain firm and determined.

Abruptly the children rose and scampered away, to rejoin their relatives under the bamboo shelters.

Inge Holz had been watching from the veranda of one of the buildings. Michael stood and crossed to her. "What happened?"

"They are afraid of that."

"Of that saying?"

"It is not a saying, Father. It is a line from the national anthem. The ARVN soldiers must sing it while marching, but in the villages singing this is dangerous crime. The NLF will cut out your tongue."

"I thought it was just a slogan."

"What is 'slogan'?"

"It's, well, just a saying."

"So. But here, nothing is just slogan."

Michael looked across the compound. The children had dispersed. He couldn't see them. He wanted to run after them and say he wasn't testing them. He wasn't trapping them. He wanted to apologize. He felt disgusted with himself.

He remembered the paper he was holding, a leaflet one of the children had given him. He held it up. "Is your Vietnamese good enough to translate this?"

She took it and read in a dead voice, but without stumbling, "The wicked Viet Cong have stored weapons and supplies in your village. Soon air force gunfire is going to be conducted on your village to destroy these Viet Cong supplies. We ask that you leave your village, as we do not wish to kill innocent people. And when you return to your village repel the Viet Cong so that the government will not have to fire on your village again."

Inge Holz handed the leaflet back to Michael and turned and walked away from him.

TWENTY-THREE

ACROSS from the hospital compound was the lake Michael had seen from the helicopter. Along its edge ran a sliver of a beach, and he was walking it, barefoot. It had been four days since he'd arrived. He'd visited the dispensaries that were still active there and he'd interviewed the Malta staff. It was time to move on, but Michael was in the grip of an unusual lethargy. He didn't understand anymore what he was doing there. His round of visitations seemed pointless.

The water lapped gently against the cuticle of sand, and Michael let it bathe his feet as he walked absently along. Perhaps half a mile from the compound he was startled to come upon a bather's towel stretched on the beach, and near it a tattered straw basket. A pair of pilot's sunglasses lay on the towel next to a propped-open book. He looked out at the water. In the glare it took a moment to spot the swimmer, a moving speck far out in the lake. Who was it?

He looked at the book. The title was in German and at first he assumed he wouldn't know it, but then he saw the author's name, Ignace Lepp, and recognized the title, in translation *The Christian Failure*. It was a book Michael had read in the seminary, an indictment of the German Catholic clergy for its willingness to cooperate with Hitler. He picked the book up. Inside the cover was written the name, in tight, European script, *Inge Holz*.

Why is she reading this? he wondered. He stared out at the lake.

She was so far away. As he watched the speck growing even smaller, he found himself imagining her body moving through the water, arms and legs working, head turning up for air, hair trailing. It was a surprise to him how easily he could call up her image — her body was lithe, not voluptuous, but lovely — and only then did he realize how her subtle womanliness had affected him.

Crazily he thought of the notorious Viet Cong ploy: maidens swimming naked in a lake, waving at passing GIs, beckoning them. The GIs drop their rifles, dash across the sand, undoing their web-belts, then fall suddenly through a punji trap, taking dung-coated razor spikes the length of their bodies. Seduce and destroy.

Michael shuddered and dismissed the image. What was happening to him?

He took off his shirt and his black chinos, stripping to his brown, army-issue boxer-shorts. Absently he touched Wiley's wooden cross at his chest as he walked into the water. When it was waist-deep he dove in and went after her. He was a strong swimmer, and before long he'd caught up with her, and simply fell into pace. They matched each other, stroke for stroke, until she turned over on her back. He did likewise and they began the return lap. They never looked at each other or spoke. Michael fixed his concentration on the fierce blue of the sky. By the time they reached the beach again they'd been swimming in sync with each other for twenty minutes. What a relief to have left behind the jarring edginess that had made their encounters so awkward. The fluidity of swimming, the instinctive common rhythm of their timing, made Michael feel as though they'd been intimate with each other.

She went ahead of him to her towel. He felt self-conscious about being in his underwear but stifled the impulse to pull on his chinos quickly, lest she think him prudish. The brown shorts in fact were perfectly modest. He sat on the sand a little apart and watched her drying herself. She wore an ordinary blue bathing suit. As she toweled her hair he saw the magical impress of her nipples through her suit; the sight stirred him, but also underscored his inexperience; nipples grew erect either through arousal, wasn't it, or cold?

Her hair was long, to her shoulders, half-brown, half-blond. It brushed at her shoulders, at her breasts. His eye fell to her deeply tanned legs, their subtle curves. He saw the flash of white between her thighs where she had not shown herself to the sun. She seemed oblivious to the effect on him of her drying herself. He stared at her as if he'd rarely seen the feminine form so displayed, which was true, of course. Inadvertently, naturally, she was outflanking his careful, measured, clerical reserve.

She offered him her towel. He declined.

She spread it again and sat.

To his regret she put on her sunglasses. He reached for his shirt, for his cigarettes. He offered her one and she accepted. He crossed to her, lit their cigarettes from one match, and then sat an arm's length and a little more away.

He couldn't think what to say. I admire your work? Why aren't you modeling fancy dresses in Berlin? Where'd you learn to swim so well?

He said finally, "I noticed your book."

She glanced at it and nodded.

"Not what I would call beach reading."

She pulled her knees close to her chest and linked her arms around them. "Difficult reading," she said, "for a German Catholic."

"Is that why you joined Malta? Is that why you are here?" How had Nicholas Wiley put it? To atone?

She shrugged, moved the book aside absently with her foot. "In Mainz, my own archbishop. He gave sermons at the cathedral. He said the Jews were termites."

"Termites?"

She thought she'd mispronounced it. "An insect that destroys a house by eating the wood. *Die Termite*. I remember the word distinctly. That week houses in Jewish Quarter of Mainz were for the first time burned."

"You remember that?"

"Yes."

They fell silent, smoking.

After a long time, Michael said, "So you're from Mainz. I'm from New York."

"Ah!" She buried the tip of her cigarette in the sand. "Cardinal Spellman."

"That's right."

"He came at Christmas to the air base at Da Nang. They wanted us to go there for his Mass. All the volunteers, to receive his blessing. To kiss his ring. I would not."

Michael stared at her. He sensed the depth of her feeling. Her strength. She reminded him of someone. Carolyn, of course.

She said, "To hear him preach against the termites."

"Cardinal Spellman doesn't speak for me on the subject of Vietnam, Fräulein."

"Oh? Who does?"

Michael had to think about it. "No one."

She nodded. "So it was with us."

He shook his head. "I understand your point of view. You think of me as just another marine, but I'm not."

"You think because you visit hospitals that makes you different. But you ride in their helicopters. You are friendly with the men who do these things." She looked at him sharply. The sun glinted off her dark glasses. "Forgive me, Father, but you are like the girls who wait outside their camps. When you are there they are happy about what they do. All the better if they can . . ." She shrugged instead of finishing.

". . . screw me."

She laughed. "Yes."

"Am I so different from you? Anybody here who tries to soften the blows becomes part of the situation that makes them possible."

"I do not like your war, Father. I do not want that you Americans do these things here, and I think you should make a stop." In her anger her English grew more confused.

"Me?"

"Yes."

"You think I should just go home and lead the rosary in a parish in the suburbs?"

"You said you wanted to help the children. So you go home and tell your people what their soldiers and pilots do to the children." She looked away. When she put her hand to her mouth, Michael saw that it was trembling.

"Fräulein . . ."

"I was four years old, but also sing 'Deutschland über Alles' in church. I see priests making the Nazi salute from the altar."

He reached his hand across to touch her shoulder. "I'm not one of those priests, Fräulein."

"You are Spellman's priest, yes?"

"And should I wear a yellow star?"

She slapped his face, hard. He ignored the blow. "Are you Germans all alike?"

"My God, I think, yes! So now some of us are here. You will also leave it to your children to denounce twenty years from now what your country is doing?"

"Fräulein, you are wrong."

"If I was wrong, you would not listen. But always you listen, though you know now what I am saying. Why is that?"

He couldn't answer her.

"You have seen it with your own eyes. You know I am right."

It was as if she'd hit him again; this time he felt it. She was forcing him to see what these months had taught him, cost him. Spellman's priest? Yes. He was back to that, at last. A man with no conscience of his own. No capacity to act. This war had the blessing of the one to whom he'd handed over his soul. Therefore he couldn't oppose the war, he could only hate it. Now it was Michael who trembled. He tried to control himself by fumbling for a cigarette, but when he struck a match he could not keep it lit.

He felt naked suddenly. This woman was staring at him. He *was* naked. He turned away, pretending to turn from the wind, to light his match.

When he had his cigarette lit he rubbed his hair, then pressed the heels of his hands against his eyes. "I ride on helicopters, yes. Once I rode with twenty American kids, GIs, just like fellows I grew up with, fellows like me. Except for one thing. They were all dead. I was the only one in the helicopter alive, the only one not in a bag." He stopped for a moment to breathe, then said, "And the Vietnamese, the *loyal* ones, the *Catholics* at your hospital, won't even recite a phrase from the national anthem! Christ! And we call it 'Winning Hearts and Minds'!" He slammed his fist into the sand. "Also known as WHAM!"

After a moment Inge Holz said softly, "They are not Catholics."

"They have pictures of the Sacred Heart and the pope hanging in their hooches."

She laughed. She reached across to squeeze his arm, the first sign of warmth she had yet shown him. Her eyes twinkled at him, to her he seemed so naive. She saw how devastated he was. "They have pictures of Ho Chi Minh too, but hidden. They know we are a Catholic hospital. They think we want those pictures everywhere."

Michael laughed and slapped his forehead. Her touch had soothed something in him. "They were so nice to me. I thought it was because I am a priest."

"They are nice to you when you are so nice to them. I have watched you with patients. You are a kind man. You are not a marine. I did not mean to say that."

Now she took off her glasses and let him see her eyes. "Father," she said, "I talk to you directly because I see you with my people. I see you are good."

He did not look away from her. Suddenly she made him feel all right. As if she knew how much he wanted her to, she touched him again, resting her hand on his arm.

He was acutely conscious of the feel of her fingers, how they had no weight, but caused sensation right to the bone. He wanted to take her into his arms and bury his face in her hair. Are you in love with someone? he would ask. And when she said no, he could ask her to be his friend. That was how he'd put it; perhaps we can be friends. He imagined her agreeing. She would stop being aloof and accusing. She would be like him; vulnerable, unsure of what such feelings meant, afraid of expressing them, yet desperate to.

Ah, poor Michael. The man's loneliness, just thinking of it, undoes me. It was of course the loneliness of a man at sea with himself, a man approaching yet another impossible choice. That loneliness we all know. But his was the further loneliness of the avowed celibate. Figments of women were as much at the center of his inner life as any man's but his figments were of a type. The love of his life, remember, had been a nun. He was immune to the charms of Saigon whores and of the pampered, bikini-clad *colonistes* of the Cercle Sportif. The tough-talking American women correspondents struck him, with their swagger, their blatant if rough-hewn sensuality, their lust for gruesome copy, as crude parodies of the male safari-jacket type. The nurses he'd encountered were noble and strong, like this German, but they lacked her attachment to the full truth. Her willingness to see beyond the victims she treated to their victimizers, and the rare ability to sustain compassion for the first while honing her fury at the second were what moved him. Michael wanted to be like her. And, yes, he wanted to possess her. He was like many priests; only purity could seduce him. When he looked down at her then, the lines of her body, the tracery of her womanliness, breasts and hips, thighs, dominated his perception. The vise-grip in which he held his desire — priest's vice — loosened for a moment. If he imagined lying with her, naked; if he imagined making love to her, it was because she, unlike the whores and *colonistes* and adventurer-correspondents, seemed the opposite of everything he'd encountered in Vietnam. But wait. Wasn't it his fear exactly that once he disavowed his place in the middle of the road — it is necessary to pursue the war, but we should do so humanely — his grip on moderation itself would slip? If he could call into question his patriotism, the bedrock virtue, what would happen to his other commitments? To his celibacy? In other words, didn't both his priestly vocation and the integrity of his fresh rejection of the American war depend on his carefully sustained detachment? Detachment from her? If he was going to place himself above the moral standard of his own people, he could do so only as a man of virtue. With this woman he could perhaps have softened the pain he felt because of the war, but wasn't it his duty now to keep that pain sharp and find a way to act on it? The thing was to stop the war, not his hurting. Thus, he steered not only their talk, but his train of thought away from his attraction to her. Ah Michael, you poor fuckless bastard!

He withdrew his arm and lit cigarettes for both of them. How do couples manage such moments now that no one smokes?

They were silent, staring off at the lake.

Michael hadn't a clue what to say, what to do.

He thought of Nicholas Wiley who seemed wise now, in his moralism, his simplicity. Michael fingered his cross, and it filled him with affection for the kid, a rare longing to see him. He said, "A friend of mine gave me this. He says about the war, 'Just stop it! That's all. Stop it.' "

"When enough people say that to them, they perhaps will."

"Maybe whether they would or not, people should say it."

Inge picked up *The Christian Failure,* looked at it for a moment, then opened to a dog-eared page. "In nineteen thirty-nine our bishops made a joint statement," she read. "Catholics must 'do their duty in obedience to the Führer, ready for sacrifice and with commitment of the whole being.' " She snapped the book shut. "I wish someone had said 'Stop it!' " She dropped the book into her bag. With her cigarette dangling from her lips, she stood and folded her towel. She dropped it in her straw bag, then withdrew a worn white lab-coat, which she donned as a robe. "I must get back."

Michael pulled on his trousers and shirt and walked with her. Neither spoke. At the entrance to the compound, she stopped. He sensed something stiffen in her, a decision made, a resolution. She held his eyes and said quite deliberately, quite carefully, "I want you to come into An Hoa with me tonight."

That was all she said, all she asked of him, but suddenly his throat was dry and he could hear the blood pulsing in his ears.

They walked in silence. The dark forms of palm trees were silhouetted against the night. The mountains beyond the lake were visible only as the black nothing above which the sky, by comparison, seemed a shade of coal blue. Ahead of them, at a distance of half a mile, were the spires of the church. No lights shone from the village. The country lived permanently in blackout.

"The cool air feels good," Michael said at last. He had to deflect the tension he felt into talk.

Inge said, "You know what happens in Vietnam at sunset, don't you?"

He heard something whimsical in her voice, something girlish, and he was drawn in by it. He was aware for the first time of her cologne. Had she worn that for its effect on him? "What?" he asked.

"The gates of the underworld are said to be opened and the souls fly out, naked and starving. They fly back to their home villages and are eating the food left for them on their family altars."

"Sounds like the Viet Cong."

"Vietnamese feed not only their children, but their ancestors."

"You love them, don't you?"

"Yes. It breaks my heart, what happens. You say that — 'breaks my heart'?"

"Yes."

The sound of helicopters in the distance stopped them. They listened as the noise grew louder. They stared up at the dark sky, but saw nothing. The aircraft flew without running lights. Soon the sound of their engines began to fade. It was impossible to say how many there were.

Michael said, "In Saigon, when there is rumbling in the distance, people in the cafés hope it isn't thunder because they don't want it to rain, they'll have to go inside. They listen and then say to one another, 'Oh good, artillery fire. Oh good, bombs.' "

Inge nodded. "Europeans and Americans."

"No. Vietnamese. I've heard Vietnamese say it."

She shook her head. "Someday soon they will bomb An Hoa."

"Why do you say that?"

"Because of the marines across the lake. They cannot have a village here. If there is a big village, always there will be NLF, what their leaflets call 'wicked Viet Cong.' "

"Are you worried for the hospital?" Michael asked, but he was thinking he was worried for her.

"Of course worried. We're in the middle, no?"

They walked on in silence then.

Once in the village they went directly to the church. Inge rapped the heel of her hand on the large mahogany door. In a matter of seconds it opened and a shadowy figure stepped aside for them. Michael recognized the form, even in the pitch-black of the church, of a cassocked priest. Once they'd entered he closed the door softly behind them, then led the way into the darkness. It took Michael a moment to realize why that darkness was wrong; not even the sanctuary lamp, indicating the Presence in the tabernacle, burned.

At an altar the priest lit a candle, then faced them. He was Vietnamese, taller than most of his countrymen but considerably shorter than Michael and extremely thin. His Roman collar hung loosely at his throat. His black hair fell across his forehead. It was impossible to say how old he was — perhaps thirty, perhaps fifty — but a certain fierce vigor showed in his face. His black eyes fixed on Inge Holz, and he greeted her softly in Vietnamese.

She responded with a whisper, and Michael sensed at once the current of their relationship.

The priest faced him. "*Mon Père,*" he said gently, "*bienvenu à l'église de Vinh Son.*"

Michael looked blank.

The priest read his small embarrassment, and said, "Welcome, Father, to the church of Vinh Son." They shook hands.

"Thank you." Now that his eyes were adjusted, Michael looked around. It was a typical Catholic church, the dominating high altar, its gaudy crucifix with painted corpus — Jesus a pale Caucasian — and two side altars, one for Joseph, one for Mary. They were standing in front of Mary's altar, and the candle the priest had lit was a small votive candle in a blue cup. "Vinh Son?" Michael asked.

"Vinh Son," the priest repeated. "Vinh Son Da Sal."

Vincent de Sales, Michael realized, as the French pronounce it. He nearly laughed. Saint Vincent. Good old Saint Vincent, patron of the order to which Carolyn had belonged, patron of the hospital in which Molly was born. *Vinh Son!* When he told me this story, he smiled. By then the Church was like a haunted house to us, and certain saints like ghosts.

The Vietnamese priest was staring at him intently, taking his measure. Finally he said, "You know of the Struggle?"

It took Michael a moment to realize what he was referring to. He said cautiously, "The Struggle; I know the word. It is used to mean 'resistance.' "

"Not 'resistance,' " the priest said softly. "In Vietnamese 'Struggle' is to rebel with all one's life-force."

"It refers to the Buddhist Struggle, no?" That movement had brought Diem down in '63 and lately it had shown signs of quickening once more.

"It is not only Buddhists who seek a third way between the Communists and the generals. Some of us do also." The priest studied Michael.

Michael showed him nothing.

"Inge told me perhaps you would like to learn. I thought to approach you as a brother priest."

Michael suddenly thought, This might be a trap! He said warily, "Every Vietnamese priest I've met is loyal to the Saigon government."

"But of course they would appear so to you. We are loyal first to God, second to the Church and third to our people. The government does not command a priest's loyalty." He smiled. The strength of his conviction communicated, but he was speaking gently. "It is the same for priests everywhere, no? Even in America?"

"It should be."

"It is so with you?"

Michael said carefully, "My government commands my loyalty as a citizen, not as a priest." He looked at Inge quickly. She was staring at him, waiting for him to declare himself. But still he felt wary. He said, "The Buddhists are tools of the Viet Cong." It was a provocative statement, one he didn't really believe, but he felt instinctively that he had to stiff-arm this priest. Why had he brought him here? What did he want? "Communists do not command my loyalty either."

"Nor mine, but the NLF is not run by Catholics. My government is. That puts me in a special position, you agree?"

Michael did not answer.

The Vietnamese priest continued to smile, inappropriately, Michael thought. Then he realized that his smile was his disguise. The priest said, "I attended seminary in Paris. My thesis was on Tocqueville. You know what he said about the Ancien Régime? 'Our government resembles the Mass for the Dead: there is no Gloria, since there is nothing to sing about; no Credo since there is nothing we believe in common; a long offertory where much money is collected, and in the end, no Benediction.' " The priest's smile was gone.

"What do you mean, 'run by Catholics'?" Michael asked. "The time of Diem is passed."

The priest made a gesture with his hand: Maybe yes, maybe no. "You remember the Ngos' Can Lao?"

"The secret organization?"

"Yes. Police, spies, provincial leaders, generals, a shadow government, all Catholics. It was the source of their power. Those men did not disappear when Diem and Nhu were killed. They simply withdrew somewhat, to wait. And now it seems the time of waiting is over."

"Why?"

"Nguyen Van Thieu," the priest said simply.

Thieu was the new chief of state. With Air Vice-Marshal Nguyen Cao Ky he had been running the government for less than a month.

"Thieu is a convert to Catholicism, a devoted, pious man, and many of the former Can Lao members see in him a new Diem. They have secretly begun a new organization, the Nhan Xa, called in English 'The Revolutionary Social Humanist Party.' Many of the old alliances have simply been struck again. Their purpose is the old one, to save Vietnam not just from Communism but from Buddhists. *They* are the ones who have convinced Lodge and Westmoreland that the Struggle for a Third Way is Viet Cong. Your government would love to have Catholics in power again. They will welcome Nhan Xa."

"What about Ky?"

"Ky is a comedian. Only Americans think of him."

"But Thieu only came to power this month. None of the others have lasted."

"He will last, I promise you, until the war is lost, or until he is dead."

"Or until the war is won."

"It won't be won."

"If Nhan Xa is secret, how do you know about it?"

"The leader is my own bishop, Nguyen Van Thuan. In our country a bishop has no secrets from his priests. Do you know him?"

"No."

The priest nodded. He was accustomed to such ignorance. "He replaced Thuc."

"Diem's brother."

"That is correct. You believe Diem's family was removed from power in nineteen sixty-three."

"It wasn't?"

"You know the myth of Hydra, the monster slain by Hercules? It had nine heads, and when one was cut off, it was replaced by two others. My bishop, Thuan, is the son of Diem's sister. The Ngos are the hydra family of Vietnam. They still control the Church. With Nhan Xa, they will control Thieu. They will control America."

And it all began, Michael thought, in the Maryknoll seminary where Ngo Dinh Diem had spent his years in exile as Cardinal Spellman's ward. Jesus Christ! he thought. Am I the only one who knows this? Michael looked at Inge again. This must sound to her like the resurgence of the Nazi party. Well, wasn't it like that?

Michael remembered that, once, his horror at what the Ngos were doing had taken him, furiously and so imprudently, to Spellman's residence. And Spellman had coopted him completely.

Michael faced the Vietnamese priest. "Why have you brought me here?"

"Because I want to tell you what I and some brother priests are going to do."

"You trust me?"

"Of course. We are eleven Catholic priests. Who can we trust if not a fellow priest? On July twentieth in all of Vietnam, in Hanoi as well as Saigon, in Haiphong and Hué, we Vietnamese will mark the Day of National Shame. On that day it is ten years since the Geneva Agreement divided our country in two. And on that day we priests from parishes all over South Vietnam will go to Saigon in behalf of our people. There will be many Buddhists in the streets, many demonstrations. The government will say the demonstrators are Viet Cong. But no one can say that about Catholic priests. We will make a simple prayer, a procession, a Way of the Cross. We will go from the president's palace to the American embassy, and we will be saying what the Buddhists say. The National Shame is what we have allowed to happen in our country. We can relieve our shame only by protesting the source of it: 'No More America in Vietnam!' No more American soldiers in our cities. No more American bombs on our villages! No more American murder of our people!"

Michael was not breathing. The priest's indictment filled *him* with shame. "And you are telling me this because . . ."

"We want you to join us."

"Making twelve."

The priest smiled. "Unintentional."

But Michael's thought was, One of the twelve was Judas. He remembered Nicholas Wiley. Judas and Peter; what made them different was how they handled their shame.

Inge Holz spoke finally, saying to Michael, "I told Pham that you are ready. If this offends you, then is my fault."

What Michael noticed was her use of the priest's name. She did not call him 'Father.' He looked from one to the other. "But I am an American. That seems wrong, given what you're saying."

The priest nodded. "In a way, that's true. But there are good reasons. You are a priest like us, and that emphasizes that we are speaking as Catholics. As priests we all object to government, you to yours, we to ours. And as priests we all proclaim the Gospel's independence from narrow, political causes of whatever kind." He paused. "And there are other reasons too. If you are with us, then the police will hesitate to move against us. We do not want our procession to be interrupted before the people see us."

Inge Holz said, "If you are not with them, the police will put them off the street at once and we may never see them again."

The Vietnamese priest ignored her, as if that was not his concern. "And your participation will attract the attention of news reporters from Europe and America. We do not burn ourselves, like the bonzes. They might therefore ignore us."

Tim O'Shea's one request to Michael: "Don't let Spelly read about you in the *Times.*"

Michael could think of a dozen reasons to say no, good ones. But his impulse — and it was to say no, to be sure — sprang from none of them. He was afraid.

"We are asking you to join us on the Day of National Shame, and on each day after that when we will repeat the procession until the war ends or until they stop us."

Michael stared at him. The gaunt, shadow-ridden priest seemed all at once an upright cadaver. Shall these bones live? But it wasn't Suu Van Pham who'd been reduced to bones. Michael saw that his own belief in his own mission, his own identity, his own position was completely collapsed. He looked out on an infinite stretch of ruins, a vast plain littered with dried, lifeless bones, the remains of all he'd once sworn by and lived for. The futility of his effort to alleviate suffering by working, timidly, within the structures of Church and government was undeniable now. The absurdity of his own life slammed him, and he felt for the first time ever disgust at what he'd become. A clerical camp follower, yes. The army's holy whore. The cardinal's. His self-loathing was surpassed only by his despair.

Dear reader, such a moment would have undone you and me, would have finished us. We'd have gone off, regarding the Vietnamese priests as foolhardy, self-aggrandizing martyrs. We'd have claimed to prefer organizing quietly among Catholic clergy and developing what we would call "authentic" opposition, "practical" dissent. We'd have refused, citing if not our vow of obedience to America's Sunshine Prelate or our obligation to the poor refugees served by the CRS, our debt of loyalty to Tim O'Shea. They couldn't undo his consecration because of us — he was a bishop forever — but they could keep him an auxiliary forever too.

And we'd have been nearly right; there were honorable reasons for men like us to say no to Suu Van Pham. Honorable reasons to pretend that nothing had changed, to insist that the invitation from this ghost of a priest was not, at last, an annunciation, a conscription, an act of God. You and I, dear reader, would have slipped away, wishing the Vietnamese dissenters well, promising to pray for them. And only we'd have known what cowards we were and how we'd just destroyed ourselves.

But Michael Maguire was not like the rest of us, any more then than he had been in Korea or would be later. His capacity for fear, and for retreat, matched ours, but when forced by events to face the truth, at last, he did so willingly. I would have deflected the truth. Perhaps you would have. Michael embraced it. Confronted with that vast plain of dry bones, the bones of the slain, the bones of his own savaged dreams, he stood with upraised arms and cried, "Live!" In him despair became hope, collapse became conversion, and fear was changed into the source of action. Such transforming will is the hero's gift, and he had it. And we remember him through these pages because, oh, we need it.

Michael nodded at Suu Van Pham. "I am honored that you should ask me to join you. *Adsum, Pater,*" he said firmly. It was the ancient declaration that each of them had made at ordination. "Send me," it means. "I am ready."

Father Suu Van Pham led Michael and Inge Holz to the rectory. In the kitchen he drew the blinds, then lit a fat, short candle on the table. He took a crucifix from around his neck and placed it next to the candle. He poured a glass of wine and set out a third of a thin loaf of bread. Then they each took seats and joined hands. For a few moments they prayed in silence. Then Father Pham raised his eyes to Michael. "You have a favorite passage of Scripture, Father?"

In Michael's mind, the pages fell open of the small New Testament Tim O'Shea had given him in Korea, and he recited from

Paul's letter to the Ephesians. " 'But now in Christ Jesus you who were once far off have been brought near in the blood of Christ. For He is our peace, who has made us both one, and has broken down the dividing wall of hostility, by abolishing in his flesh the law of commandments and ordinances, that he might create in himself one new man in place of the two, so making peace; and might reconcile us both to God in one body through the Cross, thereby bringing hostility to an end. And he came and preached peace to you who were far off, and peace to those who were near; for through him we both have access in one Spirit to the Father.' "

When Michael fell silent, Pham opened his eyes and looked at him. He completed the passage. " 'So then you are no longer a stranger or a foreign visitor. We are fellow citizens with the saints and members of the household of God.' "

The two men leaned toward one another and embraced. *"Pax tecum,"* they said.

Then each one kissed Inge Holz, whose eyes were bright. When Pham touched his cheek to hers she whispered something. Michael knew what — "I love you" — and he understood.

"Shall we say the Canon in Latin, Father? Or English?" Pham had the wine and bread arranged in front of him on the plain unfinished table.

Michael had never done the Mass so informally before. Though the mode would become trivialized in the post-Council era as "home liturgy" — that impoverished rite shorn of vestments, stripped of gesture and rubric, devoid of eloquence — one's first experience of the transcendent event so simplified, so freed from the sterile medieval accretions, called up its own special awe. The unadorned Mass could evoke magnificently that Last Meal in the Upper Room, but for Michael that night the breaking of the bread at the deal table in the blacked-out rectory was like something done in the catacombs, an act of the underground Church exactly. Wasn't the world outside raging? Wasn't it full of enemies? Weren't soldiers raising crosses on every hill? And in this shocking dispensation weren't the old loyalties replaced by a new one, modest and absolute at once? Underground, freed from trappings, the Eucharist becomes itself again, a simple meal, an act of life against death, a sacrifice. And likewise the Church. Michael felt that he was at Mass for the first time, that finally he had come home.

Latin was the vernacular of martyrs.

English was the argot of men who dropped canisters full of napalm on children.

But this was an act of communion — First Communion — with a people whose forgiveness Michael Maguire longed for.

"In your language, Father, please," he said. "In Vietnamese, let us pray."

TWENTY-FOUR

MICHAEL MAGUIRE was the tallest of the twelve, and he walked in front.

His first problem had been where to get a cassock. The Vietnamese priests were too short. Even Pham's soutane would have barely reached Michael's ankles and he'd have looked like an oafish altar boy. Ludicrous as it seems, the project of finding a cassock that would fit him preoccupied him in the days before the demonstration. If Michael Maguire was going to do this, appear in a public protest against his own government in a foreign capital, then he was going to look like what he was — a responsible, some would say important, American priest. He finally found an air force chaplain his height at Tan Son Nhut Air Base, a friendly Chicagoan who greeted Michael as if they'd been classmates. Michael told him he needed the cassock for a prayer service at the embassy.

The day itself was humid, and even in the early morning, rain threatened. July is the heart of the wet season in Saigon, and it was certain that the skies would open at some point.

Nevertheless by midmorning the streets and boulevards of the city were jammed with citizens. Few of them were demonstrators, and almost none of them had come in from the countryside. The government had coopted the move to turn the anniversary of the Geneva Accords into a protest and had declared it a national holiday. Also, soldiers were posted outside the city to prevent residents of refugee camps, displaced villagers and Buddhists from the countryside from coming into Saigon. Traditional Vietnamese had disdained Saigon when it was the French capital. Now that it had become the center of the American occupation with the degradation and corruption that brought, they hated it. And so on that day the government simply kept them out.

The Saigonese, on the other hand, were cynical and indifferent. As long as the generals kept the war in the country, and as long as the Americans stayed in the Cowboy Bars on Tu Do Street and the MPs kept the drunken soldiers away from their daughters, they ignored the government. They did business, that was all. On this day they closed their shops, though, and strolled the city as if it were Paris.

The Buddhist Struggle Movement, which had turned out hundreds of thousands of protesters against Diem, and which in a year, in 1966, would bring Saigon to the brink of chaos, was quiescent now. Thousands of its leaders were still in jail, and the Catholic opposition was wielding its power more subtly. Only students could be rallied in numbers that summer, and to them the condition of a divided Vietnam was less a National Shame than a fact of political life they had grown up with. A day of protest against the government that protected their draft-exempt status and against the Americans who brought them their beloved Everly Brothers and blue jeans was more a lark than an act of conscience.

In sum, if you weren't looking that day, you might not have noticed the earnest demonstrators, though two small groups of them were easily identifiable. A single file of saffron-robed monks snaked through throngs of white-suited men and ladies in flowing *ao-dai* dresses on Lam Son Square before the Continental Palace Hotel. Some of the monks struck shoulder-drums and others carried signs saying, "Vietnam for the Vietnamese" and "Down with U.S. Intervention in Vietnamese Internal Affairs," and "One Vietnam" and "All Life Is Suffering." The Buddhists and the students, perhaps one thousand all together, were going to spend the day chanting and praying in front of the American embassy.

The Catholic priests did not want to be taken as an adjunct to the Buddhist demonstration, as, being so few, they would have. So they changed their plan. They would avoid the embassy. It was Michael who suggested that instead they take their procession to the MACV Headquarters which that summer were still in a three-story French villa in a residential neighborhood. In fact it was a better place to make their point since their objection was not to America or Americans, but to the American military buildup. They did not know it, but no demonstrations had been conducted at the headquarters before, and because of what they started that day, it would be moved soon to a secure concrete building in the middle of Tan Son Nhut.

At the Presidential Palace they prayed the rosary in Latin before the huge elaborate gates on the other side of which deferential guards watched nervously. The guards were obviously relieved when the priests set off, in single file like the Buddhists, but behind the tall American. Michael carried the procession cross. Pham carried their only sign, which said in English and Vietnamese, "We Pray For Peace. Stop Killing Our People." Each of the other priests carried a candle and his breviary. As they walked they recited the Psalms.

The procession took them down Thong Nhut Street, a broad boulevard that had until recently been lined with graceful elms. But it was a bald street now and had a ravaged look. It had not been bombed, but the elms had been cut down early in the summer to accommodate the huge American trucks that were bringing soldiers and supplies in from Tan Son Nhut, which by July was, and would remain for years, the busiest airport in the world. "Thong Nhut" meant unification, and at the opposite end of the boulevard from the palace was the National Zoo, which gave rise to a Saigon joke; what Unification Street unified were not the halves of the country but the monkey houses at its either end.

The crowds who were long accustomed to demonstrations of Buddhist monks could not ignore these Catholic priests, not even a mere dozen of them. The people eased aside for them and craned to read their sign. The priests walked solemnly past stymied pedicabs and boys who were forced by the crush to push their Lambrettas along the sidewalks. It may have been the National Day of Shame, but in Saigon — wasn't this typical? — it had the look of a festival. The shops were closed, but at improvised stands along the curb, sellers hawked flowers, decorations and black-market goods — transistor radios, Zippo lighters and Timex watches. Even these cagey merchants gawked when the priests went by. The street urchins — the Vietnamese called them *bui doi,* the dust of life —

who pestered browsers for coins or, when they dared, picked their pockets, stood back. Catholic priests rarely left their churches or appeared in public in groups, and they never criticized the war. Old men pointed to the sign Father Pham carried and then fell to arguing about what they'd seen. Was it the funeral procession of a Spiritist sect? Were they Palm Tree Prophets? Was the man in front Caucasian? As word spread ahead of them that they were coming, people both came to the street to see and moved away from it out of certainty that such a demonstration would soon draw government riot police.

For his part Michael felt that he was enacting a dream he'd had years before. He remembered walking in single file with other POWs from one camp to the next, through Korean and Chinese villages, until finally they were brought to the prison camp at Chung Kang Djin across the Yalu. Asian faces had stared at him all along the way. In some towns they had jeered and hated. Now they were staring again, and again it was their hatred he was aware of, though no one cursed him or raised a fist. But they would have if they'd known! They'd have screamed at him and torn at his clothing. They'd have spit. "What are you doing in Asia again? Why can't you leave us alone?"

He remembered the mob of refugees rushing at him. He'd been ready with his bayonet, but had been spared using it. Once all the Americans — the Occidentals — were safe, he'd blown the Asians to smithereens. And now, fifteen years later, more powerfully than before, sorrow flowed from him. This procession was an act of penitence. This should have been Good Friday. "O my people, what have I done to thee?"

When he'd first come home from Korea, Michael had struck me as Ransom's "Tower unleaning." He was so erect, so spare, so stripped of the superfluous, so radical, so rooted! But wasn't he still? The impression those twelve priests made as they moved slowly through Saigon's streets was in large part an impression *he* made, towering above everyone in sight, setting the pace for the others with his steady cadence and holding at the level of his brow the ornate brass crucifix, the racked body of Jesus facing away from him and toward the city, toward the people and toward the army offices to which they marched.

Now they were reciting, in Latin, the Second Psalm. "Why do the nations rage and the peoples utter folly? The kings of the earth rise up, and the princes conspire together against the Lord and against His Anointed: 'Let us break their fetters and cast their bonds from us!' He who is throned in heaven laughs; the Lord derides them."

It was a new idea. To Michael Maguire the kings of the earth against whom the Scriptures railed incessantly had never included the leaders of his own country. But now that he had heard the words of the prophets as addressed to *him* and to *his* people — as opposed merely to, say, the Sodomites — revelation occurred as for the first time. America was not exempt from the judgment of God. Nor, for that matter, was the Church! The kings of the earth and the princes conspire! Nguyen Van Thieu and Nguyen Van Thuan! Lyndon Baines Johnson and Francis Cardinal Spellman!

"Serve the Lord with fear and rejoice before Him; with trembling pay homage to Him, lest He be angry and you perish from the way when His anger blazes suddenly. Happy are all who take refuge in Him!"

Michael Maguire embodied in himself, without knowing it, the end of the great American Catholic Success Story. He was, first, its crowning achievement — a Silver Star Priest. His Catholic Faith had never seemed more glorious than when it enabled him to withstand the pressures of a Chinese prison. His Catholic Faith had made him a patriot and a hero, and the Church celebrated him as if the purpose of the Incarnation was to make us better American citizens. Michael Maguire was what all those seminary estates up the Hudson and along Lake Michigan and in the hills of California were trying to, in their word, "form." He was the man with twin loyalties, *Deus et Patria,* and they were equal, matched, one at the service of the other.

But the seminaries, not understanding the risks in such exposure, had confronted him with the Word of God. It was a domesticated Word, to be sure, one that had left unmoved and unchanged generations of seminarians before. But Michael Maguire, thanks to the chance gift of Timothy O'Shea, had begun his confrontation with the Word of God in the Chinese prison, and a seed was planted well before he entered the "seed bed." It would take years to bear fruit, but when it did, it would set him apart from almost all his brothers.

He understood inchoately that the Word of God was what kept

him free in prison, and that taught him that the Word of God is freedom itself. "You cannot imprison the Word of the Lord." Paul's antiphon came back to him. You cannot imprison the Word of the Lord in a phrase like *Deus et Patria,* for the Word has nothing to do with America. Michael's anger blazed suddenly at all he'd been taught, at all he'd believed, at all he'd built his life around. His anger blazed, purifying, cauterizing.

You cannot imprison the Word of God in a national purpose, in a Cause, in a culture, in narrowly defined — nationally defined — religion. By walking in that procession with those Vietnamese priests, speaking not for Communism or Buddhism or the reunification of Vietnam or the defeat of the Dominoes — speaking only for the sacred right of innocent people not to have fire poured on their heads, Michael, having been captured by the Word, had become its instrument.

"The Word of God," Paul says, "is something alive and active. It cuts like any double-edged sword, but more finely. It can slip through the place where the soul is divided from the spirit, or joints from marrow."

It can even slip between the words "America" and "Catholic," and can declare that from now on they should be presumed to have nothing to do with each other. What had seemed our moment of glory — this is what Michael saw — had been the beginning of our disgrace. John Kennedy embodied both when he said in his great Inaugural — how we cheered him for it; these words more than any prepared us for Vietnam — "On earth God's work must truly be our own."

The eyes of every Asian that fell on Michael Maguire, who hid his own behind the blurring crucifix, flared with hatred. He seemed to hear their voices sputtering.

What has "God's work" to do with firestorms above our cities? What has "God's work" to do with throwing our sons out of helicopters? What has "God's work" to do with cutting off our ears? With herbicides, defoliants, white phosphorus or napalm? What has "God's work" to do with body-counts or "Cong catchers"? With forcing live flare rods into the orifices — mouths, anuses and vaginas — of men and women, the sons and daughters — even if you despise us as Slopes, Slant-Eyes and Gooks — of the Almighty, Everlasting, Vengeance-seeking, Justice-loving

Lord God! You dare call what you do "God's work"! You dare invoke that Name! That Word! You scum! You worm! Leave! Begone! Get out! Let my people go! Yes, *my* people! It is Yahweh who speaks! The Lord of History, Creator of the Universe, Absolute Future toward Whom all time pulses, God!

The Military Assistance Command–Vietnam Headquarters was easily distinguished from the other turn-of-the-century villas in which the French colonial elite had lived, because from its roof sprouted a forest of antennae. White and silver communications disks tilted toward the dull sky, which seemed lower. Rain was closer.

In front of the villa a sandbag barrier four feet high blocked half the street, keeping traffic in the far lane. There were no crowds on the sidewalk here, though curious, perhaps foolhardy, Saigonese were trailing along behind the procession now.

The two MPs at the villa gate saw them coming and called for reinforcements.

The priests now recited the *Te Deum,* the hymn of praise that every Catholic priest of that generation and before knew by heart because he recited it as a prayer of thanksgiving as he left the altar after Mass. "You overcame the sting of death and opened the kingdom of heaven to all believers. You are seated at God's right hand in glory. We believe that you will come and be our judge. Come, then, Lord, sustain Your people, bought with the price of your own blood, and bring us with your saints to everlasting glory."

Death, *mors.* Blood, *sanguis.* Judge, *judex.* Your people, *tuus populus.*

The words reverberated in that space between their souls and spirits, between their bones and marrow, as they closed the last distance to the American building.

By the time they reached the sandbag barrier, two squads of combat-ready American soldiers were filing out of the villa, rifles at exact angles across their breasts, obscuring their faces so that they need not look the demonstrators in the eyes.

What Michael fixed upon were the gleaming bayonets; he remembered his own and what he'd have done with it, all too willingly. A fresh wave of feeling flowed in him, but now for the first time that morning, his sorrow and anger having kept it at bay, it was fear. It flowed as cleanly as blood would once a rifle's blade had pierced him.

He began to pray, reciting numbly, "Come Holy Spirit, fill the hearts of your people. Enkindle in them the fire of your love." Then in his own voice, he whispered, "Oh Christ, help me do this."

The soldiers marched out of the compound, into the street, and as the priests stopped in a single line in front of the barrier, the soldiers split into two files and surrounded them. They were uniformly tall and burly, physically intimidating. The first blow was their appearance. There were perhaps fifty, and more than half were black men.

The sergeant barked an order, and the soldiers froze, ready.

Then a Vietnamese officer addressed a command to the priests. Disperse at once. Michael fixed his eyes upon the brass cross. It hadn't occurred to him that they wouldn't be allowed to stand peacefully in the street, for a time at least. The Buddhists conducted their demonstrations with impunity. But of course the government had learned to live with Buddhists, and the news media had long since ignored them. But Catholics! And priests! And an American!

With a high-pitched whine, a large army truck, the familiar olive canvas, backed up the street toward them. More soldiers?

Michael looked around quickly, hoping to see reporters, cameramen, American or European witnesses. None. The citizens who had been following had been stopped by a line of police a block away.

Suu Van Pham began reciting, in Latin, the Sixtieth Psalm. "Hear, O Lord, my cry . . ." The others joined in. At least if they had to be arrested, Michael thought, it would be by Americans.

"From the earth's end I call to you as my heart grows faint. You will set me high upon a rock; you will give me rest, for you are my refuge, a tower of strength against the enemy."

Even before the truck stopped, the flap was thrown back and Vietnamese Rangers began jumping out. They were carrying heavy wooden riot sticks. Immediately, though no priest resisted, they began to club them. Within seconds each priest had been bloodied, then roughly picked up and hurled into the truck.

All but Michael. A pair of American MPs had snatched the crucifix from him. Taking him by each arm, they dragged him into the headquarters building.

Within ten minutes the demonstration was over. The truck was gone. The dropped breviaries and candles, the crucifix and Pham's sign had been swept away. The bystanders, including reporters, half a block away had seen nothing, owing to the wall of burly American soldiers. The entire demonstration might have been a fantasy, a mirage. And the bystanders were dispersed then anyway when the skies opened finally, with a great clap of thunder, for the rain.

Michael was kept in a bare room, alone, for more than two hours. It was furnished with a plain wooden table and two chairs. He tried to pray but couldn't. The sound of the lock turning in his door startled him. He straightened in the chair and put his hands palm downward on the table and he watched as the door opened.

"Jack!" Michael stood. Relief surged through him, an absurd happiness. It was Jack Howe, in his white suit, his slick black hair carefully parted above his haggard face. Howe looked gaunt as ever, and stern, but the tension in which Michael had held himself so rigidly went at once. When Howe offered him his hand Michael took it in both of his and shook it gratefully.

"Are you all right, Father?"

"Yes, but you've got to get me out of here. They've arrested my fellow priests. I've got to get to them."

"Sit down, Father." Howe withdrew his hand.

"But, Jack —"

"Sit down," he ordered.

Michael stiffened. He watched in silence while Howe took a pipe from his pocket and lit it. Had he ever seen Howe smoke a pipe before? As he puffed it alive he said, "That was a stupid thing to do, Father."

"Where are my fellow priests, Jack?"

"The Viets have been taken to the Center for Political Reindoctrination at Bien Hoa."

"That's a prison! That's where V.C. terrorists are taken."

"You people didn't expect rooms at the Caravelle Hotel, did you?"

"What law did we break?" Michael stared at him; had he ever seen this Howe before?

"I thought you had more savvy than this, Father. They used you." Howe looked at Michael mournfully.

"Everybody uses me, Jack, even you." Michael was trying to stretch his mind around what, at last, it knew. "You told me once you hated the CIA. Now that I recall, perhaps you didn't explicitly deny working for it, however."

"I wish I could have told you, Father," Howe said simply.

"And now they've sent you in here because you're famous for getting me to eat out of your hand."

"Father, I asked to be the one to see you."

"Why?"

He shook his head and shrugged. "Because I know why you did it."

"I did it, Jack, because of things you taught me."

Howe stared at his pipe.

"You stayed with it too long, Jack."

Howe's eyes widened. "Maybe so. But now it's moving too fast to jump off."

"I'm off." Michael stood up. He recognized Howe's situation, that familiar despair, but it came as a surprise to find he had no sympathy for him. "Take me to Bien Hoa."

Howe stared at him.

"I mean it. If the Vietnamese priests are there, then I want to be with them."

Howe relit his pipe. It was a gesture into which he could channel his insecurity, and when the pipe was lit all traces of it were gone. He said officiously, "Father Maguire, you are being taken to Tan Son Nhut, being put on an airplane and sent home. Your visa has been revoked."

"I'm not going, Jack. Not even for you, buddy. You'll have to go back and tell your bosses that you couldn't work your magic with me this time."

"Oh, really? What are you going to do?"

Michael answered with a resolve he did not know he had. "I'm going to return to the Presidential Palace and I am going to retrace the steps that we took today, and I am going to stand outside this building until curfew. I will observe curfew because I have no intention of breaking the law. But I will repeat the procession tomorrow and the next day and the day after that and every day until my fellow priests have been freed."

"That won't be necessary, Father. Your fellow priests will be freed as soon as your plane leaves the ground. The government has no interest in making heroes of them."

"I don't believe you, Jack. I don't believe the government here. You're all fucking liars. You free the priests. Then talk to me about leaving."

Howe studied the bowl of his pipe for a moment, then turned abruptly and left the room.

More than an hour later another man came, this one in khaki. On his collar were the silver eagles of a full colonel.

He offered Michael his hand. "Father Maguire, I'm Father Paul Fitzmaurice."

Only then did Michael see the silver cross on his breast pocket. This was the Theater Chief of Chaplains.

"I have a message for you." He put a piece of paper on the table and sat.

"Already?" Michael smiled. He understood suddenly that they'd have been on the wire to New York. As he picked up the teletype sheet, he said, "Good old Tim O'Shea."

The chaplain shook his head. "Not Bishop O'Shea, Father. It's from the cardinal."

Michael's stomach constricted. Why hadn't he expected this? Had he been living in never-never land? He sat, stunned.

When he saw that the communication was in Latin, he did not breathe. The first thing his eyes fixed on were the parenthetical citations by number of canon law. He was being formally ordered back to New York under solemn obedience.

Michael looked across the table at Fitzmaurice. "It must be the middle of the night in New York! They woke Spellman for this?"

The chaplain nodded. "They want you out. Every American in Vietnam is furious at you." Especially including me, his attitude suggested.

Michael looked at the paper in his hands. "I don't think the cardinal is too pleased either."

"They're threatening to force CRS out of Asia altogether because of you."

"Good Lord."

"What did you expect?"

Michael looked sharply at the chaplain. "To be able to stand peacefully in front of an American building, to express an opinion."

"This isn't the States, Father. You're damn lucky they're not charging you with treason."

"What?"

" 'Aid and comfort to the enemy,' Father. You've heard of it?"

"Don't accuse me of treason, Colonel." Michael's anger swelled.

Fitzmaurice shrugged, backing off. "Look, you give every priest over here a bad name. You're the first American citizen to join these kooks. How do you think that looks? An American priest demonstrating against his own superiors!"

"Westmoreland and Taylor are not my superiors."

"Over here they are. This is war, Father. I don't think you understand that."

"That's one thing I do understand, Colonel. I know war when I see it, and I know when the rules of war are being violated. I've been in the countryside; have you? I've seen this war from the villages; have you? You should get your chaplains out of the officers' clubs and into the free fire zones, then tell me this is war. This isn't war, Colonel. It is mass murder. It is genocide."

The chaplain said mournfully, like a hurt mother — a common form among certain clergy — "I take your refusal to call me 'Father' as an insult, as you no doubt intend it."

"Not so. I simply find it impossible to think of you as a priest."

"You've got a nerve."

"A nerve is right! A raw nerve, involving some brother priests of ours who had the shit kicked out of them with American GIs looking on, and who are now in Bien Hoa, a torture-prison. And you know it. I'm not leaving here until they're free."

"The Viets can take care of themselves, Father. They knew well enough what they were getting into, even if you didn't." The chaplain nodded at the teletype sheet. "You don't have any choice in that matter now. That's God's Will you're holding in your hands."

Michael dropped the paper on the table. "I want you to tell whoever sent you in here I'm not leaving Vietnam until those priests are free."

"That's a solemn command you have there, Father, from your Ordinary himself. You recognize the canonical formula surely."

"Yes, I do."

"And you recall the consequences if you disobey."

"I believe the progression runs from suspension to interdiction to excommunication, doesn't it? But it's a little more complicated than my saying yes or no to a solemn order. Since they've chosen to play this canonically, Colonel, instead of, say, pastorally or even fraternally, they'll have to follow the form to its conclusion. That means they have to issue the order three times before the penalty is incurred, which gives me a little time, doesn't it?"

"And they told me you young priests didn't know your canon law."

"Some of us know it well enough to hide in it."

"But what about CRS? It won't have the benefit of canonical due process. The army can just shut it down. Do you want that on your conscience?"

Michael shook his head. "They can't do it. The Catholic Relief Service! It's the largest private foreign aid agency in America. It operates in seventy countries. It gets clothes and food to ten million people. There are three hundred CRS workers in Southeast Asia. And the board of directors has some of the most powerful men in America on it. What MACV has if they shut down CRS is bad publicity. Everybody from Uncle Walter to the *New York Times* to, maybe, the head of Caritas International comes to me to find out what happened. And do you know what? I'll tell them. And that, Colonel, is what they'll obviously do anything to avoid."

"You're pretty cocky, aren't you?"

"Not at all. I'd vastly prefer that none of this was happening. I wish I was the third curate in an upstate parish."

"You may get that wish before you're finished."

Father Fitzmaurice stood.

"And you tell them I demand to know by what authority I'm being prevented from leaving this building."

Fitzmaurice shook his head, genuinely bewildered. "This isn't the States, Father. Do you want them to turn you over to the Vietnamese?"

"That's exactly what I want."

"They can't and you know it."

"Then get our brother priests out of Bien Hoa."

Minutes after the chaplain left, Jack Howe returned. "All right, here's the deal. You're free to go. But you get the woman away from this building."

"What woman?"

"The German nurse. She's been standing outside all afternoon. Tomorrow the priests will be released. They'll be brought to the rectory of the cathedral where you can greet them. Then an army driver will take you to Tan Son Nhut, and you'll board a plane for the States. And you will never come back to Vietnam."

"You make it sound like I'm a criminal, Jack. Is that what you think after all these years? After all you've seen here? That I'm the criminal?"

Howe did not drop his eyes. Clearly he had decided that this priest wasn't going to make him feel guilty. He had his battens in place now.

"All right, Jack," Michael said, "I agree."

Howe nodded briskly and left the room.

Inge Holz was waiting beyond the sandbag barrier. The rain had stopped and the late afternoon sky was clear and bright. When Michael came out, she rushed forward and embraced him. She began to question him in a rush, but he put his finger to his lips and led her away from the headquarters building. In the middle of the next block he unbuttoned his cassock and took it off. He laughed. "I should have left this there. I borrowed it from the air force." He draped it over one arm, and put the other arm around her shoulder. "I think they let me out because they sensed you wouldn't go away."

"I wasn't certain you are still there, but where else can I go?" Her calm had never broken, but he saw how alarmed she'd been.

He told her that Pham and the others would be released the next day, and that he'd agreed to leave Vietnam.

"And you believe them?" she asked.

"I'm not going until I see them."

"But when you go they can do anything."

"They can do anything now, Inge. My being around guarantees nothing."

"But how can you leave? Without you they are there forever. Pham won't stop now. He'll need you again."

"No. He needs his own people. That's all. If I have work to

do, it's with mine. Pham doesn't need me. Maybe he doesn't need you either." Michael hadn't planned to say that. What business was it of his?

"What do you say?" She held herself against what he'd said, as if it was the first blow of many.

"He's a priest, Inge. You know what I mean."

She slipped out of his arm and ran ahead. She dodged through traffic to cross the street away from him.

By the time he caught up with her, she was sobbing.

"I'm sorry," he said, as he took her arm.

She continued to walk at a clip, but she didn't shake him off. Neither spoke. They walked as far as Lam Son Square where battered Citroëns and Pugeots competed with the motorbikes and pedicabs in the evening rush hour.

In front of the big hotel, the Continental Palace, that catered to Americans and Europeans he suggested they go in for a drink. She didn't resist. Her spirit was drained. She was exhausted, he realized, and far too vulnerable to deal with what he'd said.

The cocktail lounge was dark. Most of the tables were taken by reporters, tech-reps, embassy people, French entrepreneurs and well-to-do Vietnamese. As they took places at a small table, Michael realized that Inge Holz, even gaunt and weary, was more beautiful than any woman there. He felt ill at ease suddenly, as if he had no right to be in such a place with her.

They ordered whiskey and waited for it to be served.

Michael said softly, "I was out of line. I shouldn't have said that. I know from nothing."

"You know more than I think." She shrugged. "We have been . . ." She didn't finish the sentence. What was she going to say? Lovers? Discreet? Fools?

"I know how hard it is," he said, "to love someone impossibly." His thoughts flew to Carolyn.

Her eyes were lit with feeling when she said in a voice he could barely hear, "It is not impossible."

"Of course it is."

"Then that is because of the war."

"No, the war is what has enabled you to find each other."

After a long moment her eyes went to his and she asked, "Have you loved a woman?"

"Yes," he replied simply.

She looked away from him, tears spilling over her cheeks. She said, "For long I have wanted to talk to someone. I love him."

"I know."

"Is that wrong? Is that sinful?"

Michael knew what he'd been trained to answer, what Fitzmaurice, Spellman and even O'Shea would have answered. An absolute answer, arrived at absolutely, without hesitation. And he knew what the circumstances of his own decision to be a priest and his determination to remain one required him to answer too. The same thing.

Wrong? Sinful? Those words he applied at last to the war. But the war — ah, there was a moral dilemma, conundrum, tragic problem! Michael knew that the chaplains and bishops, having considered the war from across an infinite stretch of the ambiguous, had disqualified themselves from passing judgment because military matters were not in the area of their competence. But was love?

"You love a man," he said. "How can that be anything in God's eyes but glorious?"

TWENTY-FIVE

"MY darling Carolyn," I said, and at last she looked at me.

"Oh, Durk, I'm dying."

"But not today." I touched her cheek. Even in the fickle light of the baptistry I saw how tan she was, how beautiful. Her face was distorted, though, with feeling. We had been holding each other for a long time. The Vietnamese girl had disappeared from the shadows, and I wondered, Was she there at all? Had I invented her? "Was that your daughter?"

She looked where I was looking, at no one, but she nodded. "Yes, Thuy Thien."

"She is lovely."

"She is heartbroken." Carolyn fell against me once more. "So am I, oh, so am I."

My eye drifted to the coffin, stark and brutal box. Beyond it in the stone wall were bronze plaques, and I realized with a shudder that they marked niches for cineary urns. That was the columbarium, the vault of the dead, and it seemed suddenly so foreign, so unnatural, so Protestant — until the Renewal, Catholics were forbidden cremation — that I wondered again at Michael's being there. But was he really? I looked at the coffin once more. It holds him, I told myself, but didn't believe it. Still, I wanted to get away. Michael Maguire had been more alive than anyone I knew. If he could die, then who or what couldn't? Could the very earth live? Could God? It was a surprise to learn that for all my years, for all my books, for my eternity in the tomb of the monastery, I did not believe in death. I had been assuming like a twelve-year-old that we and the ones we love live forever. I squeezed my eyes against the truth, touched my face to Carolyn's hair. I inhaled her. "Should we go outside," I asked, "where we can talk?"

She pulled back to look at me and I was afraid her steady gaze meant she was offended. Would she drag me to the coffin, lift its lid and make me look at him? No. She nodded.

I led her by the hand, out into the ambulatory and back around the curving, becolumned passageway. And suddenly I was leading her by the hand in a different darkness. Where? What was that sound? A name? A word? A moan? It was waves breaking. It was night. We were walking along the beach at Lake George. I had escaped Saint John the Divine once more in memory. The lake's calm inland surface had been transformed by the wind. It seemed to be a bay of the Atlantic, and in the darkness the water might have stretched for three thousand miles, instead of merely three. The imported sand underfoot was difficult to walk in, made us feel drunk. The house of our friends was behind the trees. We had come out, we'd said, for air. But in fact the endless Scrabble game had bored us.

The wind whipped at our clothes. Carolyn was wearing loose white cotton bell-bottoms and a white Mexican wedding shirt. She was a summer night vision, and what light there was — the moon had set but the stars were brilliant — seemed drawn to her. When we were down the beach, utterly alone, we stopped, wordlessly, as if we'd planned to, and embraced. Her tongue was in my mouth. My hands were on the blades of her back, pressing her against me. Her hands were at my belt. And then in seconds we were naked and on the sand. I was between her thighs, moistening her with my tongue. Then I was on her. She had my prick in her hands and was taking me in. And I was crying out, Oh, God, and trying to raise my head away from her, arching involuntarily, but she was holding me, my face by her face, and as she pumped back at me, swiveling, she breathed in audibly, endlessly. When at last she exhaled, the air was a word, a whisper alive in my inner ear, as if already it had entered my body through my skin.

"Durk!" she said. But it was more than my name. It was a plea, a summons, an expression of pain that I never forgot. "Durk! Durk!" For once passion seemed to have taken over her. "I do love you!" she said, but what I heard was her emphasis; I *do* love you! As if someone had said she didn't. As if *she* had.

Michael was assigned to duties at Saint Joseph of Arimathea in Alna, a village just north of Newburgh, about a mile west of the Hudson. He was solemnly forbidden to preach or teach anything having to do with Vietnam, but that was no problem in that parish where the pressing issues had been keeping the school open and the people closed. If he participated in antiwar activities in any way, his priestly faculties would be suspended. When this was spelled out to him upon his return that summer from Vietnam, he found it impossible to respond. Something like this had happened to him before when Spellman had coopted him with the Relief Fund job. But this was not sweet persuasion. He was not given a choice this time, and frankly the old pull of priestly obedience seemed less like oppression than rescue. Once more the refuge of certitude and exemption was being offered him, no, forced on him. But now, exhausted and emotionally spent after the events in Vietnam — after seeing the hopelessness of things there — he did not reject that refuge but welcomed it. His one request was to speak in person to Cardinal Spellman. It was refused. Spellman would not see him. The cardinal, the chancellor said, would like never to lay eyes on him again. And he might not have, except for Nicholas Wiley.

But it was a while before Nicholas came back into his life. By then, Michael had grown almost accustomed to the quotidian pastoral life of Saint Joseph's. No big crises, no acts of violence, no napalm; just the early-morning Mass, offered quietly for a few old ladies before dawn; at breakfast he exchanged banalities with his fellow priests and wasn't even tempted to read the papers, as in the evening he wouldn't be tempted to watch the news on television. The world beyond Alna became less and less important as he gave himself to the oddly fulfilling tasks of parish ministry. Instead of the wounded children in primitive hospitals, there were the shy teenagers in his Religion Class. Michael taught them to feel better about themselves. Instead of frantic trekking around Vietnam, there were afternoon games of pick-up at the high school, where boys imitated Michael's slow, loose-wristed jump shot. It wasn't long before Michael was the one they came to with their problems. Instead of terrified refugees, there were addled old people in the local nursing home. Michael talked to them about the Resurrection of the Dead, and if they wanted him to he would, yes, describe heaven to them, golden boulevards, becolumned mansions and all. Instead of demonstrations in the streets of Saigon, there were wakes in the evening at which he lead the rosary or meetings of the Holy Name Society to which each month more and more of the parish men came. But always, rooting him, giving him such solace, such nurture, such pleasure, the priest's version of love-making, were those quiet early Masses, the sharp smell of candles instead of tear gas, the taste of oversweet altar wine instead of fear, and the palpable sense of God's nearness instead of loneliness. His *memento,* still, was for peace, and he always mentioned by name Suu Van Pham and Inge Holz in the prayer for the living, but the war in Vietnam was in another world than his. At Saint Joseph of Arimathea's, in other words, for the better part of a year, Michael Maguire had been condemned to the life of a small town parish priest. The truth was he loved it.

The surprise was, when Wiley showed up, Michael did not feel ashamed.

It was March of 1966. Michael was improvising a system of supports for the star magnolia that he had planted in the churchyard the previous autumn. The tree was one of his first attempts to brighten the place, but the winter had savaged it and it seemed unlikely that spring would revive it. The other priests, the pastor and the first curate, were old men who'd lost their battles years before, and the backwater church of Saint Joseph's, the emblem of their defeat, had taken on their slouch. Michael had planted several trees right away and the beginnings of a rose garden. By Christmas he had organized teenagers to paint the parish hall. This spring he'd already recruited local masons to point the brick facade of the church itself, and he was planning to turn the entire neglected churchyard into a garden. But now he wondered, Was it futile?

"Sad-looking tree," Nicholas Wiley said from behind Michael. "How'd you expect it to survive in this fresh air?"

Michael turned slowly.

The sight of Nicholas Wiley, now wearing a colorful headband and hair to his shoulders and a full beard, threw him. He had never expected to see Wiley again, as if in Alna he'd entered a world to which the likes of this by now full-blown hippie would not be admitted. In a way it was true. Wiley looked like the young people who had staked their claim to the Bancroft Fountain in Central Park. In the city his get-up was as ordinary as the business suits of lawyers, but in the churchyard of a conservative town, it seemed provocative, inflammatory. Michael himself had to stifle an instinctive repugnance at his appearance. But, when he did, when he actually looked at Nicholas Wiley then, he saw that in his own way he looked good. He looked like what he was.

He looked, of course, like Jesus. Remember how for a time America was populated with young Saviors?

Michael dropped his pliers and crossed the lawn, grinning. "You son of a gun," he said.

Nicholas Wiley opened his arms wide. Remember how men began to embrace each other that year?

Michael felt a surge of guilt as they hugged roughly, half-fighting, not about his life at Saint Joseph's but about having left it to Wiley to come to him. When he'd returned to New York he'd written to him, but the short note came back undelivered and Michael hadn't pursued it. Nicholas Wiley was part of what he'd all too willingly left behind. Already Michael's years in Vietnam had receded into the haze of memory. His sharp outrage, his intensely felt compassion for the children, his attachments to the Vietnamese he'd met were like items of contraband he had handed over to stern Customs agents upon his return. He had done it in the name of faithfulness. That irony — that he had broken faith while keeping faith — confused him. Of course he had to shut it out, along with all his feelings and convictions. The conflict implicit in his position was impossible. There could be no such thing as a defiant priest. And so, of course, he'd taken refuge in his belief that the benefit of the doubt, for priests as for married people, had always to go not to intense present feeling but to the solemn promise around which one's life was built.

"You son of a gun," he said again.

"I'd rather you called me a son of a bitch."

Michael pulled back to hold him by the shoulders, expecting to see him grinning. But he wasn't. He'd made the comment earnestly — I'm no son of a weapon — and that was Michael's first warning. "Okay, you're a son of a bitch." Michael tapped his chin. "And it's great to see you."

"It's good to see you too."

"Thanks."

"You're welcome." Now Wiley grinned, but strangely. They separated. Wiley looked around awkwardly. "Nice garden."

Michael looked at the budding trees, the grass with its first splash of green. Mulch still protected the new flower beds and burlap sacks still covered the infant boxwoods. "This is nothing. Come back in a month."

"I don't know if I'll be able to," Wiley said with abrupt solemnity.

"Why not?"

"That's what I came to talk about."

The peace movement with its full-page ads in the *Times,* its teach-ins, marches and draftcard burnings was just picking up steam that spring, and Michael was certain Wiley had come to ask him to join it. He hadn't considered that Wiley might have come to him for help. He chided himself. There was more on this young man's mind than what Michael Maguire did or didn't do to sublimate his guilt and loneliness. He studied him for a moment and read, now that he bothered to try, the signs of his pitched anxiety. Nicholas's beard obscured the facts that he'd lost weight and that his skin had a gray pallor to it. His eyes were unfocused and bloodshot. Where once only his thumbs were gnawed, now all of his fingernails had been chewed to the quick. "Come on inside," he said.

"I'd rather stay out here." Wiley looked nervously toward the grim rectory. "Could we just go for a walk or something?"

"Sure." Michael led the way. Soon they were on an unpaved lane that went up Rattlesnake Mountain, the hill at the base of which the town nestled. Neither spoke until they came to a bright meadow around a house-sized boulder. Michael scurried to the top of it, then reached back to help Nicholas up. When they were sitting, the stone cold beneath them, Michael said, "I come here to think my best thoughts."

"You're going to need them."

"Why?"

"Because I want you to tell me what to do."

"What's up?"

Wiley looked at him strangely. "You know what's up."

"No, I don't."

Nicholas pulled a creased news photo from his canvas bag. He handed it to Michael. It wasn't a picture of a child now, though, but of a Buddhist pagoda in flames. In the foreground, helmeted Vietnamese Rangers were clubbing an aged monk. It was all too familiar. The Buddhist Struggle had resumed as the war had worsened and become Americanized. The cities of South Vietnam were paralyzed daily by thousands of chanting, frenzied demonstrators. There were reports that taxi drivers and shopkeepers were shaving their heads and dressing as monks to replace those who'd been arrested. It was yet to be seen whether Ky and Thieu would be any more effective against them — though they were equally brutal — than Diem had been.

Michael folded the photograph and handed it back to Wiley. "What does it mean to you?" he asked somewhat rigidly. He resolved to keep his own reaction at arm's length until he knew what Wiley wanted.

"Just that we're back where we started three years ago. Catholic government against Buddhist people. Only now the government has three hundred thousand American mercenaries and bombers galore. They're using B-52s now."

Michael hadn't known that. B-52s? Was he so out of touch?

Nicholas shook his head. "The Buddhists don't hope to change their government anymore, you know. They're trying to change us. They know that we're the ones who have to stop the war. We're the ones who pay for it. You and I are the ones who let it happen. And it just keeps getting worse."

Michael said nothing.

Wiley looked sharply at him. "Didn't you learn anything over there?"

Michael felt the blast of the young man's disappointment — it was there after all — and tried to deflect it. "I learned always to put my chopsticks into the hot rice as soon as it was served. It was the only way to sterilize them."

"Is that what you worried about? Germs?"

Michael shook his head, but of course he had worried about germs.

"You were going to save the children! You were going to make the army take care of the wounded!"

"I was naive, Nicholas. I was wrong. You were right. The only thing to be done about the war is to stop it."

"Well, what are you doing here then?"

"I'd convinced myself that you didn't come here to guilt-trip me. You didn't come here to talk about my life; you came to talk about yours. What's going on?"

"I'm pulling out."

"What do you mean?"

"I'm going to serve the people."

"What do you mean, Nicholas? You sound like Chairman Mao." Michael waited for him to answer, but he didn't. The war had obviously possessed him, as surely as some devil, and now Michael could only try to imagine what he was contemplating.

"I have to volunteer," he said at last. "I have to cut my hair and shave and sign up."

What, the army? Did he intend to go in as a medic or something? But the army wouldn't let him within a mile of itself. Was he thinking of going to Asia with a volunteer agency? Michael knew what that impulse was like, and how futile it would be. For Nicholas it would be dangerous. "What do you mean?" he asked again.

"I have been conscripted and I have to go."

"I want to understand what you mean, Nicholas. Help me to understand."

"Is that all you can say?" He clambered to his feet. "What do I mean? What do I mean?" He raised his arms to the sky melodramatically and threw his head back. His hair rained down like an Indian's, like a prophet's. "How the hell do I know what I mean? The fucking war has got to stop! That's what I mean! The American people have got to stop it! The Catholic Church has got to stop it! 'War no more! War never again!' The pope said that! The *pope* said that!" he began screeching wildly. "Peace now! Peace now!"

Michael stood quickly. Balance was precarious on the boulder. Before Wiley could fall, Michael grabbed him and held him. The young man deflated and shrunk, falling against Michael who sensed in him an infinite relief. Nicholas began to sob. Michael remembered Inge Holz: Is this wrong? Is it sinful? Am I insane? And he had the same reaction. Was it mere rhetoric, a deflection of his own sense of responsibility for what Wiley had become? Perhaps. But he felt it nevertheless. The madness was not in this boy, but in the war.

Michael knew from his own experience that what Nicholas Wiley needed was some ordinary living, a taste of the pleasures and duties of work and friendship, a spell in the realm of the utterly unnewsworthy where alone he could be safe from the ravaging News. Death held sway over the world, after all; life over only the smallest pieces of it. Over little places like Alna and Saint Joseph's. From what Michael learned on their subsequent walks, Nicholas had become less and less connected in New York. After leaving the *Catholic Worker* he'd attached himself to a settlement house in Harlem for a time, had written for a Quaker magazine, had joined, then quit, the Newman Club at NYU in the Village. He attended demonstrations and had gone to Washington twice, once as part of a group of Quakers who held a vigil outside the Capitol while Congress debated — and passed — a special four-billion-dollar appropriation for the war. It was then he'd begun to fast, and he hadn't eaten right since. Despite all this, his part in the peace movement remained tangential. He'd made no close friends. He was no longer in touch with his family, and along the way he'd stopped seeing his therapist. So Michael offered him a job as his helper in the garden at Saint Joseph's and convinced him to take it. Surely he'd tracked Michael down hoping for such an intervention, even if he couldn't admit that to himself.

Behind the sacristy there was a room with a cot where Nicholas slept, and he stayed through the spring. At first he was too depressed to express much in the way of gratitude, but that was the last thing Michael required of him. At times he was downright sullen and at other times, often after watching the nightly news in Michael's room, he was hysterical about the killing in Vietnam. But Michael stayed at him. There was no question now of arguing about the peace movement. All Michael wanted to do was help restore the equilibrium Nicholas needed to deal with his experience creatively. Eventually Nicholas began to respond. The rectory housekeeper treated him like the son she wanted, and the hard physical work gave him an appetite for her plain food. He gained weight and a bright sunburn replaced his pallor. Even the pastor softened toward him and said that if he'd shave his beard and cut his hair, he could start taking up the collection at Mass. Nicholas refused, of course, but politely, though to Michael he joked that he was tempted because he could have used the extra income.

One morning, while Michael was taking his vestments off after Mass, Nicholas came into the sacristy from the garden. He wore an expression of pure joy and he said, "Father, you've got to come outside."

Michael followed him.

Nicholas led the way to the star magnolia and with a ringmaster's panache he stepped aside and swept his arm toward the tree's first-ever flower. "I said to the magnolia, 'Sister, speak to me of God,' and the magnolia blossomed." Wiley grinned as he watched Michael approach the branch and put his nose to the flower. "Isn't it great?" Wiley asked. "Isn't it just so great!"

It was the boy who seemed great to Michael; there was such happiness in him. Michael grinned too and said, "And this is just the beginning, Nicholas. You'll have flowers coming up all over the place before you're done."

Wiley nodded. "I think you're right, Michael. I think you're right."

"Hey, guess what?"

"What?"

"You just called me Michael."

"I did?" Wiley leaned toward him, showing his amazement.

"Just now."

"God, I never thought I'd be able to."

Michael felt as though he'd won something, a prize, an important medal. What a strange effect the use of his own name could have on him. "I knew you would, Nicholas."

"Does that mean . . . ?" He hesitated, looked down shyly, blushing.

"It means we're really friends now, Nicholas."

Nicholas looked up at him, tears brimming, relief extravagantly on his face. "Thank you, Michael. Thank you."

Michael shook his head, implying, I should thank you. He struck a pose and recited, "I said to Nicholas Wiley, 'Brother, speak to me of God,' and he called me Michael."

It was absurd, such a small thing, such happiness from it. But they both felt it. They embraced in their rough, athletic way, and they laughed and laughed.

A few days later Michael was going into Manhattan for a clergy meeting and he thought Nicholas might enjoy some time in the city too. But Nicholas didn't show for breakfast. Michael went looking for him. He knocked on the door of the little room behind the sacristy, but there was no answer. He's still asleep, Michael thought, and he opened the door quietly. But Nicholas's bed was neatly made already, army corners and all. He'd gone into Alna probably. Too bad. Michael couldn't wait. He'd have enjoyed the company. He was about to close the door when something caught his eye on Nicholas's table, a copy of the *New York Times*. That was unusual enough, since Nicholas didn't read the paper either, but in that first glance, the front page seemed wrong. Then Michael realized there was a hole in it, something had been clipped, and a clothing ad was showing through from page three. Michael wondered about it, but not for long.

The clergy meeting was at Holy Trinity in Greenwich Village and lasted through lunch. Michael enjoyed the company of priests his own age and was reluctant to return to Alna, but the other priests scattered when the meeting ended. They were big city men and all had their appointments. So Michael decided to take a long walk. It was a beautiful May day. Washington Square was full of painted hippies wading in the fountains, tossing Frisbees, passing marijuana, playing guitars. A pretty girl with hair to her waist was sitting in the grass breast-feeding her baby while her young beau serenaded them on his flute. New York, especially after Alna, seemed charmed, and he wished Nicholas had come with him. For a moment he wondered again where the kid had gone off to so early.

By midafternoon, Michael found himself at Saint Patrick's and he went in to kneel and pray while the tourists gawked and the shoppers, rattling their bags, sat and rested. He loved the place. He couldn't go there without remembering his ordination or reclaiming that sense of hope he'd felt, that sense of God's kindly touch. He knelt for a long time, offering his gratitude, his relief. He was the man, at last, he'd wanted to become.

When he came out into the bright glare he stood at the top step of the cathedral and watched the traffic of Fifth Avenue, the fancy cars and the tricked-out secretaries on their breaks, the most beautiful girls in the world. He thought of Jesus watching the gold-laden caravans from the pinnacle of the Temple. "All this I will give you," the devil had said, "if you will worship me." Michael knew for the first time why Jesus had said no. He didn't need the gold or the cars or the stunning girls. He had everything he wanted.

As he walked down the stairs he saw a group of cops on the corner near a newsstand. One of them looked toward him, and something in the man's eyes drew Michael. There were five of them, and they were craned toward a nearby motorcycle's radio.

As he walked toward them he passed the newsstand, and had to step around a stack of papers, that day's *Times*.

"What's up, fellows?" he asked.

"Hey, Father, you won't believe this one."

"What?" He cocked an ear toward the police radio, but it was all static. He let his eye fall to the newspapers. On the front page was a photograph of a Buddhist monk seated in the lotus position on a Saigon street, and he was aflame.

"Some guy," the policeman said, "over at the U.N. douses himself with gasoline and lights a match. Some peacenik kook."

Michael reeled, exactly as if that cop had jammed his nightstick into his stomach. As if he'd brought it crashing down onto his skull. No. The cops were so surprised they didn't catch him when he fell.

Nicholas Wiley died that night in the burn unit at Bellevue. Michael was with him. Nicholas never regained consciousness, and when Michael anointed him there was no place he could touch him with the sacred oil that wasn't burned. He bent over him and began to whisper into the charred hole that had been his ear the words of the Act of Contrition. "O my God, I am heartily sorry for having offended Thee . . ." Standard procedure. The idea was that the unconscious person might somehow register what was being said and assent to it.

But Michael was unable to finish the recitation. He began to sob. He wanted to rest his head on Nicholas's chest, even that scorched chest, but he was afraid to touch him for fear of causing pain. The stench of burned flesh was familiar. All too fucking familiar.

Michael began to whisper again when he could, but instead of the Act of Contrition he said simply, over and over, "I'm sorry. I'm sorry. I'm sorry."

Reporters were waiting for him outside the ward. Michael was stunned by their assumption that they had the right to question him.

"Was he your protégé?"

"What?" Michael had trouble focusing on the reporter who'd asked the question. There were a dozen or more, men and women, and some had thrust microphones at him.

"He was your employee?"

"He was my friend," Michael said, and he pushed through them.

"Dorothy Day says he was not a Catholic Worker, the Quakers say he was not a member of any meeting, and the archdiocese says they had no record of him on the Church payroll. Was he connected with your parish or not?"

Michael ignored the question. When a reporter grabbed his arm Michael pushed him roughly aside.

"The cardinal said if he was a Catholic, he's excommunicated."

"What?" Michael stopped and faced the man who'd said that.

"Because it's suicide," the reporter added.

"Suicide?" Michael glared at him.

"He burned himself to death, right?"

"When did the cardinal say that?"

"Shortly after the hospital pronounced the kid dead." The man referred to his notes. "He said, '. . . the Church condemns suicide. Anyone who commits it forfeits the right to a Church burial.' "

"He said that?"

"Well, that's the statement they issued at the chancery. His name was on it."

It was as if a pair of mailed hands reached into Michael's chest and tore his lungs out. He said, "I haven't spoken to the cardinal. I don't expect to. I will speak to Nicholas Wiley's parents, and, if they agree, he will have a Roman Catholic burial at Saint Joseph of Arimathea Church in Alna, New York. We will pray for the repose of his soul."

"You don't condemn suicide?"

A flashbulb went off in Michael's face. He was blind for a moment.

He said, "Nicholas Wiley is a martyr. He is at peace with God.

What I condemn is the war in Vietnam, and that is what the cardinal should be condemning too."

The next day Cardinal Spellman summoned Michael to his office.

He had not been in his office since the time nearly three years before when Michael had gone to him upon his first return from Vietnam. Since then, it seemed to Michael, the pin had been removed from the center of the world itself. Everything was out of kilter now. He had only one certainty as he entered the cardinal's residence, that Nicholas Wiley was going to be buried in Church.

The woman at the typewriter in the room off the entrance hall knew who he was this time. His photograph had been in all the New York papers that morning. A tourist's photograph of Nicholas Wiley in flames had been on the front page of every major newspaper in America.

"Father Maguire is here," she said into her phone.

Monsignor Dugan was waiting for him when the elevator doors opened on the second floor. He followed Michael down the hallway to the cardinal's office.

As before, Spellman was sitting at his desk, back to the window, waiting for him when he entered. Spellman did not stand. He needed the desk this time, against this man.

Dugan ushered Michael to the wing chair. Michael took it. Dugan took his place at the large Catalonian table, opened a folder and uncapped his pen.

The cardinal spoke then and his voice was steely. "You have contradicted me publicly on a grave matter of faith and morals. You have disobeyed my explicit order regarding use of the public forum. You are hereby suspended of all priestly faculties. You are not to preach, administer the sacraments, or celebrate the Holy Eucharist."

Michael did not blink. "Your Eminence, I am going to preside at the funeral of Nicholas Wiley at Saint Joseph's. After that I will obey you."

Spellman's face reddened. "You are no longer assigned to Saint Joseph's. You are now assigned to the North American College in Rome where for two years you are to pursue the Licentiate in Sacred Theology. Obviously you did not learn your lessons well enough the first time."

Michael stood. "I respectfully submit, Your Eminence, that there is little point in continuing this. I will leave Saint Joseph's when Nicholas Wiley has been buried there. I will stop preaching and go to Rome when the war in Vietnam is over."

"Consider carefully what you are saying, Father."

"I've considered it for three years, Your Eminence." Michael towered over him. The cardinal seemed small and weary. He had been defeated by the very thing — American Catholic triumph — to which he'd given the best energy of his life. It seemed no surprise at all to discover that this frightened old man could do nothing to punish Michael and nothing to stop him. Nor could Michael want to punish Spellman by denouncing that war as a monument to the man's vanity. He clung to what mattered. "I feel bound in conscience to complete my ministry to Nicholas Wiley. I cannot abandon him, not even to keep my vow to you. I wasn't with him when he needed me most, but I'm with him now."

"But you cannot have a Mass at Saint Joseph's. I will not permit it."

"Then I will do it in Central Park. Is that what you prefer? I have no intention of turning Nicholas Wiley's death into a protest rally." Michael leaned over Spellman's desk, put his hands upon it. He stared at the prelate with cold, threatening eyes and he said, "But if you refuse me access to the small church to which he devoted the last efforts of his life, that's exactly what it will become. And you will have to answer for it, to newspapers, to television, to Rome and to God." Michael straightened abruptly, and his arm shot out, his finger stabbed toward Spellman. "Believe me, Cardinal, you will have to answer."

Spellman could hardly bring himself to speak. He opened his mouth and closed it. He shook his head. Finally he said, "But we are talking about Church law! This is not a matter of my will, Father, or of yours. This is not a matter of individual conscience. You are a priest!" He gestured with both his fists at Michael. "You must condemn the sacrilege of suicide!"

"I will not!" Michael shot back. Now anger choked him too. But he reined it. "Church law on the matter of the burial of the dead — any dead — leaves room for pastoral discretion, Your Eminence. If you don't know that you should. Ask Monsignor Dugan." Michael looked back at the other prelate, who refused to raise his eyes from his notepad. He was a canon lawyer and knew that Michael was right. Michael faced Spellman again. "By your statements you have made the issue that young man's rejection of the war. You have made the issue his standing as a Catholic. You have made the issue your authority. And I am telling you — as I will tell anyone who asks — that in the matter of Nicholas Wiley I refuse to be bound by your authority. The issue is his right to a loving gesture from the Church, and he will have it. Beyond that, I refuse to yield to you in anything related to this evil war."

Cardinal Spellman's lips moved soundlessly around the only words he could think to say: "Get out!"

Michael nodded, a vestige of respect, and left.

Early the next day he prayed the Mass for the Dead, quietly, without music, in the Church of Saint Joseph of Arimathea. In front of him was the pine box containing Nicholas Wiley's remains. Michael had not made the time of the service public, but he'd notified those whom he hoped would come. Very few did. Not Nicholas's parents, not his therapist. No one from the Newman Club at NYU; the chaplain was on retreat. A seminarian and two women from the *Catholic Worker* were there, although not Dorothy Day, who would later bristle when Thomas Merton himself wrote that something was wrong with a movement that led people to kill themselves. Two Quakers with whom Nicholas had worked for a short time were there, and so was the rectory housekeeper.

Michael reminded them, as he threw the first handful of dirt onto Wiley's coffin in the parish cemetery, that Saint Joseph of Arimathea was the stranger who'd taken the body of Jesus from the cross when none of His friends would claim it. He had placed it in his own tomb.

The stone now with which to seal such a hole was in Michael's heart.

TWENTY-SIX

CARDINAL Spellman died in the last month of 1967. In his final Christmas sermon to thousands of American soldiers at Cam Ranh Bay the year before he had christened their efforts as "a war for civilization." He had said that the peace America sought could be had only through "total victory." The troops cheered him, but their applause was far from enough by then. He would return home to a people he had embarrassed, and the Holy Father himself would make clear his displeasure at what was less "faith and morals" than rank jingoism. Even Cardinal Spellman knew that he had outlived values and modes that once he had thought were absolute. His physical death was only the last of many deaths he suffered toward the end, but even so, to others it was a shock. The cardinal? Dead? As if the structures of his Church, his country and his war could not stand without his support, they immediately began to rock like runaway scaffolding in the winds of that typhoon of years, 1968.

First, in January, Tet, that decisive defeat of the Communists in Vietnam that, in the mad logic of that war, assured their victory. Then, little more than a month later, the political defeat of an upstart senator by the president in the New Hampshire primary (the president won 48 percent to Eugene McCarthy's 42 percent) that, in the same logic, sealed the defeat of LBJ and led to his withdrawal from the race. A few weeks later, in the same month, Lieutenant Calley presided over the slaughter of several hundred civilians at My Lai. Some Americans, when they learned of it a year later, would not understand the fuss, and they would be right. Calley was a victim of the army's pretense that what he did was different.

Then on a bright April day a new archbishop of New York and Vicar of the American Military was installed at Saint Patrick's Cathedral, an unoffensive Irishman named Terence Cooke whose first words from the episcopal throne were addressed to Lyndon Johnson, sitting in the front row. He thanked the president for coming and commended him warmly for his valiant search for peace in Vietnam, a search which by then was being conducted by 549,000 U.S. soldiers, none of whom could find it and many of whom, even if they lived, would never have it again. Johnson liked Catholics a lot better now than he had as a boy in Texas, for they were his diehard backers. Demonstrations of the sort paralyzing hundreds of other colleges that spring weren't tolerated on Catholic campuses, and the students weren't inclined to have them anyway. Furthermore, the Catholic bishops issued a rare formal statement about the war. Applying the principles of Vatican II and the classic moral theory of the Scholastic tradition, though not the urgent pronouncements of Pope Paul VI, they said, "It is reasonable to argue that our presence in Vietnam is justified."

No one noticed how cozy Archbishop Cooke and President Johnson were that day, however, because a few hours after the ceremony at Saint Patrick's, James Earl Ray shot and killed the clergyman who had most resolutely condemned the war. In the days and weeks following Dr. King's death, black Americans in a dozen cities set fire to their own neighborhoods. Hardly anyone noticed. But at the end of the month when students took over Columbia before going on vacation, the nation was stunned.

In France, too, the young revolted — one resists saying they were revolting — while in Germany a punk named Andreas Baader committed his first act of arson, and in Northern Ireland Catholics took to the streets for the first time in years, not dreaming how much worse their lives could get. In June, Vietnam became the longest war in U.S. history, and a lunatic Arab saw to it that the war would be as long again still when he murdered the leader of those who opposed it. Robert Kennedy was buried from Saint Patrick's Cathedral, and with him was buried any hope not only for a prompt end to the killing, but for a return to our simple faith in the goodness of our government. Carolyn and I kept the vigil on Fifth Avenue with a million others. On our radios we heard Andy Williams begin the "Battle Hymn of the Republic." A news bulletin reported that the three-month-old siege of Khe Sanh was lifted that day. The marines had held. "Mine eyes have seen the glory . . ." What should have felt like victory in that war was always more like defeat. All we could do was hold each other and sing.

In July Catholics who'd thought their Church had changed were jolted by the papal encyclical, *Humanae Vitae,* forbidding all forms of birth control except abstinence and rhythm. Well, it *had* changed because immediately thousands of Catholic priests in Europe and America publicly rejected the pope's authority in the matter. Bishops on the other hand, who had found it possible the year before to ignore Paul's radical criticisms of capitalism, private property and the profit motive in *Progressio Populorum,* now fell in behind His Holiness with a vengeance. When the large majority of seminarians signed a dissenting letter in Boston, Cardinal Cushing fired them without discussion. In Los Angeles Cardinal MacIntyre forced his clergy to take a solemn oath of fealty, and in Washington Cardinal O'Boyle imposed an oath of his own and suspended more than forty of his priests for refusing to take it. Many priests didn't wait to be suspended. In large numbers — tens of thousands eventually — they began to resign their ministry altogether. Meanwhile millions of Catholic lay men and women who had long since decided for themselves in the matter of contraception regarded the squabbling of celibates over other people's sex lives with distaste and a kind of embarrassed pity. So much for the triumph of American Catholicism.

In August the police — Catholics again — rioted in Chicago and the Russians sent tanks into Prague. The first event guaranteed the defeat of the Democratic candidate and the second meant that the Republican candidate — or so he said — could not reveal his secret plan for ending the war. In China the Red Guard had begun their rampage, but we didn't care about China yet.

In October Jacqueline Kennedy married Aristotle Onassis, a divorced man. The Vatican newspaper called her "a public sinner." But now even cardinals began to dissent — authority was in shambles everywhere — when Cushing of Boston countered, "Leave the poor woman alone."

November gave us Nixon.

On December 10 Thomas Merton, with whom we began, having left his Kentucky monastery for the first time in over twenty years, was in Bangkok for a meeting of Zen and Christian monks and masters, an effort toward East-West reconciliation. He was electrocuted while trying to plug in a fan. By now even the most benign American contact with Southeast Asia seemed dangerous, tragic, violent and absurd.

And on Christmas Eve, the last week of the year, the American military elite, our astronauts, preached the homily from the moon. "In the beginning God created the heaven and the earth," one of them read, looking back at us, a blue ball hanging in nothing. "And the earth was without form, and void; and darkness was upon the face of the deep."

Some people were undone by that string of jolts and others were made by it, their energies focused and the essentials of their lives revealed. Michael was one of these, though perhaps he would not have been, frankly, but for me and Carolyn.

After leaving Saint Joseph's, he'd lived with us in Brooklyn. The suspension of his faculties as a priest disoriented him, and he turned to us for the support and friendship he was not getting from his fellow clergy. Oh, there were always a few renegade Jesuits hanging around, junior editors from *America* or young faculty and graduate students whom I'd bring over from Fordham thinking the clerical company would cheer him up. But the radical priests, as Paul Simon called them, were hotshots, hypnotized by their own flamboyance. What seemed to attract them to Michael was his bad standing. The New York press had made much of his conflict with Spellman, and the young antiwar priests and seminarians who sought Michael out seemed to regard such ecclesiastical disapproval as a high achievement. Michael didn't feel that way about it. He was never comfortable with rebels, and he hated it when events made him one.

It was during that time, when he was our guest and before he moved into a small apartment of his own in the East Village, that he and I began to sit up late at night, rediscovering the things that had made us friends. We were both drinking too much, but the booze helped.

During those late-night sessions, Michael talking with an abandon I'd never experienced in him, I first began to perceive the shape of this story. Korea, Lennie Pace, Tim O'Shea, the seminary, the flap with Robert Moses, Vietnam, Spellman, Jack Howe, Nicholas Wiley, Inge Holz and Suu Van Pham. I began to understand what had happened to Michael and why his confrontation with the cardinal, so long postponed, had left him at the mercy of a paralysis of guilt. During that period of his living with us I watched him struggle to fight it off.

One night we were sitting in the living room. Carolyn had gone to bed. Michael and I were sprawled in opposite corners of the same couch because it faced the window that framed the skyline of Manhattan, on which each of us let his eyes play. Surreptitiously I looked at him occasionally. He wore his gauntness more easily by then. His thin, ascetic visage had become the essence of his good looks. I, on the other hand, having quit smoking, had entered a period of overweight. His leanness, like his boldness, represented a kind of rebuke to me. His dark hair was longer than mine, and it made me feel foolish that this priest should have been handsomer, more stylish than I was. I didn't like how he made me feel. Sometimes the silences that fell between us were awkward ones and it had been so repeatedly that night.

"What's wrong, Durk?" he asked at last.

I shook my head. "Nothing's wrong, Michael."

"Have I overstayed my welcome?"

"Hell, no, you kidding?"

"Something's bugging you."

I smiled at him. "There was a time when you'd have let it bug me. You used to believe in holy reticence."

"So anyway . . ."

I worked on my drink for a few minutes and considered whether to say it. Hell, Michael Maguire was a city-wide symbol of integrity. He had his problems with Church authority, and his defiance of it had very nearly derailed him emotionally, but to a lot of the rest of us he'd become the focus of moral opposition to the war. He was already an exemplar. And what did that make me? I was a two-bit professor at a second-rate college, a sometime contributor to small-circulation journals. My professional and even personal concerns, which ordinarily seemed worthy of the best energy of my life, seemed at times like that with Michael, when the silence was on us, utterly trivial. How noble he was! How pure! How unfettered by the banalities of raising a family or earning a living! My job was to correct papers and hire instructors and chair committees and pen scathing insights so that I could pay plumbers and keep my child in barrettes and give my wife the rent money for her studio. Carolyn's work was just being noticed by the midtown galleries. One of my main jobs was to encourage her. I knew what a rare artist she had become. I considered it a privilege to pay her bills. But that was a further clamp on me, wasn't it? And clamps Michael would not have understood. His job, after all, was to speak the truth to power. I forced a smile. "You're a hard act to be in the same ring with, Michael. First a fucking war hero. Now you're threatening to become an antiwar hero. Or is it war antihero?"

"Come off it, Durk. What am I doing? A little draft counseling, what's that?"

"Maybe it's not what you're doing, Michael, but what you *are*. Tell me the truth. You think I'm just a wad of intellectual pretension, don't you?"

"No."

I laughed. "You're just afraid I'll throw you out if you say it."

"I'm not afraid of that. You know how I feel about those diehard resisters, Durk. Come on. They drive me crazy. *They* think you're bourgeois, sure. But I don't. Shit, I'm bourgeois!"

"No, you're not. You're a radical now, Michael, whether you like it or not. And folks like me feel a little uncomfortable around folks like you. A little judged."

"I don't judge you. Who the fuck am I to do that? You know the truth about me."

"What truth?" I stared at him. I was going to make him say it, admit it. Of course I knew.

"That I should have taken on the cardinal seven years ago."

If Carolyn had set herself on fire, I thought, he would have. That I nearly said that revealed to me how drunk I was. I checked myself and forced yet another laugh. "But if you had, then you and Caro would be the couple whom I was visiting. There's the irony, Michael. Is that the regret you feel?"

He shook his head. "What's the point of a regret like that? I'm just saying that I'm not judging anybody. We all have to live with the choices we make, eh?"

"Right. But see, I live with mine, *and* I live with yours. That's all I mean. I build a life that I think is mine, or mine and Carolyn's, or mine and Carolyn's and Molly's, and then, lo and behold, I see that I've built it on a little raft that bobs along in your wake. I'm a raft, Michael, see? And you're a fucking battleship."

He grinned. "But we're in the same bathtub?"

"I guess so."

"I won't be here forever, Durk. I promise."

"That's not what I'm talking about, Michael. If I feel uneasy it has to do with me, not you. I want you here. So does Carolyn. We love you, Michael."

Michael looked away from me, I thought because I'd embarrassed him. But then I realized he was staring at someone. I turned. Carolyn was standing in the doorway, in her bathrobe. Her hair was down to her shoulders. How long had she been there?

"You fellows going for the record?"

"Are we keeping you awake?" Michael asked.

I resented his solicitude. It was easy for him to be gracious because she wasn't his wife. She wasn't the symbol of his domestication. Of course I loved her, and of course I pitied him for not having her, but also — and powerfully at that moment — I hated the feeling of being hemmed in, bound by a hundred responsibilities. Sure, I'd have liked to stop the war. I'd have liked to open myself more fully to the great dramas of the time. But I couldn't and, finally, she was why. I couldn't even shoot the shit with my old buddy. Who the hell was she to sneak up on us? Who the hell was she to criticize our drinking? How I wished, for that moment, to be free of her, of Molly, of my chairmanship, of my house, of my wry, aesthetic, essentially passive sensibility. I wanted to be like Michael: free, pure, simple, direct, alone.

Carolyn shook her head. "Molly was up." She crossed to our couch and sat between us. She rested a hand on each of us.

"The Blessed Trinity," I said, and crossed myself.

Carolyn looked at me with disarming warmth, and I felt guilty for resenting her. "Can I get you a drink?" I asked.

"I'd love some wine."

I stood and started for the kitchen. Michael said, "Bring some bread, would you?"

"Sure."

I didn't think anything of his request. I brought bread and cheese, together with Carolyn's wine. When I'd put the tray on the coffee table Michael said, "Would you guys mind terribly? Praying with me?"

Carolyn and I exchanged a quick glance. The Mass? Bread and wine? Did he mean the Mass?

"Jesus, I'm a little drunk, Michael. So are you."

He sat up and leaned across us, a hand on Carolyn and a hand on me. "You two are so good to me. I love you so much. I never thank you."

"Sure you do," I said, backpedaling. I couldn't handle the confusion of modes. I was a liberal Catholic. My faith was more important to me than ever, and I wasn't cowed by rubrics or regulations. Home liturgies were common among our circle, particularly with Michael as celebrant since he was not allowed to offer Mass publicly, but not in the middle of the night, not as an act of real intimacy, not shorn of everything but a French roll, a glass of muscatel and sentimental blurry-eyed gratitude. Why couldn't he just thank us, kiss us on our cheeks and pass out like other drunks?

But Carolyn said, "That would be nice, Michael."

He took a piece of the bread I'd brought. "Just something simple," he said. He lifted the bread. We all stared at it. After a long silence, a silence that transformed our mood, he spoke softly, naturally, as if to someone who was really there. "Blessed are you, Lord God of the Universe, for through your goodness we have this bread to offer, fruit of the earth and the work of human hands. Let it become for us a spiritual food." He paused and looked at each of us. I could feel my reluctance falling away. What was it that drew me in? His intensity, perhaps. His feeling. His, well, holiness. He halved the bread and said, "He took bread and broke it and gave it to his friends, saying, 'Take this and eat it. This is my body. It will be broken for you.' "

Then he gave it to us. I ate it and felt as I did a calm come over me. I hadn't known how hungry I was until he fed me.

Carolyn ate and leaned against me. I put my arm around her and felt the relief of one whose only love has returned from a long journey. We watched and listened while Michael blessed the wine. When we drank, the three of us, so quietly, so tenderly, each from the one glass, it was possible to believe that, yes, God was with us.

When Michael first threw himself into work against the war, his purpose was simple and relatively uncontroversial. He was not drawn to street demonstrations or to giving great speeches. He was invited to be on the platform in Washington in October of '67 with Robert Lowell and Norman Mailer, Dr. Spock and William Sloane Coffin, but he refused. He attended the demonstration, but as one of the thousands. Nor was he among those who chose to get arrested at the Pentagon. The self-celebration of the leading resisters made him uneasy. It was to the practical and undramatic activity of draft counseling that he gave almost all of his energy. He spent long hours every day in conversation with young men in a small room in the Protestant chaplain's office at NYU. Ministers, and eventually even priests, from all over the city referred their "Greetings"-panicked boys to him. In his mind they were a procession of Nicholas Wileys, and if he was compulsively at their service it was only in part to oppose the war. In their trying to decide whether to be objectors or to fake their medicals or to claim to be homosexuals or simply to refuse induction and split, he wanted to give them the support and constructive advice that no one had given Nicholas; that lack, Michael thought, was what had killed him.

He became an expert in the Selective Service laws, which were toughened several times in that period, and he began to train other draft counselors. As the Justice Department, even under Ramsey Clark, who would come to seem wildly left-wing after John Mitchell, became more aggressive in enforcing draft laws — the army needed more than a million young men in its draft pool now and could not allow the system to break down — Michael became more adept at finding ways to draw out the appeals process and to outflank the VFW fogies who sat on local draftboards. The situation heated up when indictments started coming down not only on the radicals who burned their draftcards and on the ministers, like Coffin, who supported them, but also on kids who, unable to get C.O. status, were laying low, hoping to avoid having to choose between Vietnam and Canada. Pushed by indictments or the threat of them, Canada was it, of course, for thousands, and Michael became part of the network of clergy who helped boys get there. He told me one night that every time he drove back from Montreal he felt he was returning to a damned country that had decided in some perverse, unconscious way to punish itself by banishing the very best of its children.

They were his children, his sons, his Lennies and Nicholases, terrified kids with the balance of their lives in jeopardy. He could not simply watch them, in that primordial image of our generation, falling from the cliff or being pushed from it, from the field of Rye. He had to find a way to catch them. He had to find a way to share their jeopardy and he had to find a way to strike real blows, at last, against the war.

Hence draftboard raids. Hence the destruction of Selective Service files.

It was after midnight, the early hours of December 17, 1968. Merton was dead a week, Bobby Kennedy six months, Spellman a year, JFK and Ngo Dinh Diem five years, and Pope Pius XII ten. Michael and three others, another New York priest and two young Catholic peace workers, were, for their parts, more alive, more alert, more pumped with hunter's nerve than ever. They were inside the federal building in downtown Newark, New Jersey. It had been closed for hours.

The Selective Service office was on the fourth floor, two floors above the office of the U.S. Attorney for Northern New Jersey. There had been draftboard raids by Catholics in Baltimore, Catonsville, Milwaukee and the Bronx already, but this was the first one conducted at night by people who did not intend to be arrested. It was not their purpose to make one grand gesture before going to jail. They wanted to do as much damage to the Selective Service system as they could, for it had dawned on people by then that it was the war machine's one exposed and vulnerable gear. Thousands of young men in various cities had already been reprieved when their files were destroyed by having blood or homemade napalm poured on them, and Michael Maguire and his coconspirators wanted to multiply that number by tens and hundreds.

Michael was the first to leave his hiding place. He had been huddled since before the building closed in a rarely used and flimsily locked mop closet in the men's room off the main post office lobby. Now, following the thin beam of his flashlight, he crossed that lobby quickly, went into the stairwell and down to the basement snack bar. He rapped on a storage room door once. The lock was thrown and the door opened quickly. Father Pete Bryant raised a hand, then followed. They were both dressed clerically, blacks and collar, unusual for priests like them by then, but their clothing was the color of night, and if they were arrested they wanted to be taken from the start for what they were. They were also wearing surgical gloves, the clerical dress of burglars.

They went back up the stairs quietly and quickly. On the second floor were postal offices where clerks worked. Michael knocked once on the ladies' room door. Jerry Dunne and Joe Reilley had crouched for the hour before the building closed on the same toilet in a booth they'd marked with an out-of-order sign. Now they came out promptly, young men in their mid-twenties. Jerry was a draft counselor whom Michael knew well, and Joe was his roommate, a math teacher in a Catholic high school in Queens. Pete Bryant worked in a parish in Harlem, and he was the one who'd made the point that by hitting the draftboard in downtown Newark, it would be young blacks, mainly, whose files the government would lose. Why should white kids be the only ones spared a vicious death in Asia?

Another advantage Newark had — the main one — was that the federal building, like many in the centers of older cities, was not alarmed or guarded at night, and the locks were common ones. Both Bryant and Maguire had learned what they could about picking them and were in fact by then as proficient at it as the average petty burglar. The doors to the offices, also, were paneled in the old-fashioned style, with frosted glass. Jerry Dunne carried tools and suction cups to cut through it if they had to.

They didn't. In minutes they were on the fourth floor and seconds later, having picked a simple tumbler lock — there was a dead-bolt lock that might have stymied them, but the last clerk out had neglected to throw it — they were inside the sprawling, cabinet-lined mammoth room of the Newark Selective Service office. The two younger men had cased the place with visits and they knew what they were after. They led the way to the bank of files where the 1-A forms were stored. Each of the four took a separate cabinet and began to empty its contents into one of the two laundry bags he'd brought; then on to the next cabinet and the next until, within minutes, each man had both his bags stuffed with the papers that identified the thousands of New Jersey boys who were even then in the process of being drafted. Hauling their bags on their shoulders, like Santa's helpers, they left the office. On the glass Michael scrawled with a grease pencil, "Stop the killing! Stop the war!"

The next morning Michael, still dressed as a priest, though now wearing street gloves, went to the *Newark Star-Ledger* and asked the receptionist to take the box he gave her to the city editor. It contained one undamaged Selective Service file from which the draftee's name had been excised, and a plastic bag full of ashes and a letter describing what they'd done. It ended, "If this was Vietnam instead of New Jersey these would be the remains of people instead of paper," and it was signed, "The Catholic Conspiracy to Save Lives."

In the next weeks they took advantage of the Christmas and New Year's lull, which slowed the bureaucracies' ability to respond. Michael, Pete Bryant, Joe Reilley and Jerry Dunne repeated the action in Camden, Albany, Wilmington and Harrisburg. In each case they were able to enter the Selective Service office — in Harrisburg it was only a floor above the FBI field office — seize the files and get out. Each morning after, Michael presented the ashes of the burned files to a local newspaper or radio or television station. The Catholic Conspiracy to Save Lives was suddenly notorious. In Portland, Oregon, during the night before Richard Nixon's inauguration, another group unknown to Michael raided the Selective Service office in the same way and signed itself, "The West Coast Conspiracy to Save Lives." By the end of January, draftboards in Joliet, Illinois, and San Diego were similarly hit by other groups.

In Washington several things happened. The Selective Service received a special appropriation to begin the immediate microfilm duplication of its records. The General Services Administration issued new guidelines for security in federal buildings and created an emergency fund for twenty-four-hour patrols of buildings housing Selective Service offices. J. Edgar Hoover made the arrest of the draftboard conspirators a top priority for the FBI.

Michael shouldn't have shown himself at the newspapers, perhaps. The FBI had a good description of him and, since his conflict with Spellman and his participation in various demonstrations had been well publicized, he was an obvious suspect. But while his purpose was not to get arrested, neither was it to avoid arrest at all cost or indefinitely. He knew what he was doing. And he knew that if their raids succeeded, the draftboard offices would quickly be made invulnerable anyway to amateurs like him and his friends, both the ones he knew and the ones he didn't.

The FBI, on the other hand, wanted more than Michael. Hoover wanted everyone. Agents were convinced that Michael Maguire was the leader of at least two dozen raiders, and that he had orchestrated the recent burglaries in the Midwest and on the West Coast too. In fact there had already been that many Catholics arrested and freed on bail, and by the end of 1969 forty or fifty more would be. Most of them were priests and nuns, some like Michael in bad standing and some formally defrocked. They participated in draftboard raids not out of subservience to any leader or as part of a centralized organization, but out of subservience to what they'd have described as a vocation to end the war. They were disparate groups, only in the loosest sense conspirators, but they embraced the word *conspiracy* nonetheless. Like true Romans, they loved its Latin etymology, for it means "breathe together." Like true Romans, they liked the draftboard raid for its liturgical simplicity and its moral purity. They were destroying paper to save children.

But governments everywhere fail to understand the spontaneously expressed moral urges of the people. Always governments are fingering agitators and uncovering master plans and tracking down ringleaders. There were a dozen priests like Michael; well known, articulate, charismatic, capable of inspiring boldness in the tame. But the FBI singled him out. Eventually they made him famous. They could simply have arrested him with the evidence they had, and however the trial came out that would almost certainly have ended his aggressive resistance. But, prodded by Hoover and supported fully by the new attorney general, they embarked upon a plan to break the back of what they regarded as the core of the kooky Catholic war resistance.

She came to his office at NYU in early February. Celia Zack, a startlingly pretty Jewish woman in her late twenties. She had lustrous dark hair and eyes dark enough and deep enough to draw anyone in. But her eyes' constant rapid blinking undercut their effect and belied her intelligence, her nerve, and made her seem slightly vacuous. She blinked like that because of her contact lenses.

Michael knew her slightly. She was a board member of RESIST, which had its offices in the same building as his. The antiwar crowd had moved into the religious centers of universities as the alienated kids had moved out. RESIST had sponsored the early draftcard burnings and had more recently focused its efforts on helping draft-dodgers get to Canada. Michael had obtained false papers for a dozen or more of his clients from Celia Zack.

She stood in the doorway of his office.

"Come in," he said.

She shook her head. "Let's go for a walk." She turned the fur collar up on her heavy afghan coat.

When he didn't respond, her eyes went meaningfully to the corners of his ceiling; the room might be bugged.

Michael nodded and got his coat. On their way out he whispered, "You movement heavies flatter yourselves."

It was a brittle day, midmorning, and the only people they passed were walking purposefully, tilted into the cold air.

Celia didn't speak until they'd cut into the park at Washington Square, which was empty even of winos. The fountain in front of the great arch was full of leaves, and on its plaque someone had sprayed, "Ho! Ho! Ho Chi Minh! NLF Is Going To Win!" The trees scratched at the gray sky.

"I know that you're the mystery priest, Michael," Celia Zack said finally.

They kept walking. Michael decided to say nothing.

"Don't you want to know how I know?"

"What's the mystery priest, Celia?"

"Skip it, Michael. Come on. You know what I'm talking about. Newark, Albany, Wilmington, Harrisburg. I suspected you right away. When you weren't around the office I figured there'd be a raid within a few days and there always was."

"Smart. You should be with the FBI."

"I have a proposal to make."

Michael said nothing.

"Well, do you want to hear it or not?"

"Look, Celia, if you have something to say to me, say it." There was something about this woman Michael didn't like. Was it an assumption of superiority? Secular condescension?

"Okay. Let me lay it out for you. I have a friend who works as an office manager at the Selective Service Building on Canal Street. That's the central records depot for the local offices all over the city. It's the largest in the country. It's where the One-A forms are transposed onto IBM, the last step before induction notices are sent out. My friend has helped us a few times by lifting files of particular draft-eligibles and destroying them. It's the best way to beat the system. Without duplicates, it takes them a year to track a kid down again, and then the delay gives him the perfect basis for a complaint in court."

"Why does your friend do that for you?"

"I've been cultivating him for a couple of years."

"What's his name?"

She hesitated, but only for a moment. "Malcolm Dodd. I always thought of him as my trump card, but now he tells me they're going to start microfilming files next week."

"Good things don't last forever."

"And then when I put two and two together about you I realized I'd been thinking much too small. Why not take out all the One-A files for the whole city? We could bring the whole system here to a halt. They'd have to start from scratch."

It was a stunning thought. Michael answered carefully, "How would that work exactly?"

"My friend hands over plans and keys to the offices, codes for the alarm systems, keys and combinations to the cabinets, and the patrol schedule of the night guards. To do the job right would take a lot of people. There are a lot of files."

"And that's why you're talking to me? Because I'm the 'mystery priest'?"

" 'The Catholic Conspiracy to Save Lives,' right?"

"But there are dozens of people in RESIST who'd do it. Why

don't you organize them? Imitation, after all, is the sincerest form of flattery."

"I would, but there isn't time. The microfilming will be done in a couple of weeks. An action like this takes discipline obviously, and a group that's been weeded out and tested. A group like yours."

"What do you mean 'cultivating'?" he asked.

"What?"

"You've been 'cultivating' this office manager. How so?"

She shrugged. "I let him fuck me."

Michael looked across the park. No birds, no hippies, no derelicts. "So now we fuck him," he said.

"They probably can't finger him. There are three hundred clerks in that office, and maybe thirty of them could get the keys and plans."

"Filching a file now and then is small potatoes compared to this. Are you sure he'll do it?"

"He loves me."

Michael nodded. "It can make a man pathetic, can't it?"

She looked up sharply. "Yes." She conveyed for an instant only, but effectively, her hatred. And Michael realized what he didn't like about her. He stifled it and said, "I'll have to talk to my people. We'd move on it this weekend."

"How many?"

"Could it handle twenty-five?"

She smiled. Could it ever.

Saturday night, Sunday morning. Two o'clock, then three. Canal Street, a canyon of offices and warehouses and loft-factories, was deserted. A careful observer who knew what to look for could see the figures in the shadows. Michael watched the windows of the old stone building from across the street. In cars and vans up the block and down, people sprawled on seats and floors to be invisible. From a casket warehouse behind him people watched. He could feel their eyes.

He watched. He was waiting for the flashlight beam of the GSA guard to pass by the windows of the stairwell between the third floor and the fourth. It had passed already seven times at intervals of roughly twenty minutes, intervals prescribed in the schedule of rounds he'd memorized. Now when it passed, it was go.

There it was.

He turned his jacket collar up against the cold and stepped into the street. Then he was across and at the door. The key worked. Inside he applied another key to a metal panel and opened it. A maze of wires and toggles, it took a moment to make sense of it. He threw the numbered switches in sequence, then closed the panel. The alarm for floors one through five was deactivated.

Through three sets of locked doors, each key worked. He took the stairs two at a time. On the fifth-floor landing he opened another panel and threw a second set of switches. Now the alarm was off everywhere. He looked at his watch. Four minutes. The guard was in the basement.

On the seventh floor, he entered the main file room. He waited for a moment to let his eyes adjust to that less severe darkness. He had to work without a flashlight there because of the large uncurtained windows, but they admitted sufficient light from the street. Finally he saw the bank of cabinets that he wanted and approached it. He had the small key ready. It took him a second to find the hole, but then he inserted the key. It made a noise. And then he was ripping sheets of paper furiously. The noise of his destruction resounded through the room.

"Freeze!" a man cried.

Lights blinked on.

In quick succession, two burly men hit him, one with his fist just at the kidneys, and another with a vicious chop between his shoulder and his neck. It dropped Michael to his knees, but immediately he was hauled up. His hands were cuffed behind him. And an agent hooked him under the chin and lifted him with the muzzle of a shotgun.

"Where the fuck are the others?" the agent demanded.

Michael said nothing.

Agents crashed into the room behind them. A dozen others already present were poised with their weapons behind desks and cabinets, ready to shoot. There were shotguns everywhere.

"Where the fuck are the others?" A note of hysteria in the man's voice surprised Michael. He himself felt remarkably calm. Everything was going as he expected, although the weapons surprised him. The shotguns. Was he Dillinger? Didn't they know they didn't need weapons?

The agent pressed the gun barrel into Michael's gullet, against his Roman collar. Michael said, "I'm alone."

The agent eased the pressure with the gun. "What?"

"I'm alone," Michael repeated.

A supervisor, one of those who'd been waiting in the casket warehouse, came in. Altogether he had forty-two men in the operation that night, and he didn't like what he saw. He'd pulled people off six squads for this raid, the biggest in New York since the Joe Columbo takedown, and he was going to have to show for it. "Where the fuck are the others?" he bellowed. It was the exact phrase Hoover would use — though without "fuck" — in the morning. "There were going to be twenty-five. Where the fuck are they?" He glared at the agents.

One said, "He was the only one who came in from the street." Another said, "No one came up the back stairs or the freight elevator. No one came in from the alley." The other agents began to holster their guns and to check their watches.

"He says he's alone," one offered.

The supervisor let his eyes fall to the papers that Michael had ripped and strewn. He saw at once that the pages were blank.

The agents had been cued to wait until the perpetrators had actually destroyed documents before arresting them. The charge would be destruction of government property. But what if the fucker had brought his own paper in? What in hell was going on here? If he hadn't actually destroyed draft files, the charge wouldn't even be B&E since he'd come in with keys. All this trouble for illegal entry? Since the federal government did not own the land on which the building sat, it wouldn't even be crime on a government reservation. It would be a local charge, tried in local courts, a step above trespassing! All this trouble for one fucking son of a bitch? For a month's probation? Heads would roll! His head would roll! If the newspapers got it, he'd be sent to Dubuque.

The supervisor yelled, "Out! Everyone out! Check the building again! Every corridor, closet and toilet! Find them if they're here! Goddamnit, find them!"

When the other agents had left, he said to the two who had Michael, "Uncuff him." They did so. "Wait outside." They left too.

Then Michael was alone with the supervisor in the brightly lit cavernous room. They stared at each other for a long time, then the FBI man bent and picked up one of the torn blank pages. At the top were printed the words "The Catholic Relief Service, 350 Fifth Avenue, New York, N.Y." The agent smiled. "Very clever, Father."

"I'm glad you appreciate it."

"I'm the only one who will." The agent gathered the papers, a third of a ream perhaps, and carefully stuffed them inside his coat. Then he fastidiously pulled on his leather gloves. He opened several file cabinet drawers, then withdrew a file folder from one of them. It was about two inches thick. He offered it to Michael. "I think you'll find this material more interesting, Father."

Michael did not answer him, nor did he take it.

The supervisor nodded. "That would have been too easy, wouldn't it? I understand your purposes, Father. Frankly, you're a little naive if you think anyone's going to believe your version of events here. Now I'll have to ask you to understand my purposes."

Suddenly his right fist shot into Michael's abdomen. Michael doubled over, clutching himself. Before he could stop him, the agent had opened Michael's hands and forced the folder between them. Pages fell to the floor. The FBI man brought both his fists down on Michael's neck. As Michael went down, he kicked him in the groin. Michael fell, hands open, on the scattered Selective Service forms. Fingerprints. Not many, but enough.

The supervisor picked up a sheaf of papers and carefully ripped them in two. His hands were perfectly steady. No hysteria or threat of it in this man. He dropped the pages, then retrieved another sheaf and ripped those. He let them fall like leaves. He knocked Michael aside, then picked up the pages on which his hands had rested. He ripped those and let them fall. Destruction of government property. Not much, but enough.

When Michael, gasping and still clutching himself, looked up, the FBI man said calmly, "Sorry, Father. It's all in the job."

The next morning the *New York Times* had the story on the front page of its late edition. "Priest Arrested by FBI in Draft Office," the headline read. And the subhead: "Priest Charges Entrapment."

The second paragraph of the story read, "A package delivered to the *New York Times* early this morning contained a letter describing the one-man draftboard raid and the reasons for it. The letter was signed, 'Father Michael Maguire,' although its source has not been verified. The package also contained a set of wax impressions of keys purported to fit doors and cabinets in the Canal Street Selective Service Building and which the letter claims were supplied to Father Maguire by an FBI agent provocateur. The package also contained a tape recording of a conversation between a woman identified as Celia Zack, an antiwar activist, and a man identified as Father Maguire. In the conversation, which was apparently recorded without the woman's knowledge, she does raise the subject of the raid on the draftboard that took place last night. She can be heard describing keys and building diagrams that she says were supplied by a Selective Service employee named Malcolm Dodd and that were apparently being handed over to Father Maguire. The woman also details the patrol schedule of the building guards. If the tape is authentic and if Miss Zack does in fact work for the FBI as the letter asserts, then there may be some basis for Father Maguire's claim. According to *New York Times*'s legal sources entrapment occurs when a criminal act takes place that could not otherwise have taken place without the material assistance of government agents. *New York Times*'s sources maintain that it is illegal for law enforcement officers to actively further the commission of a crime even for the purpose of gaining evidence against a suspect. The FBI had refused comment on Father Maguire's charges as of this writing, although the *New York Times* was able to learn that no one named Malcolm Dodd is employed at the Selective Service office on Canal Street. A spokesman for the U.S. Attorney denied that Miss Zack works for the government and that there was entrapment in this case. The spokesman said, 'The accused can make his case, whatever it is, to the judge and jury.' "

The final paragraph of the news story was a quotation from what it doggedly called "the letter alleged to have been written by Father Maguire." Looking at it now, I find it moving, as I did then, although also somewhat ingenuous. When he wanted to the son of a bitch could croon the *Ave Maria,* warble and all.

"Though as a Catholic priest and the son of a New York City policeman who died in the line of duty I have an inbred respect, even reverence, for the law, I decided to allow myself to be entrapped in this way to expose the illegal and immoral methods used by a desperate government against its own people to keep them from protesting the infinitely more illegal and immoral war it continues to wage against the Vietnamese people. In their name and in God's name and in America's, we say, 'End this evil war before it destroys us all!' "

TWENTY-SEVEN

CAROLYN and I were sitting on a stone bench in the Biblical Garden, a small, tidy plot nestled against the Cathedral Choir and containing with floral fundamentalism only plants mentioned in the Bible: fig trees, mustard plants, lilies, papyrus and the star-of-Bethlehem. Trellised between the buttresses of the cathedral were ten cedars of Lebanon, evergreens that one never sees in the Holy Land now. They were overharvested eons ago, and I was thinking for the first time since leaving Israel of the war in Beirut, the overharvesting of blood.

Another tree caught my eye, a small redbud, the Judas tree. I touched Carolyn's sleeve. "They say that tree descends from the one on which Judas hanged himself. Its flowers are crimson because it blushes with shame."

Carolyn did not speak. I left my hand resting on her sleeve. I remembered sitting self-consciously in a garden like that with Michael at the Cloisters above Inwood. I remembered our laughing hysterically because Jesus cast demons into some poor bastard's swine.

I remembered our sitting on that hill overlooking the river and the bridge.

Carolyn and I had bought our house years later because it overlooked the other river, the other bridge. "Do you remember," I asked quietly, "how we used to have supper on our balcony overlooking the river and the city?"

She nodded. The bright sun and its heat swaddled us.

She took my hand.

"I used to think on those evenings that we would live forever."

"I thought Michael would," she said simply.

Four fruit trees grew in the center of the garden. I could not read the small sign in front of them. Apple trees? Apricot? But of course it was the Tree of the Knowledge of Good and Evil. From one of those Adam plucked fruit and therefore death came into the world.

A large pigeon pecked at gravel near us. What a miserly life! I thought. A few desperate years, odd grains, bread crumbs, the discards of squirrels, then a solitary grotto under shrubs somewhere and a pigeon's heart attack. And is it different for us? The fucking outrage of it! It made me want to kick that bird, kick God.

Michael died of a heart attack. He was just fifty, as I was at that point. He'd been in perfect health, Molly told me, a jogger. He'd quit smoking as a wedding gift to Carolyn.

I knew nothing of the last years of his life, how he earned a living, how he was changed by federal prison, how he was as a father, whether he took up golf, whether he could fix the gutters himself or had, like me, to hire people.

"Where do you live?" I asked.

"In Brooklyn."

"Our house?"

"Yes."

"Good." Could I possibly have meant that? Michael had usurped me utterly. I must have known they were living there. Shouldn't I have been surprised? Had I been a ghost to him around that house? I hoped so suddenly. I hoped I had haunted him. I hoped when the wind blew doors shut in the middle of the night he had thought it was me coming after him. "Did the two of you have supper on the balcony?"

"Not alone, the way you and I did. It's different when the children are older."

"Molly looks wonderful, Carolyn. She fills me with pride."

Carolyn smiled, drew back from her grief.

"And I met your handsome son. You have a Vietnamese daughter. You've been busy." I covered her hand, cupped it between my two. "And you kept painting."

She nodded, but absently. She had no real capacity for talk about such things, as if her painting, her house, her children even, could have sustained her then. I saw that it would have been wrong for me to steer away from Michael. Memory alone assuages loss, and that was what I was there to help with. It shocked me to realize that I was the one person who could help her navigate that weather. I was there to put heart into that woman. Yet what heart had I? And if I could give her, finally, nothing, wouldn't it be because she had long since taken from me all I had?

We sat in the stillness of the garden. I saw the shadow of the great cathedral creeping toward us, the stillness and the shadow of death.

Finally she said, "Frank, thank you for coming."

"No, Carolyn. I'm the one to thank you. How could I ever have not been here?" I must have shown her more of my feelings than I intended, because all at once she took me in her arms and pressed my face to her breast. *She* consoled *me!*

After a time I pulled away from her. "Carolyn," I said somewhat formally, stifling my emotion, "I want to help you, to be your friend."

"Oh, Frank, I need you! I went to pieces and sent Molly for you, as if you lived in Philadelphia. It was crazy." She shook her head. "What made me wild was when they said we couldn't bury him in sacred ground. It made me crazy when they used that word about him."

"Excommunicated?"

She nodded. "As if he were Hitler or someone. And I didn't know what to do. Someone suggested Saint John's and Dean Evans here has been wonderful . . ." She looked up at the soaring cathedral, the buttresses, the windows, the great bulk of stone. ". . . but it's not . . ." She didn't finish.

"Catholic."

"I didn't think it would bother me, but it does. I can't put his ashes in a wall, a safe-deposit box. I have to commit him to the earth! I have to bury him the way he buried people! This isn't where he belongs, Frank. It's a Protestant church. We can't leave Michael here."

"We could try to think about it in a new way, Caro. So much has changed. Catholics and Episcopalians are so much alike now . . ."

"Oh, but Frank . . ." Her eyes glistened. ". . . none of that matters. This isn't Michael's place."

I'd had the same reaction at first, but I'd put it aside. Now I felt the depth of her pain, her shock. "We're still Catholics, aren't we?" I said it smiling, hoping to bring out the irony — we'd thought ourselves so worldly, but we were just mackerel snappers after all — so we could savor it together.

But her eyes overflowed. I was not prepared for that show of desolation. She had displaced her great distress, loading it on that detail of obsolete ecclesiology. It didn't matter to the dead where they were buried, and did God care if it was Saint John's and not Saint Patrick's? But God was not sitting by me, shattered. What did God know of exile or excommunication or the loss of home?

If it mattered to her, it mattered.

"Molly said you spoke to the chancellor."

"That's when I went to pieces. He was awful to me, cold and legalistic. And when I became so upset no one understood. They said it meant nothing, what bishops think. But I was destroyed, and I knew that no one would understand but you. No one would help me but you." She clutched at me. "Oh, Frank, we have to bury Michael in the Church! We have to!"

"I know it, Caro."

She had my shirt in her fists and was shaking me. "Oh, Frank, I'm the reason he's excommunicated! It's me, Frank! I'm the one they blame! It's me! That's what they think! It's me!"

Of course it was; an undispensed priest marries an ex-nun divorcée, flouting all values, all the holiest traditions. What did she expect? Baby's breath?

She should never have been the one to approach the chancellor. What latitude he might have had — what capacity for compassion — had surely been swamped in his clerical resentment, however clothed it had come in canons.

For myself, I had taken shelter both from that desolation of hers and from my own long-nursed wound in the one unclouded feeling I had. In its womb there was nothing of anger, despair or grief even; not even grief. There was only loving that woman and longing to soothe her.

"Carolyn, I'll talk to him. What time is it? I'll call him now."

She raised her hand, her wrist. The movement drew my eye along her arm to her bosom. A vision of her nakedness filled my mind again. It was the image to which instinctively and, yes, lustfully I returned repeatedly, as to a memory of the house that gave me shelter from my first storm. I saw her thighs open, her pelvis tilting at me, her offered cunt.

"It's three-thirty." She fell back against the bench and laughed crazily. "This is nuts! What's wrong with me? The service is all set, just four hours from now. The dean of the cathedral is presiding. It was in the paper. We can't change it."

"Let me talk to them, Caro. Maybe there's something we can do." Weren't there dispensations? Rescripts? Absolutions? Annulments? Weren't there miracles? Was there no way — I refused to believe it suddenly — for the Roman Catholic Church to manifest God's mercy toward that man? "I'll call the chancellor. What's his name?"

It was exactly as if I'd slapped her. "You don't know?"

"No."

"It's Archbishop O'Shea, Frank. Tim O'Shea."

"Michael's friend?"

Tears once more burst out of her.

"Take me to the Catholic chancery."

The taxi driver looked at me dully through the cloudy plastic shield.

"Behind Saint Patrick's Cathedral," I explained, "on Madison."

He popped the clutch and punched a button on his meter, a digital readout. Where was the meter flag? I wanted to ask. We jolted into traffic.

On the telephone in Dean Evans's office I had learned that Archbishop O'Shea was there. His secretary wouldn't put me through unless I stated my business. It had been easy to picture her, upright in a severe wooden chair in front of an antique Underwood, the dark reaches of the high-ceilinged old mansion looming above her. The chancery office of the archdiocese had been in the south wing of the Villard Mansions since 1948. Fit for a Borgia prince, the building was a Roman Renaissance palazzo full of Tiffany glass, Saint-Gaudens sculpture and the murals of John Lafarge. One of the grandest houses in all New York, it had been the vain indulgence not of an Italian aristocrat but of a nineteenth-century railroad baron. It had matched Spellman's position as the drum major of the Church's arrival in America that he should have bought the place and dubbed it the Cardinal Farley Building. It dwarfed his own residence across the avenue, and it seemed almost vengeful when he turned the mansion into the offices of his chancellor. He would not, of course, have grasped the irony that once more Catholics were scooping up the leavings of Protestants. The descendants of Henry Villard and his successor proprietor, Whitelaw Reid, who entertained the Prince of Wales in the house, had long since moved farther north. The fashionable Upper East Side had come into its own. Midtown was fit now only for commerce and for Catholics.

The cab, after cutting through Central Park, went down Fifth Avenue. The traffic was like traffic in Jerusalem, but the people on the sidewalk, their clothing, their lack of it, the shoulders and thighs of women, the glittering store windows in which their bodies were reflected, windows behind which the bodies of mannequins took tribute in glances, plaster nipples stretching plastic blouses, wreaked havoc with my concentration. I wanted to remember everything I could about Timothy O'Shea. I wanted to remember what I'd read in canon law. I was certain the bishop had discretion about who was buried where and how. In death, everyone is excommunicated; therefore no one should be. But I could not think. My mind was taken up utterly by the pretty girls in their summer dresses. Oh early Irwin Shaw!

At Fiftieth Street the driver slowed for a turn. We passed in front of Saint Patrick's, then cut and swerved and were driving along the side of it. An unexpected affection for the spired church surged in me, but I was amazed how small, how ungrand it seemed. Saint John's, even incomplete, was more than twice Saint Patrick's size, and standing as it did on the promontory of Morningside Heights it had a monumentality Saint Patrick's, in the shadow of the skyscrapers of Rockefeller Center, lacked.

New York's nineteenth-century Catholics had been outraged when they heard about plans for the heretics' cathedral in their city. It would be — and was — the largest cathedral in the world. Ingenuously, in making that claim the Protestants did not include in the comparison Saint Peter's in Rome, which, at nearly twice the size again, was the only edifice bigger. Technically they were right, though, because Saint Peter's was not a cathedral, but a basilica. Still Catholics in New York over the years had refused to be cowed by the relative modesty of their cathedral. It may not have been designed and furnished by America's great architects and artists, and it may have been only the size, they would admit, of Chartres and Notre Dame de Paris, but at least it was finished. The churches were begun within a decade of each other. In less than two decades, Saint Patrick's, paid for by the pennies of millions of immigrants, was completed. Saint John the Divine, paid for by the sporadic benefactions of the richest people in America, would probably never be completed. The house of worship for a dwindling elite, Saint John's, even at solemn services on Sundays, seemed always nearly empty. Saint Patrick's, even between Masses on any weekday, seemed always nearly full. And there was the difference, the oldest one, the one that mattered. There are fifty million Catholics in America, two million Episcopalians.

We Catholics have long memories. Take your thumb out of our ingratiating joviality, of our worldly liberalism, and you will loose a flood of bitterness. Then watch what we do with it. In the new age in which neither layman nor priest, progressive nor conservative, chancellor nor cardinal nor pope, even, want to be thought unecumenical, small-minded or parochial, we spare the ancient Protestant enemy and pour the old acid on ourselves.

Hence my taxi ride. Hence my purpose as the cab swung north on Madison, cut across the avenue to the far curb and jolted to a stop in front of the Renaissance palace; I had come to ask the Roman Catholic archdiocese of New York to lift its sanction, to ask Holy Mother the Church to have mercy on her son.

"This place?" the cabbie asked.

"That's right." I was counting bills out for him. The feel of the money was alien, and not because it was American. I had not even so much as paid a cab fare in a decade. The bubble of unreality in which I had been living touched ground but did not break.

"This is a hotel, Mac, not the archdiocese."

"What?"

Even in daylight, even in August, the courtyard trees were lined with white Christmas twinkle lights.

"The Helmsley Palace Hotel."

I craned toward the mansion. The windows sparkled. The entranceway glimmered with brass. At a polished revolving door a uniformed man was taking someone's suitcase. And above the three stories of the nineteenth-century masterpiece loomed a huge, gleaming skyscraper.

I paid the cabbie and got out.

At the door the uniformed Hispanic — in earlier days he'd have been Irish — gave me the once-over. What's with the denim shirt and sandals, man? I nodded at him and went in.

The Villard Mansions now served as a showplace narthex — grand staircase, polished pink marble, restored paneling, flashing chandeliers, Oriental runners with brass fasteners — for a piggy-backed run-of-the-mill behemoth hotel. New York's Industrial Brahmins had abandoned their palazzo to upstart Catholic clergy who had bequeathed it now to expense account admen from Dayton and accountants from Houston who wore English suits, knew their *nouvelle cuisine* and preferred a Continental ambience. This was the best Olde World Palace Hotel yet. I made a quick round of the public rooms to convince myself I was not dreaming. Where were the portraits of Farley, Hughes, Hayes and Spellman? In niches where once stood statues of Frances Cabrini, Mother Seton and Isaac Jogues were now flamboyant floral displays. Against the elaborately carved oak wall at the top of the grand staircase where once the huge seal of the archdiocese — the tassled hat, the Greek Cross, the flame, the motto *Fiat Voluntas Tua* — had hung there was now a mammoth portrait of the unsmiling, waistcoated, mustachioed Villard. His successors still displeased him.

In the stunning second-floor library that had served as the office of the chancellor — I had been in it once and remembered the twin fireplaces with Italian marble mantels and the barrel-vaulted ceiling — afternoon tea was being served on tables covered with pink damask. A lady touched her napkin to her mouth and eyed me suspiciously. Would I come over to her table and sell her a sign-language card? Suddenly I sensed that she would have bought one. She might have taken me to her room.

It was the building I remembered, but the gloom was gone, that cinctured repression, that overhanging threat that swamped light and life, sucking oxygen from the rooms and spirit from their occupants. Now, as in all hotels, infidelity was in the air, the faint smell of sex. Even that matron from Ohio at her tea knew it, exuded it. She had that Last Chance look in her eyes and flashed it at me because I was not dressed right, because I did not belong.

She would have been in charge. She would never have had to see me again. With a shock I realized she was younger than I was and, yes, I would have loved to screw her, not in her husband's company's room upstairs, but in *this* room where once an archbishop of the Church had sat up to his ass in anathemas. Anathema shit! Tempus fuck!

I left the room for the corridors and stairs again. The restoration, the polish, the carpeting and gold leaf had turned the intimidating shadows of God's offices in New York into the living illustration of a slick travel brochure. Amenities and ambience! It was the perfect end for that counterfeit Roman masterpiece, that New York version of a Hollywood backlot front. From its beginning that house had offered its lonely, uprooted American owners the illusion of a past, of a culture, of a tradition. Ironically, a *Catholic* past, culture and tradition — as in Michelangelo, as in Dante Alighieri. Its first owners had stayed most of a century. Its second, the Irish clergy to whom the Italian Renaissance, however Catholic, had been as alien, finally, as it had been to the Protestants who aped it, had stayed a few decades. Now its owners were guests who stayed the night, had coffee and *brioche* in the Gold Room and left, pleased with the place and with themselves.

When a bellboy — no, *concierge!* — saluted me, I wanted to intone the benediction in plain chant for him. Instead I asked where to find a phone book and he told me.

I looked up "Chancery," then "Archdiocese" and found nothing. I looked up "Catholic" and found a listing, with multiple departments and centrex dialing, for the New York Catholic Center at 1011 First Avenue, and I understood even before going there what had happened.

It was a new twenty-story rectangular office building with aluminum window frames, beige Levolor blinds and gray facing stone. Unpainted aluminum letters above the entrance identified it straightforwardly: "The New York Catholic Center," and a good thing too, for otherwise I could have taken it for one of the other seven million clone-buildings in this city, the Arco Building, Random House, Lever Brothers. It was the perfect emblem for the new Church. Having rejected as unmodern and antidemocratic the trappings — if not the political structure — of the feudal aristocracy, the archdiocese had embraced the trappings of the American corporation. The clergy who worked in this building did not aspire to be princes but managers. The cardinal was the president and the chairman of the board, and Archbishop O'Shea was "Senior V.P. for Ops," or perhaps "Assistant CEO."

Good, I thought, crossing the street and going in. I slipped by the distracted security guard — not spinster secretary — and into the elevator. The floors were identified by their offices: Catholic Guardian Society, Hospital Apostolate, Insurance Division, Pension Division, Catholic Relief Service, Marriage Tribunal, Communications, Catholic Home Bureau, Catholic New York. At the top, floor twenty, not a palace but the executive suite, the sign said "Chancellor." I wanted to say, No, that's wrong! You can't have it both ways. Thomas More was a chancellor. An absolutist, he drew lines and refused to cross them, but you can't do that. Not in this place, not in this business. You are an American executive, paid to accommodate and compromise. You cannot pronounce anathemas against your middle management. This building professes the new faith, Your Excellency, even if you don't. It is efficient, computerized, unionized, organized, socialized and banalized. In its sterile fluorescent glare we see episcopal arrogance, clerical vengeance and vestigial medieval tyranny — and this is why, finally, one accepts this otherwise tragic transformation as the work of God — for the devils-on-the-loose they are.

The elevator doors opened and, as if by magic I was standing in front of a desk at which a plain young woman sat. She looked up from a ledger with an expression of mild curiosity. On the wall behind her was yet more aluminum, but that was an abstract figure of the Risen Christ, which I recognized only because of the legend below it: "I am the Resurrection and the Life."

The sculpture was an unexpected reminder that that building, like the Villard Mansions before it and like Saint Patrick's and Saint John the Divine, was supposed to be a mere shell, casing, glove of that truth. But what was the Resurrection to me? And what was the Life? They were words from the homily I'd stopped listening to, as easily ignored as the tawdry piece of modern sculpture. I looked away from it, thinking, What complete shit.

"I'd like to see the archbishop, please. My name is Francis Durkin. Tell him I'm an old friend of Michael Maguire's."

The young woman did not see it as her place to screen me. Probably some monsignor in the inner office would do that. She disappeared behind a pair of walnut doors. A moment later she returned, stood at the door and said, to my surprise, "Archbishop O'Shea will see you now."

His office was plushly carpeted, paneled and carefully lit, modern in all respects. A gray hopsack sofa sat adjacent to a polished ebony desk. On a glass and brass coffee table was arranged a selection of the best magazines. The wall behind the desk was entirely glass, and the view of the East River and the Fifty-ninth Street Bridge was stunning.

Archbishop Timothy O'Shea in black shirt and collar, not robes and skull cap, not even suitcoat, was coming toward me with his hand extended. He was in his early seventies. The crown of his hair was white, longish, setting off his bald head. His skin was tanned and he was not fat. He looked like a cabinet secretary. "My goodness," he said with enthusiasm, "Frank Durkin, how are you? Welcome! Welcome!"

It was not what I expected.

We sat on the sofa together. He offered me coffee, tea or sherry, and I took sherry. So did he.

I raised my glass. "Will you drink to Michael?"

"Of course I will."

We did.

"It's why I'm here."

"I heard you were in a monastery in the Holy Land."

"That's true." I indicated my shirt, my baggy trousers and sandals. "This is Benedictine street garb. I came back today for the funeral. I'm here because I can't believe you won't let him be buried in the Church. I've just come from Saint John the Divine. His family is distraught and so am I."

"I understand. It's thoroughly regrettable." He let his gaze drift to the view. After a moment he said wistfully, "I wish it wasn't like this."

My earlier expectation, of an Orson Welles prelate denouncing permissiveness, attacking infidelity and broken vows, had been off the mark. I sensed at once O'Shea's sadness, and it disarmed me.

He said, "It came as a great shock, Michael's death. I'd always hoped to see him again. I missed him."

All at once my heart flowed toward the man. For a moment I laid aside my argument. Perhaps I should have understood what it was from his side. "You were his mentor. Your gift to him in Korea of that little New Testament changed his life."

"Ah!" His eyes widened and he looked at me with such unwalled unhappiness that I realized I had inadvertently touched a nerve. "That New Testament, my God, what a mistake that was."

"What do you mean?"

He shook his head. "How can I tell you without your thinking . . . ?" He put his glass down and pressed the heels of his hands against his eyes. When he uncovered them they were red. "I gave him that New Testament the night before a battle. He'd seen action the day before . . ."

"He blew up that bridge."

"That's right, and I was worried about him."

"That book was just the thing. He said it was what got him through."

"I know, and it made him want to be a priest, and then it made him the best priest any of us knew."

"Well?"

"But when I gave it to him I told him that that particular copy of the New Testament had been my brother's. I said that my brother had it with him when he was killed at the Battle of the Bulge. That was a lie. It wasn't my brother's at all. I had already given my brother's Bible to another GI, and it moved him so that, well, I used the story with other fellows. I gave away a lot of Bibles and I always said the same thing. You could call it a pastoral technique. I wanted them to treasure the book and I thought it was all right to . . ." He stopped, breathed deeply. "It was an awful thing to do. It didn't matter with the others because I never saw them again, but with Michael, who always treasured that little book, I felt that our friendship was based on a deception of mine, and I was afraid that somehow it would go wrong. And then, of course, it did."

Now when he pressed the heels of his hands against his eyes he seemed like the old man he was, the old fox, the old manipulator. I had to stifle my disgust at his trick, his sodding "technique." I felt sorry for him despite myself.

After a moment he said, "It was the worst thing that ever happened to me, when Michael left the priesthood. He was my son."

"I know that. I know that he considered you his father. But

you disavowed him before he left. You broke with each other over the war."

"Yes, but he was right about Vietnam. And now I see that he was right even to break the law, even to go underground the way he did. America needed the moral witness, and so did the Church. If we pulled through that period with our soul intact, perhaps it was due to him and others like him. Michael was a hero to many priests. They were destroyed when he turned his back on them."

"I think he felt they'd already turned their backs on him. You had. And so had the cardinal."

He nodded. "It was a terrible time. Some of us were wrong." He fell silent, then said suddenly, "Now, of course, the leading Catholic pacifists are all bishops. The Catholic Church may end up a Peace Church."

"If it does, Michael will have started it."

"That's true. I'll tell you something. If he was alive today, he'd be a bishop."

"No, he'd be a husband and a father."

O'Shea blushed. "I mean if he was still a priest."

"But in any case, at some point he'd be dead, wouldn't he? And it wouldn't matter what he was. He'd still stand naked and alone before God, in need of mercy."

"That's right."

"Well, why can't he have mercy from the Church?"

Archbishop O'Shea did not answer me, and so I asked it another way. "Can you explain to me why Michael can't have the funeral Mass, the last blessing and burial in sacred ground?"

"You know why." His voice was barely above a whisper.

"No, I don't. I truly don't."

"He's excommunicated."

"By whom?"

"By himself. You know how these things work. He violated his solemn vow, and he did so publicly."

"Your complaint is that he didn't apply for a proper dispensation, or what? From what we hear in the desert, priests rarely obtain papal dispensations anymore, and well-known priests never do."

O'Shea was stiffened now. This was ground on which the moves came naturally. "Excommunication follows *ipso facto* when rejection of authority in a solemn matter is culpable, obstinate and externally manifested."

"All right. Grant that. He broke his vow. He's excommunicated. But he's also dead. Isn't it time to lift the penalty? I know there are rules and canons and proscriptions, but there are also exceptions, and rescripts and absolutions."

He shook his head.

"Why?"

"Because the order of the priesthood is at stake, that's why. Pope John Paul has reestablished discipline on the issue and just in time. Priests everywhere were confused and demoralized. Men like Michael by the thousands had let them down, and Paul VI had no idea how to deal with it. His ambivalence — his desire to be compassionate — only made things worse. This pope is not ambivalent." O'Shea gestured easily and I realized that he had retreated to a rote explanation of the Church's position. Did bishops take seminars in how to pontificate on this shit? "The priesthood is the spine of the Church, and it is forever. It is a radical, absolute vocation, and the Church must proclaim it as such. It is not a mere job or a career, an occupation to pursue for a while or for a phase of one's life. It is a sacred compact with God, a Covenant. 'Thou are a priest forever!' That is what Michael's excommunication means, and if the archdiocese is observing it scrupulously it is doing so not punitively, but, as the Constitution on the Church says, 'for the edification of the flock.' Only by a rigorous, one could even say heartless, observance of this point can this truth be protected and understood."

"But many ex-priests receive the sacraments."

"They did not flout authority. When they die their funerals won't be reported in the *New York Times*."

"So it's a matter of publicity? Forgive me, but I'm trying to understand. It isn't that he flouted authority, because you just said he was right about that."

"About the war. Not about marrying your wife."

His thrust stopped me. I should have known it would come, of course.

He saw his advantage and pressed it. "I'd have expected you of all people to understand our point of view. There are consequences to human acts. Some acts must simply not be condoned in any way."

"That's how I feel about what you are doing. Yes, Michael took my wife. And no, I don't condone it. But he is dead. She's alive. She is the one who is being punished now."

"She is not entirely innocent, it seems to me."

"Who the hell are you to throw that stone?"

"I'm a member of the Church. We loved Michael Maguire and she took him from us."

"You had already failed him! A deception at the heart of your friendship, yes! But not about a little volume of Scripture. The lie that destroyed his priesthood — and my marriage, damn you! — was the one that you priests tell each other, that you are brothers, that you care for one another, that you love each other. You never mistreat each other or exact vengeance upon each other or degrade each other. You only act for the edification of the flock. What shit! You make me sick!" O'Shea was staring at his hands obsequiously, and his willingness to sit there passively in the blast of my anger only stoked it. "Why am I surprised at your rejection of him now? You treat the dead like you treat the living. No wonder Michael began to wither! No wonder he refused finally to shrivel like the rest of you and become a gutless, conscienceless husk, a walking, Mass-saying, golf-playing, war-blessing carcass! A sacred compact with God? Bullshit! You people are in covenant with privilege. Everything is sacrificed to that, especially members who dare to challenge it. Michael woke up, that was his offense. I saw, when he did, what he was on his way to becoming. He fought it from within, but he was losing and he knew it. I saw his loneliness. It scorched him. It dried the blood in his veins. And do you know what? The Vietnam war saved him." O'Shea looked up at me, a look of confusion on his face. He *was* hearing me. But really, I didn't care. This was my moment to say what had happened and I was at its mercy. "The Vietnam war was probably the best thing that ever happened to Michael. It made him remember that he was a man before he was a priest. It made him remember his first ideals, and it forced him to make his compact with people again. The war destroyed his aloofness and his smugness. It brought him back. All he wanted after that was to be a man and a priest both. But it's impossible. You with your fancy new office and your mild regret at what stiffening the spine of the Church requires — what shit! — are the best evidence of that. He was your son, you said. But when the world fell down around his ears, when he needed support and love and solace and strength for that incredible, heroic resistance of his, could he get it from you? No! Or from the cardinal? No! Or from his fellow priests? No! Or from the Church herself? No! Of course he had to turn to someone else!"

"You were his friend. Why didn't he turn to you?"

The archbishop's second thrust. He had no idea why, but it undid me.

TWENTY-EIGHT

BEGINNING with Michael's trial, this story becomes Carolyn's story and mine too. She and I were stunned by the news of his arrest, and even before we saw him we knew that it would profoundly affect us. In fact it set in motion the events that changed everything.

Carolyn supported him immediately. It took me longer to work through my good-citizen bias, but eventually I too got the point. By the time his trial formally opened in May 1969 — it was the month the war peaked; 539,000 GIs were in Vietnam — I had come to see what he'd done as an elegant ethical gesture and I wrote as much for *Commonweal*. My piece on his trial was reprinted in newspapers all over the country. Michael had the article framed, together with an ancient snapshot of the two of us looking like members of the Gashouse Gang.

I was not surprised that so many people were moved by what he'd done. But not everyone was. When he was arrested, the archdiocese issued a statement saying Father Maguire was a previously suspended priest who had acted purely as an individual and in no way as a representative of the Church. The archdiocese would not censure him, but neither would it post his bail.

His bail was set at twenty thousand dollars. Carolyn and I didn't hesitate to post it, though it meant emptying our bank accounts and cashing in our bonds and my life insurance. I had been looking forward to extending an upcoming sabbatical by a year with those savings. I am chagrined to admit it, but I was going to write a novel about growing up in Inwood.

Carolyn and I went to the courthouse together. We delivered the cashier's check to the proper clerk and then went in the company of a federal marshal to the jail. The marshal served the jail-officer with the court order and left. A few minutes later doors clanged and Michael appeared, looking gaunt in his black clothing. Carolyn ran to him and embraced him. Even while he held her Michael stared at me. The desolation in his eyes seemed familiar. When he embraced me in turn, he whispered, "Thanks. It was awful. It was like China."

His terror of confinement had taken him by surprise, and he said that if he'd known what a nightmare recapitulation of his POW experience it would be, he'd never have walked willingly into the FBI ambush. After dinner — we ate in a small Italian restaurant in the Village — Carolyn and I suggested he come home with us. He seemed not to want to. He could go back to his nearby studio apartment. But we insisted. We both insisted. When he agreed, his relief was palpable. He lived with us then again, while preparing for the trial. Our house became the headquarters of his defense committee. Carolyn set aside her painting and arranged for babysitters for Molly in order to work full-time publicizing the trial and raising money to pay the lawyers. I was up to my ears at the university, but I gave every minute I could. I stifled my ambivalence, and found it possible, to my surprise, to see beyond the posturing and self-righteousness of the war resisters. Hell, in my own, didactic way, I became one of them. I wrote against the war every chance I got. Sometimes my desk felt hot beneath my hands. It was a frenzied, anxious, but exhilarating time. Michael had invitations from colleges and church groups all over the country. Even I took to the platform. I was particularly adept, it turned out, at debating the government lackeys who showed up at teach-ins. They were fodder for me. To speak at an antiwar rally, I discovered, was nothing like lecturing in the classroom. About literature I was wry and circuitous, carefully discursive, deliberately understated. I did not display myself in public. But about the war, to my own surprise, I spoke with unrestrained emotion, particularly as we discovered that spring that our new president was not winding down the violence, but intensifying it.

I'll always be grateful to Nixon, that worm. Thanks to him even I could feel pristine. It was glorious, how in hating the war and the warmakers, we could love ourselves. Praise the Lord and pass out pompous leaflets! Right on, Mother!

The antiwar movement was a perfect mix of the ridiculous and the profound, of true nobility and blatant solipsism. And its most memorable moments held both elements in tension.

I remember, for example, a rally at Boston University, the self-styled "Berkeley of the East." It was held at the football stadium and students from Boston's half-dozen large colleges had filled the stands to overflowing. It was a balmy spring day, and the kids were tricked out in tie-dyed T-shirts, flowing hair and moccasins. Frisbees sailed to and fro above their heads and, between speakers, a blues band wailed away on amplified harmonicas. Michael and I had driven up from New York and we arrived late. A kid at the gate who didn't recognize Michael said that Dave Dellinger and Tom Hayden had already spoken, but that everybody was waiting to hear Father Maguire. Michael winked at me. The note of deference was a surprise from this kid, at least to me. B.U. wasn't Notre Dame or Fordham. I didn't think a priest, even the celebrity-resister-priest, would make much of a dent there. But that was because I had yet to grasp that draft-age boys particularly regarded Michael as their great defender. And kids who wouldn't have thought of going into a church were as susceptible to the Great American Romance of the Priest as their parents had been. Michael was their Bing Crosby. As we walked into the stands, students began to recognize him. He had taken to wearing a black turtleneck sweater and a black windbreaker, a costume other priests would imitate, and, with his height, his leanness, he was a striking figure. As we walked through the stands toward the platform, students began to applaud. Frisbees stopped flying, though the music continued to blare. The closer we came to the platform the more students recognized him and began applauding. They stood. The ovation crossed the stadium like a wave, following us. By the time we reached the platform the band had stopped playing. The musicians were a scruffy, ill-groomed bunch with the studied look of nihilists, but they were applauding too. Michael looked at me, helpless. Thousands of college kids were cheering him. I clapped my hands theatrically toward him and bowed. As he mounted the stairs to the platform he leaned into me. I could sense that he was moved, but also embarrassed. Who was he? Bob Dylan? This was wacky. "Fuck peace," he whispered.

In May, Michael's case was finally heard. It was a simple procedure, quick and anticlimactic. The judge refused to admit into evidence the tape-recording that had been supplied to the *Times*, and when Michael's lawyer subpoenaed Celia Zack, he learned that she had disappeared. In the end Michael's defense consisted of little more than his own testimony. On the stand he was utterly credible, and it seemed to me the prosecutor's inability to shake his story would be decisive. When he sought repeatedly to refer to the war, the judge interrupted him. The war was not on trial. But when the prosecutor repeated the irrelevant slander that Michael had encouraged Nicholas Wiley to immolate himself, the judge allowed it. In his instruction to the jurors, the judge ordered them to disregard all arguments having to do with entrapment. The government was not on trial either. In fact, Michael had succeeded in making an issue, whether the judge allowed it or not, of abusive patterns the government would repeat against other Catholic resisters, against radicals, against genuine hoodlums and eventually against members of the U.S. House and Senate.

It took the jury less than an hour to bring back its verdict. Michael was guilty of willful and malicious destruction of government property. A week later the incensed Irish Catholic judge handed down a sentence of two to five years in prison.

When that sentence was announced there was a gasp in the courtroom. One of the jurors, present now as a spectator, cried, "No!" And Michael's shoulders sagged. When given a chance to speak, he only shook his head. A moment later, after the judge had left and people had begun to clear the room, Michael turned in his place, looking for us. Carolyn's face was buried in her hands. I knew it was her eyes he wanted. I touched her. She uncovered her face and Michael took refuge in what it showed him.

At a time like that friends stand without defenses in one another's company. I knew that the level of feeling between Caro and Michael was more intense than ever, but the context for their feelings, their love, had been radically altered. How can I indicate our states of mind, or the common state I presumed we shared? It is important that you understand. We had all been softened by the years. Once, perhaps, even they would have romped into an affair, believing implicitly, as the young do, that there is only one possible form of expression for such feelings. But it was different for them now because their love for each other — I knew this with primordial certainty — existed inside their love for me. It was therefore radically chaste. It was a love I could encourage. Though we were two sides of a love triangle, Michael was not my competitor. It was as likely that Carolyn should have been, in fact. In that courtroom, after his sentencing, the three of us embraced. We stood together for a long time. *That* was the expression we wanted. Carolyn, Michael and I shared a sense of having come home again in one another.

He continued to live with us during the months it took the courts to dispose of his appeal. Though his coming jail term loomed above us, we found it possible to live happily, as one family. Summer came. In August, to escape the rat-race of antiwar work — Michael was more in demand than ever — we rented a cabin at Lake George. At night after Molly was asleep, we would sit on the porch looking up at the stars. Sometimes I read poetry aloud. One verse of Eliot's became a theme of ours, a joke, but more than a joke because it hinted at the mysteries there were and would always be among us.

Who is the third who walks always beside you?
When I count there are only you and I together
But when I look ahead up the white road
There is always another one walking beside you
Gliding wrapt in a brown mantle, hooded
I do not know whether a man or a woman
— But who is that on the other side of you?

During the period leading up to our "vacation," Carolyn had worked herself to a frazzle too. Once she'd laid aside her painting, it was as if all her creativity was channeled into organizing, and she had done it with great success. She shunned the celebrity mode that Michael, like it or not, fell into, and she didn't function as a pinch-hit speaker as I did. Instead she spent long hours arranging events, benefits at art galleries, concerts at which the heroes spoke and cocktail parties at which the rich radicals could make donations to Michael's rich lawyers. At all of these occasions Carolyn would hover at the edge of things, making sure the microphones worked and the bartender had ice and the girl at the table by the door had pens with which the chic supporters could write their checks. And Carolyn always looked lovely. She'd developed a style of dressing that was fittingly unconventional; she was surely no lawyer's wife, no socialite, no BonWit DimWit. But she never embraced the counterculture cult of ugliness — uniform unisexuality; workboots, overalls, fatigue jackets, torn flannel shirts — that held sway in the movement. I remember her in long, high-waisted dresses, sandals, but still with heels, bangles at her wrists, no makeup but her luxuriant blond hair cinctured in bright, trailing silk like Louise Nevelson or Isadora Duncan. You knew she was an artist, just looking at her. It didn't matter that she hadn't painted in months.

Well, it mattered to her. And the fact that she'd fallen into a role, that of an antiwar hostess, that she despised mattered too. Stokely Carmichael had said a woman's place in the movement is on her back. Carolyn's place, she said, with bitterness that shocked me, was at the door, smiling. We were alone in our room one night at Lake George. It was the first time we'd talked to each other about what those months had really felt like. Her alienation, her weariness, were different from mine, and had led her to a vastly different conclusion.

"I've decided to do a raid, Durk."

"What?" I sat forward. I'd been propped against the headboard of our bed. I was wearing pajamas. She wore a T-shirt, no bra, and shorts. A blue engineer's bandanna was tied around her head.

"On the Dow Chemical offices at Rockefeller Center next month. A symbolic burning of napalm against its creators. We're going to burn some files."

"You're not serious."

"I am. There are seven of us. I have to do it, Durk. I haven't done anything."

I stared at her, unbelieving. This was the most insidious thing about the antiwar movement, how it could make such generous, dedicated, zealous workers feel as though they'd done nothing. Shit, she'd done nothing *but,* for months. For the crazies who were always within an inch of taking over, the only contribution to peace that counted was the act of going to jail. It was self-aggrandizement through self-punishment. It was madness. I'd never expected Carolyn to fall for it. I had to control my anger, I had to work at understanding her, at listening. I said quietly, "Why am I only hearing about this now?"

"Well, there wasn't any point to both of us being in on it, was there? We couldn't both do it."

"Because of Molly, you mean."

"That's right."

"Well, I'm glad you thought of her to that extent."

"Don't use Molly against me in this, Durk. Don't be angry at me. I need your support."

I took her hand in mine. "Caro, I think it's brave of you to want to do it. But you can't. You simply can't. They'd use it against Michael."

She shook her head. "He doesn't know about it. We've kept him out of it on purpose. Obviously the court would use any involvement on his part to extend his sentence."

"And when you and who — Jack? Sonny? Kate? — when you get busted in Dow Chemical they're going to think Michael's not involved? He got two to five years, remember? You want to make sure he serves every possible day, is that it?"

"Of course not. But we do want him to know that what he's begun will continue."

"Sweetheart, it can't continue. Not that way. There's only one Michael Maguire. There's only one hero."

She withdrew her hand from mine and looked away. What a disappointment I was to her. It was true. There was only one Michael. I was a disappointment, of course, to myself. But, hell, I was used to that. Nevertheless, I pressed the point, because I was right. "We have to work against the war, Caro, in the ways that *we* can. That means not making Michael's situation worse. And it also means, by the way, staying close to Molly. You'd be in jail a year."

She looked down at the thin bedspread, smoothed it with her hands. "But, Durk," she said finally, "I haven't done anything against the war. And I haven't helped Michael."

"You want to take his place in jail, don't you?"

She looked up and I saw the flicker of her recognition. She nodded slowly and I could read her worry. "I think I would handle it better than he will."

I was about to say, "You would. You're stronger than any of

us." But before I could I had a recognition of my own. She didn't want to take his place in jail. She just wanted to be with him. The truth stopped me cold. Before I maneuvered past it, Molly cried out sharply from the next room, the panic of a bad dream in her voice. Carolyn went to her at once.

I was alone with unwanted knowledge. Carolyn was far more like Michael than like me. If she'd been a nun still, instead of my wife, she'd have been his virgin princess, his Saint Joan at the head of his army. It did not occur to me to think of her as his Magdalen.

When Carolyn returned she stopped short in the doorway of our room and leaned against the jamb. Wearily she unknotted her bandanna and shook her hair free. Then she looked at me pensively. "You're right, Durk. I couldn't leave Molly. She's what's kept me from becoming even harder."

"You're not hard, darling."

"I hate the war. I hate what it's doing to us. Don't you feel it?"

"Yes. But I didn't know it was the war."

"What else is it?"

I shrugged. "Quotidian Distraction, darling." I could be so insufferably blasé. I patted the bed, Come sit. She crossed to me. I said, "Once Michael is gone, you and I can withdraw somewhat from all that antiwar shit." She started to protest. I stopped her. "You know we can. We're both in it because of him. He drafted us, didn't he?" She nodded. "You simply *must* start painting again, Caro. You're an artist. That's the longing you feel, the unhappiness. You're not *working*. You must work. Your paintings are the opposite of war. That's how you resist. That's how you keep faith. You are an artist, Caro!"

She leaned against me, and I felt the tension drain out of her. "You mean I can?" she asked. "I really can?"

"What, go back to painting?"

She nodded.

"Darling, you must."

Her arms went around me. "Oh, Durk, you know me, don't you? You take care of me. No one takes care of me like you do."

"That's my job, love. I'm your husband."

"You're my best friend."

"Same thing."

"It's why you put up with me."

"I put up with you because I love you, Caro."

"Oh, Durk." She surprised me then by kissing me passionately. We fell back upon the bed, at the mercy of her emotions, which I took to be gratitude, relief, and the old affection.

"I love you," she said. "I've never loved you more." She clung to me so fiercely I believed her.

Of course I was conscious of Michael's presence in the room beyond Molly's. I was both grateful to him — he had drawn from both of us entirely new capacities for feeling — and sorry for him because he would never experience with either of us the fullness of intimacy that Carolyn and I, to our mutual surprise, shared then. I remember restraining myself at orgasm that night and subsequent ones at Lake George so that he wouldn't hear, so that he wouldn't feel bereft.

That August Michael and I climbed Black Mountain, one of the highest peaks in the Adirondacks. Carolyn and Molly had gone down to Westchester to see her parents. The heat was ferocious and by the time we arrived at the top of the mountain we were soaked with perspiration and too weary at first to bother with the view. In our packs we had liquor. We sat against the rocks and traded swigs. When I finally looked out across Lake George the vista — a spine of mountains running north — made my mind reel. In my dehydrated state, the gin helped, of course. I felt instantly drunk. I faced away, but behind us was an even grander view, the Green Mountains of Vermont. I faced west, nestled in the crevice of the rock and tried to focus, for sobriety's sake, on the sun. It had fallen to within two or three hands of the horizon.

We sat in silence for a long time. Maybe we did get drunk. Maybe that was why we said those things.

He began, "All of this I will give you."

"If?" I knew the phrase, the opening of the devil's temptation of Christ. If you will fall down and worship me.

But he said, "I'll just give it to you. There."

"Thanks."

"I would though, Durk. I'd give you the whole goddamn world if I could, for what you've done for me."

"Michael, it's been a privilege. You're a fucking hero. Have a drink."

"Don't say that."

"But it's true."

"I'm not interested in being a hero to you. One time we sat in the Cloisters. Do you remember that?"

"Sure."

"We covered the same ground."

"You were a hero then too."

"Do you remember the Unicorn Tapestry?"

"The Unicorn in Captivity."

"That's right. I pointed out to you that what looked like the blood of the Unicorn was actually the juice of the pomegranate tree dripping down on it. Do you remember?"

"Yes."

"Guess what."

"It was blood after all."

"That's right. And if it wasn't for you I'd have bled to death."

"Get out of here."

"I would have, damnit. I still might." He took my sleeve. "Durk, I've got to tell you, I'm bleeding right now. I'm scared shitless. I think prison is going to do me in."

"Come off it, Michael. You know about fear. It's a reflex. It just gets you ready. Fear's your friend."

"No." He draped my neck. He was drunker than I was. "You're my friend."

"We're all your friends, hero!"

"Goddamnit, listen to me! Don't call me that. I'm telling you I'm afraid. I'm afraid because I know the stakes now. I didn't before. When we were kids, you and me, we hadn't a clue how fucking easily things get lost."

"What, like youth?"

"Like faith." He hesitated, took a breath, then declared, "I think I'm losing mine."

Michael was serious. Even in my fog I sensed that he was talking about something important, something more profound than his alienation from Church authority. Michael Maguire was nothing if not a believer. "You mean in God?" I asked carefully.

"I don't trust Him to sustain me. Isn't that the point of faith?"

"I guess." My mind went blank. After all the months of being at the mercy of this man's ordeal, of being, however willingly, at the service of his vaunted integrity, this was impossible to take in. Michael had to believe in God, he was that kind of priest, of man. He had thrown himself over Kierkegaard's edge where there was either grace or nothing. If God did not sustain him — we knew the Church wouldn't — who would or could? Then I panicked; not me, I thought, no way, bud! I can be your friend, but not the Ground of Your Being.

"In China," he said, "the guards told me that World War Three had started, remember that?"

"Yes."

"They told me New York had been hit with the A-bomb and for a time I believed them. I believed that everyone I knew and loved was dead and that half the cities of Europe and America were ash and that a cloud of radiation was hanging over the world. I believed all that, Durk, but I still believed in God. I still believed He loves us and takes care of us. But now . . ." He fell silent.

I became increasingly desperate. He gave me the feeling that somehow I had to rescue him — his faith! — with what I said. I wanted to recite a whole litany of reasons for belief, but I could not think of one. After several swallows of gin I swept my hand toward the horizon grandly. "But look at the view, Michael. It's the fucking world at our feet. You see any fucking radiation cloud? Hey, you wanted to give it to me as a token of your gratitude, right?"

"That's right."

"Well, that's how God feels. There it is. Mountains, valleys, rivers, trees, animals, Vermont, New-fucking-York, Cana-fucking-da, the whole fucking earth!" I slugged his shoulder. "And God puts it there for you, hero! Out of gratitude!"

"You're not listening to me."

"Because you manifest His conscience for Him, hero. Nobody does that like you do it. That's why He put you here."

"Durk, listen to me, will you? None of that means shit to me!"

"So you're having a little Dark Night of the Soul, that's all."

"No, that isn't all."

I put my hand on his shoulder. "Look, Michael, if I were you I'd be sick thinking about what's coming up. But I'm not you. More to the point, you're not me. You can deal with it."

"And you couldn't? Why the hell am I special?"

"I don't know. But you are. That's the fact of it, Michael. You have a strength the rest of us lack. You're stuck with it. And that's why more is asked of you."

"No, more is asked of everybody. If we filled the jails the war would end."

"If we filled the jails we'd fill the jails, that's all."

"Well, that makes me a chump, doesn't it?"

"Why? For manifesting God's conscience on earth? What better thing for a priest to do? You're a *priest,* Michael! That's the difference between you and me. It's a big difference. Priests sustain the rest of us. We draw on you for courage and for gentleness and for moral example. Maybe we suck life out of you. That's what we need you for. I see the problem; I see *your* problem. Who do priests draw on? Who do priests suck life out of? Who sustains the sustainer? Well, you have to answer that one. I can't."

"In theory, God does."

"He always has, right?"

"Yes."

"Well?"

"It's different this time."

"Why?"

This was when he could have told me. He was silent for some moments, then took a hit of gin. "I guess because I'm older. I don't know. Maybe I'm afraid of dying. I told you. When we were kids we didn't know how easily things get lost."

I put my arm around his shoulder. "Michael, you won't lose me."

He looked at me sadly. This was the last time we got drunk together. "Just don't call me 'hero,' all right?"

When the appeals process had finally run its futile course, Michael was ordered to begin serving his sentence on the first day of December 1969.

And he might have.

But in late November news stories began appearing about an "alleged massacre" of civilians that was reported to have taken place in a Vietnamese village variously referred to as "Pinkville," "Songmy" and "My Lai." The story came out in disjointed pieces and at first without sensation. Courts-martial of certain junior officers were discreetly under way, and that was what began attracting the attention of reporters. At first the civilian death toll was put at forty-three, then at "somewhat over a hundred." By the end of November more than ten American GIs who admitted participating had given reporters their accounts of the incident.

For most of a day in late March of 1968, dozens of American soldiers, acting under orders of officers, had herded more than five hundred old men, children and women into the village square, into fields and into a large drainage ditch where they fired their automatic weapons on them at close range. This was not the act of frenzied, panic-stricken boys, but of lucid soldiers who had come to regard every Vietnamese person — every "Dink" — of whatever age or position as the enemy. There was one American casualty, a GI who shot himself in the foot rather than obey. The "Combat Action Report" about the incident, filed by the lieutenant colonel who supervised from his helicopter, called it an "attack that was well-planned, well-executed and successful."

When *Life* magazine, the last week in November, published nine gruesome photographs, eight in color, showing corpses of babies piled on one another, of toothless old women and Pappa-san men strewn in paddies, of hundreds of villagers stretched along a ditch, the world was stunned. The photographs had been taken secretly and held back until now by a disgusted but frightened army photographer. His pictures and his testimony were the most damning revelations of the whole war.

Only two weeks before, on November 15, a quarter of a million Americans had marched on Washington, the largest demonstration in the capital's history, demanding an immediate end to the war. They had thought that they grasped its horrors in full dimension, but they didn't. Now suddenly the rhetoric of the radicals, crazy youngsters who threw stones at cops and broke windows at peace marches, seemed justified. The first shock of My Lai would lead to others, and it would take months before the full story of that and related atrocities became known. But in those first weeks of the My Lai disclosures Americans grasped viscerally, finally, what the Vietnamese had long known. The war itself was the atrocity.

Still, I was surprised that that was what Michael wanted to talk about. It was snowing lightly, but neither of us paid much attention to the weather. I was aware of Michael's weighty mood and thought he had a right to one, since this was his last day of freedom. We were walking across the plaza at Lincoln Center. It was where we habitually strolled when he came to see me at my office in the new Fordham building on Sixtieth Street. The huge Chagall tapestries dominated the square even from inside the glass facade of the Met. Ahead of us snowflakes dusted Henry Moore's reclining nude, that massive stolid sculpture which I'd come to think of as the steely heart of New York City. It was noontime.

Why the hell was he going on about the war? He was on his way to jail! Wasn't Vietnam someone else's problem now?

"Did you read that about Calley? How he tore that infant from the Buddhist priest's arms so that he could shoot the priest? And then how he shot the infant? His M-16 must have cut that baby in half."

Michael's agitation made me impatient, but it alarmed me too. I hadn't felt it at such a pitch since Nicholas Wiley's death. We turned the corner at the far side of the reflecting pool in front of the Vivian Beaumont. In reply I was reduced both by my concern for him and by my despair at the war to saying simply, "It's grotesque."

"No, no, Durk! You miss the point if you think of it as grotesque. Don't you see, it's ordinary! It's commonplace! Calley is what this war has become. The army is full of Calleys now. He's no exception."

"Come on, Michael. Don't go SDS on me."

"Calley does it up close, that's all. But it's the same thing."

"I don't think it's quite —"

"Ask the Vietnamese! It's the same to them!"

"The point is, Calley's being court-martialed, isn't he?"

"Yes, because some kid blew the whistle and forced the issue. So they string up an imbecile lieutenant and a few Pfc's from Tennessee . . ."

"And Captain Medina."

". . . when it's the generals who should be hung, especially Sennett."

"Who's Sennett?"

"Brigadier General David Sennett, the commander of Fort Hamilton in Brooklyn."

"I don't get it."

"He was the Eleventh Infantry Brigade commander in March of sixty-eight. Calley was his boy. My Lai was his operation."

"Look, Michael, if you think the brass will be held accountable for this thing you're wrong. You might as well hope they bring Agnew and Nixon to court for it. Somebody has to be tried for shit like My Lai. Why not the animals who actually did it?"

"Durk, listen to me!" He took me by the arm and pushed me to a low, concrete parapet. We sat. "My Lai gives us a brand-new chance to force the American people to look at what this war has become, what it's been for years. I'll tell you who's responsible for My Lai: *we* are! Goddamnit, isn't that the point, finally? We rejected this war as a people two years ago, but it's worse than ever! So everyone marches on Washington. But Nixon ignores it. Thieu uses his army against his own people. Agnew rants about the kooks. A few of us timidly break the law and get locked up. And we all throw our hands in the air and say, 'Well, we tried!' But meanwhile our boys keep going over there by the thousands after raising pet rabbits in boot camp so the DI can snap their necks. And yes, then they're animals! And they *will* do anything! To anyone! Do you hear me? That's what this war has done! Our soldiers will do anything to anyone! Do you hear me?"

"Yes. So does half of Manhattan."

We stared at each other. Steam puffed from his mouth and nostrils. Finally he said, "West Point is playing basketball against Saint John's tomorrow night at Madison Square Garden. The local commander always attends Army games as a kind of presiding officer. General Sennett's going to be in the front row at mid-court. There's going to be a demonstration and I am going to be a part of it."

"But you can't! You go into custody tomorrow!"

"That's what I wanted to tell you. I'm not turning myself in. I'm not cooperating with the government anymore, Durk. Authority has to be legitimate." Michael smiled. "Even Saint Thomas said that. If this government wants me to obey it, then they can stop the war. If they won't call the real criminals to account, then we will. If they want me tomorrow, they can come to Madison Square Garden."

At first, so domesticated — housebroken — was my mind that I did not understand what he was saying. Had his lawyer obtained an extension from the court? Of course not. Even before I spoke I grasped in its full dimension the enormity, the audacity, of what he'd said. "You mean you're going to . . . ?" I didn't have a word for it.

But he did. "Resist, Durk. I'm going to resist. Not out of rebelliousness. You know me. I'm no revolutionary. I hate what I've come to. But I see now what we have to do — challenge and if we can, destroy America's faith in people like General Sennett and General Abrams . . ."

"And Nixon?"

"As far as the war goes, yes. GIs have to stop obeying their officers. Teenage boys have to stop obeying their draftboards. And peaceniks have to stop obeying the courts."

"Michael, you've lost me. Honest to God, you've lost me. The last time we talked you told me you'd had it. You were through. You'd done your part."

"I was indulging myself, Durk. I'd become obsessed with my anxiety about prison. What's that next to the sacrifice of the Vietnamese? My Lai reminded me, that's all. At first I thought I was doing this because I *am* afraid of prison, but that's not it. I'll go to jail eventually, but not before I strike a real blow at the war. Americans, if you face them with it, won't tolerate this thing. And that's what I'm going to do, face them with it. Before we're through, Durk, it won't be that kids refuse induction, but that their mothers and fathers won't let the army near their kids."

"Where will you go?"

"To America," he said, utterly without self-consciousness. "If the government wants me they can come out there and catch me, where everyone can see."

The melodrama of his statement, the cartoon-talk about "America" so typical of the time, stands out starkly now as I repeat it, but then it seemed eloquent. His bravado simply took my breath away. My God, I thought, it's the old Michael Maguire, the boy-soldier hero hurtling down a hill against an enemy patrol to save his wounded buddies and their priest, the young idealist handing over the rest of his life in one wrapped package to the Lord, the priest off to Vietnam to rescue children, then defying the cardinal to bury Nicholas Wiley. Yet now Michael seemed readier, as if every previous act of boldness — "*L'audace! Toujours l'audace!*" — was practice for this one.

"And this means," he said, "I'm going to owe you a lot of money. I'll be forfeiting bail. That's your twenty thousand dollars. That's what I'm here to talk about. I'm telling you right now that somehow, someday I'll see that you're repaid."

For a moment I felt sick at the thought of all that money, which was *all* of my money, going up in smoke, the smoke of his sacrifice. I couldn't reply.

He said, "I feel terrible about it," and I saw that he did.

But then it hit me, what was money, even that sum, in such a context? Michael was talking about an ultimate act. He had become, in a way, an ultimate man.

And I? At that moment I was like everyone. I forgot what he'd shown me in secret, the cost of his world-saving, charismatic integrity, the cost in loneliness and self-doubt. I rejoiced instinctively to see him large again, unyielding, the rock of our rejection. My reservations — I thought his decision was quixotic, foolhardy and dangerous — were obliterated by the pride I felt just to be his friend. I thought him right about the war, about America and about My Lai as the turning point we'd been awaiting.

"Forget the money, Michael," I said, "I mean, please. And tell me now exactly what I can do to help."

TWENTY-NINE

And when our work is done
Our course on earth is run
May it be said, "Well done;
Be thou at peace."
E'er may that line of gray
Increase from day to day,
Live, serve and die we pray,
West Point, for thee.

After the robust, throaty rendition of their alma mater, the cadets, a thousand strong and concentrated, a gray mass, in the upper seats, let out one of their startling, sustained roars. The noise, like a balloon expanding in a box, pressed against the walls and girdered ceiling of the Garden. West Point cadets make the best roars in sport because of all that pent-up energy and their acquired knack for unison. Only seminarians could match them in those traits. Seminarians, of course, do not learn to roar since they are not, most of them, being trained for battle.

The roar did not fade until the referee tossed the ball into the air at center court. The Redmen snagged it and immediately moved on Army's basket; three quick passes, a feint, a shot, swish! Saint John's would never lose the lead. By halftime the score was 42–28. Even the automated cadets in the stands had gone slightly limp. The Saint John's fans across the arena looked like long-haired hippies next to the Corps, though in fact they were relatively conservative Catholic kids from Queens and would have looked downright square at Dupont Circle or Haight-Ashbury or, for that matter, in Greenwich Village. But by now even to most of them, the army was the enemy of their generation, and the cadets were traitors to it. They wanted their ballplayers to beat West Point mercilessly.

It was because of the abuse Military Academy teams regularly took at other colleges during the late sixties that the local commanders compulsively attended the games. They always sat, bedecked and accompanied by aides, in a prominent seat. It was like setting up a commandpost on a ridge so that both your enemy and your own forces would behold your nerve and be, in one case, shaken and, in the other, reinforced. At halftime General Sennett stood in his place in the first row at center court and greeted well-wishers, old friends, retired officers and celebrities.

When the priest walked out onto the court with a microphone in his hand, the general assumed, as the guards had, he was some functionary from Saint John's about to begin the halftime program. He looked innocuous in his Clark Kent spectacles, black suit and Roman collar.

"Ladies and gentlemen," he said, "may I have your attention, please." At first the crowd ignored him. Sennett took his seat, however, and the cadets, seeing that, fell silent. Soon the quiet spread across the Garden. The priest was alone in the middle of the court. "Please come forward," he said. Suddenly from seats and aisles in all parts of the arena, men and women filed onto the court. They moved with ceremonial dignity, donning white conical hats as they did so. Sennett was among the first to recognize those as stylized Vietnamese peasant hats, and he was close enough to read what was written on them: "Old Woman," "Infant," "Buddhist Nun," "Village Elder," and so on. The priest, Sennett realized, was staring at him as he said, "Think of these four hundred and twenty-two people as the old men, women and children who lived in a small village in Quang Ngai Province until March 16, 1968. That was the day that you, General Sennett, as the commanding officer of the Eleventh Infantry Brigade, sent Task Force Barker, led by Lieutenant Colonel Frank Barker, including Charlie Company, led by Captain Ernest Medina, including a platoon led by Lieutenant William Calley, against their village, which was called My Lai." By this time the several hundred demonstrators had joined the priest on the court. They stood rigidly, like figures in a mime, pointed in every direction, their faces obscured by their conical hats. After a long silence during which there was no sound from anyone in Madison Square Garden, the priest said, slowly and distinctly, the sound system carrying every nuance of his voice, "General Sennett, we accuse you of and charge you with the murder of these people."

At that all four hundred and twenty-two demonstrators — the "infants," "elders" and "nuns" — fell to the floor, limp. Like that, snap! They were a mass of corpses! Only the priest remained standing.

After an initial gasp, the crowd was absolutely still, too stunned to react, with the exception of photographers, whose cameras clicked and whirred.

Sennett stared at the priest. His face was a blank mask.

The priest said, "May God forgive you. We do not." And then he took off his glasses, his gesture toward disguise. He walked off the court, stepping around the "corpses" as he did so.

The newspapers the next day made much of the fact that at the very moment Michael Maguire was confronting the army general in front of twelve thousand people, the FBI was searching for him in New York rectories. As of noon that day he had become a fugitive priest.

It was a powerful myth for Catholics of the old school. The priest on the run, the outlaw celebrant, the Jesuit with a price on his head. Fugitive priests had founded the Church in the Catacombs while Caesar's legions hunted them. Fugitive priests had kept the last flicker of the true faith alive in Elizabethan England while the queen's men stalked them. They hid in priest-holes, in secret rooms behind fireplaces. They went about disguised as lawyers or teachers, and the people revered them. Their legends grew even while they lived, and when at last they were caught and martyred, the Church remembered them as saints. They were Thomas, James and Peter, Edmund Campion, Robert Southwell and John Fisher. There were fugitive priests in Ireland and then, in our own time, in Europe under the Nazis, in China under Communists, and in Latin America under military regimes. As children my generation of Catholics read comic books about them, and articles in *Our Sunday Visitor*. We celebrated their feast days and prayed to grow up with their courage and their willingness to risk everything for God. We sang how sweet 'twould be if we "like them could die for Thee." Now there was a priest-fugitive in our own country, hounded not by Caesar or the queen, Hitler, Stalin, Mao or some generalissimo, but by that other company of our heroes, the FBI.

Michael taunted them. Within a week of having "gone underground" he began the dramatic series of surprise appearances at rallies and in churches, making speeches, preaching sermons, and giving interviews, stealthily, to reporters. A network of dozens of people from Washington to Boston sprang up to help him, to hide him, to arrange his meetings with students and with antiwar and church groups. Brave strangers drove him from one rendezvous to another.

Carolyn and I were not among that network and neither were his other close friends. For the most part, during his months underground, we did not know where he was. Obviously we were being watched and our phones were surely tapped. Michael was in the hands, mainly, of Jewish professors, ironically, and that was why he succeeded beyond anyone's expectation. The FBI, lumpishly, concentrated on us Catholics.

Still, we heard stories about him. Not many days would pass without some report from that unlikely outlaw subculture about his latest escapade. There we were, sophisticated academics, journalists and professionals all up and down the East Coast, but we were like kids with ears to the radio. *Gangbusters! The FBI in Peace and War! The Shadow!* In the snatches of what we heard we knew that a legend was being made. A legend, unbelievably, for the likes of us.

In Washington in late January there was a meeting of top leaders from around the country of CALC, Clergy and Laity Concerned About Vietnam. About seventy of them, men and women of various denominations, gathered to coordinate plans for the upcoming campaign to lobby congressmen to cut off funds for the war. They were meeting in the basement auditorium of a Baptist church in Northeast Washington, not far, ironically, from Catholic University where Michael had done his training. At the start of their morning session the chairman melodramatically promised the group that before the meeting adjourned that day they would be hearing from, as he put it, "the priest-prophet of the peace movement." No one at that meeting had to have it spelled out that that meant Michael Maguire, and the anticipation that even those hard-boiled activists felt at the prospect of his coming was a distraction of the first order all day.

Sure enough, late in the day, after their workshops and small group meetings, the people reassembled in the auditorium. Word had spread to other local clergy and activists. Even seminarians from Catholic U. showed up, filling the corridors and stairwells outside the basement hall. The uninvited overflow were ushered into the unheated church upstairs, and soon even it was full. There the people stared at an empty sanctuary, the cold air showing the vapor of their breath, and they listened closely to the proceedings downstairs through the squawky sound system. The CALC meeting had turned into an ad-hoc rally. A folksinger led choruses of "Blowin' in the Wind" and "If I Had a Hammer." A black poet in Muslim dress read verses that asked questions of the Vietnamese. (Do you not curse us in your sleeping and your waking?) A gospel choir sang three rousing numbers. A minister from Indian Territory in South Dakota spoke feelingly about the old American custom of genocide. And then silence fell over both groups, down and up, as the CALC chairman took the podium.

No sooner had he introduced Michael than Michael's voice, cutting short the applause, filled the auditorium and the church with heartfelt exhortations addressed expressly to the organizers. "CALC exists to save lives!"

No sooner had his speech begun than half a dozen men, some bearded and wearing fringe-leather jackets and some clean-shaven, dark-suited, looking like clerics, left the pews of the upper church hurriedly. They dashed down the stairs to the auditorium and burst into it, with guns drawn, crying, "Freeze! FBI!" Their FBI colleagues who had infiltrated the auditorium ahead of them looked sheepishly back from their chairs. Those agents hadn't moved because they knew the truth, that Father Maguire's ringing antiwar speech, which had not stopped or slowed or broken cadence despite the interruption, was even then being delivered by a large, reel-to-reel tape machine balanced precariously and quite visibly on the otherwise vacant podium.

Another time Michael appeared at a so-called Celebration of Resistance at the University of Connecticut at Storrs, a typical college town in the farming area north of Hartford. The weekend festival, with music, speeches, "political theater," slide-shows and movies, was held in the huge university fieldhouse. The place was packed for the Saturday night rally because Jane Fonda was appearing. That Father Michael Maguire unexpectedly joined her was like Mick Jagger showing up at a Janis Joplin concert. Fonda embraced the renegade priest chastely when he walked onto the stage. When she turned then and introduced him to the crowd, most of whom had recognized him and were already cheering, the seven widely scattered, overweight and nervous campus policemen got orders from their chief through their walkie-talkies to converge on the platform and arrest him. Students saw the cops moving and spontaneously, good-naturedly, spilled into the aisles, slowing them. Michael spoke only for a moment — "Resistance, yes! Violence, no!" — and then disappeared backstage. He made good his escape inside one of the giant puppet heads of the mime troupe that had preceded Jane Fonda on the evening's program. The papier-mâché head that enabled him to slip by the police was, in fact, a dreary, gray monster, the writhing face of death.

Between these dramatic, much-discussed appearances, Michael shuttled from place to place driven by strangers, people whose names he made a point not to know. In the cities, his movements and contacts were orchestrated by a handful of organizers, four or five at the most, whose identities I never knew. Obviously, given his success, they were people Michael had reason to trust. The longer he was at large — and it had never occurred to them in the beginning that he would elude capture for so many months — the more smoothly the network functioned. He hid out in little attic rooms or apartments over garages. His attitude toward the strangers who harbored him was one of utter trust, a kind of abandon, although he refused to stay with families with young children, who would not understand why their parents and a priest would break the law. He did not go out in daylight even when he was in small towns that seemed far removed from the controversies of the day. Mostly he was sheltered in the nicer suburbs where lived the professors, ministers, rabbis, psychiatrists and social workers his hosts tended to be: Newton outside Boston, Columbia near Baltimore, Summit, New Jersey, Media outside Philadelphia. He avoided New York, where he was so well known, and places like New Haven, Cambridge and Princeton, which the FBI were sure to stake out. Though he was on the platform often with antiwar celebrities, he never hid out with them. And he had nothing whatever to do with the anarchistic underground of the SDS and its spin-off groups of crazies. Instead he lost himself among an anonymous mass of average, essentially moderate people. They were no "underground" at all, but had simply come to hate the war passionately and now welcomed Michael, despite the risks, as a way of turning up the volume on their "no" to it. In the evenings, Michael habitually encouraged his hosts to have friends over so they could talk. Just being exposed to him in such informal settings, knowing that that huge posse of Hoover's agents was outside looking for him, realizing what risks he was taking and most of all experiencing up close his compelling, single-minded but strangely relaxed and self-accepting dedication was enough to change people in fundamental ways. It was commonly said by men and women who met him in such circumstances — I heard this second and third hand often — that for the first time since they'd turned against the war they believed they could make a difference to it, they could help stop it. Michael Maguire, by example, by manner, by what he said and especially by how he lived, was shattering the paralysis of doubt, futility and frustration people felt. When they asked him, as they always did, "But what can *we* do?" he would smile, raise his shoulders and say, "You've already broken the law by being here with me. You are in resistance now. So keep resisting." An act of disobedience had freed him once so that when the opportunity came to strike a real blow against the war he could take it. Now he had become himself the occasion of disobedience for others, and many of those, in fact, found it to be as freeing for action as he had. He left a trail of recruits to the antiwar movement behind him, men and women who would give it their best energy for years.

Ironically, because of him, some of those liberals found themselves reconsidering their attitudes toward that most reactionary of impulses, belief, and that most conservative of institutions, the Church. For whatever else Michael was during that time, he was never more a priest. Perhaps only the unchurched who did not take such things for granted could fully appreciate that the driving force of his resistance was his spirituality. Those who were sensitive to it were moved, and those who weren't still knew that this man had depths they couldn't touch. He was rarely with religious people, and so mostly he prayed by himself. Prayer, the hagiographers would say, became his one steadfast companion.

In the interviews he gave and in his short talks in that variety of settings he hammered away at what My Lai revealed. The story of that massacre and the subsequent army cover-up that was exposed that winter gave him his theme and made his message accessible to a broad public. Not even staunch supporters of the war were unaffected by the news of My Lai. Even military men professed repugnance. Sennett himself was eventually censured, reduced in rank and stripped of his DSM. Horror at the war spread to average people, and Father Michael Maguire gave voice to it. His hit-and-run appearances were widely covered in the media, though not with universal approbation. Editorials blasted him regularly, but the average journalists who wrote the news stories about him hardly disguised how enthralled they were. A surprisingly large segment of viewers and readers followed the dramatic unfolding of his defiance with sympathy. Groups, including apolitical and patriotic ones, began passing resolutions of support for the fugitive priest. Vestries and parish councils began inviting him to their churches to preach. At times organizers of antiwar rallies deliberately began rumors that Michael was coming as a way of drawing television coverage for their demonstrations, and that made it seem as if he was capable of a kind of omnipresence; Father Maguire, more than once, was reported to have been in Washington and Boston on the same night. Hadn't he become like Superman?

Cardinal Cooke steadfastly refused all comment about the notorious priest, although a Vatican spokesman in Rome said the pope was praying for him. Reports from Stockholm had it that he was a candidate for the Nobel Peace Prize (which had yet to be given to Henry Kissinger). It was a period when the sixties ended and the seventies began, and though Michael Maguire's defiance seemed to embody a massive national repudiation of the war, the brutal bombing of the North was resumed in those months and plans were laid for the invasion of Cambodia. We had no idea how utterly immune from influence, moral or political, the warmakers always were.

In January, despite its own condescension toward him, the *New York Times Sunday Magazine* ran a long, dramatic interview with Michael. The reporter described having been searched, blindfolded, and driven in successive cars to a farmhouse well outside of New York City. It was like *Breathless, Bonnie and Clyde* or

Easy Rider, only this criminal was no psychopath, no weirdo, no loser, but, in the reporter's estimate, an accomplished, intelligent, admirable man. In February his picture appeared on the cover of *Time* and the accompanying article was entitled "Wanted and Needed." If his appeal among Catholics grew out of the myth of the fugitive priest, his appeal to the people as a whole — it seemed eventually that the entire country was rooting for him — grew out of the classic American romance with the decent outlaw — Who was that masked man? — who challenges the crooked sheriff not for his own ends but for the town's.

The door bell rang. Carolyn looked up sharply from her book.

I looked at the clock. It was nearly midnight, a Saturday in February. The house was utterly still. Molly was asleep in her room at last. A school friend was sleeping over and they had drawn out the goodnights endlessly. Carolyn and I had each made trips to silence giggles.

I waited for the bell to ring again. It didn't. Finally I put my own book aside, took my glasses off, and stood. Carolyn stayed where she was.

I opened the door. No one was there. When I stepped out onto the stoop to look down the street I think I half-expected someone to jump on me. No one did. I went back into the house and shut the door. On the floor below the mail slot was a piece of paper the size of a business card. I might have missed seeing it. I picked it up, but was afraid to read it, as if the FBI could see through wood. I went into the living room. The curtains were drawn, as they always were that winter. By Carolyn's lamp I squinted at the piece of paper. "Come to the eleven o'clock at Saint John the Divine," it said, and nothing more. No signature, no peace sign, no Chi-Rho. But the handwriting was as familiar to me as my own. I let Carolyn read it. We did not exchange a word. Then I dropped the note onto the embers in the fireplace and watched it flame.

We left the house the next morning at eight-thirty and spent an hour and a half riding various subway trains, hopping on and off at the last minute the way Cary Grant and Audrey Hepburn would have. We came up at Times Square, caught a taxi to Columbus Circle, walked to the Paulist church, went in one door and out another, and caught another taxi to Saint John's. We arrived feeling exhausted and nervous at ten minutes before eleven.

The organ was playing softly, far from full out, but the tones filled the vast church. On the wooden chairs and needlepointed cushions — not pews with kneelers, the Catholic notes — several dozen people sat and knelt. But in that space dozens counted for nothing. Others arrived as we did, shaking their heavy coats open and walking with a certain timidity into the overwhelming Gothic nave. The mammoth piers, curving stone pillars rising one hundred feet in a single, stark leap, dwarfed everything human. It took an act of intellect to recall that those columns themselves were made by men too; the sacred space itself was human. I watched the other arriving worshippers, hoping they would make the cathedral seem less empty. They were older and well, but not flashily, dressed. The men wore their hair slick and the women wore hats. Except for an occasional young person wearing blue jeans and an angelic expression, the gathering congregation seemed like establishment Episcopalians, as one might have expected. Of course, establishment Episcopalians by then, led by their outspoken Bishop Paul Moore and theologians like Pike and Stringfellow, were resolutely against the war. Still, that the pulpit of this cathedral might be offered to Michael Maguire, the fugitive priest, amazed me. As I walked well to the front of the center aisle, clutching Carolyn's arm, my anxiety, like the architecture, soared. We took our places. I knelt at once and tried to pray. My mind was whirling along, and in the end, like a schoolboy, I mumbled my Hail Mary and sat.

At the appointed time a blast from the trumpets behind us reverberated the full length of the cathedral. As we rose, I held a hymnal for Carolyn, but neither of us sang. We turned to watch the ranks of choir, clergy and attendants enter. How sparse the congregation seemed! There may have been several hundred, but they seemed a paltry number and the strains of their singing were lost in the vaulted shadows. Still the procession was impressive, with boys carrying medieval banners ahead of the choir. The paired singers passed pompously, and then came the candle-bearers, the crucifer and thurifer whose incense pot spewed forth a pungent, billowing cloud through which strode the subdeacon, deacon and presiding priest. The smoke stung my eyes. There was no sign of Michael.

The last time Carolyn had attended a Solemn High Mass had been at Michael's ordination in Saint Patrick's a decade before.

Such liturgy, with chanted prayers, the Gregorian music, the incense, the hierarchy of officiants — as opposed to concelebrants — in old-fashioned fiddleback vestments, was rarely seen in post-Council Catholicism. It seemed strange to think of it as a Protestant service, since it was more familiar to me, and more beautiful, than anything I'd seen in a Catholic church in years.

It was the first Sunday of Lent and there was no *Gloria.* After singing the *Kyrie,* the choir sat and the Scriptures were read by lectors. And then the celebrant, identified by the program as the dean of the cathedral, the Reverend Thomas Reid Evans, mounted the elaborately carved white marble pulpit. Father Evans was a huge man — he had to be in that space — and his head was crowned dramatically with white hair, though he did not impress as old. He wore spectacles, but took them off with a flourish as he began to speak.

"For reasons that will be obvious to you in a moment, it was not possible for me to consult in advance with either the liturgical committee or the standing committee of the board of trustees, and for the sake of limiting possible legal jeopardy, I decided not to consult with the bishop but used my own discretion — my *sole* discretion — as the pastor of this community to invite into our pulpit this morning, on this first Sunday of the Penitential Season, a priest of the Church who has restored to us in all its power the commission priests receive from the Lord Himself to go forth into the world preaching the Gospel of Peace."

Abruptly, with no further comment, he turned and descended the pulpit and resumed his chair in the sanctuary. After a moment a bearded man robed in white and wearing a purple stole walked from behind the carved choir stalls up the length of the Choir. He bowed at the altar as he crossed in front of it, then walked to the pulpit and mounted it.

The beard threw me. He looked like an English actor. But when I heard his voice as he blessed himself and pronounced the sign of the cross, I wanted to cry out with joy for the sight of him. The old son of a bitch! My dearest friend!

Carolyn seized my hand and squeezed it. As we listened to him, I knew that I would never forget what he said.

He recited first this verse from Luke: "And when he drew near and saw the city he wept over it saying, 'Would that even today you knew the things that make for peace.' "

He paused. He seemed to look at each of us in the congregation singly.

"My dear friends," he said softly, "a brief word about the things that make for peace. There are three, Faith, Hope and Love. Faith is the easiest of these because it is an act of God's, not ours. The question is not whether we believe in Him, but whether He believes in us. And we have the absolute promise — the Flesh of His Son — that He does. God is the Faithful One. He is faithful even to us. Therefore we can, as Paul says, move mountains. We can even, perhaps, end wars.

"And Hope. Hope is the ability to see more than is before our eyes. We look at all the damned of this century, a hundred million killed needlessly in war, and know that we have turned the earth itself into the village of My Lai. Yet instead of seeing mere victims, reasons to hate the living, Hope sees in that host of war-dead a Communion of Saints who even now prepare to swoop down on us and seize us and shake us from our complacency. Live! they say. Stand! they say. Be what you are, creators of the future with God! Despair is the conviction that we can do nothing to end the war. And that is the last sin, the most costly sin. It dooms not just the one who commits it, but, in this century, the fragile world itself. In Hope, therefore, we tear that despair from our bosoms, our stony hearts, and we hurl it at heaven, crying to all those men, women and children, the victims of our recent history, 'Come you holy spirits! Renew the face of the earth!'

"And Love. Love, as Dorothy Day insists, is a harsh and dreadful thing. It is not romance or infatuation or an ocean of warm feelings. Love is radical communion with all those who have been forgotten or condemned or brutally massacred. Love, in our dispensation, is a crucifixion. How can we end the war? We have been told and told again. Each of us in his or her own way must take up the Cross and follow. Its road leads outside the city, away from comfort and security and the nurture of those who cherish us. The Cross, remember, puts us in the company of criminals, of fugitives, of those on whom presidents and generals, tribunes and centurians only spit. We have never been in better company in our lives.

"Faith, Hope and Love. The things that make for peace. And the greatest of these, Paul wrote, is Love. It was the discovery he made while in prison. With chained hands Paul wrote his messages — his love letters — to those who sustained him, who held him dear. They feared for him. But he said, 'No! Do not be afraid! Do not lose faith! Do not despair! Work for peace! We have the promises of Christ! We have His Word! The presidents and generals, the principalities and powers pursue me and will imprison me. But they can never imprison the Word of the Lord!' "

Michael turned in the pulpit toward me, and his eyes found mine. It was the first indication that he knew I was there. His sermon until this point had been delivered in a quiet voice, but his voice rose now as he ringingly repeated the last sentence. "They can never imprison the Word of the Lord!" He raised his hand to his mouth. I thought he was going to bless himself, but instead he touched his finger to his lips, a kiss, and then he threw it to us, to Carolyn and to me. And he turned, went down from the pulpit, and was gone.

There was silence for a moment and then the congregation burst into muted but amazed conversation. "My God," someone behind us said, "that was Father Maguire!" He said it in the awed tone of the cow-town barber: "That was the Lone Ranger!"

Carolyn leaned against me. I felt how drained she was. We clung to each other. I loved her more than ever. Michael — I could admit this at last — was what bound us.

After the Creed Dean Evans knelt and led us in prayer. He prayed for peace, and he prayed for "Our dear brother Michael. Carry him, O Lord, in the palm of Thy hand. Protect him from violent men. And open the ears of all who hear him. And open our hearts, that we too might be instruments of Thy Peace. We pray in the name of Christ."

"Amen," the people answered resoundingly.

By the time the offertory hymn was finished and the wine and bread were prepared, FBI agents had arrived. The congregation had not been unanimously edified after all.

The agents, eight that I counted, walked along the side aisles eyeing us sheepishly. Their hair was close-cropped and they carried their hats in their hands. They were ill at ease and for good reason; they were Catholics. You could feel them itching to genuflect. How strange their business must have seemed to them suddenly. How they'd have preferred to raid a gambling den or a chop-shop. How bizarre that setting must have seemed to them, the Roman liturgy, the Gothic church, the incense, candles, holy water, vestments. Were these Protestants or not? And was their quarry a criminal or a saint? Why weren't such distinctions sharp like they used to be?

I wanted to call out to them, "Sorry, G-Men! You missed him again!"

But all at once I felt sorry for them.

At the *Sanctus* we said with one voice, and it seemed to me defiantly, "Blessed is he who comes in the name of the Lord!"

Carolyn and I wanted to meet Dean Evans and thank him, so we went to the coffee hour at the Cathedral House, a Gothic château on the south side of the cathedral compound. The reception was in a splendid room with a gnarled timber ceiling and huge leaded windows and rare carpets on the floor. I was told that originally it was the bishop's house, and when someone faulted it for being too elegant, J. P. Morgan, a trustee, defended it by saying, "Bishops should live like everyone else."

Dean Evans greeted us cordially and introduced us to his handsome, confident wife. To them we were just two of several hundred worshipers. I wanted them to know we had come expressly to hear Michael. I said, "We're friends of Father Maguire. We're Catholics." In another context that would have been a stupid identification, an offensive one, but in that context it was exactly right. The Episcopal dean knew what I was saying. At his ordination Michael had given my faith in God back to me, and now, after a decade in which such distinctions had been blurred, he'd given me back my affiliation. For the first time since my days as a Good Shepherd altar boy, I could take pride in calling myself a Catholic.

"He is the jewel of the Church," the dean said. "I'm glad that you were here."

"Will you be in jeopardy now?" Carolyn asked.

"I hope so."

The dean's wife put her arm through her husband's. "Father Maguire has changed things here," she said.

The dean smiled. "She means he's changed some sheep into lions. It was people like us who began this war. Well, maybe it's time people like us ended it."

Their sense of themselves, so large, though not precisely arrogant — we start, we finish — was what struck me. It wouldn't have occurred to my people to feel responsible for Vietnam, though given its peculiarly Catholic origins, we should have. But in Good Shepherd High School in all its incarnations we learned to feel responsible only for our sex-weakened souls if at all. At Groton, Exeter, Saint Paul's and Choate, which indeed spawned the National Security Clique who ran the war, they were taught to feel responsible for the world. The dean was right. And so was Michael to go after him and his kind. Turn them against the Vietnam war, mobilize *their* anger, unstop *their* impotence and you will have more than torn draft files and burned cards, more than riots in the streets, more than teach-ins and demonstrations. You will have peace.

"Smug, aren't they?" I said to Carolyn as we left. I couldn't quite stifle my inborn Irish resentment.

She shook her head. "I wish Michael got support like that from his own people."

"His own people are chasing him."

We went out into the raw day and were crossing the broad garden, "the Cathedral Close," that was enclosed on one side by the imposing Synod House, yet another Gothic masterpiece, and on the other by the buttressed flank of the cathedral itself. As we walked toward Amsterdam Avenue we had to lean into the wind. It was Lenten weather. I hated it.

At the towering monument in the center of the Close, the platform crowned by the classic spire, Carolyn stopped. "What is that?"

It was the elaborate pulpit, the focus of the outdoor services that had been common before the nave was built, but I teased her. "It's the topmost spire of the Underground Church."

She laughed and opened her arms. I went into them. "Oh, Frank, let's not go home. Let's spend the afternoon together."

"I'd love that. We could ride the ferry like we used to and then get plowed at Desmond's."

"Yes, that's it! Let's!" Her face broke into a smile. "I'd love that. I'll go call Emily and see if she'll stay with Molly through the afternoon."

"I'll wait here," I said. I was glad to have left the Cathedral House crowd behind. I watched Carolyn retrace our steps. She was wearing a dark sheepskin coat and boots. She looked like a Russian princess. I felt a surge of affection for her. How her impulse pleased me!

"Mister Durkin?" A familiar man approached from the direction of the Synod House. He was wearing a dark overcoat and hat and as he drew near I saw him reach into his inside pocket. I knew even before he flashed it at me that he was pulling out his badge. "I'm Special Agent Finnegan, the Federal Bureau of Investigation."

"I remember you. You were at Father Maguire's trial."

"Yes."

"You testified."

"That's right."

"You were the agent in charge."

"I'm not wild about our work right now, Mister Durkin. I gather you're not either."

"That's right."

"Can we talk for a minute?"

"I'm just waiting for my wife."

"She's a pretty lady."

"Thank you."

"Look, Father Maguire is not doing himself any good this way. They're going to throw the book at him, you know."

"Someone has to catch him first, don't they?"

"Oh, we'll catch him."

"People are beginning to wonder, Mister Finnegan. How do you fellows do against Russians or the Mafia if this is how you do against a priest?"

"A priest has certain advantages. Especially if he's right."

"You think he's right?"

"About the war? Yes."

"I find that surprising, frankly."

"We're not numbskulls, you know. Who supports the war at this point? The question is how to end it. I think Father Maguire is keeping it going. Why should the NLF negotiate seriously if they think the U.S. is about to fold?"

"Wait a minute, I thought you said he's right?"

"His ends are right. Not his means."

"A nice Jesuit's distinction. Where'd you go, Fordham?"

"Georgetown."

"You should have heard his sermon. Even the rich old ladies were very moved."

"Where is he now, Mister Durkin?"

"You come right to the point, don't you?"

"You're his oldest friend. Obviously you knew ahead of time he would be here. Or do you always come here on Sundays?"

"Sometimes. It brings back memories of the Tridentine Mass, you know? They have everything but sixteenth-century underwear."

"I thought you might see things a little more reasonably than he does. I thought you might help us for his sake."

"Father Maguire's welfare is your main concern, I guess, huh?"

"Obviously not. But I do think the man is hurting himself."

"I'm not interested in discussing this with you further, Mister Finnegan. I simply can't help you." I saw Carolyn coming out of the Cathedral House toward us.

"Do you know where he is?"

"No. Obviously he'd be a fool to let me know. Your boys have me in their sights all the time."

"Except when you shake them in the subway. On that count alone I could take you downtown, you know."

"Feel free."

The agent stared at me. I read his disdain all too easily. What contempt he had for the likes of me! He made me feel guilty, but how could I have explained to him that my true crime till then had been good citizenship?

"I'm going to come back to see you, Mister Durkin. No one will know but you and me." He glanced toward Carolyn and stepped back, blocking her view of himself with a shrub. "And until I do I want to leave you with something to think about." He paused. Was he waiting for me to ask what? I said nothing. He looked toward Carolyn again and withdrew farther. "Your lovely wife," he said, "and your oldest friend, the famous Father Maguire — they've been fucking their heads off together for years."

"Who was that?" she asked.

I was so relieved to turn toward her, to bathe my eyes in the sight of her. The agent's words had jolted me, but not in the crude way he wanted. I saw his ruse for what it was. He was a desperate man, and with reason. Michael had made him the Bureau buffoon. Obviously Finnegan would try anything now.

But without intending to he'd just done me an enormous favor. He'd put my oldest, worst, fear into words and I was grateful to him because I saw at once, at last, it was impossible. Impossible.

"A derelict," I said, hugging her. "A bum who wanted a handout. Churchyards are full of them."

THIRTY

ARCHBISHOP O'Shea put his sherry glass down with a definitive flourish. In his view our conversation had ended and it remained only for him to shepherd me as gracefully as he could, given the spilled acid between us, toward the door.

But I refused to move. I was staring into the amber liquid of my own glass, and I saw in its swirl the miniature of my face. A pathetic figure, mine. Why did I feel more strongly than ever the need to win him over? Why did I want so desperately to prolong our talk? He was right; it was pointless. His position, the position of the Church, was clear and fixed. And mine? I was a child having crawled back to be domineered again. I wanted the approval of my rigid father, the worship of my unforgiving mother. And it was not for Michael I craved these goodies, or for Carolyn, but for myself.

"Archbishop," I said carefully, "if Michael Maguire cannot be buried in the Church, is there leeway for some other solution? Another gesture?"

"Like what?"

"I thought perhaps you'd want to come to the service. Perhaps you'd offer a prayer."

He shook his head.

Suddenly a vision of what Michael's funeral would look like filled my head: that vast, dark cathedral and, lost in its shadows, the scrawny company of mourners. Who would be there? A few dozen neighbors, the parents of his children's friends, a handful of co-workers. But more evident than who was there would be who was not. Even a hundred in attendance would seem like no one, and the empty chairs of the mammoth church would stand like rebuking ghosts.

As altar boys Michael and I had served at countless funerals at Good Shepherd. We vied for funerals for unworthy reasons — to miss morning classes, to earn the dollar tip, to ride in the priest's limo out to the cemetery in the Bronx — but also because in that parish nothing edified, nothing affirmed, nothing made us cherish who we were more than that large demonstration of loyalty and loss. Perhaps because the Irish are emotionally inhibited, particularly when it comes to the expression of simple affection, they respond to funerals compulsively, as a last, though often first, opportunity to stand with a friend *as* a friend. Funerals in Good Shepherd were jammed, and the numbers — not the liturgy, not the eulogy, not the holy water or the benediction, just the numbers — were what we cared about. And we, imagining our own funerals, knew that one day the aisles would be crowded with our cronies too. *They* would be weeping by the hundreds. *They* would be clutching rosaries. *They* would be passing hats for our wives and children. Their multitude would represent the finest achievement of our lives, that we had accumulated such abundant love. This dream was one of many we had before we realized to our horror and then relief — or was it the other way around? — that Good Shepherd Parish had everything a man could want: comely wives, cozy taverns, rent control, ball fields and cheap transport to the job; everything but oxygen. When we left Inwood our parents were crushed and their friends regarded us as traitors and the guys in the bars swore that we'd be sorry. And now, finally, I was.

I put my glass by his and stood. He stood. When our eyes met I realized I did not remotely understand him. Despite myself I pressed, "There is one other question, Archbishop."

He blinked at me.

"I'm thinking of Korea. You were on a hill waiting for the enemy to come and kill you. Michael stopped them. He saved your life at a huge cost to himself. Did you ever pay him back for that?"

"No. Once I thought he was asking me to, but he never really did."

I shook my head. "Archbishop, he did just now."

For a moment it seemed he was going to respond, but he did not. I imagined him standing in the hatchway of that helicopter firing an officer's sidearm down at the Chinese soldiers, a killer priest. It was impossible to tell now what if anything he felt, and it seemed ludicrous to me that earlier I had found something in this man to pity. But now the secret in this iciness, in this absolute rejection, revealed itself, and at last I understood. "How he must have hurt you."

A moment later I was on the steaming street.

Alone with my panic.

Panic? you ask. Why panic?

Because I had to return then to Saint John the Divine Cathedral, which was empty of people but full of ghosts. Ancient ghosts: Martin Luther, Henry VIII, Edmund Campion, John Fisher and Thomas More. There were the ghosts of Morgans, Potters and Huntingtons who wanted worthy monuments to their own munificence, and there were the ghosts of the Irish coolies on whose backs their colossi rose. There were ghosts with names I knew: Lennie Pace, Mary Ellen Divine, Sister Anne Edward, Dorothy Day, Cardinal Spellman, Tom Dooley, Thomas Merton, two Kennedys and two Ngos. There were the ghosts of Korean refugees and Chinese soldiers, of Inge Holz, Suu Van Pham, of My Lai and of a legion of slaughtered Vietnamese. There were the ghosts of the American dead. There was the ghost of Nicholas Wiley. And in a room behind the great facade, like a room behind the fireplace, a priest-hole, there hovered above his own coffin the ghost of Michael Maguire. Each awaited the tri-une word that I knew had been refused; no "*Requiescat in pace*" here. The Church had spoken. The anathema had been pronounced. The benediction was withheld not from one man or several, but from an age, a generation, a people, an entire world.

It fell to me to be for the dead and for the living a sign of peace, of mercy, of forgiveness, and I knew I could not do it.

By now, of course, you know why. The FBI man came back as he promised he would, and like some Arthurian alchemist, with a mere flick of his finger, he changed the gold of my life to lead.

He turned on the tape-recorder, then left me alone in the interrogation room. Until then I had thought I was under arrest. I had thought they'd brought me to their headquarters to threaten me or bribe me, neither of which would have worked. They could have tortured me and I would not have helped them. I would have died first and my last thought would have been of Michael, my last feelings love for him and joy that I too, after all, had become a hero, a martyr for the faith. But, alas, they didn't kill me.

They only made me listen.

I watched the reels spinning and waited for the sound to crackle on.

A man's voice broke the silence abruptly. "Maguire, tape forty-seven, Lake George, August nineteenth, nineteen sixty-nine. Two seventeen P.M."

The silence then was of a different kind. It was the silence of our summer, of our cabin, of our nights and days, the three of us together. I remembered climbing Black Mountain with him. I remembered her clinging to me and saying, "I've never loved you more."

A door banged open and a woman spoke. Why did it shock me that it was Carolyn? The door slammed closed and I heard then the familiar creak of floorboards and the swarming rustle of bedclothes being torn back.

Michael's first words were, "Oh Christ!"

I listened as to the sounds of a city being razed, the destruction of all future, all faith, all things, in his phrase, Luke's phrase, that make for peace.

When Carolyn cried out as she never cried out when I was in her, it was the Master's "Epheta!" His mud and spittle were on my eyes. I opened them and I saw their story whole.

Though it spanned twenty-two years, including one of the most tumultuous decades of the century, and though it swept across the full range of human experience, from war to childbirth to death, from virginity to adultery, from celibacy to parenthood, from sanctity to excommunication, their love remained until the end what it was in the beginning: the innocent love between a priest and a nun. Once the epitome of what is tragic in life, it is the most ludicrous of romances now and commentators always wink when they speak of it. Priests and nuns when they fall in love recapitulate the absurd Victorian melodrama of fully grown men and women fumbling through an excess of clothing toward their first nakedness. We are supposed to laugh at them as their habits fall. How superior they make us feel, those of us who succeeded at an early age in purging sex of awe and love of all transcendence. And how smugly do we imagine the desolation of their guilt, those who surrender principle and violate vows and cuckold God Himself. Priests and nuns think love means all things — salvation and damnation both — while for us it is the way, as our music puts it, to make it through the night.

Silence. *This* priest and *this* nun — my dearest, dearest friends. The silence in which they came together deafens me even now. Can the cuckold-husband narrate such a scene? And how could he possibly know of it? Oh, it is so simple; this is the hard-won prize of my work, the very center of the story I have struggled to bring you. I have played it over and over in my imagination, never fussing over diction, over voice, over the length of sentences. It is the curse of sensitivity that we behold more than we want, the blessing that we see the truth. Truth! What is truth? Mere rhetoric? But rhetoric, in Yeats's definition, is will doing the work of the imagination. Alas, I am a man of no will when it comes to this. I am at the mercy of what I have continually imagined. Nay, conjured. Nay, witnessed. Silence. This is what happened. Silence. This.

See him walking across the Brooklyn Bridge on its fabled scaffold high above the black river, a solitary figure in the middle of the night. In daylight and with good binoculars Carolyn could have watched him coming from the balcony not a dozen paces from the bed where she was asleep alone. I was in Cambridge, Massachusetts, delivering a paper on Hopkins at an important Harvard symposium. I'd been honored to be asked and had thought of it as my lucky day. Oh cruel irony. Oh the inscape, the instress, the asshole of Inwood.

It was the night of the day in May 1966 that Nicholas Wiley died.

Michael had left Bellevue, having run the gauntlet of reporters — "You don't condemn suicide?" — from whom he learned of the Church's condemnation of Nicholas. He had found it impossible to return to his parish and had instead walked aimlessly through Manhattan. He went to Chrystie Street, thinking to talk to Dorothy Day — had she renounced Wiley too? — but at the last moment he knew it was impossible to talk to her. From

Chrystie Street to the Brooklyn Bridge is no distance, and instinctively he made for it. He could have as easily been coming to me as to her, and there is the irony, the particular pain. What chaos followed from the accident that at the moment of his most brutal desolation, I was away and Carolyn was not.

He rang the bell.

Carolyn stirred, but did not wake up.

He rang again, although he almost decided not to.

Carolyn was frightened by the bell when it finally woke her, and she went immediately into Molly's room. Molly was two and a half years old. She was fast asleep.

When Carolyn saw through the glass that it was Michael, she was afraid at first that he had come with news of me, that I'd been killed in a car wreck. How much simpler for everyone if that had been the case.

"Michael, what's wrong?"

It startled him to see her in her robe and nightgown, her long hair falling over her shoulders, and he realized only then what rudeness it was to present himself at that hour. He didn't answer at first. They stood looking at each other on opposite sides of the threshold.

He shook himself. "I'm sorry, Carolyn. Something awful happened. A young friend of mine burned himself today."

"Oh Michael, I heard about it. He was a friend of yours? Oh God!" She took his hand and pulled him into the house, and in that movement he went into her arms. She held him for some moments, but like a mother would have.

"Come have a drink," she said.

He looked at his watch. "God, Carolyn, I had no idea it was so late. I'm sorry."

"Don't be silly. I'm glad you came."

"I know," he said, following her into the kitchen, "but Durk will kill me."

"He isn't here," she said over her shoulder. "He's in Boston until Friday."

If you imagine Michael shuddering with anticipation at that revelation, you have misunderstood him. He was capable of all the inner urges, of course, but his virility was a function of restraint. He was thirty-four years old and had been faithful to his vow of celibacy, remained in fact a virgin. He had been ambushed on occasion by desire, and masturbation was not unknown to him, but he had not allowed himself in years consciously to fix upon Carolyn's image as the object of his lust, as he would have surely were she not still the owner of his heart.

In the kitchen he sat at the Formica counter while Carolyn brought glasses and the gin. They sipped quietly. Michael told her Nicholas's story. She listened carefully for what it revealed about his own.

Michael was adrift in the aftermath of his futile time in Vietnam. His final surrender to Spellman's tyranny, his upstate banishment to Saint Joseph's and his too-easy embrace of the tranquillity of exile left him profoundly vulnerable to feelings of guilt. The guilt was appropriate because he violated his conscience brutally when he chose to obey the bark of the Church rather than the cry of the Vietnamese. And then he had tried to draw Nicholas Wiley into exile with him, but the young pacifist's conscience was more ruthless. The mistake had been to dam its torrent with the trivialities of life in the country parish. When the dam burst, poor Nicholas was at the mercy of that flood, the rage of it.

"I know it seems silly, Caro, given his age and mine, but I felt like a father to Nicholas. I never felt like a father before."

She touched his arm. "You're a good father, Michael. Only good fathers make good priests."

Michael shook his head slowly. "If I'd been more attentive to him, to what he was feeling . . ."

"Michael, how could you know? He didn't know himself."

"But I did know, Caro." He leaned against her. She caressed him. And they were still.

After a time he said, "It's as if I was forbidden to."

"What?"

He straightened, moved away slightly. She withdrew her hand and each fussed with the gin. "To pay attention to feelings."

"Well, in a way you are forbidden to do that, aren't you?"

He smiled. She was bitter about her convent experience, and the religious life was a topic they avoided. "I guess I am," he said. "If so . . ." He took a hefty drink. "I'm in the state of disobedience now."

"Because you're feeling . . . ?"

"Like getting drunk."

"Now there's a feeling priests are allowed to have."

He laughed and poured more gin into his glass. "Not 'allowed,' encouraged!" He drank again.

Carolyn watched him. "Which is sad," she said quietly.

"It's the only way, love. As Saint Paul said, it's either that or burn."

"I thought he said, 'Marry or burn.' "

That stopped him. He looked at her abruptly. "That's the issue, isn't it?"

"Is it?"

"I mean that's the point of renouncing feeling. It's the only way to live like this."

"That's the saddest thing I ever heard, Michael."

"But you know it's true."

She wouldn't look at him.

"Don't you?" he pressed.

"Then why live like that?"

"You know why."

"No, I don't, Michael. I honestly don't."

"Well, you did."

Now she faced him squarely, and when their eyes met, he had an impulse to shield his from hers. "Yes, I did," she said. "I knew about the 'Come follow me!' and the 'Not my will but Thine!' and the 'Be ye perfect!' and the '*Fiat Voluntas Tua*.' But I also know about the man who put the Pharisees in their place. And I know who the Pharisees are today. And I know how they maintain their control over good people like you. They make you think that the most precious experience possible to a human being is an evil one. Nicholas Wiley has offered you a chance, Michael, because he's made you *feel* something. Well, don't drown that feeling! And don't talk it away with your Bible quotes!"

"But Carolyn, Nicholas Wiley burned himself to death because of his feelings."

"Is that what you're afraid of, immolating yourself?"

"No." He looked away from her. "But I am afraid of lunacy."

Carolyn lifted her gaze to the window. The lights of Manhattan shone in the black, but it was to a reflection in the glass her eyes were drawn. On Michael's face the lines were taut, fierce, unbecoming. She had never seen him in the grip of cowardice before. "Your refusal is the lunacy," she said harshly.

It was the truth between them, the very heart of it. He knew, as I would have, that she meant, beneath the generalities about "feelings," his refusal of her.

He said quietly, "I wish I could change it."

"You can," she said simply.

Michael waited for her to look at him. "I'm afraid," he said.

"I know."

Neither breathed. Already they had crossed the threshold; he closed a door behind them by saying, "Of you."

Silence, what silence then between them. Michael stared at the counter, Carolyn bowed her head. They could still have drawn back. Each small step required another, bolder one. The wind from the river rattled lightly at the window. The wall clock hummed.

Michael raised his eyes to look at her. The nightgown was closed at her throat. Its white cotton shimmered against the navy blue of her robe, a kimono, full sleeved without lapels. She had belted it tightly. Her waist and bosom were defined, not erotically but with unabashed womanliness. He pictured her as she had been when he first knew her, in the black habit of a Sister of Charity, and then he pictured her stepping from the terrace in Dobbs Ferry, in the near nakedness of an ordinary bathing suit, her long legs, her cropped blond hair, her thighs. Was it possible that first vision of her beauty had occurred only six years before? Those six years, with a marriage, a child, a house, a resolute pursuit of painting, had been for her a long time, but for him they had been an eternity, an infinite stretch in which, while worlds ended outside, nothing happened inside. It had been that long since anyone touched him, since she had.

He reached his hand toward hers where it rested by her glass. Shyly he covered it.

When she looked up at him, tears spilled from her eyes. Her crusty assertiveness had evaporated. When she spoke he could barely hear her. "I have been wanting you to do that."

Michael knew that if he continued touching her all was lost, yet he could not remove his hand. This was what he'd feared — being outdistanced by his racing heart. But Carolyn was ahead of him, she was waiting for him. She at least had been consistent from the start.

He leaned toward her and she brought her face to his. He kissed a tear. He raised his other hand to touch her hair. Suddenly that hand closed on the back of her neck and pressed her face against his. Their kiss was like a blow, stunning them both. Carolyn's lip bled at once, and the taste of her blood made Michael wild. Lunacy, he thought, yes, lunacy! This could make a man set fire to himself. But this had nothing to do with Wiley.

Against the image of a man aflame he buried his face between her shoulder and her neck. "Oh Caro!" Immolation of another kind.

The chair fell out from under him. She took his weight and her hands pulled at him passionately. She brought his face up to kiss him again, pushing her tongue into his mouth, but she began to fall too. They went together to the floor, roughly. Their arms and hands never faltered, hers pulling him on top of her, his pressing through her robe and the thin cloth of her nightgown.

"Stop!" she said, "Stop!" and rolled her face away.

He raised himself on one knee, off her. Oh Christ, what are we doing? This is impossible!

But that was not her meaning.

She stood and took his hand and led him to her bedroom. To our bedroom.

He followed mutely.

She closed the door behind them and by our bed she turned toward him. She opened her robe and let it fall. "We should be undressed," she said. "We should be naked for each other."

Michael unbuttoned his black shirt. No woman would have done that for him. At his bare chest, hanging from a string around his neck, was a small plain cross of wood, Wiley's cross.

He went to her, understanding that this must happen slowly, deliberately. He would have preferred it that way himself, but preference had nothing to do with it. The storm of his arousal broke. He kissed her, pressed her body against his, and the sensation of her breasts rising beneath the thin cotton against his skin unleashed him. He tore at her nightgown, pulling it down feverishly, even while pushing her away to look, to see those breasts, her waist, the hair of her crotch, to see that she was after all the fulfillment of his lust. She fell back onto the bed, and her legs opened.

He threw off his clothing and was on her, but he was too frantic, too new, too at the mercy of his passion, and he could not find her. All at once he was terrified that he would ejaculate outside her. "Help me!" he said. "Help!"

And didn't that plea of his sum up everything? Why he was afraid; why the suicide of his protégé drove him into her arms, her legs; why this moment had been so long in coming, so terrifying. He was the man who helped others. He had never needed help himself. There was his true virginity.

She knew just what to do and did, guiding his penis successfully, seizing it in the mouth of her womb so that when, seconds later, all that he withheld began to pump violently like Gatling rounds, a new terror took hold of him — many first-time lovers have it — that he would kill her.

When she screamed, how could he have known it was not with pain? In his dream of copulation, brutality was muted but there. But now when she thrashed below him, all was violence. Her arms held him as the walls of her cunt held his prick. Her constrictions came in spasms; she gave what she got. She strangled him.

Then he cried out like a gored beast. They were both killers. Was that the recognition that freed him?

He stopped caring finally what would happen if he fucked her, and simply did.

Remorse, when it came, was gentle. They spoke of me, of course, and would surely have felt horror at their betrayal, but their postcoital happiness reduced it to something like regret. It was as if I was a passenger in a car one of them was driving — it didn't matter which — and then the other's car came out of nowhere. Perhaps it was the highway's fault or the weather's. In the collision I was the only victim. What else could they do but console each other for what they'd done? At least I would never know.

Michael dressed before dawn and at the door he said to her, his finger under her chin, "I love you." Then he left. He went to his rectory in Alna, showered, put on fresh clericals and said the early Mass for the repose of the soul of Nicholas Wiley. Later that morning, in his fateful, final meeting with Francis Cardinal Spellman — "I refuse to yield to you in anything related to this evil war!" — he remembered what, on the scale of moral conduct, was the true blasphemy, not disobedience or adultery, but genocide.

Still he felt an overpowering remorse at having failed Nicholas and at having broken his priestly vows and at having, yes, betrayed me. But the bite of those sorrows was nothing compared to the passion set loose in him at last. There was a woman now, and there was a war, and in relation to each he found the precious treasure that he'd counted lost forever, not the Kingdom of God, but his own manhood. His memory and his manhood had been returned to him by Wiley's soul and Carolyn's body.

I have had twelve years to understand, and I think I do, although I have perhaps accepted less than I have understood.

It was not their purpose to hurt me. On the contrary, they always sought to lull me in the cat's cradle of their lies. And there were times when they even offered me a crack at the truth, but I rigorously avoided that. When Michael spoke to me on Black Mountain of his dread, his discouragement and sense of doom, I chose to hear him always as the hero of resistance, as if the dread was of prison and not of hell, as if what doomed him was his faithfulness and not his betrayal. I was a cooperator in their adultery, and even a beneficiary of it. I'm certain it was true, as Carolyn said, that she loved me more than ever, even while she deceived me. It was Michael who opened her fully, not me. When at last she had him, her joy overflowed. She could not have feigned her happiness, and I, with Molly, saw more of it than anyone.

Surely at some level I knew what had happened. They were secret lovers for three years. I have described already times when the truth — "I *do* love you!" — all but raped me. But I never allowed it entrance to the center of my heart. It was writing in the sand in the wind, and before the last letter was formed the first was always gone. I refused to hold the literal image in my mind; Michael and Carolyn naked with each other? Fucking? Not once in a fit of passion, but every chance they got? Every chance I gave them? Settling into a long, easy liaison that made them not less loving, as the "old morality" swore it would, but more? Carolyn became a great wife and mother, and Michael became a hero-priest because of — who could have explained this? — in a word, sin.

When at last I was made to face what was obvious, I simply could not do so as myself. I became someone else. I became what the FBI man thought I was, and what he wanted.

I watched the tape reels spinning, silent now except for the *flick flick flick* of the tailing brown ribbon. The room, stark white, unornamented, the light glaring fiercely above me, was like the set of a play. One of those modern things, Pinter or Beckett, in which the antagonist representing absolute evil or absolute good —

it is never clear and doesn't matter — inflicts his torment from outside the room. He never enters.

But if I was a Pinter character, I would have dismissed what I had just heard with an ironic remark — "Golly, but the good Father paid close attention in Confession all these years!" — and I'd have resumed my life with Carolyn, my friendship with Michael, as if nothing happened. But I'd have become the absolute antagonist outside *their* stark white room.

But I am out of Ibsen, not Pinter. I had no choice but to shake heaven, to bring it down, even if on myself. This was the betrayal I'd foreseen, expected, made possible. Yet it was the one event — even including, say, the arrival on our cities of Russian missiles — for which I was utterly unprepared. There had been no air-raid drills for this.

My reaction watching those reels was no more a matter of choice than it was for the end of the audio tape to go *flick flick flick*. I was possessed by the simplest reflex, the oldest one, an absolute impulse. It taught me the only wisdom I would need in Israel when I got there, the only relevant truth of the Nuclear Age: that when the enemy strikes and we are defeated totally — our cities razed, our future ash — it will not matter that no purpose is served by our destroying in return and with our last effort a Beirut or a Moscow or a My Lai for that matter. Retaliation is the rule of life. That's all.

The door of the interrogation room opened — theater of the absurd now utterly — and the mode of mine walked in.

THIRTY-ONE

MONHEGAN Island is a whale-shaped rock twelve miles off the coast of Maine, only a few miles around and reaching perhaps a hundred and fifty feet above the sea. For three hundred years it has maintained a cruel, stolid indifference to the pounding waves of the Atlantic, to the shrouding weather, to the fierce fishing people who have made it home, to the artists and rare summer tourists who defy the twin hostilities of nature and native, and to the hardy traffic of lobster boats, trawlers and cargo ships for which it remains a fearsome navigational hazard. Nearly a hundred vessels have piled up on its rocks. The story of Monhegan's wild shore is the story of shipwreck.

No savvy fugitive would have gone there, and I could not imagine why Michael would have chosen it. Carolyn and I were clinging to the same stanchion, the upright pipe that supported the flimsy roof of the lobster boat we'd hired to take us out from Boothbay Harbor. It was early in April, much too soon for tourists, and the lobsterman had eyed us warily when we'd approached him. But for fifty dollars he swallowed his qualm. He could be out and back in four hours. It was a Sunday and he couldn't haul traps anyway. What was it to him that the island's one small hotel didn't open up until June? What was it to him that the Monhegan people would shun us? We didn't explain that we had reason to think that a friend of ours was out there already, expecting us.

I pressed the ends of my collar together at my throat. The spray had saturated my citified raincoat, and I dearly wished for a hat. I was freezing, though the day had begun as balmy and bright. I tried to focus on the island, which seemed to undulate mystically ahead of us, though we were the ones who rose and fell. Our boat was at the mercy of swells and I considered it a miracle that I had not gotten sick yet. For the first hour it had frightened me that I could not see the island through the fog, and all that time the lobsterman's boat had seemed less seaworthy the farther from land we got. How I wished for radar. I did not trust his compass or his skill until suddenly the island appeared ahead of us, like an apparition. I looked at the man to offer the homage of a nod, but he ignored me. Carolyn raised her eyebrows with relief. We were strictly Circle Line sailors. This was fucking awful.

I said, "Why the hell would he come out here?"

"This is why." Carolyn grimaced as the boat dropped.

"But if they came after him, there's no escape. It's a corner. He's put himself in a corner."

"You just wish he'd stayed in Manhattan, the island with bridges."

"Damn right I do. Maybe this is the wrong Monhegan Island. Maybe it's the name of a nice resort in North Carolina."

Carolyn shook her head. The message that fell through our mail slot, in Michael's writing, had said only, "Monhegan Island, Palm Sunday morning."

"Besides," she said, sliding her arm through mine, "they'd never think to look for him out here."

"They have their ways." I pressed her arm between my elbow and my ribs. The wind feathered the wisps of her hair, tugging them one after the other out of her scarf. Beads of water clung to her lashes.

One time we took the boat from Galway to the Aran Islands. The sea became rough and then rain began to fall. Neither Caro nor I became sick, but many of our fellow passengers did, and to escape the cramped, putrid space below we went up on deck and stood huddled by a lifeboat. The rain lashed us and the boat bucked like a bronco, but we loved it. When the tourists came crashing up from below to be sick, they rushed one after the other for the nearest rail, but that had them puking into the wind with predictable results. Perhaps it was cruel of us, but we laughed and laughed. We were on the largest of the Aran Islands for three days. It never stopped raining, but that did not faze us because we spent the entire time in bed. Our Irish hosts — we stayed in a small, child-ridden B&B — eyed us suspiciously during our rare forays downstairs for meals. That we scandalized them heightened our pleasure. What a surprise to both of us that a gloomy, puritanical outpost of the Kingdom of Repression should have been the scene of our greatest coital excess. Talk about broncos! Carolyn and I rode each other like champions. Because that dreary little world held nothing for us we could focus for a change entirely on each other. In that foreign place we could become the other people we wanted to be. We came together like sex-starved strangers. The weather, having transformed our tourist weekend into a tryst, was a problem in only one regard. Owing to the pervasive dampness, our sperm-soaked sheets never dried out and we were too embarrassed to ask the Missus for fresh ones.

Carolyn leaned toward the lobsterman. "How do local people get out here, if there's no ferry?"

He shrugged. His gaze was fixed on the island. His hands played the wheel, the spokes of which were welded bolts. "Not much call. Local people stay put. Mail boat on Tuesdays. That's it."

"Do they get television out here?"

"Nope. No phones either. Just two-way radio."

Carolyn looked at me and said quietly, "So he can walk around without worrying about being recognized. That might be worth being in a corner."

I asked the lobsterman, "What about newspapers? What about *Time* magazine?"

He shrugged.

"You ask him," I whispered to Carolyn. "He won't answer me."

The boat wallowed as we hit what seemed to be a wake, a wave distinctly larger than what we'd been through. Then the boat's propeller bit again and we steadied. Carolyn hugged me. "I hate this," she said. "I hate it. I wouldn't do it for anyone else."

"Me neither," I said.

Irony does not feature in my recollection of that morning. Obviously my true feelings toward Michael and toward what I had done, was doing, were coated over by numbing layers. My mind was entirely taken up with the details of our journey, although I do recall thinking that my nausea, once I began to feel it, was fitting. Otherwise it seems to me I was moving through events the way a sleepwalker does, with no sharp sensations of anticipation, fear, bitterness, or guilt.

As we approached the small harbor nestled in the gut between Monhegan and its tiny satellite, Manana, the noise of our boat's engine grew louder, not that our reticent skipper gunned it, but that the sound bounced back at us from the island's looming mass. The irregular, insistent clanging of a floating gong filled the air with tension, then faded as we left it behind. Even before I could distinguish between the gray rock of the shore and the sharp line of scraggly green pine above it, the boat slowed. Inside Manana the water was smooth. When I leaned over the boat's edge I could see the reflection of my own face, which I barely recognized.

I saw no houses until we swung around the tip of a promontory. On the hill above were separate small clusters of rugged-looking cottages. A large white clapboard building with a covered porch and shuttered windows must have been the summer hotel. Poking up from the trees at a higher elevation were a church steeple and the round white tower of the famous lighthouse.

We were cutting through a fleet of moored lobster boats essentially like the one in which we were riding. On their transoms were names like "Lu-Ann," "Beth-Marie" and "Sally-Jo." I nudged Carolyn. "Do you think the women out here have hyphenated names, or do the fishermen credit their wives and girlfriends together?"

Carolyn stared at me as if she hadn't understood. I was thinking that if she had a boat, it would be the "Michael-Frank."

Tied to the pilings at the single thrusting pier was a large oceangoing trawler, the only boat of its size in the harbor. It dwarfed us as we pulled in beside it.

"Goddamn!" the lobsterman said when he saw it. "What's she doing in here?"

There was an emotion in his voice — anger? alarm? — that disturbed me. "What do you mean?"

"These trawlers wreck our traps," he said. "They got no business in this close."

Close? It seemed to me we were halfway to Europe.

"She just better get out of this harbor before the tide goes. Ever seen a whale on the rocks? That's what she'll be."

With effortless skill he slipped in behind the trawler. I reached out to fend us off when we bumped the pier, but the boat slid up to it gently and stopped, just kissing the pilings.

I looked up at the trawler's looming black stern. Rust-stained white letters two feet high arched across it: "Sea Witch. Halifax."

A young man dressed for weather in a yellow slicker and watch cap greeted us from the pier. We clambered out of the boat, which slipped away then as smoothly as it had come in. I turned to thank the lobsterman, but he was intent on the helm and headed out with no farewell. As I watched him leave it was with a pang. Why didn't I just go with him?

The young man led us off the pier and up a dirt road that was lined with open oil drums. An unbearable stench came from them. They were full of rotten fish, lobster bait, and it was then that my nausea got the best of me. I turned away and vomited violently on the side of the road. Carolyn tried to help but I shrugged her off. For perhaps two full minutes, though it seemed like hours, I retched. When the heaves subsided and I recovered some sense of myself, of my situation, I looked around expecting to see unfriendly men laughing at me the way I had laughed on the boat to Aran. But there were only Carolyn and our guide.

I followed them miserably.

I was quite aware that Carolyn could hardly contain her excitement, and only then did the bile coating my mouth seem truly bitter.

The young man led us up the steep hill behind the village, along a rutted dirt path. If there were cars or trucks on Monhegan I didn't see them, and I can't call the trail we followed a road. At the top of the hill was the lighthouse we'd seen from the water, a great phallus fifty feet high. At its base stood a neglected shed. No sooner had we come upon it than our guide turned and left us.

Michael came promptly out of the shed, walking vigorously. He too was dressed like a seaman, and his beard enhanced the ruddy image, but I knew him at once. Despite everything — what I'd learned and what I'd done — my first surge of feeling was of the old affection, the need.

When my father lay dying in a dreary Queens hospital in 1964, Michael never left us. My father had a terrible time. He knew he was dying, and when he was awake he was crazy with fear. His piety had failed him when my mother died several years before, and if it had been up to me to console him, he would have died in the throes of despair. But Michael knew how to help him, with a combination of silence and muted reassurance. Michael talked simply and directly of the Christian faith. He told my father, and me who listened, about the death of Lazarus, about the anguish of Jesus. Another priest had glibly begun describing the Streets of Heaven to my father, who had cursed him in a seizure of panic and railed, "Don't talk to me about heaven! Talk about my dying!" And that's what Michael did. Only when the full terror of that loss — Lazarus', ours — had been plumbed did he broach the subject of resurrection, but by then my father was ready to hear of it.

Eliciting faith from the wary is like getting a wounded bird to walk into your hand, but Michael, a natural priest if I ever knew one, could do it effortlessly. When my father died Michael was holding his hand and they were praying together the Hail Mary. It was the first prayer my father had uttered since my mother's death. He released his grip on life because Michael made him ready to. He believed in God, like me, because Michael did. If he had not been my friend, if he had only been the priest who sent my father on his way, I'd have been in his debt for the rest of my life. But with Michael, as with a brother, it was never a question of owing. At my father's graveside he said to me, "Now we really have to stick together."

I watched Carolyn go into his arms.

They kissed the way I'd seen them kiss dozens of times before, not with great passion certainly — no one's mouth opened — but with forthright affection. Their bodies were pressed together, but not sensually. Still I saw their kiss and embrace differently, and though even then I could not have identified its signals explicitly I recognized the unmistakable reality of their intimacy.

I lowered my eyes. Was that an act of deference? Of bashfulness? Reluctance to intrude upon lovers? Wasn't it my acknowledgment of their right to be together? From the very beginning I'd been the outsider in the ill-fated trio. I was the interloper, the one who'd come between. Perhaps that knowledge was what kept my jealousy at bay. If I trembled it was with the weak-kneed vertigo of one who'd just puked his guts out. I was sicker than I'd felt in years. But emotionally I was in space, floating weightlessly, not like an astronaut, but like an astronaut's tube of toothpaste.

When Michael turned to me I found it possible to go to him and embrace him. I did not kiss his cheek.

Hey, I told myself, no big deal. These things happen. What the hell, he fell in love with the wrong woman, or I did. It wasn't the end of the world. Just a bit of nastiness between two mortals. He slugged me; now I was slugging him. It had been going on since Cain and Abel. No, since Eve left Adam for the snake. No big deal.

Then why were my legs trembling?

The lighthouse was in the middle of a clearing, but ringing it were wild, weather-beaten shrubs and vine-tangled trees. The undergrowth was too thick to see into. Where was the goddamn FBI? I wanted this shit over with.

Michael took my arm firmly between his two hands. "Durk, what's wrong?"

When I looked at him, the concern in his eyes, the friendship, was what set off the charge at last. This fucker! This son of a bitch! This self-proclaimed saint! How dare he manifest love to me! Or rather pity! Or was it mere guilt? Out with it, Fuck! Show me what you really feel, the smug superiority of the usurper! Oh, you tortured soul! How you condemned yourself for flourishing a bayonet at those Korean peasants, but what of the bayonet you plunged in me? My wife's betrayal is nothing to yours! My first friend, the one who taught me trust! But what is trust now? Now I feel it, that blade between my breast and its bone, cutting cleanly, opening a hole in which to bury all past and future, a hole . . .

I caught myself before I cried, "*Et tu!*" No melodrama, no display. I would show the fucker nothing. I covered one of his hands. "I've been sick," I said.

"I think he may be dehydrated," Carolyn explained.

"There's a tap in the cabin. Come in." Michael led me into the shack and Carolyn followed. I put my mouth at the faucet and drank, an act full of history, for as boys we were always finding faucets to drink from. He might have slapped me on the back, "It's my turn, Durk, come on!" But he let me drink my fill. I remembered the Inwood summer ritual of opening the fire hydrants and dancing in the spray. This man was in the middle of every happy memory I had. He'd taken those from me too.

The water tasted of rust, but it soothed me and my stomach felt better at once. When I straightened I was less lightheaded, and I looked around the small shadowy room. Rampant cobwebs held the corners. In the center were two chairs at a plain table, the only furniture, and I took one of them. Carolyn and Michael remained standing, but I didn't care.

"A lighthouse?" I asked, "Won't the coast guard find you?"

Michael shook his head. "They run these things from Portland or someplace now. They're automated. These cabins haven't been lived in for years."

"How long have you been here?" Now when I looked around I noticed that there was no cot, no toilet, no sign of food. A blanket was bunched in a corner.

"Last night. I came out on a boat like yours."

"But you'll be staying here?"

He shook his head. "This was just a rendezvous. I'm pulling out right away."

"What do you mean?" Suddenly I didn't know what to feel or think. Would it be good news or bad if he escaped the FBI? Were they even then watching from hiding places in the woods?

"I'm going away." He looked toward Carolyn. He was explaining himself to her, not me. "That's why I wanted to see you. I'm leaving the country."

"For Halifax?" she asked. She'd been paying attention too.

"Yes."

"Then it's over?" I asked. "Your resistance is over?" Was it possible that the great hero had reached his limit? That the antiwar priest, having spent his passion for peace, would become just another convict on the lam?

No.

He said, "I'm going to Vietnam. This Friday, Good Friday, Suu Van Pham and thirty-two other Vietnamese priests are going to occupy the cathedral in Saigon. They're going to offer it as a sanctuary to anyone who will refuse to fight anymore. I'm going to join them."

"Oh Michael!" Carolyn crossed to him. She did not bother to

disguise her impulse now as she embraced him, resting her head on his shoulder. Light glistened off tears in her eyes.

"You'll be a martyr yet," I said with a show of bitterness, despite myself. I was sick of his fucking virtue, his righteousness, his crusade against evil. I was sick of his hypocrisy. Was I the only one who had to suffer it?

But he took me literally. He shook his head. "As usual the risk is mostly someone else's. If I go, though, some American GIs might be moved to join us."

I was impressed despite myself. It was the perfect way to bring his resistance to a close. No mere surrender, but the most dramatic challenge yet to the war and, finally, a fully *Catholic* act of atonement for its Catholic origins. A Good Friday protest against the crucifixion of a people that began with the holy righteousness of Tom Dooley, Ngo Dinh Diem and Cardinal Spellman. Sanctuary in Saigon! Michael Maguire strikes again! His arrest in Saigon and the long transfer back to the States for prison would attract the attention of the world.

Suddenly I felt sorry for Carolyn. No matter what had gone on between them, no matter what understanding they had, he was still putting her second to his sacred vocation. So what that his sacred calling now was to political opposition instead of ecclesial subservience. But clearly Carolyn had accepted second place in his heart. Why shouldn't I have accepted second place in hers?

It was not a question I was interested in answering.

Michael said, "I just wanted to see you both before I went."

He meant me too. "Oh Jesus, Michael . . ." I began, but I had to stop because my voice cracked. Perhaps I was going to tell him what I'd done. Perhaps I was going to accuse him of what he'd done. It doesn't matter, because he interrupted me.

"And I wanted someone in the States to know where I was going in case . . ."

He stopped short of statement because the implication carried. If he was found by the government in Vietnam before the press knew he was there, anything could happen. He could simply disappear forever. He had come a distance from fun and games with the Fordham boys of the FBI.

"You haven't told anyone else?"

"You're the only ones I trust enough."

At last I faced what I was doing. Compared to what rose in my throat then, the vomit had been lemonade. The first full knowledge of the meaning of my act choked me, and I realized that whatever happened to him, I had already destroyed myself. I had committed moral suicide, or in the more familiar phrase, mortal sin. I had made myself over into what he and Carolyn were in relation to me — liars, traitors, egotists. But I lacked utterly the element that mitigated their offense: they at least were driven by love, not hate. And when the coming events laid the truth bare — I saw this clearly for the first time — they would have each other still. I would have not even my own soul. I was disemboweled. Like an Oriental warlord I had, with ceremony but no dispatch, sliced open my own soft middle. It only remained to press against the wound until the flow of blood rescued me from the awareness of what I'd done. Faced with doom like that, there was nothing to do but surrender to it.

But in truth I was not dying. Maybe moral suicide is never fatal. The chasm inside me, having swallowed everything I valued, began to close. Soon all would be smooth again. Air would purify my lungs. The bile would recede. And I could claim like everyone — like Michael, like Carolyn, like the FBI and like the men who ran the war — that life's cruelties force us all too regularly to do what we abhor.

He looked at his watch. "I'm sorry to say it's time to go."

"You have to leave before the tide goes out," I said.

"That's right."

"And from Halifax?"

"To Montreal, then Paris, then Saigon."

"But how? What about visas?"

He smiled. "Vatican diplomat, Durk. I'll be an Irish monsignor with Caritas International as of Wednesday." He laughed raucously. "They still leave the clergy alone, especially if they have a little red at their throats."

"Unless it's lipstick," I said. Carolyn started, but Michael laughed easily.

"Come on," he said. He put his arms out, one to drape each of us. Carolyn and I fell into step with him, and like three chums we strode down the rough trail toward the harbor.

Michael saw it before I did.

He stopped abruptly as we came around the last curve a few dozen yards above the pier.

Sitting in the middle of the harbor, dominating it, was a large white boat, seventy-five feet or longer. On its bow was the red diagonal slash that identified it as a coast guard cutter; on the forward deck was a large weapon, a machine gun or a cannon, at which a man sat. It was aimed at us. A dozen other men in orange life vests stood at various stations on the boat holding rifles.

On the pier were four men dressed like duck hunters. One of them was Finnegan. He was holding his badge aloft. "FBI, Father!" he called. "You're under arrest."

Michael did not move. He did not lessen the pressure of his arm on my shoulder. I stared straight ahead, not breathing, terrified that I would have to look at him.

Someone stirred behind us. Out of the corner of my eye, only a dozen yards away, I saw two more duck hunters by a shack. These had shotguns aimed at us.

"Keep walking!" Finnegan ordered. "We don't want anyone to get hurt."

Michael dropped his arms from me and Carolyn and without a word to either of us stepped away and began to walk to the pier.

Carolyn ran after him, crying his name. She clung to him. Michael tried to pull away from her but couldn't.

I went to them and tried to pull her back. She fought me, but Michael made her release him. When he looked at me I found it possible somehow to meet his gaze. I saw the recognition at the very moment it came to him. "Jesus Christ!" he said, "You!"

Carolyn looked at me. Her realization grew more slowly but with deadlier effect. I watched the flood of horror rising as she stared at me.

Michael turned immediately and walked to Finnegan, who began reading him his rights while the others handcuffed him. I heard one of the agents call him "Father." Later, leaving the cutter in Portland, he would be photographed smiling broadly, like a lottery winner, between two glum agents. He would be flashing the peace sign despite his handcuffs. The fucker was indomitable. The photograph would appear everywhere. I would be certain that he flashed that "V" just for me, to say, "Michael Maguire withstands everything, even you, Durkin!"

Carolyn pulled away from me slowly and backed down to the pier. It was as though she was staring at the Man With No Face. I see that expression of hers vividly, its shock and disbelief. I had done this to Michael, she saw at once, because of what she had done to me. This nightmare began with her, and she knew it. But it ended with me. Shock and disbelief bound us, and also, finally, guilt. Looking at her was like looking in a mirror. Hers was the face, the desolation of that moment and the despair, I had turned on myself ever since. It was what I had fled from and what, even in the desert, in the fourteenth century, I had never escaped.

The agents took her back to the mainland with them. They offered to take me too, but I refused. When the cutter pulled out of Monhegan Harbor, Michael was already below. I never saw him again.

Carolyn was at the railing, staring back at me. I had her full attention at last.

The funeral would begin in less than an hour. Carolyn was napping in the guest room of the dean's house when I returned from the Catholic Center, and so I went to see Molly. While her brother and sister explored the Biblical Garden, my daughter and I sat together in silence on a stone bench. She held my hand. I held hers. That seemed enough. When it came time for me to go to Carolyn, Molly hugged me fiercely, and I knew that I would never be without her again.

I waited for Carolyn in the austere parlor where visitors were received. The maid had the impression I was someone's brother.

The door opened and it was she.

I stood.

There was no sign of sleep in her eyes, but a subtle luster had been restored to them. Her hair was even more tightly pulled back than before. She had changed into a simple black dress, and it enshrined her grief. Her grief had become part of-her loveliness. It displayed the fullness of her love and therefore, curiously, made her seem as gifted as bereft.

Without a word she sat on the sofa and I joined her. She looked at me expectantly. I hated that I had failed her. I wanted to report that the cardinal himself was coming. "I'm sorry, Caro. They're adamant."

"Did you see Archbishop O'Shea?"

"Yes. If he wasn't so personally involved . . ."

She looked away. "Well then."

"It doesn't matter," I said without conviction. "The Church is different now. Charismatics, Encounters, Journal Groups, Christian Zen. Michael wouldn't recognize it anyway."

She nodded. "But I can't have him cremated, Frank."

"Caro, even the Catholic Church permits cremation now."

She shook her head. "I can't leave him here. I have to bury him in the ground someplace." She took my hand suddenly. "Will they let him be buried in sacred ground?"

"No, Caro, they won't."

"Oh." She exhaled, dispirited.

Because I thought it would help her to address the detail of where to bury him — isn't concreteness what rescues us? — I pressed it. "Do you go to the country?"

She nodded, then looked at me. "Lake George."

The words pierced me. How I'd cherished our time there. Michael had simply replaced me in my house, in my vacation place, in my daughter's life and in my wife's arms. Did they pretend I never existed? Did they come to think I was simply the part of Michael's personality he outgrew? Had my function only been to save his place until he was ready for it? But my function now, to find him a new place, did not allow such questions. "I recall an old cemetery in Bolton Landing. Do you?"

She nodded. "We went there for stone rubbings." The memory saddened her. The wave of emotion endeared her to me, completed the resurgence of my love.

"Would that be a place?"

For a moment she didn't react. Then she nodded vigorously, decisively. Her teeth cut into her lip.

"It's his remains that will make the ground sacred, Caro."

"I know." Her acknowledgment of my banality made it seem quite true.

Sadness, and with it silence, took over both of us.

I looked at the clock above the mantel. It was nearly six-thirty. I listened to it ticking. Two minutes went by, then five.

Caro whispered my name. I looked at her. She was staring at

her hands. "Frank, I wanted you to come because Michael and I both hoped that someday . . ." It frightened me when she stopped. I wanted desperately to talk about it before going into the cathedral, before seeing Michael's face.

"Don't stop, Caro."

"We hoped we could find a way to . . . We . . ." She faced me at last. "Oh, Frank, I'm sorry. I'm so sorry."

It was my impression that tears had come into her eyes, but I was unsure because tears had blinded mine. "You, Caro? You're sorry? But what I did was so much worse."

"Frank, I loved you." She fell against me.

"I know it, Caro. You loved both of us. I understand about that now."

"Will you forgive me?"

"I did that long ago. That's why I came when you asked me to. It's Michael I never finished with. Did he ever indicate how he felt? I mean about what I did?"

She dropped her eyes. "He never spoke of it, Frank."

"Did he speak of me?"

"No."

"Oh, God."

"But that's only because his feelings about you ran so deep. I know that he wanted to be reconciled with you more than anything. He wanted it as much as I did."

"And now he's gone before we . . . Time has healed a lot, but it never healed that."

"But it would have, Frank."

"Do you think?"

"Yes, I'm sure." She stroked me. The gentleness of her touch acknowledged *my* grief, my right to it.

"I feel completely lost, Caro. I've been suspended all this time, floating in space. Now I'll never . . . Michael was like the earth to me. I think I'll never get down to it again."

"But you have to be on earth, Frank, for me. I need you, and so does Molly."

How I wanted to reassure her, to say she had me. But I was telling her the exact truth. The loss of Michael had left me incomplete, like an amputee. Of what use could I be to her or Molly or anyone?

She sat upright, but left her hand on my arm. "It helps just having you here." She was pulling back from the edge. Had she seen over it too? Into that pit, that emptiness? "I appreciate it. I know you've put us first. I appreciate it very much. Now if we can just get through the service."

"As long as we don't have to sing 'A Mighty Fortress Is Our God.' "

We both laughed. In his great hymn, Luther called the pope the Devil.

"You know what?" I said gamely. "We don't need the Catholic Church. We have each other." I punched her shoulder lightly. Even as I said that I knew how untrue it was. The final loss of our Catholicism — for what did the archdiocese's rejection mean if not that? — was as devastating at that moment as the loss of Michael. What was our religion but the cluster of rituals, formulas, beliefs and learned responses by which, *precisely,* we were able to finish the business that every death interrupts? The Church existed to help us say a final word of love or, as in my case, forgiveness. If our religion — our Catholicism — was useless to us then, having become a sign of recalcitrance instead of reconciliation, when would it ever be of use? We were like victims of a shipwreck clinging to each other on an alien shore. Who asked in such a situation whether the compass was at fault or the navigator or the captain? Or was it the fault of the dumb rock we ran upon? All we knew was desolation. We consoled ourselves by insisting that we didn't need the only vessel that could have carried us home.

At that moment, as if to underscore the poignancy of our exile, there was a rap on the door and an oh-so-Anglican clergyman, a canon of the cathedral, opened it.

He was as tall and lean as those upper-class clerics with the best jobs always are. Though he was middle-aged, his face was boyish and his hair was closely cut, giving him the look we once associated with marines, but now with homosexuals. Not that he was one of *those;* his wedding ring flashed. His foppishness was a function of mere breeding, not sexual preference. It was no longer considered bad form to look like what he was. In the sixties men like this let their grooming go and pretended they were the sons of plumbers like the rest of us. But not anymore. In his clerical collar and striped seersucker suit he looked like a chaplain of the

British Raj, and I realized it had been glib sophistry to assert that little remained to separate Episcopalians and Roman Catholics. In that "little," revealed in meaningless details like the color of a priest's clothing, were buried millions of colonized and murdered people, many of them Irish and many Catholic. In that "little" were buried my own ancestors and Michael's. In that "little" was lost the distinction between the people who built the Cloisters and the people who clean it. Nothing separated us but history. It was a whole new reason to resent our own Church, that its intransigence abandoned us to the exquisite civility of the rich. For the point was that, at that moment, we would go anywhere and embrace any heritage and accept any offer of hospitality, even the smuggest one, if it included a simple, direct proclamation of the Gospel of Jesus Christ.

"Carolyn?" he began familiarly. Then, seeing me, he put his manicured hand out. "Hello, I'm Martin Putnam, the dean's assistant."

I stood and shook hands with him. I felt oafish in my monastic mufti. I needed a shave and a shower. "I'm Frank Durkin," I said. The priest stared at me so intently I had to look away. And then my discomfort exploded into humiliation when for the first time it occurred to me that, after all those years, I had a part in Michael's legend too. I was the FBI informant.

Canon Putnam turned back to Carolyn. "I hate to bother you with this, but there are television people outside. I've told them no interviews, of course. But I wanted to know your feelings about letting them film the service."

Carolyn looked at me.

"No," I said without hesitating. "Absolutely not."

Putnam ignored me and continued to stare at Carolyn. "The more dramatic their footage, the more likely they'll use it. What better way to memorialize Michael than to draw attention to the killing in Beirut? Wouldn't he seize the opportunity to denounce . . . ?"

"I beg your pardon, Canon Putnam." I touched his shoulder. "But we don't want camera crews in church." Did I have to explain myself? Did I have to say it's against our religion? The man had the instincts of a publicist. So would you if you had the largest cathedral in the world and no congregation to fill it. No wonder he offered it to aerialists and jazz musicians and renegade Catholics.

Carolyn said, "Television? Why is television here?"

The canon touched her. "Because Michael is still news, my dear. He was a great American when America needed one." How did he manage to make even that tribute seem condescending? I pictured him, years before, as a seminarian who'd gone into the ministry, instead of the family investment firm, to avoid the draft. Nicholas Wiley would have been about his age by now.

He waited for Carolyn to contradict me. When she didn't he said, "All right. But we can't stop them from filming outside." He looked at me. "Just so you'll know."

I nodded at him, but the image of stars arriving at some premiere seemed ludicrous to me. No one would be coming to Michael's funeral. Television was there because Canon Martin Putnam, the Impresario Priest, had called them.

"Dean Evans has mentioned you," he said. "You were a friend of Michael's, weren't you?"

"Yes, I was his friend."

It was easy to read the canon's expression, and he wanted me to: *What friends poor Michael had, you and Archbishop O'Shea.*

Somehow I found it possible to continue looking at him this time. A surge of anger rescued me from my embarrassment. *You Anglicans don't believe in excommunication, do you? And you never betray your best friends either. You have manners.* If he says something ingratiating, I told myself, I will hit him.

When Carolyn took my hand I was surprised. It was a manifestation of her loyalty, and I was grateful for it.

Canon Putnam said to her, "Dean Evans will keep his remarks brief of course. He asked me to tell you that he intends to draw the connection between Michael's ministry and what's happening in Lebanon. Is there any other particular point you want him to make?"

"His remarks?"

"The eulogy."

"Oh."

Why was it a surprise to her? Clearly she had been unable to anticipate in any way the details of the service. Distress distorted her face, but instead of making her seem helpless, it girded her. She was still the strongest woman I had ever known. "Dean Evans has been wonderful to me, but he can't speak for Michael. I'm sorry, but he can't."

"Well, I . . . whatever you . . ."

She turned to me. "Frank, will you?"

THIRTY-TWO

WHEN we were children nuns told us that Pentecost was the birthday of the Church. The silliness of that notion, the banality of it, struck me even as a boy in the overheated classrooms of Good Shepherd School. I am not inclined, like so many, to mock the memory of those earnest women. Such easy targets; my instinct is always to defend them. Nuns made the Church possible, and many of their ludicrous images — the Baby Jesus pretending to a drooling helplessness — made great mysteries available in ways the obtuse categories of theologians — Homoiousian — never could. But the birthday of the Church? I remember squirming at the idea of the Apostles gathering around a cake with one candle. Was I supposed to think of its flame as the fiery manifestation of the Holy Ghost? Was the noise they made with their Gift of Tongues the group's off-key singing of the Happy Birthday song?

Now of course I am an informed Christian and I know what Pentecost really was. I refer to it here not for the sake of some blatant, facile comparison between the lives of Jesus and Michael Maguire, as if finally my point is to make Michael a latter-day Christ, but because at Pentecost was revealed the structure of human hope, which begins, of course, in despair. The followers of Jesus had disgraced themselves. They had all abandoned him, or, as Mark put it, rather more mercilessly, "They all forsook him and fled." They left a stranger, a centurion, one of the crucifiers, to finally and formally acknowledge Jesus: "Truly this man was the Son of God."

Those who claimed to love Jesus simply disappeared. They were terrified that what happened to him was going to happen to them. And so they hid. They dispersed. They went their separate ways. Only one thing could have brought them together again — a miracle. Only a miracle could have changed them from confused, inarticulate, and beleaguered peasants into a company of preachers who would in a generation ignite an empire. Pentecost is the day on which the miracle happened. Not a mountain being moved, not the sun being stopped in the sky, the miracle was a eulogy. A eulogy of Jesus.

The eulogist was no orator, and he was no hero. Of all the disciples he had the least right to stand in the main street of Jerusalem and speak of the Lord because, like Judas, who'd had the decency to kill himself, this man had not merely abandoned Jesus, but had explicitly betrayed him. He was Peter. When he stood up — had Mary asked him to? — and told the simple story of Jesus of Nazareth, everything changed. He told how Jesus went around doing good and how his words and actions fulfilled the promises of Scripture; how he came, like a good Jew, to Jerusalem for Passover, though he knew the leaders of the people plotted against him there; how he was arrested and, though the Romans offered to release him, how the people themselves demanded that he be put to death; how he was crucified among thieves; but also how His Father was faithful to him even in death and so raised him up to glory. In the exposition, the telling of the story itself, those who'd been a part of it were able to grasp its meaning at last, and those who hadn't been a part of it were able nevertheless to see its relevance to their lives.

People from all over the world — Parthians, Medes and Elamites — heard Peter's words as a new language, but one they understood. And in the recitation of facts with which they were familiar but had never seen whole, as forming like every story a coherent structure with a beginning, a middle and an end, the people recognized the narrative that bound them together, that made them a community, that made them what came to be called the Church.

What came to be called the *kerygma,* the Good News, the Gospel, began — and this is the miracle — as the coward's eulogy of the only man he ever loved, the one whom he betrayed.

I was in the huge Gothic cathedral alone, walking the aisles. Michael's funeral was to begin in half an hour. A few people had taken places in pews at great distance from each other. Once more I felt the pang of disappointment for him. In that vast space it would seem that no one came, no one cared. He would have passed from the earth unnoticed, unmourned by all but a meager remnant. If the death of this man was insignificant, whose wasn't?

Yet also, at the same time, the space itself, however it dwarfed us or because it did, was exactly right for that particular liturgy. In the end that structure overpowered its own history, and its associations with class and denomination meant nothing. It was a Gothic cathedral, and to a Catholic its stones were sacred. Its aisles, its nave, its narthex, its crossing, its transept and choir formed the geography of memory. At first I'd felt entrapped by it, but memory is what saves us when we are faced with death. These were the darkened, mysterious aisles along which I'd run with Michael as a boy. Actually I'd run *after* him, for he was the one who led the way in all our explorations, our adventures. He was the one who'd pushed first into tunnels or who leapt into quarries or who sallied forth on the winter's first ice. I, with others, had stood outside those tunnels, back from those cliffs, on those shores, waiting to see if he made it, to see if it was safe. And we'd cried after him, "Go, Michael, go!"

The pointed patterns of color splashing the stone floor from the stained-glass windows signaled the coming of nightfall, for this was evening light, not morning. Yet my memories had not, as I'd feared, condemned me to an end-of-the-day nostalgia. The sun was gone behind the buildings of the city, but its last light and warmth filtered into that immense yet intimate enclosure. The feelings I had for him filled it, and like angels whose wings could be heard fluttering in the reaches, so also did the memories we'd inherited from our people, of *their* adventures. In this place we'd recognized that those adventures going back eons were ours. That communal memory suggested that *we* had hidden from barbarians behind these pillars; *we* had taken the spiraling stone stairways at a clip, yeomen rushing to the battlements; *we* had crept from cavern to cavern, from vigil light to lantern; *we* had attended coronations and installations and heard anathemas pronounced from the great Chair; *we* had been present when saints were named and kings wed and cardinals invested and nonconformists banished; and *we* had lowered our heads and struck our breasts countless times when the anointed one high above us held for all to behold the broken Body of Our Lord. The Gothic cathedral is the Catholic's Holy Land, and even those of us who were raised in pale parish churches carried in our minds, as Jews did Palestine, the image of that homeland. You see, as Catholics we knew that we, like that very place — and isn't this what's gone now? — were made for worship.

I had been grieving for Michael, but for so much more than him. He was the flower of Catholic life, the best we had, the one who went before us and showed that it was safe. Against the numbing sameness of secular culture even as it had encroached upon the Church, he had stood as our champion in exactly the way, as a boy-soldier, he had stood against the enemy for the sake of his friends. He could risk his life because he believed innately that life is made for more than itself. That innate knowledge — what made him a hero — became the conscious religious affirmation — what made him a priest — of his maturity. The world is made for more than itself: that is what Michael meant. That is what the structure of the cathedral meant. No mere achievement or act of heroism could have justified or explained his life, as no organizational function, no bishop's throne, no social or aesthetic purpose could have justified or explained that church. Michael Maguire was the Gothic cathedral of men. He and it were made — I hesitate to introduce the word after all this time in the telling — for God.

If God did not exist, then that building was a cruel, pompous joke on itself. If God did not exist, then Michael Maguire, war hero, resistance leader and priest-against-the-Church was a figure of the absurd. I did not think, in beginning this story, that it would end religiously. I had thought rather that religion was that cluster of false notes we had left behind. I had gone, perversely, to a desert monastery to escape it. And hadn't Michael abandoned his religion to love a woman and make a family? The Catholic Church, like a good Roman, had fallen on its sword. Hence the unarticulated grief of a generation of sophisticates. We were exactly like the sons and daughters of a suicide, with anger for the past and fear for the future, each so intense we never consciously entertained them. If the Church could not maintain the loyalty of men like Michael, then surely — and wasn't this to be our theme? — God's work on earth had failed.

As it had when His Son was crucified, his disciples having fled. As it had until Peter stood among strangers and told the story.

Is it the core Christian insight that just when we free ourselves from the spell religion casts, we come face to face with God? When we confront failure we succeed? When we die we live? Doesn't the inbuilt tension between forgiveness and sin provide the drama of every human narrative? Aren't the stresses between, in Simone Weil's phrase, gravity and grace what keep the Gothic masterpieces standing?

Michael was dead, but God lived.

Was that enough for me?

Could one believe finally in the Resurrection of the Dead? That is the question this story puts. As it was the question Peter's put. It is the only question left, and has always been.

I was ready now to be with him.

His coffin waited, still, in the baptistry, the priest-hole, and as I crossed in front of the high altar toward that octagonal chamber in which the marble font sat like God's crown, I genuflected, right knee to left heel with an altar boy's precision. The physical gesture reassured me, restored me, reminded me.

On the coldest mornings of winter in Inwood the place we loved to be was in the sanctuary — steaming radiators, undulating linoleum tile, threadbare orientals — of Good Shepherd Church. Each pair of altar boys thought of themselves as halves of one person. Since they, together, held the corners of the priest's chasuble while he genuflected and raised up the Sacred Host, it was natural for altar boys to come to think that together they were worthy of almost anything. But let a morning come when one of the pair did not appear; the other was struck with terror at what he had to do alone. What if the Host fell to the floor? What if the finger-towel got wet? What if he forgot the secret Latin phrases that the priest's hocus pocus — "*Hoc est Corpus* . . ." — required?

I always served Mass with Michael because he never failed to come and he always knew exactly what to say and when to move the Book. And if the unexpected happened, a tabernacle key missing or a shortage of sacred wafers or a blown-out paschal candle, I knew that Michael could deal with it. At those times, I anticipated terrified GIs and Vietnamese priests and American draft-dodgers, crying after him as he moved decisively to do whatever had to be done, "Go, Michael! Go!"

A tower shaped like a lantern and supported by rounded arches overhung the baptistry. It was nearly dark in there, shadows dominated, and at first I did not see the coffin. Had attendants moved it already? But no, for I had just crossed the intersection of aisles where it would sit during the funeral. The coffin would be carried into the nave in the opening procession. As my eyes adjusted I saw the oblong shape against the arched doorway that led to the columbarium, the room where ashes were interred in stone, the final prison. Caroly was right to want the earth for him, not walls.

Slowly I approached.

I wanted to cast aside our personal history. I wanted to exchange the end of our friendship for the beginning. Couldn't we have been two boys lifting up the corners of a golden chasuble forever? That close to God? That close to one another? Instead we were two men on a weather-beaten desperate island, separated forever by the woman who united us. I saw him looking back at me, amazed, through that fog of pathos which was to blur, then stain, the entire chronicle of our time. Even the most cherished memories of our innocence had become polluted by the knowledge of what happened. It was like wanting to be rid of our *national* history. Oh, if we could only have been the heroes of the world, vanquishers of Hitler, defenders of freedom, forever. Oh, if we could only have had our Kennedy, our Pope John, our Tom Dooley, Tom Merton, our Cardinal Spellman in his prime, our Martin Luther King. If we could only have had the Holy Catholic Church we'd first believed in. If we could only have had "America."

Instead we had Vietnam. That evil war forms the center of this narrative, not as the source of all the evil that befell us, but as the great reminder that no nation is holy — not even ours; no Church is sacred — not even this one; any more than a single one of us is free from sin — not even Michael Maguire. The shadow of the Fall has been upon this story from the start, and that, not references to cathedrals, cardinals or the infidelity of priests, is what has made it Catholic. The bronze cock stands on every paragraph, as if it were a barn, a basilica, and like the memory of My Lai, it rattles each time the wind blows. It crows each time we deny who we are. And for every denial there is later put the question, thrice, "Do you love me, friend, more than these others do?" In every paragraph I have tried to answer.

I tell you, Michael, dead as you are, that you and I *ourselves* embodied the age without knowing it. We were the town that had to be destroyed to be saved. We were the immolations and the gunships and the body bags. We were the naked girl running down the road with napalm bubbling her skin. We were the dark-eyed campus beauty at Kent State, screeching above the corpse of her youth. We were the scar on LBJ's belly, and we were the coonskin on the wall. We were what made Cassius Clay change his name. We were the stonewall around Nixon and we were Washington aflame. Instead of in truth or God we believed in our innocence, then in our sorrows, and that is what made us dangerous. You were going to end the war. I was going to create a mansion of literature, love and loyalty.

We had handfuls of each other that we carried like treasures until the day we turned and found that all we carried were stones. What else to do but set them rolling? How did it feel to be all alone? To be on your own? How did it feel? Oh, dear reader, by now dear friend, don't ask me. I could never tell you. Ask Anne Sexton, John Berryman, Delmore Schwartz, Cesare Pavese, Randall Jarrell, Sylvia Plath, Marilyn Monroe, Janis Joplin, Papa Hemingway, William Inge, and why shouldn't our souls be disquieted?

"Go, Michael!" I cried. But also, "Wait for me!" You didn't. You forgot what my life was, and you became hard while I grew soft. You were too far ahead to see it happening when I became totally — overly — dependent on one thing. Not you, God or booze. Just her. She was all I needed and all I had. And no one in the world — not Nixon, Mao or J. Edgar Hoover — could have destroyed our love but you. You took Carolyn from me, you bastard. And I repaid you without a kiss.

And now I was touching the gleaming wood of your coffin, at the end of my recitation.

How could I believe in God, Church or the Resurrection of the Dead when I did not believe you were in that box? You, Michael, in the throes of decay? You, Michael, with a waxen face? A rosary through your fingers? All you ever had were bones and flesh, fleet feet and that fierce conscience of yours. Now they were separated? If flesh was falling from your bones, why did mine adhere? If you were dead, Michael, how could I believe that I was alive? The box alone did not convince me.

And so with a finger under the lip of wood I lifted the cover of your coffin expecting anything — a staring mask, plasticene, lipstick, rouge, a pirate's skull — but you.

Ah. Ah. I had nothing then but silence. Only emptiness. The void. Nothing. And nothing. And nothing.

Later — only moments, but it might have been all of time — Dean Evans interrupted me. He was as imposing as I'd remembered, that great shock of white hair, that physical self-assurance. Also, that quiet earnestness.

"Mister Durkin," he said sadly, "it is nearly time to begin."

"May I have a moment more, please?"

He looked at me, not as if I was ridiculous, which I expected, but as if he'd known I was going to ask. He nodded, and threw a glance at the pallbearers behind him. They withdrew.

"Where's Carolyn?" I asked.

"She's in the pew with her children."

"Is Molly there?"

"Yes."

"Then would you ask Carolyn to come here a moment? Just for a moment?" To help me break the grip of that nothing, which had me, that paralysis.

He nodded and turned.

Then, again after no time or all time, she was standing in the arched entrance of the baptistry.

Her eyes went to the open coffin, and she drew back, shaking her head.

I offered my hand, but said, "Caro, help me make my peace with him. Please help me."

When she looked at me I saw in her eyes finally the glint of understanding. She came and stood by me.

Over his remade, lifeless face.

"Michael, it's me and Caro." I had no idea whether I was speaking this aloud or only in my head. "You died before I said to you that I am sorry, and I so wanted your forgiveness. I wanted to give you mine. Is it too late?"

Carolyn took my hand, pressed it like a dead flower.

He did not speak to me.

I leaned toward him, thinking to kiss those lips. But when he did not breathe on my face I stopped, suspended just above his frozen skin.

Oh, he is dead!

This is death!

There was no kissing now. No forgiving.

Organ music behind me. And a congregation resonant but removed, as if in another sphere, singing, "The strife is o'er, the battle done; Now is the victor's triumph won. O let the song of praise be sung, Alleluia!"

Dean Evans, vested in black cope, motioned at the pallbearers and they came forward.

Carolyn and I stood aside. We should have slipped out then to join the laity, to let the clergy splice their rubrics, but we could not, either of us, leave him.

One of those strangers closed Michael's coffin.

When the pallbearers had it hoisted and began the slow unsteady procession out into the ambulatory, Dean Evans gestured toward me and Carolyn. "Walk with us," his hand said. Holding each other we fell into step behind the gleaming box.

I was numb. I was as a man upright but asleep. I merely followed, with only one sensation, that of a chill on my face, a frosted patch where I'd expected the warmth of Michael's breath. Outside the baptistry, in the main body of the cathedral, the procession suddenly became elaborate. Ahead of the coffin were dozens of robed choir members, and ahead of them was a huge borne cross, a pair of torches and a white banner emblazoned, "Blessed are the Peacemakers." Interspersed between the choir and the coffin and between the coffin and us were a thurifer carrying a smoking incense vessel and two pairs of surpliced acolytes. And waiting to walk with Dean Evans were vested deacons and more acolytes, candles flickering off every face.

And they were all singing with rolling robust voices, "On the third morn he rose again, Glorious in majesty to reign; O let us swell the joyful strain, Alleluia!"

Slowly we moved. Instead of cutting directly across the near aisle to the sanctuary, however, the procession wound into the north aisle, into the nave, among the pews where the mourners sat.

And it was there that the first jolt hit me, the first surprise, the first miracle. The frontmost dozen rows of chairs — not pews — were full of albed priests, some with stoles crossed on their breasts and gathered in cinctures, some with stoles hanging in stripes from their shoulders. Others wore the vestigial Benedictine cowls, that serve professors now and low church preachers. As the coffin appeared, their eyes displayed their loss. They were like firemen, policemen, soldiers gathered by the death of a brother. After the choir passed they began to file out into the aisle ahead of the coffin. As I watched I could feel my concentration slowly coming back, a focus of mind, to grapple with this mystery. Who exactly were they? But at once, recognizing the cut of the albs and stoles, the flash of cassocks and habits under outer vestments, I understood that they were Jesuits, Paulists, Franciscans, defiant priests of the Roman Catholic archdiocese, as well as Episcopal vicars and canons, Lutheran pastors and Baptist ministers. I saw familiar faces, priests from Michael's seminary class — Gene O'Mally — and veterans of antiwar demonstrations. They were clergy of every stripe from New York, but not only New York. Monsignor Egan, the famous Chicagoan, was there. Interspersed among the men were women, similarly vested, the new *ordinandi,* the new prophets of several denominations. There were parish priests and teachers, pastors, curates and missionaries. There were the famous ones whose names came back easily as they passed: Harvey Cox, Daniel Berrigan, William Sloane Coffin, Monsignor Fox, Bishop Alcott of the Episcopal diocese, John Ferris Smith, Robert MacAfee Brown, Henri Nouwen, Paul Lannan, and Michael Hunt. There were more than a hundred, ordained all, brother and sister priests of the excommunicant.

And with full strong voices they were singing, "O Risen Lord, all praise to you, Who from our sin have set us free, That we may live eternally, Alleluia."

The second jolt — miracle — came when our part of the procession resumed, behind the concelebrating clergy, and I saw at last, moving into the heart of the darkened nave, that the vast cathedral, the second largest church in the world, was full.

Full of people. Men, women, children, students, nuns, old, young, ex-priests, journalists, politicians, peace workers; a dominance surely of the middle-aged, looking slightly worn, faded, but above their hymnals, looking also strong, clear-eyed, resolute. They were Parthians, Medes and Elamites. They were Jews. There were thousands of them.

And I was stunned. Archbishop Timothy O'Shea was not there. Terence Cardinal Cooke was not there. Pope John Paul II was not there. But their people were. People come to bury Michael Maguire; come to send him on his way.

Who, therefore, were the outcasts? Who the excommunicants?

"Alleluia, the strife is o'er, the battle done . . ."

The song soared above us.

The procession turned the first corner and then the second.

"Who from our sin have set us free."

And we were striding now down the main aisle, toward the altar and the pulpit. Carolyn had both her hands linked in the crook of my arm and when I looked at her, I saw those eyes, brimming over, fixed upon the coffin.

I saw also, for the first time, what we were doing here, why she had sent for me.

Yes, Michael was dead.

And yes, we were alive. The Church, having died, was reborn. We were the Church, that throng gathered in memory, and also by it. We had been remembering ourselves, becoming part of each other once more. This had been the work of Michael's ghost and the work — Ah, Bright Wings! — of the Holy Ghost. That alleluia there and then outweighed all unfinished business, every anathema and each harbored wound of betrayal. That alleluia outweighed what we had done or not done, what we had lost, had found or had forgot. That alleluia outweighed death.

Yes, we believed in the Holy Catholic Church, the forgiveness of sin, the resurrection of the dead and life everlasting.

Into life everlasting we had gathered to commit our friend. Into life everlasting we wanted to release him.

I had been using memory and remorse to cling to him. He was my saint, my sinner, my hero, my great friend, my last enemy. He was none of these. He was a man. And as a man, not God, he stopped the world for a moment to speak of peace. And if the world had not heard him, we had heard him.

As we approached the altar on which we would break bread, a communion of the living and the dead, of Catholics and Protestants, of Jews and gentiles, of believers and unbelievers, of the reborn and the fallen-away, of Americans and Asians, of the saved and the damned, a communion, in that precious phrase, of saints, I sensed at last — oh gratitude! — the Presence of the One from whom Michael heard the call and toward whom even then Michael, steadfast marcher, was striding. He was striding as always, just ahead of us. And we had come to that act of remembrance and of worship out of the old habit of following him. We yet believed — and this is what our priests must do for us! — because he did.

As my eye fell to the magnificent carved pulpit, the shrine of the eternally unimprisoned Word of God, I knew at last what I would say. That throng needed no sermon, no homily, no eulogy, no explanation or confession, nothing more from me. Michael Maguire's story had been enough. It had brought us here to earth again, and him to the threshold of heaven. It was my place, my privilege just to end it, crying with my fist raised at his remains, "Go, Michael! Go, Michael! Go in peace, dear Michael! Go!"

AFTERWORD

SINCE I wrote this book in the early 1980s, so many entirely unanticipated things have happened. And many things you would perhaps consider much more likely have *not* happened.

More than ten years after this book appeared, twenty years after the fall — or liberation — of Saigon, Robert McNamara published a memoir in which he acknowledged that early on he saw that the Vietnam War was unwinnable and that the further pursuit of it was a terrible mistake. (He also said that Ngo Dinh Diem's Catholicism was part of what led to the first fatal errors: "we totally misjudged that.") Yes, McNamara's silence after reaching that conclusion seems unforgivable — but where, at least, is any comparable statement of conscience from Henry Kissinger or the others who kept the war going?

I could not have imagined in 1984, when *Prince of Peace* was first published, that the United States would maintain its punitive embargo of Vietnam for ten more years. In that period, the black flag of the POW/MIA movement became ubiquitous in America, sprouting on flagpoles outside post offices, VFW posts, union halls. Yet while the hundreds or thousands of missing American soldiers and fliers would understandably haunt us, little was made of the Vietnamese MIAs, whose numbers were counted in five digits or six. And this "nonreckoning," as I see it, goes to the heart of the matter.

Prince of Peace was written around a nut of outrage that still sits in my throat. I first claimed that feeling as my own upon learning of the massacre of more than five hundred civilians at My Lai by American soldiers. The massacre occurred in 1968, although we did not hear of it until 1969 because of an army cover-up. By 1984 it was clear that the cover-up was continuing: thirteen soldiers were indicted for war crimes, and twelve for carrying out the cover-up, but only one man was convicted of anything: Lieutenant William L. Calley, who was found guilty of twenty-two murders. He was given a life sentence but served only six months in prison. On the thirtieth anniversary of the massacre, in March 1998, at ceremonies in Washington, three veterans were honored for having tried to stop the berserking GIs of Charlie Company. "The army has finally come to terms with what was a black day," a U.S. senator said. But had it? What does it say about the army and the country that this anniversary was observed by honoring true, but decidedly exceptional, heroism when we have never held responsible the perpetrators of that crime?

It is this ongoing inability to "come to terms" with Vietnam that I could never have imagined as I wrote about the war in this novel. Our nation remains cursed and haunted by Vietnam. Why? Because we lost? Because those who fought in the war were so unfairly scapegoated when they returned home? Or could it be that the Vietnamese dead — perhaps two million of them — weigh anonymously on our conscience.

Not long after publishing *Prince of Peace,* my wife and I brought our daughter to the Vietnam Veterans Memorial in Washington, that stark symbol of what the war did first to the dead and then to all of us.

"The Vietnam War?" Lizzy asked, taking in the names etched in black granite.

"Yes," we answered.

"Then where are the Vietnamese names?"

The question hangs above this nation. Where are the names of the 504 women, old men, and children who died at My Lai? Like Kissinger, we have never really acknowledged what we did in Vietnam. If you had told me in 1984 that eight years later this country would elect as president a man who had responded to the Vietnam War by resisting the draft, I would have been consoled and proud. But if you had then told me that he would cooperate with his right-wing critics in treating that resistance as a thing to be ashamed of, I would have been mystified.

The failure to "come to terms" with Vietnam has been part of a broader failure to come to terms with America's Cold War militarism. Nothing demonstrates that more clearly than our refusal to significantly reduce our dependence on nuclear weapons. In 1984 the United States possessed more than thirty thousand nuclear weapons. Ronald Reagan had dispatched Pershing missiles to Europe, and announced the Strategic Defense Initiative, which, if implemented, would have violated the crucial Anti–Ballistic Missile Treaty. That same year, the *Bulletin of the Atomic Scientists* moved the hands of the Doomsday Clock, the symbolic timepiece tracking the likelihood of nuclear war, to three minutes before midnight, the closest the world had come to the zero hour in more than thirty years.

The antinuclear movement was born. Millions took to the streets demanding, as it was called, a nuclear freeze. And they were heard. When Mikhail Gorbachev became the Soviet leader in 1985, he and Reagan formed an unexpected partnership to turn the tide against the arms race. Their 1987 Intermediate-Range Nuclear Forces Treaty led to START and START II. George Bush followed Reagan's lead to cut the American nuclear arsenal by half. In 1991 the Doomsday Clock was moved "off the scale," to seventeen minutes before midnight. The danger seemed past.

Amazingly enough, under Bill Clinton, a president with a history as a war protester, that process has not only stalled but, with the outbreak of nuclear testing in India and Pakistan, reversed itself. As this edition of *Prince of Peace* is published, the U.S. nuclear arsenal is stuck at fifteen thousand warheads, many of which remain on a hair trigger. The president has refused to embrace a policy of No First Use, or even the ultimate goal of nuclear abolition. The hands of the Doomsday Clock were moved forward in 1995, and again in 1998 — to nine minutes before midnight.

On the Mall in Washington, one might also wonder where the names of the Vietnam War protesters are. No monument stands to the peace movement. With few exceptions, this nation still behaves as if the mass outpouring of revulsion and anger at McNamara's terrible mistake and at Richard Nixon's unconscionable prolongation of it remains something to be ashamed of. Perhaps we are ashamed, finally, of having failed so utterly to leave behind our Cold War militarism.

"Come to terms"?

Prince of Peace is a political novel, but it is a religious novel too. So I will end with a prayer. May the men, women, and children who died in those towns and hamlets and jungles — ours and theirs — rest in peace. Peace. Peace. But there will be no rest for those of us who live, forgetting what we learned. "No more war!" said Pope Paul VI at the United Nations in 1965. He says it again in this novel, the act that sets the story in motion. "War no more! War never again!" We will not have peace until Peace becomes our purpose.

J.C.
Boston, Massachusetts
June 1998